HD 304491
69 Toliver,
.T54   The select series.
.T655

The Select Series: Microsoft® Outlook® 2002

Pamela R. Toliver

LIBRARY
WEST GEORGIA TECHNICAL COLLEGE
303 FORT DRIVE
LAGRANGE, GA 30240

Upper Saddle River, New Jersey

LIBRARY OF CONGRESS CATALOGING-IN-PUBLICATION DATA

Toliver, Pamela R.
　　The select series. Outlook / Pamela R. Toliver.
　　　　p. cm.
　　Includes index.
　　　　ISBN 0-13-064572-9 (alk. paper)
　　　　1. Microsoft Outlook. 2. Time management—Computer programs. 3. Personal
　　information management—Computer programs.　　I. Title: Outlook.　　II. Title.

HD69.T54 T655 2002
005.369—dc21　　　　　　　　　　　　　　　　　　　　　　　　2002010410

Publisher and Vice President: Natalie E. Anderson
Executive Acquisitions Editor: Jodi McPherson
Senior Project Manager: Thomas Park
Assistant Editor: Melissa Edwards
Editorial Assistant: Jasmine Slowik
Developmental Editor: Samantha Penrod
Media Project Manager: Cathleen Profitko
Marketing Manager: Emily Williams Knight
Production Manager: Gail Steier De Acevedo
Project Manager, Production: Tim Tate
Associate Director, Manufacturing: Vincent Scelta
Manufacturing Buyer: Natacha St. Hill Moore
Design Manager: Pat Smythe
Interior Design: Lorraine Castellano and Proof Positive/Farrowlyne Associates, Inc.
Cover Design: Lorraine Castellano
Full-Service Composition: Black Dot Group/An AGT Company
Printer/Binder: Banta Book Group, Menasha

Credits and acknowledgments borrowed from other sources and reproduced, with permission, in this textbook appear on the appropriate page within the text or at the end of the respective project.

Microsoft, Windows, Windows NT, MSN, The Microsoft Network, the MSN logo, PowerPoint, Outlook, FrontPage, and/or other Microsoft products referenced herein are either trademarks or registered trademarks of Microsoft Corporation in the U.S.A. and other countries. Screen shots and icons reprinted with permission from the Microsoft Corporation. This book is not sponsored by, endorsed by, or affiliated with Microsoft Corporation.

Microsoft and the Microsoft Office User Specialist logo are trademarks or registered trademarks of Microsoft Corporation in the United States and/or other countries. Pearson Education is independent from Microsoft Corporation, and not affiliated with Microsoft in any manner. This text may be used in assisting students to prepare for a Microsoft Office User Specialist Exam. Neither Microsoft, its designated review company, nor Pearson Education warrants that use of this text will ensure passing this relevant exam. Use of the Microsoft Office User Specialist Approved Courseware logo on this product signifies that it has been independently reviewed and approved in compliance with the following standards:

Acceptable coverage of all content related to the Expert Level Microsoft Office exam entitled "Outlook 2002"; and sufficient performance-based exercises that relate closely to all required content, based on sampling of text.

Copyright © 2002 by Prentice-Hall, Inc., Upper Saddle River, New Jersey, 07458. All rights reserved. Printed in the United States of America. This publication is protected by copyright and permission should be obtained from the publisher prior to any prohibited reproduction, storage in a retrieval system, or transmission in any form or by any means, electronic, mechanical, photocopying, recording, or likewise. For information regarding permission(s), write to: Rights and Permissions Department.

10 9 8 7 6 5 4 3 2 1
ISBN 0-13-064572-9

Series Authors

Pamela R. Toliver and Yvonne Johnson

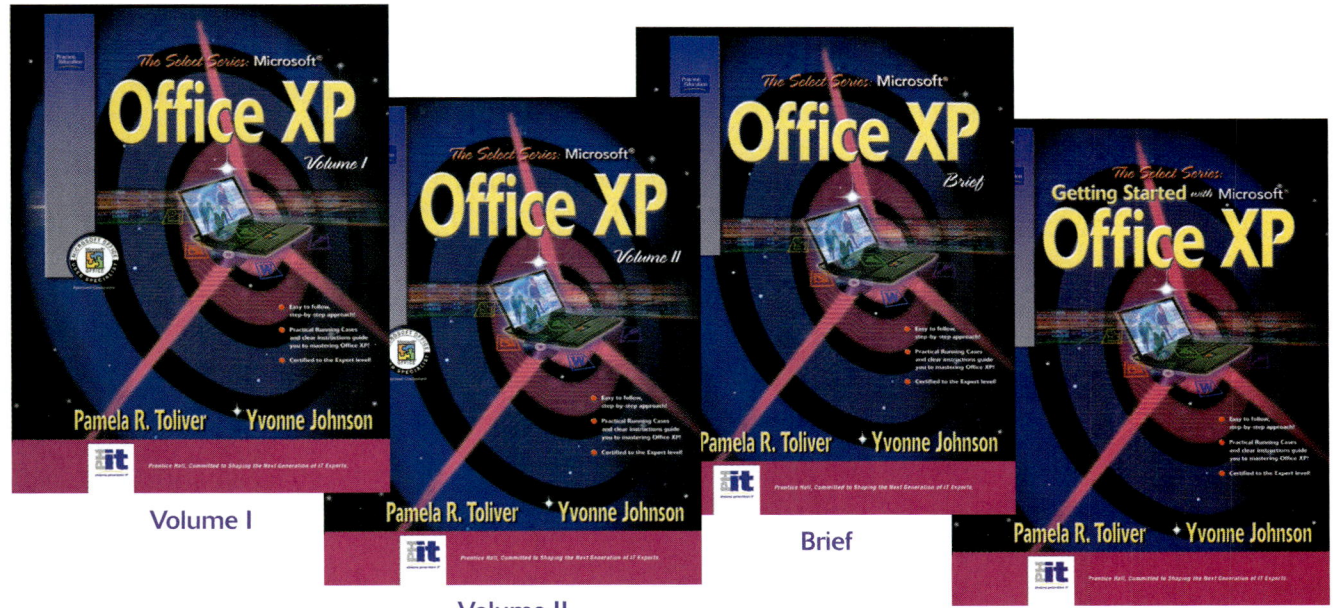

Volume I

Volume II

Brief

Getting Started

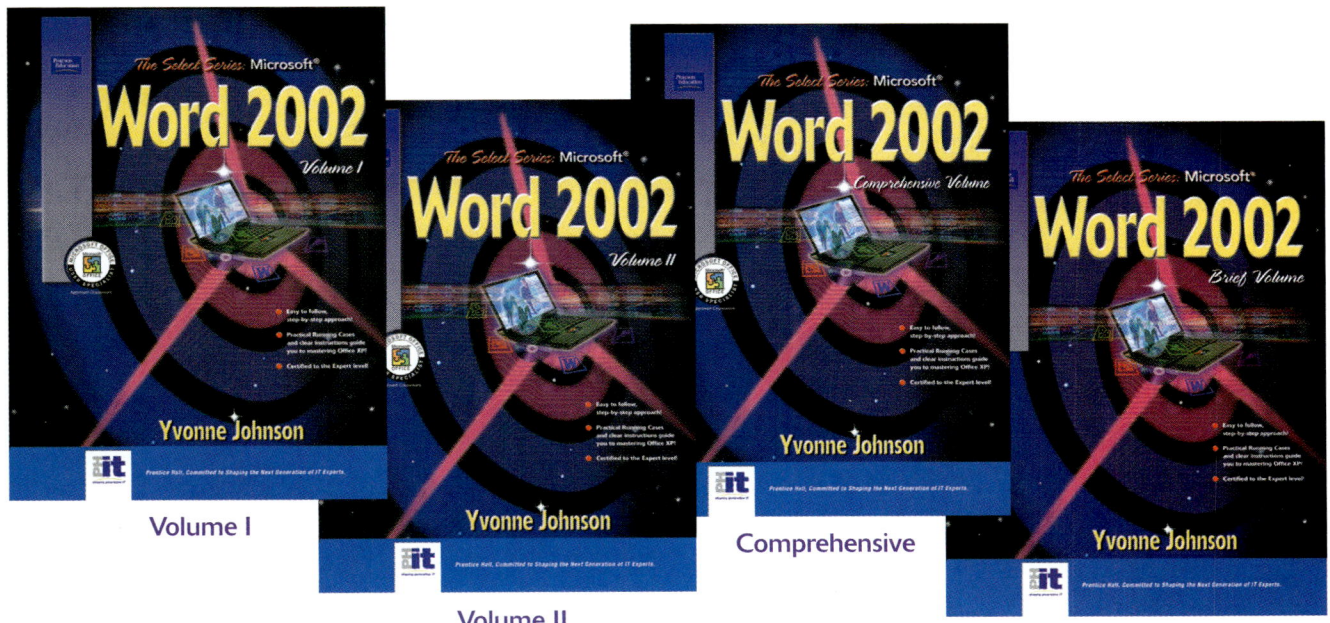

Volume I

Volume II

Comprehensive

Brief

Dedication

This book is dedicated to the driving force of educators who struggle with the challenge to keep up with the ever-changing field of technology.

Acknowledgments

Completing a work of this magnitude is like a snowball rolling downhill, gathering speed and picking up so much help along the way. Without the support and growth, this work would not have been completed:

To the development staff, I say thank you for keeping us on track.

To the technical reviewers, thanks for trying to keep us accurate.

To the copy editors, thanks for keeping us consistent.

To production and design, thanks for laying it all out, expanding and compressing to make it fit so beautifully within the boundaries.

But most of all, thanks to educators everywhere for creating the impetus that made this work necessary.

Pam

Preface

About this Series

The Select Series uses a class-tested, highly visual, project-based approach that teaches students through tasks using step-by-step instructions. You will find extensive full-color figures and screen captures that guide learners through the basic skills and procedures necessary to demonstrate proficiency in their use of each software application.

The Select Series introduces an all-new design for Microsoft Office XP. The easy-to-follow design now has larger screen shots with steps listed on the left side of the accompanying screen. This unique design program, along with the use of bold color, helps reduce distraction and keeps students focused and interested as they work. In addition, selectively placed Tip boxes and Other Ways boxes enhance student learning by explaining various ways to complete a task.

Our approach to learning is designed to provide the necessary visual guidance in a project-oriented setting. Each project concludes with a review section that includes a Summary, Key Terms & Skills, Study Questions, Guided Exercises, and On Your Own Exercises. This extensive end-of-project section provides students with the opportunity to practice and gain further experience with the tasks covered in each project.

What's New in the Select Series for Office XP

The entire Select Series has been revised to include the new features found in the Office XP suite, which contains Word 2002, Excel 2002, Access 2002, PowerPoint 2002, Publisher 2002, FrontPage 2002, and Outlook 2002.

The Select Series provides students with clear, concise instruction supported by its new design, which includes bigger screen captures. Steps are now located in the margin for ease of use and readability. This instruction is further enhanced by graded exercises in the end-of-project material.

Another exciting update is that every project begins with a **Running Case from Selections, Inc.**, a department store that has opened shop online as e-Selections.com. Students are put in an e-commerce–based business environment so that they can relate what they are learning in Office XP to a real world situation. Everything is within a scenario that puts them in the department store where they perform tasks that relate to a particular division of the store or Web site.

About the Book

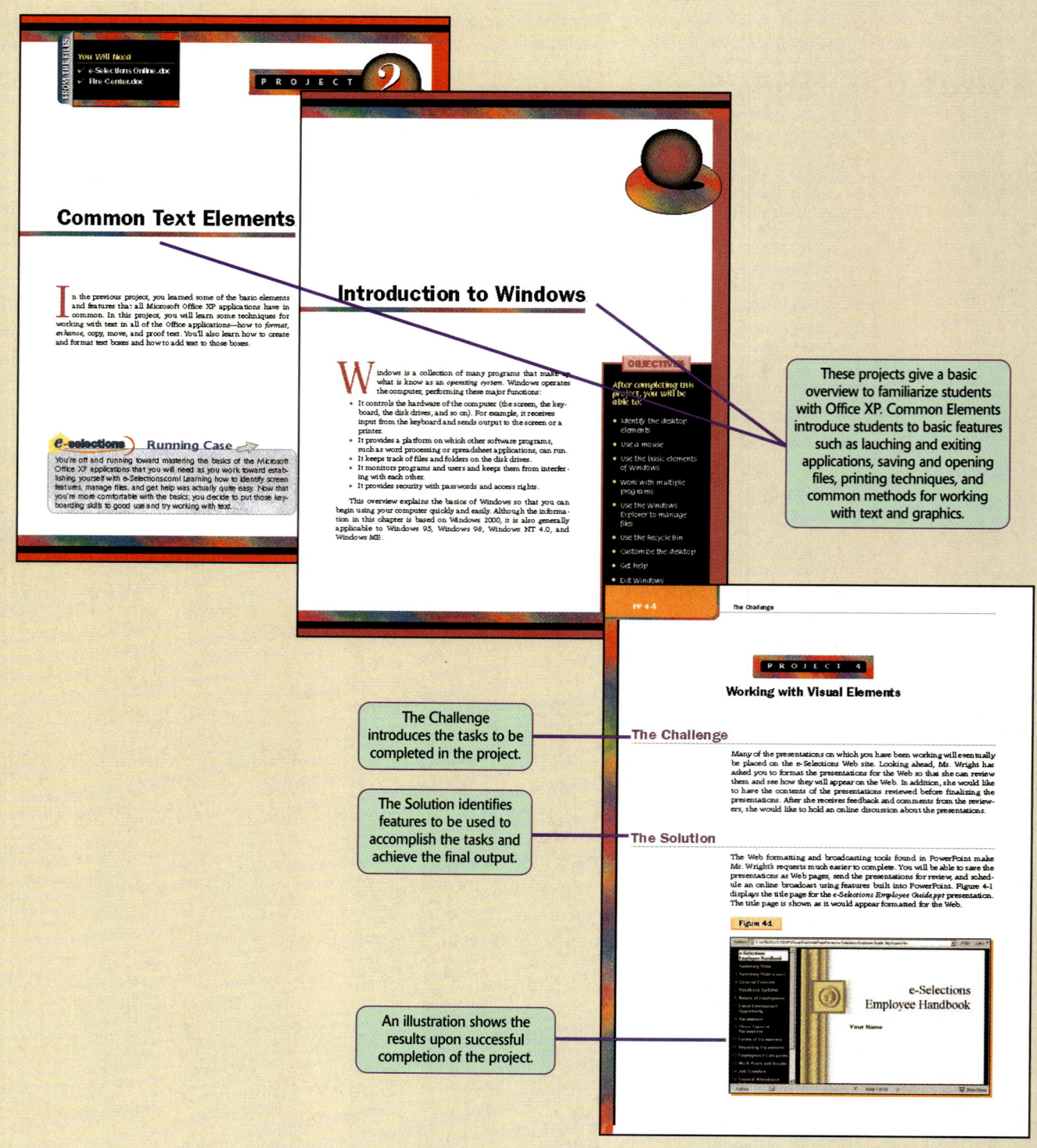

These projects give a basic overview to familiarize students with Office XP. Common Elements introduce students to basic features such as lauching and exiting applications, saving and opening files, printing techniques, and common methods for working with text and graphics.

The Challenge introduces the tasks to be completed in the project.

The Solution identifies features to be used to accomplish the tasks and achieve the final output.

An illustration shows the results upon successful completion of the project.

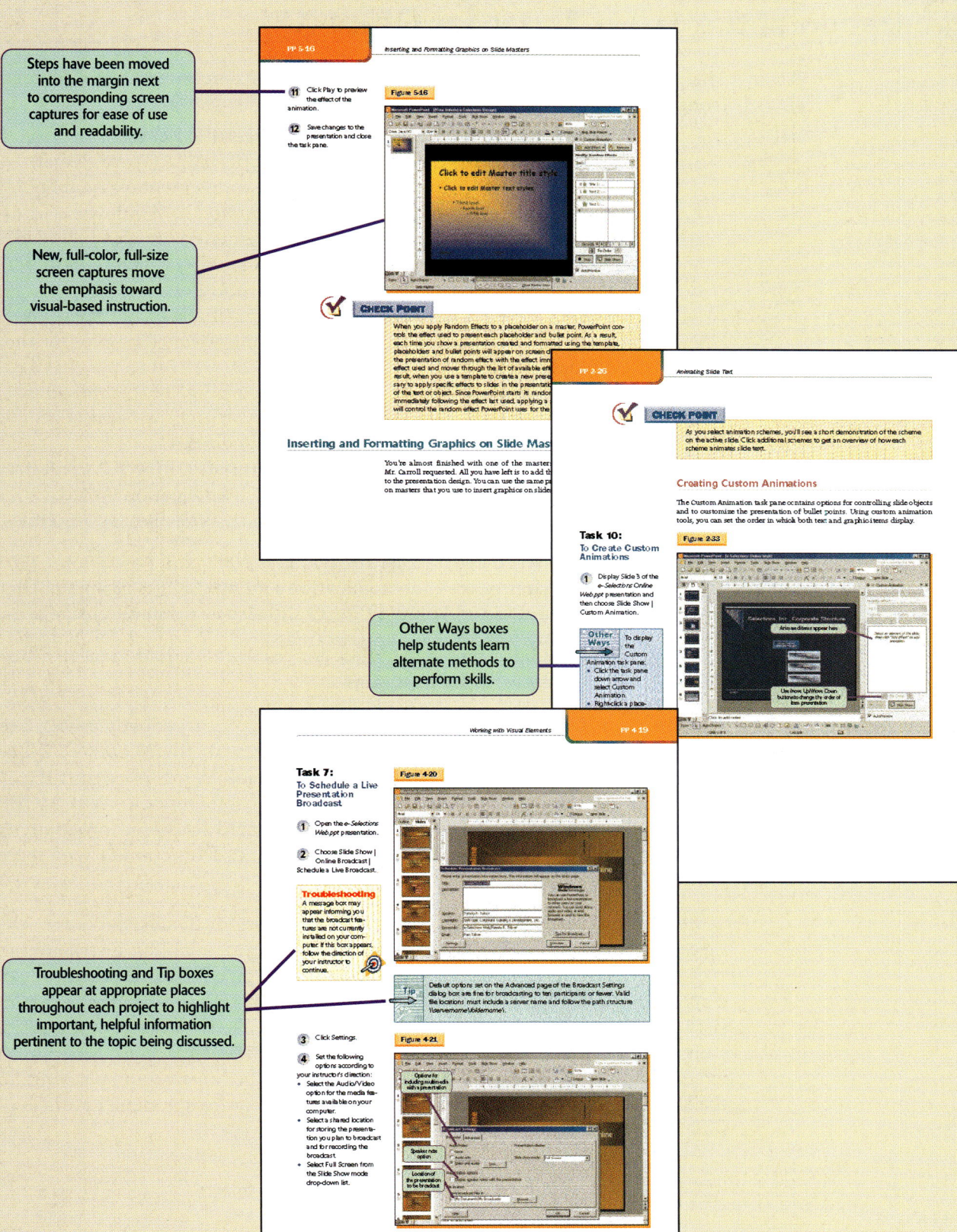

Organization of the Select Series for Office XP

The new Select Series for Office XP includes four combined Office XP texts from which to choose:

- **Microsoft Office XP Volume I** is MOUS certified at the Core level in each of the major applications in the Office suite (Word, Excel, Access, and PowerPoint). Four additional supplementary modules (Introduction to Internet Explorer, Introduction to Windows, Introduction to Outlook, and Common Elements) are also included. In addition, three integrated projects are included which integrate files and data among Word, Excel, Access, and PowerPoint.
- **Microsoft Office XP Volume II,** MOUS certified at the Expert level, picks up where Volume I leaves off, covering advanced topics for the individual applications.
- **Microsoft Office XP Brief** provides less coverage of the individual applications than Volume I (a total of four projects as opposed to six). The supplementary modules are also included.
- A new volume, **Getting Started with Microsoft Office XP,** contains the Introduction and first chapter from each application (Word, Excel, Access, and PowerPoint) plus the four supplementary modules.

Individual texts for Word 2002, Excel 2002, Access 2002, and PowerPoint 2002 provide complete coverage of each application and are MOUS certified. They are available in Volume I and Volume II texts and also as Comprehensive texts.

This series of books has been approved by Microsoft to be used in preparation for Microsoft Office User Specialist exams.

APPROVED COURSEWARE

The Microsoft Office User Specialist (MOUS) program is globally recognized as the standard for demonstrating desktop skills with the Microsoft Office suite of business productivity applications (Microsoft Word, Microsoft Excel, Microsoft PowerPoint, Microsoft Access, and Microsoft Outlook). With MOUS certification, thousands of people have demonstrated increased productivity and have proved their ability to utilize the advanced functionality of these Microsoft applications.

Customize the Select Series with Prentice Hall's Custom Binding program. The Select Series is part of the Custom Binding Program, enabling instructors to create their own texts by selecting projects from Office XP to suit the needs of a specific course. An instructor could, for example, create a custom text consisting of the specific projects that he or she would like to cover from the entire suite of products. The Select Series is part of PHit's Value Pack program in which multiple books can be shrink-wrapped together at substantial savings to the student. A value pack is ideal in courses that require complete coverage of multiple applications.

Instructor and Student Resources

Instructor's Resource CD-ROM

The **Instructor's Resource CD-ROM** that is available with the Select Office XP Series contains:

- Student data files
- Solutions to all exercises and problems
- PowerPoint lectures
- Instructor's manuals in Word format that enable the instructor to annotate portions of the instructor manual for distribution to the class
- A Windows-based test manager and the associated test bank in Word format

Companion Website www.prenhall.com/select

This text is accompanied by a companion Website at *www.prenhall.com/select*.

Features of this new site include the ability for you to customize your homepage with real-time news headlines, current events, exercises, an interactive study guide, student data files, and downloadable supplements. This site is designed to take learning Microsoft Office XP with the Select Series to the next level.

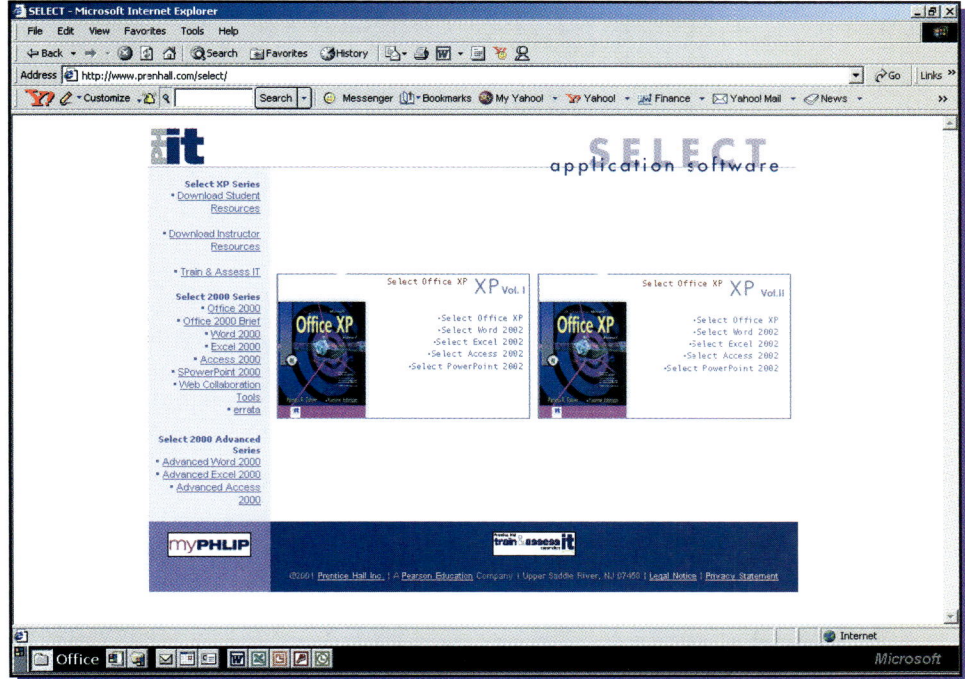

Now you have the freedom to personalize your own online course materials!
Prentice Hall provides the content and support you need to create and manage your own online course in WebCT, Blackboard, or Prentice Hall's own Course Compass. Choose "Standard" content to enhance the material from this text or "Premium" content, which provides you with even more lecture material, interactive exercises, and projects.

Training and Assessment   www.prenhall.com/phit

Prentice Hall offers Performance Based Training and Assessment in one product, Train&Assess IT. The Training component offers computer-based training that a student can use to preview, learn, and review Microsoft Office application skills. Web- or CD-ROM delivered, Train IT offers interactive, multimedia, computer-based training to augment classroom learning. Built-in prescriptive testing suggests a study path based not only on student test results but also on the specific textbook chosen for the course.

The Assessment component offers computer-based testing that shares the same user interface as Train IT and is used to evaluate a student's knowledge about specific topics in Word, Excel, Access, PowerPoint, Windows, Outlook, and the Internet. It does this in a task-oriented environment to demonstrate proficiency as well as comprehension of the topics by the students. More extensive than the testing in Train IT, Assess IT offers more administrative features for the instructor and additional questions for the student.

Assess IT also allows professors to test students out of a course, place students in appropriate courses, and evaluate skill sets.

CourseCompass   www.coursecompass.com

CourseCompass is a dynamic, interactive online course-management tool powered exclusively for Pearson Education by Blackboard. This exciting product allows you to teach market-leading Pearson Education content in an easy-to-use, customizable format.

BlackBoard   www.prenhall.com/blackboard

Prentice Hall's abundant online content, combined with Blackboard's popular tools and interface, result in robust Web-based courses that are easy to implement, manage, and use—taking your courses to new heights in student interaction and learning.

WebCT   www.prenhall.com/webct

Course-management tools within WebCT include page tracking, progress tracking, class and student management, gradebook, communication, calendar, reporting tools, and more. GOLD LEVEL CUSTOMER SUPPORT, available exclusively to adopters of Prentice Hall courses, is provided free-of-charge upon adoption and provides you with priority assistance, training discounts, and dedicated technical support.

Brief Table of Contents

Preface	**v**
Introducing Outlook 2002	**OU-1**
Project 1: **Setting up Outlook 2002**	**OU 1-1**
Project 2: **Organizing Outlook Contacts**	**OU 2-1**
Project 3: **Maintaining the Outlook Calendar**	**OU 3-1**
Project 4: **Corresponding Using Outlook Mail**	**OU 4-1**
Project 5: **Recording Tasks and Writing Notes**	**OU 5-1**
Project 6: **Managing Outlook Files, Folders, and the Journal**	**OU 6-1**
Project 7: **Integrating, Customizing, and Sharing Outlook Files**	**OU 7-1**
Project 8: **Using Outlook with the Internet**	**OU 8-1**
Glossary	**OU G-1**
Index	**OU I-1**

Table of Contents

Preface	**v**

Introducing Outlook 2002	**OU-1**
THE CHALLENGE	OU-2
THE SOLUTION	OU-2
THE SETUP	OU-2
Launching Outlook	**OU-3**
Task 1: To Launch Outlook	OU-3
Identifying Outlook Features	**OU-4**
Using the Outlook Bar	**OU-4**
Task 2: To Access Outlook Features	OU-5
Displaying the Folder List	**OU-9**
Task 3: To Use the Folder List	OU-9
Getting Help	**OU-10**
Task 4: To Ask a Question	OU-11
Task 5: To Use the Office Assistant	OU-13
Exiting Outlook	**OU-15**
Summary and Exercises	**OU-16**
SUMMARY	OU-16
KEY TERMS	OU-16
SKILLS	OU-16
STUDY QUESTIONS	OU-17
Multiple Choice	OU-17
Short Answer	OU-17
Fill in the Blank	OU-18
For Discussion	OU-18

Project 1 Setting up Outlook 2002	**OU 1-1**
THE CHALLENGE	OU 1-4
THE SOLUTION	OU 1-4
Customizing Outlook Today	**OU 1-4**
Task 1: To Customize Outlook Today	OU 1-5
Setting a Launch Feature	**OU 1-7**
Task 2: To Change the Default Feature Window	OU 1-7
Creating Folders	**OU 1-8**
Task 3: To Create a Personal Folder and Add it to the Outlook Bar	OU 1-9
Customizing the Outlook Bar	**OU 1-11**
Task 4: To Add an Outlook Bar Group	OU 1-12
Task 5: To Reposition Folders on the Outlook Bar	OU 1-13
Task 6: To Add a Shortcut to the Outlook Bar	OU 1-14
Task 7: To Change the Outlook Bar Shortcut Icons Size	OU 1-15
Customizing Toolbars and Menus	**OU 1-15**
Task 8: To Set Menu Options	OU 1-16
Task 9: To Add Buttons to Toolbars and Commands to Menus	OU 1-17
Setting Time Zones	**OU 1-19**
Task 10: To Change Time Zone Settings	OU 1-20
Task 11: To Add Time Zones	OU 1-21
Setting Options and Changing Views	**OU 1-22**
Task 12: To Change the View	OU 1-22
Task 13: To Resize Feature Panes	OU 1-25
Finding Items	**OU 1-26**
Task 14: To Find Outlook Items	OU 1-26
Summary and Exercises	**OU 1-28**
SUMMARY	OU 1-28
KEY TERMS	OU 1-29
SKILLS	OU 1-29
STUDY QUESTIONS	OU 1-29
Multiple Choice	OU 1-29
Short Answer	OU 1-30
Fill in the Blank	OU 1-30
Discussion	OU 1-30
GUIDED EXERCISES	OU 1-31
ON YOUR OWN	OU 1-33

Project 2 Organizing Outlook Contacts	**OU 2-1**
THE SETUP	OU 2-4
THE CHALLENGE	OU 2-4
THE STRATEGY	OU 2-4
Creating Contacts	**OU 2-5**
Task 1: To Create Contacts	OU 2-5

Opening, Editing, and Deleting Contacts — OU 2-9
- **Task 2:** To Open, Edit, and Delete Contacts — OU 2-9

Sorting and Finding Contacts — OU 2-10
- **Task 3:** To Sort Contacts Using Views — OU 2-10
- **Task 4:** To Apply Advanced Sort Techniques — OU 2-11
- **Task 5:** To Find Contacts — OU 2-14

Printing from the Contacts Folder — OU 2-15
- **Task 6:** To Print Contacts — OU 2-15

Flagging Contacts for Follow-Up — OU 2-17
- **Task 7:** To Flag Contacts for Follow-Up — OU 2-18

Creating Personal Distribution Lists — OU 2-19
- **Task 8:** To Create a Personal Distribution List — OU 2-19

Tracking Contacts Activities — OU 2-21
- **Task 9:** To Track Activities Involving Contacts — OU 2-21

Setting Contacts Options — OU 2-22
- **Task 10:** To Set Contacts Options — OU 2-22

Copying Contacts — OU 2-23
- **Task 11:** To Copy Contacts to Create New Contacts — OU 2-23

Summary and Exercises — OU 2-25
- SUMMARY — OU 2-25
- KEY TERMS — OU 2-25
- SKILLS — OU 2-25
- STUDY QUESTIONS — OU 2-26
    - Multiple Choice — OU 2-26
    - Short Answer — OU 2-27
    - Fill in the Blank — OU 2-27
    - Discussion — OU 2-27
- GUIDED EXERCISES — OU 2-28
- ON YOUR OWN — OU 2-31

Project 3 Maintaining the Outlook Calendar — OU 3-1

- THE CHALLENGE — OU 3-4
- THE SOLUTION — OU 3-4

Displaying and Navigating the Calendar Window — OU 3-4
- **Task 1:** To Display the Calendar Window — OU 3-5
- **Task 2:** To Use Calendar Navigation Tools — OU 3-7

Scheduling Appointments — OU 3-8
- **Task 3:** To Schedule Appointments in the Calendar — OU 3-9
- **Task 4:** To Set Appointment Reminders — OU 3-11
- **Task 5:** To Schedule and Label an All Day Event — OU 3-13
- **Task 6:** To Move, Copy, and Delete Appointments — OU 3-14

Scheduling Recurring Appointments — OU 3-16
- **Task 7:** To Schedule a Recurring Appointment — OU 3-16

Scheduling Meetings Involving Others — OU 3-18
- **Task 8:** To Invite Others to Meetings and Schedule Resources — OU 3-18

Editing Meeting Participants and Sending Updates — OU 3-21
- **Task 9:** To Edit the Meeting Participants and Send Updates — OU 3-21

Canceling a Meeting — OU 3-22
- **Task 10:** To Cancel a Meeting — OU 3-22

Printing the Calendar — OU 3-23
- **Task 11:** To Print Calendars and Appointments — OU 3-23

Customizing the Calendar — OU 3-25
- **Task 12:** To Set Calendar Options — OU 3-26
- **Task 13:** To Apply Conditional Formatting to Appointments — OU 3-28

Summary and Exercises — OU 3-30
- SUMMARY — OU 3-30
- KEY TERMS — OU 3-31
- SKILLS — OU 3-31
- STUDY QUESTIONS — OU 3-32
    - Multiple Choice — OU 3-32
    - Short Answer — OU 3-33
    - Fill in the Blank — OU 3-33
    - Discussion — OU 3-33
- GUIDED EXERCISES — OU 3-34
- ON YOUR OWN — OU 3-36

Project 4 Corresponding Using Outlook Mail — OU 4-1

- THE SETUP — OU 4-4
- THE CHALLENGE — OU 4-5
- THE SOLUTION — OU 4-5

Displaying the Inbox and Identifying Inbox Features — OU 4-5
- **Task 1:** To Display the Inbox and Identify Inbox Features — OU 4-6

Opening and Responding to Messages and Meeting Requests — OU 4-7
- **Task 2:** To Retrieve and Open E-Mail — OU 4-7
- **Task 3:** To Reply to and Forward Messages — OU 4-8
- **Task 4:** To Respond to Meeting Requests — OU 4-10
- **Task 5:** To Propose a New Meeting Time — OU 4-12

Saving Messages in Different File Formats — OU 4-14
- **Task 6:** To Save Messages — OU 4-14

Printing Inbox Items — OU 4-15
- **Task 7:** To Print Outlook E-Mail Messages — OU 4-15

Modifying Message Formats and Creating Signatures — OU 4-15
- **Task 8:** To Change Message Format Settings and Create a Signature — OU 4-16

Creating and Sending E-Mail Messages — OU 4-18
- **Task 9:** To Create an E-Mail Message — OU 4-19

Setting Message Tracking Options — OU 4-20
- **Task 10:** To Set Message Tracking Options and Send the Message — OU 4-21

Formatting Messages Using Stationery — OU 4-22
- **Task 11:** To Format a New Message Using Stationery — OU 4-22

Flagging Messages for Follow Up — OU 4-23
- **Task 12:** To Use Message Flagging Features — OU 4-24

Sorting and Searching for Messages — OU 4-25
- **Task 13:** To Sort and Find Messages — OU 4-25

Setting E-Mail Options — OU 4-26
- **Task 14:** To Set E-Mail Options — OU 4-27

Working with Mail Attachments — OU 4-29
- **Task 15:** To Attach, Open, and Save Files Using E-Mail — OU 4-29

Summary and Exercises — OU 4-32
- **SUMMARY** — OU 4-32
- **KEY TERMS** — OU 4-33
- **SKILLS** — OU 4-33
- **STUDY QUESTIONS** — OU 4-33
  - Multiple Choice — OU 4-33
  - Short Answer — OU 4-34
  - Fill in the Blank — OU 4-34
  - Discussion — OU 4-35
- **GUIDED EXERCISES** — OU 4-35
- **ON YOUR OWN** — OU 4-37

Project 5 Recording Tasks and Writing Notes — OU 5-1
- **THE CHALLENGE** — OU 5-4
- **THE SOLUTION** — OU 5-4
- **THE SETUP** — OU 5-4

Creating Task Lists — OU 5-5
- **Task 1:** To Record Tasks and Create Tasks Lists — OU 5-5

Updating and Modifying Tasks — OU 5-7
- **Task 2:** To Edit and Update Tasks — OU 5-7

Changing the Tasks View and Organizing Tasks — OU 5-8
- **Task 3:** To Change Tasks View and Organize Tasks — OU 5-9

Creating and Updating Recurring Tasks — OU 5-9
- **Task 4:** To Create and Update Recurring Tasks — OU 5-10

Assigning Tasks and Sending Task Requests — OU 5-11
- **Task 5:** To Assign and Send a Task Request — OU 5-12
- **Task 6:** To Accept, Decline, or Delegate Tasks — OU 5-13
- **Task 7:** To Send Task Updates — OU 5-14

Tracking Assigned Tasks — OU 5-15
- **Task 8:** To Track Assigned Tasks — OU 5-15

Printing Tasks — OU 5-16
- **Task 9:** To Print Task Items — OU 5-16

Setting Task Options — OU 5-17
- **Task 10:** To Set Task Options — OU 5-18

Creating and Editing Notes — OU 5-19
- **Task 11:** To Create Electronic Notes — OU 5-19

Viewing, Organizing, and Reading Notes — OU 5-20
- **Task 12:** To View, Open, and Edit Electronic Notes — OU 5-21

Assigning Notes to Contacts — OU 5-21
- **Task 13:** To Assign Electronic Notes to Contacts — OU 5-21

Setting Notes Options — OU 5-23
- **Task 14:** To Set Notes Options — OU 5-23

Saving, Forwarding, and Printing Notes — OU 5-24
- **Task 15:** To Share Electronic Notes — OU 5-24

Summary and Exercises	OU 5-27	Summary and Exercises	OU 6-32
SUMMARY	OU 5-27	SUMMARY	OU 6-32
KEY TERMS	OU 5-28	KEY TERMS	OU 6-33
SKILLS	OU 5-28	SKILLS	OU 6-33
STUDY QUESTIONS	OU 5-28	STUDY QUESTIONS	OU 6-33
Multiple Choice	OU 5-28	Multiple Choice	OU 6-33
Short Answer	OU 5-29	Short Answer	OU 6-34
Fill in the Blank	OU 5-29	Fill in the Blank	OU 6-34
Discussion	OU 5-29	Discussion	OU 6-35
GUIDED EXERCISES	OU 5-30	GUIDED EXERCISES	OU 6-35
ON YOUR OWN	OU 5-33	ON YOUR OWN	OU 6-37

Project 6 Managing Outlook Files, Folders, and the Journal   OU 6-1

THE SETUP	OU 6-4
THE CHALLENGE	OU 6-4
THE SOLUTION	OU 6-4

Creating and Assigning Categories to Items   OU 6-4

Task 1: To Create New Categories and Assign Categories to Items   OU 6-5
Task 2: To Modify the Master Category List   OU 6-8

Sorting Items by Category   OU 6-9

Task 3: To Sort and Find Items by Category   OU 6-9

Customizing Outlook Views   OU 6-11

Task 4: To Customize Outlook Folder Views   OU 6-12

Creating Rules to Organize Outlook Items   OU 6-14

Task 5: To Color Code Messages and Move Items to Folders   OU 6-15
Task 6: To Create an Inbox Rule Using the Rules Wizard   OU 6-19

Creating Associations between Outlook Items and Contacts   OU 6-23

Task 7: To Link Outlook Items Manually   OU 6-23

Using the Journal   OU 6-24

Task 8: To Turn On and Set Options to Track Journal Activities   OU 6-25
Task 9: To Record Journal Entries   OU 6-26
Task 10: To Assign Contacts to Existing Journal Entries   OU 6-28
Task 11: To Modify Journal Entry Types   OU 6-29

Archiving Items   OU 6-29

Task 12: To Archive Files   OU 6-30
Task 13: To Restore Archived Items   OU 6-31

Project 7 Integrating, Customizing, and Sharing Outlook Files   OU 7-1

THE SETUP	OU 7-4
THE CHALLENGE	OU 7-4
THE SOLUTION	OU 7-5

Sending, Exporting, and Importing Contacts   OU 7-5

Task 1: To E-Mail and Export Contacts   OU 7-6
Task 2: To Export Contacts to a File   OU 7-7
Task 3: To Save vCards as Contacts   OU 7-9
Task 4: To Import Contacts from a File   OU 7-11
Task 5: To Create a Contact from an E-Mail Message   OU 7-12

Sharing Outlook Folders   OU 7-13

Task 6: To Assign Delegates and Set Delegate Permissions   OU 7-14
Task 7: To Set Folder Permissions   OU 7-16

Opening Folders Belonging to Other Users   OU 7-17

Task 8: To Open Another User's Folder   OU 7-18

Creating Office XP Files from Outlook   OU 7-19

Task 9: To Create a New PowerPoint File from Outlook   OU 7-19
Task 10: To Create a New Letter to an Outlook Contact   OU 7-21

Creating E-Mail Stationery   OU 7-24

Task 11: To Create Custom E-Mail Stationery   OU 7-24

Creating Custom Outlook Forms   OU 7-27

Task 12: To Create a Custom Message Form   OU 7-27
Task 13: To Use a Custom Form   OU 7-30

Summary and Exercises   OU 7-32

SUMMARY	OU 7-32
KEY TERMS	OU 7-32

SKILLS	OU 7-33
STUDY QUESTIONS	OU 7-33
Multiple Choice	OU 7-33
Short Answer	OU 7-34
Fill in the Blank	OU 7-34
Discussion	OU 7-34
GUIDED EXERCISES	OU 7-35
ON YOUR OWN	OU 7-38

Project 8 Using Outlook with the Internet — OU 8-1

THE SETUP	OU 8-4
THE CHALLENGE	OU 8-4
THE SOLUTION	OU 8-5

Saving a Calendar as a Web Page — OU 8-5

Task 1: To Save a Calendar as a Web Page	OU 8-6

Sharing Free and Busy Schedules — OU 8-8

Task 2: To Set Free/Busy Options	OU 8-9
Task 3: To Join the Internet Free/Busy Service and Publish a Schedule	OU 8-10
Task 4: To Authorize Access to Your Schedule	OU 8-12
Task 5: To View a Free/Busy Schedule	OU 8-14

Assigning Folder Home Pages — OU 8-15

Task 6: To Assign a Home Page to the Notes Folder	OU 8-16

Sending and Receiving Information Using a Newsreader — OU 8-17

Task 7: To Subscribe to a Newsgroup	OU 8-18
Task 8: To Open and Read Newsgroup Messages	OU 8-20

Scheduling NetMeetings — OU 8-20

Task 9: To Schedule an Online Meeting Using NetMeetings	OU 8-21

Using Outlook Instant Messaging — OU 8-21

Task 10: To Enable Instant Messaging in Outlook	OU 8-22
Task 11: To Activate Instant Messaging and Send a Message	OU 8-23

Using Remote Mail — OU 8-25

Task 12: To Create and Specify an Offline Folder	OU 8-27
Task 13: To Synchronize All Folders	OU 8-28
Task 14: To Switch Between Online and Offline Mode	OU 8-29

Setting Security — OU 8-29

Task 15: To Modify Security Zone Settings	OU 8-30

Obtaining a Digital ID — OU 8-32

Task 16: To Obtain a Digital ID	OU 8-32

Digitally Signing or Encrypting Messages — OU 8-33

Task 17: To Send Secure E-Mail	OU 8-33

Summary and Exercises — OU 8-35

SUMMARY	OU 8-35
KEY TERMS	OU 8-36
SKILLS	OU 8-36
STUDY QUESTIONS	OU 8-36
Multiple Choice	OU 8-36
Short Answer	OU 8-37
Fill in the Blank	OU 8-38
Discussion	OU 8-38

Glossary — OU G-1

Index — OU I-1

Introducing Outlook 2002

Microsoft Outlook 2002, a personal desktop organizer, is installed as an integral part of Microsoft Office XP. The features in Outlook 2002 help you track appointments, send and receive e-mail messages, maintain a list of To Do tasks, monitor computer activities, and instantly update business and personal contacts.

OBJECTIVES

After completing this project, you will be able to:

- Launch Outlook
- Identify Outlook features
- Use the Outlook Bar
- Display the folder list
- Get help
- Exit Outlook

e-selections Running Case

As an employee of e-Selections, a division of Selections, Inc., you will be sending and receiving e-mail, scheduling appointments and meetings, and keeping track of clients and Selections, Inc., personnel. The e-Selections division uses Outlook 2002 as its primary desktop organizer. It is time for you to learn the basics about each Outlook feature.

Introducing Outlook 2002

The Challenge

e-Selections employees use Outlook to communicate information about meetings, record updates to client information, and send electronic copies of documents; almost everything that requires your attention can be monitored with Outlook. It is vital that you know the basics of working with Outlook to help you keep abreast of what is going on in the division.

The Solution

Ms. Amber Wright, e-Administration Manager, has asked Ms. Elisa Sandoval, Selections, Inc., Corporate Trainer, to spend an hour with you, introducing you to the Outlook navigation tools and features you will need to use frequently. The focus of the session will provide you with an overview[md]just the basics for now. You will return for training on individual features as both time and need require.

The Setup

Options set in other Office XP applications rarely affect the way Outlook appears when you launch it. As a result, the features displayed in the Outlook window may vary, depending on the setup in the lab, computer classroom, or office you are using. Figures shown in this book are based on the default settings that appear with a typical Outlook 2002 installation. Settings on your computer may be different from those shown in the figures in this book. Table 0-1 identifies the settings that are used to get you started in Outlook. When these settings are active, your screen will appear as shown in Figure 0-1. As you move through the different Outlook projects, you will customize settings and folders along the way.

Introducing Outlook 2002

Table 0-1	Outlook Default Settings
Default Feature	**Setting**
Launch Folder	Click the Inbox icon on the Outlook Bar to switch to Inbox.
Office Assistant	The Office Assistant is hidden. Right-click the Office Assistant and select Hide.
Toolbars	Only the Standard toolbar is active. Choose View	Toolbars	Standard to display the toolbar.
Outlook Bar	The Outlook Bar appears down the left side of the window. Choose View	Outlook Bar to display the bar.
Preview Pane	The Preview Pane appears at the bottom of the Inbox window. Choose View	Preview Pane to display the pane.
Folder List	The Folder List is hidden. Choose View	Folder List to hide the list.

Launching Outlook

Tip In Windows XP, you can launch Outlook by double-clicking the desktop icon or by choosing **Start | E-Mail (Microsoft Outlook)** or by choosing **Start | All Programs | Microsoft Outlook**.

Launch Outlook using the same techniques you use to launch other applications. The typical installation of Microsoft Outlook 2002 creates a desktop shortcut to Outlook for easy access. There are three ways to launch Outlook:

- Double-click the Microsoft Outlook shortcut icon on the Desktop.
- Click the Launch Microsoft Outlook icon on the Quick Launch toolbar.
- Choose **Start | Programs | Microsoft Outlook**.

Task 1:
To Launch Outlook

1. Double-click the Microsoft Outlook shortcut icon on the desktop.

2. Click the Maximize button on the Outlook title bar to maximize the application window.

Tip Because of installation and customization differences, the Outlook window on your computer may vary from the one pictured here.

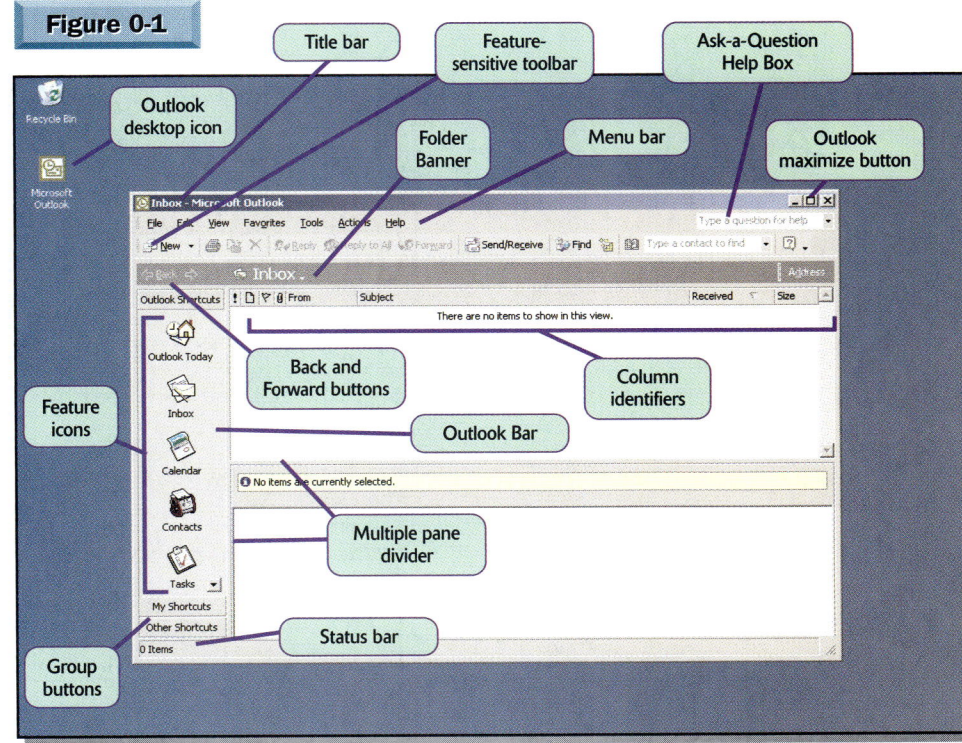

Figure 0-1

Identifying Outlook Features

Each Outlook feature—Calendar, Contacts, Tasks, and so forth—is designed to help you organize different types of information. Outlook stores each type of feature in a separate folder. By leaving Outlook open as you work in other applications, it becomes an effective reference and tool for accomplishing tasks in other Office XP applications. Table 0-2 identifies Outlook navigation items and how to use them.

Table 0-2	Outlook Navigation Features
Use	**To**
Outlook Bar	Access Outlook features by clicking their associated shortcut icons.
Back button	Display the previously viewed feature or item.
Forward button	Return to a feature or item after clicking the Back button.

Using the Outlook Bar

The Outlook Bar organizes Outlook features in folders and places the folders into three different shortcut groups: Outlook Shortcuts, My Shortcuts, and Other Shortcuts. These group names appear on the Outlook Bar as buttons. When you click a group button, icons representing shortcuts to different Outlook features within the group appear. When you click one of the icons, the folder containing items for the selected feature opens, and the Outlook window changes to display information appropriate to the feature.

Table 0-3 identifies folders and features available in the Outlook Shortcuts group and how to use them.

Table 0-3	Folders in the Outlook Shortcuts Group
Folder	**Contents**
Outlook Today	Preview a summary of your appointments and tasks and keep track of the number of new e-mail messages on the same screen.
Inbox	Store e-mail messages you receive.
Calendar	Schedule appointments and meetings.
Contacts	Record business and personal contacts on a Rolodex™-type file for easy access.
Tasks	Record things to do, prioritize the list, and check tasks off as they are completed.
Notes	Store notes during phone conversations and meetings on electronic sticky notes.
Deleted Items	Retrieve "thrown out" items from the wastebasket as long as it has not been emptied.

Introducing Outlook 2002

OU-5

Table 0-4 identifies folders and features available in My Shortcuts group and how to use them.

Table 0-4	My Shortcuts Group
Folder	**Contents**
Drafts	Save items you have not finished yet.
Outbox	Store items you create offline or items not sent yet.
Sent Items	Keep copies of items you have previously sent.
Journal	Monitor computer activities as they happen and create a timeline of events for projects.
Outlook Update	Connect to Microsoft's Web site to update your Outlook installation.

Task 2:
To Access Outlook Features

1. Click the **My Shortcuts** group button at the bottom of the Outlook Bar to display folders in the group.

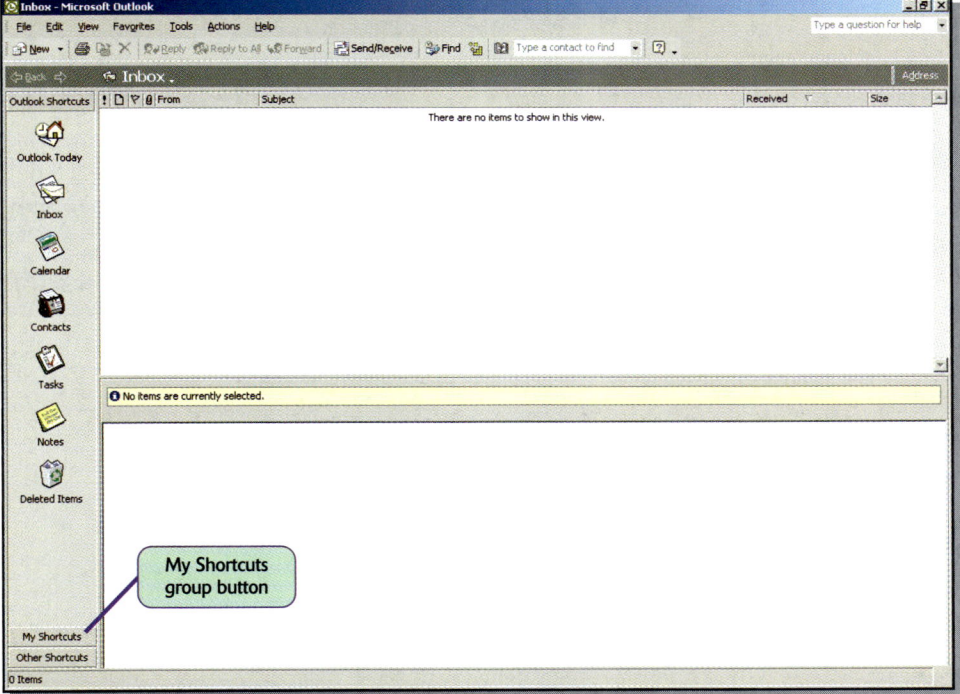

Figure 0-2

Using the Outlook Bar

2 Click the **Drafts** Drafts icon to open the folder and change the folder banner.

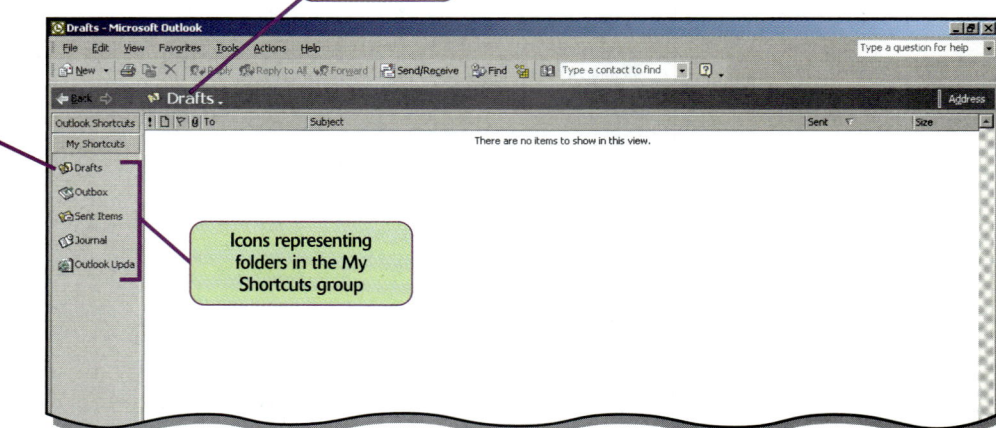

Figure 0-3

- Folder Banner changes to *Drafts*
- Drafts icon
- Icons representing folders in the My Shortcuts group

Tip The folder banner changes only when you click a different icon on the Outlook Bar to open a different folder rather than when you click a different group button.

3 Click the **Other Shortcuts** group button at the bottom of the Outlook Bar and review the Outlook Bar icons contained in the group.

4 Click the **Outlook Shortcuts** group button on the Outlook Bar to display shortcuts to main Outlook features and click the Restore  button to restore the window to its original size.

Figure 0-4

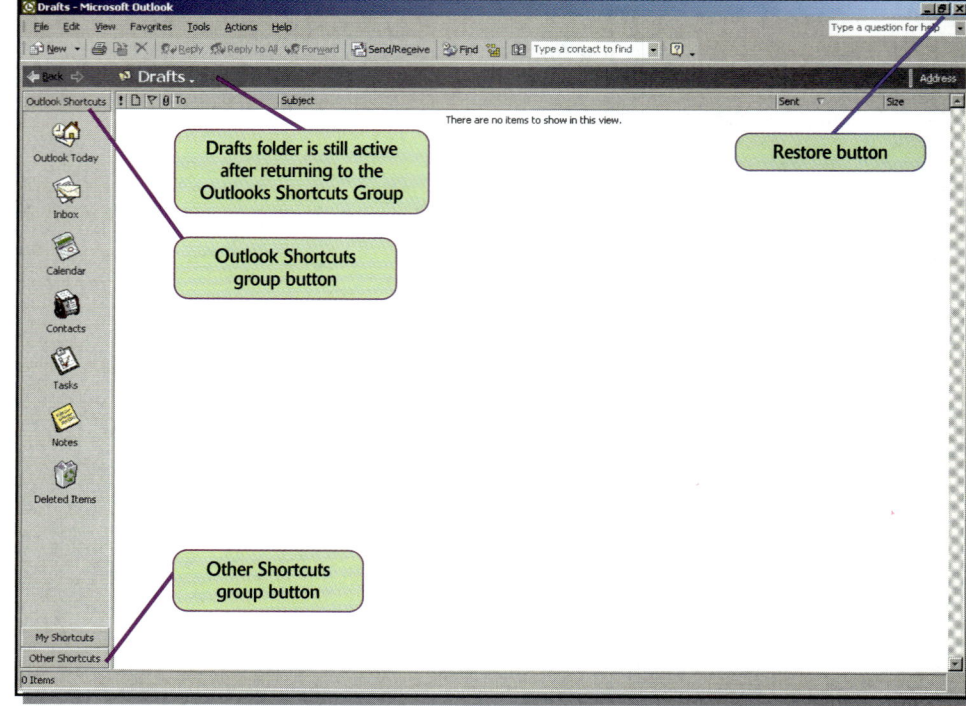

- Drafts folder is still active after returning to the Outlooks Shortcuts Group
- Restore button
- Outlook Shortcuts group button
- Other Shortcuts group button

5 Click the **Scroll Down** ▼ button at the bottom of the Outlook Bar repeatedly to see icons that are hidden and until the button disappears.

> **Troubleshooting**
> If If no Scroll Down button appears on your Outlook Bar, resize the Outlook application window by dragging the lower right corner of the window diagonally to make it smaller. Continue to reduce the size of the Outlook application window until you see the scroll button in the Outlook Bar.

Figure O-5

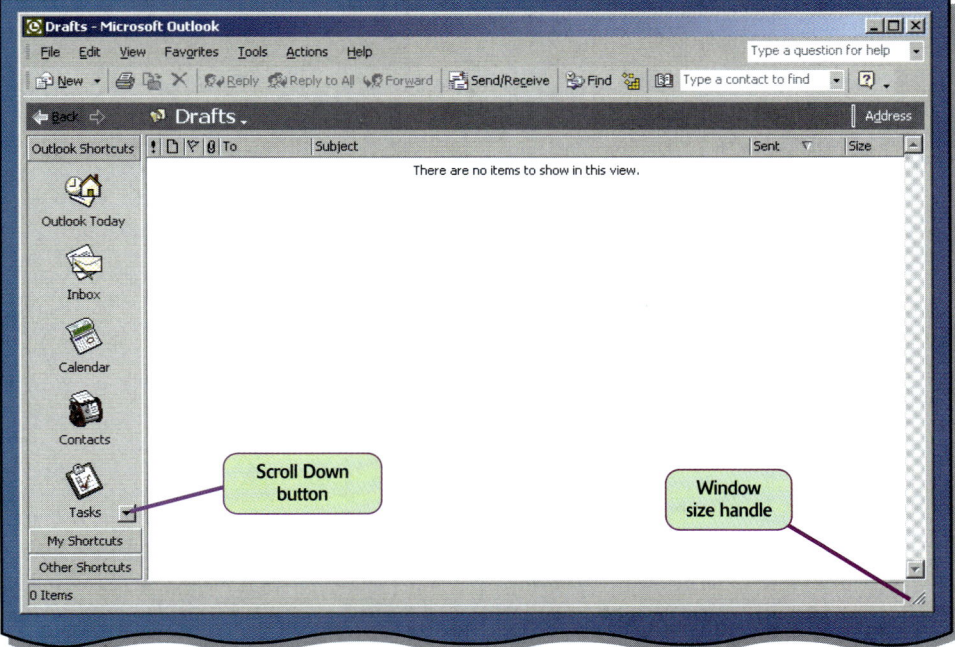

Tip Notice that the Scroll Down button disappears from the bottom of the Outlook Bar when the last icon is displayed. In addition, a Scroll Up button appears at the top of the Outlook Bar, indicating that additional icons are hidden at the top of the bar.

6 Click the **Scroll Up** ▲ button until the Calendar shortcut appears and the Scroll Up button disappears.

Figure O-6

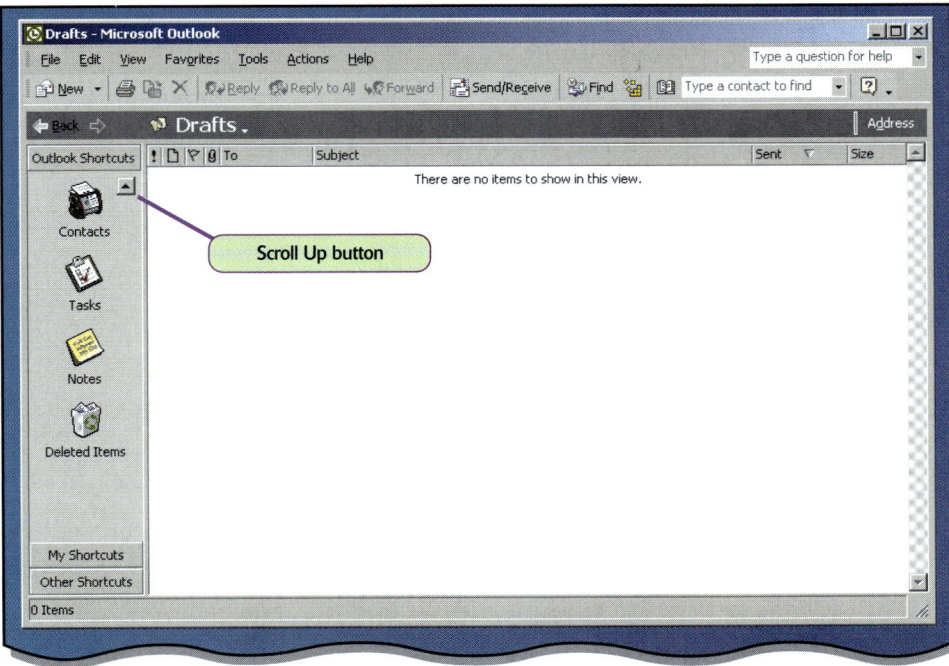

Using the Outlook Bar

7 Click the **Calendar** icon on the Outlook Bar to open the Calendar folder and review Calendar screen features.

8 Click the **Tasks** icon in the Outlook Bar to open the Tasks folder and then click the **Back** button on the banner bar above the Outlook Bar to redisplay the Calendar folder.

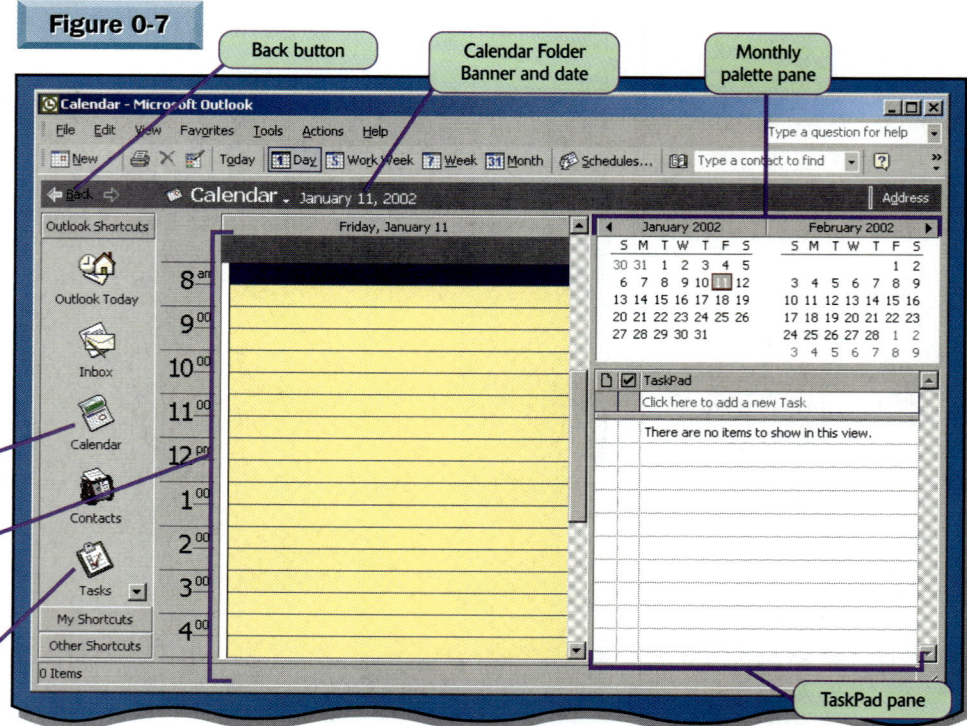

Figure O-7
- Back button
- Calendar Folder Banner and date
- Monthly palette pane
- Calendar icon
- Daily palette pane
- Tasks icon
- TaskPad pane

Troubleshooting The Back button is available only after you have clicked other icons on the Outlook Bar; the Next button is available only after you have clicked the Back button.

9 Click the **Outlook Today** icon on the Outlook Bar to open the Outlook Today folder.

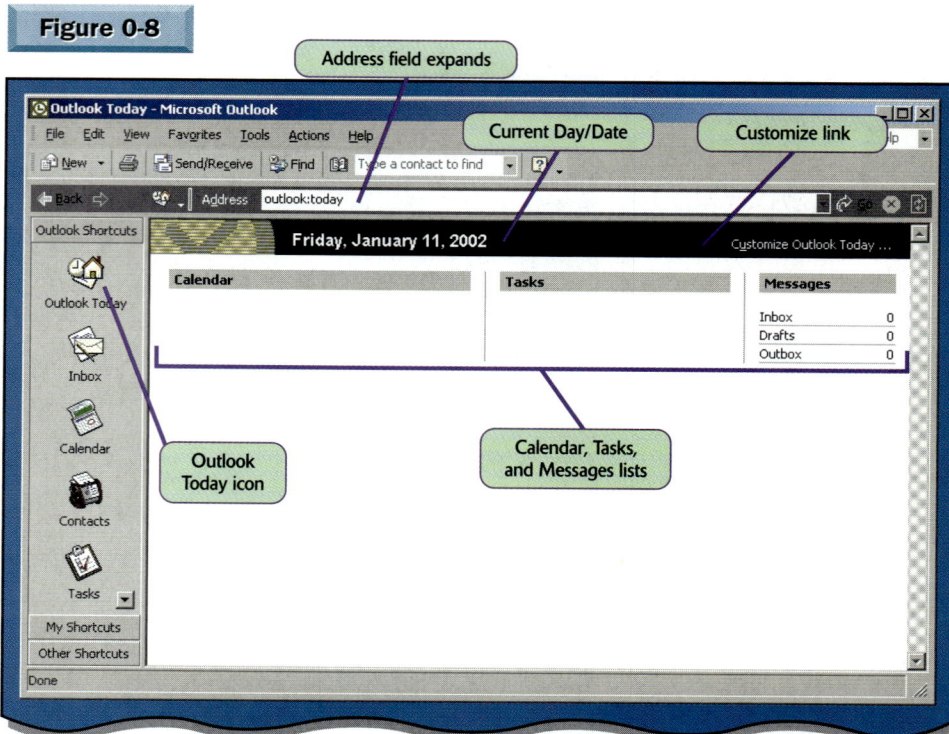

Figure O-8
- Address field expands
- Current Day/Date
- Customize link
- Outlook Today icon
- Calendar, Tasks, and Messages lists

Displaying the Folder List

Outlook items—mail messages, calendar appointments, tasks, and so forth—are stored in separate Outlook folders. Each of the main Outlook folders is represented by an icon on the Outlook Bar, allowing you to efficiently display folder contents. In addition to the icons found on the Outlook Bar, you can display the Folder List to access folders.

Task 3:
To Use the Folder List

1 Display Outlook Today, if necessary, and click the down arrow on the Outlook Today folder banner.

2 Click the **Pushpin**  to anchor the folder list in a separate pane.

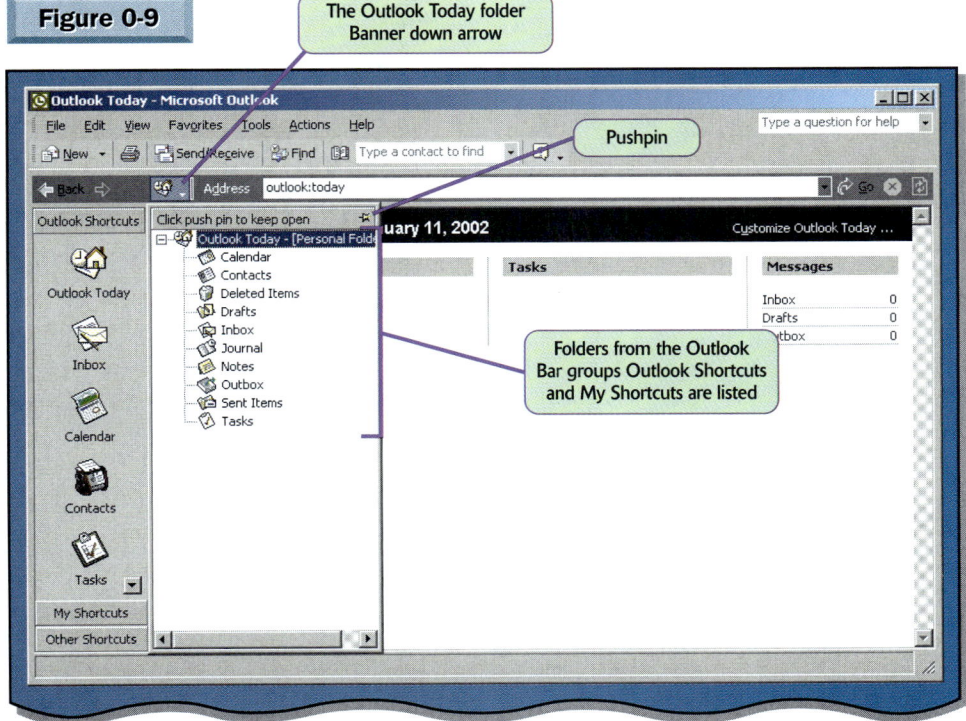

Figure O-9

Tip If the Folder List pane is too narrow to show complete folder names, drag the right border of the pane to the right.

3 Click the **Folder List Close X** button to close the folder list.

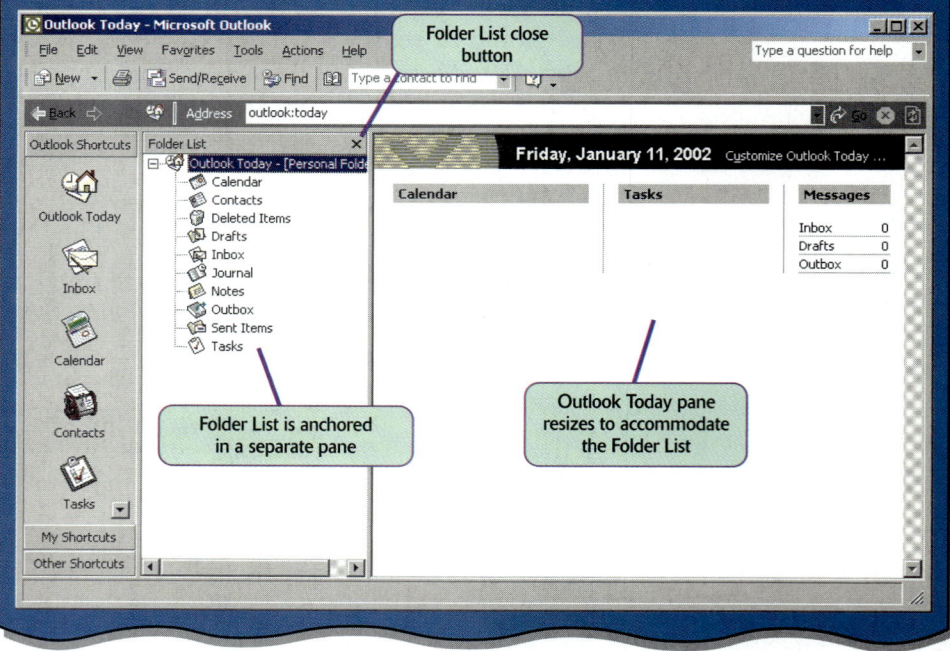

Figure O-10

Getting Help

In the Windows section, you learned how to use Windows Help and how to locate information about specific topics. Outlook comes equipped with a variety of help features that allow you to get help right on your computer as you work.

Tip

As you work with dialog boxes in different Windows applications, you will often see a question mark button in the upper right corner of a dialog box title bar. This button provides access to context-sensitive help about features and options contained in the dialog box. Just click the question mark button, point to the item or option you want to know more about, and click. Information about that item will be displayed.

Introducing Outlook 2002 OU-11

WEB TIP

If you are connected to the Internet, you can access one of several Web sites maintained by Microsoft to provide up-to-the-minute help online. The Web provides information directly from Microsoft support team members as well as information and helpful hints from other Office users. To access the Microsoft Web site directly from Outlook, choose **Help | Office on the Web**. Your default Web browser launches and displays the Microsoft Office Update page.

Asking Questions

A new *Ask a Question* tool has been added to the right end of the menu bar in all Office XP applications, including Outlook 2002. Using the Ask a Question text box, you can type a question and receive a list of possible topics related to answering the question. The questions you type in the Ask a Question text box should be related to the application that is active at the time you ask the question. For example, if Outlook is the application you are using, then the question you ask should relate to Outlook rather than to Word, Excel, or some other application. While there appears to be no limit to the length of the question you ask, the Ask a Question text box can actually hold a maximum of 256 characters. To make searching for help more efficient, short questions are preferred.

Task 4:
To Ask a Question

1 Click the **Ask a Question** text box on the menu bar.

2 Type **How do I display the Office Assistant?**, press Enter to display a list of help topics, and click **Display tips and messages through the Office Assistant**.

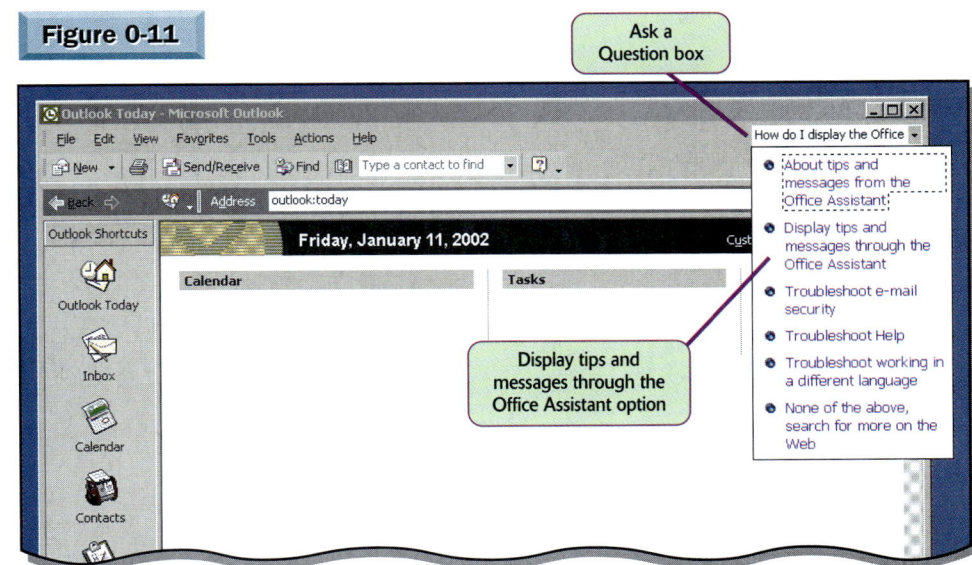

Figure O-11

Troubleshooting Because the Help files are updated frequently, the list you see when you search for help may be different from the list shown here.

3 Click the Show button on the Help window toolbar, if necessary, to expand the Help window.

4 Click the Help pane Close button. The Help pane closes and the Outlook window repositions on screen.

> **Tip** After you click the Show button to expand the Help window, the button appears as a Hide button on the Help window toolbar.

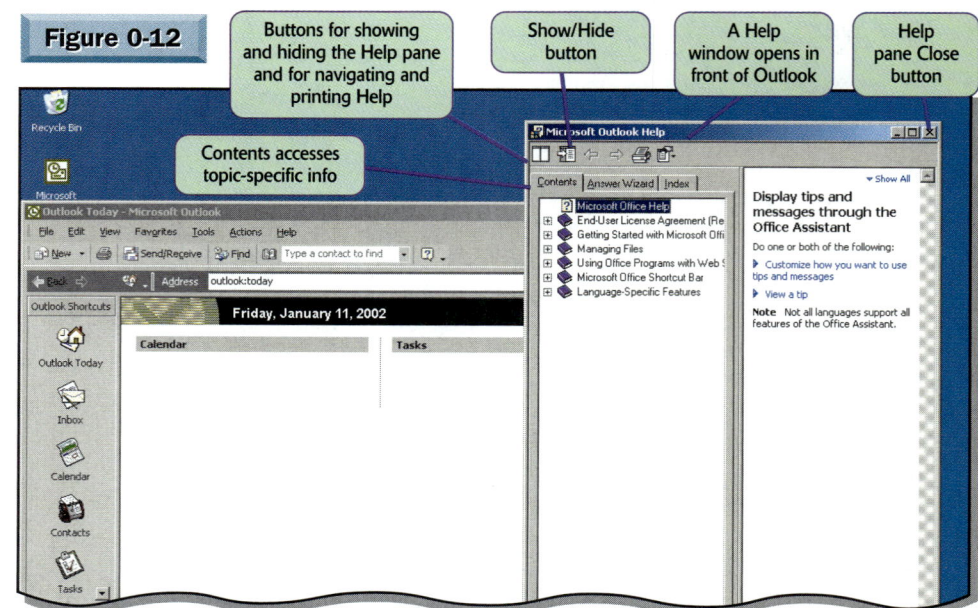

Figure O-12

- Buttons for showing and hiding the Help pane and for navigating and printing Help
- Show/Hide button
- A Help window opens in front of Outlook
- Help pane Close button
- Contents accesses topic-specific info

> **Tip** When you expand the Help window, you will notice three tabs that you can use to access different Help features. The *Answer Wizard* enables you to search for topics related to the question you type and the *Index* displays an alphabetic list of topics contained in Help.

CHECK POINT

Having trouble finding your way around Help? You are not alone. Help is a valuable tool, but as you work with Help, you will discover that the format of information displayed after you select a topic varies. Here are some of the formats you will see in the Help window and what they represent:

- A list of step-by-step instructions for performing a task
- Green words that provide a definition when you click them
- Blue arrows ▶ that expand a topic to provide a list of subtopics or step-by-step instructions when you click them

Using the Office Assistant

The Office Assistant is a help feature that is growing in popularity. The Office Assistant is easy to use, is personably animated, and provides a focused list of help topics related to questions you "ask."

Introducing Outlook 2002   OU-13

If the Assistant was displayed the last time one of the Office applications was used, it will appear onscreen when you launch Outlook. When closed, the Assistant waits on the Standard toolbar and appears when you call it to look up information about topics for which you need help. After you start the Office Assistant in one application, it remains onscreen until you close it—even when you open another Office application. However, if Outlook is the active application when you ask the Office Assistant a question, the list of topics the Office Assistant displays relates to Outlook.

Task 5:
To Use the Office Assistant

Figure 0-13

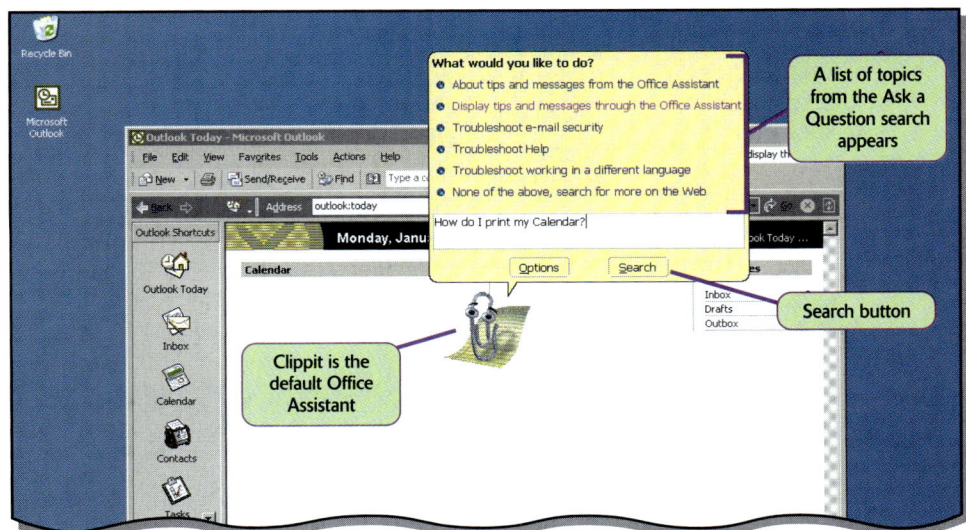

1 Choose **Help | Show the Office Assistant**, and then click the Office Assistant.

2 Type **How do I print my Calendar?** and click **Search** to start the search. The Office Assistant takes notes as you type.

 As you type a question in the Office Assistant text box, it also appears in the Ask a Question text box on the menu bar.

Other Ways
To display the Office Assistant:
- Click the **Microsoft Outlook Help** [?] button on the Outlook toolbar.

 The Office Assistant dialog box opens in different shapes and sizes, depending on how it was last used. In addition, the topics listed reflect the results of your last search, regardless of which Outlook Help feature you used. If you have conducted no searches for information, no listings will appear in the Office Assistant list until you conduct your first search.

③ Click **Print a calendar** to display help about printing.

Figure 0-14

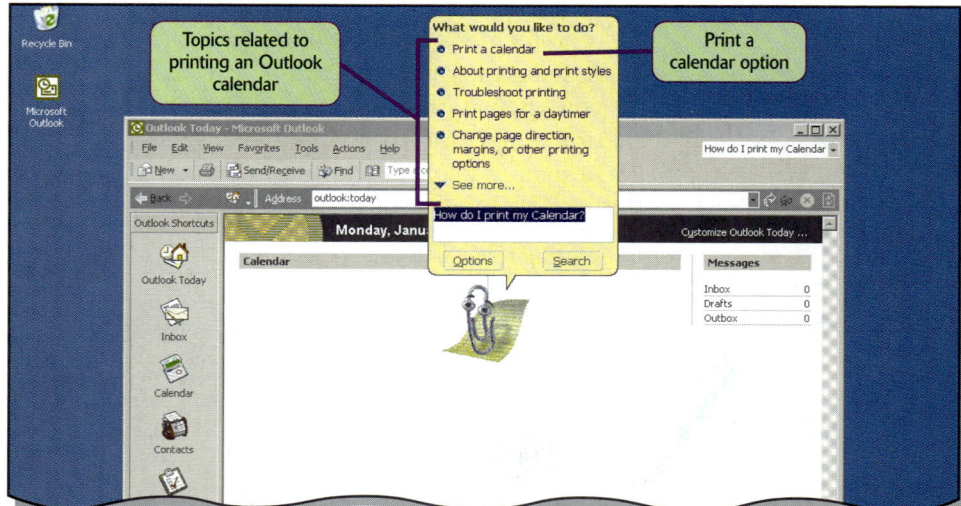

Topics related to printing an Outlook calendar

Print a calendar option

Troubleshooting The list of related help topics may vary, depending on the Microsoft programs you have installed and the Outlook setup on your computer. As a result, the list of topics you see may be different from the topics shown in Figure 0-14.

④ Close the Help window, right-click the Office Assistant to display a shortcut menu, and select **Hide** to close the Office Assistant.

 To hide the Office Assistant:
- Choose **Help | Hide the Office Assistant**.

Tip The Help window is sized as it was when you last closed it. If it was expanded on closing, it opens expanded.

Figure 0-15

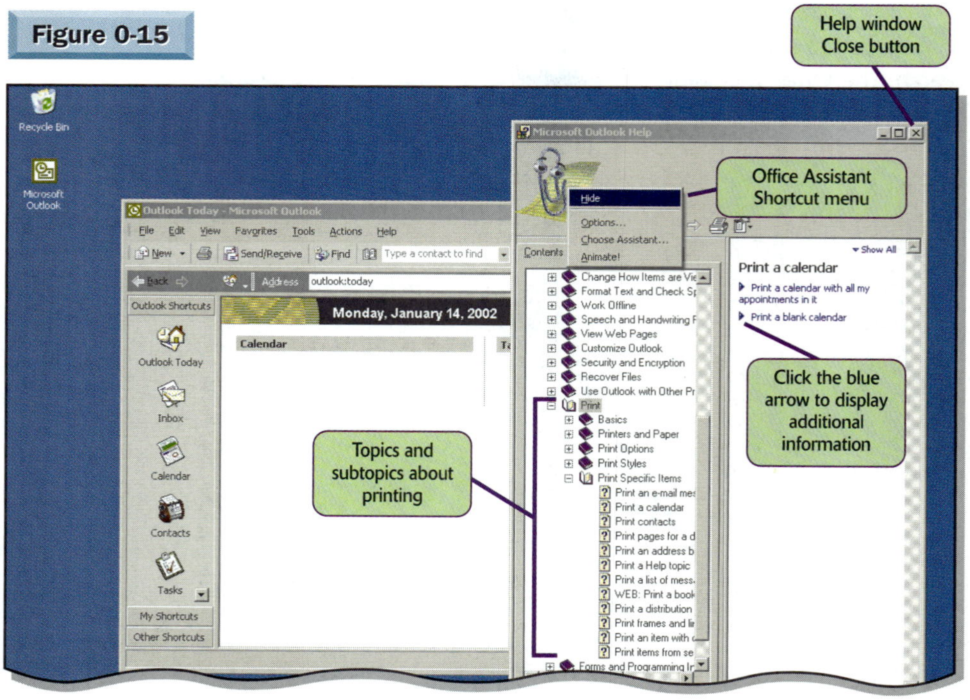

Help window Close button

Office Assistant Shortcut menu

Topics and subtopics about printing

Click the blue arrow to display additional information

 Troubleshooting After you choose Hide the Office Assistant several times, a dialog box will appear asking if you want to deactivate the Office Assistant. Read the options carefully and choose the option that best represents how you want to use the Office Assistant.

Exiting Outlook

Because Outlook is an application, you exit Outlook using the same techniques used to exit for exiting other applications. Use one of the following techniques to exit Outlook:

- Click the application Close button.
- Choose **File** | **Exit**.
- Double-click the application control menu icon that appears at the left end of the title bar.
- Press [Alt] + [F4].
- Right-click the Outlook feature button on the Windows taskbar and choose **Close**.

If you have messages in the Outbox when you close Outlook, a message window appears. Read the message carefully and take the appropriate action:

- Choose **Yes** to log on and deliver the messages.
- Choose **No** to close Outlook without delivering messages.
- Wait until the counter completes the countdown and closes Outlook automatically.

CHECK POINT

Outlook and other Office XP applications contain two features designed to help you restore the application should it hang up during use or fail to launch properly. Each of these features is described in Table 0-5.

Table 0-5	Recovery Features
Feature	**Description**
"Hang Manager"	A feature designed to "break" into a nonresponding application. You will find this feature by choosing **Start**	**Programs**	**Microsoft Office Tools**	**Microsoft Office Application Recovery**.
Office Safe Mode	Office-specific tools designed to fix and troubleshoot failed application startups. When Outlook fails to launch, a prompt should appear explaining the error and presenting start alternatives.

SUMMARY AND EXERCISES

SUMMARY

- Outlook 2002 helps you track appointments, send and receive messages, maintain a list of to-do tasks, monitor computer activities, and instantly update business and personal contacts.
- The e-mail feature enables you to send and receive electronic mail.
- The techniques you use to launch Outlook are similar to those used to launch other applications.
- You can keep Outlook open as you work in other applications so that you can use it as a reference.
- The Outlook Bar groups Outlook features into three shortcut categories: Outlook Shortcuts, My Shortcuts, and Other Shortcuts.
- Appointments are recorded in the Calendar.
- Contacts stores information such as names, addresses, phone numbers, and company names.
- Each Outlook feature stores items in folders.
- Numerous help features are available. The Office Assistant and the Ask a Question features enable you to ask questions about the active application.

KEY TERMS & SKILLS

KEY TERMS

Calendar (p. 4)	Folder List (p. 3)	Outlook Bar (p. 3)
Contacts (p. 4)	Inbox (p. 4)	Outlook Today (p. 4)
Deleted Items (p. 4)	Journal (p. 5)	Tasks (p. 4)
e-mail (p. 3)		

SKILLS

Access Outlook features (p. 5)	Launch Outlook (p. 3)
Ask a Question (p. 11)	Use the Folder List (p. 9)
Exit Outlook (p. 15)	Use the Office Assistant (p. 13)

STUDY QUESTIONS

MULTIPLE CHOICE

1. To change from one Outlook feature to another,
   a. click the feature icon on the Outlook Bar.
   b. press [Ctrl] + [F6].
   c. double-click the feature on the Outlook Bar.
   d. press [Enter].

2. The Outlook feature designed to keep track of the things you need to do is the
   a. Inbox.
   b. Tasks.
   c. Schedule.
   d. Journal.

3. The Outlook folder that stores messages you want to send is the
   a. E-mail folder.
   b. Inbox folder.
   c. Outbox folder.
   d. Sent Items folder.

4. To exit Outlook,
   a. click the application Close button.
   b. press [Alt] + [F6].
   c. choose File, Close.
   d. press [F4].

5. The Ask a Question text box appears on the
   a. title bar.
   b. menu bar.
   c. toolbar.
   d. Task Pane.

6. To launch Outlook, use any of the following techniques *except*
   a. double-clicking [icon].
   b. choosing Start | Programs | Microsoft Outlook.
   c. clicking [icon] in the system tray.
   d. All of the above can be used to launch Outlook.

7. To return to the previous Outlook window, click
   a. ⇐ Back.
   b. [icon].
   c. [icon].
   d. [X].

8. Icons on the Outlook Bar represent
   a. folders.
   b. programs.
   c. groups.
   d. categories.

SHORT ANSWER

1. In which Outlook Bar group does Outbox appear by default?
2. Which Outlook features might you use to record notes during a telephone conversation?
3. How can you turn off the Office Assistant?
4. What is Office Safe Mode and when will it be used?
5. What feature holds e-mail messages?

FILL IN THE BLANK

1. The Outlook feature designed to keep track of meetings is the _____.
2. The Outlook feature designed to store names and addresses of business associates is _____.
3. Features are arranged on the _____ in three different shortcut groups.
4. The default Office Assistant looks like a(n) _____.
5. The Outlook feature that automatically tracks activity in Office programs is _____.
6. When Outlook "freezes," use the _____ to try to recover the program.

FOR DISCUSSION

1. List and describe the items displayed on the Outlook Shortcuts group of the Outlook Bar.
2. Describe the Outlook features you believe you would use most often.
3. Briefly discuss when, how, and why you would use the Office Assistant.

PROJECT 1

Setting up Outlook 2002

Outlook contains tools that enable you to set up different features to accommodate personal preferences. Using these tools, you can create new folders in which to store Outlook items, add folders to the Outlook Bar to make them easier to access, and set up folder windows to display items in the format you prefer.

OBJECTIVES

After completing this project, you will be able to:

- Customize Outlook Today
- Set a launch feature
- Create folders
- Customize the Outlook Bar
- Customize toolbars and menus
- Set time zones
- Set options and change views
- Find items

e-selections) Running Case

Now that you have explored some of the basic features available in Outlook, it is time to turn your attention to setting up Outlook for the way you work.

Netstalking

"As more and more Americans are going online, particularly our children, it is critical that they ar protected from online stalking. Cyberspace should be a place for learning and exploration, not a place for fear," said Vice President Al Gore in a statement issued in September 1999.

Many people think they are pretty anonymous as they surf the Internet. Not so...everywhere you go on the Net leaves electronic footprints. By analyzing these footprints, others might find out more about you than you want them to know.

Unscrupulous people can use the information obtained to impersonate someone else, gather information about another person, or contact someone. What's really scary is that many times information is gathered from someone without that person realizing it. What do they do with this informtion? Here are a few examples:

- Joe disagrees with Jim's response posted in a newsgroup or on a bulletin board and humiliates him in the public area of the Usenet forum—a process sometimes known as "flaming."
- Mary accesses Ivy's web page and sends an extremely large file to Ivy that crashes Ivy's e-mail server.
- Sean subscribes Amy to hundreds of mailing lists.
- Albert locates Julie's phone number and calls at odd times of the day and night—collect!

Sound scary? Of course it is! And that's just the beginning of how dangerous the Internet can be.

But the question remains: How do people find information about others on the Internet? Here are just a few ways people gather information about others:

- E-mail addresses posted with messages and responses on newsgroups and bulletin boards
- 'Finger' programs that convert e-mail addresses into a person's real name

False Identity

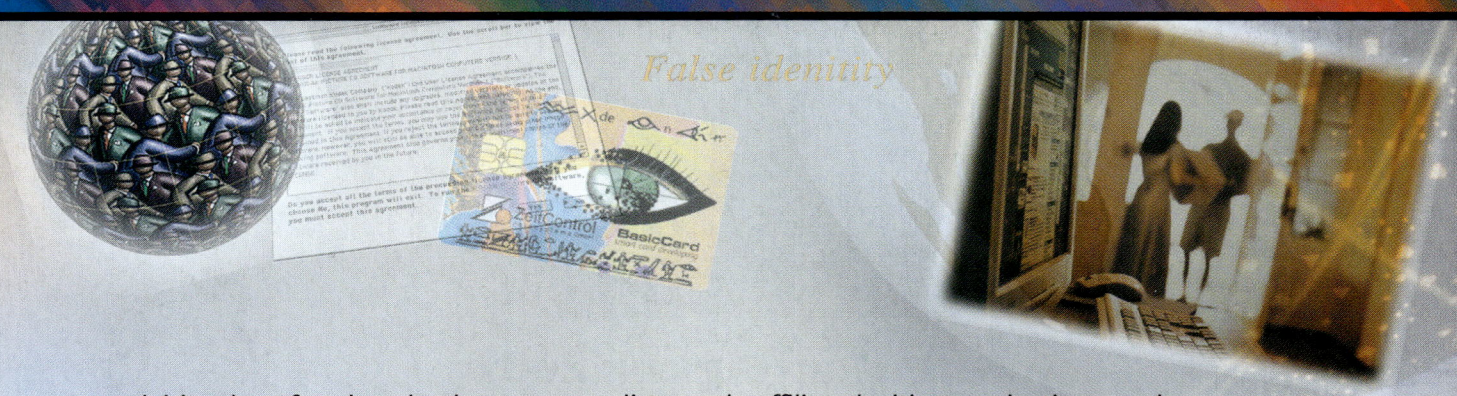

- 'Ph'—short for phonebook—programs list people affiliated with organizations, such as universities.

- 'Whois' queries within common Internet Service Providers (ISP) return personal information about the general vicinity in which a person is located and sometimes where a person works.

- Internic—the official registration company for .com, .org, .net, and .int domain names—makes available the contact names, addresses, and phone numbers of the people who registered domain names.

- Real-time IRC where visitors "talk" with strangers in a seemingly anonymous environment, provide access to e-mail addresses and potentially provide access to more personal information.

- Accessing Web pages opens the door for the Web page owner to identify an IP address and location.

Simply turning off the computer doesn't necessarily put an end to netstalking. The fact is, the same rights apply on and off the Internet; nobody has a right to hassle or threaten someone else. Harassing other users breaks the ISP Code of Conduct; therefore, it could result in termination of the account. When carried too far, it provides the basis for legal action. There are a number of tips for staying anonymous as you surf the Web. Here are just a few:

- Withhold as much personal information as possible when you sign up for Internet access.

- Set up an e-mail address with a "coded" or fictitious name.

- Download tools that "stalkers" use and see what personal information they can access.

- Use an Anonymizer to go through a special server to reach sites on the Web. Anonymizers strip away personal details and retrieve the page.

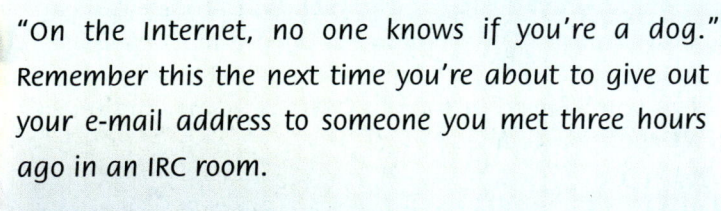

"On the Internet, no one knows if you're a dog." Remember this the next time you're about to give out your e-mail address to someone you met three hours ago in an IRC room.

Unscrupulous actions

PROJECT 1

Setting up Outlook 2002

The Challenge

During your first session with Ms. Elisa Sandoval, Selections, Inc., Corporate Trainer, you identified a number of Outlook features that can help you better manage your work schedule and help keep you organized. While the Outlook default settings on many of these features are adequate, there are a number of changes you would like to make on specific features to better meet your needs for the way you work. You would like to implement some setup changes and create some special folders to help you organize your work and also explore some of the pros and cons for the settings you believe you want to implement. Because you will be traveling to each regional office of Selections, Inc., you are also curious to know whether you can track appointments at different offices using a different time zone setting.

The Solution

Settings for each individual Outlook feature are, of course, determined after you have worked with the program for a while. There are a number of features that are basic to Outlook that you can adjust as you begin working with the product. Ms. Sandoval can help you identify some of the advantages and disadvantages of changing settings for some of these default features.

Customizing Outlook Today

Outlook Today was designed to present a preview of your day. It displays a summary of your appointments, a list of tasks that need to be completed, and new e-mail messages you receive. From Outlook Today, you can open appointment windows, mark tasks completed, open e-mail messages, and so forth. You can customize Outlook Today to display each time you launch Outlook, select folders you want to include in Outlook Today, and select a style for the layout of the Outlook Today window.

Setting up Outlook 2002 OU 1-5

Task 1:
To Customize Outlook Today

1 Launch Outlook and click the **Outlook Today** icon on the Outlook Bar, if necessary, to open the Outlook Today folder.

2 Drag the **Address** bar handle to the right to display the **Personal Folders–Outlook Today** folder banner.

3 Click the **Customize Outlook Today** button to open the Customize Outlook Today window.

Figure 1-1

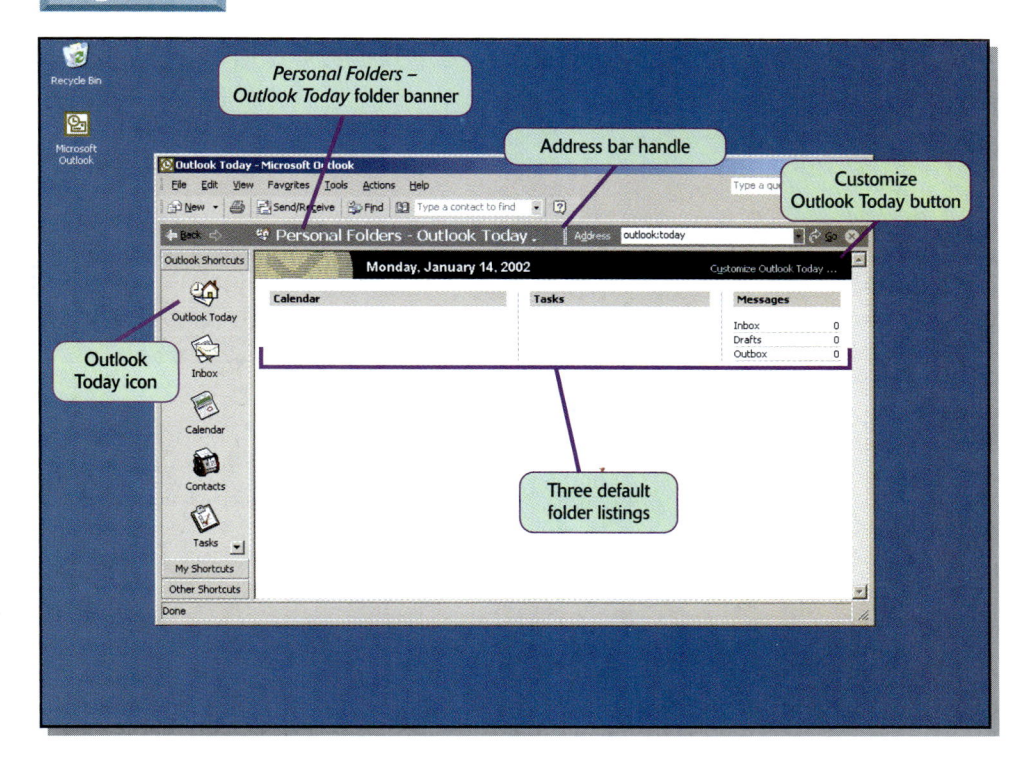

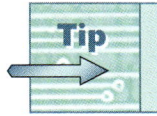

Personal Folders – Outlook Today folder banner
Address bar handle
Customize Outlook Today button
Outlook Today icon
Three default folder listings

Tip When the mouse pointer is properly positioned on the Address bar handle, the mouse pointer shape changes to a two-headed black sizing arrow.

4 Maximize the Outlook window and click the **Choose Folders** button in the **Messages** area to open the **Select Folder** dialog box.

5 Clear the check marks in all folders except the **Inbox** folder and click **OK**.

Tip Checking the *When starting, go directly to Outlook Today* check box tells Outlook to display Outlook Today each time it is launched instead of displaying the Inbox or another folder.

Figure 1-2

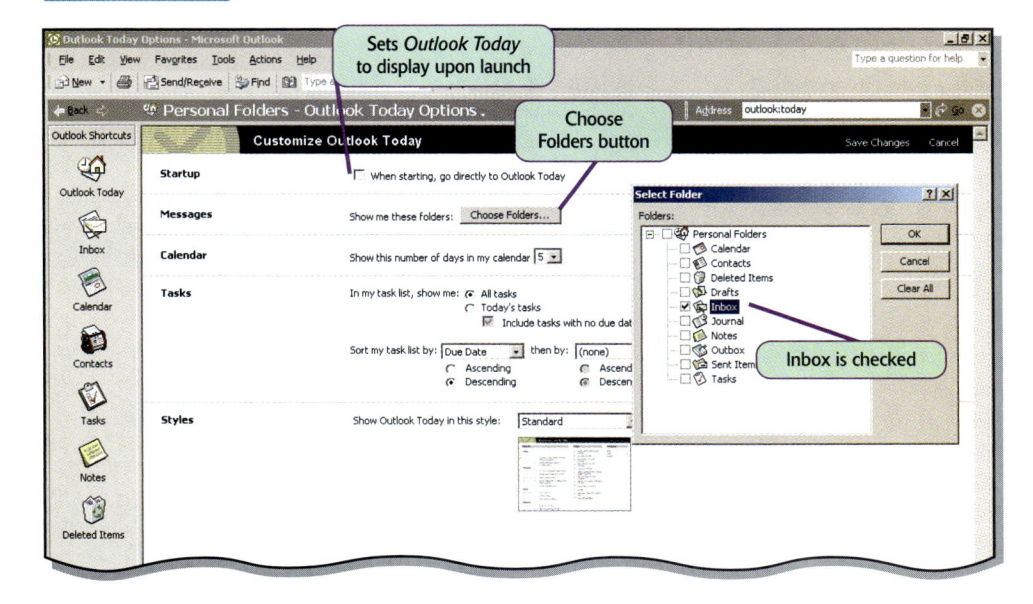

Sets Outlook Today to display upon launch
Choose Folders button
Inbox is checked

Customizing Outlook Today

> **Troubleshooting** If there is a scroll bar in the Folders list, be sure to scroll through the entire list to see that only those folders you want to select are checked. If other folders are checked, click the **Clear All** button and then select the Inbox check box.

6 Click the **Show this number of days in my calendar** down arrow and select **7** from the list of days to show, select the **Today's Tasks** option, and ensure that the **Include tasks with no due date** check box is selected.

7 Click the **Sort my task list by** down arrow and select **Due Date**, click the **then by** down arrow and select **Creation Time**, and ensure that **Descending** is the sort direction for both options.

8 Select **Standard (two column)** from the **Styles** drop-down list and then click **Save Changes** at the right end of the Customize Outlook Today bar.

9 Review screen changes.

Figure 1-3

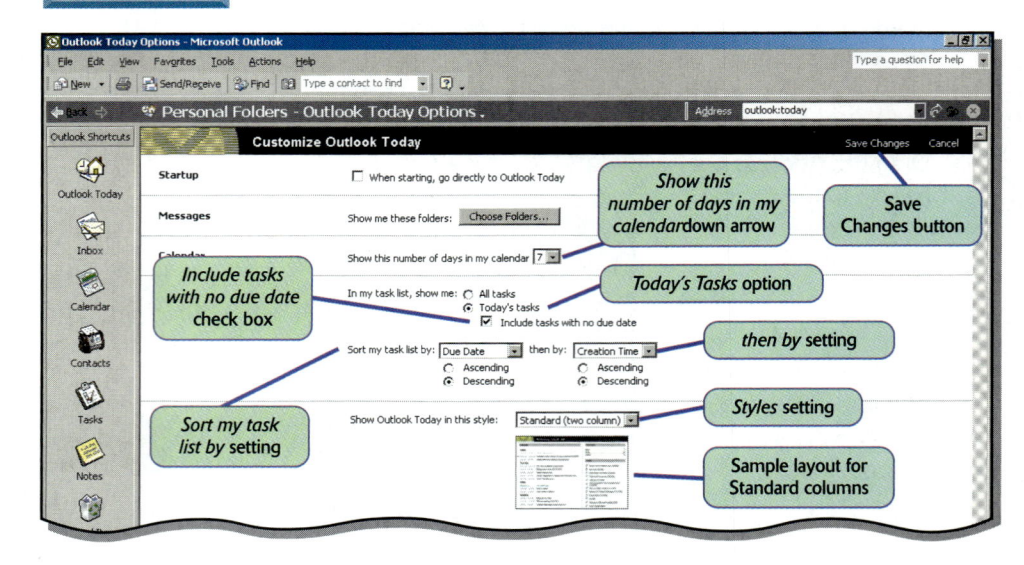

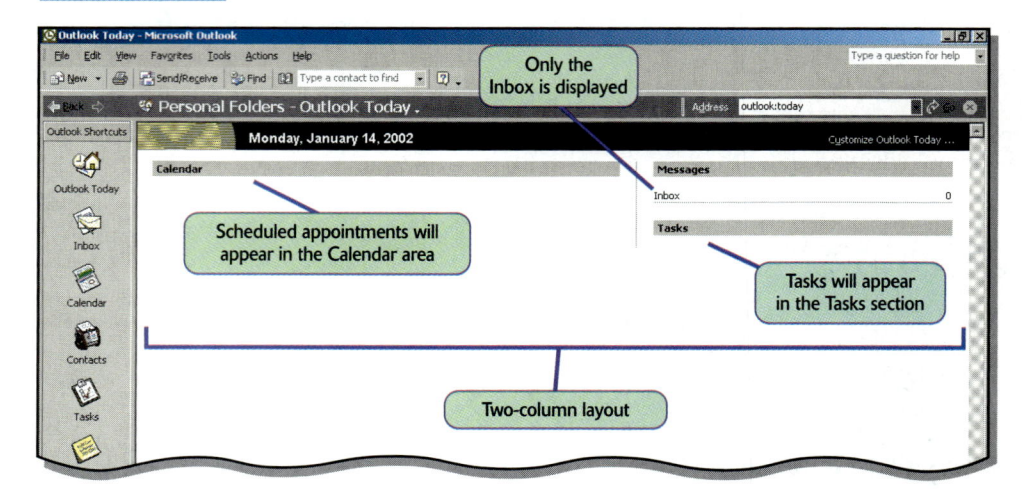

Figure 1-4

Setting up Outlook 2002

Setting a Launch Feature

The option to display Outlook Today as the default launch window appears among the Customize Outlook Today options. What if you want another window to appear by default each time you launch Outlook? You can also set Outlook to display the Inbox, Calendar, Contacts, or Tasks list each time you launch Outlook.

Task 2:
To Change the Default Feature Window

1 Choose **Tools | Options** to open the Options dialog box and click the **Other** tab.

2 Click the **Advanced Options** button to display additional options.

Figure 1-5

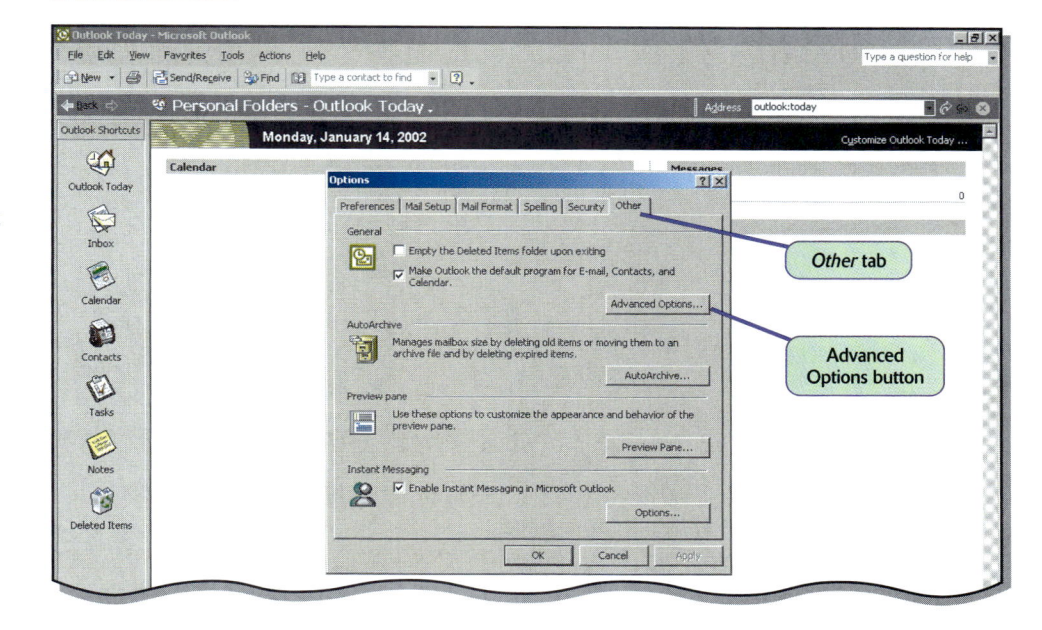

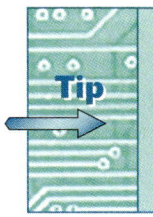

Other tab

Advanced Options button

Tip If you have right-to-left foreign languages, such as South Asian languages, installed on your computer, you may see a **Right-to-Left** tab when you display the Advanced Options dialog box. Options on the Right-to-Left page enable you to set options that affect text displayed in the foreign language.

3 Click the **Startup in this folder** down arrow, select **Calendar**, and then click **OK** twice to close the dialog boxes.

4 Exit Outlook and launch it again.

Figure 1-6

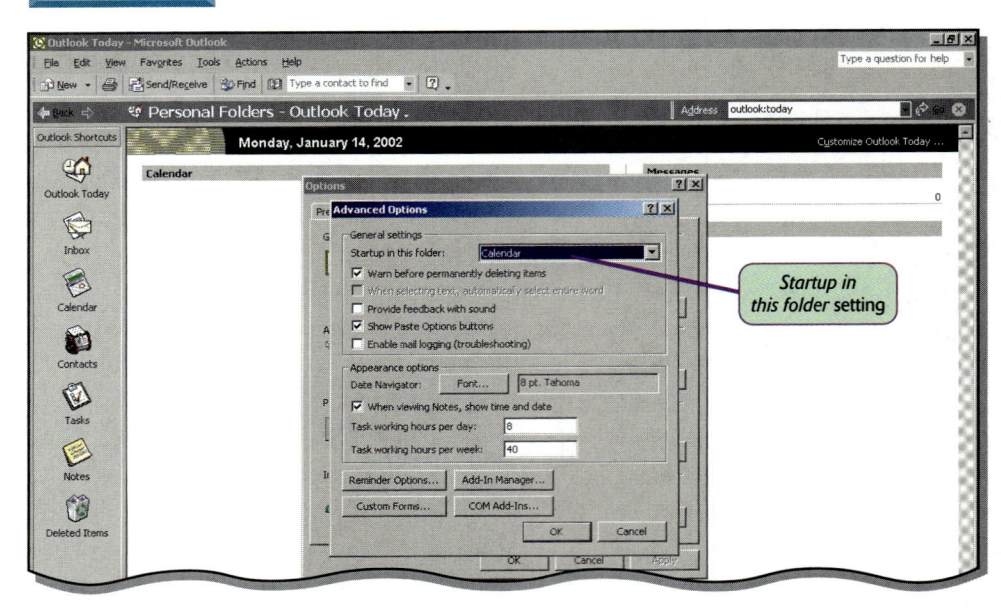

Startup in this folder setting

5 Click the **Outlook Today** icon on the Outlook Bar to return to Outlook Today.

Figure 1-7

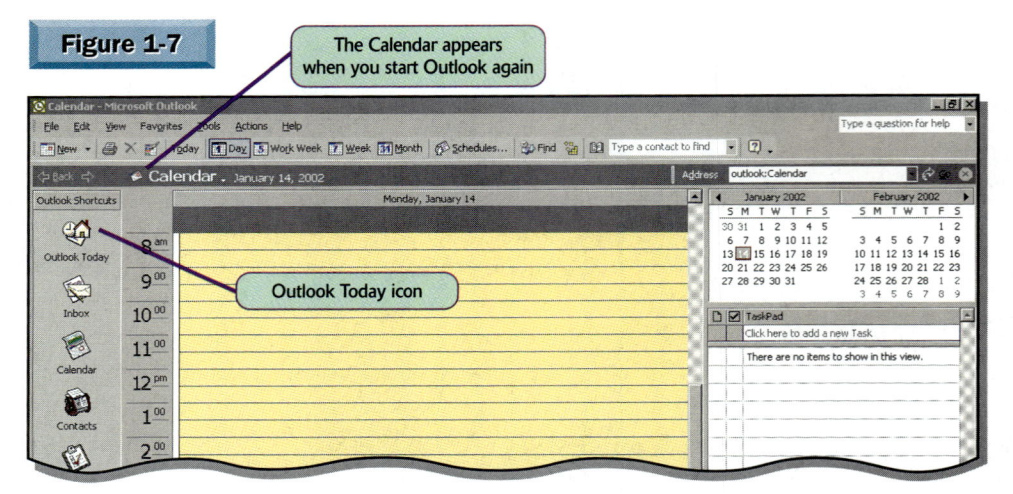

The Calendar appears when you start Outlook again

Outlook Today icon

Creating Folders

Although Outlook comes with a set of default personal folders in which it stores items associated with different features, creating special topic-specific folders enables you to store items related to specific projects and events. Sorting items into special folders will help keep you organized. As you create new folders, Outlook presents a message box that enables you to choose whether or not you want to add the folder to the Outlook Bar. Folders are added to the My Shortcuts group on the Outlook Bar.

Setting up Outlook 2002

Task 3:
To Create a Personal Folder and Add it to the Outlook Bar

1 Click the **Outlook Today** icon on the Outlook Bar to redisplay Outlook Today, if necessary.

2 Choose **File | Folder | New Folder** to open the **Create New Folder** dialog box.

3 Click the **Personal Folders** expand button to display a list of folders.

4 Position the insertion point in the **Name** field, type *Your First Name*, substituting your real name for the text that appears here, and click **OK** to create the folder.

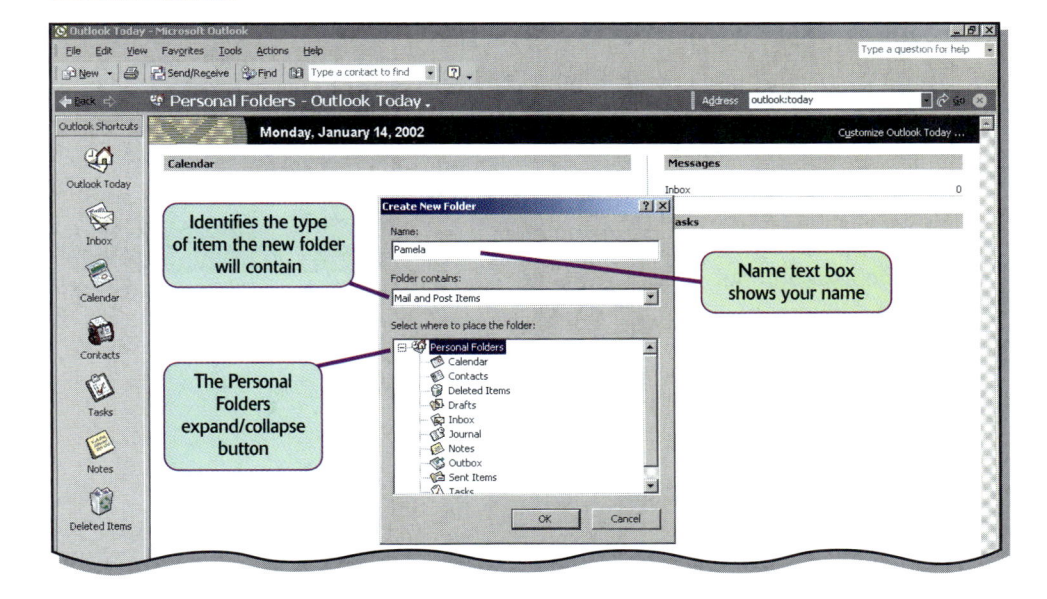

Figure 1-8

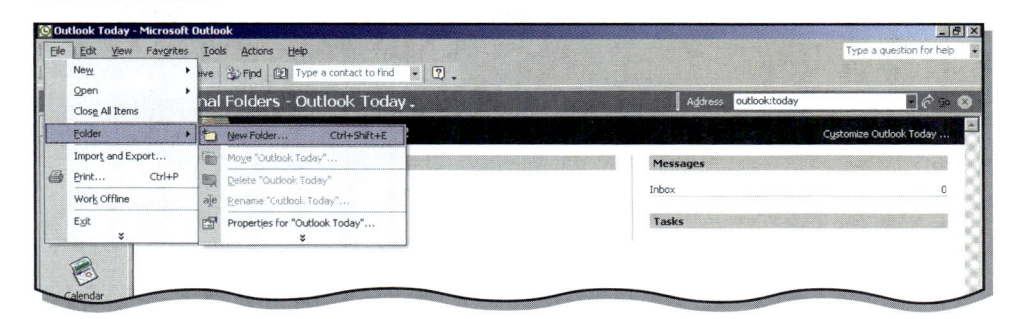

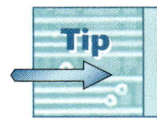

Tip You do not have to display Outlook Today to create a new folder; it just ensures that everyone is starting at the same spot.

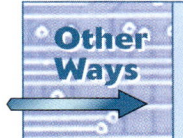

Other Ways
To create a folder:
- Choose **File | New | Folder**
- Press Ctrl + Shift + E.

Figure 1-9

Creating Folders

5 Read the message contained in the message box and then click **Yes** to add the folder to the Outlook Bar.

Troubleshooting

Selecting the **Don't prompt me about this again** check box bypasses the *Add shortcut to Outlook Bar?* message. As a result, if this check box was previously checked, you may not see the message and can skip Steps 5–7. You can still add the folder to the Outlook Bar using techniques described in Task 6.

Figure 1-10

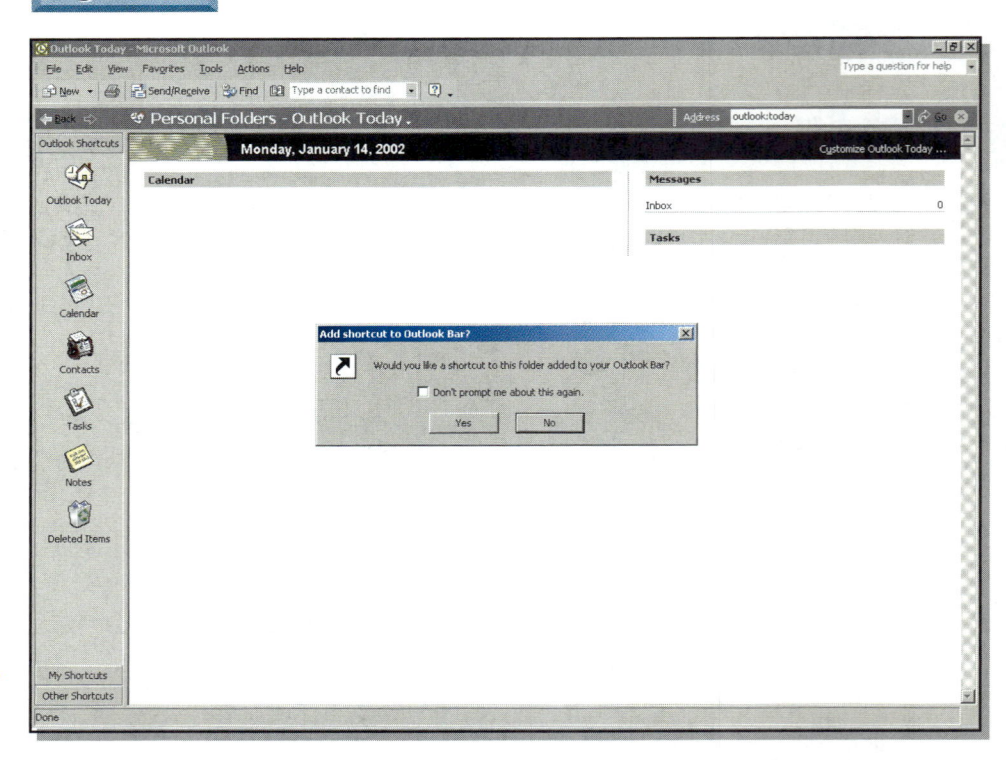

Tip Notice that the **My Shortcuts** group button blinks after you add the folder to the Outlook Bar.

6 Click the **My Shortcuts** group button to display the group folders.

Figure 1-11

The My Shortcuts group button blinks to indicate the group containing the new folder

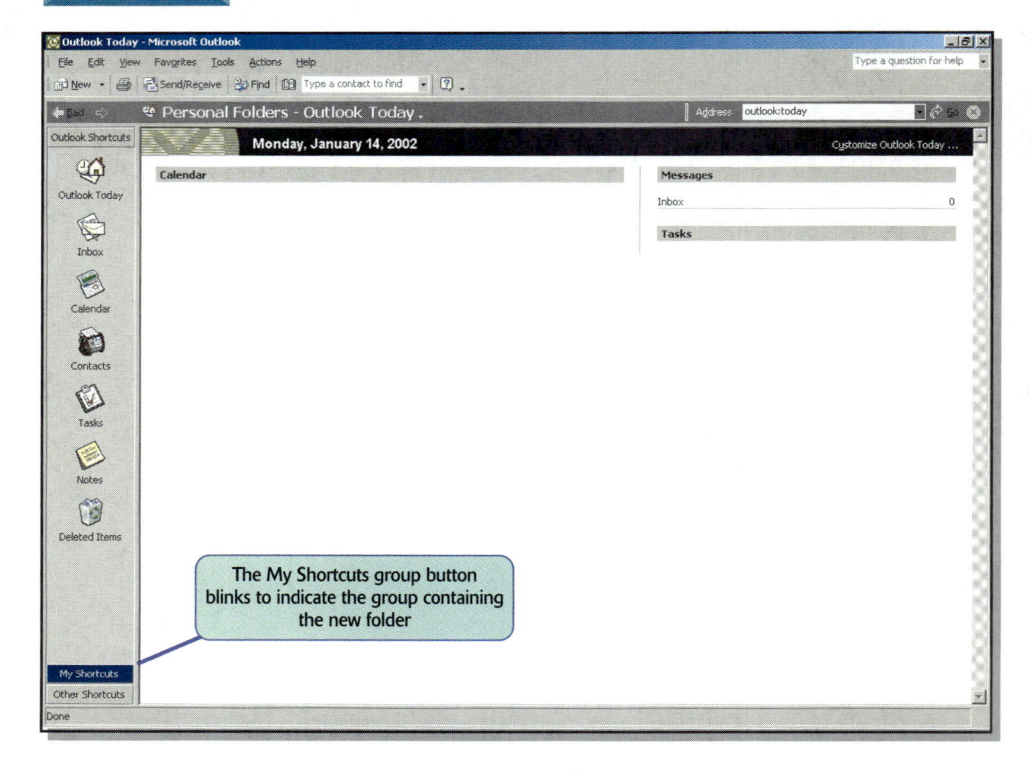

7 Click the new folder name to open the folder.

Figure 1-12

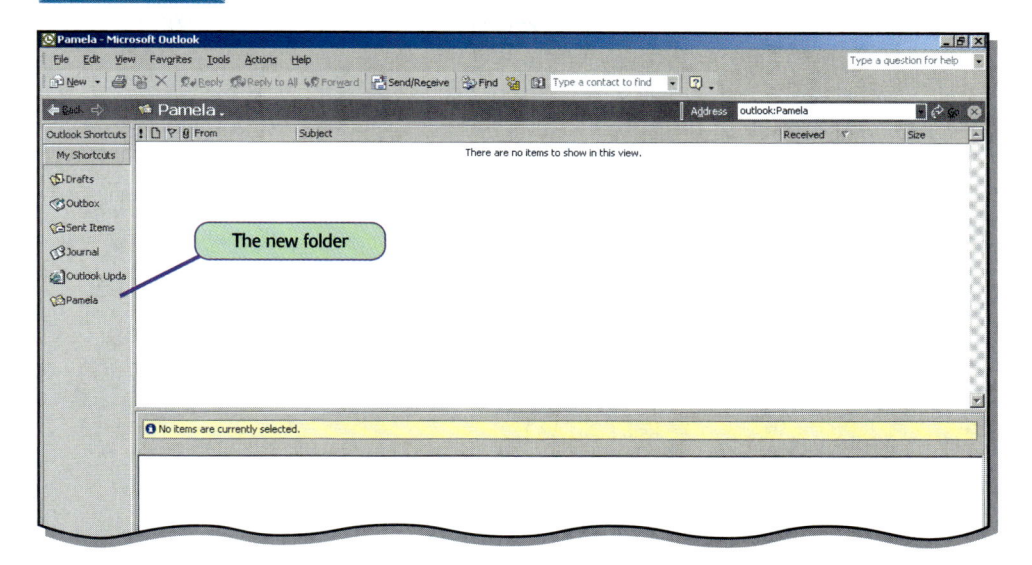

The new folder

Customizing the Outlook Bar

The Outlook Bar contains shortcut icons that provide easy access to Outlook folders and other items you access in Outlook. Because the icons are simply shortcuts rather than files or folders, you can customize the Outlook Bar without affecting Outlook and other folders by:

- Repositioning folders
- Adding, renaming, and removing groups
- Creating Outlook Bar shortcuts
- Changing the size of the Outlook Bar shortcut icons

Adding Outlook Bar Groups

As you work on projects and other events or topic-related activities in Outlook, you may want to store shortcuts to related folders in groups by themselves. You can add the Outlook Bar groups as you need them and then move folder shortcuts into the groups.

> **WEB TIP**
>
> Check the Web for free personal desktop organizer programs and compare them to Outlook. Which of these programs is the most powerful? Do the free programs meet your basic needs?

Task 4:
To Add an Outlook Bar Group

1 Click the **Outlook Shortcuts** group button to display the group contents.

2 Point to a blank area of the Outlook Bar, right-click, and select **Add New Group**.

3 Type **Outlook Class** and press Enter. The new group appears at the bottom of the Outlook Bar.

Figure 1-13

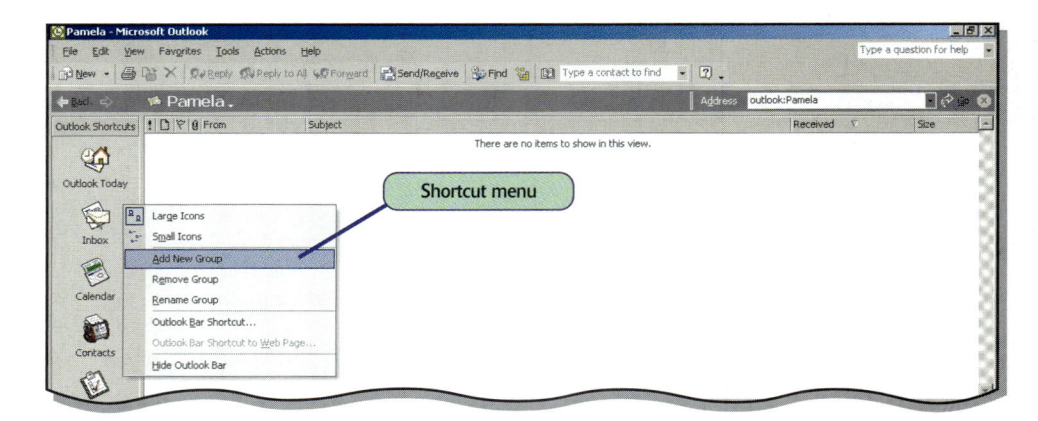

Shortcut menu

Figure 1-14

The new group appears at the bottom of the Outlook Bar

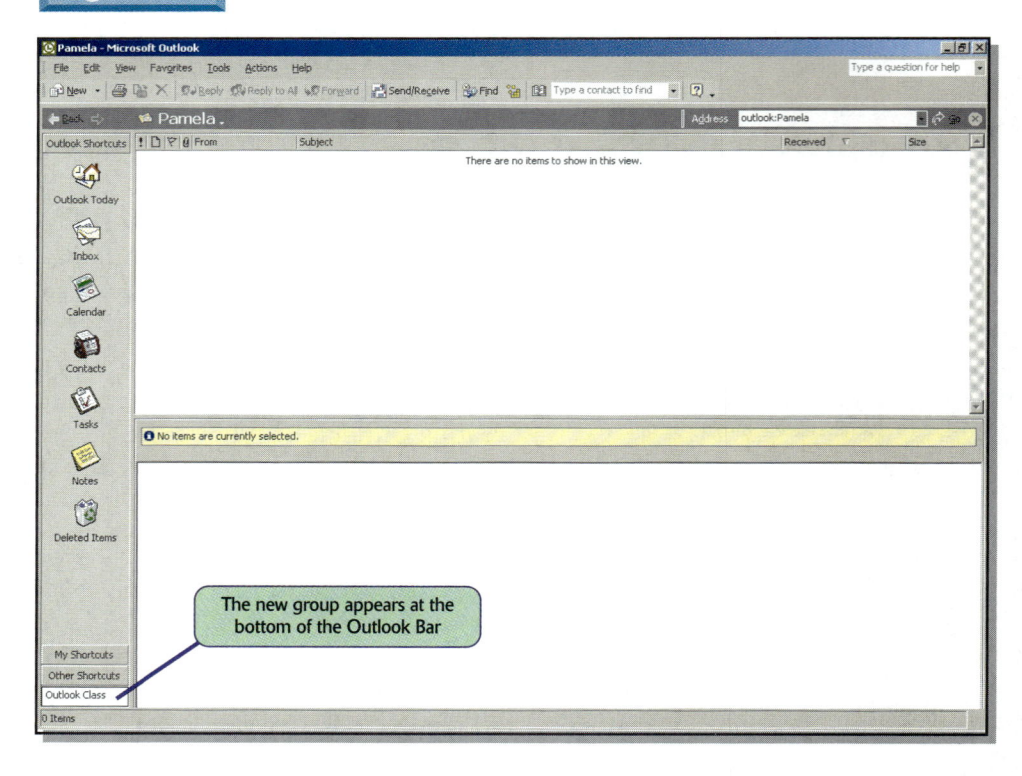

CHECK POINT

Now that you have created a new Outlook group and placed it on the Outlook Bar, what happens if you no longer need the group? You can either rename the group and create new folders to appear in the new group or you can simply remove the group from the Outlook Bar. Because the Outlook Bar holds shortcut icons to Outlook folders and other items, folders remain available from the Folder List after you remove the group and the folder shortcuts it contains from the Outlook Bar.

Repositioning Outlook Bar Folders

The primary objective of creating new folders is to help keep your work organized. To make accessing the new folder more efficient, you can move the folder to the Outlook Shortcuts group.

Task 5:
To Reposition Folders on the Outlook Bar

Figure 1-15

The Outlook Class group opens

A black bar identifies folder position

1 Click the **My Shortcuts** group button to display group folders and select the folder shortcut with your name on it.

2 Drag the folder to the bottom of the Outlook Bar and pause when the mouse pointer is positioned on the **Outlook Class** group button until the Outlook Class group opens.

3 Release the mouse button to place the folder in the group.

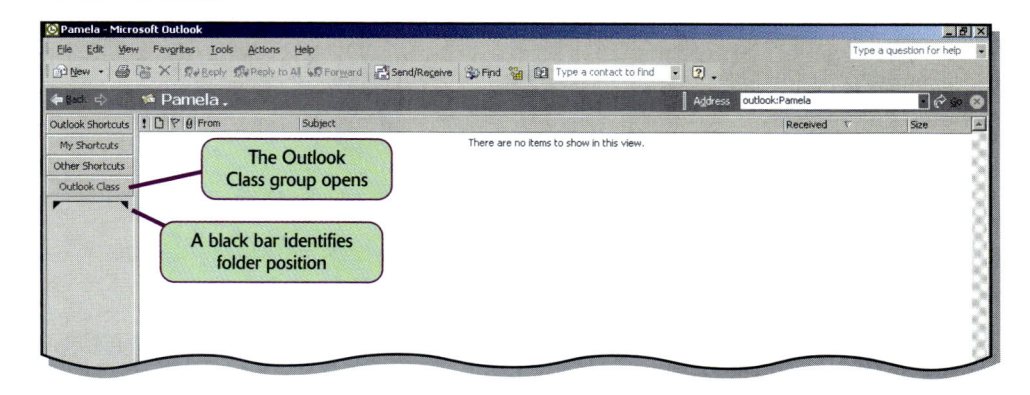

Tip: Notice, as you drag, that a black bar appears when the mouse pointer is positioned between folder icons. When you point to the Outlook Class group button, the group opens and a black bar appears at the top of the group bar.

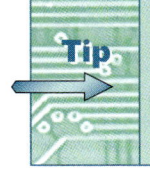

Creating Outlook Bar Shortcuts

In addition to adding new folders to the Outlook Bar as you create them in Outlook, you can add folders containing other items, such as document folders that you use frequently. If you choose not to add a shortcut for a folder to the Outlook Bar at the time you create it, you can use the techniques outlined in Task 6 to add it at any time.

Task 6:
To Add a Shortcut to the Outlook Bar

1 Display the **Outlook Class** group on the Outlook Bar, if necessary.

2 Point to a blank area of the Outlook Bar, right-click, and select **Outlook Bar Shortcut**.

Figure 1-16

3 Click the **Look in** down arrow and select **File System** to display folders contained on disks and drives available on the computer.

4 Expand the **My Documents** folder, select the **My Documents** folder (or another folder you want to add to the Outlook Bar as directed by your instructor), and click **OK**. The folder name appears with the folder on the Outlook Class group of the Outlook Bar.

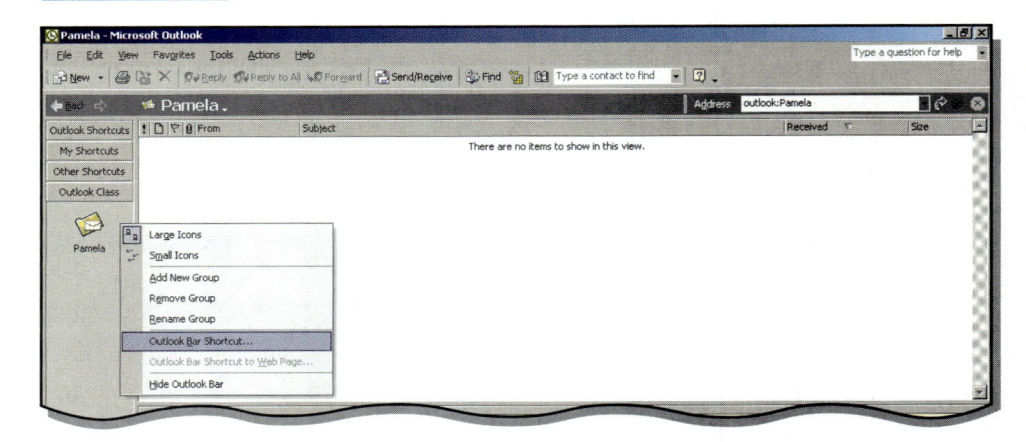

Figure 1-17

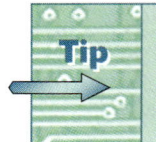

Tip: If you store your student files in a different folder or on a different disk, you may want to select the appropriate drive name and then select the folder to add it to the Outlook Class group on the Outlook Bar.

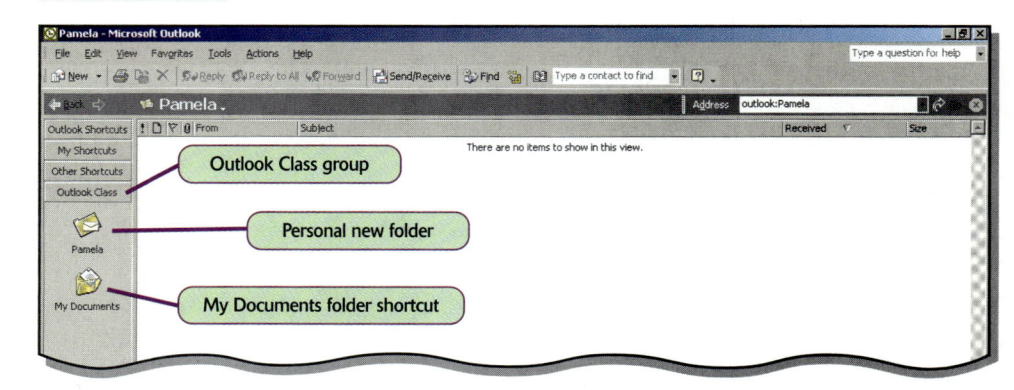

5 Review the Outlook Class group folders.

Figure 1-18

Setting up Outlook 2002

OU 1-15

Changing the Size of the Outlook Bar Shortcut Icons

As you work with different Outlook Bar groups, notice that the Outlook Shortcuts group displays large shortcut icons while the My Shortcuts group displays small shortcut icons. As you add shortcuts to different Outlook Bar groups, you may want to change the display of shortcuts to make them easier to access. Changing the format for shortcuts in the Outlook Shortcuts group to display as small icons makes them more accessible. It also removes the need for scroll buttons for accessing shortcuts that appear offscreen.

Task 7:
To Change the Outlook Bar Shortcut Icons Size

1. Click the **Outlook Shortcuts** group button on the Outlook Bar and click the **Inbox** icon to open the Inbox folder.

2. Right-click a blank area of the Outlook Bar and select **Small Icons** to change the icon size so that they appear similar to those in the My Shortcuts group.

Figure 1-19

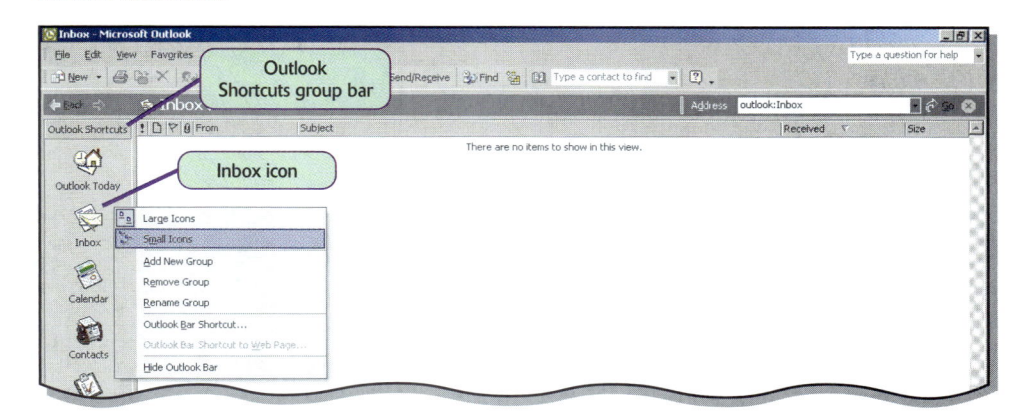

Outlook Shortcuts group bar

Inbox icon

Tip You do not *have* to open the Inbox; you can actually open any Outlook folder. Opening the Inbox just ensures that your screen will match the figures in this task.

WEB TIP

You can find anything from movie listings to hotels online. Check out the movie listings in your area to see if they are up to date.

Customizing Toolbars and Menus

The most frequently used toolbar buttons and menu items are the ones Outlook displays by default. As you switch between Outlook features, such as from the Calendar to the Inbox, the toolbar and menu options reflect tasks and options relative to the chosen feature. You can customize the toolbars and menus to your own personal needs.

Changing the Menu Settings

By default, Outlook menus initially display only the most frequently used commands. A full list of menu commands appears after pointing to the menu for a few seconds. You can change the menu setting to always display the full menu by setting options in the Customize dialog box.

Task 8:
To Set Menu Options

1. Choose **Tools | Customize** to open the Customize dialog box and click the **Options** tab, if necessary.

2. Select the **Always show full menus** check box, if necessary, select the **Large icons** check box, and view the results at the top of the screen.

3. Clear the **Large icons** check box and then click **Close**.

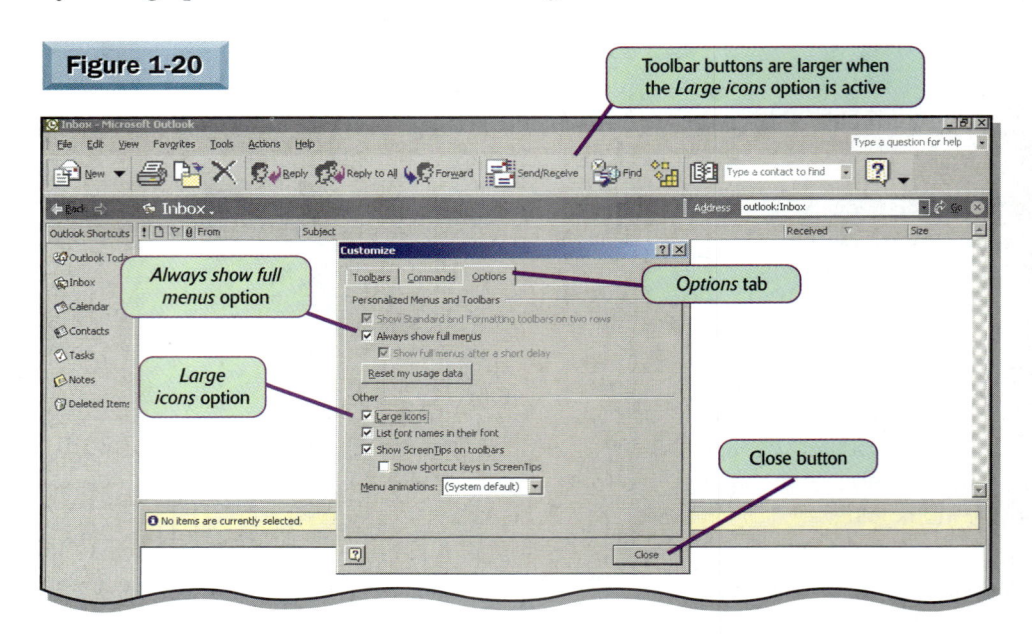

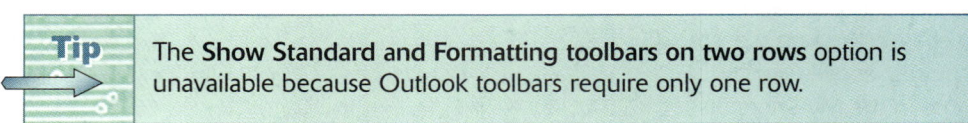

Figure 1-20

Tip: The **Show Standard and Formatting toolbars on two rows** option is unavailable because Outlook toolbars require only one row.

Adding Buttons to Toolbars and Commands to Menus

The default toolbars and menus contain most of the buttons and commands you will use as you work. When you identify buttons and commands that you want to add, remove, or reposition to make them more accessible, you will want to customize Outlook toolbars and menus. You have already identified a number of additional buttons you want to add to the default toolbar and a command that you want to reposition on the menu to make it more accessible. Ms. Sandoval will show you the basic procedures to follow so that you can customize additional toolbars and menus as the need arises.

Setting up Outlook 2002

Task 9:
To Add Buttons to Toolbars and Commands to Menus

1 Click Outlook Today, choose **Tools | Customize**, and click the **Toolbars** tab.

Figure 1-21

- Toolbars tab
- Checked items are active
- Option for creating a new toolbar
- Option for resetting all toolbars back to the default settings

2 Click the **Commands** tab, select **File** in the **Categories** list, if necessary, and scroll the **Commands** list until you see the **New Folder** command.

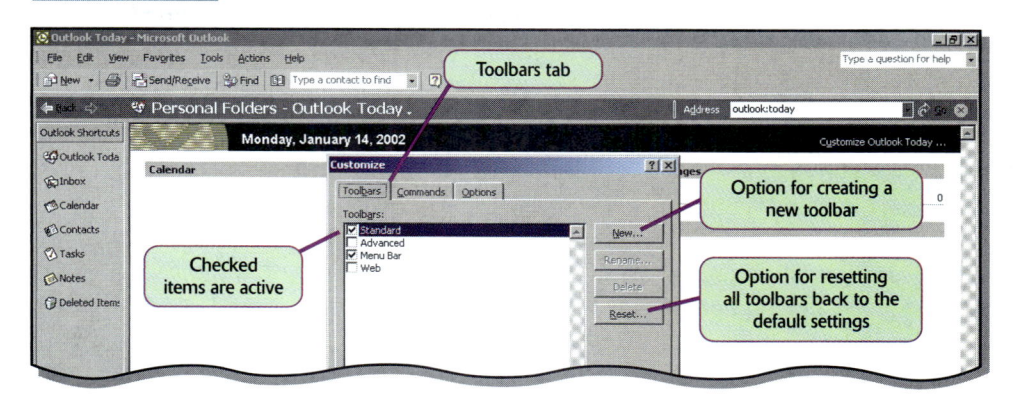

Figure 1-22

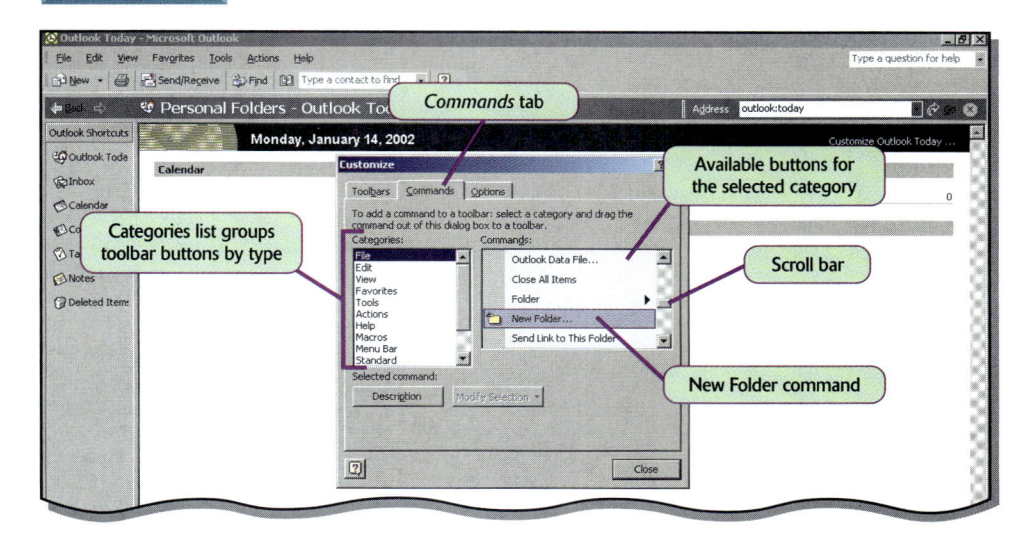

- Commands tab
- Categories list groups toolbar buttons by type
- Available buttons for the selected category
- Scroll bar
- New Folder command

3 Drag the **New Folder** button from the **Commands** list and position it on the toolbar between the Print button and the Send/Receive button. Then release the mouse button to drop the new button into position.

Figure 1-23

- A bar identifies the active button
- A button and (+) appear with the mouse pointer
- New Folder icon on the Commands list

Tip As you drag the mouse across the dialog box, the mouse pointer appears to carry an X. The X changes to a plus after you move the pointer onto one of the toolbars.

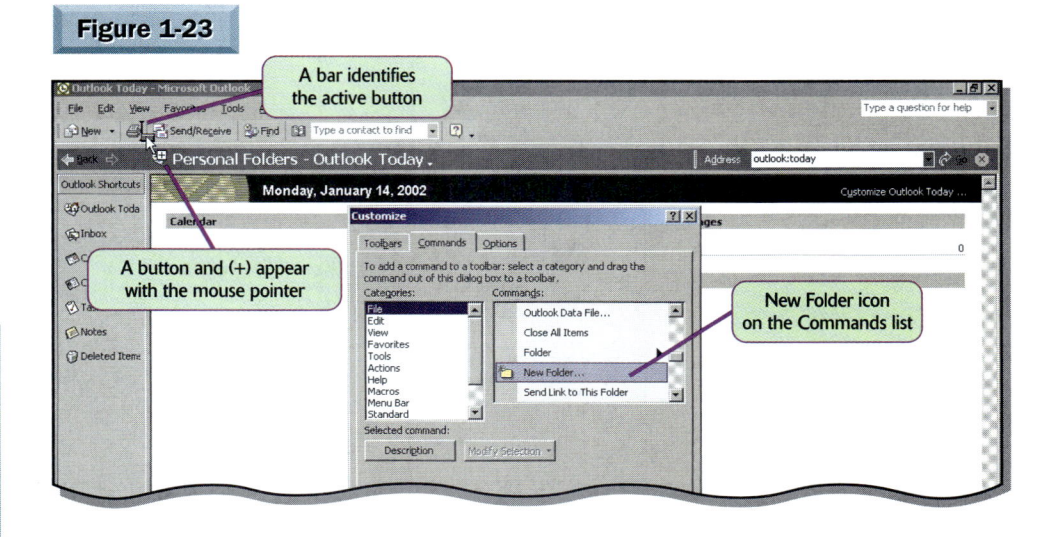

Customizing Toolbars and Menus

> **Troubleshooting** After you drop the new button into its position on the toolbar, a dark border appears around the button. The border will disappear when you close the Customize dialog box or perform a different customize action.

4 Click and drag the **New Folder** button from the **Commands** list in the Customize dialog box, point to the **File** menu until the full menu appears, if necessary, and position the command between the **New** and **Open** commands on the menu to add the new command to the menu.

5 Click the **Close** button in the **Customize** dialog box.

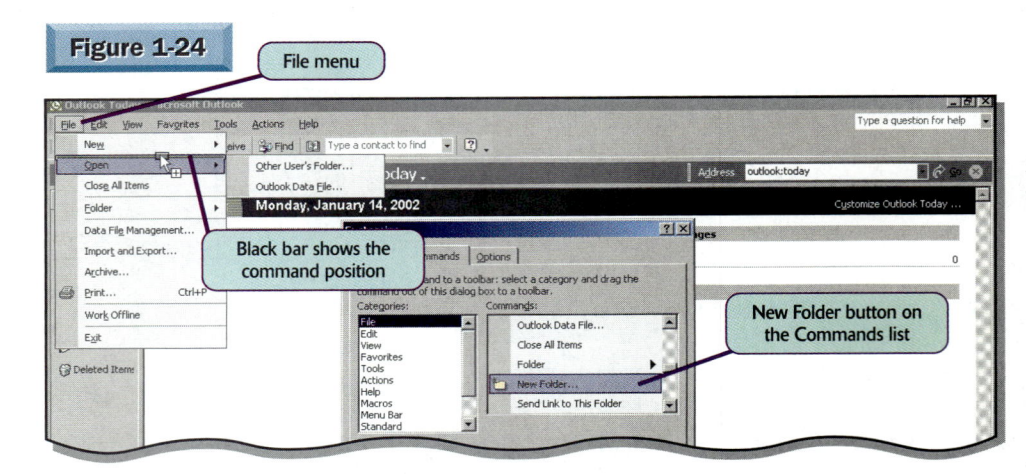

Figure 1-24

Callouts: File menu; Black bar shows the command position; New Folder button on the Commands list

> **Troubleshooting** As you move the mouse pointer over File menu commands, cascading menus will appear. They will have no affect on the position of the New Folder command on the menu.

> **Tip** To add a totally new menu to the menu bar, display the Customize dialog box, click the **New Menu** listing in the Categories list, and drag the New Menu command to the desired position on the menu bar.
>
> To change the name of a menu on the menu bar, display the Customize dialog box, right-click the menu, double-click the text beside **Name** on the shortcut menu, and type the new menu name.

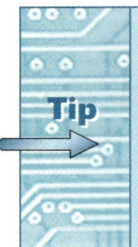

6 Click the **New Folder** button you just added to the toolbar to test its action and to open the Create New Folder dialog box, and then click **Cancel** to close the **Create New Folder** dialog box without creating the folder.

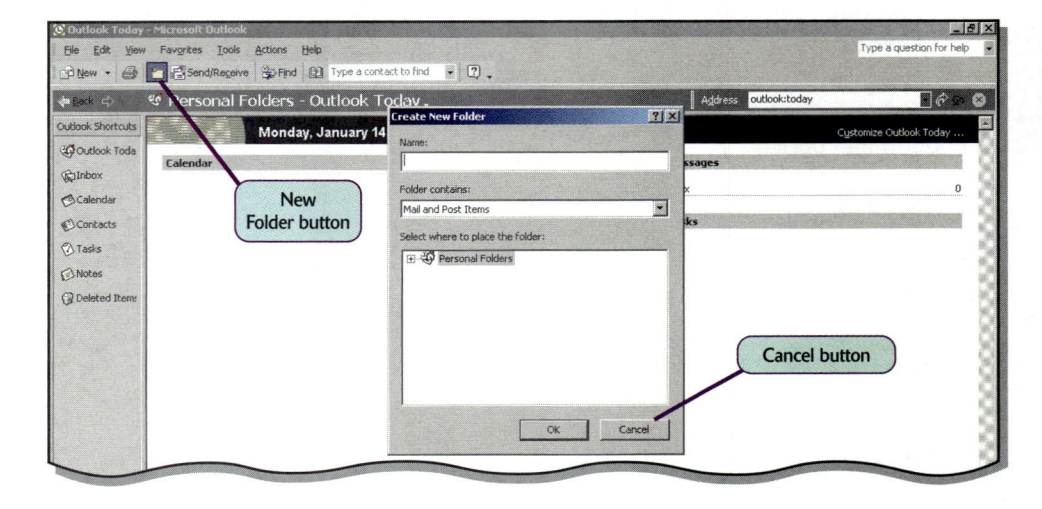

Figure 1-25

Callouts: New Folder button; Cancel button

> **CHECK POINT**
>
> The same basic techniques used to add buttons to toolbars and commands to menus can also be used to remove buttons and commands. Simply display the Customize dialog box, drag the icon you want to remove from the toolbar or the command you want to remove from a menu, and drop it at any position away from a toolbar or menu. Because the buttons on the toolbars and menu commands are copies of those contained in the Customize dialog box, you do not have to worry about accidentally permanently deleting the button or command from Outlook.
>
> You can actually remove buttons from the toolbar without displaying the Customize dialog box. Just press and hold the [Alt] key as you use the mouse to drag a button from the toolbar. Be careful, or you might accidentally remove a button and wonder where it went!

Setting Time Zones

Travelers who use Outlook will find tracking appointments in different *time zones* an efficient way to ensure that they arrive at appointments and meetings, as well as at the airport, on time. You can change your time zone to display a new time zone or add an additional time zone that is displayed next to the standard time zone setting.

Changing Time Zone Settings

Changing the time zone setting in Outlook affects the time zone setting of all other Windows-based programs on the computer. As a result, changing the time zone setting to a different time zone records all information as if you were actually in that time zone. For example, if you created a spreadsheet after changing the time zone setting in Outlook, the creation date and time of the spreadsheet would reflect the date and time of the active time zone setting.

Task 10:
To Change Time Zone Settings

1 Click the **Calendar** icon on the Outlook Bar to open the Calendar folder.

2 Choose **Tools | Options** and click the **Calendar Options** button.

3 Click the **Time Zone** button.

Figure 1-26

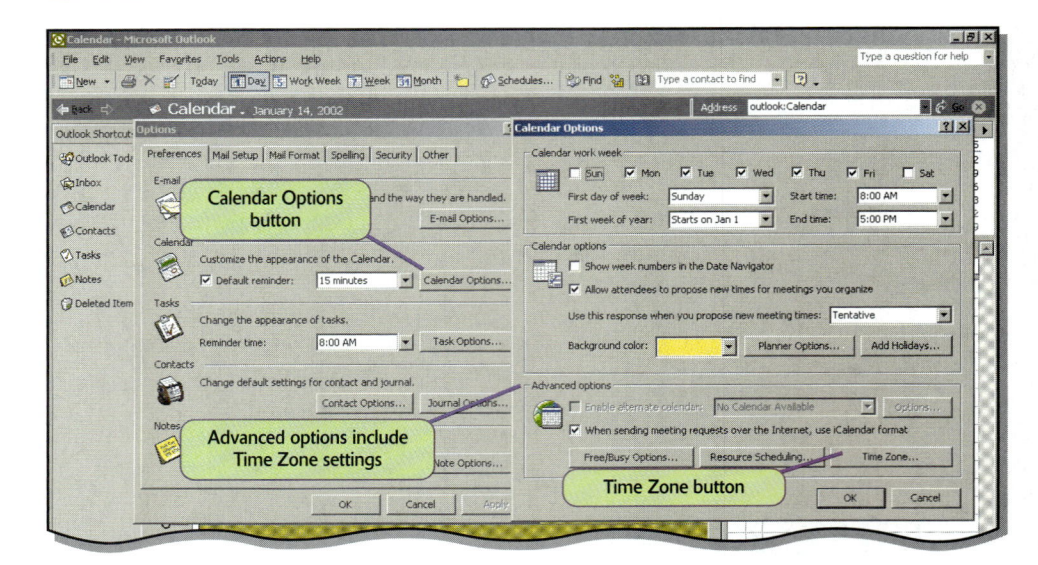

Callouts: Calendar Options button; Advanced options include Time Zone settings; Time Zone button

Tip: You can change time zones from any Outlook feature, but changes appear in the Calendar.

4 Click the **Time zone** down arrow, scroll the list of available time zones, and select the time zone in which you are currently located.

5 Click **OK** three times to close all dialog boxes.

Figure 1-27

Callouts: Current time zone setting; Option to adjust for time changes in April and October; Options for adding time zones; Time zone down arrow

Setting up Outlook 2002

OU 1-21

> **Tip** You can change time zones "on the fly" from the Calendar Day palette. Just right-click the blank area above the time bar and select **Change Time Zone**.

Adding Time Zones

Most people who travel frequently prefer to leave their standard time zone set on their computers and add additional time zones when they travel. When additional time zones are added to Outlook, the standard time zone is used as a reference point and the new time zone appears beside the default time zone.

Task 11:
To Add Time Zones

1 Choose **Tools | Options**, click the **Calendar Options** button, click the **Time Zone** button, and select the **Show an additional time zone** option.

2 Click the **Time zone** down arrow for the additional time zone and select the time zone immediately west of your current location.

3 Type **My Home** in the **Current time zone Label** field, type **Travel Zone** in the **Label** field for the additional time zone.

4 Click **OK** three times to close the dialog boxes.

> **Tip** If you have foreign languages installed on your computer, you may see a foreign language symbol beside the date at the top of the daily palette.

Figure 1-28

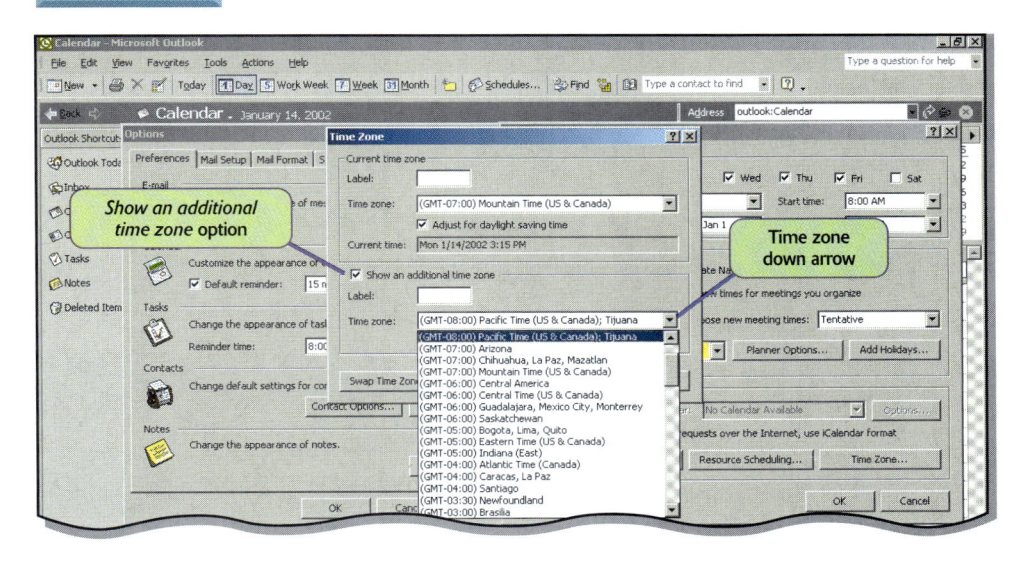

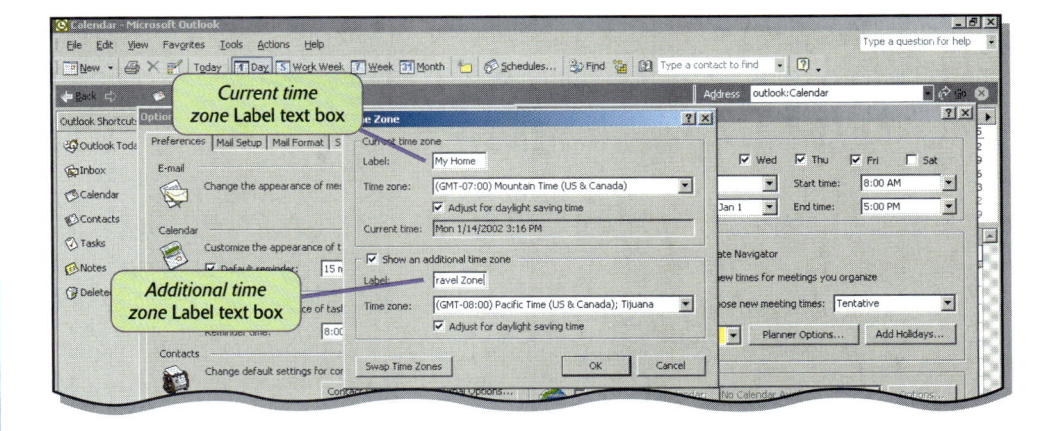

Show an additional time zone option

Time zone down arrow

Figure 1-29

Current time zone Label text box

Additional time zone Label text box

Setting Options and Changing Views

Each Outlook feature has a set of standard *views* that change the arrangement of information onscreen. While the views for each feature vary due to the nature of information and the items displayed for the feature, the procedures for changing the view are the same for all features.

Task 12:
To Change the View

1 Launch Outlook, display the Calendar, if necessary, and choose **View | Current View** to display a list of views.

2 Select **Active Appointments**.

Figure 1-30

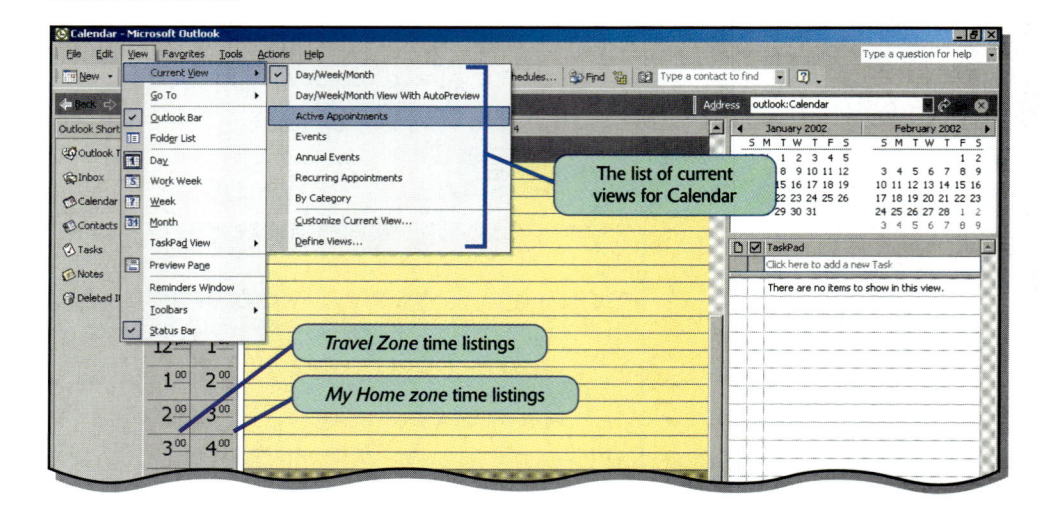

- The list of current views for Calendar
- Travel Zone time listings
- My Home zone time listings

> **Tip:** The list of current views varies for each Outlook folder. For example, views available for the Calendar include Day/Week/Month and Active Appointments while views available for the Inbox folder include Messages and Unread Messages.

3 Choose **View | Preview Pane** to display detailed information about the selected appointment.

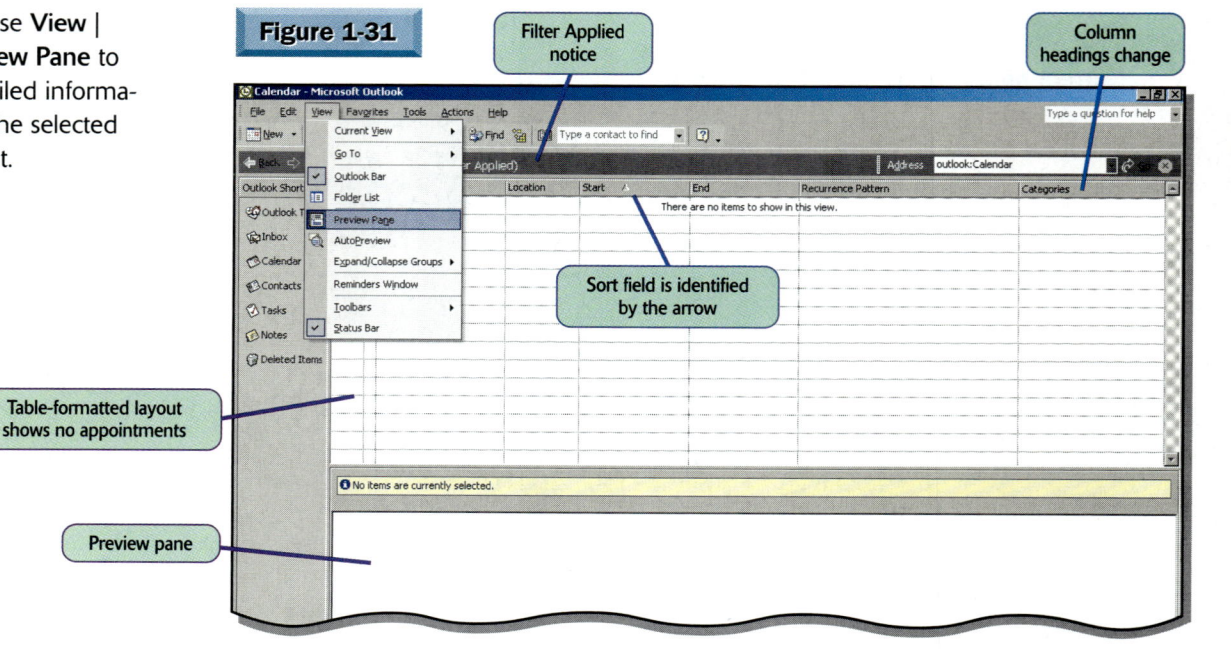

Figure 1-31

- Filter Applied notice
- Column headings change
- Sort field is identified by the arrow
- Table-formatted layout shows no appointments
- Preview pane

Setting up Outlook 2002   **OU 1-23**

4 Click the **Inbox** icon on the Outlook Bar to open the Inbox folder and choose **View | Preview Pane** to close the preview pane.

Figure 1-32

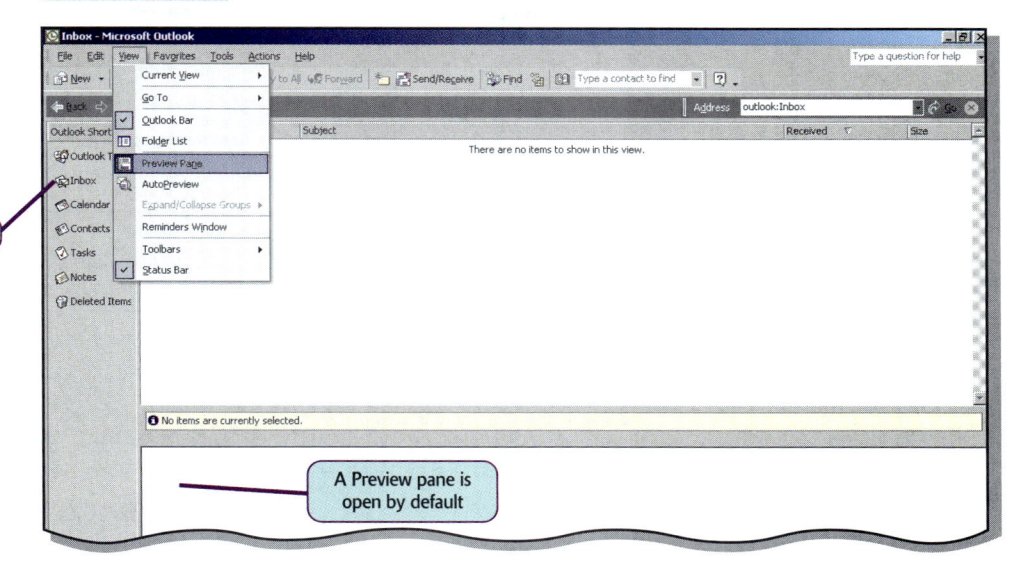

Inbox icon

A Preview pane is open by default

5 Choose **View | Current View | Message Timeline** to change the Inbox folder view.

Figure 1-33

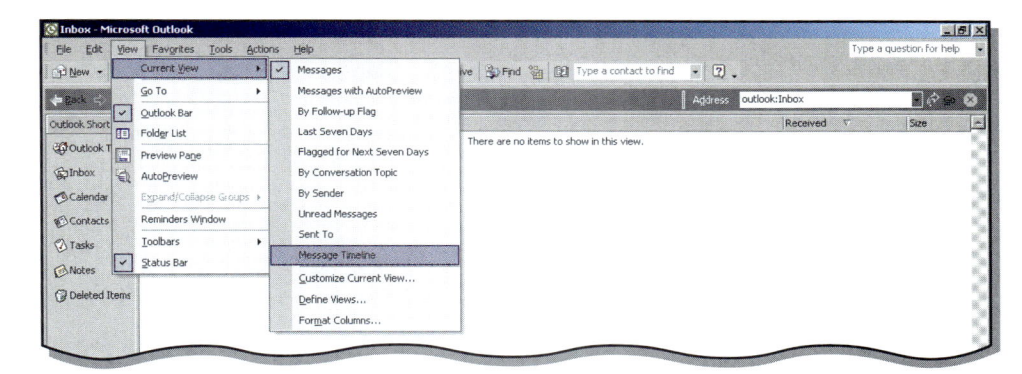

6 Click the **Calendar** icon on the Outlook Bar and then choose **View | Current View | Day/Week/Month** to restore the default Calendar folder view.

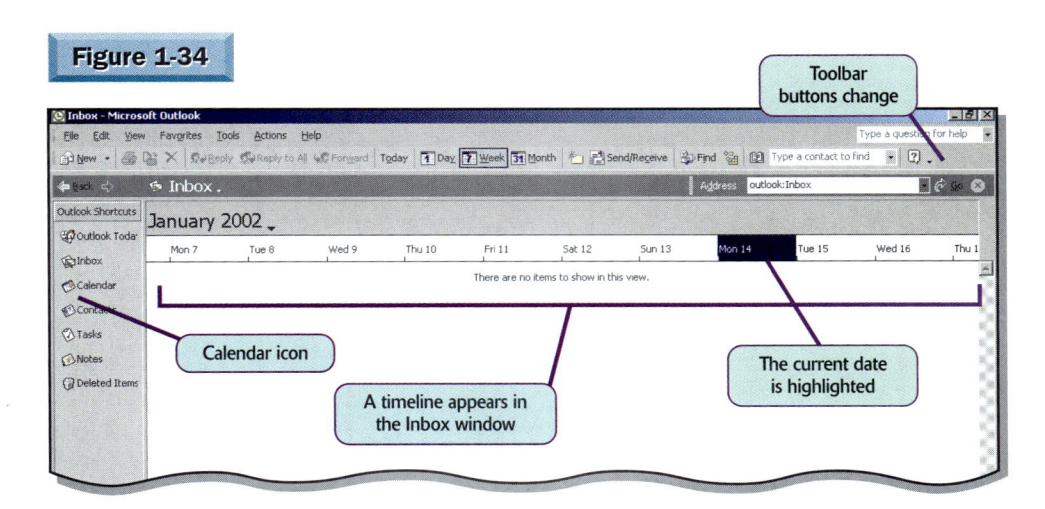

Figure 1-34

Toolbar buttons change

Calendar icon

A timeline appears in the Inbox window

The current date is highlighted

CHECK POINT

You have most likely already learned the different techniques for copying and moving text, but it never hurts to review information. As you continue your work in Outlook, you will create items and receive messages from which you will want to extract information that you can use in other items or files. Here are some facts about copying and moving:

- The *Cut* command is used to remove text from its current position.
- The *Copy* command leaves text at its current position.
- The *Paste* command places the items contained on the Clipboard at the position of the insertion point.

Office XP offers three different techniques for moving and copying text:

- Click the **Cut**, **Copy**, or **Paste** button on the Standard toolbar.
- Choose **Edit | Cut/Copy/Paste**.
- Press Ctrl + X to Cut, Ctrl + C to Copy, or Ctrl + V to Paste.

The last body of text or object that you cut or copy is stored on the Windows Clipboard so that you can paste it in any Windows file as many times as you want. When you cut or copy the next body of text or object, the previously stored text or object is replaced. However, because Outlook is an Office XP application, the text or object remains on the Office Clipboard until you log off or power down the computer. Because the Office Clipboard can hold up to 24 snippets of cut or copied text, when you cut or copy the 25th item, the first item on the Office Clipboard moves off the clipboard to make room for the new item.

Sizing Feature Panes

Many of the windows displayed in Outlook contain multiple panes. You can adjust the size of each pane by dragging a pane border and customizing the window to meet your needs.

Task 13:
To Resize Feature Panes

1 Display the Calendar, if necessary, and position the mouse pointer on the vertical border between the Date Navigator palette and the daily calendar palette.

2 Drag the vertical pane border that appears between the daily calendar and the Date Navigator/TaskPad pane to the right.

> **Tip** The sizes of the three panes in this Calendar view are controlled by the number of months displayed in the Date Navigator palette.

3 Position the mouse pointer on the border between the monthly palette and the TaskPad and drag the border down until it jumps once into place.

> **Tip** By releasing the mouse button when the border first "jumps" into place, there will be room for one additional monthly palette in the Date Navigator pane.

Figure 1-35

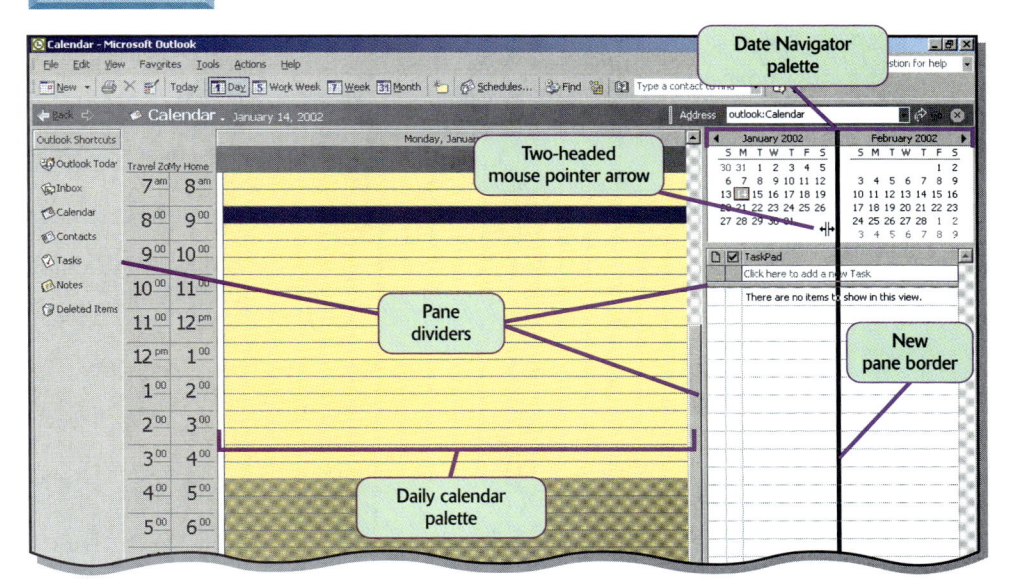

Figure 1-36

> **Troubleshooting** As you drag, the border does not appear to move until you cross the halfway point on the first monthly calendar in the Date Navigator. Then the border jumps and appears between the two monthly calendars.

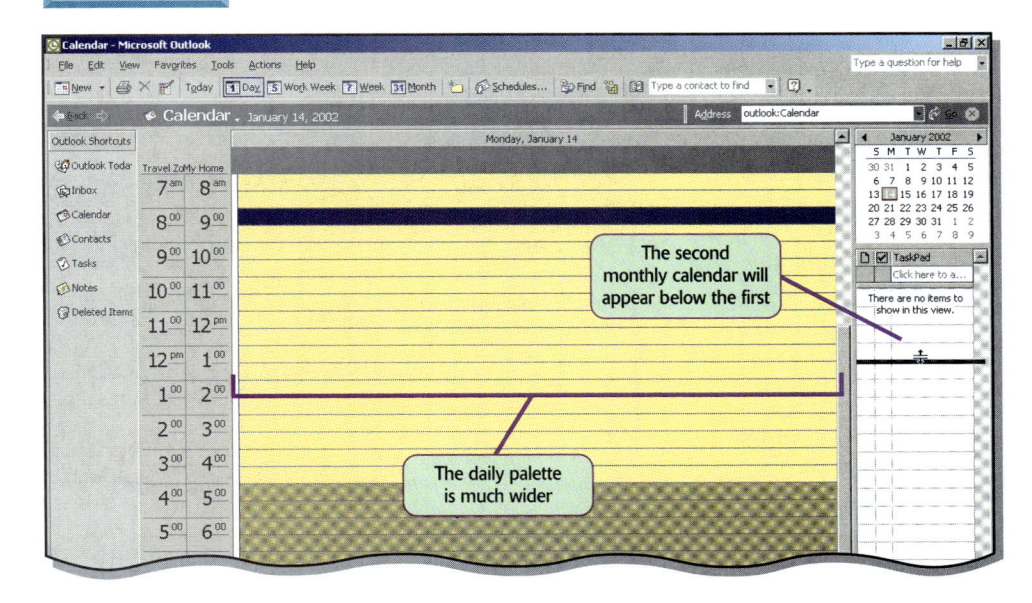

Finding Items

4 Drag the border between the Outlook Bar and the daily calendar palette to the right until all shortcut icon names are fully displayed.

5 Restore the Date Navigator and TaskPad panes to their original sizes.

Figure 1-37

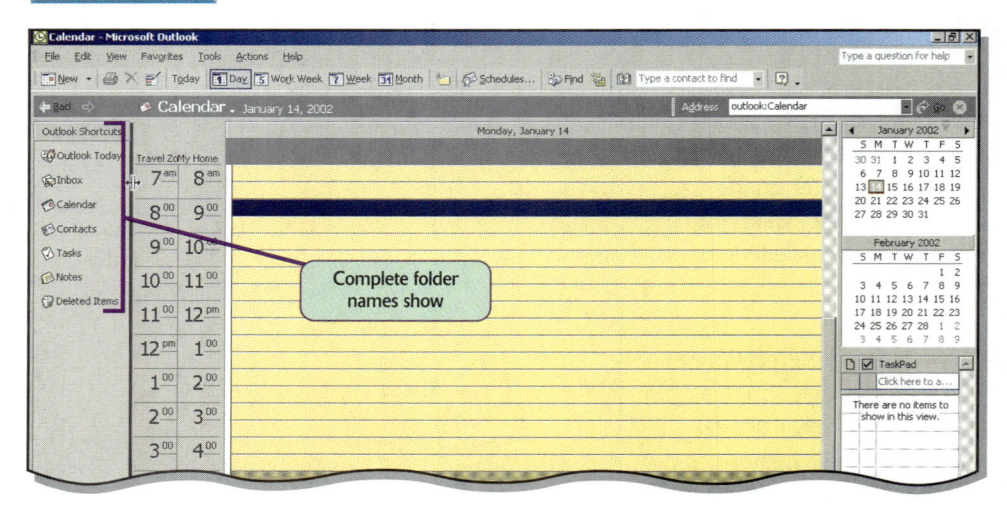

Complete folder names show

Finding Items

Outlook contains a sophisticated Find feature that makes locating items—e-mail messages, contact listings, tasks, appointments, and so forth—from different features a snap! The Find feature enables you to for various types of items based on the words or phrases contained in them. Outlook automatically assumes you want to search the active folder, but the Find feature is available for all folders. If you want to search folders other than the active folder, for example, you can select the folders of your choice. Learning how to use the Find feature will simplify your tasks as you progress through the projects in this book.

Task 14:
To Find Outlook Items

1 Display the Calendar and then click the Find button on the Standard toolbar.

2 Type *Your Name* in the **Look for** text box, click the **Search In** down arrow, and select **Choose Folders**.

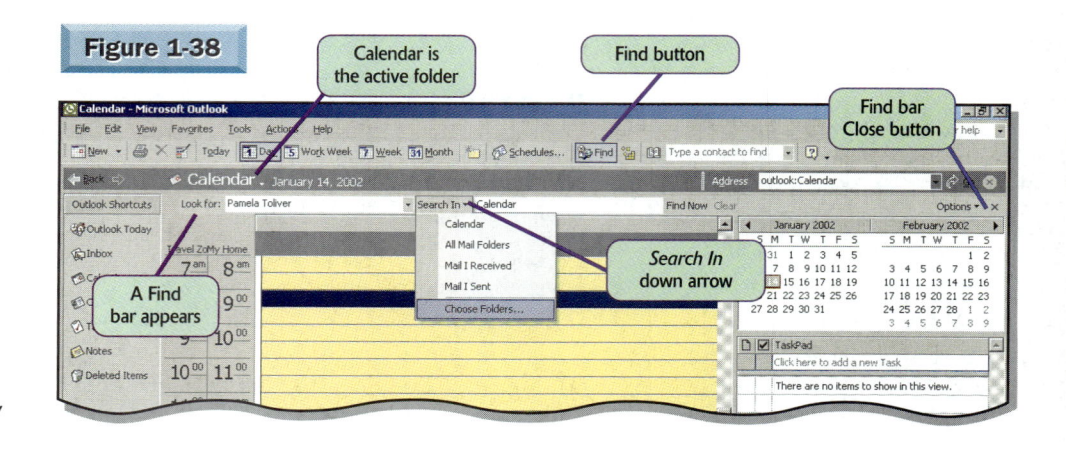

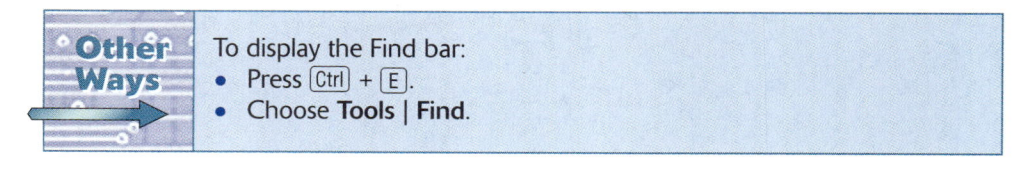

Figure 1-38

Calendar is the active folder

Find button

Find bar Close button

A Find bar appears

Search In down arrow

Other Ways
To display the Find bar:
- Press Ctrl + E.
- Choose **Tools** | **Find**.

Setting up Outlook 2002

3 Select the check boxes for each of the folders so that Outlook will search all folders for items containing your name, and then click **OK**.

Figure 1-39

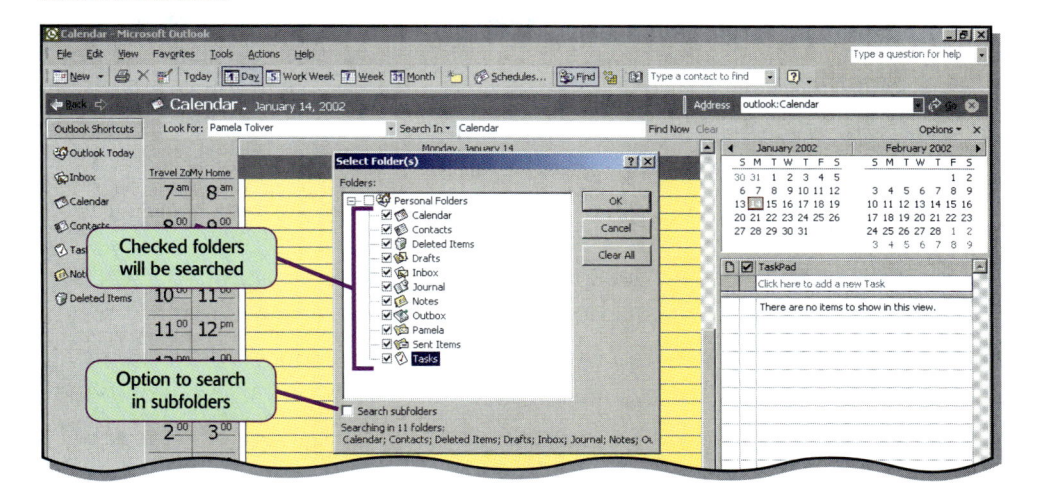

Checked folders will be searched

Option to search in subfolders

4 Click **Find Now** to start the search.

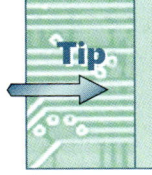

Figure 1-40

The list of folders appears in the Search In list

Find Now button

> **Tip:** To match the case of text during a search, click the Find Bar **Options** down arrow, select **Advanced Find** to display the Advanced Find dialog box, click the **More Choices** tab, and select the **Match case** check box. Then click the **Find Now** button in the Advanced Find dialog box.

5 Click the Find bar **Close** ✖ button to close the bar and then choose **View | Current View | Day/Week/Month** to return to the default Calendar window.

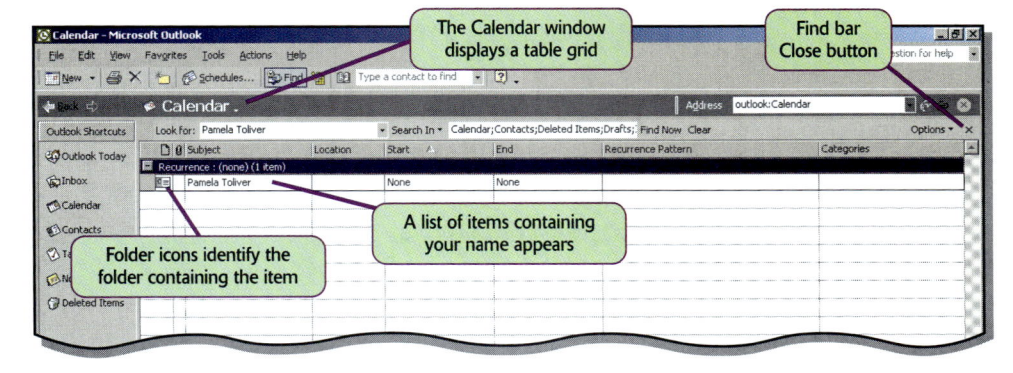

Figure 1-41

The Calendar window displays a table grid

Find bar Close button

A list of items containing your name appears

Folder icons identify the folder containing the item

SUMMARY AND EXERCISES

SUMMARY

- Outlook Today displays a summary of your appointments, a list of tasks that need to be completed, and new e-mail messages you receive.
- You can customize Outlook Today by selecting folders you want to include and selecting a style for the layout of the Outlook Today window.
- You can set Outlook to display Outlook Today, the Inbox, Calendar, Contacts, or Tasks each time you launch Outlook.
- Outlook comes with a set of default personal folders in which it stores items associated with different Outlook features.
- New folders can be added to the Outlook Bar My Shortcuts group.
- Creating special topic-specific folders enables you to store items related to specific projects and events and helps keep your work organized.
- You can add Outlook Bar groups as you need them and then move folder shortcuts into the groups.
- You can add folders containing other items, such as document folders that you use frequently, to the Outlook Bar.
- Changing the format for shortcuts in the Outlook Shortcuts group to display as small icons makes more of the shortcuts visible.
- The default toolbar contains most of the buttons you will use as you work but you can add or remove toolbar buttons as needed.
- Changing the time zone setting in Outlook affects the time zone setting of all other Windows-based programs on the computer.
- When additional time zones are added to Outlook, the standard time zone is used as a reference point and the new time zone appears beside the default time zone.
- Each Outlook feature has a set of standard views that change the arrangement of information onscreen.
- Find enables you to search for items based on the words or phrases that they contain. You can select the types of items you want to locate from any folder.

KEY TERMS & SKILLS

KEY TERMS
Message Timeline (p. 1-23)
time zone (p. 1-19)
views (p. 1-22)

SKILLS
Add an Outlook Bar group (p. 1-12)
Add a shortcut to the Outlook Bar (p. 1-14)
Add buttons to toolbars and commands to menus (p. 1-17)
Add time zones (p. 1-21)
Change the default feature window (p. 1-7)
Change the Outlook Bar shortcut icons size (p. 1-15)
Change the view (p. 1-22)
Change time zone settings (p. 1-20)
Create a personal folder and add it to the Outlook Bar (p. 1-9)
Customize Outlook Today (p. 1-5)
Find Outlook items (p. 1-26)
Reposition folders on the Outlook Bar (p. 1-13)
Resize feature panes (p. 1-25)
Set menu options (p. 1-16)

STUDY QUESTIONS

MULTIPLE CHOICE

1. Each Outlook feature stores items
   a. in the feature window.
   b. on the Outlook Bar.
   c. in Outlook files.
   d. in folders.

2. You can set all of the following items to display upon launch *except*
   a. Inbox.
   b. Calendar.
   c. Contacts.
   d. custom folders.

3. One technique for copying text to the Clipboard is to
   a. press Ctrl + C.
   b. press Ctrl + X.
   c. press Ctrl + V.
   d. click 📋.

4. Shortcut icons added to the Outlook Bar for new folders appear in the
   a. Outlook Shortcuts group.
   b. My Shortcuts group.
   c. newest group.
   d. Outlook Bar frame.

5. Outlook Today displays information for all of the following *except*
   a. appointments.
   b. new mail messages.
   c. notes.
   d. tasks.

6. To remove a button from a toolbar without displaying the Customize dialog box, what key do you press as you drag the button off?
   a. Shift
   b. Ctrl
   c. Alt
   d. Delete

7. To locate items in the Inbox, use the
   a. Find feature.
   b. Search and Replace feature.
   c. Go To feature.
   d. Copy feature.

8. The Windows Clipboard can hold up to
   a. 12 items.
   b. 24 items.
   c. 1 item.
   d. unlimited items.

9. You can customize the Outlook Bar in all of the following ways *except*
   a. adding and deleting shortcuts.
   b. creating, renaming, and deleting groups.
   c. deleting the Outlook Bar.
   d. changing the size of shortcut icons.

10. To customize the size of individual sections of a feature window,
    a. add a button to the toolbar.
    b. first use the Find feature to find the item.
    c. drag a pane border.
    d. you must use the View menu.

SHORT ANSWER

1. What are the procedures to create folders in Outlook?
2. What determines the items that appear on the Current View list?
3. How do you display the Find bar?
4. What is the easiest way to move shortcut icons on the Outlook Bar?
5. What other items can you add to Outlook Bar shortcuts besides folders created in Outlook?
6. Buttons available in Outlook that you can add to toolbars appear on what page of the Customize dialog box?
7. What folder name appears in the Look For text box on the Find bar?
8. What types of items can folders that you create in Outlook hold?
9. How do you display the Outlook Bar shortcut menu?

FILL IN THE BLANK

1. Shortcut icons appear on the Outlook Bar in _____.
2. The _____ is the default Outlook launch feature unless you change it.
3. To change time zones, display the _____ dialog box.
4. _____ appears in the feature banner for Outlook Today.
5. Tools used to customize menu display actions appear on the _____ page of the Customize dialog box.
6. The Office Clipboard can store up to _____ items.
7. Icons on the Outlook Bar represent _____.
8. The _____ displays item text and information in a separate pane when certain view options are set.
9. To access options for customizing Outlook, display the _____ menu.
10. A(n) _____ identifies the active location of folders as you reposition them on the Outlook Bar.

DISCUSSION

1. Identify at least three tasks that you expect to perform frequently and for which you might want to add a button to the Outlook toolbars.
2. What are the advantages of creating special folders for storing Outlook items?

3. What is the difference between adding and changing time zones and the impact of each option?
4. What technique do you find yourself using most frequently to copy, cut, and paste information among Windows programs?

GUIDED EXERCISES

1 CLASSIFYING ASSIGNMENTS

Keeping your class appointments straight and separate from your other meetings and appointments you record in Outlook can become a tedious task. To help you organize your work, you can create a folder, add it to the Outlook Class group, and then drag class appointments into the class folder. You can also add the floppy disk drive (A:) to the Outlook bar to make it easier to locate student files that are stored on the disks you place in the floppy drive. By changing the size of icons shown on the Outlook bar you will be able to view more folders without having to click the down- or up-arrow icons. You can then search for all items—e-mail messages, appointments, meetings, contacts, and so forth—from your Instructor and copy the appointments to the *Class Due Dates* folder. Follow these instructions to complete this task.

1. Click the **New Folder** button you added to the Outlook toolbar.

2. Select **Calendar** from the **Select where to place the folder** list, name the folder *Class Due Dates*, and click **OK**.

3. Click **Yes** to add the folder to the Outlook Bar and display the My Shortcuts group.

4. Drag the new folder to the Outlook Class group button and position the folder at the bottom of the group.

5. Click the **Find** button, type your instructor's last name in the **Look for** text box, click the **Search In** down arrow and select **Choose Folders**, select all folder check boxes, and click OK; then click **Find Now** to locate all items with your instructor's name on them.

6. Select only those items identified by a Calendar folder icon, drag them to the *Class Due Dates* folder, and close the Find bar.

7. Add the A:\ drive to the Outlook Bar Outlook Class group and size the Outlook Bar pane to display all text contained in all folders.

8. Set the Outlook Bar to display small icons by right-clicking a blank area of the Outlook bar and selecting Small Icons.

2 ZONING IN ON THE TOOLBAR

Because your schedule becomes so complex, you schedule appointments into the future quite regularly and would like to be able to quickly filter the view without having to use the menu. Being able to switch views quickly from the toolbar would be a great help when you are in a hurry. In addition, using Outlook Today to present an overview of scheduled appointments for the day can be extremely useful. Follow these steps to set up a view drop-down list on the toolbar and add the Calendar to the Outlook Today view.

1. Display the Calendar and choose **Tools | Customize**.

2. Select **Advanced** in the **Categories** list and scroll the **Commands** list until you see **Current View**.

3. Drag the **Current View** box to the toolbar and position it between the **Calendar Coloring** button and the **Today** button.

4. Close the Customize dialog box and click the Current View down arrow to review the filters you can apply from the list.

5. Open the **Outlook Today** folder, click the **Customize Outlook Today** link, click the **Choose Folders** button, select the **Calendar** check box to display the Calendar in the pane and click OK.

6. Select the **When starting, go directly to Outlook Today** check box to make Outlook Today the default start feature and then save changes to close the customize window.

3 DEREGULATING THE TIME ZONES AND TOOLS

You are back at your home office now and want to restore the Calendar window daily calendar palette to its original layout. Removing the second time zone will accomplish this task. You would also like to restore the File menu and toolbars to their default settings. Follow these steps to make these changes.

1. Choose **Tools | Options** and click the **Calendar Options** button.

2. Click the **Time Zone** button and clear the check mark from the **Show an additional time zone**.

3. Choose **OK** three times to close all dialog boxes.

4. Display Outlook Today, press and hold the [Alt] key, and drag the **New Folder** button off the toolbar.

5. Choose **Tools | Customize**, display the **File** menu, drag the New Folder command from the menu, and close the **Customize** dialog box.

6. Display the Calendar, press and hold the [Alt] key, and drag the Current View feature from the Calendar toolbar.

ON YOUR OWN

The difficulty of these case studies varies: ⚑ are the least difficult; ⚑⚑ are more difficult; and ⚑⚑⚑ are the most difficult.

1 GETTING BACK TO "NORMAL"

⚑ Whew! The Inbox window is quite a conglomeration of mysterious times! The problem with the current window display is that messages will be a challenge to find. Change your Current View setting to a view that lists messages and click the **Received** column heading to sort messages by date and time received. Then remove the extra time zone from the Calendar, if necessary. Create a new folder formatted to hold Inbox messages, and name the folder *Outlook Class Messages*. Add the folder to the Outlook Bar and move the folder to the Outlook Class group. If no Outlook Class group is available, create it.

2 DE-CLASS-IFYING OUTLOOK

⚑⚑ Now that class is over, you no longer need the Outlook Class group. You would, however, like to maintain the folders that appear in the group. Move the folders contained in the Outlook Class group so that they appear at the bottom of the Outlook Shortcuts group. Set the folder icon view in the Outlook Shortcuts group to show large icons. Then remove the Outlook Class group from the Outlook Bar. Set the menu options to display full menus after a short delay and large icons for toolbars. Remove the Calendar from Outlook Today, if it is displayed, and change the settings for Outlook Today to show only today's tasks.

3 SETTING SAIL

Summer is a great time to be assigned to work in Paris, France! You have just learned that you have been assigned to a special one-month project in Paris and want to get Outlook set up and ready to work while you are away from your home office. The following changes need to be made to Outlook to set up folders and customize Outlook so that it will be ready when you start the project:

- Add a time zone for Paris, France, to the Calendar.
- Create a new Outlook Bar group named *International Enterprise* and add at least 3 folders to the group, one folder to hold messages related to the project, a folder to hold calendar appointments and meetings for the project, and a folder to hold tasks associated with the project. The name of each folder should contain the word *Paris*.
- Size the Outlook Bar to display full text of the new group and folders you add to it.
- Format the Calendar window to display only one month in the Date Navigator.
- Finally add a new menu named *Project* to the menu bar and add the Appointment, Task, and Mail Message commands to the new menu.

4 PREPROJECT PLANNING

Many of us know well in advance when special events will occur. As a result, we can set up special filing systems or folders in which to keep files and information associated with the event organized. A Board of Directors meeting is scheduled for the end of next month. You have been assigned the task of organizing the event and assigning tasks associated with the event to other office personnel. To help you maintain an organized Outlook program, you decide to take some preliminary preparation steps before things become too hectic. Create a new Outlook Bar group named *Board of Directors*. Then switch to Windows Explorer and create a new folder in which to store different document files associated with the meeting. Create additional folders in Outlook, one to hold each of the following types of items: Messages from Board Members, Tasks, and Notes. Create shortcuts for all three folders and place them in the *Board of Directors* group on the Outlook Bar. Finally, create a new menu named *Board* on the menu bar and add the Appointment, Distribution List, and Mail Message commands to the menu. Because the meeting will be held in Hawaii, change the existing second time zone or add a time zone to show the time zone for Hawaii.

Photospread credits pages 1-2 & 1-3

©R.W. Jones/Corbis; ©FPG: ©Mark Adams 1999; ©Tony Stone: ©John Lund, ©Ed Honowitz; ©Pearson Education; and ©Lorraine Castellano

PROJECT 2

Organizing Outlook Contacts

The Contacts list stores information—such as names, addresses, phone numbers, and company names—about your personal and/or business contacts. As your list of contacts grows, you will find it useful for sending e-mail messages, assigning tasks, creating documents, merging with other Office applications, and recording new activities. In addition, you will find that storing contacts electronically is more efficient for editing, updating, and deleting contact information.

OBJECTIVES

After completing this project, you will be able to:

- Create contacts
- Open, edit, and delete contacts
- Sort and find contacts
- Print from the Contacts folder
- Flag contacts for follow-up
- Create a personal distribution list
- Track contacts activities
- Set contacts options
- Copy contacts

e-selections Running Case

As you explored the basic features available in Outlook and set up feature windows to best meet your needs, you identified a number of people with whom you expect to communicate on a regular basis. In addition, you have gathered a number of cards from business and personal associates that you would like to get set up in Outlook before you lose their cards. What better way to get started than to learn the ins and outs of the Outlook Contacts feature.

PDAs are PDQ

The hype about wireless Web was recently summarized in an article by John Yaukey of the Gannett New Service. He wrote:

"Trading stocks from an Everest base camp. Web surfing at 30,000 feet. Ordering pizza while sky diving. Not!"

So is he trying to say that the wireless Internet access tools were a bust? No. He was simply saying that the advertisers went a little extreme when they first started promoting the concept of wireless Internet and Web access. While the cost of personal digital assistants (PDAs) that enabled you to connect using wireless technology were at first not worth the cost, they've come a long way. Now hundreds of companies are working to improve the wireless experience and millions of technophiles eagerly await.

Admittedly, the small screens limit data displays and data transmission speeds are significantly slower than the standard PC dial-up connection. But you can also have fun with these little units. Just imagine:

You find yourself debating a topic about which you know nothing. You whip out your handy-dandy PDA, access your favorite encyclopedia site, and, voila, you win the debate!

You're in an airport and catch the tail end of a news broadcast that you're certain mentioned an earthquake in your home town. Connect using your wireless unit to a continuous news service and relax when you discover the quake didn't affect your family.

Download e-mail from 35,000 feet and watch all those around you clench their teeth in envy. Access important messages instantly—and let your friends keep you up-to-date on important happenings in their lives.

But how do you make this kind of connection? There are a number of different ways and tools to get you set up:

The Hardware

To connect to the Wireless Web, you'll need some hardware. There are a variety of different styles and types of all shapes and sizes on the market.

Personal Digital Assistants (PDAs)

Perhaps one of the most popular units with which to go wireless is the personal digital assistant or PDA. You've seen them everywhere and perhaps even have one of your own. They come in different shapes and sizes and cost anywhere from $150 to $900.

Web Phones

Probably one of the most versatile mobile Internet units is the Web phone. These units are capable of transmitting both voice and data and limit the number of separate units you carry when you also want a cellular phone. What's more, they are less expensive than most PDAs—anywhere from $100 to $400.

Pagers

The most expensive type of wireless access hardware unit is the pager because these units are considered business tools rather than fun toys.

Wireless Modems

Some PDAs come with built-in wireless modems—others don't. You'll need a wireless modem to connect just as you need a regular modem to connect from your home PC. What you won't need is a cord connected to a wall. The cost of the modem itself is about $100. Most of the time the modem is supplied by the service provider. Web phones, of course, enable you to connect by calling a special dial-Alex Loeb, the project manager, says she envisions taking the Tablet PC "into meetings, but also crawling into bed with it at night, reading my e-mail and switching over to a novel. And when my husband reminds me of our big weekend coming up, I make my reservation online." Lampson says, "Delivering the idea of the Dynabook means that all your information, and the information from the world around you, won't be limited to your desk, but be available at your fingertips."

PROJECT 2

Organizing Outlook Contacts

The Setup

Figures in this Project appear with some customizations set during tasks and exercises completed in other projects. As a result, the Outlook Bar you see may be different from the bar shown in figures in this Project.

The Challenge

The stack of business cards that you have accumulated during your brief tenure at e-Selections has grown to such an extent that you are losing track of whose cards you have collected. In addition, you have a number of cards from people at your previous place of business with whom you want to maintain contact. You have been told that Outlook provides a feature for electronically storing names and addresses of business associates and personal contacts and would like to enter the information contained on the cards.

The Strategy

Because Ms. Sandoval is unavailable and you have short periods of time available for entering data into Outlook, you decide to explore the Contacts feature on your own. As you work, you can record questions and interesting discoveries and discuss them with Ms. Sandoval during your next session.

Creating Contacts

Many offices today have a corporate list of business associates that is installed when an employee's computer is set up. This corporate list of contacts is often called a Global Address List or something similar, and it is usually maintained by a central authority. When you add contacts to the Contacts feature in Outlook, the listing is stored in the Contacts folder—one of the Personal Folders in Outlook. The first contact listing you want to add contains your personal and business data, and you will eventually want to send this information to colleagues outside the company.

Task 1:
To Create Contacts

1 Launch Outlook, maximize the application, and click the Outlook Bar **Contacts** icon.

2 Click the **New Contact** button to open a new **Untitled–Contact** window.

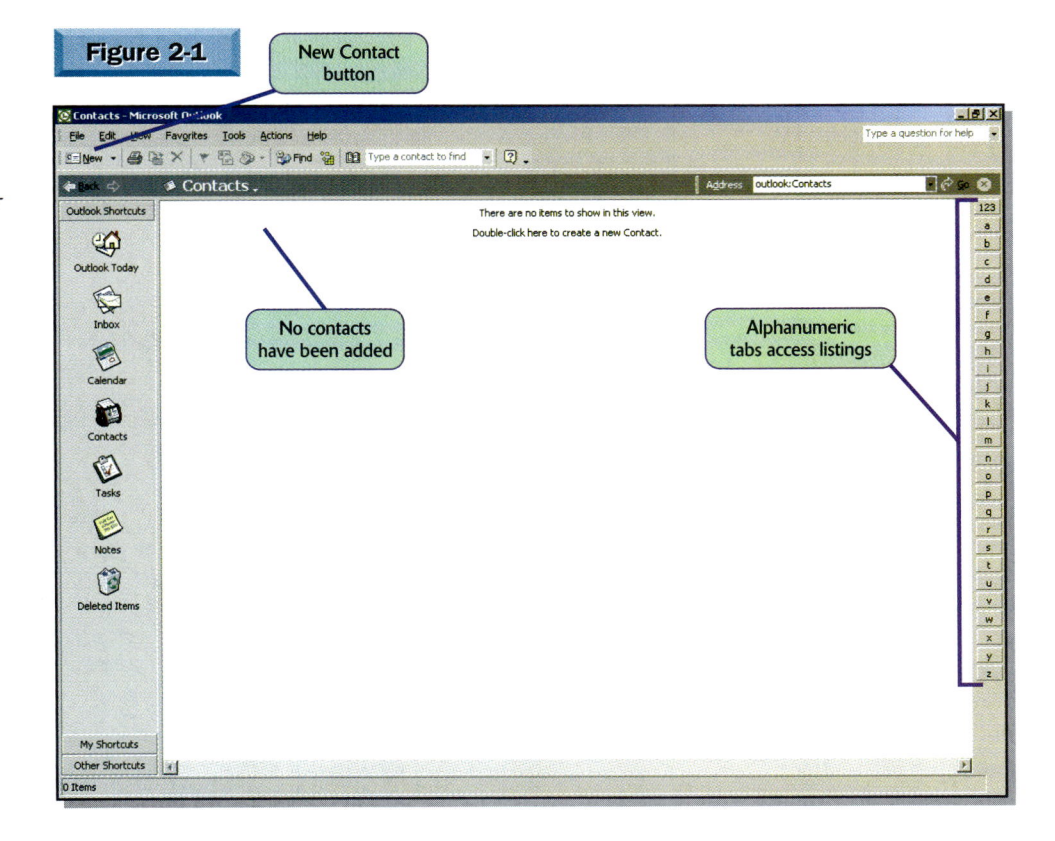

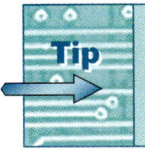

Figure 2-1

Callouts: New Contact button; No contacts have been added; Alphanumeric tabs access listings

Tip Organizations often add company contacts to each new installation of Outlook. As a result, there may already be contacts listed in your Contacts folder.

Creating Contacts

3 Type the following information into the corresponding dialog box fields, substituting your real data for this generic data:

Full Name:	Your Name
Job title:	Student
Company:	Your College/University
Address:	Your school address
Business:	Your school phone number
Home:	Your home phone number
E-mail:	Your e-mail address

Figure 2-2

Save and Close button
Contact name replaces *Untitled* after you type the name
Arrows display lists of field names
Fields of information to type
Buttons access additional dialog boxes
Fields of information to type

Tip Press Tab to move from field to field or click to position the insertion point in the appropriate field. Press Enter to add additional lines for fields such as the Address field.

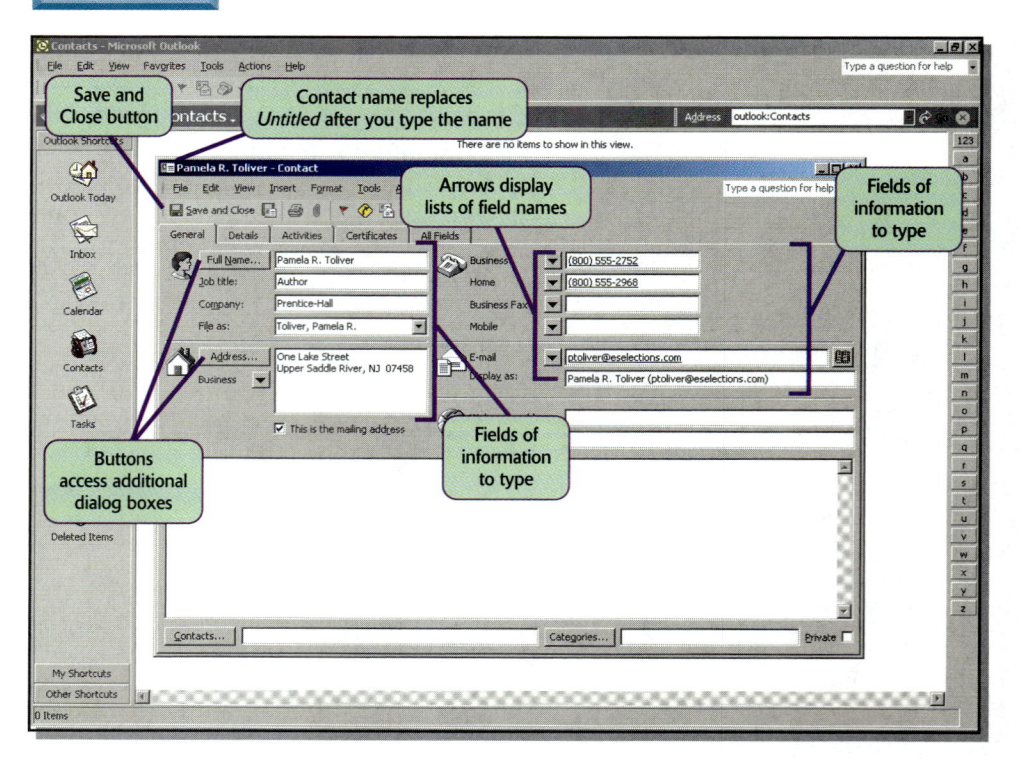

Tip Field names displayed in the New Contact form identify information, such as name, address, phone numbers, and e-mail addresses, used most frequently by people who maintain address books. The down arrows that appear beside some fields of information enable you to select from a list of field names that describe the data typed in the field text box.

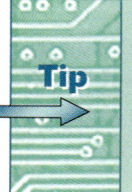

4 Click the **Save and Close** button to save the contact and return to Outlook Contacts.

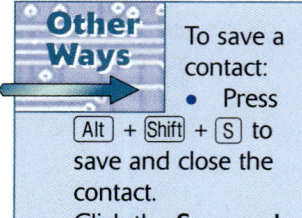

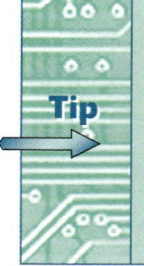

Tip The icon that appears at the right end of the e-mail text box represents the Outlook Address Book. The Address Book is a collection of different address books that are provided by Microsoft. It is created automatically in Outlook so that listings from the Contacts folder also appear in the Address Book. Depending on how your network is configured, the Address Book may also contain listings from an Exchange Server or Internet Directory services.

Other Ways
To save a contact:
- Press Alt + Shift + S to save and close the contact.
- Click the **Save and New** button to save the current contact and display another blank contact form.
- Choose **File | Save** to save changes to the contact and leave it open.

5 Create a new contact for your instructor and save and close the contact.

Figure 2-3

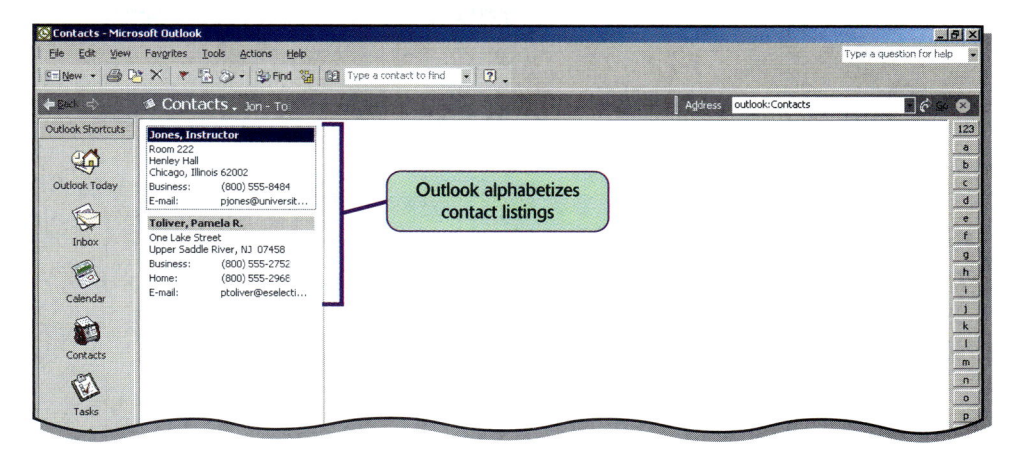

Outlook alphabetizes contact listings

CHECK POINT

As you type information into fields for new contacts, you may notice a few unusual dialog boxes and buttons popping up. As you type information into Contact fields, Outlook checks the data and information to determine whether or not it conforms to the standard format for the type of information fields normally contain. For example, when Outlook checks the information you type in the Full Name field and finds only one word, Outlook displays the Check Name dialog box to tell you that unusual data appears in the Full Name field. You can type the contact name into the individual fields shown in the Check Name dialog box or click OK to close the dialog box without making changes. When you type telephone numbers in the phone fields without including an area code, a Check Phone Number button appears at the right end of the active field. Click the button to display a Check Phone Number dialog box and make the necessary changes to the phone number or edit the number in the Contact form. The advantage of having the Check Phone Number dialog box display for contacts from foreign countries is that you can select the country and let Outlook provide the country code for the phone number.

Troubleshooting Depending on the settings that are active on your computer, Outlook may display a message box asking if you want to make this a business contact. Click **No**.

6 Create a new contact for Ms. Elisa Sandoval, the corporate trainer, whose business card is shown in Figure 2-4.

7 Create contact listings for two of your computer classmates that contain their names, job titles, university name, school phone number, and e-mail address, saving and closing each contact as you complete it.

Figure 2-4

e-selections

Elisa Sandoval
Senior Corporate Trainer

Selections, Inc.
240 W. Prospect Rd.
Omaha, NE 77485

Phone: (201) 555-1231
Fax: (201) 555-1010
E-mail: eSandoval@eSelections.com

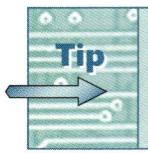

Tip: Because e-Selections is the online division of Selections, Inc., you will notice that the logo on the business card represents the division while the mailing address is the home office.

8 Create a new contact for **Sam Togej** and click the **Address** button to open the Check Address dialog box.

9 Type **17 Simbe Way, The Cottswolds, UK** in the fields shown in Figure 2-5, select **United Kingdom** from the **Country/Region** list, click **OK**, and then save and close the contact.

10 Create a new contact, type **AAA** in the **Company** field, and then save and close the contact. You will use this contact for an activity later in this Project.

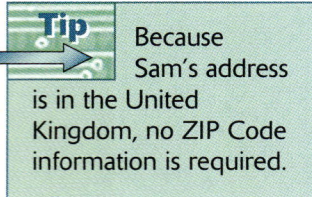

Tip: Because Sam's address is in the United Kingdom, no ZIP Code information is required.

Figure 2-5

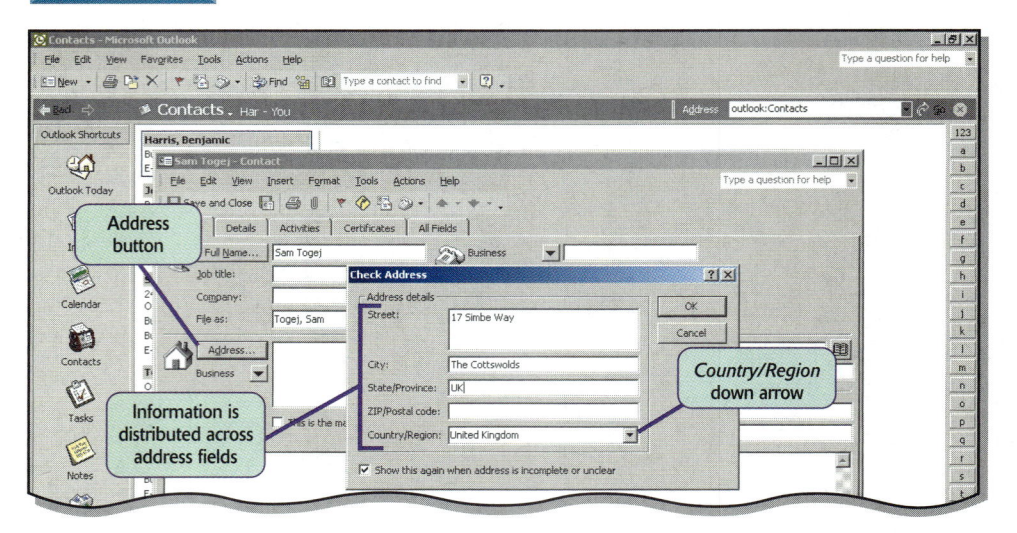

Tip: The Check Address dialog box presents text boxes for entering each part of a contact address. In one of the text boxes, you can enter different countries. Outlook displays this dialog box automatically when you enter incomplete information in the Address box of the contact form.

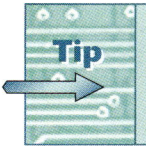

Tip: When information is typed in the Company field and no information is typed in the Full Name field, the contact is filed alphabetically using the company name.

Opening, Editing, and Deleting Contacts

One of the nice things about storing data electronically is the ease with which you can edit the information to bring it up to date—without all the erasing and crossing out associated with editing written data. You might find yourself editing listings in Contacts and deleting records that become out of date more frequently than you expect.

Task 2:
To Open, Edit, and Delete Contacts

1 Double-click the title bar for your personal listing and click the **Details** tab.

2 Complete personal details that apply, adding your major area of study in the **Department** field and the department chairman's name in the **Manager's Name** field, and then save and close the contact.

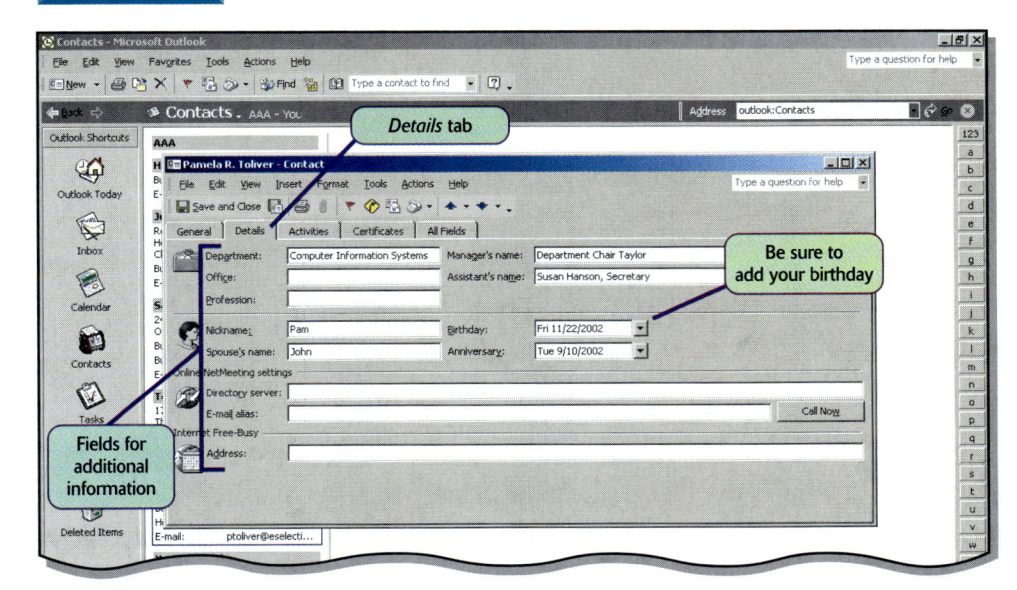

Figure 2-6

Details tab

Be sure to add your birthday

Fields for additional information

> **Tip** Outlook adds birthdays and anniversaries in your Calendar if you enter them on the Details page.

3 Double-click the title bar for AAA, click in the **Address** field, type **123 Main Street, Sarasota, FL 12345**, and save and close the contact.

4 Click the title bar for one of the computer classmates you entered and click the **Delete** ✕ button to remove the contact.

5 Choose **Edit | Undo Delete** to restore the contact.

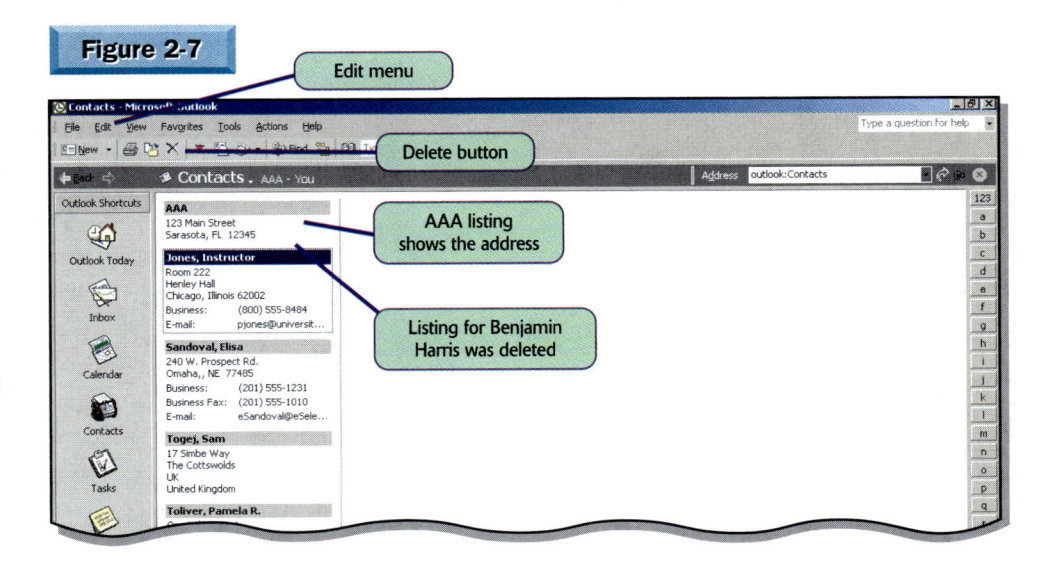

Figure 2-7

Edit menu

Delete button

AAA listing shows the address

Listing for Benjamin Harris was deleted

WEB TIP

Did you know that there are now several different services that offer free Internet connection? Search the Web for *Free Internet* and see how many you can find.

Sorting and Finding Contacts

Outlook provides searching and sorting tools that enable you to find a contact from any Outlook folder. To sort contacts, you can change the Contacts folder view to change the arrangement of field information in the window or apply advanced techniques for setting additional sort orders using the View Summary dialog box.

Tip Arrows appear beside column headings to identify the current field on which the view is sorted. In addition, when the arrows point up, the field is sorted in ascending order; when the arrow points down, the field is sorted in descending order.

Task 3:
To Sort Contacts Using Views

1 Choose **View | Toolbars | Advanced** to display the Outlook Advanced toolbar.

2 Click the **Current View** down arrow on the toolbar to display a list of available views and select **By Company**.

3 Click the **Full Name** column heading to sort the contacts alphabetically by the Full Name field within each company. Arrows now identify *Full Name* and *Company* sort fields.

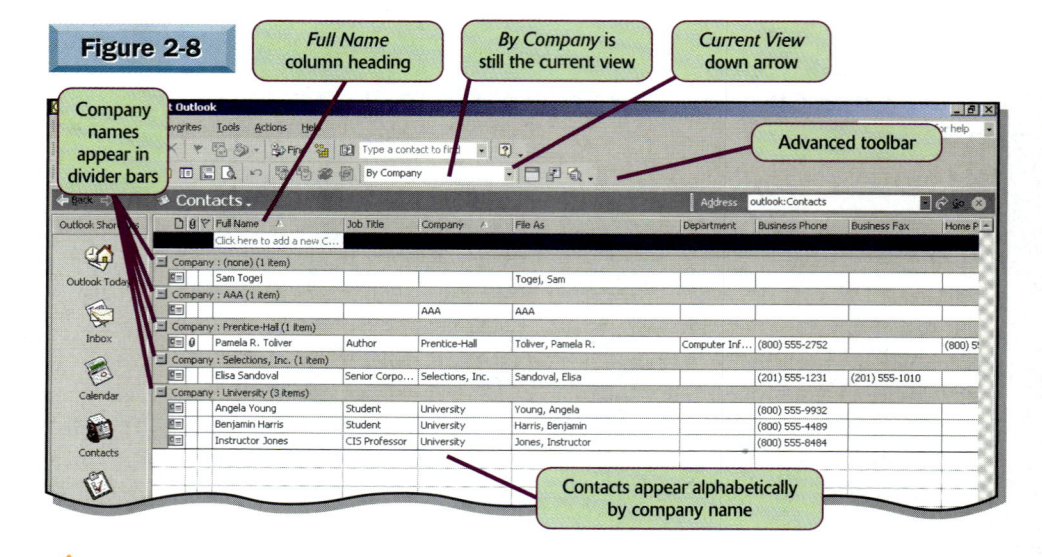

Figure 2-8

Callouts: Full Name column heading; By Company is still the current view; Current View down arrow; Company names appear in divider bars; Advanced toolbar; Contacts appear alphabetically by company name

Troubleshooting Because the names and addresses of your classmates will vary, the display you see will be different from the listings shown in Figure 2-8.

Organizing Outlook Contacts OU 2-11

4 Click the **Current View** down arrow again and select **By Location**.

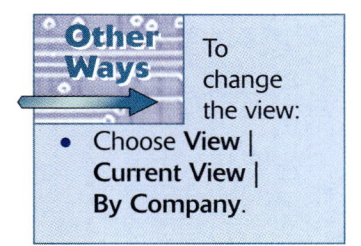

Figure 2-9

- *Country/Region appears in divider bars*
- *By Location appears in the Current View box*
- *Country/Region appears with an arrow to indicate that it is the sort field*

Other Ways

To change the view:
- Choose **View | Current View | By Company**.

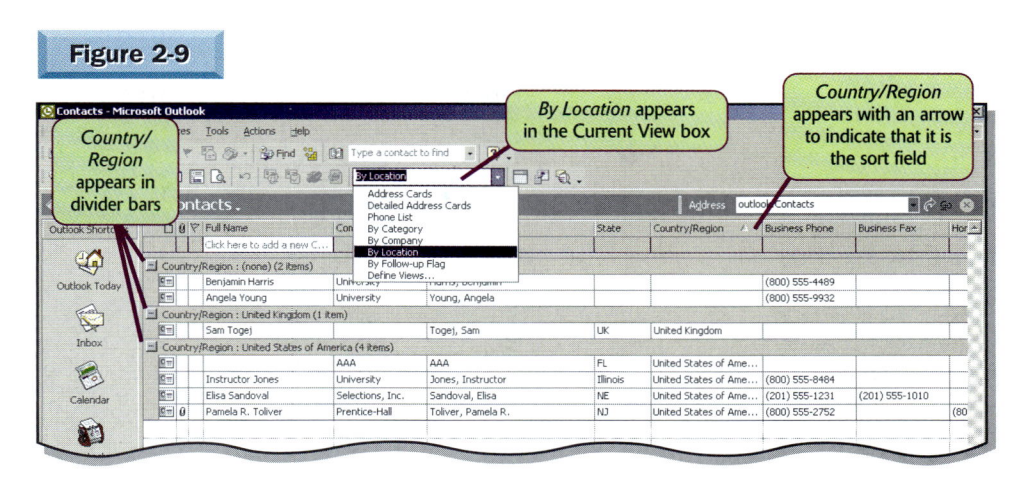

Using Advanced Sort Techniques

Changing the Contacts folder view provides an easy way to sort contacts in the most frequently sorted orders. As your contacts list grows, you may have numerous contacts with identical data in various fields—same last name, the same company name, or both. To arrange these listings more precisely, you may want to identify additional sort fields. When special sort order needs arise, you can customize the view using the Sort dialog box.

Task 4:
To Apply Advanced Sort Techniques

Figure 2-10

1 Display Outlook **Contacts** in the **By Location** view, if necessary.

2 Choose **View | Current View | Customize Current View** to open the View Summary dialog box.

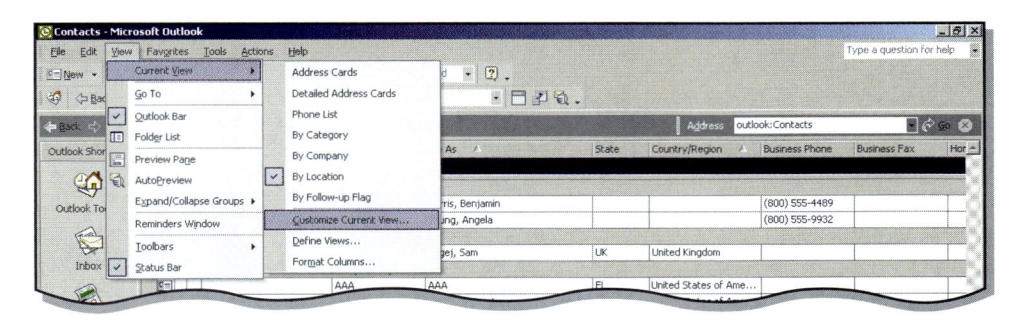

Other Ways

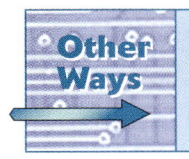

To display the View Summary dialog box:
- Right-click a blank area of the window and select **Customize Current View**.

3 Click the **Sort** button.

> **Tip** The Other Settings and Automatic Formatting buttons displayed in the the View Summary dialog box control font, font size, font color, and other settings specific to the active view.

Figure 2-11

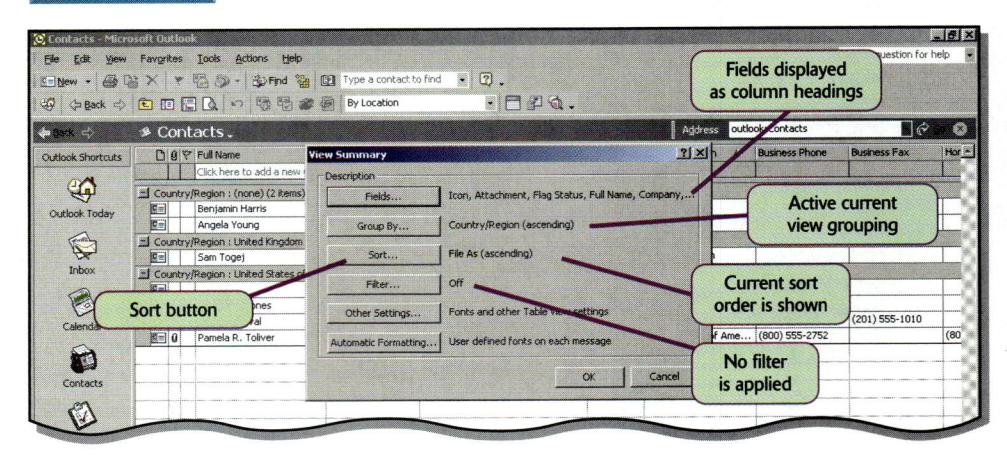

- Fields displayed as column headings
- Active current view grouping
- Current sort order is shown
- No filter is applied
- Sort button

4 Click the **Then by** down arrow and select **Business Phone** to set a second field on which to sort.

> **Tip** After you select one additional field, the next *Then by* field becomes active.

Figure 2-12

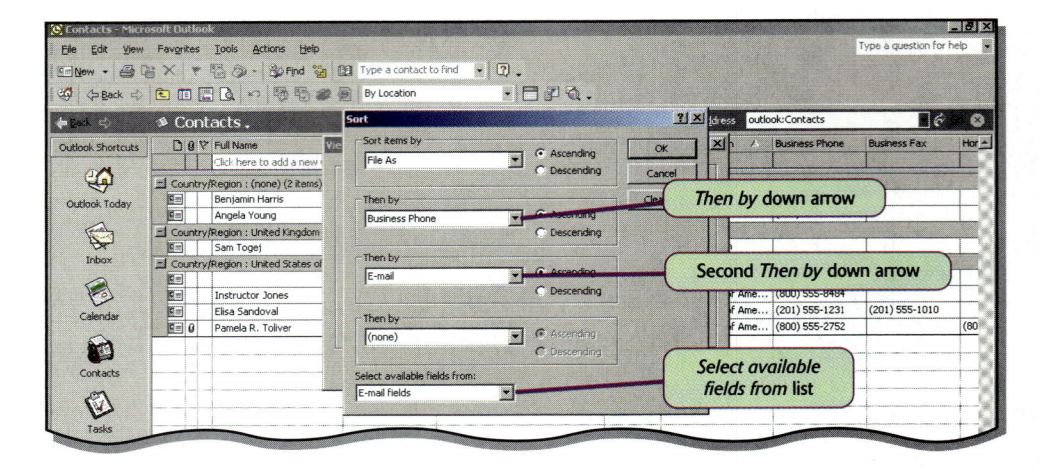

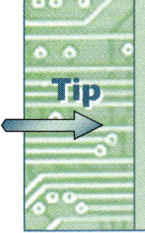

- Then by down arrow
- Second *Then by* down arrow
- *Select available fields from* list

5 Click the **Select available fields from** down arrow and select **E-mail fields** to change the list of fields on which you can choose to sort.

6 Click the second **Then by** down arrow, select **E-mail** as the third sort field, and click **OK**. A message box notifies you that the e-mail field is not shown in the view and asks if you want to show it.

> **Tip** By default, the fields available for sorting appear on the *Frequently-used fields* list. When *Frequently-used fields* is set as the *Select available fields from* list, a list of fields most commonly used for sorting contacts is available for setting sort order. Because the e-mail field does not appear on the *Frequently-used fields* list, changing the list of available fields to *E-mail fields* makes it possible to select the e-mail field for sorting.

7 Click **Yes** to add the **E-mail** field to the current view and then click **OK** to close the View Summary dialog box.

Figure 2-13

8 Scroll to the right until the **E-mail** field appears in the view window.

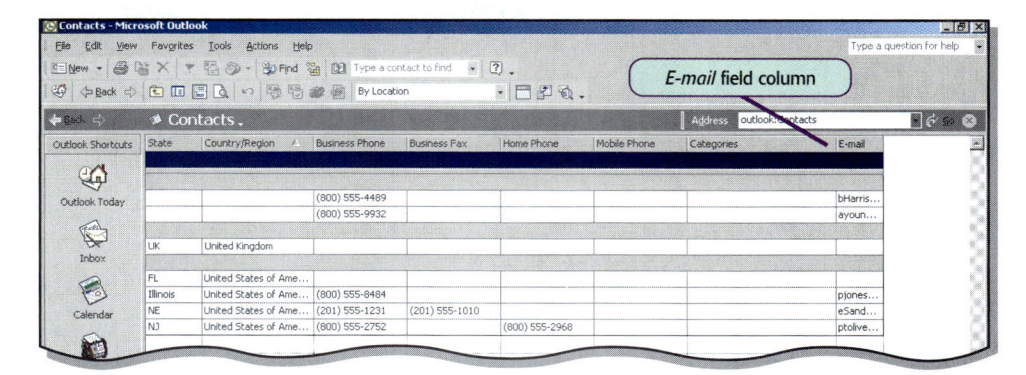

Tip Outlook places new fields added to a view in the first available space at the far right of the view.

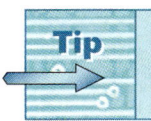

9 Drag the **E-mail** column heading to the left of the table and position the heading just to the left of the **State** field.

Figure 2-14

Troubleshooting
If you drop the field in the wrong position, pick it up and drag it to the correct position or choose **Edit | Undo** and start over.

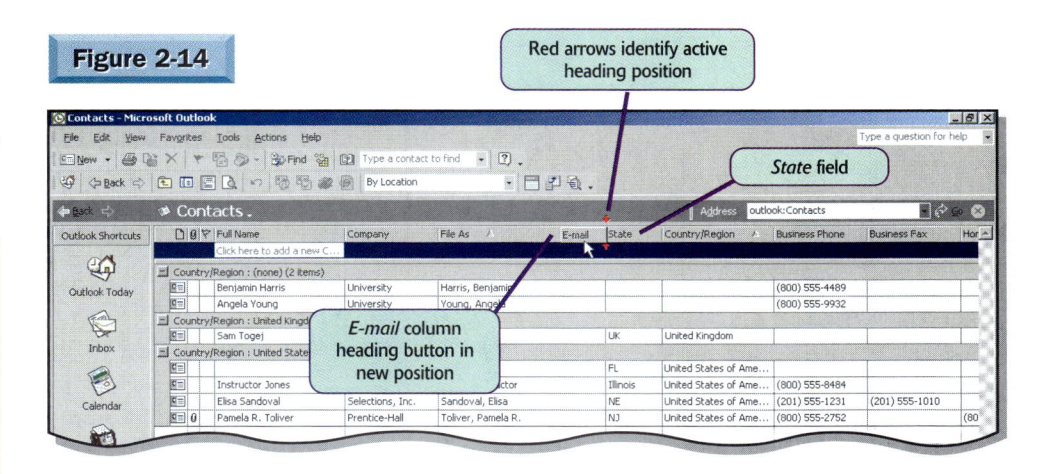

Finding Contacts

Most contact lists grow to include so many listings that locating contacts becomes increasingly more complex. You can, of course, use the Find feature to locate a contact along with all other items that contain the contact's name. As you become more familiar with Outlook features, you will find that you can select contacts and integrate contact information with other Outlook features—to perform such tasks as generating e-mail messages, assigning tasks, inviting contacts to meetings, and so forth. You will also discover that you can use contacts to automatically add information to files in other applications. Because of the wide variety of ways you can use contact information, the Outlook Find feature helps you locate contacts from any Outlook feature.

Task 5:
To Find Contacts

1 Change the current view to display **Address Cards**.

2 Click the **Find a Contact** text box on the Standard toolbar, type your last name, and press [Enter] to open the contact.

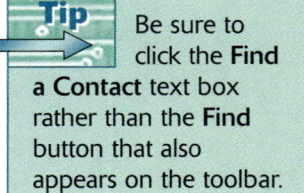

> **Tip** Be sure to click the **Find a Contact** text box rather than the **Find** button that also appears on the toolbar.

Figure 2-15

Find a Contact text box

Address cards view

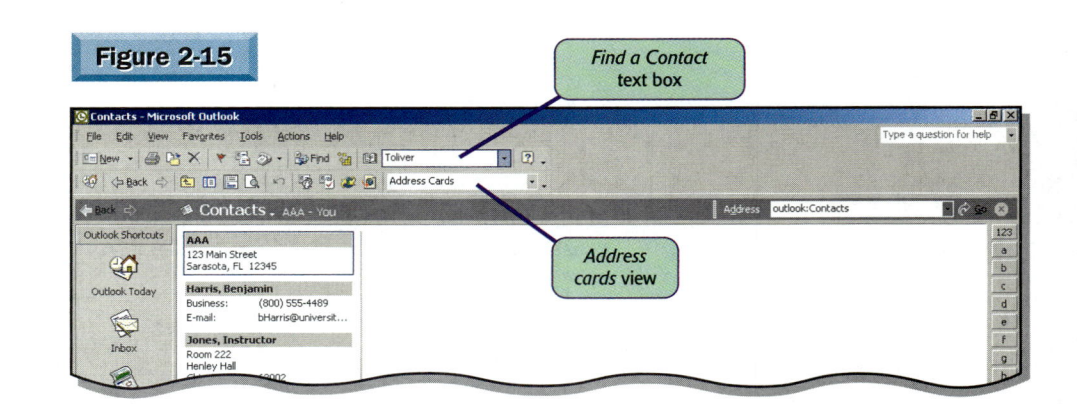

Troubleshooting If Outlook finds no listings, your system may not be set to display Contacts in the Address Book. Check with your instructor to be sure that changing the setting will have no detrimental affects on other settings. Then right-click the Contacts icon on the Outlook Bar, select **Properties**, click the **Outlook Address Book** tab, and select the **Show this folder as an e-mail Address Book** check box.

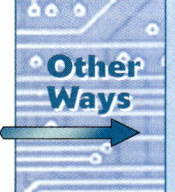

Other Ways

To find a contact:
- Choose **Tools | Find** and type the contact name in the **Look for:** text box in the Find bar.
- Press [Ctrl] + [E] and type the contact name in the **Look for:** text box in the Find bar.

> **Troubleshooting** If you have more than one contact with the same last name, the **Choose Contact** dialog box opens. Select the name of the contact to open and then click **OK**.

3 Close your contact listing and switch to Outlook Today.

4 Type **sa** in the **Find a Contact** text box on the Standard toolbar and press [Enter] to open the Choose Contact dialog box.

5 Select **Sam Togej**, click **OK** to open the contact listing for Sam Togej, and then close all open contacts windows.

Figure 2-16

sa appears in the Find a Contact text box

Outlook found two contacts containing sa in the name field

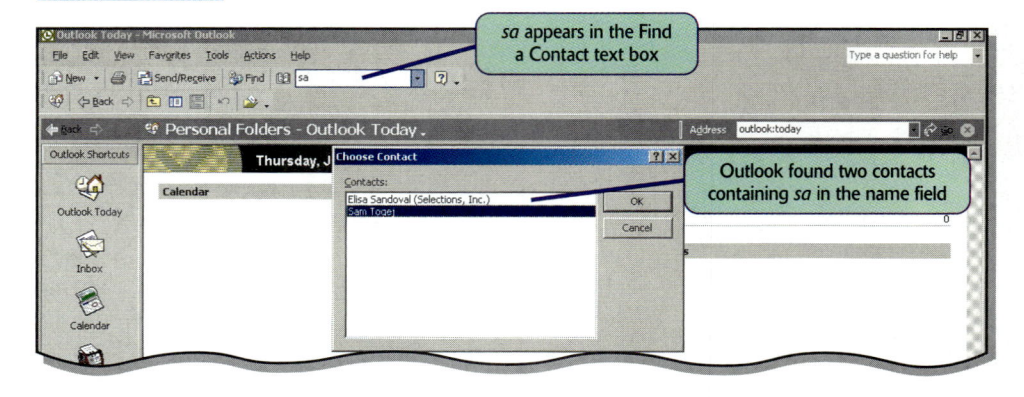

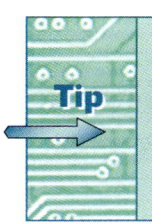

Tip: Typing only a portion of a name or other information expands the search so that more contact listings will appear in the Choose Contact dialog box. When the list in the Choose Contact dialog box is too long to efficiently find the contact you want to open, you can narrow the search by typing additional text in the Find a Contact text box.

WEB TIP

Portals are Web sites that act as guides to other Web sites and Web services. Many portals specialize in different types of information. See if you can locate Web portals that specialize in providing government or college information.

Printing from the Contacts Folder

Basic procedures for printing in Outlook are the same as the procedures for printing in other Windows applications. Because of the unique field names and information stored in different Outlook folders, the printing options, windows, and dialog boxes within each feature will vary.

Task 6:
To Print Contacts

1. Switch to the Contacts folder and choose **File | Print** to open the Print dialog box.

2. Scroll down the **Print style** list, select the **Phone Directory Style**, and click **Preview**.

Other Ways
To open the Print dialog box:
- Press Ctrl + P.
- Click the Print button.

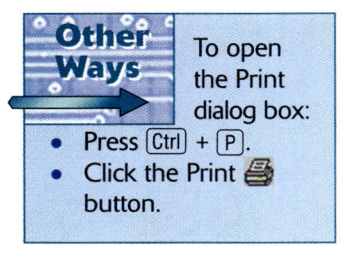

Figure 2-17

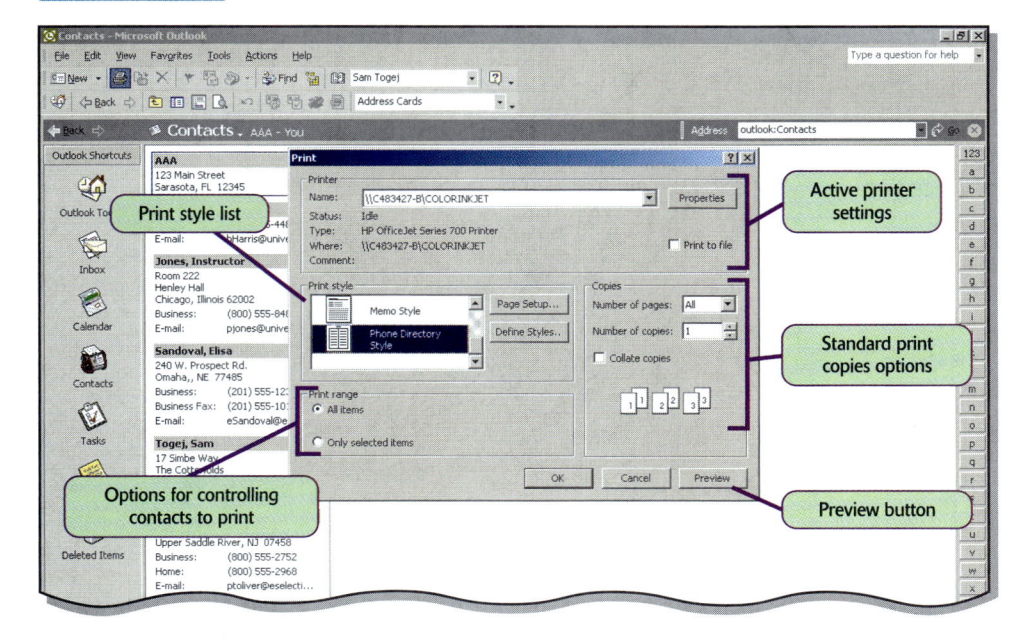

Callouts: Print style list, Active printer settings, Standard print copies options, Preview button, Options for controlling contacts to print

Tip: The folder containing the items you want to print must be active.

Printing from the Contacts Folder

3 Press `Esc` to close the Preview window; then choose **File | Print Preview**.

4 Click the **Page Setup** button on the Print Preview toolbar.

Figure 2-18

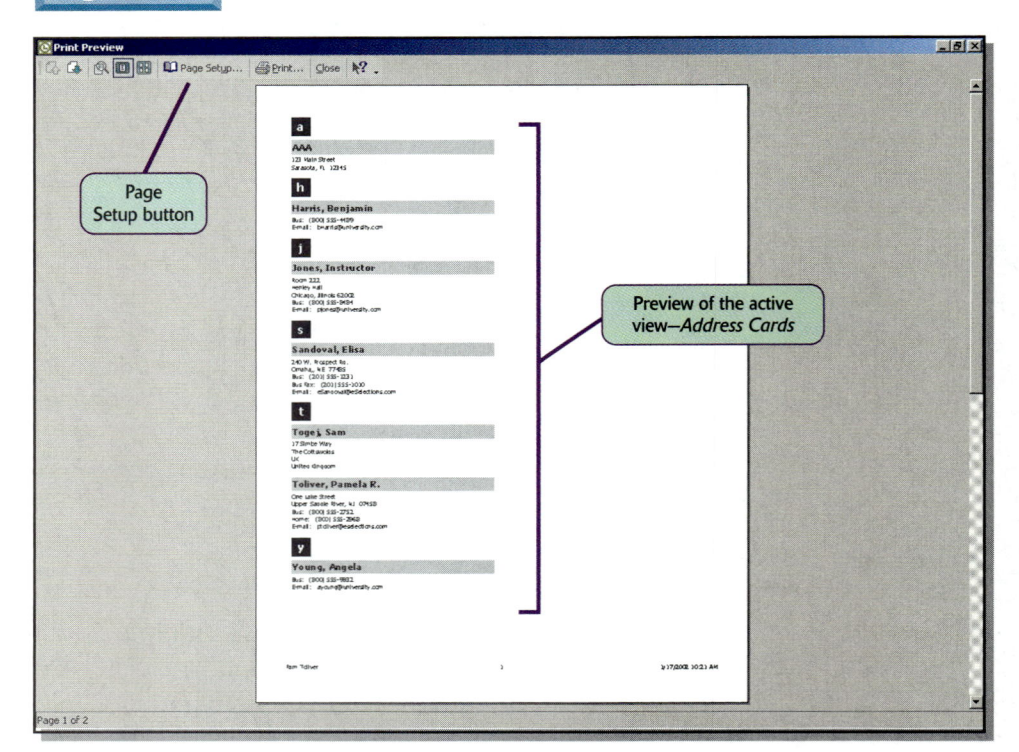

- Page Setup button
- Preview of the active view—*Address Cards*

5 Set the following options on the **Format** page of the Page Setup: Card Style dialog box:
- Click the **Number of columns** down arrow and select **3**.
- Click the **Blank forms at end** down arrow and select **None**.

Figure 2-19

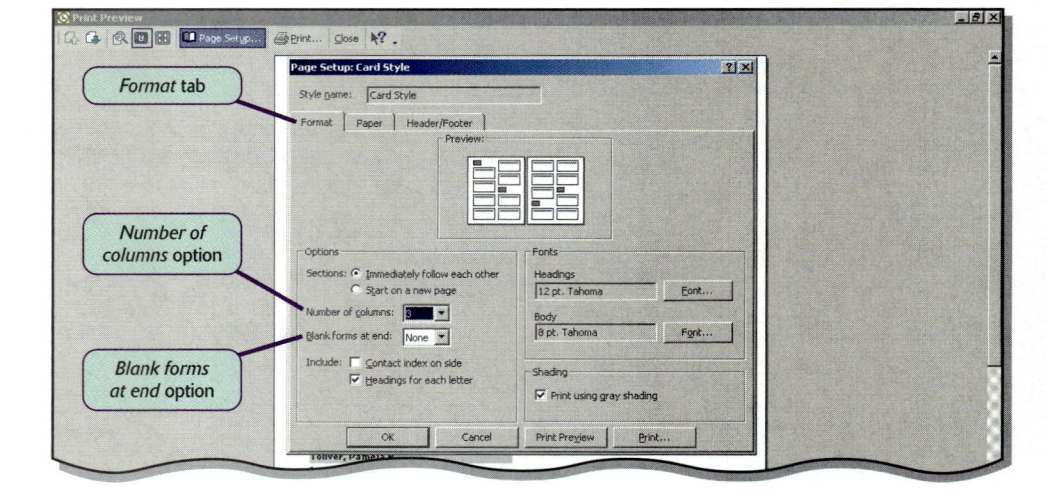

- Format tab
- Number of columns option
- Blank forms at end option

Organizing Outlook Contacts OU 2-17

6 Click the **Paper** tab, select the **Landscape** orientation option, and click the **Print Preview** button.

Figure 2-20

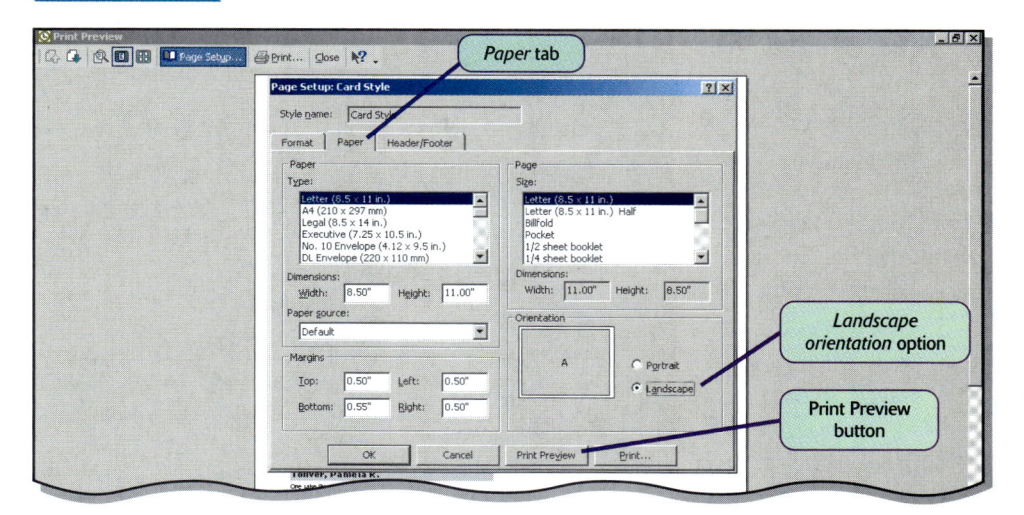

7 Press [Esc] to close the preview window and double-click the title bar of your contact listing to open your contact form.

8 Choose **File | Print** from the menu bar in the open contact window.

9 Click **Cancel** and then close your contact form.

Figure 2-21

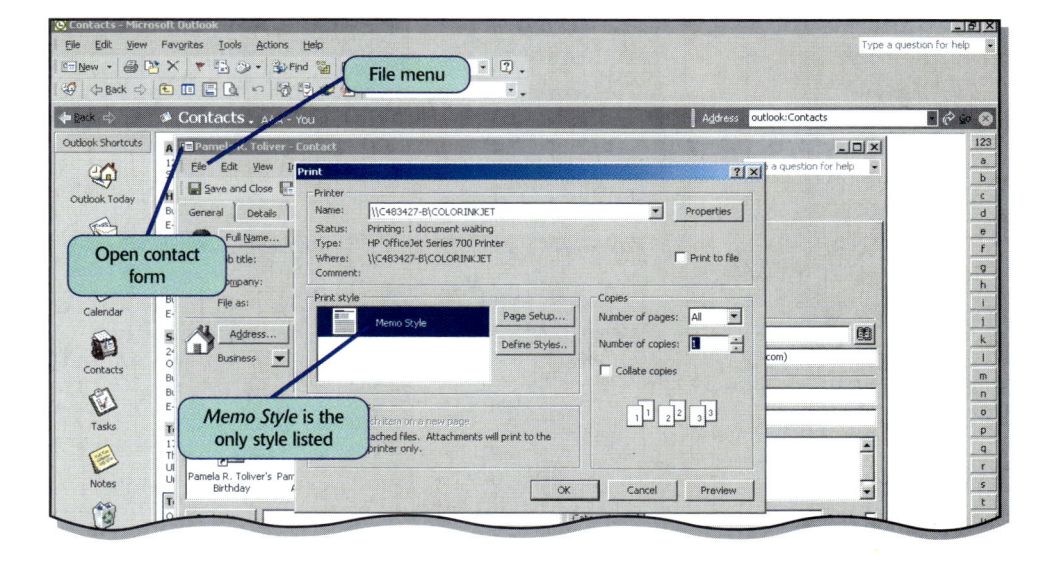

Flagging Contacts for Follow-Up

As you enter information for new contacts, there will be times when you are uncertain about the correct spelling of a person's name, do not have their phone number, or want to verify other information and edit the contact at a later date. In addition, you may want to set up an appointment or meeting involving a contact or want to call the contact later. You can set a reminder to follow up on these types of activities by *flagging* the contact for follow-up.

Task 7:
To Flag Contacts for Follow-Up

1 Open the contact listing for your instructor and click the **Follow Up** button on the Standard toolbar to open the Flag for Follow Up dialog box.

2 Set the following options in the Flag for Follow Up dialog box.
- **Flag to:** Send E-mail.
- **Due by:** Select the date for next Wednesday.
- **Time:** 5:00 PM

3 Click **OK**.

4 Save and close the contact.

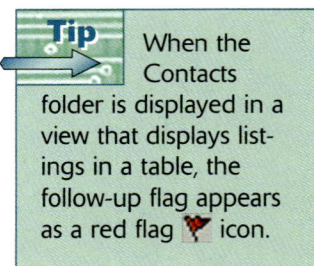

Tip When the Contacts folder is displayed in a view that displays listings in a table, the follow-up flag appears as a red flag icon.

Figure 2-22

- Follow Up button
- Instructor's contact form
- Flag to setting
- Due time
- Due by setting

The flag message appears in the InfoBar at the top of the contact General page

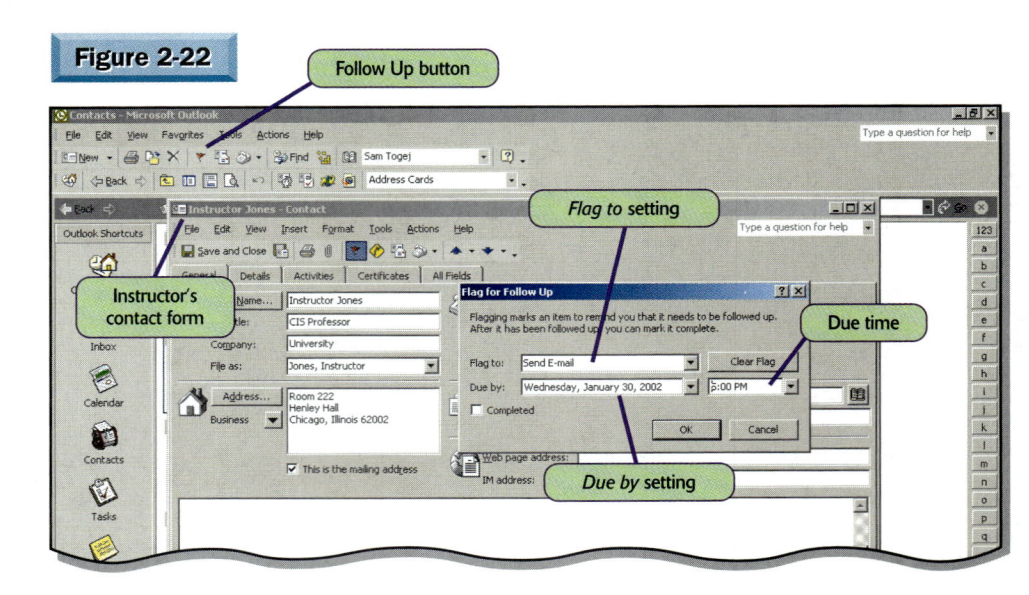

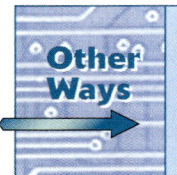

Other Ways

To flag an item:
- Choose Actions | Follow Up.
- Press Ctrl + Shift + G.
- Right-click the item you want to flag and select **Follow Up**.

Figure 2-23

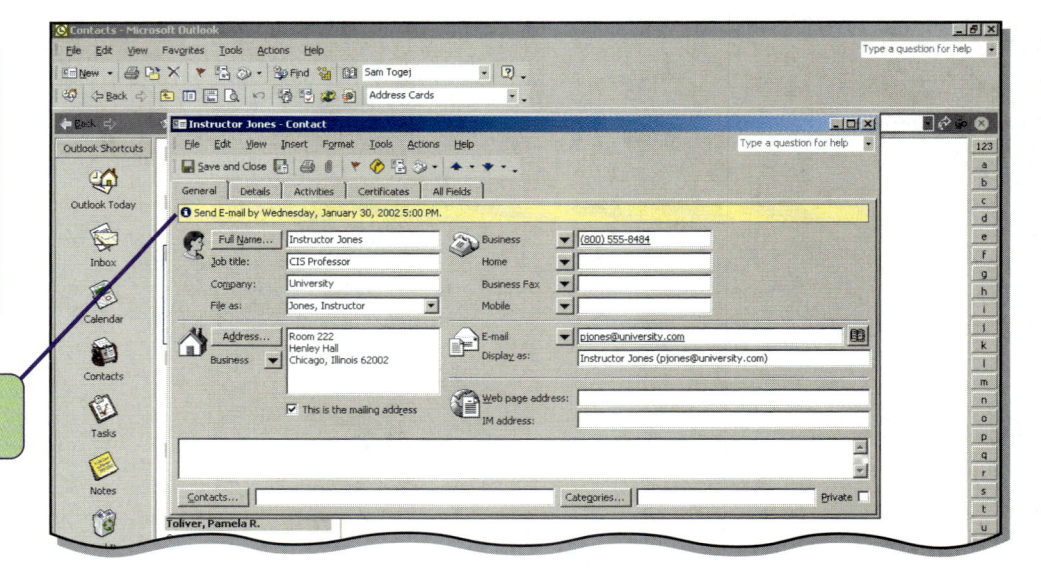

Organizing Outlook Contacts   OU 2-19

Creating Personal Distribution Lists

People who work for the same company, associates who work in your department, and other contact listings that share a common element can be grouped together to form a *distribution list*. Creating distribution lists can reduce the amount of time spent selecting individual contacts for communications as well as time spent sorting and finding contacts who share the common element.

Task 8:
To Create a Personal Distribution List

1 Display the Contacts folder, right-click a blank area of the Contacts window to open the shortcut menu, and select **New Distribution List** to open the Untitled–Distribution List dialog box.

Figure 2-24

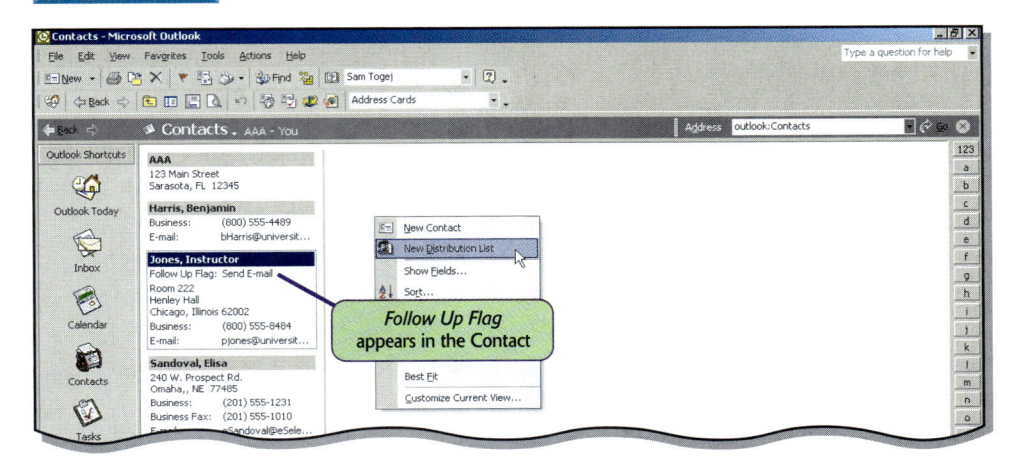

Follow Up Flag appears in the Contact

Other Ways

To create a distribution list:
- Choose File | New | Distribution List.
- Press [Ctrl] + [Shift] + [L].
- Click the **New** button down arrow and select **Distribution List**.

2 Type **Outlook Class** in the **Name** field, click **Select Members** to open the Select Members dialog box, and select **Contacts** from the **Show Names from the** list, if necessary.

Figure 2-25

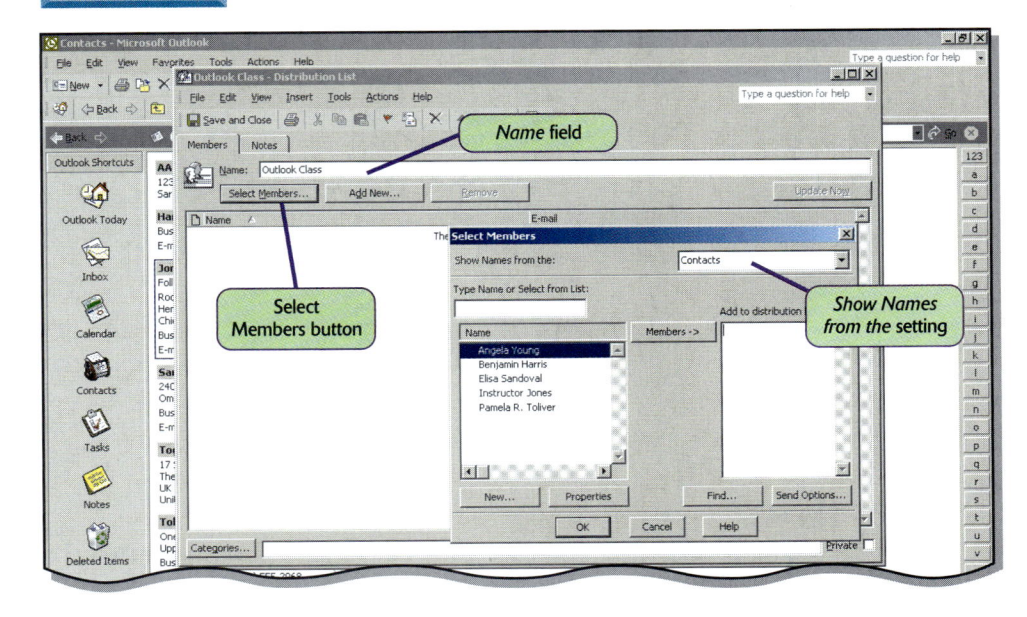

Name field

Select Members button

Show Names from the setting

Creating Personal Distribution Lists

3 Select your instructor's name in the list on the left, press the Ctrl key and click the contact listings for both classmates as well as your own listing, and then click the **Members** button.

> **Tip** Only contacts for which you have recorded e-mail addresses appear in the list of available names.

4 Click **OK** to place all four names in the distribution list.

5 Select your name in the distribution list names, click **Remove**, and then save and close the distribution list.

> **Tip** Removing a contact from a distribution list does *not* remove the contact from the Contacts folder.

Figure 2-26

- Distribution list name appears in the title bar as you type it
- Members button
- Selected contacts are highlighted
- Contacts added to the distribution list

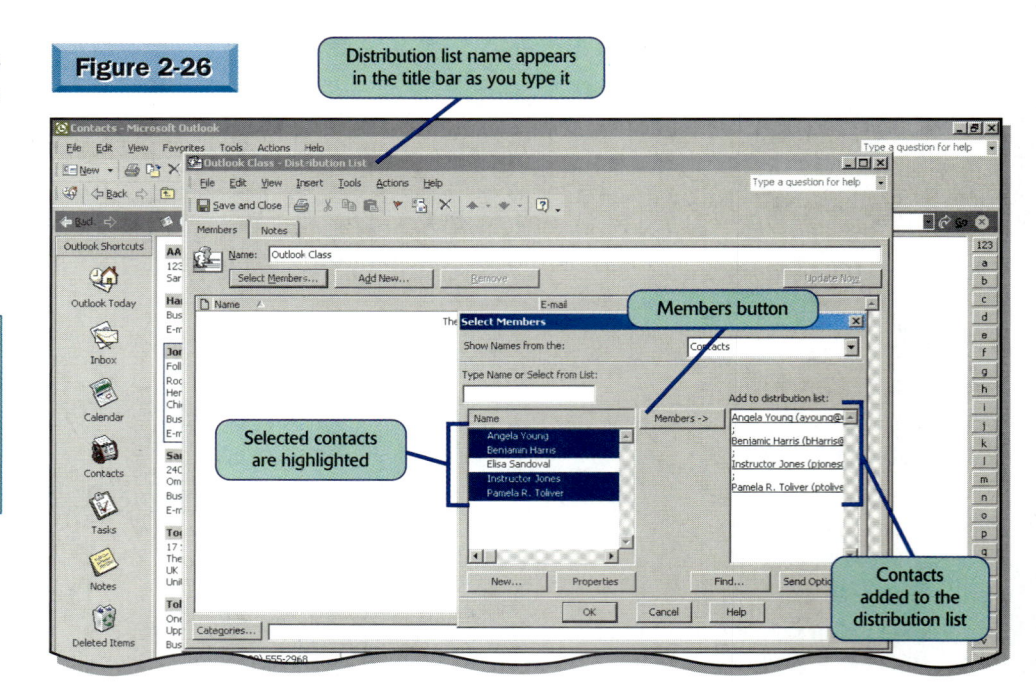

Figure 2-27

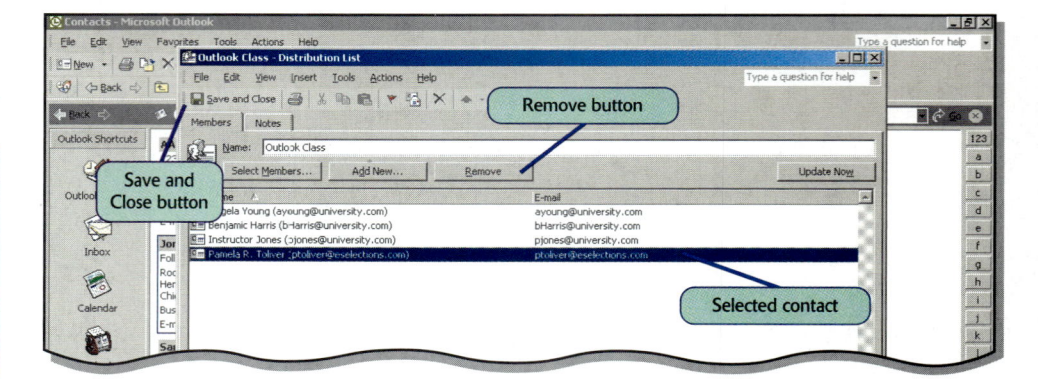

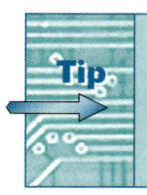

- Save and Close button
- Remove button
- Selected contact

> **Tip** It is easy to identify distribution lists when the Contacts folder is open. The distribution list title appears in a contact title bar and an icon showing multiple faces appears at the right end of the distribution list address card title bar.

Tracking Contacts Activities

Each task you complete that involves a contact is recorded in the activities for the contact. Tasks that Outlook automatically records in the activities list include adding a contact to a distribution list, sending a letter or e-mail message to a contact, and scheduling birthdays, appointments, and meetings with contacts. You can track activities involving contacts from the contact listing form.

CHECK POINT

Tired of using the Find feature to locate items associated with people you have listed in your Contacts folder? Use the Activities page of the dialog box to filter Outlook items by contact. For example, to locate e-mail messages you have received from your supervisor, open the contact for your supervisor and review items listed on the Activities page.

Task 9:
To Track Activities Involving Contacts

1 Open your personal contact listing and click the Activities tab.

2 Click the **Show** down arrow and review items you can display.

3 Close the contact.

Figure 2-28

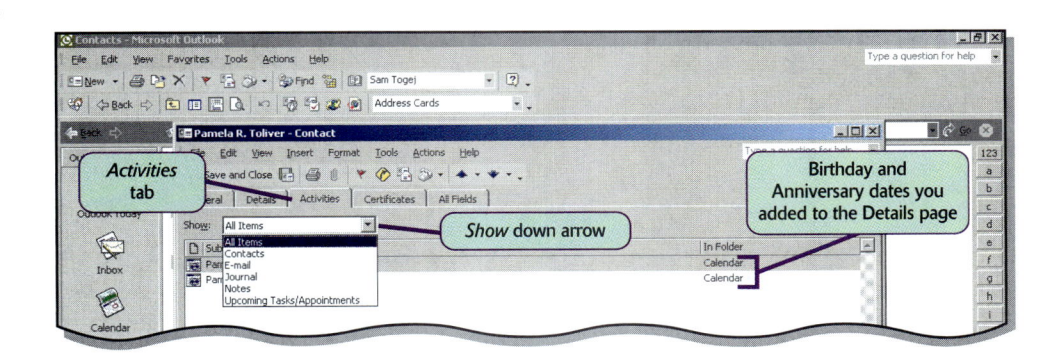

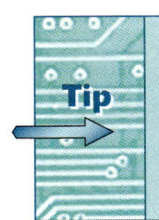

Activities tab

Show down arrow

Birthday and Anniversary dates you added to the Details page

Tip

If you have been using Outlook for some time, you may see a long list of activities associated with your personal contact listing. All activities involving you will appear on the Activities list, including e-mail messages you have sent and received, calendar appointments, tasks, deleted items, and items in personal folders you have on your computer.

CHECK POINT

Wondering why the birthday you added to the Details page of the contact listing says that it is in the Calendar folder? A straight answer is simply because you entered a date in a field named *Birthday*. The fact of the matter is that information in all Outlook features is interconnected to form an extensive web that links items from one Outlook folder to other Outlook folders. You will see this "information sharing" frequently as you explore other Outlook features.

Setting Contacts Options

The Contacts screen settings you have seen and worked with are, for the most part, the default settings established by Outlook designers. When you moved the e-mail column to a new location in Task 4, you customized the Contacts By Location view. You can also change settings that affect the name format and name display format for new contacts.

Task 10:
To Set Contacts Options

1 Choose **Tools | Options**, click the **Preferences** tab, if necessary, and click the **Contact Options** button.

Figure 2-29

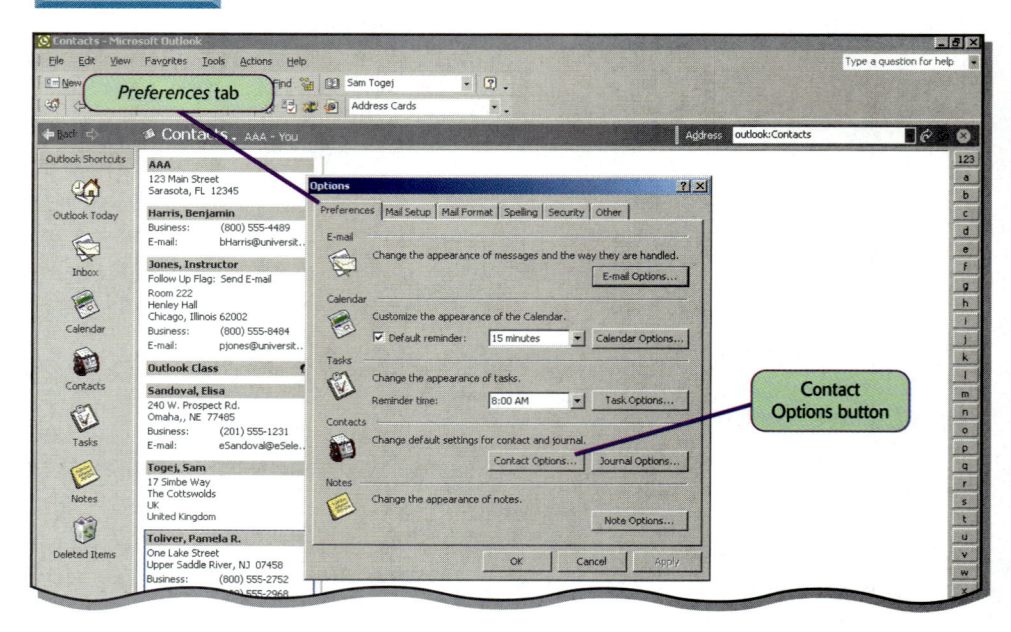

2 Click the **Default "File As" order** down arrow, select **First Last**, and click **OK** twice.

> **Tip**
> Changes made to the Contact Options affect new contacts only. No adjustment is made to existing contacts. To change the "File As" order for existing contacts, open the contact, click the **File as** down arrow, and select the format for each contact individually.

Figure 2-30

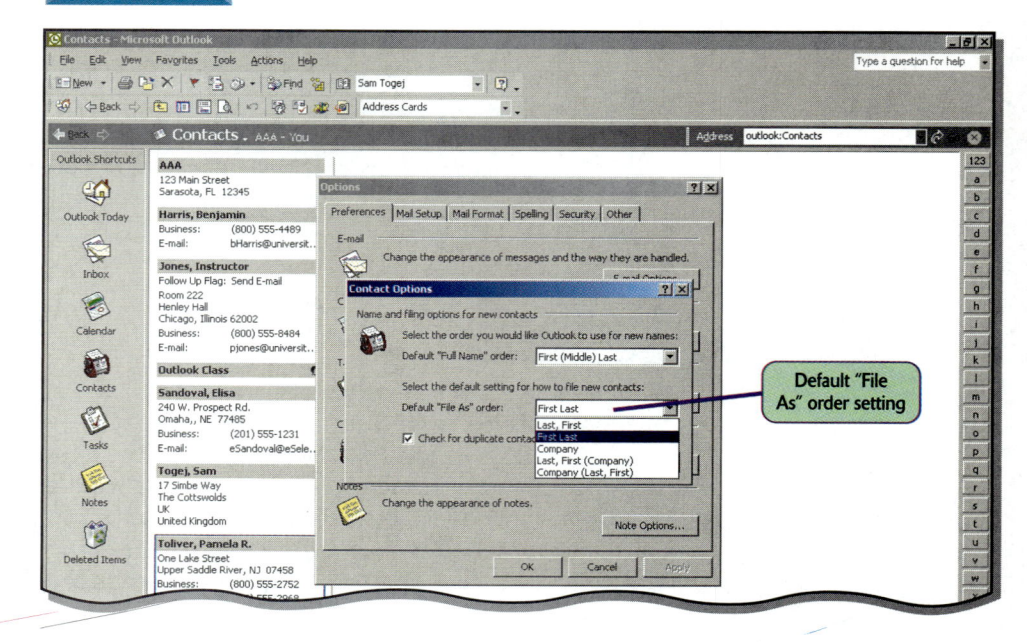

Copying Contacts

When the data associated with new contacts duplicates data contained in an existing contact, you can copy the existing contact and edit it to reduce the amount of data entry required.

Task 11:
To Copy Contacts to Create New Contacts

1 Click the title bar of the **Elisa Sandoval** address card to select it.

2 Press Ctrl and drag the card to the end of the last address card.

Figure 2-31

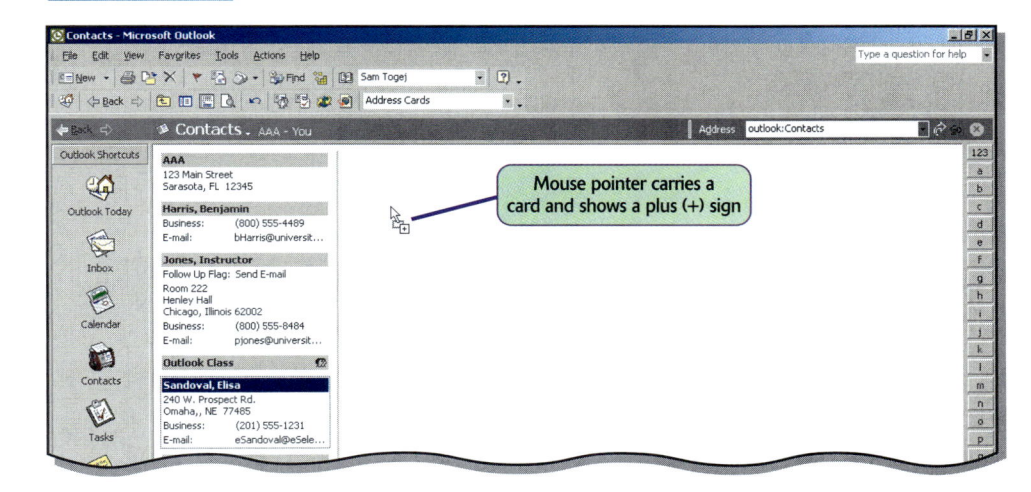

Mouse pointer carries a card and shows a plus (+) sign

Troubleshooting As you drag the contact, the mouse pointer appears to carry a new page and has a plus (+) beside it. If you do not see a plus (+) symbol, you need to press the Ctrl key before you drop the address card.

3 Open one of the **Elisa Sandoval** contacts and edit the data to create a contact for the business card shown in Figure 2-32.

4 Save and close the edited contact.

Figure 2-32

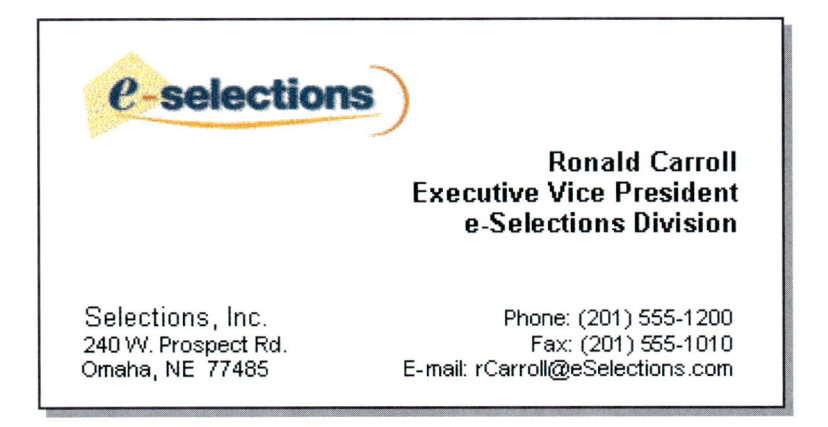

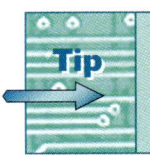

e-selections

Ronald Carroll
Executive Vice President
e-Selections Division

Selections, Inc.
240 W. Prospect Rd.
Omaha, NE 77485

Phone: (201) 555-1200
Fax: (201) 555-1010
E-mail: rCarroll@eSelections.com

Tip Even though you dropped the copy of the contact at the end of the list, Outlook automatically alphabetizes all contacts. As a result, you can find both listings together with other contacts starting with *s*.

5 Exit Outlook.

Figure 2-33

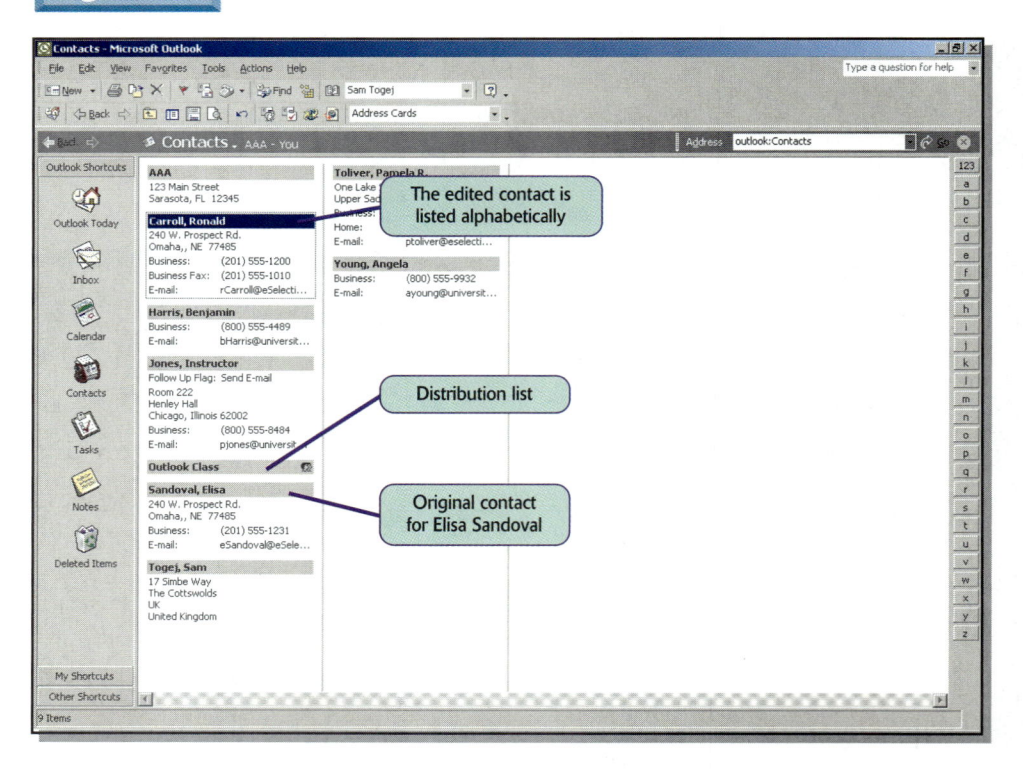

SUMMARY AND EXERCISES

SUMMARY

- The Contacts folder stores information, such as names, addresses, phone numbers, and company names.
- Contacts added to Outlook are stored in the Contacts folder—one of the Personal Folders in Outlook.
- Storing data electronically makes it easier to edit the information and keep it current.
- Changing the Contacts folder view provides an easy way to sort contacts in the most frequently sorted orders.
- When special sort order needs arise, you can customize the view using the Sort dialog box.
- The Find feature locates a contact along with all other items that contain the contact's name.
- The Find a Contact text box on the Standard toolbar acts as a tool for locating contacts from any Outlook feature.
- Because of the unique field names and information stored in different Outlook folders, the printing options for each feature vary.
- You can set a reminder to follow up on activities such as sending e-mail messages by flagging the contact for follow-up.
- Distribution lists provide an efficient way to group contacts containing common elements into one listing.
- You can track activities involving contacts from the contact listing form.
- You can change settings that affect the name format and name display format for new contacts.

KEY TERMS & SKILLS

KEY TERMS distribution list (p. 2-19)   Flagging (p. 2-17)

SKILLS

Apply advanced sort techniques (p. 2-11)
Copy contacts to create new contacts (p. 2-23)
Create a personal distribution list (p. 2-19)
Create contacts (p. 2-5)
Find contacts (p. 2-14)

Flag contacts for follow-up (p. 2-18)
Open, edit, and delete contacts (p. 2-9)
Print contacts (p. 2-15)
Set contacts options (p. 2-22)
Sort contacts using views (p. 2-10)
Track activities involving contacts (p. 2-21)

STUDY QUESTIONS

MULTIPLE CHOICE

1. Most large corporations and organizations maintain a company-wide list of contacts that they distribute to all company personnel that is sometimes known as
   a. System Contacts.
   b. Global Address List.
   c. Personal Contacts.
   d. Corporation Clients.

2. All of the following fields on the new contact form access additional dialog boxes *except*
   a. Full Name.
   b. Save and Close.
   c. Address.
   d. Check Phone.

3. When you edit a contact listing,
   a. replaced information appears with a line through it.
   b. original information disappears and the new information takes its place.
   c. a new contact containing the new information is added.
   d. you must first remove the old contact and create a new one.

4. You can find a contact from any view by
   a. clicking the **Find** button and entering the contact name.
   b. choosing **Tools | Find** and typing the contact name.
   c. choosing **Edit | Go To** and typing the contact's last name.
   d. clicking in the **Find a Contact** text box on the Contacts folder toolbar and typing part of the contact name.

5. To open a contact listing,
   a. double-click the listing title bar.
   b. right-click the listing and press Enter.
   c. click the **Open** button on the toolbar.
   d. click the **New** button on the toolbar.

6. When you need to sort contacts by different fields, select the sort fields from which of the following dialog boxes?
   a. Sort.
   b. Advanced.
   c. View Summary.
   d. Settings.

7. The View Summary dialog box contains buttons to access all the following features *except*
   a. Fields.
   b. Group by.
   c. Find.
   d. Filter.

8. Which of the following layout styles is available to print an open contact listing?
   a. Card Style.
   b. Small Booklet Style.
   c. Memo Style.
   d. Full-Page Style.

9. To flag a contact for follow-up, click
   a. [icon].
   b. [icon].
   c. [icon].
   d. [icon].

10. You can set all of the following pieces of information when you flag a contact for follow-up *except*
    a. type of follow-up.
    b. due date.
    c. time due.
    d. start date.

SHORT ANSWER

1. How do you access a blank form to add contacts to the Contact list?
2. What is the purpose of the Full Name button on a contact form?
3. What does the Activities page of the Contact listing show?
4. How does the Global or company-wide contacts list vary from the contacts you add to your Contacts folder?
5. What happens if you fail to enter a complete address for a contact?
6. What happens when you save a contact?
7. How do you delete a contact?
8. What determines the layout styles displayed in the Print dialog box?
9. How many different fields can be used to sort contacts?
10. What does the down arrow beside the **Home Phone** field on the New Contact form access?

FILL IN THE BLANK

1. The Outlook feature designed to store names and addresses of business associates is _____.
2. Most contacts that you add to Outlook appear in the Contacts folder which is a(n) _____ folder.
3. To save a new contact and display the contact in the Contacts window alphabetically among other contacts, click the _____ button on the contact form toolbar.
4. _____ provide a quick way to sort contacts.
5. Marking contacts for follow-up is called _____.
6. A contact listing that contains a number of additional contact listings is called a(n) _____.
7. All messages, letters, and other entries involving contacts appear on the _____ page of the contact listing form.
8. Distribution lists are identified in the Contacts folder by _____.
9. The _____ field controls whether contact listings appear alphabetically by first or last name.
10. To copy a contact, press the _____ key as you drag the contact and drop it at another location on the Contacts folder window.

DISCUSSION

1. What is the difference between a Global Address List and Personal Contacts?
2. What controls the available options in the Print dialog box?
3. Why would you want to create a distribution list when you have already created individual listings for the same people?
4. How do you change the field name for a phone number or other fields on the Contacts form?

GUIDED EXERCISES

1 PUTTING FAMILY FIRST

Parents and other relatives have a way of making us feel guilty when we fail to communicate regularly, don't they? Now that you will be using Outlook, you can increase your communication frequency by adding entries to your contacts list so that you can zip off a letter, note, or e-mail to family members more regularly. Storing the contacts in a separate folder helps you keep the listings for relatives separate from business contacts so that you can locate them more efficiently. Follow these steps to create a folder in which to store relative contacts and then add contacts to the folder

1. Launch Outlook and display the Contacts folder.

2. Choose **File | New | Folder**. The Create New Folder dialog box opens.

3. Type **Family Contacts** in the **Name** field, ensure that **Contact Items** appears in the **Folder Contains** field, click **OK**, and click **Yes** to add the folder to the Outlook Bar.

4. Click the **My Shortcuts** group button and then click the **Family Contacts** shortcut icon to open the folder.

5. Create new contact listings for at least three family members, changing the field names for phone numbers and addresses to identify the information as either home or office.

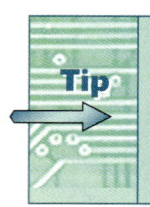

> **Tip**
> To change the field names for specific fields, click the down arrow beside the field name and select the appropriate listing.
>
> As you add the new listings, they appear in the active folder—Family Contacts—rather than in the main Contacts folder.

> **Tip**
> When you have a number of consecutive contacts to enter, click the **Save and New** button on the toolbar to save each contact as you complete it and display a blank contact form all with a single click.

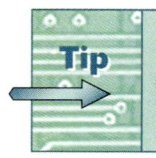

2 CREATING AND PRINTING RESUME GETTERS

Starting to think about looking for a job? You will need to get your resume in order and that usually means identifying past employers as well as people you can use as references. Why not start by adding these people to your Contacts list. That way you can print the listings and take them with you when you go to an interview when having to complete an application on-site. Follow these steps to add suitable contacts to your Contacts folder, flag the contacts for follow-up, and print the references.

1. Create new contact listings for all previous employers. Be sure to include their complete address and telephone and fax numbers. Add the dates you were employed to the comments area for each listing.

2. Create new contact listings for each person you want to use as a reference on your resume. Be sure to include a variety of different references so that you can vary references according to the job for which you are applying. Again, be sure to include full names, addresses, and telephone numbers. Add the job types for which each person would best serve as a reference to the comments area of the contact form. Leave blank any information you do not have available; you can look it up and fill it in later.

3. Open the references and former employers whose information is incomplete and click the **Flag for Follow Up** button. Set the due date for a week from Monday. Then be sure to look up the information for each incomplete employer and reference so that you can go back and edit them to complete their information.

4. Close all open contacts, press [Ctrl] and click the title bar for each employer and reference you entered to select all the contacts.

5. Choose **File | Print**, select **Small Booklet Style**, select the **Only selected items** option, and click **OK** to print the selected contacts.

3 BUILDING UP OFFICE CONTACTS

Creating contacts for many people within an organization with whom you communicate regularly can become tedious work, especially when you are new to a company. Because so much information that you need to add to each contact is the same as the information contained on other company contacts, you can reduce the amount of time spent creating contact listings by copying existing listings and editing them. You can also reduce the amount of time you spend adding names to electronic messages you send by creating distribution lists for each group of people with whom you communicate regularly. Follow these directions to add three new contacts for the e-Selections division of Selections, Inc., to your contacts folder.

1. Open the Contacts folder, click the contact title bar for *Elisa Sandoval* to select the contact, and choose **Edit | Copy** to copy the contact.

2. Choose **Edit | Paste** twice to add two new contacts for Elisa Sandoval to the folder.

3. Open the Elisa Sandoval contacts and edit the data to create the contact for e-Selections personnel listed in Table 2-1, saving and closing each edited contact as you complete it.

Table 2-1   e-Selection Personnel

Name	Job Title	Business Phone	E-mail
Amber Wright	Administration Manager	(201) 555-4454	aWright@eSelections.com
Dave Martin	Image Control Manager	(201) 555 4487	dMartin@eSelections.com

4. Choose **View | Current View | By Company** to change the Contacts folder view.

5. Choose **File | New | Distribution List**, name the new distribution list *e-Selections Managers*, click the **Select Members** button, add Elisa Sandoval, Ronald Carroll, Amber Wright, and Dave Martin to the distribution list, and close the distribution list.

6. Choose **File | Print**, select the **Table Style**, and click **OK** to print a listing of all entries in the Contacts folder sorted by company.

ON YOUR OWN

The difficulty of these case studies varies: ♪ are the least difficult; ♪♪ are more difficult; and ♪♪♪ are the most difficult.

1 STAYING IN TOUCH

♪ Keeping in touch with friends you had in high school as well as friends you make in college is a challenge. Even if you do not know a person's e-mail address, you can still record the person in your Contacts list. Create a new Outlook Contact folder named *Personal Friends*. Add Contact listings for a close friend from high school, a friend you have made in college, and a friend from work or a social organization. In addition, add the contacts shown in Table 2-2. Then print copies of the *Personal Friends* folder using the Phone Directory Style.

Table 2-2	Personal Friend Contact Information		
Name	**Address**	**Telephone**	**E-mail**
Carla White	1526 Hedgwood Drive	970-555-2752	cWhite@isp.com
Harry Burley	4480 North Allen	970-555-9570	hBurley@isp.com
Sara Bonnell	302 South Rob	970-555-7015	sBonnell@isp.com

2 CLASS-IFYING CONTACTS

Some of the contacts you have created are strictly part of in-class assignments, so you want to isolate them to make them easier to access. Create a new contacts folder named *Class Contacts* but do not add the folder to the Outlook Bar. Display the Folder List and expand the Contacts folder to display the custom folders. Drag copies of contacts associated with class into the new *Class Contacts* folder. Be sure to place a copy of your instructor's contact in the new folder. Print a copy of the new folder listings using the Small Booklet Style. Use the Find a Contact text box to locate contacts with the same last name as your instructor to see if Outlook locates both copies of the listing. Display the main Contacts folder and preview a copy of the folder using the Small Booklet Style. Finally, delete those contact listings from the Contacts folder that you copied to the new *Class Contacts* folder and then print a copy of the Contacts folder.

3 WORKING WITH PERSONAL CONTACTS

Because there will be times when you want to communicate with relatives and friends at work as well as at their home or school addresses, you want to add additional information to the listings of all your relatives and friends. If you have not yet created contacts for your family members, create at least three family contacts. Then edit the listings by doing the following:

- Print a copy of the contact listing for at least three relatives using the print style you prefer.
- Then edit the three listings so that they show business information on the General page of each listing and personal information on the Details page for each listing.
- Be sure to include each relative's birthday; you will want to send a card.
- Print a copy of the edited listings using the Memo Style.
- Finally, edit the listings for the contacts shown in Table 2-3 to add the information to the Details page. If you have not yet created contacts for the people shown in Table 2-3, refer to Table 2-2 for initial contact information.

Table 2-3	Additional Contact Information		
Name	**Profession**	**Birthday**	**Spouse's Name**
Carla White	Medical doctor	December 22	Robert White
Harry Burley	Insurance adjustor	March 1	Janet Burley
Sara Bonnell	Teacher	June 19	Timothy Bonnell

Organizing Outlook Contacts

4 LOCATING FRIENDS ON THE WEB

▶▶ The World Wide Web not only stores information about companies, Web sites for bidding on items, and so forth, but it also contains telephone book information as well as e-mail addresses for many people. Search the Web for the Web sites for three computer companies whose products—computers, printers, and so forth—you use regularly. Search the company site for mailing address information, telephone numbers, and the e-mail address of a person to whom you could send inquiries about their products or to whom you could send requests for technical assistance. When you have located the information for at least three companies, record the information in a new contacts folder named *Computer Companies*. Then create a distribution list named *Computer Companies* that contains all three of the company names you added. Print a copy of each contact form along with a copy of the *Computer Companies* distribution list window.

5 PREPROJECT PLANNING

▶▶▶ When you know in advance that a special event will occur, you can begin getting organized and setting up for the event in advance. A Board of Directors meeting is scheduled for the end of next month. You have been assigned the task of organizing the event and assigning tasks associated with the event to other office personnel. You may have already started getting Outlook prepared for this event by creating a new Outlook Bar group named *Board of Directors*. If you have, great—if you have not, then you need to create the group now. Then create a new *Board of Directors Contacts* folder to contain contact listings, place the folder on the Outlook Bar, and move the folder to the *Board of Directors* group. Add contact listings for the six Board members listed in Table 2-4 to the new *Board of Directors Contacts* folder. Sort the list of Directors by State, and then by City.

(continued)

Copy your instructor's listing into the Board of Directors folder. Because you want to be sure that you send meeting information to each board member, flag each contact in the folder. Print copies of the listings as a phone directory. Then set the Contacts folder options to display the Default "File As" order to Last, First (Company), display your instructor's listing in the main Contacts folder, and print a listing of the activities page of the listing.

Table 2-4	Board of Directors Members		
Name	**Address**	**Telephone**	**e-Mail**
Donald Koontz	802 North Allen Robinson, IL 62454	618-555-3964	dkoontz@isp.com
Norma Rule	Rt. 1, Box 884 Naperville, IL 64544	217-555-3384	nrule@isp.com
Tamara Patterson	448 Blarney Stone Way Bloomington, IL 61704	217-555-2701	tpatterson@isp.com
Lee Lowell	2471 Spring Lane Indianapolis, IN 46268	317-555-7521	llowell@isp.com
David Steele	889 Seventh Avenue Pekin, IL 61554	309-555-3234	dsteele@isp.com
Pamela Ayers	18822 Flakewood Court Little Rock, AR 72207	501-555-2807	payers@isp.com

Photospread credits pages 2-2 & 2-3

©Tony Stone: ©Andreas Pollok; ©2002 Nokia, Inc.; ©2002 Handspring, Inc.; ©Pearson Education; and ©Lorraine Castellano

PROJECT 3

Maintaining the Outlook Calendar

The Outlook Calendar feature is designed to help you track appointments and manage meetings. Whether the appointments and meetings are private or require the attendance of others and the booking of resources, you can use the Outlook Calendar to set them up, cancel them, and edit them. Outlook even provides special tools that enable you to schedule appointments and meetings that occur on a regular basis and publish your calendar so that others can view your schedule.

e-selections) Running Case

You recently received a flyer listing a number of different positions open at the e-Selections Division of Selection, Inc., and identified one position in which you are interested. After learning that the position requires a degree in computer information systems, a degree that you have not quite completed, you decided to enroll at the local college on a part-time basis and plan to complete the requirements for your degree while continuing to work for e-Selections. The college offers a number of different courses that can help you meet the degree requirements while learning some of the applications you use at work. After noting the little bits and pieces of paper and sticky notes containing phone messages and appointment reminders, you decide to take a course in electronic time management. You are delighted to discover that the first application you will learn is Outlook.

OBJECTIVES

After completing this project, you will be able to:

- Display and navigate the Calendar window
- Schedule appointments
- Set reminders and label appointments
- Move, copy, and delete appointments
- Schedule recurring appointments
- Schedule meetings involving others
- Edit meeting participants and send updates
- Cancel meeting requests
- Print the calendar
- Customize the calendar

Smartcards—Take the Money and Run

A new wave of smart cards is making its debut in the market place these days. Smart cards in the form of credit cards that know you—they know all about you! And experts say they will change the way you live and shop. In fact, universities, such as the University of Michigan, are issuing smart cards to students.

Smart cards are essentially plastic cards that have 32-bit computer chips set in them. These chips store about 80 times more data than the magnetic strips found on the backs of other credit cards currently in use.

Smart cards can serve as ID, credit card, debit card, phone card, rail passes, and much more, because personal and account information—even PIN numbers used to authorize purchases—is stored on the smart card in encrypted format, making it more difficult for thieves to obtain account numbers.

By storing so much information on one small card, the number of cards you have to carry is significantly reduced. Fat wallets are slimmed down, and the need to carry cash becomes a thing of the past.

Students carrying smart cards issued by their schools can enter dorms, use the school library, pay for meals, make phone calls, and shop by presenting the same small card.

But the concept of smart cards is not all that new. They made their debut way back in the 1970s in the form of TMRs (an acronym for "Take the Money and Run"). You guessed it—these are the cards that were first used to draw funds from your bank at the bank money machines.

cashless society

Smart cards progressed from the early 1970s through the decade to the 1980s where they became more popular, especially for interfacing with banks. During the 1980s, the use of magnetic strips became more popular for use with consumer cards, and smaller chips that hold more information were integrated with cards used by organizations.

Throughout the 1990s, the technology was perfected to resemble what we're seeing today. And the trend appears to be growing. A number of organizations currently offer smart cards—Visa International and American Express were among the first. As the cost associated with making smart cards drops, more and more companies are looking to implement smart cards, but there are still drawbacks.

One of the biggest challenges facing smart card users is retailers' hesitation to accept them. Because they are new and store data in a different format, they require special card readers not yet in place.

In addition, current computer systems that record point-of-sale information will require upgrades to accommodate the smart card format.

Nevertheless, the number of companies and organizations offering smart cards is growing, and experts believe that it's only a matter of time before smart cards become widespread throughout the United States.

Is there a smart card in your future? Perhaps—in fact, probably. Smart cards are getting smarter, and the increasing need for transaction security along with the move towards a "cashless society" almost guarantee it!

Smart cards progressed from the early 1970s

PROJECT 3

Maintaining the Outlook Calendar

The Challenge

Sticky notes seem to be cropping up all over your desk and computer monitor as more and more people call to set up appointments, invite you to attend meetings, and notify you of regularly scheduled and mandatory meetings. Keeping track of these appointments and meetings has been a real challenge. Now that you have started classes, you have additional appointments and classes that you need to schedule. You would like to get all these appointments organized to reduce the number of potential appointment conflicts.

The Solution

The Outlook Calendar feature is just the tool you need to help track meetings and appointments to prevent double-booking yourself. As luck would have it, it is also the first application you will learn in your college applications class. As you explore the Calendar feature, you can begin entering those meetings and appointments you have already made and set up your class meetings, too. You will also learn how you can use the Outlook meeting invitation features to invite others to attend meetings. Because you have already explored the Calendar feature when you set time zones and learned how to change views, you feel confident that you will breeze right through learning how to schedule appointments.

Displaying and Navigating the Calendar Window

The default Calendar window is a busy, tri-paned window that enables you to keep track of appointments, view two full months, and view your task list all in the same window. As you work in the Calendar, the window changes, and it is important to be able to identify screen features and how to use them.

Displaying the Calendar

Outlook offers the same procedures to display the Calendar window that are used to display other Outlook features. The Outlook Bar provides the easiest access to the Calendar window.

Task 1:
To Display the Calendar Window

1. Click the Outlook Bar **Calendar** icon.

Troubleshooting
The Calendar toolbar on your computer may contain buttons different from those shown here because of customizations completed in previous Projects.

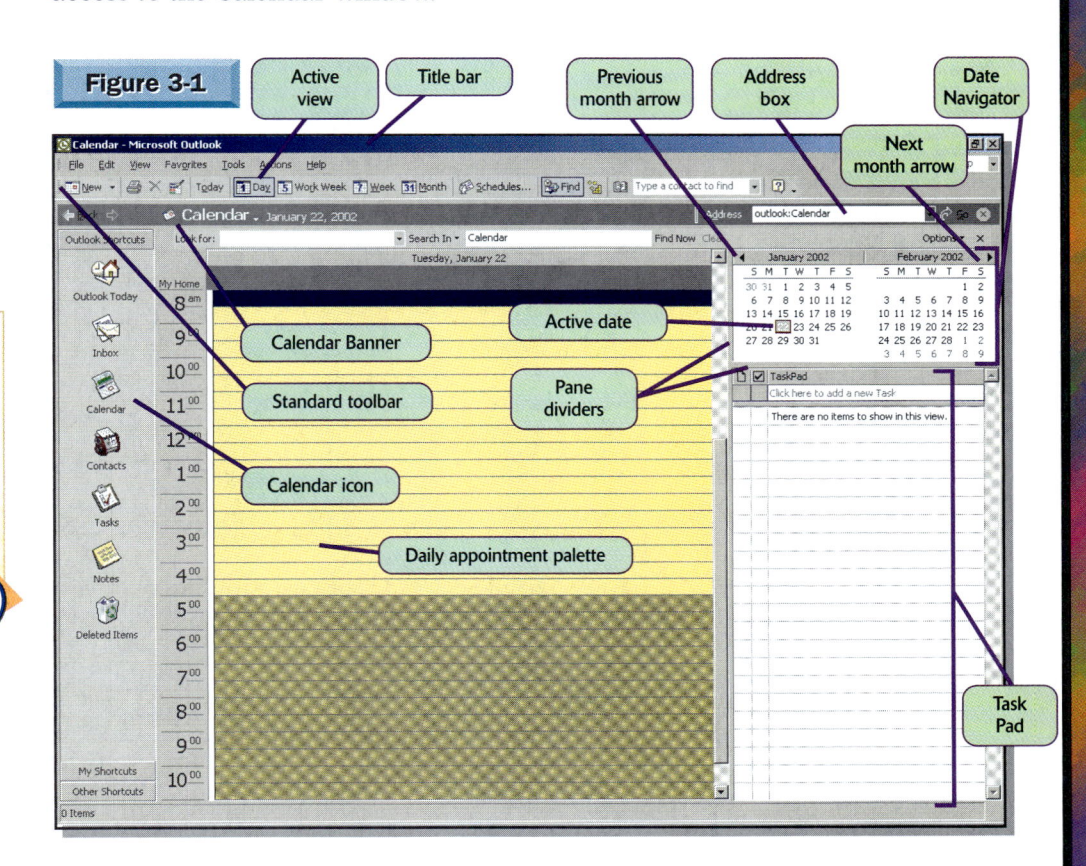

Figure 3-1

Labels: Active view, Title bar, Previous month arrow, Address box, Date Navigator, Next month arrow, Calendar Banner, Active date, Standard toolbar, Pane dividers, Calendar icon, Daily appointment palette, Task Pad

Identifying Calendar Window Features

Because of the close integration between calendar appointments and tasks, the Calendar window combines navigation tools with a calendar navigation palette and task pad that displays active tasks. Each of the features shown in Figure 3-1 is described in Table 3-1.

WEB TIP

For travelers on the go, you will find that many hotels have initiated fast Internet connections from their guest rooms. Simply connect from your laptop or *PDA* and complete those tasks normally accomplished at the office.

Table 3-1	Calendar Window Features
Feature	**Description**
Application title bar	Identifies the program and feature that is open
Calendar Banner	Folder banners appear at the top of the active window and identify the folder that is open—in this case, the Calendar. Clicking the folder name in the banner displays the Folder List.
Date Navigator	Displays a full-month palette for one or more months depending on the size of the pane. Use the palettes to navigate to different months and dates.
TaskPad	Displays active tasks and their status.
Pane dividers	Control the portion of the window each pane uses. Drag a border to adjust the pane size.
Standard toolbar	Provides shortcuts for performing most common tasks.
Active view	Identifies the portion of the calendar that appears in the window.
Address box	Displays the active location and can be used to type a URL for accessing a Web site.
Active date	The date displayed in the calendar window.
Daily appointment palette	Shows the active date and time slots for the active view. Appointments appear in this palette after they are scheduled.
Next month	Displays the next consecutive month palette.
Previous month	Displays the previous consecutive month palette.

Navigating the Calendar Window

In Project 1, you learned how to change the Calendar views and drag *pane borders* to adjust screen display. Navigating the Calendar involves learning how to use views to change the screen display, how to use the date navigator tools to change dates, and other tools to move among Calendar window panes.

Maintaining the Outlook Calendar   OU 3-7

Task 2:
To Use Calendar Navigation Tools

1 Launch Outlook and click the **Calendar** shortcut on the Outlook Bar to open the Calendar folder, if necessary.

2 Click the **Next** button or **Previous** button until the Date Navigator displays January 2002 and February 2002.

3 Click **17** on the January 2002 palette.

4 Press [Ctrl] + [G] to open the Go To dialog box.

5 Type **5/9/2003** in the **Date** field and click **OK** to display Friday, May 9, 2003, in the Calendar.

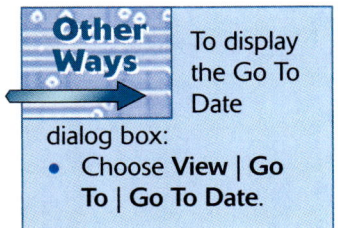

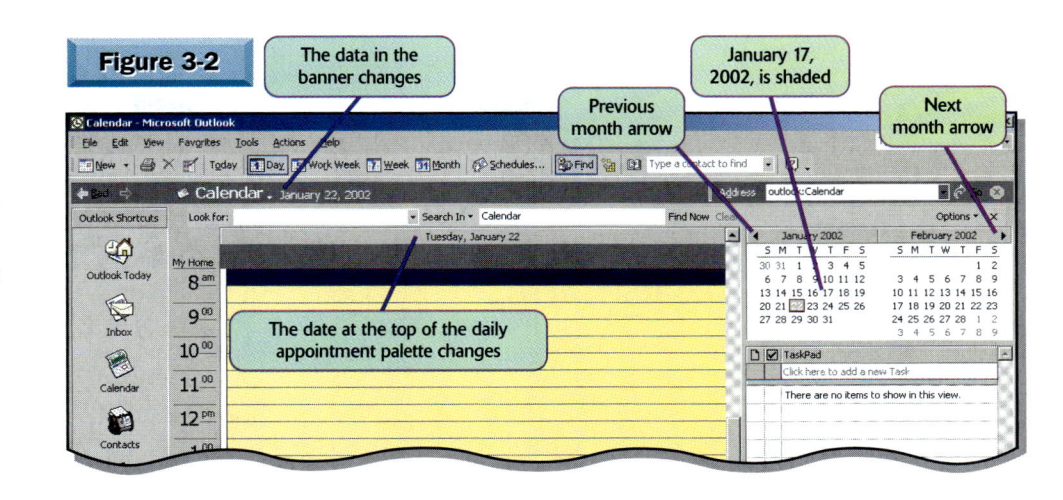

Other Ways
To display the Go To Date dialog box:
- Choose **View | Go To | Go To Date**.

Figure 3-2
- The data in the banner changes
- January 17, 2002, is shaded
- Previous month arrow
- Next month arrow
- The date at the top of the daily appointment palette changes

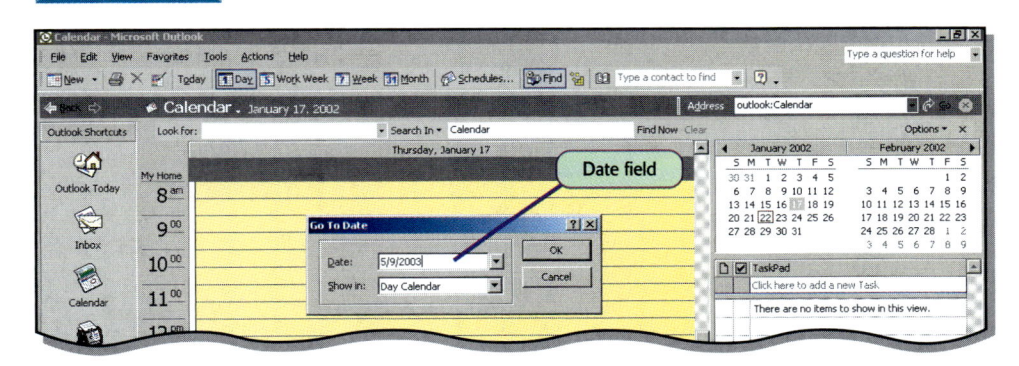

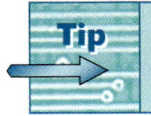

Figure 3-3
- Date field

Tip If you click the **Date** field down arrow, a date palette appears. You can use the date palette to navigate to the date you want to display.

6 Drag the mouse over the dates for Monday through Wednesday, May 12–14, 2003, on the monthly date navigator.

7 Click the **Today** button on the Standard toolbar to return to the current day.

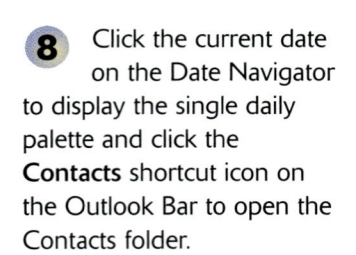

Figure 3-4

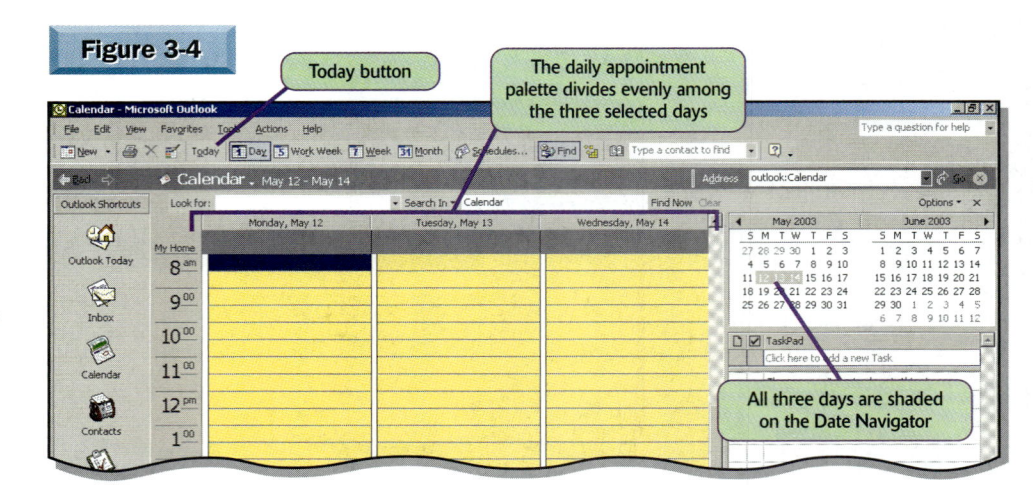

- Today button
- The daily appointment palette divides evenly among the three selected days
- All three days are shaded on the Date Navigator

8 Click the current date on the Date Navigator to display the single daily palette and click the **Contacts** shortcut icon on the Outlook Bar to open the Contacts folder.

9 Click the **Back** button to return to the Calendar.

Figure 3-5

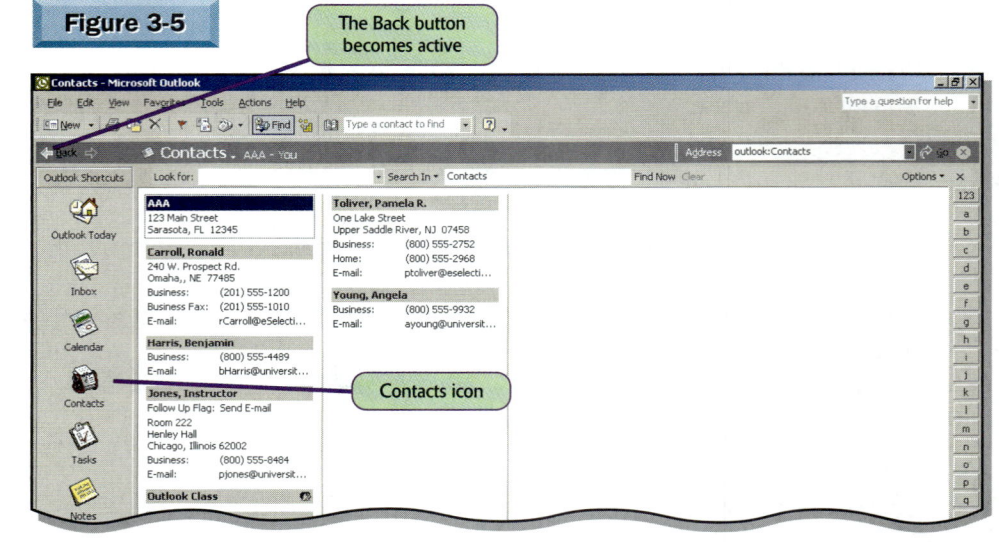

- The Back button becomes active
- Contacts icon

Troubleshooting The contacts listed in your Contacts folder may be different from those shown in Figure 3-5 due to contacts entered during previous projects and assigned exercises.

Scheduling Appointments

Whether you use the Calendar to keep track of appointments, assignments, or other *events*, recording entries in the Calendar is easy. You can schedule simple appointments in the calendar by typing the appointment directly on the daily calendar palette. When you need to include detailed information about an appointment, you can open the new appointment dialog box and set the appropriate options.

Maintaining the Outlook Calendar

OU 3-9

Task 3:
To Schedule Appointments in the Calendar

Figure 3-6

Callouts in Figure 3-6:
- February/March, 2003
- The bell indicates that a reminder is set
- Wednesday, February 5, 2003
- 11:00 time slot
- The appointment appears with a blue border

1. Click the Outlook Bar **Calendar** icon and display February and March, 2003, in the Date Navigator.

2. Click the date on the Date Navigator for **Wednesday, February 5, 2003**.

3. Click the **11:00** time slot on the daily appointment palette, type **Pick up forms from the Placement Office.** and press Enter.

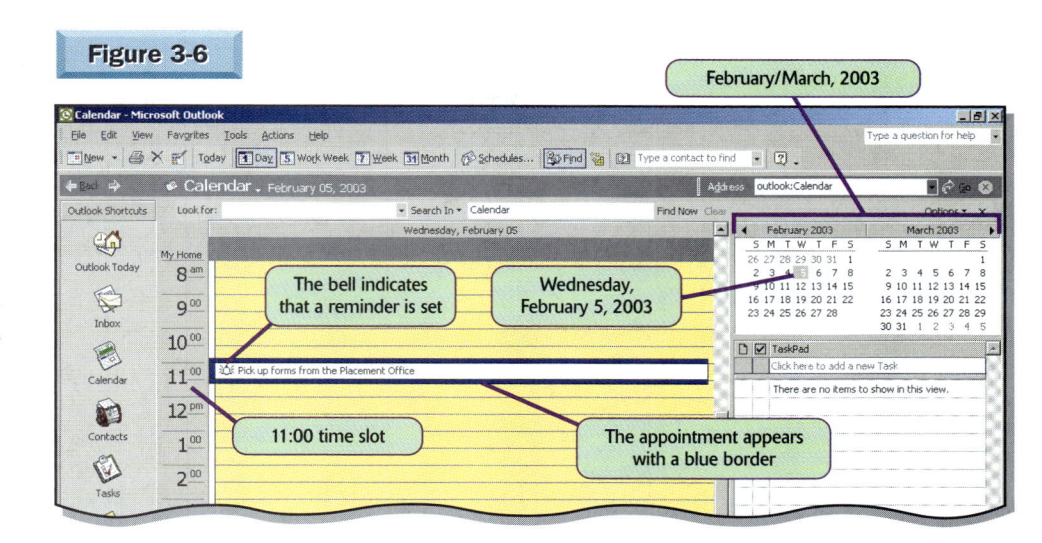

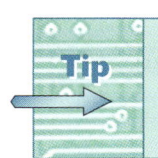

Tip: The default setting in Outlook schedules half an hour for appointments. You can drag the blue border on the bottom of the appointment to extend the appointment length.

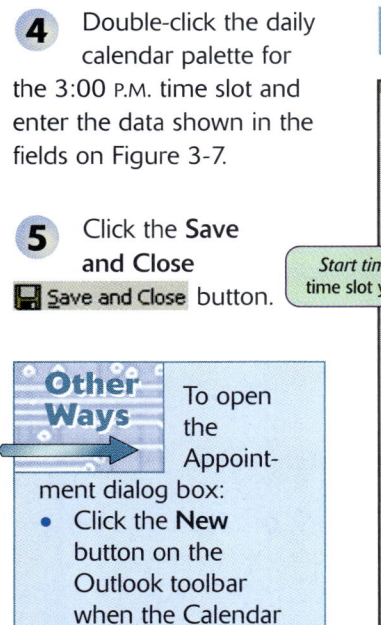

4. Double-click the daily calendar palette for the 3:00 P.M. time slot and enter the data shown in the fields on Figure 3-7.

5. Click the **Save and Close** button.

Figure 3-7

Callouts in Figure 3-7:
- Save and Close button
- Appointment title and subject are the same
- *Start time* is the time slot you chose
- *Location* can be entered
- *End time* is selected from the drop-down list
- Time marked as busy to prevent double-booking
- Clear the *Reminder* check box
- Area for adding notes and appointment information
- Hides appointment contents from other viewers

Other Ways

To open the Appointment dialog box:
- Click the **New** button on the Outlook toolbar when the Calendar is active.
- Choose **File | New | Appointment**.
- Choose **Actions | New Appointment**.
- Press Ctrl + N.

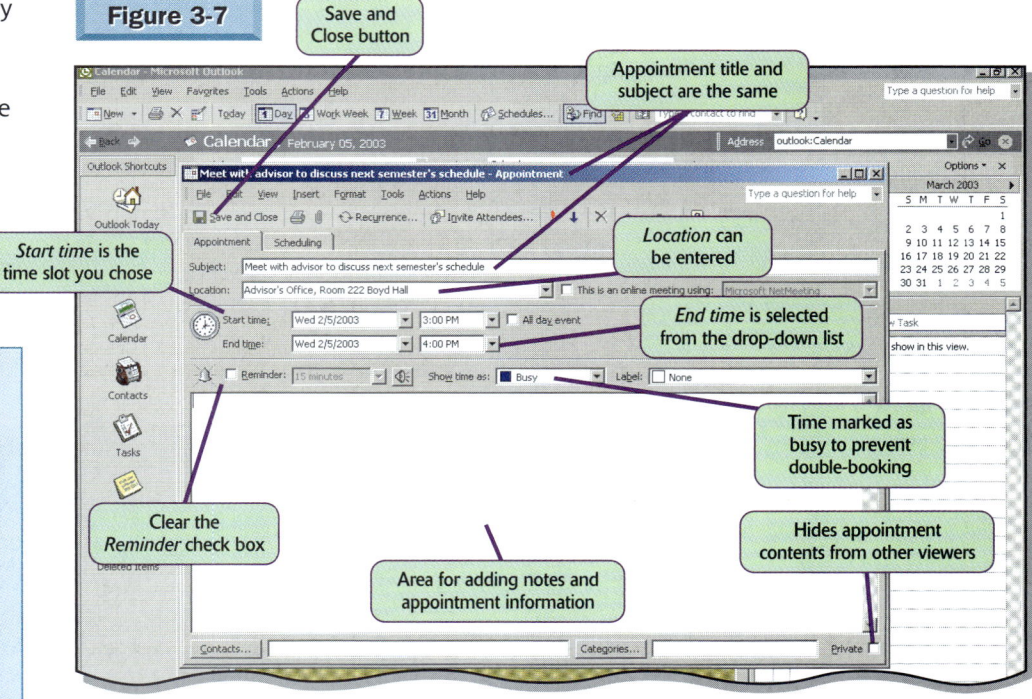

LIBRARY
WEST GEORGIA TECHNICAL COLLEGE
303 FORT DRIVE
LAGRANGE, GA 30240

6 Click the **Today** button to return to the current date.

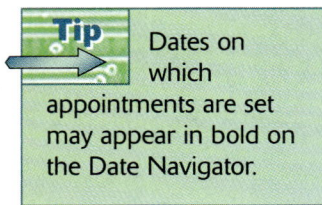

> **Tip:** Dates on which appointments are set may appear in bold on the Date Navigator.

Figure 3-8

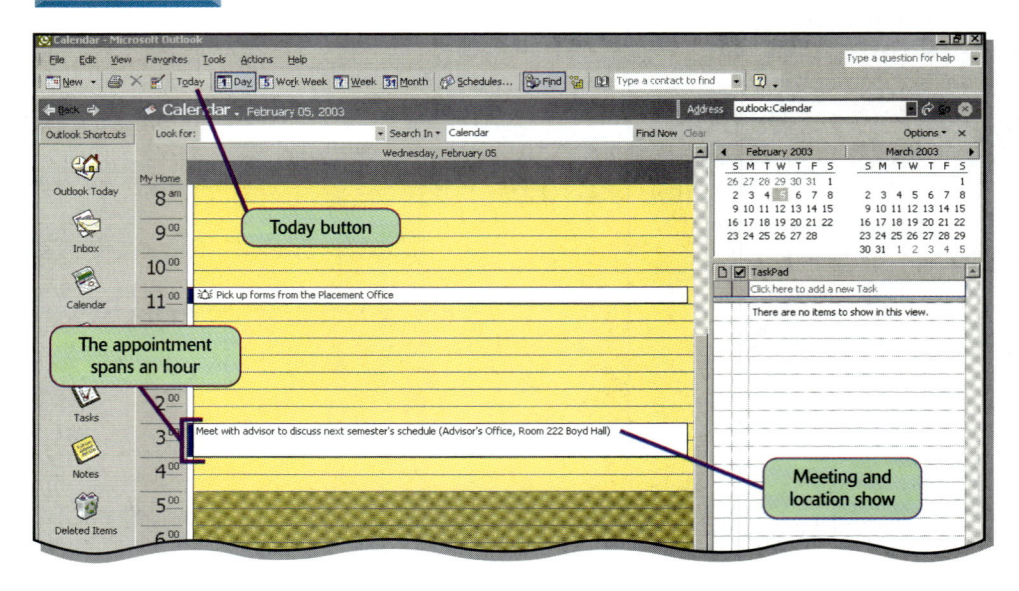

[Screenshot of Calendar - Microsoft Outlook showing Wednesday, February 05 with callouts: "Today button", "The appointment spans an hour", and "Meeting and location show". The 11:00 slot shows "Pick up forms from the Placement Office" and the 3:00 slot shows "Meet with advisor to discuss next semester's schedule (Advisor's Office, Room 222 Boyd Hall)".]

Setting Reminders

Setting *reminders* is a great way to prompt Outlook to remind you of important meetings and appointments. Before setting a reminder, determine how much time you need to get ready for or to travel to an appointment or meeting so that you can set the reminder timing.

> **Tip:** Outlook must be running for the reminder to appear, and if you are nowhere near the computer, you will miss it!

CHECK POINT

As you have discovered by now, selecting text in Word, cells in Excel, and items in all applications requires special text and item selection techniques. Outlook is no exception. Selecting appointments in the Outlook Calendar without positioning the insertion point within the appointment text can be tricky, but it can be narrowed down by considering the mouse pointer shapes. Table 3-2 identifies different mouse pointer shapes in the Outlook Daily Calendar view and their uses.

Table 3-2   Calendar Mouse Shapes

Mouse Shape	Icon	Position and Use
Four-headed arrow	✥	Appears when you point to the left border of a scheduled appointment and is used to select the appointment.
Two-headed arrow	↕	Appears when you point to the top or bottom borders of a scheduled appointment and is used to extend the start or end time for the appointment.
Selection arrow	↖	Appears when you point to the middle of a scheduled appointment and is used to position the I-beam within the appointment text for editing.
I-beam	I	Appears after clicking the center of a scheduled appointment and is used to position the insertion point for appointment text editing.

Maintaining the Outlook Calendar

OU 3-11

Task 4:
To Set Appointment Reminders

1 Open the **Calendar** folder and display the appointments for **Wednesday, February 5, 2003**.

2 Position the mouse pointer on the blue border to the left of the three o'clock appointment.

Figure 3-9

The mouse pointer appears as a four-headed arrow

3:00 appointment

3 Double-click the blue border to open the appointment in a separate window.

4 Select the **Reminder** option, if necessary, and click the **Reminder** down arrow.

5 Select **30 minutes** and then click the **Reminder Sound** button.

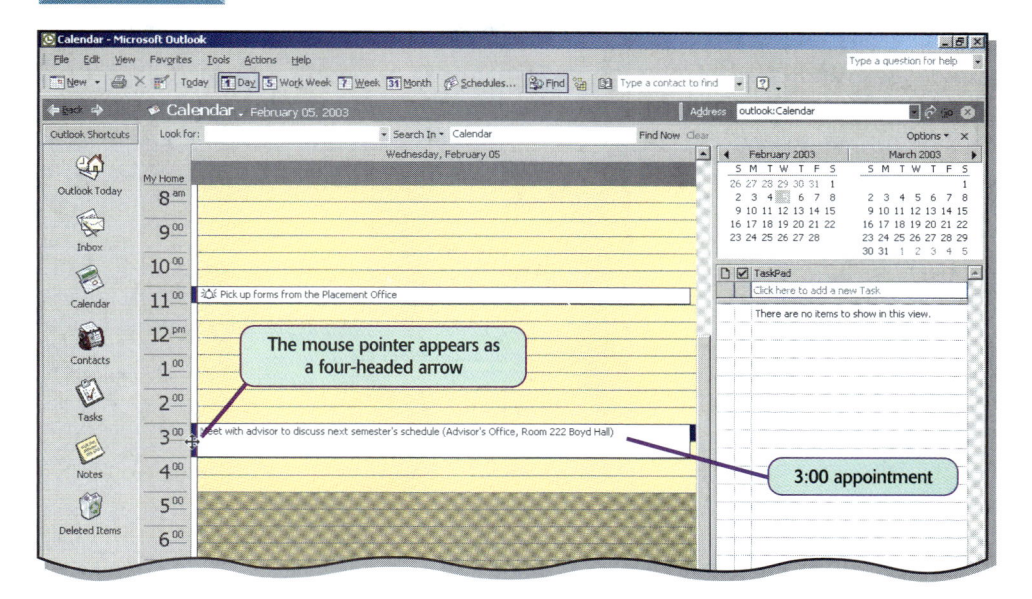

Figure 3-10

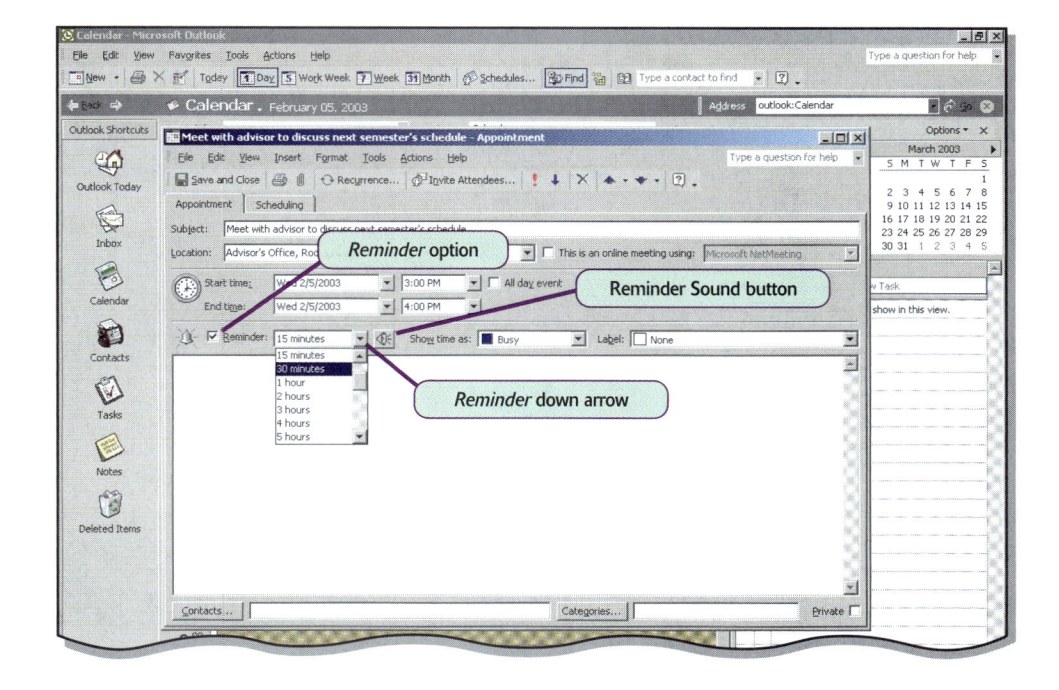

Reminder option

Reminder Sound button

Reminder down arrow

> **Tip**
> Reminders set for appointments in the main Calendar folder and for tasks in the Tasks folder appear onscreen in advance of the appointment according to the time you set for the reminder. However, if you set reminders for appointments or tasks that you schedule in custom calendar or task folders, Outlook displays a warning message telling you that only reminders set for items in the main Calendar and Tasks folders will display. To ensure that the reminders you set appear onscreen, be sure to save them in the main folders.

Scheduling Appointments

6 Select the **Play this sound** check box, if necessary, click **OK**, and then click the **Save and Close** 💾 Save and Close button.

Figure 3-11

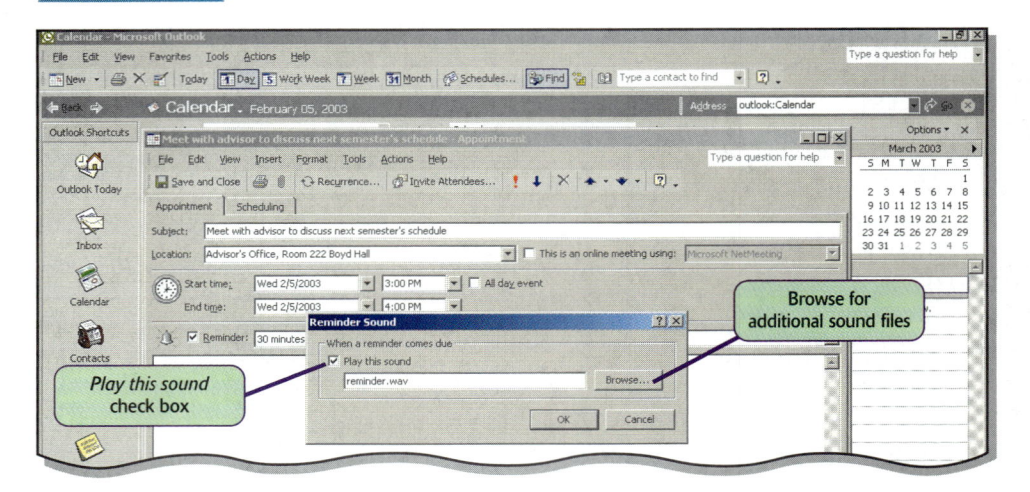

Play this sound check box

Browse for additional sound files

CHECK POINT

Periodically, as you work, reminders you have set for appointments will appear. The first time you see a Reminder dialog box, be sure to read the options carefully. Figure 3-12 displays a sample Reminder dialog box for your review.

Figure 3-12

Maintaining the Outlook Calendar

OU 3-**13**

Scheduling and Labeling All Day Events

Meetings and events that encompass a complete workday as well as those events that span multiple days can be scheduled as all day events. When you schedule an appointment as an all day event, Outlook places an event banner just below the day/date banner on the daily appointment calendar for each day reserved for the event. In addition, Outlook automatically schedules the days as busy.

Labels in Outlook help you organize your appointments using color coding to draw attention to the different types of appointments. You can apply a label to any type of appointment, but labeling all day events can be particularly effective.

Task 5:
To Schedule and Label an All Day Event

1 Go to March 17, 2003, point to the blank area between the day/date banner and the daily appointment calendar, and double-click.

2 Type **Spring Break** in the **Subject** field and type appropriate information in the **Location** field.

3 Click the **End time** down arrow, select the last day of Spring Break, and select other options shown in Figure 3-13.

Figure 3-13

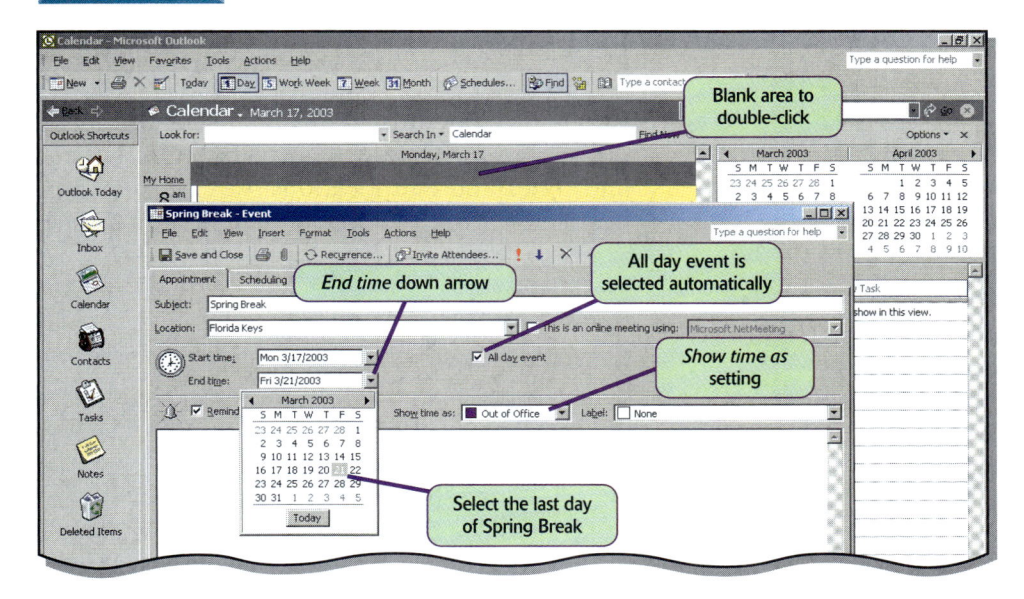

Callouts: Blank area to double-click • End time down arrow • All day event is selected automatically • Show time as setting • Select the last day of Spring Break

Other Ways
To open the new all day event appointment dialog box:
- Choose **Actions | New All Day Event**.

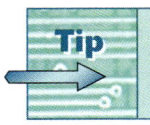

Tip
To change the **Show time as** setting, click the down arrow and select the appropriate option from the drop-down list.

4 Save and close the appointment window.

Tip Dates on which full day events are scheduled do not appear in bold.

Figure 3-14

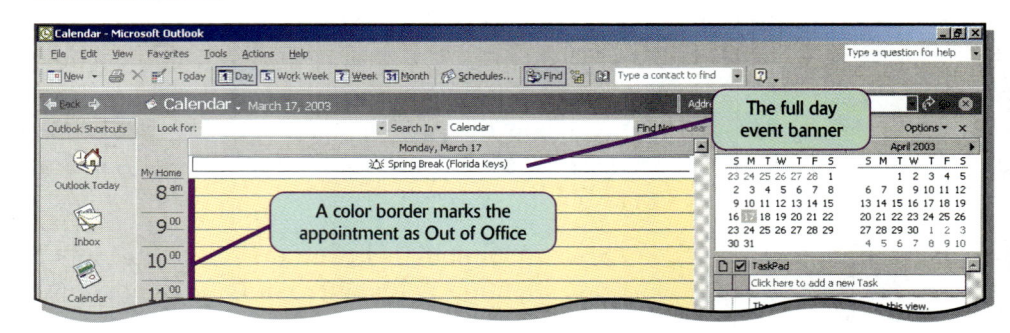

The full day event banner

A color border marks the appointment as Out of Office

Moving, Copying, and Deleting Appointments

Scheduling appointments and meetings on your electronic calendar is a great way to manage your time. When those meetings are cancelled or rescheduled, electronic scheduling makes rescheduling all types of appointments and events more efficient. You can simply drag the appointments to different dates and times and edit locations, when necessary, or open the appointment and change the time and date. Cancelled appointments can simply be deleted.

Task 6:
To Move, Copy, and Delete Appointments

1 Display **Wednesday, February 5, 2003**.

2 Position the mouse pointer on the blue band on the left side of the 11:00 appointment until you see a four-headed mouse pointer, then drag the 11:00 appointment to **Friday, February 7, 2003**, in the monthly Date Navigator.

3 Move to the date on which Spring Break is scheduled to begin, point to the middle of the event banner, and then drag the event banner to Monday, March 10, 2003, to move the week of Spring Break.

Figure 3-15

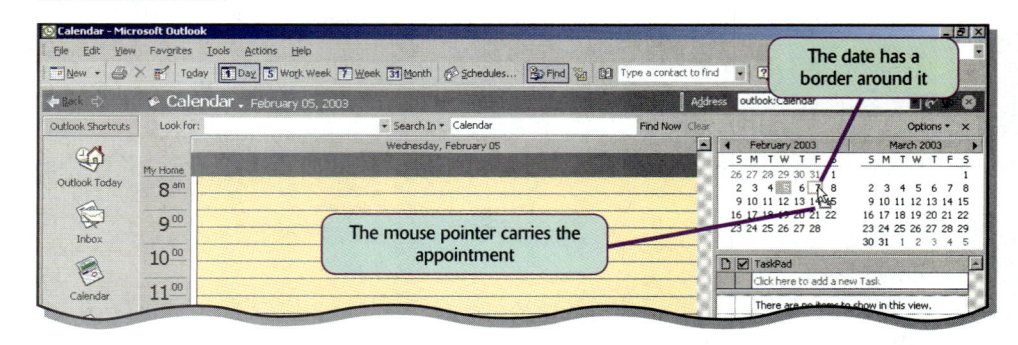

The date has a border around it

The mouse pointer carries the appointment

Tip The appointment appears in the same time slot on the new day that it occupied on the original date.

Maintaining the Outlook Calendar

OU 3-15

4 Display **Wednesday, February 5, 2003**, again, press Ctrl and drag the 3:00 appointment to **February 13, 2003**.

Tip Pressing and holding the Ctrl key as you drag the appointment to a different date copies the appointment rather than moving it.

Figure 3-16

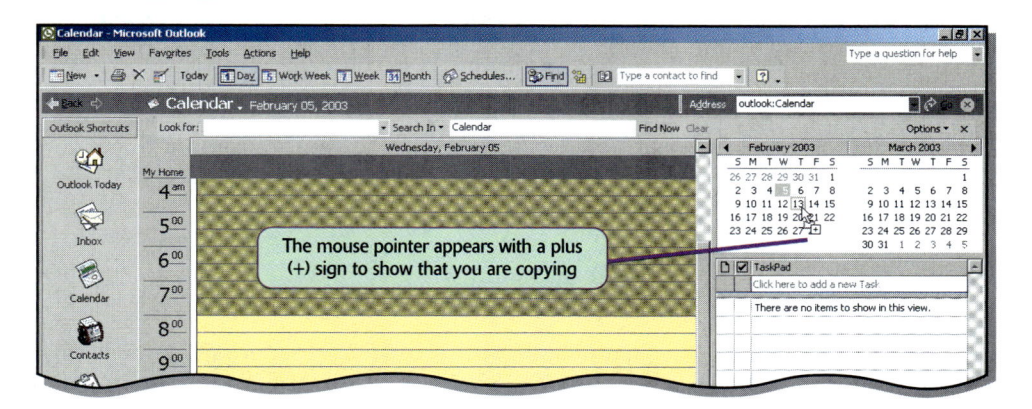

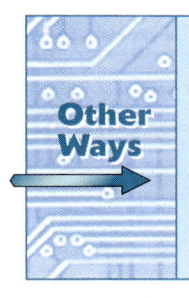

The mouse pointer appears with a plus (+) sign to show that you are copying

Other Ways

To move or copy appointments:
- Press Ctrl + X or click the **Cut** to cut an appointment and place it on the clipboard.
- Press Ctrl + C or click the **Copy** to copy the appointment and place it on the clipboard.
- Press Ctrl + V or click the **Paste** to paste the appointment contained on the clipboard to a new date.

5 Position the mouse pointer on the bottom border of the 3:00 appointment, drag the border down to 5:00 to extend the appointment end time, and press Enter to complete the appointment change.

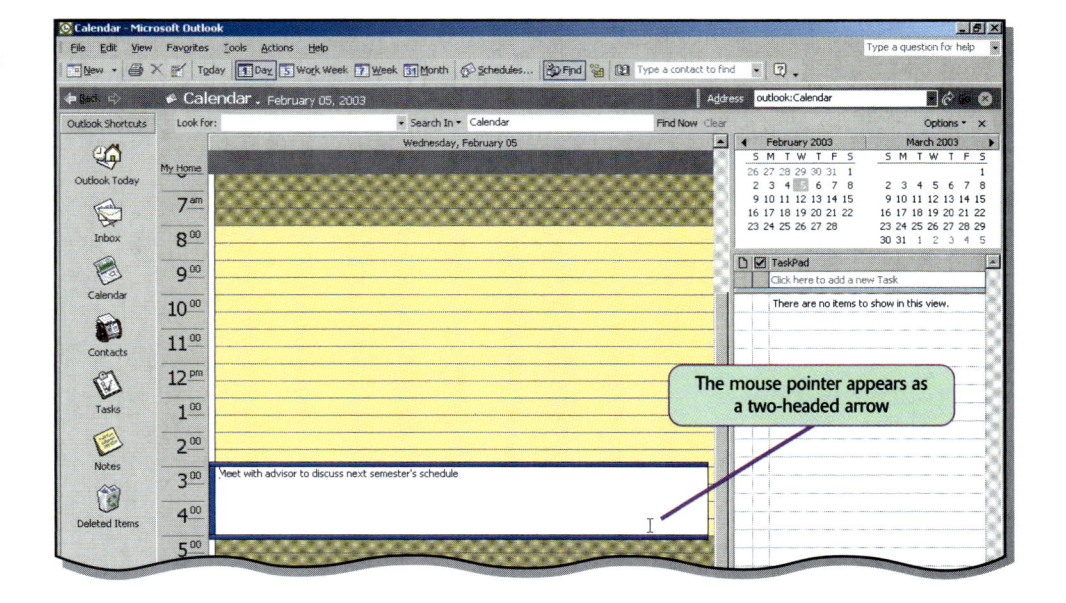

Figure 3-17

The mouse pointer appears as a two-headed arrow

Scheduling Recurring Appointments

Most companies have meetings that occur on a regular schedule that you are required to attend. Rather than move to each date on which such appointments occur to enter the appointments individually, you can schedule a *recurring appointment*. By identifying the pattern by which the recurring appointment repeats, you schedule the appointment for all dates by entering it only once.

Task 7:
To Schedule a Recurring Appointment

1 Open the **Calendar** folder and move to the day on which your next Outlook class is scheduled to occur.

2 Double-click the time that class is scheduled to start and type the appointment information shown in Figure 3-18, substituting your class dynamics as necessary.

Figure 3-18

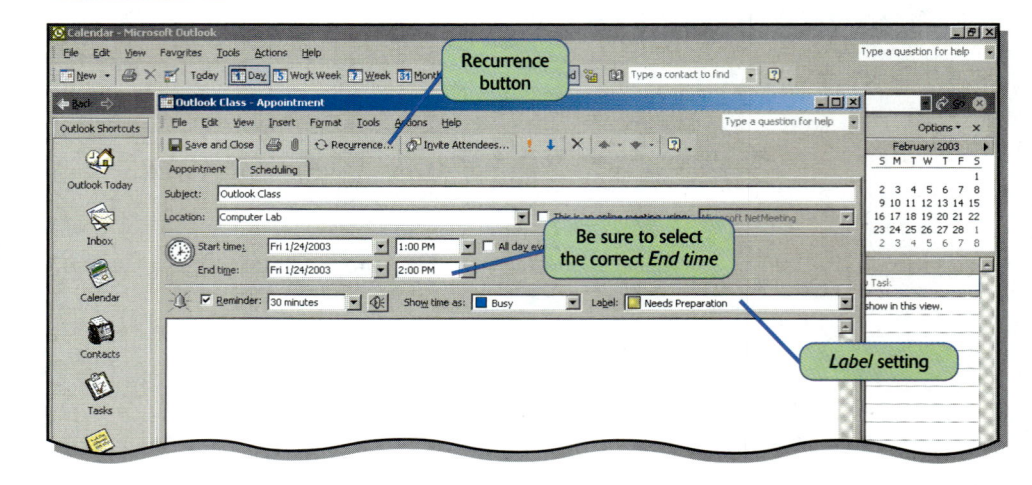

Callouts: Recurrence button; Be sure to select the correct *End time*; *Label* setting

> **Tip** To change the **Label** setting, click the **Label** down arrow and select the appropriate option from the drop-down list.

3 Click the **Recurrence** button.

> **Other Ways** To open the Appointment Recurrence dialog box:
> - Choose **Actions | New Recurring Appointment**.
> - Press [Alt] + [Shift] + [U]

4 Verify the **Start**, **End**, and **Duration** times, select **Weekly** in the **Recurrence pattern** list, and then select the days of the week on which your class occurs.

5 Select the date of the last regularly scheduled class from the **End by** drop-down list.

6 Click **OK** and then save and close the appointment.

Figure 3-19

> **Tip** Values set in Figure 3-19 are provided as examples. Follow the direction of your instructor to set your class recurrence values.

> **Troubleshooting** After you save and close the appointment, a message box may appear advising you that there is a conflict between the Spring Break event and class dates. Delete the classes for the week of Spring Break.

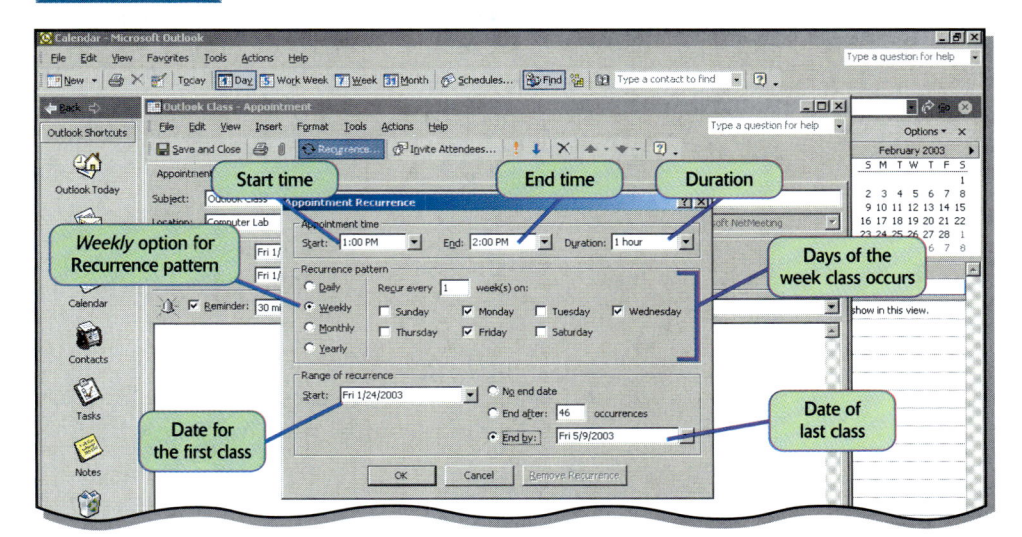

7 Move to the last class scheduled to occur, select the appointment, and press Delete to delete the class.

Figure 3-20

> **Tip** Remember, to select an appointment, point to the left border of the appointment until the mouse pointer appears as a four-headed arrow, and then click the border.

8 Select **Delete this occurrence** and click **OK**.

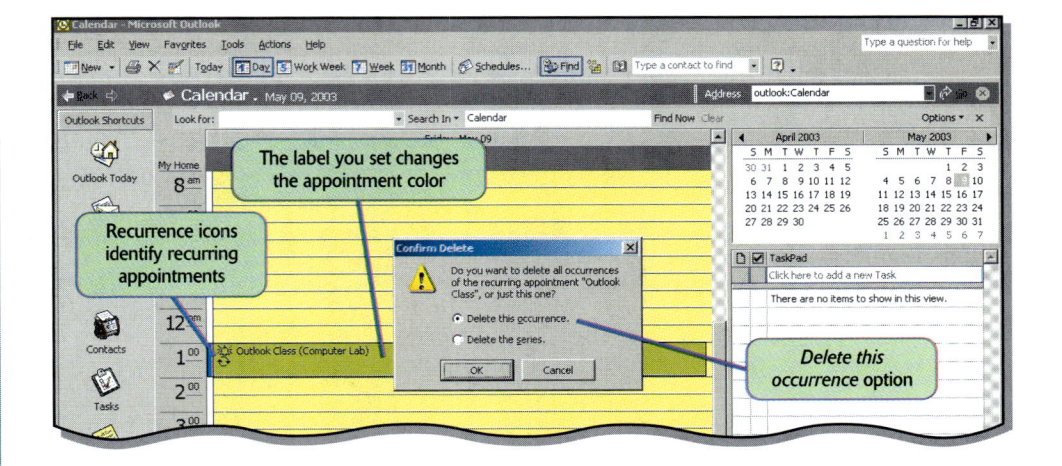

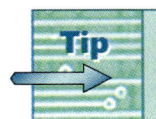

> **Tip** Depending on the settings active on your computer, dates on which appointments occur may appear in bold on the Date Navigator.

Scheduling Meetings Involving Others

Many organizations use Outlook to schedule conference rooms, audio-visual equipment, supervisors, and other *resources* for meetings, as well as to invite others to attend meetings. When those invited to attend a meeting receive their invitation, they can respond or suggest a time that is more convenient for the meeting.

Creating and Sending Meeting Requests

When you schedule a meeting in Outlook, you can send a notice of the meeting to other users whose names and e-mail addresses are stored in Contacts and invite them to attend the meeting.

Task 8:
To Invite Others to Meetings and Schedule Resources

1 Click the **Today** button on the Outlook Calendar toolbar to return to the current date, tap the → key to move to tomorrow, and then click the **New Appointment** button to create a new appointment.

2 Click the **Invite Attendees** button to change the appointment to a Meeting.

Figure 3-21

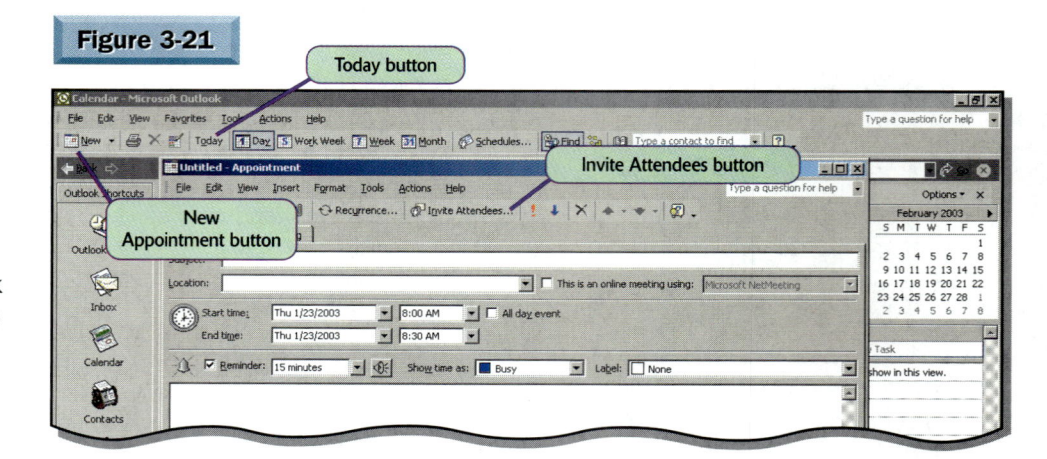

Today button
New Appointment button
Invite Attendees button

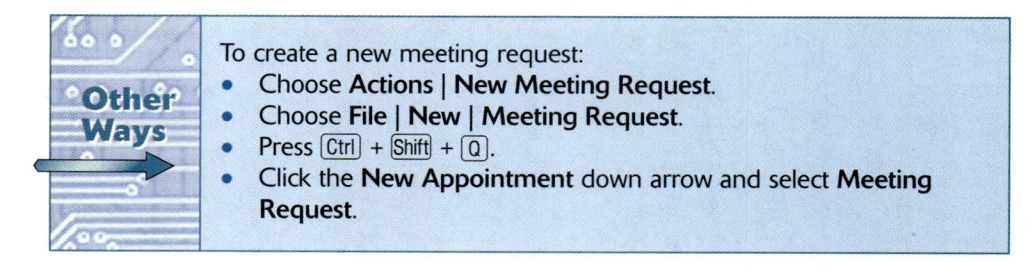

Other Ways

To create a new meeting request:
- Choose **Actions | New Meeting Request**.
- Choose **File | New | Meeting Request**.
- Press Ctrl + Shift + Q.
- Click the **New Appointment** down arrow and select **Meeting Request**.

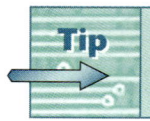

Tip The date that is active on your screen will be different from the one shown here.

Maintaining the Outlook Calendar   **OU 3-19**

3 Click the **To** button at the top of the Appointment dialog box to open the Select Attendees and Resources dialog box.

4 Select the two classmates you added as contacts and then click **Required**. Selected classmates appear in the Required list.

5 Select your instructor's name, click **Resources**, and click **OK** to return to the Meeting dialog box.

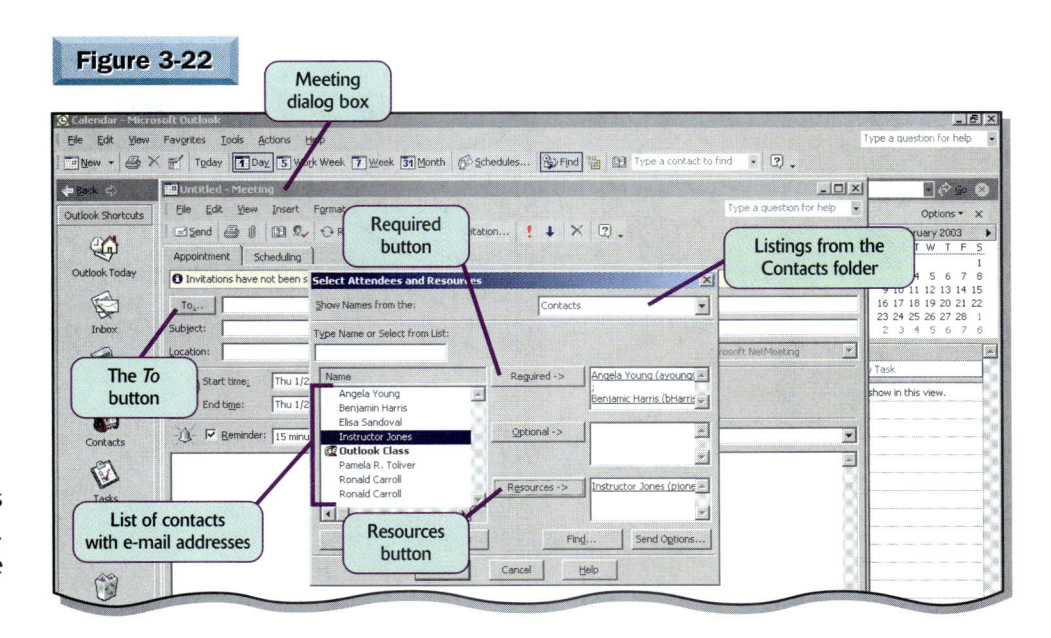

Figure 3-22

Troubleshooting If you have not yet added two classmates and your instructor to your Contacts list, click the **New** button on the Select Attendees and Resources dialog box, select **New Contact** from the New Entry dialog box, click **OK**, and enter information for the first classmate in appropriate fields. Be sure to include an e-mail address. Then repeat the procedure for the second classmate and your instructor, if necessary.

6 Set additional options as shown in Figure 3-23 to schedule the meeting as an all day event for Saturday.

7 Click **Send** and then display the calendar for **Saturday**.

Figure 3-23

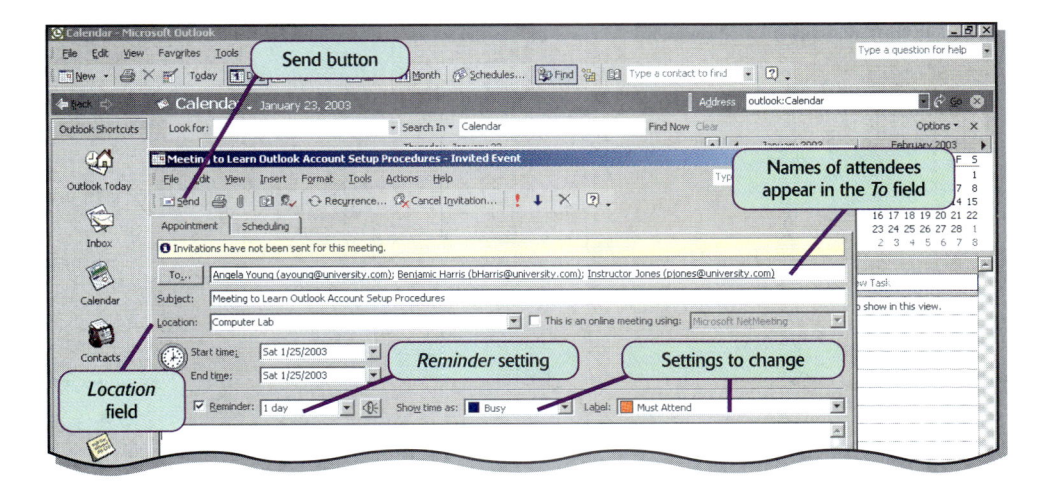

Troubleshooting Outlook assigns resources to the **Location** field of the Meeting dialog box. To change the location to Computer Lab, select the existing data in the **Location** field and then type the meeting location shown in Figure 3-23.

Scheduling Meetings Involving Others

8 Review the newly scheduled appointment.

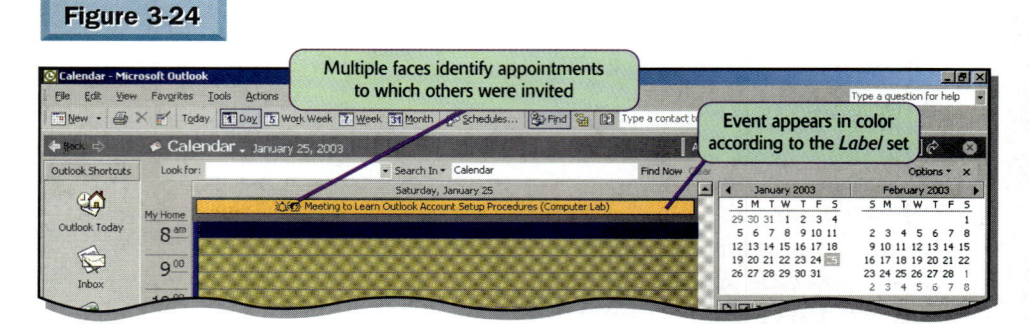

Figure 3-24

Multiple faces identify appointments to which others were invited

Event appears in color according to the *Label* set

CHECK POINT

The *Scheduling* page of the appointment dialog box provides an overview of your schedule. If you are connected to an intranet or Web site where others you invite to meetings have posted their schedules, you can hone in on a time that is mutually convenient to most of those you plan to invite by adding their names to the invitation and then clicking the *Scheduling* tab. Outlook even posts a message when you access the *Scheduling* tab to let you know that the schedules for all attendees may not be available. The schedule for those invited to the meeting appears similar to the one shown in Figure 3-25.

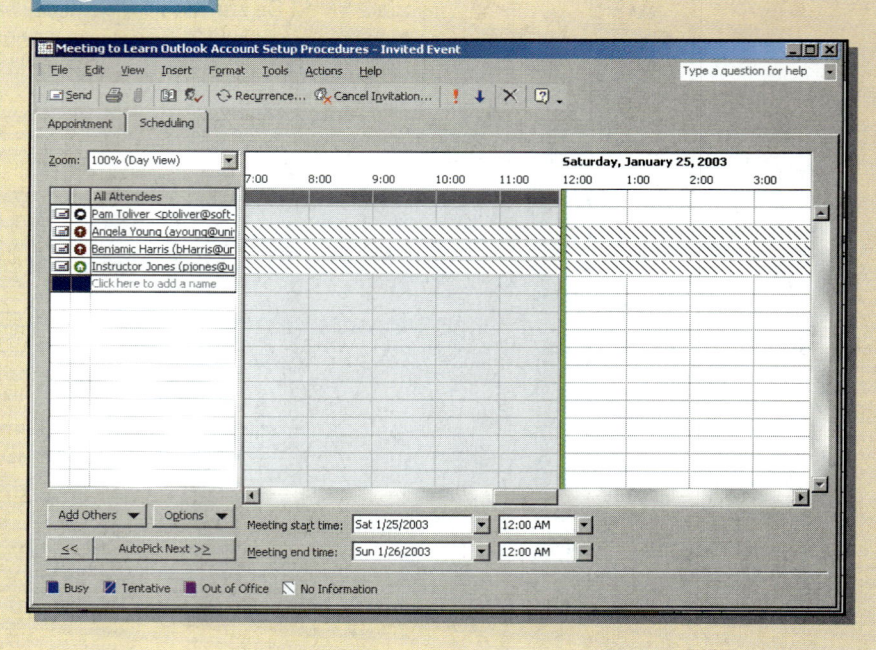

Figure 3-25

Editing Meeting Participants and Sending Updates

As those invited to attend meetings respond to the meeting invitation, you may find that others need to be added to the list of participants to substitute for those who cannot attend. Each time you edit the list of meeting attendees, Outlook prompts you to send an update.

Task 9:
To Edit the Meeting Participants and Send Updates

1 Double-click the banner for the meeting scheduled for Saturday to open the meeting appointment.

2 Choose **Actions | Add or Remove Attendees** to open the Select Attendees and Resources dialog box.

3 Select the listing for one of your classmates in the **Required** list, press Delete to remove the listing, and then click **OK**.

4 Save and close the meeting.

Figure 3-26

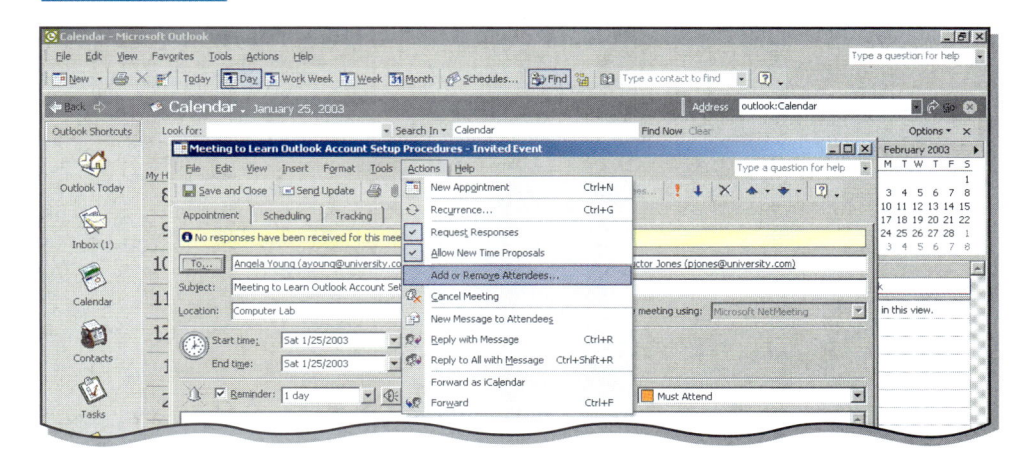

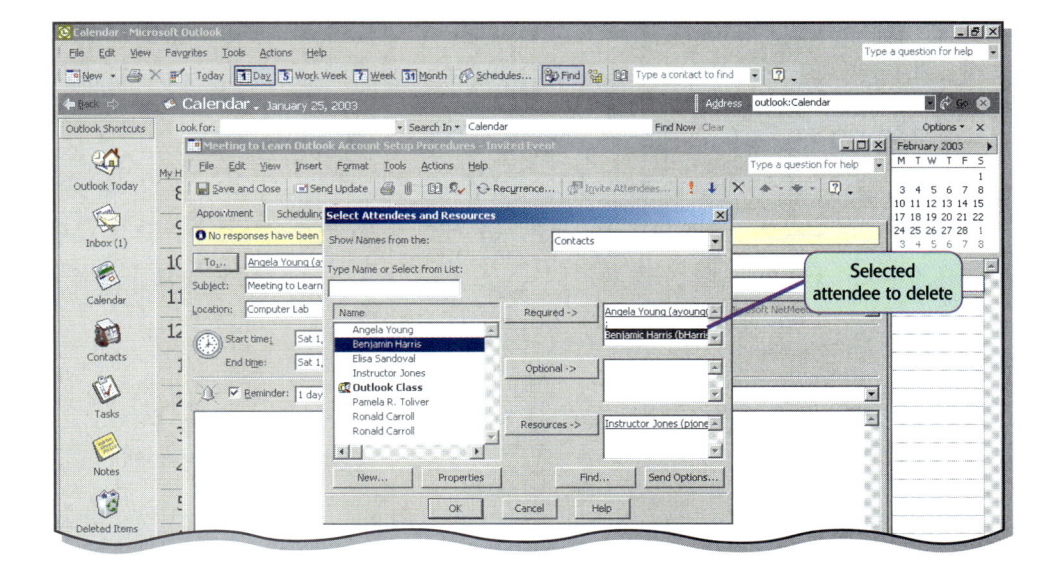

Figure 3-27

Canceling A Meeting

5 Select **Send updates to all attendees** and click **OK**.

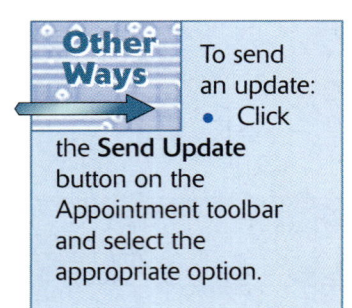

> **Other Ways**
> To send an update:
> - Click the **Send Update** button on the Appointment toolbar and select the appropriate option.

Figure 3-28

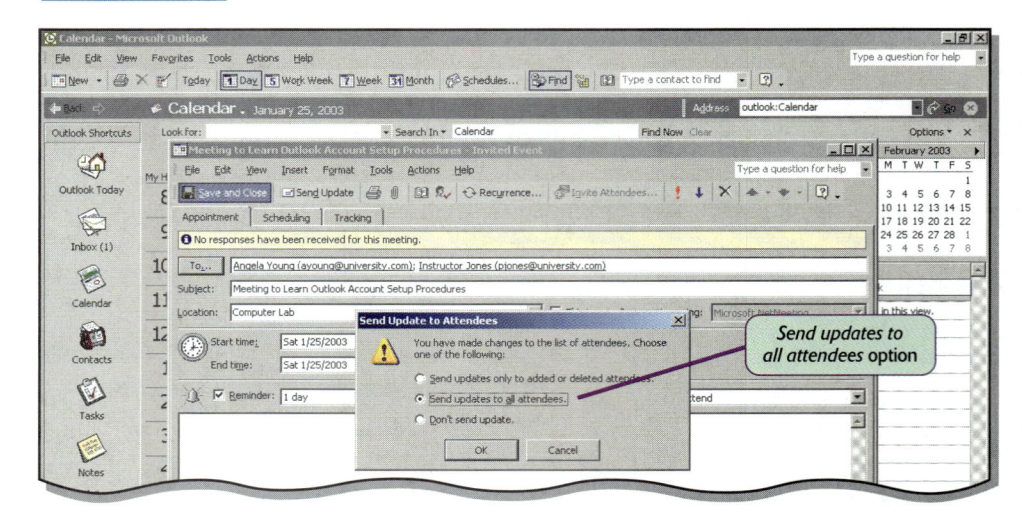

Send updates to all attendees option

Canceling a Meeting

As you begin to receive responses, you may discover that there are too few people planning to attend the meeting to make it worthwhile. When this happens, you can cancel the meeting and instruct Outlook to automatically send meeting cancellations to those invited to attend the meeting.

Task 10:
To Cancel a Meeting

1 Double-click the meeting banner for Saturday's meeting.

2 Choose **Actions | Cancel Meeting**.

3 Select **Send cancellation and delete meeting**, click **OK** to return to the Invited Event dialog box, and click **Send**.

Figure 3-29

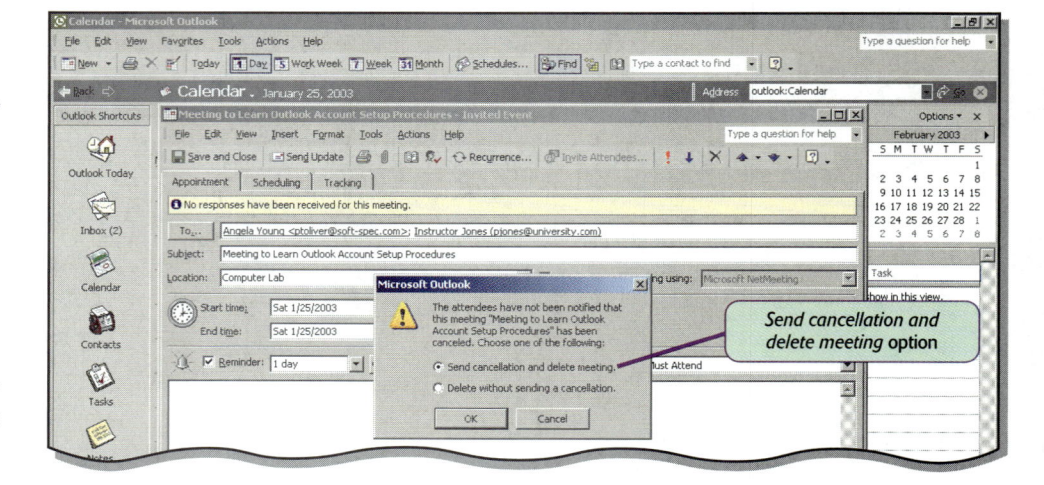

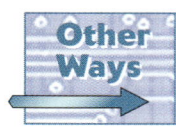

Send cancellation and delete meeting option

> **Other Ways**
> To cancel a meeting:
> - Click the event banner and select **Delete** to cancel a meeting.

Maintaining the Outlook Calendar

CHECK POINT

When you schedule an appointment and invite attendees, you can use the meeting window to send additional e-mail messages to those invited to the meeting. Simply open the meeting appointment window and choose **Actions | New Message to Attendees**. This is a quick and easy way to keep all those invited to the meeting up to date on information regarding the meeting without having to create a distribution list in the Outlook Contacts folder.

Printing the Calendar

Like most files created electronically, you can print appointments and calendars in a variety of different formats. The procedures for initiating the Print command are basically the same as those used to print files in other applications as well as from other Outlook features. However, clicking the **Print** button on the Standard toolbar from the Calendar folder opens the Print dialog box in Outlook. The view that is active when you print controls the print layout styles in which you can print the information.

Task 11:
To Print Calendars and Appointments

1 Display February 2003 and March 2003 in the Date Navigator pane and select **February 7, 2003**.

2 Click the **Print** button on the Standard toolbar to open the Print dialog box and select the options shown in Figure 3-30.

3 Click **Preview**.

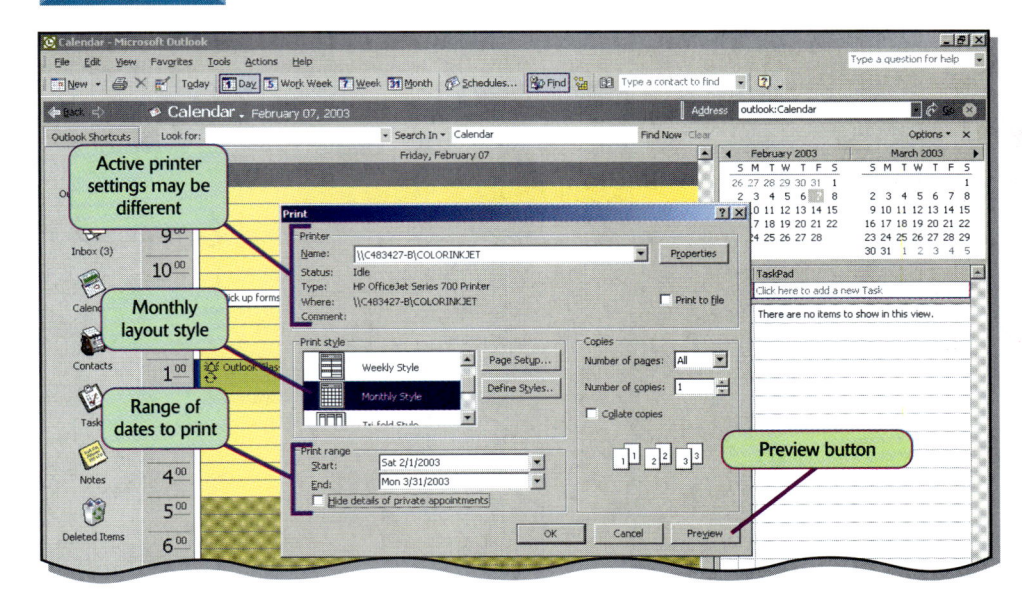

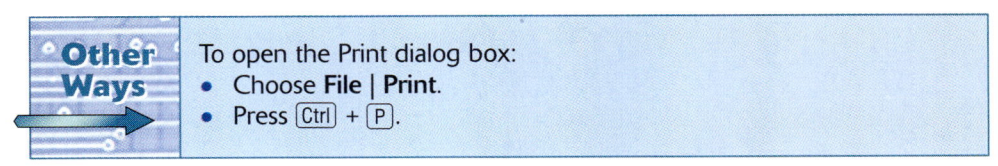

Figure 3-30

Active printer settings may be different

Monthly layout style

Range of dates to print

Preview button

Other Ways
To open the Print dialog box:
- Choose **File | Print**.
- Press [Ctrl] + [P].

4 Click **Close** on the **Print Preview** toolbar to close the preview.

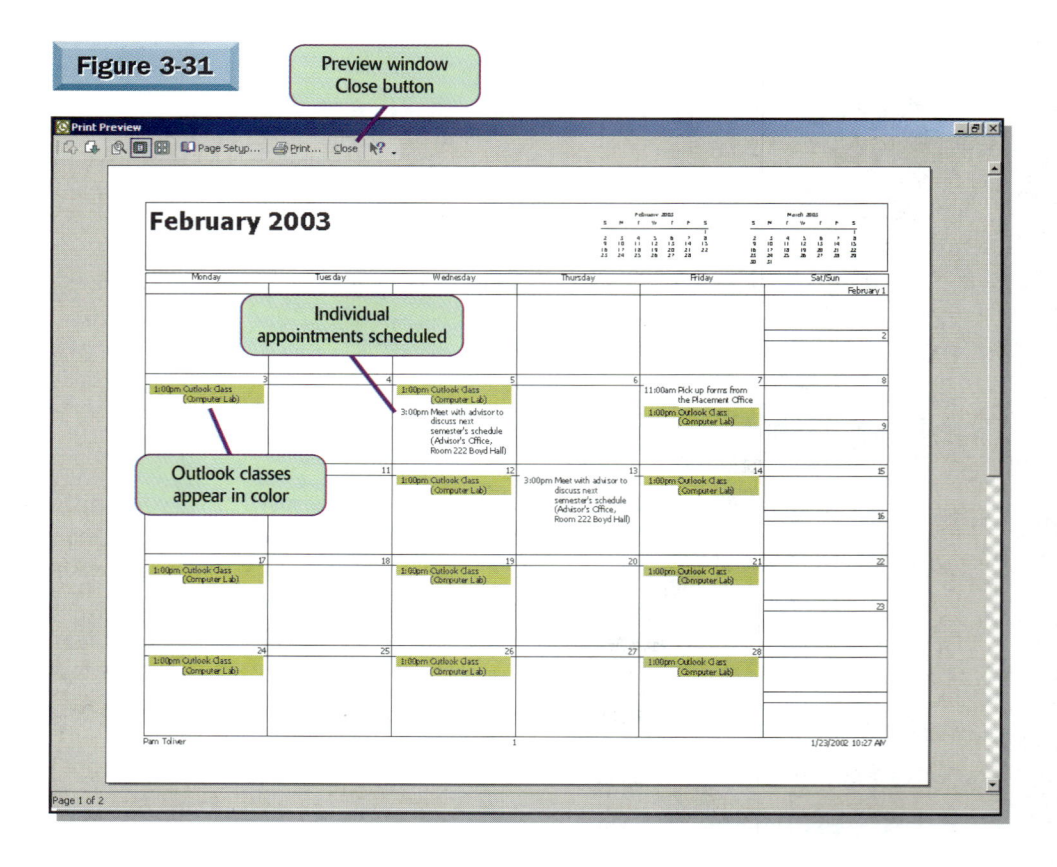

Figure 3-31

Preview window Close button

Individual appointments scheduled

Outlook classes appear in color

5 Choose **View | Current View | Active Appointments**, click the **Print** button to open the Print dialog box, select the **Table** style, and click **Preview**.

Figure 3-32

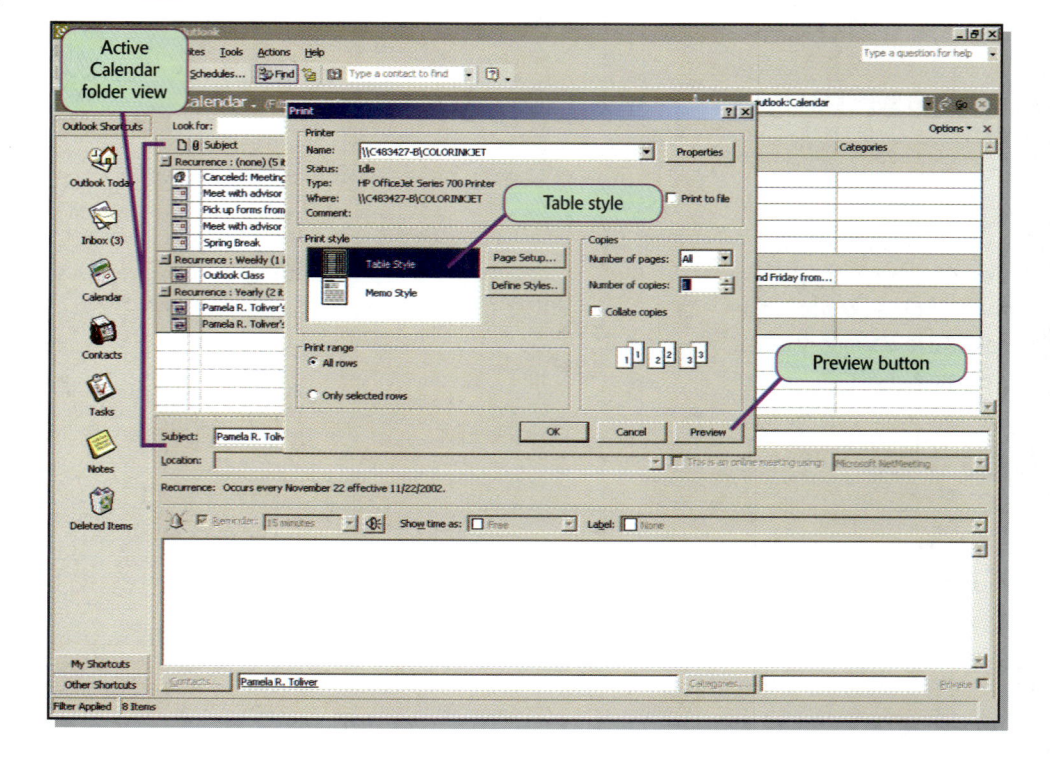

Active Calendar folder view

Table style

Preview button

6 Close print preview and choose **View | Current View | Day/Week/ Month** to restore the default view.

Figure 3-33

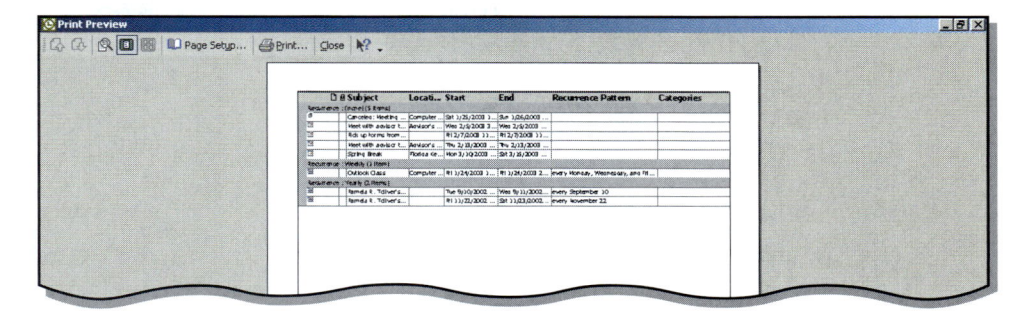

WEB TIP

Personal Digital Assistants (PDAs) are bustin' out all over and provide a great way to connect on the go. Simply add a modem in the form of a PCMCIA card and you can connect to your online calendar or send and receive e-mail. Many PDAs come equipped with full-size keyboards so that you can create documents and other files using special versions of Office products such as Word and Excel.

Customizing the Calendar

Throughout this project, you have been working with the default settings available in Outlook Calendar. You can customize the settings for the way you work by setting options for the Calendar as well as by creating "rules" that control formatting applied to special appointments.

Setting Calendar Options

The Calendar Options dialog box contains options for setting a number of different Calendar features.

- The time scale on the Calendar window
- A default reminder and reminder timing
- The Calendar work week
- Meeting response options

Additional dialog boxes display options for controlling special Calendar features. Each of these special features is described in Table 3-3.

Customizing the Calendar

Table 3-3 Advanced Calendar Options

Access these options	To
Planner Options	Set options for using the online scheduling feature or when you are responsible for maintaining a group calendar.
Add Holidays	Select different countries' national holidays you want to add to your calendar. The holidays appear as event banners.
Free/Busy Options	Publish calendar free and busy times to a company intranet site or to a public Internet site.
Resource Scheduling	Maintain the schedule for resources, such as conference rooms, within your organization that can be scheduled by others in the organization.
Time Zone	Add or change the active time zone.

Task 12:
To Set Calendar Options

1 Open the **Calendar** folder and choose **Tools | Options**.

2 Select the **Default reminder** option, set the reminder time to **30 minutes**, and click the **Calendar Options** button.

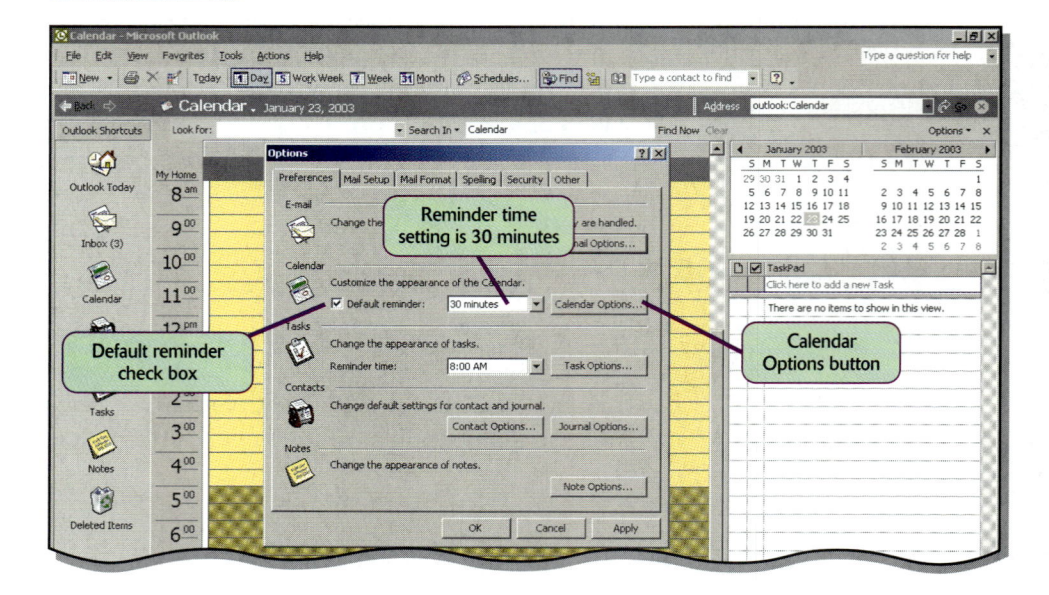

Figure 3-34

Maintaining the Outlook Calendar

OU 3-27

3 Click the **Background color** down arrow and select a different color.

Figure 3-35

4 Select the **Show week numbers in the Date Navigator** check box, and then click **OK** twice to return to the Calendar window.

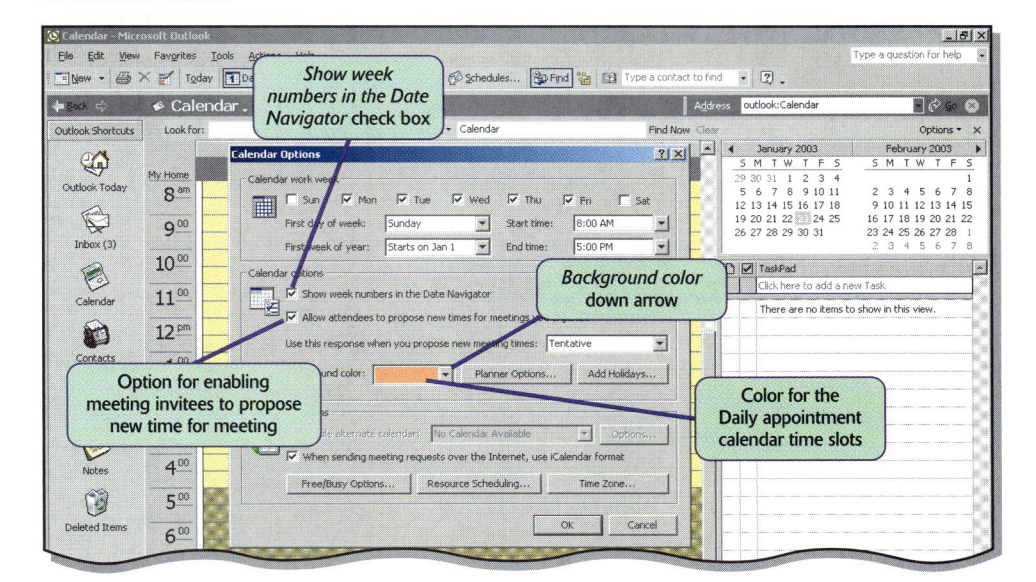

5 Review Calendar folder changes.

Figure 3-36

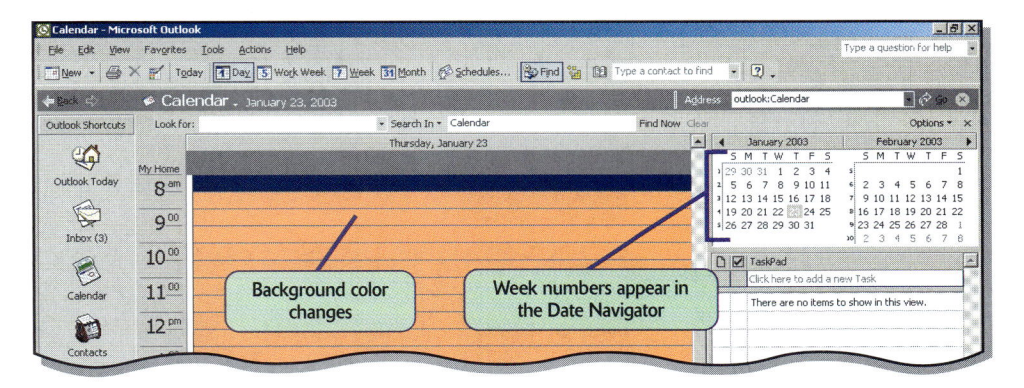

CHECK POINT

Outlook comes with sets of holidays already planned and outlined and organized by country so that all you have to do is import them. Here is how to add them to your Calendar. Choose **Tools | Options**, click **Calendar Options**, and then click **Add Holidays**. Select the countries whose holidays you want to add to your calendar and click **OK**. Outlook imports the holidays and places them as banners on the appropriate days—and these holidays span years into the future!

Apply Conditional Formatting to Appointments

Another way to customize Outlook Calendar is to create rules that format appointments and other items automatically. You could, for example, set a rule that automatically formats any meetings involving your instructor by labeling the meeting as Important. Each formatting rule you create is named and you control the conditions set as well as the formatting you want to apply to the rule.

Task 13:
To Apply Conditional Formatting to Appointments

1 Open the **Calendar** folder, if necessary, and choose **Edit | Automatic Formatting**.

2 Click the **Add** button.

Figure 3-37

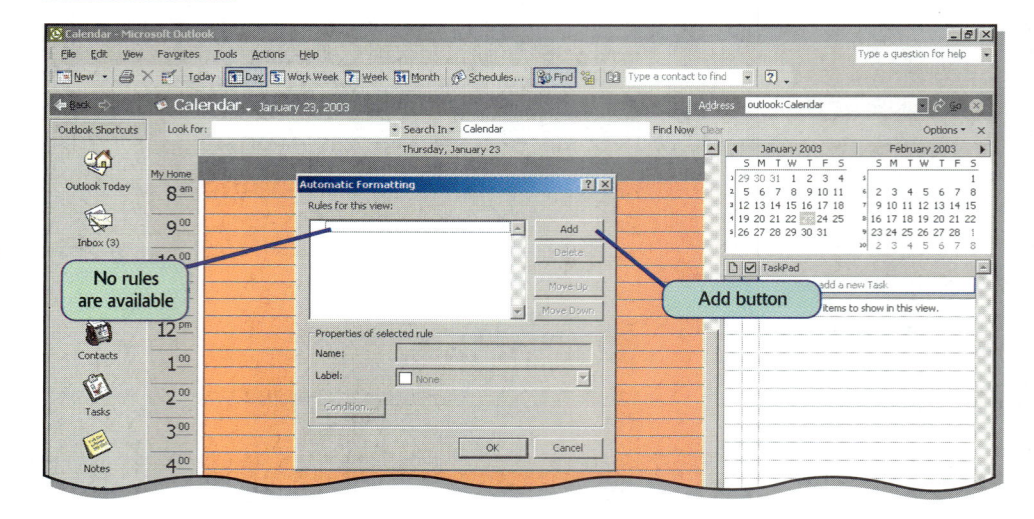

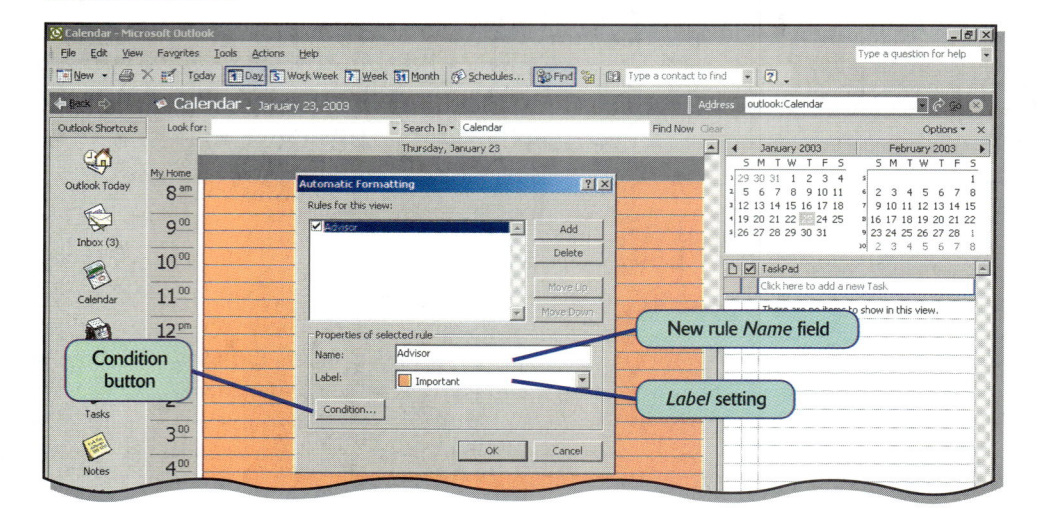

3 Type **Advisor** in the **Name** field and select **Important** from the **Label** list.

4 Click the **Condition** button.

Figure 3-38

Maintaining the Outlook Calendar

OU 3-29

5 Type **Advisor** in the **Search for the word(s)** field, select **frequently-used text fields** from the **In** list, and click **OK**.

Figure 3-39

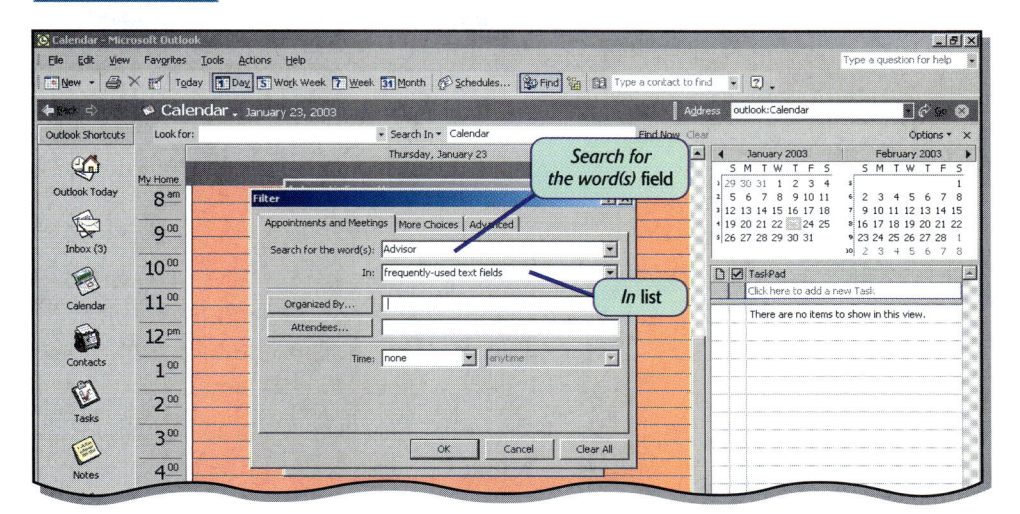

6 Click **OK** to return to the Calendar window and change the Daily Calendar palette color back to the default color.

7 Display **February 2003** in the Date Navigator, and click **13** to view the changes in the appointment with your advisor.

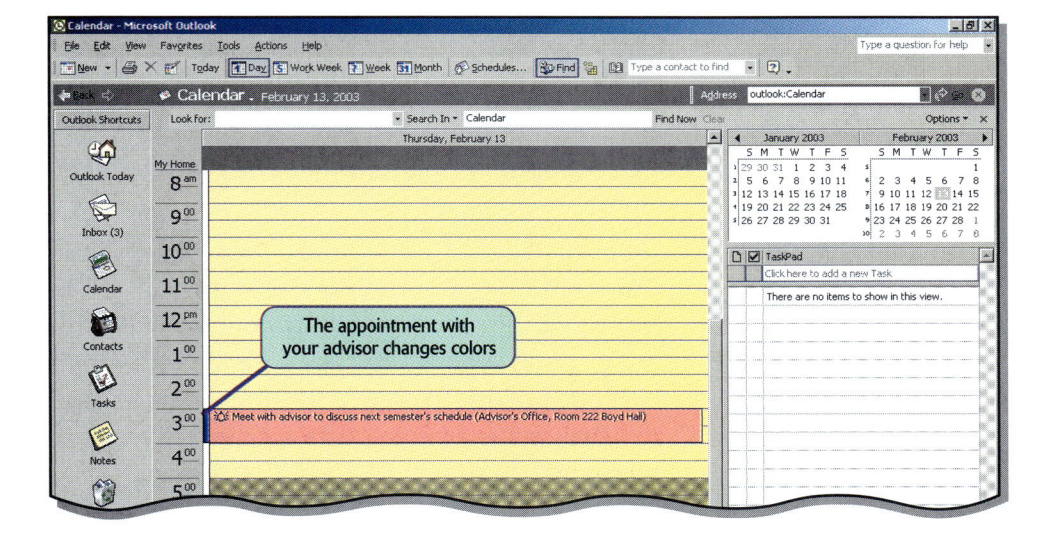

Figure 3-40

SUMMARY AND EXERCISES

SUMMARY

- The Outlook Calendar folder displays a tri-paned window containing the appointment palette to help you track appointments and manage meetings, a Date Navigator palette to help navigate dates, and a TaskPad to track a list of "to do" items.
- Display the Go To Date dialog box to move to a specific date. You can schedule simple appointments in the calendar by typing the appointment directly on the daily calendar palette.
- When you need to include detailed information about an appointment, use the new appointment dialog box and set the appropriate options.
- Setting reminders is a great way to prompt Outlook to remind you of important meetings and appointments.
- Outlook places an event banner just below the day/date banner on the daily appointment calendar for each meeting and event that encompasses a complete workday as well as those events that span multiple days.
- Outlook automatically schedules days on which full day events are scheduled as busy and labels can be used to color code appointments to draw attention to different types of appointments.
- You can edit appointments, move them to different dates, copy them by dragging them to different dates and times, open the appointment and change the time and date, or cancel the appointment by simply deleting it.
- By identifying the pattern by which a recurring appointment repeats, you schedule the appointment for all dates by entering it only once.
- When you schedule a meeting in Outlook, you can send a notice of the meeting to other users whose names and e-mail addresses are stored in Contacts and invite them to attend the meeting.
- Each time you edit the list of meeting attendees, Outlook prompts you to send an update.

- You can cancel meetings and instruct Outlook to automatically send meeting cancellations to those invited to attend the meeting.
- The view that is active when you print controls the print layout styles in which you can print the information.
- You can customize the settings for the way you work by setting options for the Calendar as well as by creating "rules" that control formatting applied to special appointments.
- The Calendar Options dialog box contains options for setting a variety of different Calendar features.
- One way to customize Outlook Calendar is to create rules that format appointments and other items automatically.

KEY TERMS & SKILLS

KEY TERMS

attendees (p. 3-18)
Calendar Banner (p. 3-6)
conditional formatting (p. 3-28)
Date Navigator (p. 3-6)
events (p. 3-8)
I-beam (p. 3-10)
label (p. 3-13)
pane borders (p. 3-6)
PDA (p. 3-25)
planner (p. 3-26)
private (p. 3-34)
recurring appointment (p. 3-16)
reminders (p. 3-10)
resources (p. 3-18)
scheduling (p. 3-14)
TaskPad (p. 3-6)
updates (p. 3-21)

SKILLS

Apply conditional formatting to appointments (p. 3-28)
Cancel a meeting (p. 3-22)
Display the calendar window (p. 3-5)
Edit the meeting participants and send updates (p. 3-21)
Invite others to meetings and schedule resources (p. 3-18)
Move, copy, and delete appointments (p. 3-14)
Print calendars and appointments (p. 3-23)
Schedule appointments in the calendar (p. 3-9)
Schedule and label an all day event (p. 3-13)
Schedule a recurring appointment (p. 3-16)
Set appointment reminders (p. 3-11)
Set calendar options (p. 3-26)
Use calendar navigation tools (p. 3-7)

STUDY QUESTIONS

MULTIPLE CHOICE

1. All of the following tools enable you to navigate a calendar *except* the
   a. Outlook Bar.
   b. Date Navigator.
   c. Go To dialog box.
   d. View menu.

2. Selecting multiple dates in the Date Navigator
   a. makes all selected dates active.
   b. enables you to enter an appointment on all selected dates at one time.
   c. displays selected dates in the Daily calendar.
   d. displays only selected dates in the Date Navigator.

3. To display the Go To Date dialog box,
   a. press →.
   b. press Ctrl + G.
   c. choose **Edit | Go To | Go To Date**.
   d. both b and c.

4. Clicking the **Back** button
   a. displays the last active date.
   b. opens the last active Outlook folder.
   c. displays the last active dialog box.
   d. displays the previously accessed application.

5. To send a notice of a meeting to people who should attend,
   a. click the **Notify** button.
   b. you must switch to the Inbox and create a new message.
   c. click the **New Meeting To** button.
   d. click the **Invite Attendees** button.

6. When you schedule an event, the event banner appears
   a. in the event start time on the daily palette.
   b. only in the Date Navigator palette.
   c. at the top of the daily appointment palette.
   d. in the TaskPad window.

7. If you add a person to the list of meeting attendees,
   a. Outlook enables you to send updates to all meeting attendees.
   b. you have to call the new people to advise them of the meeting.
   c. Outlook notifies you if the new people are available.
   d. Outlook displays an error message because you cannot edit the list of meeting attendees.

8. The command to cancel a meeting appears on the
   a. appointment window Actions menu.
   b. Outlook Inbox Actions menu.
   c. Outlook Inbox Tools menu.
   d. Outlook Inbox File menu.

9. You can open the Print dialog box with the Calendar folder open by doing all the following *except*
   a. clicking 🖨.
   b. pressing Ctrl + P.
   c. choosing **File | Print**.
   d. choosing **Actions | Print**.

10. Use the main Calendar Options dialog box to change
    a. background color.
    b. time zones.
    c. holidays.
    d. print settings.

Maintaining the Outlook Calendar

SHORT ANSWER

1. What are the two basic techniques for entering appointments in the Calendar?
2. How does Outlook remind you of appointments if the computer is turned off?
3. What happens if you set an appointment reminder in a Calendar subfolder?
4. What happens when you delete one appointment in a recurring series?
5. If you move or copy an appointment to a different date, what time slot does Outlook put it into?
6. Unless you change the settings, what happens when you send a meeting request?
7. What button can you click to notify meeting attendees of a change in meeting time?
8. What happens when you click the **Print** button from the Calendar folder?
9. What does conditional formatting enable you to do?
10. How do you display a new appointment window with the all day event option already checked?

FILL IN THE BLANK

1. The mouse pointer appears as a(n) _____ when positioned to select an appointment.
2. A(n) _____ appears beside appointments when a reminder is set.
3. Use _____ to color code appointments by type.
4. All day events appear as _____ in the daily appointment calendar.
5. Appointments that occur at regularly scheduled intervals are called _____ appointments.
6. The _____ page of the new appointment dialog box displays your free and busy times.
7. Holidays that you can add to your Calendar are grouped by _____.
8. The _____ displays the active folder and is used to type a URL to access a Web site.
9. The _____ displays a list of To Do items in the Calendar window.
10. The _____ dialog box can be used to move to specific dates.

DISCUSSION

1. What is the advantage of labeling appointments?
2. What Calendar feature do you think you will use most?
3. What type of messages and information might you use the **Actions | New Message to Attendees** command to send?

GUIDED EXERCISES

1 SCHEDULING PERSONALS

While many companies frown on using corporate equipment for personal tasks, recording personal appointments in your Outlook Calendar and marking the time as busy will prevent trying to maintain two separate calendars and reduce the chance that you will overcommit. As you know, Outlook contains an option that enables you to mark personal appointments as *private*. Private appointments show the time as busy but hide the nature of the appointment so that others viewing your schedule see only that you are unavailable. As a result, you can schedule that dental appointment you have been putting off. Follow these steps to create a folder in which to store relative contacts and then add contacts to the folder:

1. Launch Outlook, open the Calendar folder, and use the Date Navigator to move to November 5 of the current year.

2. Double-click the 8:00 A.M. time slot, type **Dental Appointment** in the Subject field, type **Dr. Hurt's Office** in the Location field.

3. Select the **Private** option and then click the **Save and Close** button to save the appointment. A key appears beside the appointment in the Daily calendar to identify the appointment as private and locked.

2 CLASSY APPOINTMENTS

One way to organize appointments is to set up different folders to hold different types of appointments. You can create the new folders and then add new appointments to the folder or you can move existing appointments from one calendar folder to another. Follow these steps to move some of the class appointments into a Class Appointments folder. If you already have a folder named **Class Appointments**, skip steps 1 and 2.

1. Open the **Calendar** folder and choose **File | Folder | New Folder**.

2. Type **Class Appointments** in the **Name** field, ensure that **Calendar Items** appears in the **Folder contains** field, click **OK**, and click **Yes** to add the item to the Outlook Bar.

3. Move the *Class Appointments* folder to the Outlook Shortcuts group, if necessary, and then display the main Calendar folder.

4. Move to the date of your next Outlook class using the Date Navigator, select the **Outlook Class (Computer Lab)** assignment, and drag it to the **Class Appointments** folder.

5 Click the **Find** button to display the Find Bar, if necessary, type **class** in the **Look for** field, and click **Find Now**. Drag the appointment that appears in the table to the **Class Appointments** folder.

6 Change the Calendar folder view back to **Day/Week/Month**.

7 Open the **Class Appointments** folder and navigate to the month containing your next class, if necessary, to view the appointments.

3 CELEBRATING ANNUALLY

When you add birthdays and anniversaries to the Detail page of a contact listing, Outlook automatically places the event in the Calendar. You can check the recurrence of a birthday or anniversary to be sure that it is scheduled to appear on the appropriate date each year. Follow these steps:

1 Move to the date on which your birthday occurs this year.

2 Double-click the event banner and select **Open the series**.

3 Click the **Recurrence** button and review the options displayed in the **Appointment Recurrence** dialog box.

ON YOUR OWN

> The difficulty of these case studies varies:
> ⚑ are the least difficult; ⚑⚑ are more difficult; and ⚑⚑⚑ are the most difficult.

1 DATING MAJOR PROJECTS

⚑ Keeping track of major class assignments and projects can be a snap, using features available in Outlook. Record due dates for at least three major class projects, ten different assignments, and at least two special appointments or assignments that are due outside the regularly scheduled class times for all your classes. If you have fewer than the required number of projects, assignments, and special appointments for this exercise, make up fictitious entries to meet the number requirements. Then print a copy of your calendar using the Monthly style to carry with you to your next computer class.

2 SCHEDULING TIME OFF

⚑ One of the rules you learn after you start working is that it is important to pay yourself first so that you are always setting aside some amount of money for a "rainy day." The same can be said about scheduling time for yourself to do some of the things you like to do. Add an appointment to your calendar that schedules at least three hours each week to do something besides study and work. Set reminders for these appointments, and be sure to specify, in the appointments Subject field, the type of activity you plan to enjoy. Then print a copy of your calendar for one week that shows the planned activities.

3 MORE CLASSY APPOINTMENTS

Each class you take probably meets on a different schedule with different intervals between classes. Record recurring appointments for each of your classes, setting the recurrence for each class that shows the appropriate interval. Print a copy of the monthly calendars for each month of the semester. Then delete appointments in the series for each class period that the class(es) will not meet, such as on holidays and breaks from school. Finally, record appointments for each final exam you will take this semester, setting the appropriate time and exam length as you set up the appointment. Label each test using the *Needs Preparation* label. Add reminders to the calendar for each test so that you are reminded in plenty of time to complete the necessary study for the test. Then print a copy of your calendar for finals week.

4 FAVORITE THINGS

Outlook makes a great tool to help keep you in good graces with relatives and friends. By scheduling the birthdays of your closest relatives and friends, you can set reminders that will notify you far enough in advance so that you remember to send a card. Record the birthdays for five of your closest relatives and five friends whose birthdays you want to remember and make them all-day events. Set a reminder for each birthday. Create a conditional formatting named *Birthdays* that labels birthdays a specific color and apply the formatting to the new birthdays you have set. Print the calendar in Calendar Details Style for each day on which you recorded a birthday. Then access the Internet and locate a resource that provides free electronic birthday greeting cards. Add the resource to your Contacts list so that you can find it easily when you need to send a birthday card at the last minute.

5 KICK BACK TIME

Have you ever had trouble getting organized enough to notify your friends of get-togethers during the semester? Outlook makes this task easy. Send a meeting request to at least three friends and your instructor notifying them of a get-together at your place two weeks from Friday. Add the names and addresses of three friends to your Contacts list using the tools available in the Invite Attendees dialog box, if they are not yet listed in the Contacts folder. Word the meeting request so that those who receive it know whether you are *really* planning for them to attend this get-together or if you are just fulfilling a class assignment. Then identify an additional person to be invited, change the time for the get-together, and send an update. Ask each person to reply to the invitation so that you will have additional e-mail messages to use in the next Project. Print a copy of each invitee's response. Finally, send out a cancellation notice to each invitee to cancel the get-together.

6 MEETING WITH THE BOARD

The meeting of the Board of Directors that you have been organizing is fast approaching. It is time to send out the invitations to the board members advising them that the meeting is tentatively scheduled for Thursday and Friday, May 21–22, 2004, from 9:00 A.M. on Thursday until 4:00 P.M. on Friday. Create contact listings for the six members of the board that are identified in Table 3-4. If you have already added these names to the Board of Directors Contacts folder in a previous project, access them using the information already entered. Then create a distribution list named *Board of Directors* and add the names of each board member shown in Table 3-4 to the distribution list. Send meeting invitations to the *Board of Directors* distribution list and ask the board members to reply as soon as possible so that the tentative dates can be set and the necessary reservations made for the meeting location. Copy the names and e-mail addresses of each board member listed in Table 3-4 into the meeting request form so that each board member will have up-to-date e-mail addresses for all board members. Print a copy of the meeting invitation.

Table 3-4	Board of Directors Members
Name	**e-Mail**
Donald Koontz	dkoontz@isp.com
Norma Rule	nrule@isp.com
Tamara Patterson	tpatterson@isp.com
Lee Lowell	llowell@isp.com
David Steele	dsteele@isp.com
Pamela Ayers	payers@isp.com

Photospread credits pages 3-2 & 3-3
©Tony Stone: ©John Riley; ©FPG: ©VCG1997, ©Mark Adams; ©Pearson Education; and ©Lorraine Castellano

FROM THE FILES

You Will Need
✓ e-Selections.doc

PROJECT 4

Corresponding Using Outlook Mail

In today's fast-paced world, the importance of communicating over the Internet has become vital to the success of most businesses. As a result, perhaps the most-used Outlook feature is the e-mail Inbox. Outlook e-mail contains tools that enable you to send, receive, respond to, format, and customize the look of messages you send, whether you are communicating with people on a local area network (LAN) or with people on the Internet.

OBJECTIVES

After completing this project, you will be able to:

- Display the Inbox and identify Inbox features
- Open and respond to messages and meeting requests
- Save messages in different file formats
- Print mail
- Modify message formats and create signatures
- Create and send e-mail messages
- Set message tracking options
- Format messages using stationery
- Flag messages for follow-up
- Sort and search for messages
- Set e-mail options
- Work with mail attachments

e-selections Running Case

In your roles as a student and as an employee of e-Selections, you will be sending and receiving e-mail, scheduling appointments and meetings, and keeping track of e-Selections clients and personnel. The e-Selections division uses Outlook 2002 as its primary e-mail program. As a student at the local college, you will learn most of the things you need to know about e-mail in class and transfer that knowledge to your work environment.

E-Mail Overload!

*"You've Got Mail!"…Cha Ching…
Wa, ha, ha, ha, ha!…Ding dong…
New mail has arrived. Would you like to read it now?…*

These are the sights and sounds of new mail arriving on different e-mail programs. Do you recognize any of them? The number-one reason most people connect to the Internet, or "go online," is to send and receive e-mail. In today's world of business, it's also a vital link to clients and vendors. So, what's the catch? One day you may wake up and find yourself on E-MAIL OVERLOAD!

"E-mail has become a double-edged sword: an extremely efficient tool that can quickly overwhelm if it's not properly handled," said John Yaukey of the Gannett News Service in a recent article. Imagine returning to your office after being away for a few days and finding over 500 e-mail messages awaiting your return.

Could you be one of the over 80 million people whose inbox is starting to look a bit like your garage? If so, here are a few good rules for helping to manage your e-mail and inbox:

- **Discipline:** Deal with each message only once; when it arrives respond to it, delete it, or file it.

- **Organize the Inbox:** First, create specific folders and storage spaces for each type of message. It will make it easier to find your messages and keep the Inbox cleaned out and uncluttered. Then, delete the messages you don't need to keep.

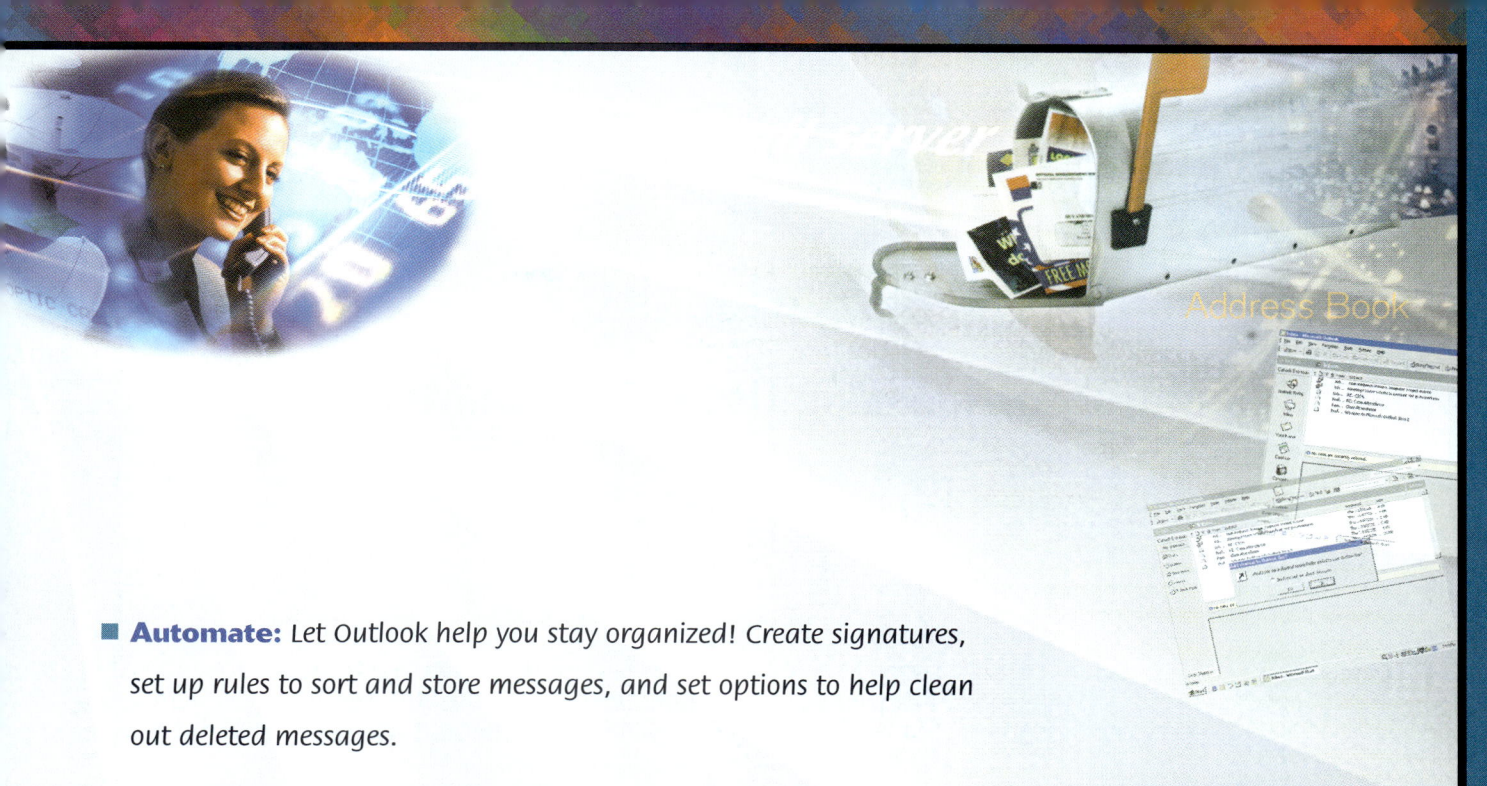

- **Automate:** Let Outlook help you stay organized! Create signatures, set up rules to sort and store messages, and set options to help clean out deleted messages.

- **Preview messages:** Most e-mail programs are equipped with a preview pane that enables you to scan messages when the subject of a message is vague. Open only those that you need to read more thoroughly.

- **Go wireless:** To prevent e-mail from backing up when you're away from your computer, you could get a cell phone or personal digital assistant (PDA) that includes built-in, wireless e-mail access. Then you can handle the messages as they arrive.

- **Consider a universal inbox:** A universal inbox enables you to access voice-mail and e-mail messages over the Web or by calling a toll-free number. When you dial in, you can have a virtual assistant read your e-mail messages and retrieve your voice-mail messages.

- **Separate business and personal e-mail:** Keeping personal and business e-mail separate helps prevent ugly problems—especially when businesses monitor e-mail. Currently, 45% of all businesses monitor their employees' e-mail and that number is expected to rise. Set up a separate, personal e-mail account.

By managing and using e-mail wisely, you'll avoid becoming a slave to it!

PROJECT 4

Corresponding Using Outlook Mail

The Setup

Before starting this Project, it is a good idea to reset some of the customizations you may have set as you worked your way through other Projects in this book. Launch Outlook and follow the instructions identified in Table 4-1 to restore system defaults and to ensure that the screen you see will match the figures in this Project.

Table 4-1	Outlook Settings
Feature	**Setting**
Office Assistant	Hide the Office Assistant.
Preview Pane	Hide the preview pane by choosing **View	Preview Pane** if it is open.
Outlook Bar	Right-click an empty space on the Outlook Bar and select **Large Icons**.
Toolbars	Choose **Tools	Customize	Toolbars**, select the **Standard** toolbar, click **Reset**, click **Yes**, and click **Close** to restore the toolbar to its default settings.
	Choose **Tools	Customize	Options**, select the **Show Standard and Formatting toolbars on two rows** check box, and click **OK**.
Outlook Start Feature	Choose **Tools	Options	Other**, click **Advanced Options**, select **Inbox** from the **Startup in this folder** list, and click **OK** twice.
Deleted Items Folder	Choose **Tools	Options	Other** and clear the **Empty the Deleted Items folder upon exiting** option, if necessary, and click **OK**.
Mail Editor	Choose **Tools	Options	Mail Format**, select the **Use Microsoft Word to edit e-mail messages** option, select **HTML** from the **Compose in the message format** list, and click **OK**.
Find Bar	Close the Find Bar by clicking the **Close** button at the right end of the bar.

The Challenge

e-Selections employees use the Outlook mail feature to communicate information about meetings, update client information, transmit electronic copies of documents, and communicate many other types of information with other personnel as well as with clients outside the company. Ms. Amber Wright, e-Administration Manager, is delighted to learn that you have enrolled in the CIS program at the local college. As part of the employee development program, she has approved your application for time away from the office to attend classes and has sent the approval using Outlook e-mail. Along with the approval, she has asked you to identify those features associated with e-mail that you believe can benefit others in the organization and has asked you to summarize those functions upon completion of the course.

The Solution

In order to complete the report requested by Ms. Wright, it is vital for you to learn your way around Outlook e-mail. You have figured out some of the elementary features associated with e-mail, and plan to use your course to explore additional e-mail functions. As you progress through the e-mail unit, you will learn how using e-mail will help you keep abreast of what is going on in the division and enable you to communicate in a timely manner with company and college personnel.

WEB TIP

Looking for a free e-mail program to use outside the classroom or school? There are a number of them available; Juno, HotMail, and Xoom are just a few. Each of these services also has a fee-based Internet access program as well, so be careful when you contact the sites to ensure that you are getting the free stuff!

Displaying the Inbox and Identifying Inbox Features

The Outlook Inbox stores messages you receive from others, and, unless you change the settings, the Inbox is the default feature that appears each time you launch Outlook. The Inbox contains other unique features that help you review messages and identify information about the message. The Inbox window displays a relatively simple arrangement of e-mail information.

Task 1:
To Display the Inbox and Identify Inbox Features

1 Launch Outlook and click the Outlook Bar **Inbox** icon to display the Inbox, if necessary.

Tip Inbox items displayed in Figure 4-1 are messages delivered as a result of tasks performed in other Outlook 2002 Projects. The messages and variety of items you see will be different.

Troubleshooting
Depending on the settings that are active on your computer, the Inbox window may contain two separate panes—a message list at the top of the window and a preview pane at the bottom of the window. When messages are displayed in the preview pane, viruses attached to the messages are more easily spread to your computer. As a result, closing the preview pane helps protect your computer from infection. To close the preview pane, choose **View | Preview Pane**.

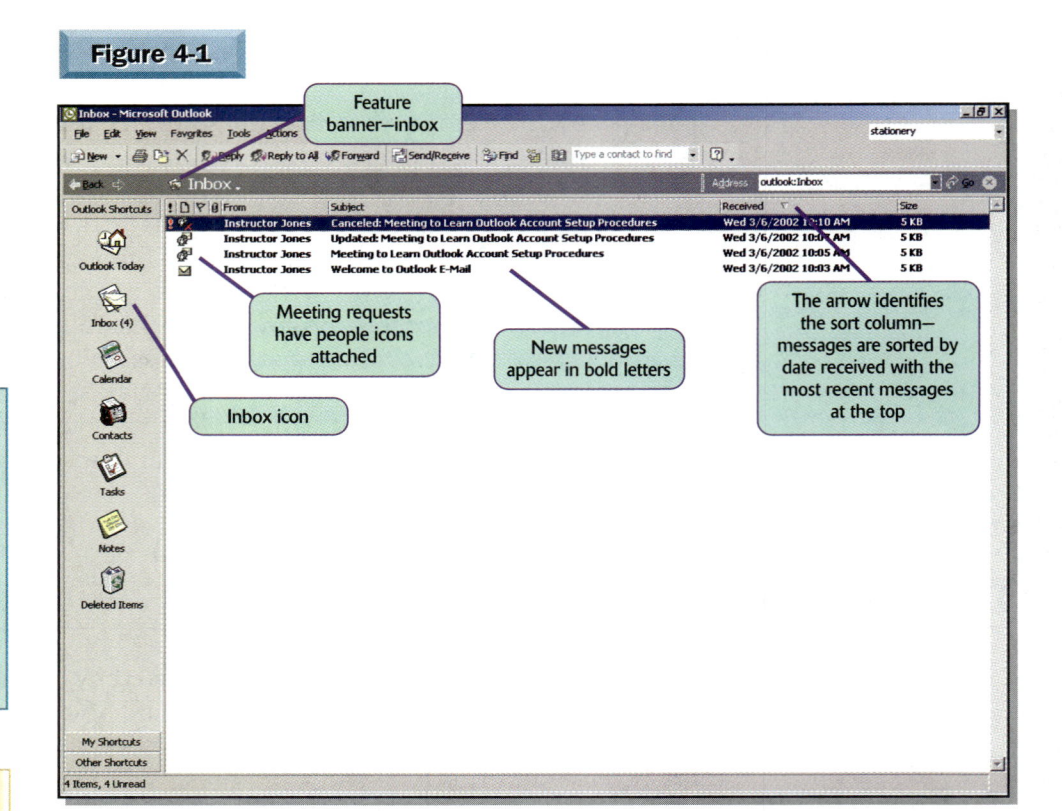

Figure 4-1

Callouts:
- Feature banner—inbox
- Meeting requests have people icons attached
- Inbox icon
- New messages appear in bold letters
- The arrow identifies the sort column—messages are sorted by date received with the most recent messages at the top

Identifying Message Icons

The icon that appears beside messages in the Inbox helps identify the message or item by type. Table 4-2 identifies different icons that may appear beside messages and items in the Inbox.

Table 4-2	Inbox Item Icons
Icon	**Description**
✉	Identifies new messages that have arrived but have not yet been opened
✉	Identifies messages that have arrived and have been opened
	Identifies new meeting requests that have arrived
	Identifies new task requests that have arrived
	Identifies receipts for messages that you have sent that the recipient has opened
	Identifies responses to meeting requests that you have sent
	Identifies messages to which you have replied
	Identifies messages you have forwarded to others
	Identifies meeting invitations that have been accepted
!	Identifies meetings that have been canceled

Opening and Responding to Messages and Meeting Requests

Messages, meeting requests, task assignments, and notifications appear in your Outlook Inbox. Figure 4-1 points out some of the icons that identify different types of message items. You can change Outlook settings so that Outlook checks for new messages regularly, or you can tell Outlook when to check for messages. Each time you check for messages, Outlook connects to the mail server (either your school network server or your Internet Service Provider, depending on how you are connected) to see if new messages are waiting to be delivered.

Checking for and Opening Messages

Regardless of what type of message is delivered to your Inbox, the procedures for opening the message and viewing its contents are the same. Most mail servers hold incoming mail on the mail server and distribute e-mail to Inboxes of all personnel periodically, depending on system settings. You can also check for new messages manually when you want to.

Task 2:
To Retrieve and Open E-Mail

1. Click the **Send/Receive** button on the Inbox toolbar to tell Outlook to check for new messages.

2. Double-click the new **Welcome to Outlook E-Mail** message from your instructor to open it.

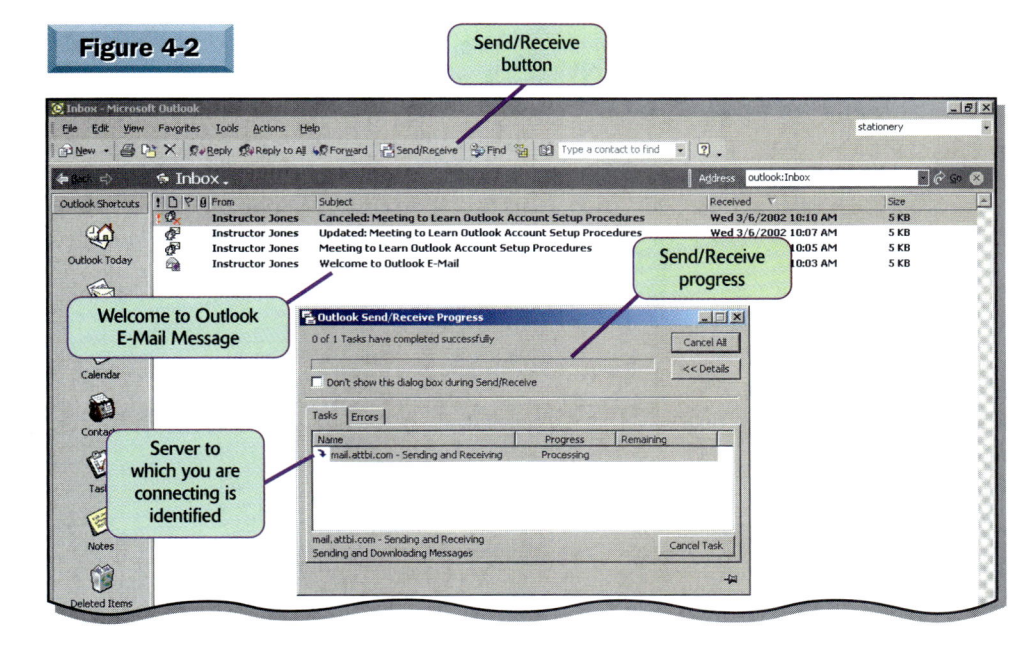

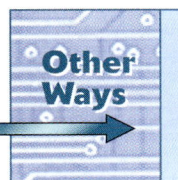

Figure 4-2

Send/Receive button

Welcome to Outlook E-Mail Message

Server to which you are connecting is identified

Send/Receive progress

Other Ways

To retrieve messages not yet delivered:
- Choose **Tools | Send/Receive | Send and Receive All**.
- Press F5.
- Press F9.

3 Read the message and leave it open for the next task.

Troubleshooting
If your message window opens maximized, click the **Restore Down** button to make your screen look like Figure 4-3.

Figure 4-3

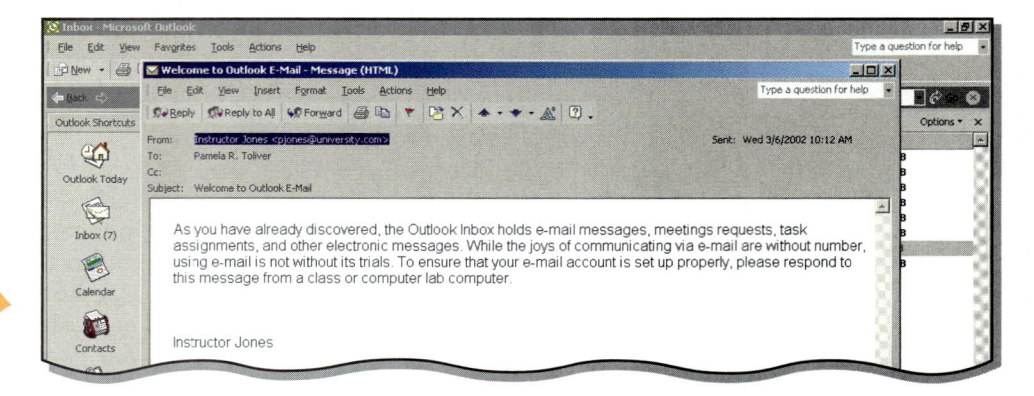

Responding to Messages

The Outlook Inbox stores a number of different types of messages; standard e-mail messages that you receive from others, invitations to meetings, and task assignments are just a few of the different message types. The procedures you will use to respond to different message types vary somewhat.

Replying to and Forwarding Standard Messages Outlook provides easy access to features that enable you to reply to messages you receive and to forward messages on to others when the information may be important to them. You can choose to reply only to the sender of the original message or to reply to all message recipients. When you reply to or forward messages, Outlook provides space in the e-mail message box for you to include additional comments or information.

Task 3:
To Reply to and Forward Messages

1 Open the message **Welcome to Outlook E-Mail** that you received from your instructor, if necessary.

2 Click the **Reply** button and type the message shown in Figure 4-4.

3 Click the **Send** button to send the reply.

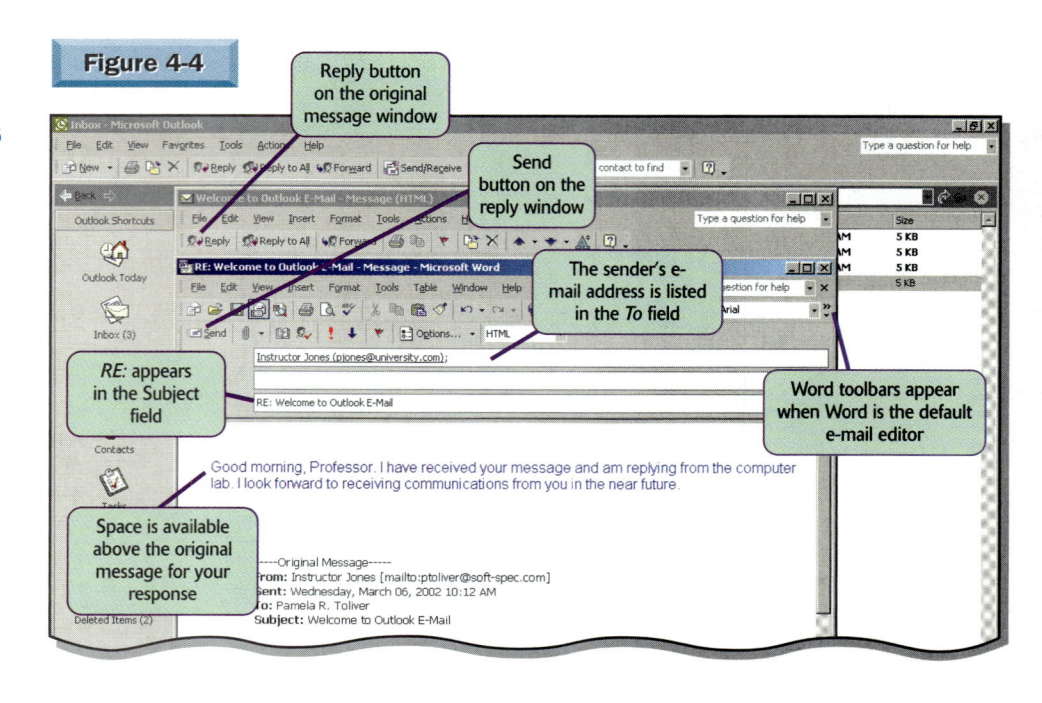

Figure 4-4

- Reply button on the original message window
- Send button on the reply window
- The sender's e-mail address is listed in the *To* field
- Word toolbars appear when Word is the default e-mail editor
- RE: appears in the Subject field
- Space is available above the original message for your response

Other Ways

To open a reply window:
- Press Ctrl + R.
- Choose **Actions** | **Reply**.

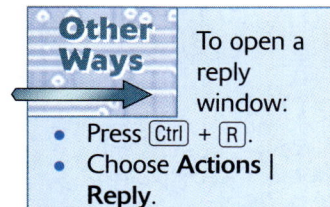

Troubleshooting If you do not see the Word toolbars on your reply window, check the mail editor settings on your computer that were identified in the Setup section at the beginning of this Project and take the necessary action to change the setting.

Tip Always check the *To* field to ensure that you are sending your message to the person you want to receive it. Messages that have been forwarded to you or to someone else before landing in your Inbox may redirect your reply to the wrong person—and that can be embarrassing!

4 Open the **Welcome to Outlook E-Mail** message from your instructor again and click the **Forward** button to open a Forward Message window.

5 Type the e-mail address for one of your classmates in the **To** field and type This message is being forwarded to you from class in the message area above the original message.

6 Click the **Send** button to send the message and then close all open message windows.

Figure 4-5

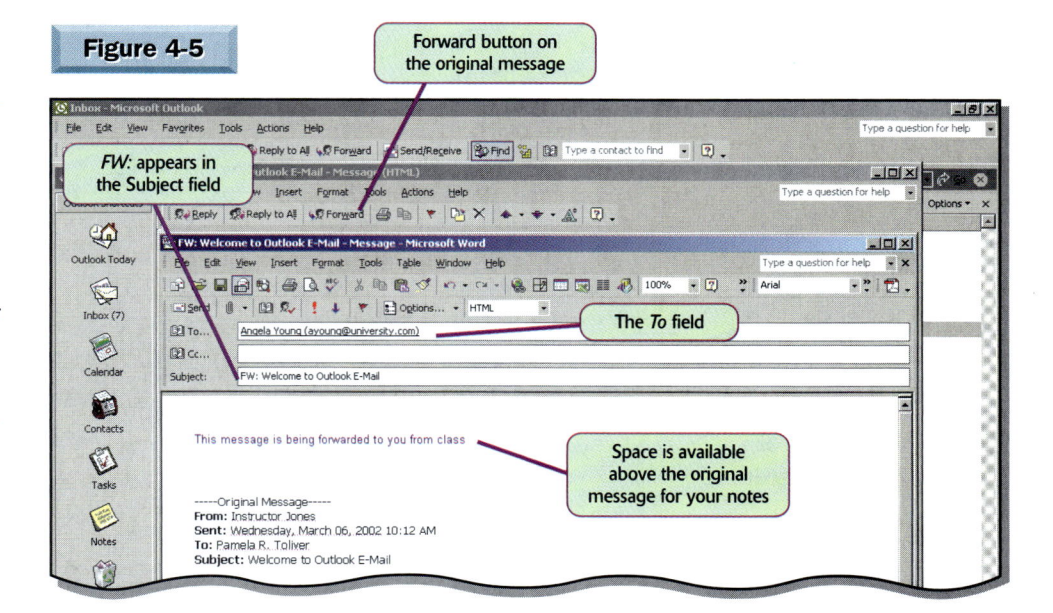

- Forward button on the original message
- *FW:* appears in the Subject field
- The *To* field
- Space is available above the original message for your notes

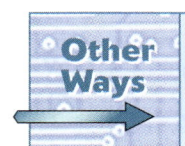

Other Ways

To forward a message:
- Press Ctrl + F.
- Choose **Actions** | **Forward**.

Responding to Meeting Requests Tools for responding to meeting requests appear on the message toolbar. In addition, when the Inbox Preview pane is displayed, response buttons appear on the pane separator. Outlook provides four different options for responding to meeting requests, and Outlook takes specific action depending on which response you choose, as described in Table 4-3.

Table 4-3	Meeting Request Responses
Response	**Description/Action**
Accept	Presents a dialog box containing options for sending a message with the response: sends the acceptance to the sender, schedules the meeting in your Calendar, and deletes the meeting request from your Inbox and places it in the Deleted Items folder
Tentative	Presents a dialog box containing options for sending a message with the response: sends the tentative acceptance, schedules the meeting in your Calendar folder as tentative, and deletes the meeting request from your Inbox and places it in the Deleted Items folder
Decline	Presents a dialog box containing options for sending a message with the response: sends the decline to the sender and deletes the meeting request from your Inbox and places it in the Deleted Items folder
Propose New Time	Presents the Propose New Time dialog box, listing the names of those invited to attend the meeting and their posted schedules so that you can select a time that appears to be free for all attendees; enables you to send the proposed new time to the meeting organizer and marks the suggested time as tentative on your calendar

Tip The Propose New Time option is available only if the sender left the option active when sending the meeting request.

Task 4:
To Respond to Meeting Requests

1 Double-click the Inbox **Meeting to Learn Outlook Account Setup Procedures** request message to open it.

2 Close the message, open the **Updated: Meeting to Learn Outlook Account Setup Procedures** message, notice that this message, too, is out of date, and close the message.

3 Open the **Canceled: Meeting to Learn Outlook Account Setup Procedures**.

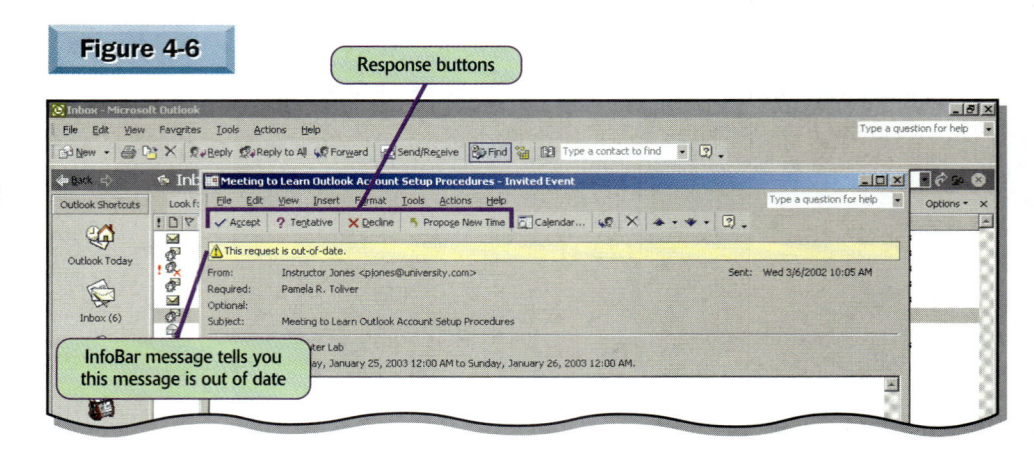

Figure 4-6

Response buttons

InfoBar message tells you this message is out of date

Tip Depending on the e-mail option settings that are active on your computer, closing one message may automatically open the message that appears above it in the Inbox.

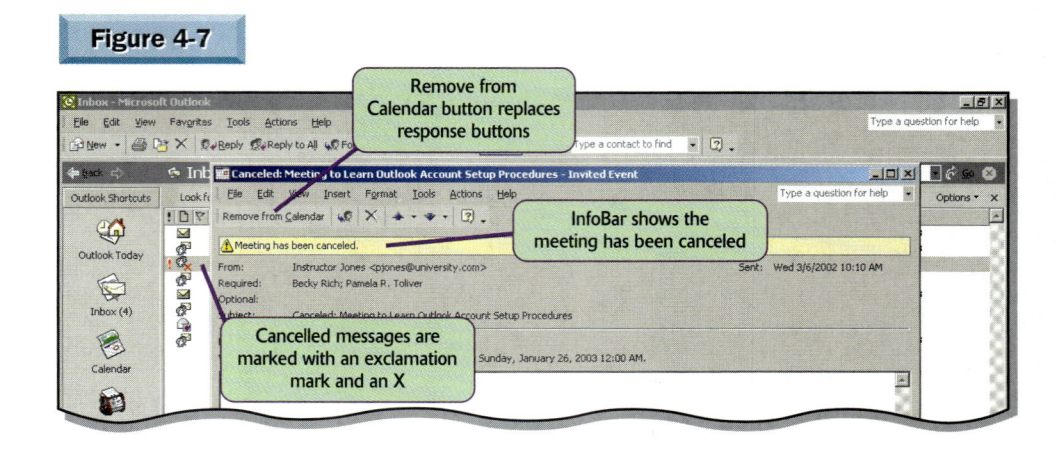

Figure 4-7

Remove from Calendar button replaces response buttons

InfoBar shows the meeting has been canceled

Cancelled messages are marked with an exclamation mark and an X

4 Close the message and open the **Meeting Regarding e-Selections Job Opportunities** message from your instructor.

5 Click the **Accept**, **Decline**, or **Tentative** button to reply to this message as directed by your instructor.

Figure 4-8

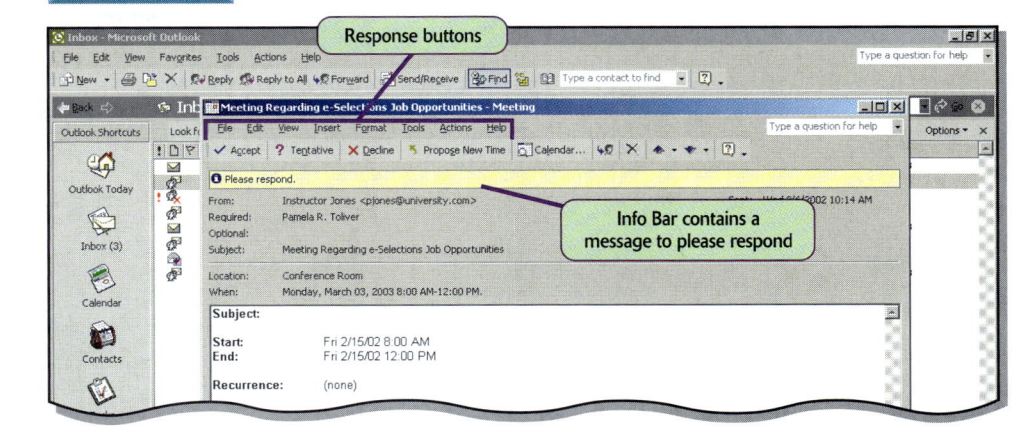

Response buttons

Info Bar contains a message to please respond

> **Tip:** To check your calendar appointments from the message window to determine if you are available, click the Calendar button on the message toolbar.

6 Select the **Send the response now** option and click **OK** to send the message.

Figure 4-9

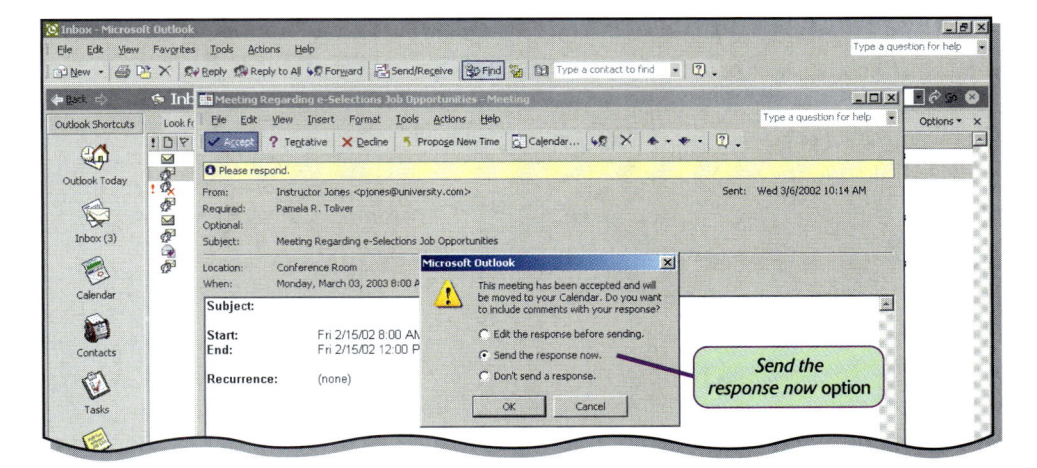

Send the response now option

CHECK POINT

Did you notice that the meeting request message no longer appears in your Inbox?

The default setting in Outlook automatically removes meeting requests from your Inbox when you respond to the invitation. To keep meeting requests in your Inbox, choose **Tools | Options | E-Mail Options | Advanced E-Mail Options** and clear the check mark from the **Delete meeting request from Inbox when responding** option.

Proposing New Meeting Times Outlook responses to meeting invitations provide an option for proposing an alternate time when you are unavailable for the time set in the meeting request. When you click the Propose New Time button, Outlook displays the Propose New Time dialog box that shows the schedules of each person invited to the meeting so that you can pick a time that appears to be available for all meeting attendees. Of course, the schedules you see are only as up to date as the people who post their calendars keep it. As a result, you may find that others are not as available as the calendar might suggest!

Task 5:
To Propose a New Meeting Time

1 Open the **Guest Speaker** meeting request you received from your instructor and read the message.

2 Click the **Propose New Time** 🏹 Propose New Time button on the message toolbar.

3 Click the **Zoom** down arrow and select **50% (Week View)** to display additional days in the schedule window.

Figure 4-10

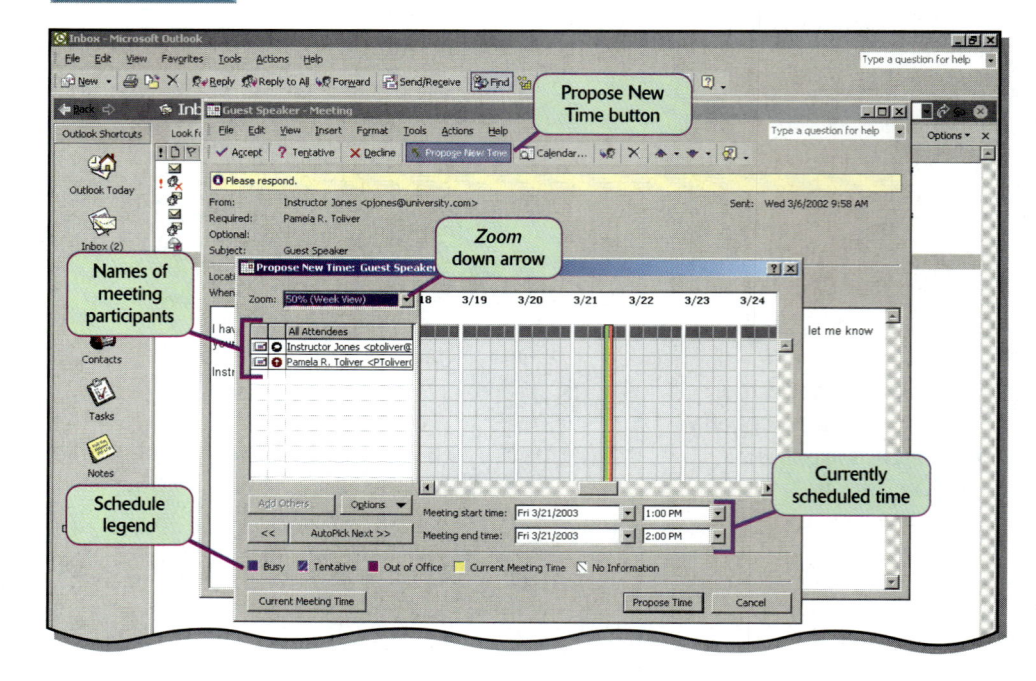

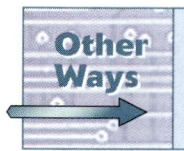

- Propose New Time button
- Names of meeting participants
- Zoom down arrow
- Schedule legend
- Currently scheduled time

Other Ways

To propose a new time:
- Choose **Actions | Tentative and Propose New Time**.
- Choose **Actions | Decline and Propose New Time**.

🎯 **Troubleshooting** If you have not yet joined the Microsoft Office Internet Free/Busy Service, Outlook displays a message box each time you propose a new meeting time, asking if you want to join. Click the response button for the action you want to take: **Join** to join the service, or **Cancel** to continue without joining. (See *Sharing Free/Busy Schedules* in Project 8 for information on your free and busy schedule.)

Corresponding Using Outlook Mail OU 4-13

4 Set the **Meeting start time** to 2:00 P.M. and the **Meeting end time** to 3:00 P.M.

5 Click the **Propose Time** button to open the Propose New Time dialog box.

Figure 4-11

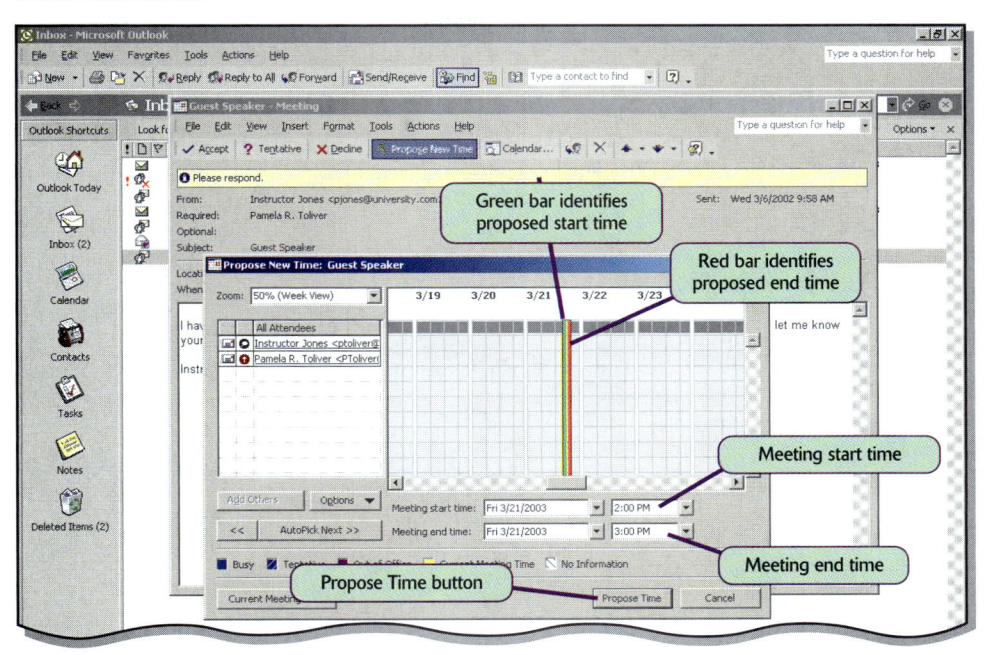

6 Complete the message and click **Send**. The message goes to the meeting organizer and the meeting request moves to the *Deleted Items* folder.

Figure 4-12

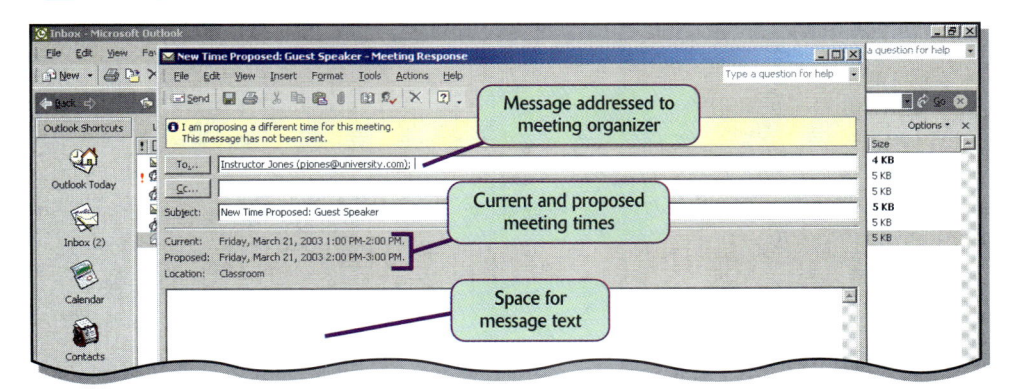

CHECK POINT

So what do you do if responses to meeting requests leave you in a muddle about what to do?

It is conceivable that others to whom you send meeting requests will propose new times for the meetings while others will either accept or decline the request. As a meeting organizer, you receive all responses to the meeting request. Outlook tallies these responses, and you can view a list of all those who have accepted, declined, etc., by opening any of the meeting responses you receive or by opening the appointment window and reviewing the information in the InfoBar. After you collect responses from all attendees, you may decide that a new time is required for the meeting or decide to remove those who cannot attend from the list of attendees and invite new people to attend. Each time you make a change to the meeting time or attendees, you can distribute an Updated Meeting Request form to those invited to the meeting. The cycle repeats until the meeting and participants are set.

Saving Messages in Different File Formats

E-mail messages may contain information that you want to keep and perhaps use in documents and files created using applications such as Word, Excel, and PowerPoint. You can save the messages in different formats including HTML, text formats, and message format to make them easier to access and read outside of Outlook.

Task 6:
To Save Messages

1 Open the **Welcome to Outlook E-Mail** message you received from your instructor.

2 Choose **File | Save As** and type **Welcome Message Text** in the **File name** text box.

3 Click the **Save as type** down arrow, select **Text Only**, and click **Save**.

4 Open the *Welcome to Outlook E-Mail* message, if necessary, and repeat the procedures outlined in Steps 2-3 to save the message in HTML format using the file name *Welcome Message HTML*.

5 Close all open messages.

Figure 4-13

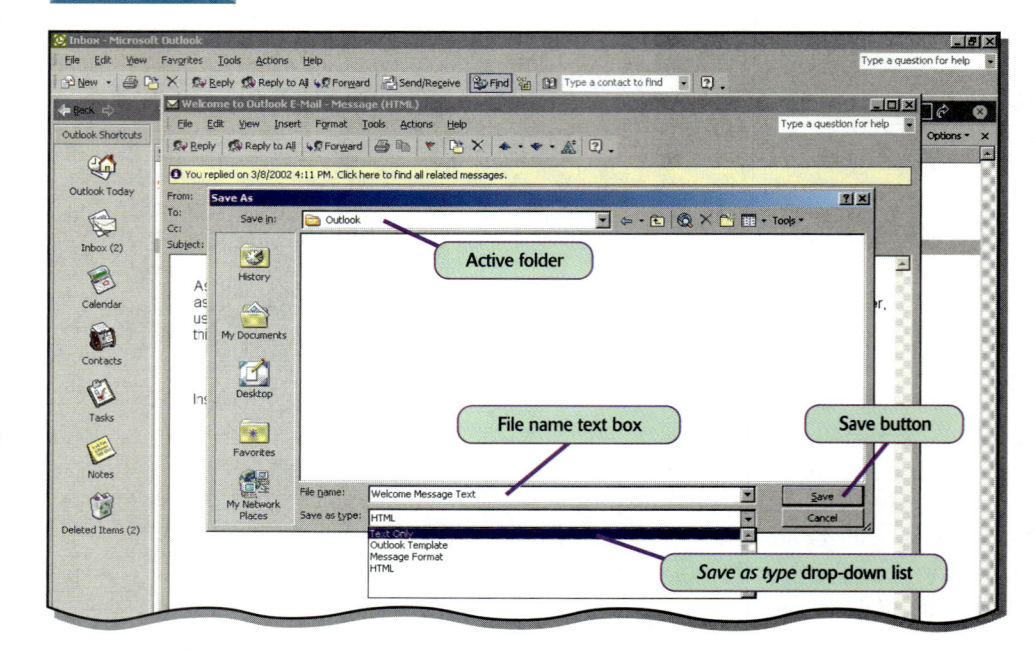

Active folder
File name text box
Save button
Save as type drop-down list

Tip The text message is saved in the My Documents folder unless you have a different default folder or change the save location.

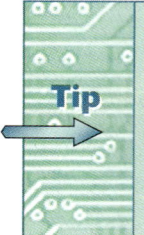

Tip Outlook adds a *.txt* extension to files saved in Text Only format and an *.html* or *.htm* extension to messages saved in HTML format. To open messages saved in alternate file format and display them in different applications such as WordPad, Microsoft Word, or Internet Explorer, launch the application in which you want to display the file and then open the file.

Printing Inbox Items

Because the format of information as well as the information content for each Outlook feature is so different, options for printing items in each feature vary. You will use basically the same procedures to access the Print dialog box that you used to print items in other features. If a message is open when you print, only the active message prints. If the Inbox is active when you print, you can select to print a list of messages in the Inbox or the selected item.

Task 7:
To Print Outlook E-Mail Messages

1 Display the Outlook Inbox, choose **File | Print**, and select **Table Style** from the **Print style** list.

2 Click the **Preview** button to preview a printout of the Inbox list and then click the Preview window **Close** button to close the preview.

3 Open the *Welcome to Outlook E-Mail* message again and click the **Print** button to print the active message in Memo style.

Figure 4-14

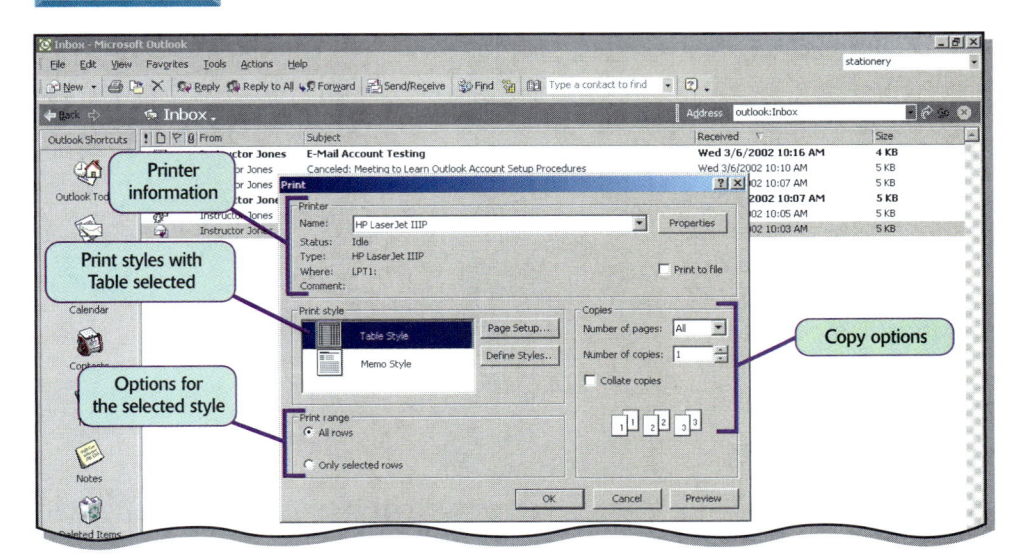

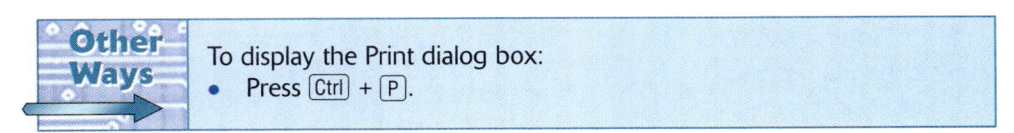

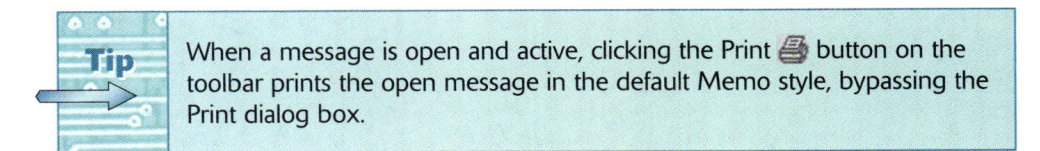

Callouts: Printer information; Print styles with Table selected; Options for the selected style; Copy options

Other Ways
To display the Print dialog box:
- Press Ctrl + P.

Tip
When a message is open and active, clicking the Print button on the toolbar prints the open message in the default Memo style, bypassing the Print dialog box.

Modifying Message Formats and Creating Signatures

Outlook contains options that enable you to identify the format and text editor you want to use for creating and responding to e-mail. When Microsoft Word is set as the e-mail editor, you can create plain text messages or format messages using a template and other Word tools—document formatting tools, spell checker, and so forth. Outlook also contains tools for creating *signatures*—blocks of text that contain information you want to transmit with messages you send. Signatures typically contain information similar to the information that appears on business cards so that message recipients know how to contact you. Using signatures to insert the information reduces the amount of time required to enter repetitive information on each new mail message.

Modifying Message Formats and Creating Signatures

Task 8:
To Change Message Format Settings and Create a Signature

1 Launch Outlook, if necessary, and display the Outlook **Inbox**.

2 Choose **Tools | Options** and click the **Mail Format** tab.

3 Clear the **Use Microsoft Word to edit e-mail messages** check box and click the **Signatures** button to open the **Create Signature** dialog box.

Figure 4-15

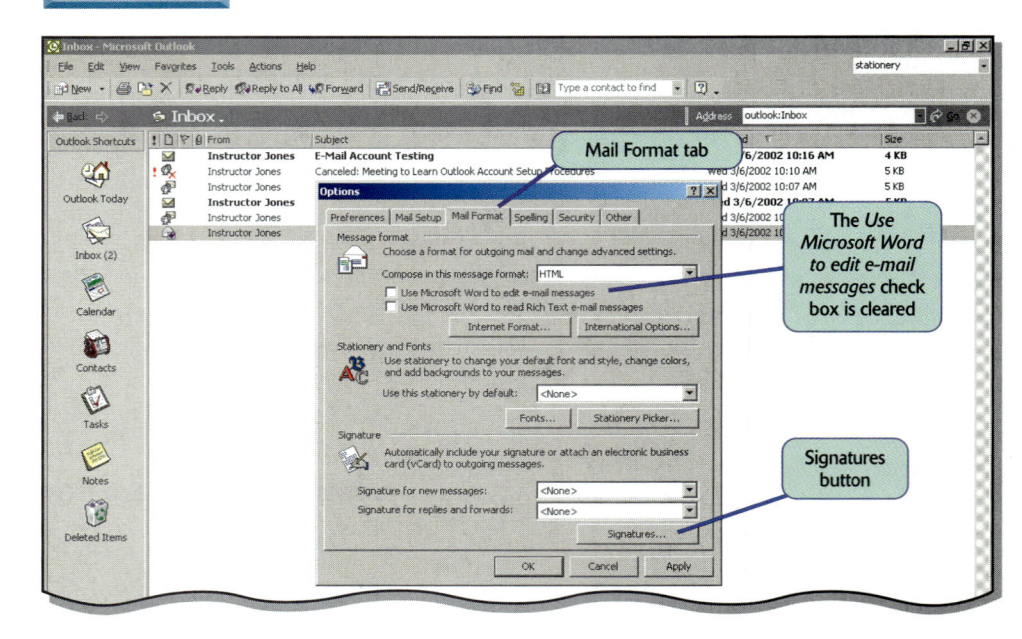

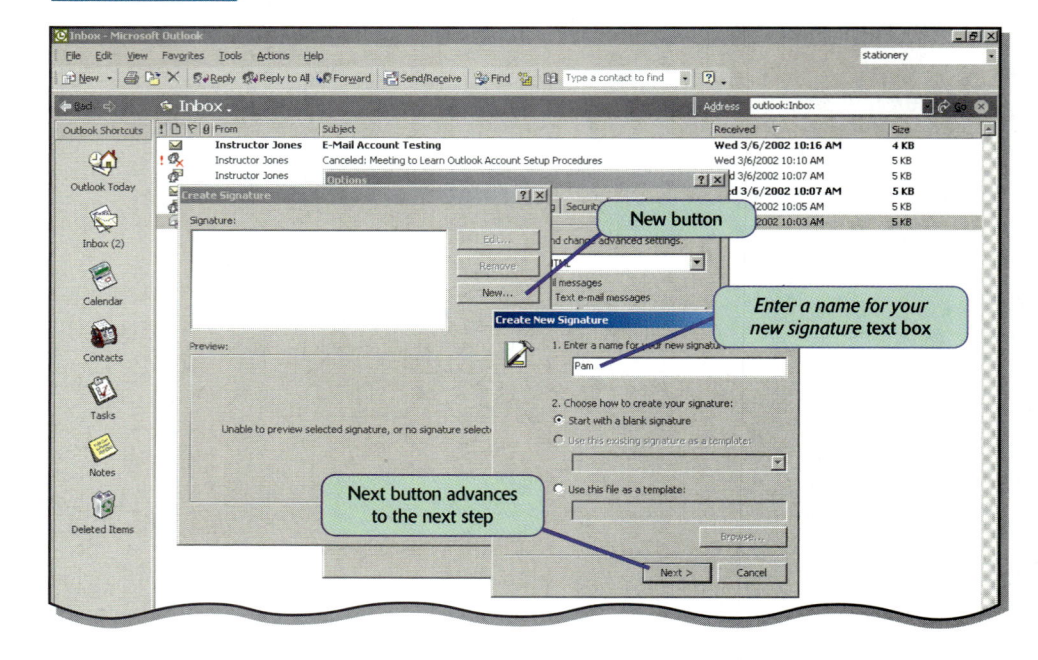

Mail Format tab

The Use Microsoft Word to edit e-mail messages check box is cleared

Signatures button

4 Click **New** to open the **Create New Signature** dialog box.

5 Type *Your Name* in the **Enter a name for your new signature** text box, substituting your real name for the *Your Name* text, and click **Next**.

Figure 4-16

New button

Enter a name for your new signature text box

Next button advances to the next step

Corresponding Using Outlook Mail   **OU 4-17**

7 Create the signature that displays your name, your class, and your section number on separate lines, and then click **Finish**.

Figure 4-17

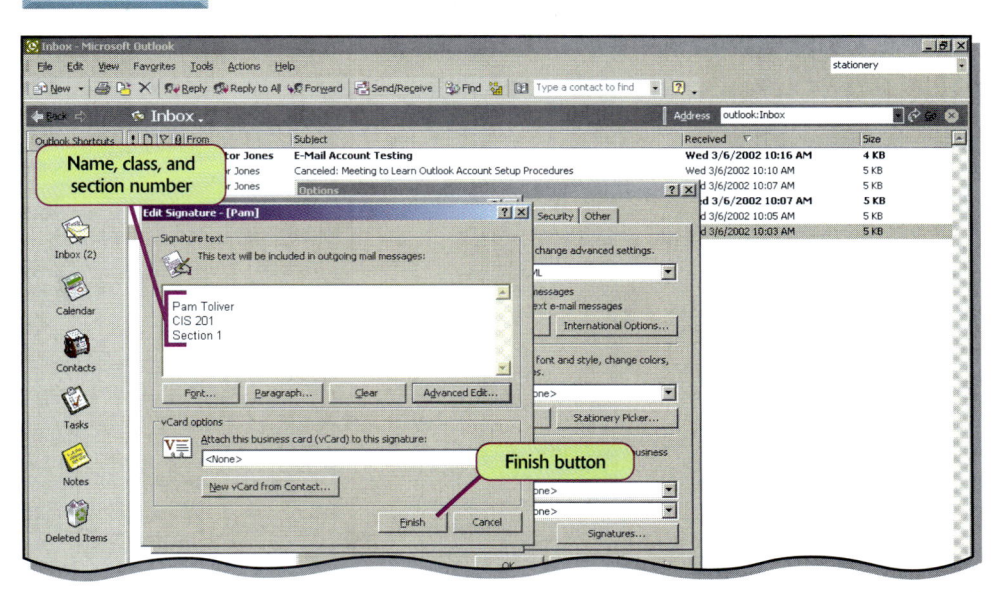

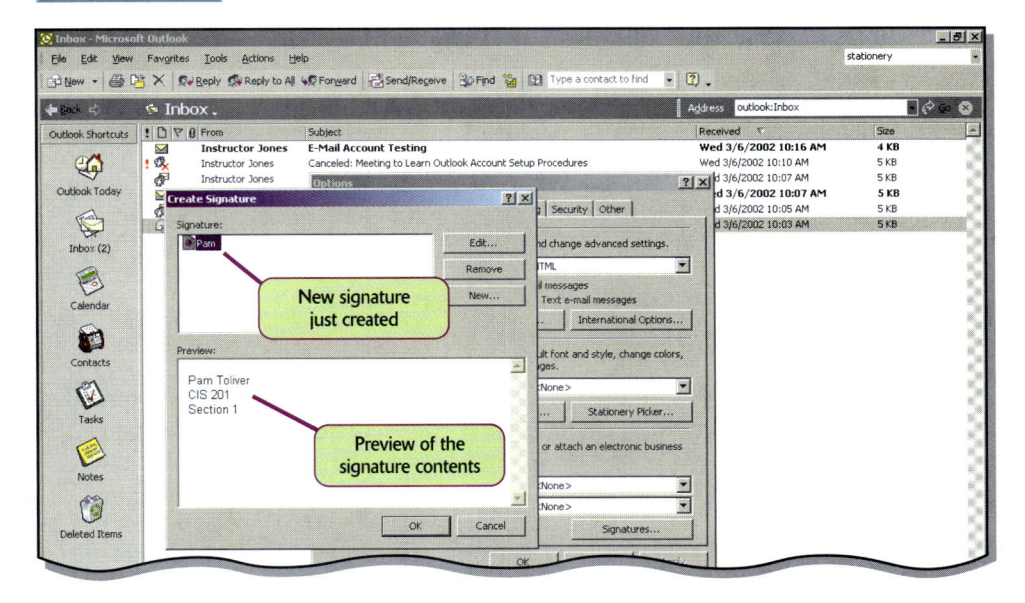

> **Tip** Outlook places a blank line at the beginning of the signature to ensure that there will be a blank line before the signature in e-mail messages. Without a blank line before the signature, you would have to remember to enter a blank line before every e-mail message you send.

8 Click **OK** to close the Create Signature dialog box.

Figure 4-18

9 Click the **Signature for new messages** down arrow and select your signature, if necessary, and then click **OK**.

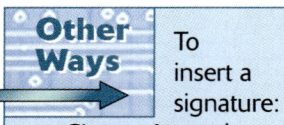

Figure 4-19

> **Other Ways**
> To insert a signature:
> - Choose **Insert** | **Signature** | *Signature Name* on the new message window when using Outlook as your e-mail editor rather than Word.

Signature for new messages down arrow

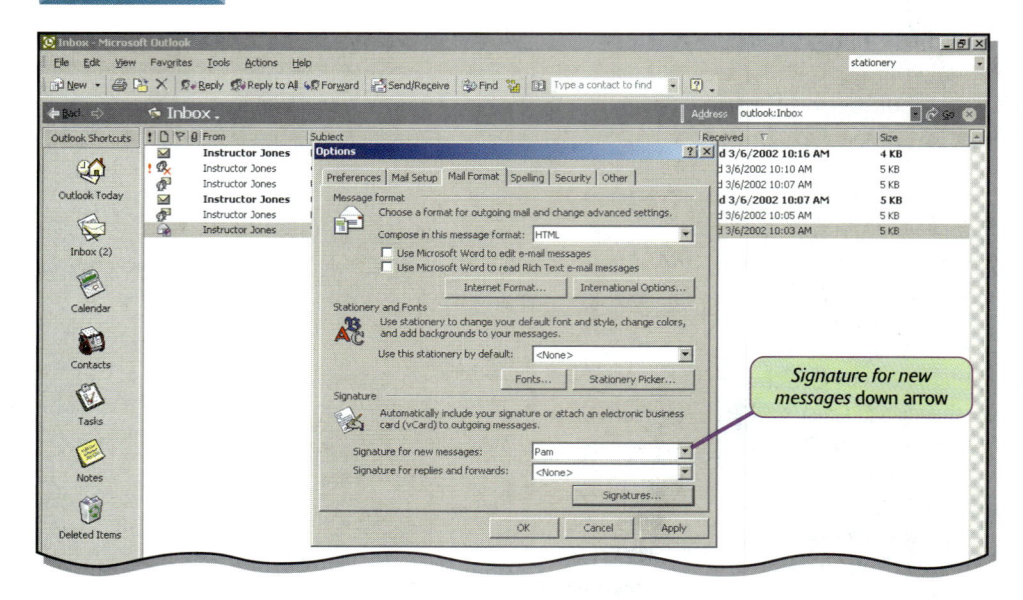

Creating and Sending E-Mail Messages

WEB TIP

Did you know that there is a strict etiquette associated with e-mail? It is called netiquette, and you will find great netiquette tips on the Web. Search for a list of netiquette resources.

Outlook offers a variety of different ways to create new e-mail messages from different Outlook features. However, creating new mail messages from the Inbox is the most intuitive starting point. As you have already discovered, the New button on the Standard toolbar changes for each feature to make creating new items more efficient. Because you have created and activated a signature, Outlook places the signature at the bottom of each new message you create. You can, of course, remove the signature manually from a message or reset the signature option so that it does not appear automatically. Because the default mail editor was changed in the last task, you will use Outlook tools to format e-mail messages.

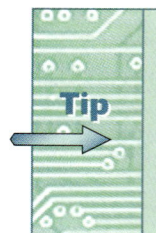

Tip Use the Cc field to copy a single e-mail message to more than one person. For example, you could send an e-mail message to your department manager letting him know that you must leave town due to an emergency, and then add one or more of your coworkers' names to the Cc line so that they receive a copy of the same message. This saves you from having to e-mail each person individually with the same information.

Task 9:
To Create an E-Mail Message

1 Display the Outlook **Inbox** and click the **New Message** 📧 New ▼ button on the Outlook toolbar.

Troubleshooting
If your system requires that you log on to the network to display a list of valid e-mail users, log on now—you will need to be connected to continue.

Figure 4-20

New Message button

Your signature appears automatically

Other Ways
To create a new mail message:
- Choose **File | New | Mail Message**.
- Choose **Actions | New Mail Message**.
- Click the **New Message** 📧 New ▼ down arrow and select **Mail Message**.
- Press **Ctrl** + **N**.

2 Click the **To** button, double-click your own personal e-mail address in the contacts list on the left, and then click **OK** to place your name and e-mail address in the To field.

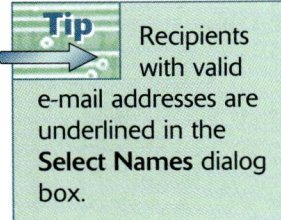

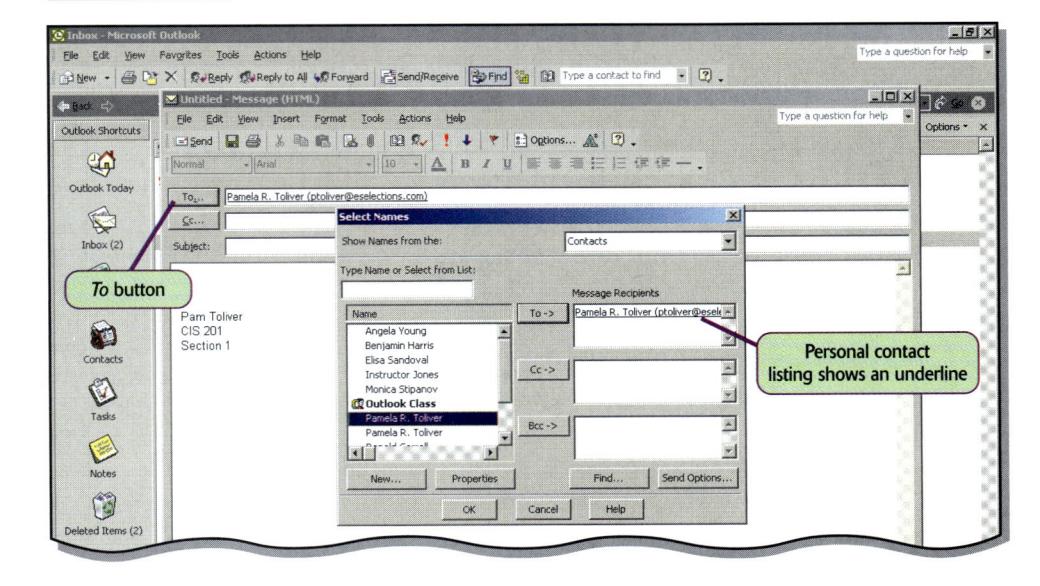

Tip Recipients with valid e-mail addresses are underlined in the **Select Names** dialog box.

Figure 4-21

To button

Personal contact listing shows an underline

3 Press **Tab** and type the e-mail address of one of your classmates in the **Cc** field.

4 Complete the message shown in Figure 4-22 and click the **Save** 💾 button to save the message. You will send the message after completing the next task.

Figure 4-22

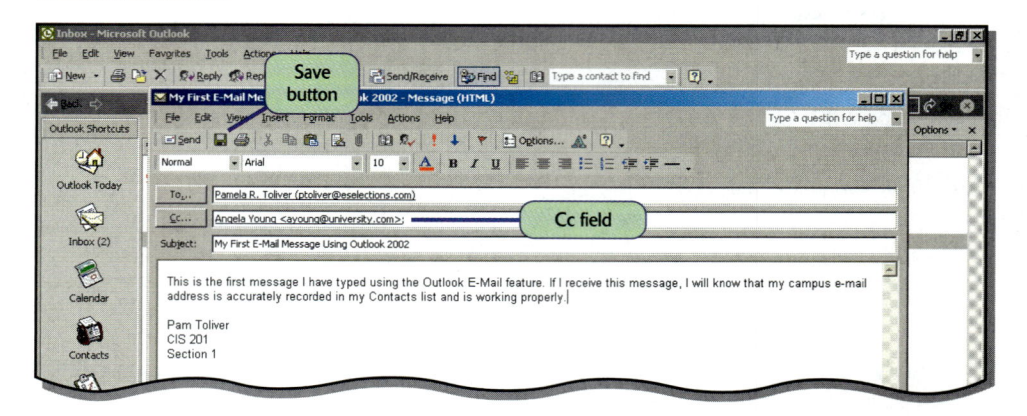

Save button

Cc field

Troubleshooting
If the **Save** 💾 button does not appear on your toolbar, check the toolbar settings identified in the Setup section of this project to display toolbars on two rows.

Tip To change the message font settings, choose **Format | Font**, and select font settings that you want to use. To change the paragraph settings, choose **Format | Paragraph**, and select the paragraph alignment setting that you want to use. Changes you make apply to the active message only.

Setting Message Tracking Options

By default, Outlook sends messages you create to message recipients immediately, but it is often difficult to know when each recipient opens the message. You can set delivery options for your messages that identify the message level of importance and also to request a receipt when the recipient opens the message.

Troubleshooting If the message created in Task 9 is closed, you can open it by clicking the **My Shortcuts** group button on the Outlook Bar, click the **Drafts** icon, and then double-click the saved message.

Task 10:
To Set Message Tracking Options and Send the Message

1 Display the message created in Task 9 and choose **View | Options** from the message menu bar.

2 Click the **Importance** down arrow and select **High**.

3 Select the **Request a read receipt for this message** check box, click **Close** to close the **Message Options** dialog box, and click the **Send** button to send the message.

Figure 4-23

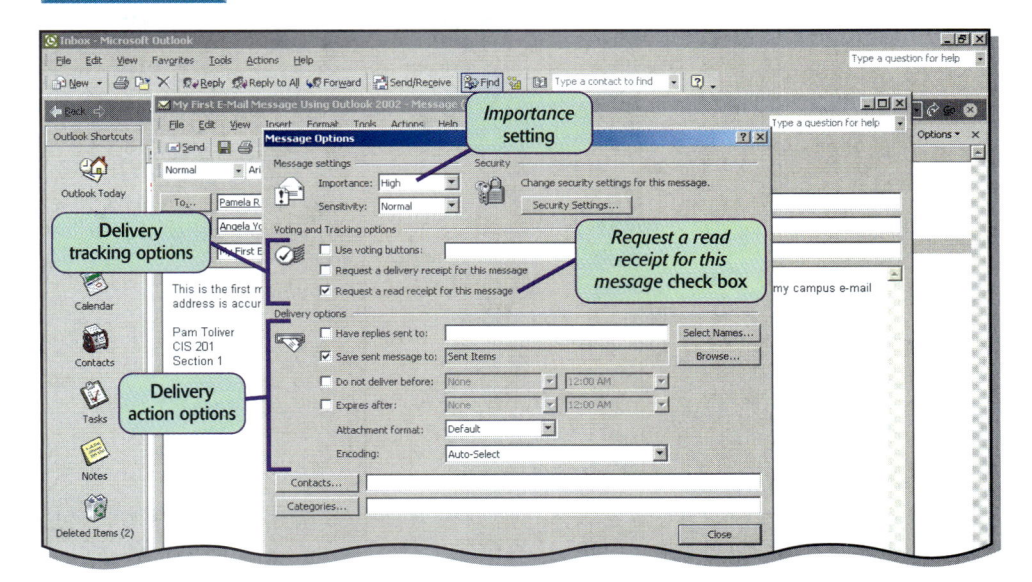

Callouts: Importance setting; Delivery tracking options; Request a read receipt for this message check box; Delivery action options

Troubleshooting Default settings in the Message Options dialog box depend on the Outlook setup on your computer and may vary from those shown in Figure 4-23.

Tip If you are logged on to the e-mail system when you click Send, your message is sent immediately. If you are working offline, your message is stored in the Outbox and will be sent the next time you log on.

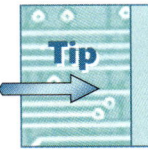

Tip Message options appear next to messages received in recipient Inboxes when recipients are using Outlook. Recipients using other e-mail programs may see no importance indicators nor be able to send a read receipt.

CHECK POINT

When you receive a *Read receipt*, can you be sure that the recipient actually *read* the message?

Of course not. The message option *Request a read receipt for this message* can be misleading. What Outlook really determines is when the message has been opened; whether the recipient reads it or not is a different matter. It is the old "You can lead a horse to water, but you can't make him drink" concept.

Formatting Messages Using Stationery

Microsoft Outlook comes with a "box" of stationery designs that you can use to format e-mail messages you create. Formatting messages using stationery dresses up your messages and makes them more aesthetically pleasing to the recipient.

Troubleshooting Formatting messages with stationery designs increases the size of messages. As a result, the time required to send and receive may be longer on some machines. In addition, mail recipients using e-mail programs other than Outlook may see the design as an *attachment* to their message and wonder what it is.

Task 11:
To Format a New Message Using Stationery

Figure 4-24

1 Display the Inbox and choose **Actions | New Mail Message Using | More Stationery** to open the Select a Stationery dialog box.

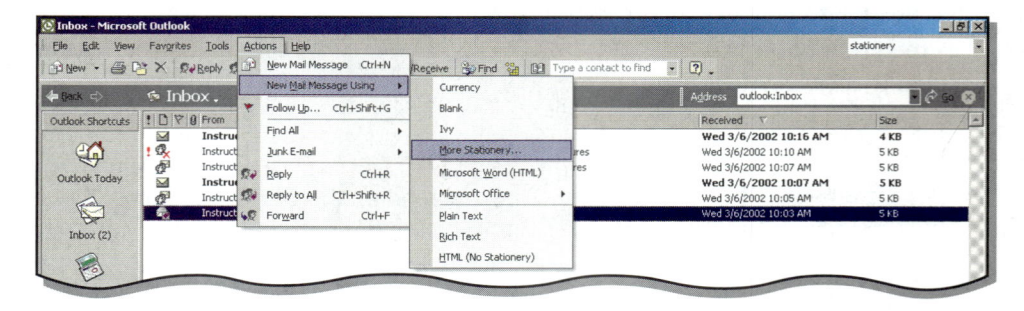

Tip The stationery titles that appear above the **More Stationery** command reflect the names of the most recently used stationery on your computer. As a result, the stationery names shown on your list may be different from those shown in Figure 4-24.

2 Scroll the list of available designs and select the one you want to use to format the message and then click **OK**.

Figure 4-25

Troubleshooting
Because stationery layouts are updated regularly, stationery available on your machine may be different from the stationery displayed in Figure 4-25.

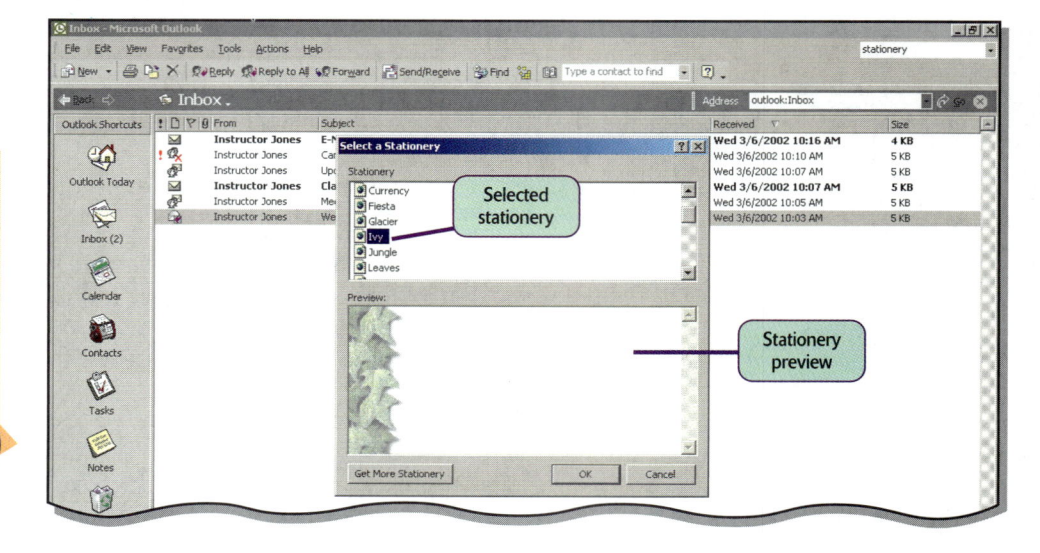

3 Address the message to your instructor, type **Message using Stationery** in the **Subject** field, and type a short message explaining why you chose the stationery design you used.

4 Click the **Send** button to send the message.

Figure 4-26

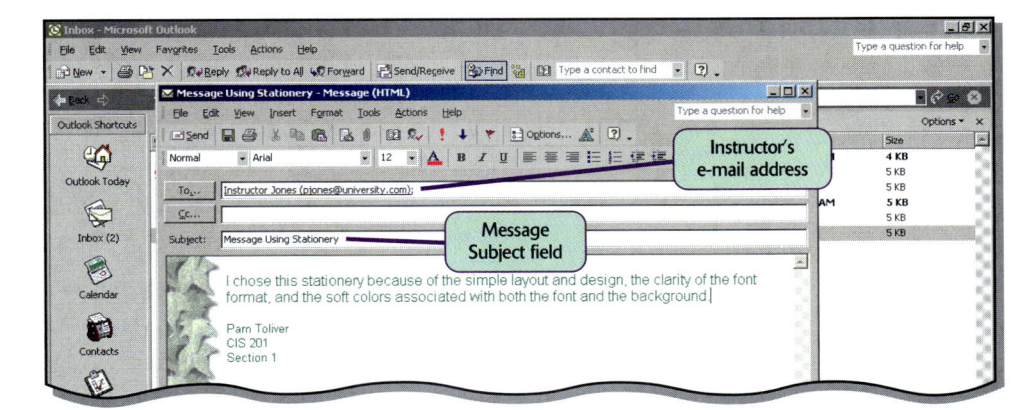

Instructor's e-mail address

Message Subject field

CHECK POINT

When you locate a stationery that you really like and want to use it for all messages you create, you can set the stationery as a default using techniques similar to those you used to set up your signature. Choose **Tools | Options | Mail Format** and then click the **Stationery Picker** button. Select the stationery you want to use for all new messages and choose **OK** twice.

Flagging Messages for Follow Up

When more time is required to adequately respond to an e-mail message and you want to respond later, you can flag messages so that you can locate them quickly. Flagging messages places a red flag icon in the Flag Status column. You can set the required follow-up activity, set a due date, and mark flagged items complete all from the Flag for Follow Up dialog box.

Task 12:
To Use Message Flagging Features

1 Open the *Welcome to Outlook E-Mail* message in your **Inbox**.

2 Click the **Follow Up** button to open the Flag for Follow Up dialog box.

3 Click the **Flag to** down arrow and select **Reply**, click the **Due by** down arrow and select tomorrow's date, and click **OK** to save the flag settings.

4 Click the message **Close** button to return to the Inbox window.

Figure 4-27

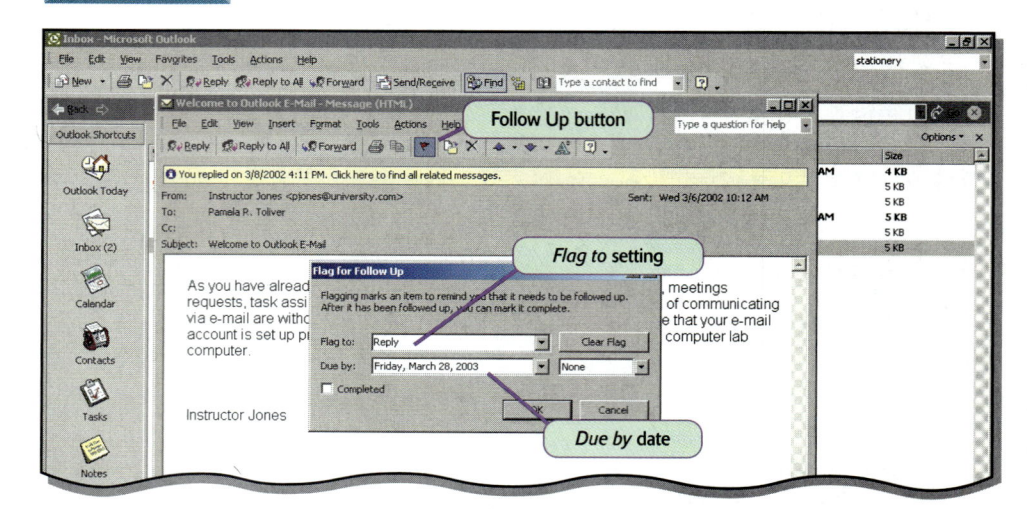

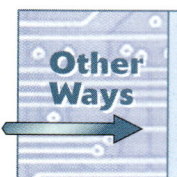

Follow Up button
Flag to setting
Due by date

Other Ways

To display the Flag for Follow-Up dialog box:
- Choose **Actions | Follow Up**.
- Press Ctrl + Shift + G.
- Right-click an unopened item and select **Follow Up**.

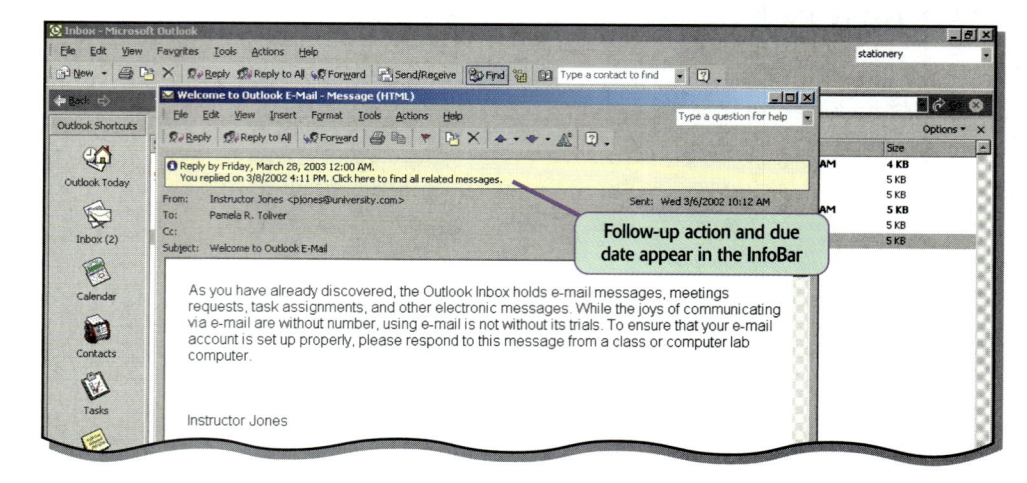

Figure 4-28

Follow-up action and due date appear in the InfoBar

5 Right-click the flag in the Inbox and select **Flag Complete**. The flag changes to white to show that it is complete

Figure 4-29

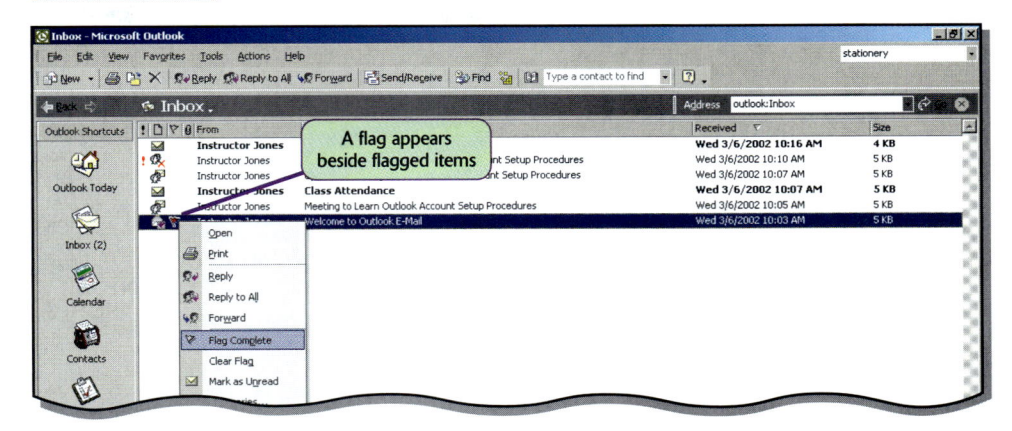

A flag appears beside flagged items

Sorting and Searching for Messages

The arrangement of Inbox information into columns makes sorting messages and other items in the Inbox quick and easy. As the number of items—messages, meeting requests, and so forth—stored in the Inbox increases, however, you may have to use the Find feature to locate particular message items. The Find feature in Outlook enables you to search for items based on the words or phrases contained in any part of the message.

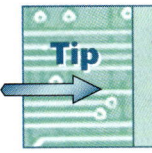

> **Tip** Outlook automatically assumes that you want to locate items contained in the current folder, but you can select the folder you want to search by selecting it from the **Search In** drop-down list on the Find Bar.

Task 13:
To Sort and Find Messages

Figure 4-30

Subject column heading

An arrow identifies the sort column

1 Open the Inbox and then click **Subject** column heading button to sort the messages alphabetically by subject.

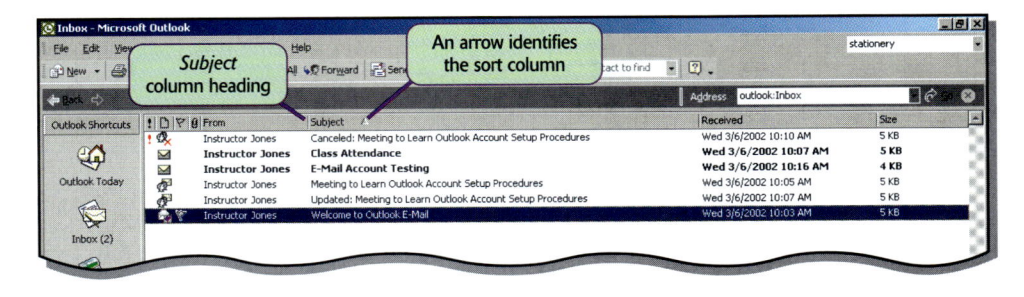

2 Click the **Received** column heading button to sort messages chronologically with the most recent items at the top.

3 Click the **Find** button on the Outlook toolbar to open the Find Bar.

4 Type **Respond** in the **Look for** text box and click **Find Now**.

Figure 4-31

5 Click **Clear** on the Find Bar to display all messages and then click the Find Bar **Close** button to close the Find Bar.

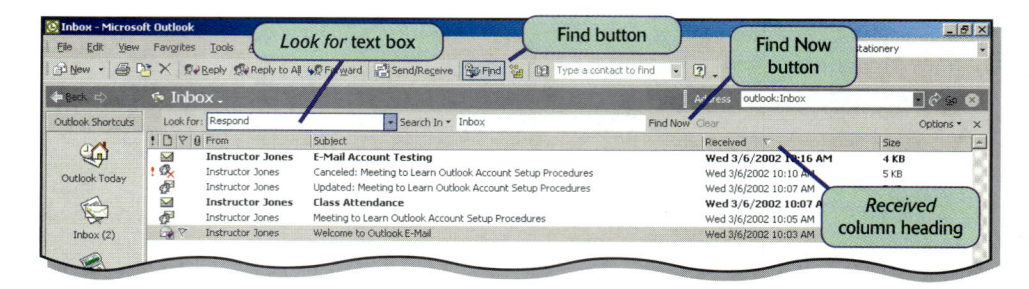

Figure 4-32

Setting E-Mail Options

In addition to the mail format and signature options you set earlier, Outlook contains a number of mail options for controlling mail delivery, tracking options, and so forth. The options appear on various pages of the Options dialog box.

Tip Outlook applies options set in the E-mail Options dialog boxes as default settings to all messages you send. You can change the options for individual messages without affecting the default settings.

Task 14:
To Set E-Mail Options

1 Display the **Inbox** and choose **Tools | Options**.

2 Click the Preferences tab, then click **E-mail Options** to open the **E-mail Options** dialog box.

Figure 4-33

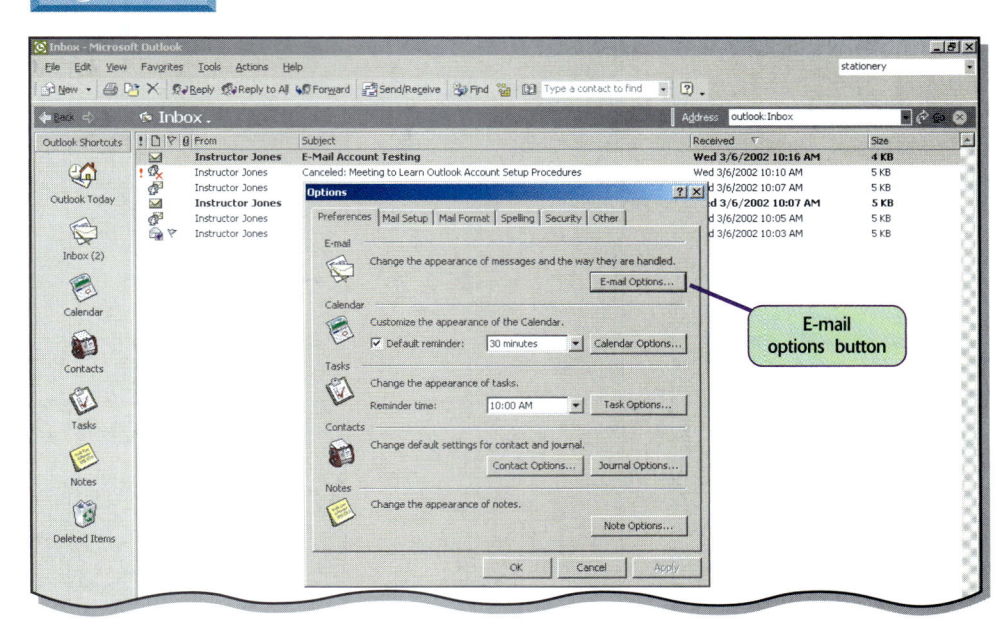

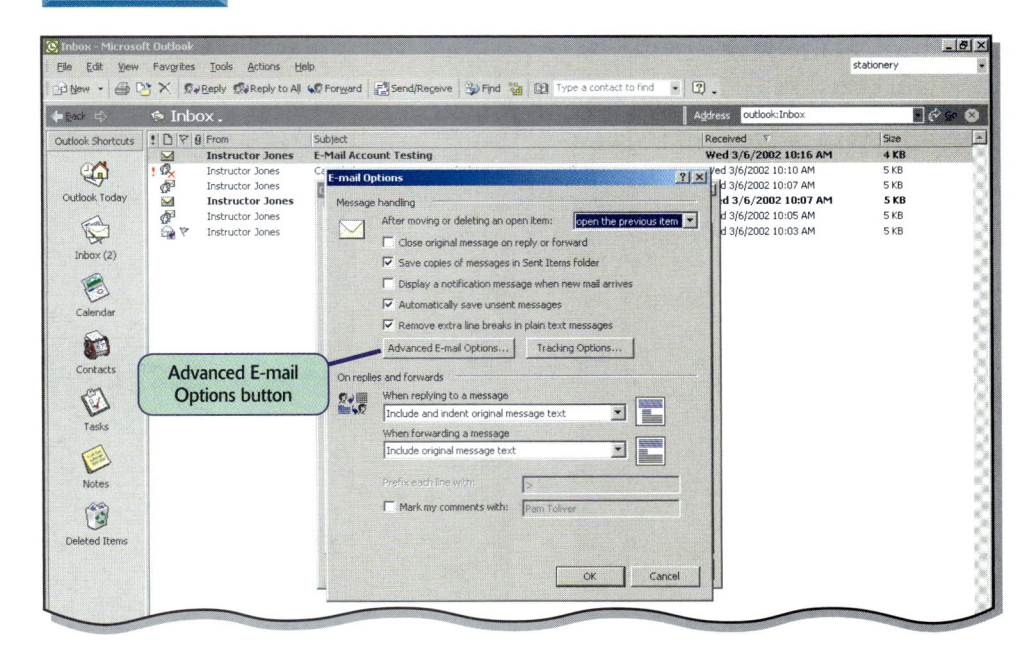

3 Click **Advanced E-mail Options** to open the **Advanced E-mail Options** dialog box.

Figure 4-34

Setting E-Mail Options

4 Review each option and select options identified by your instructor.

5 Click **OK** to close the Advanced E-mail Options dialog box and then click the **Tracking Options** button to open the Tracking Options dialog box.

Figure 4-35

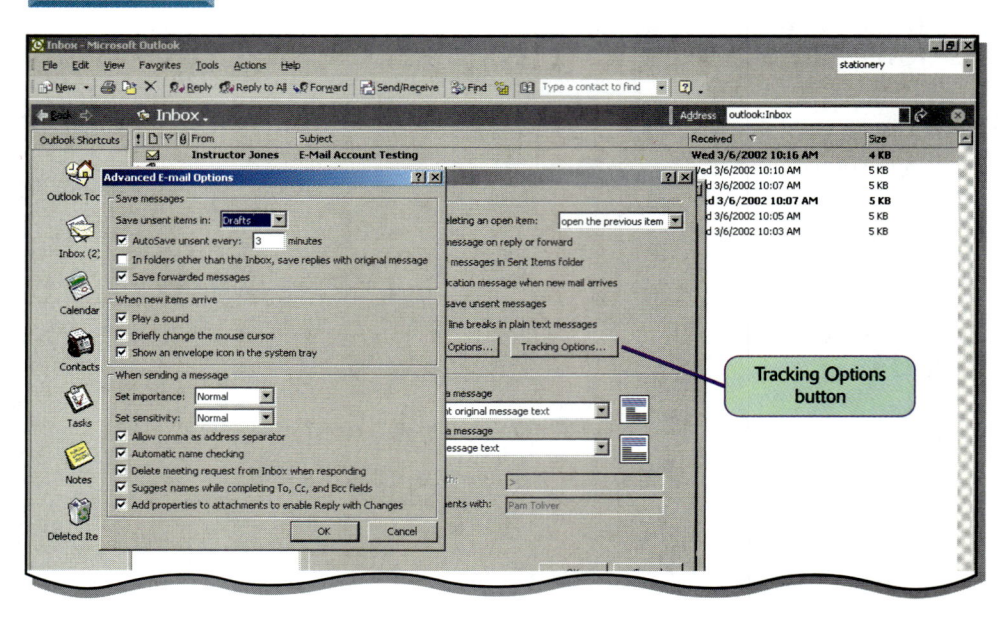

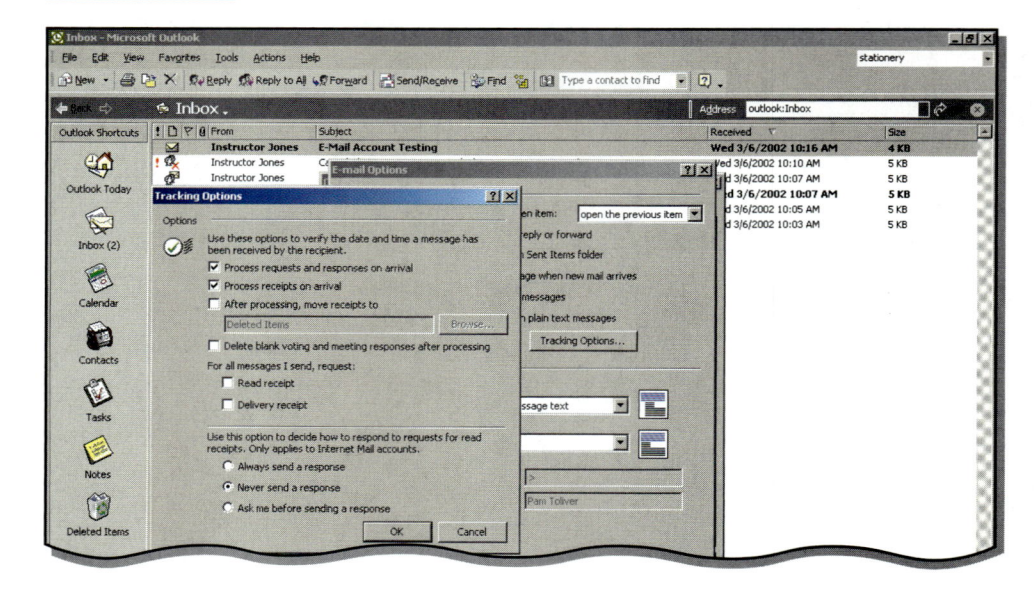

> **Tip** Not certain what the impact of setting an option might be? Click the **Help** ? button, point to an option you want information on, and then click the option to display a tip about the option.

6 Review each option and select options identified by your instructor.

7 Click **OK** three times to set options selected in each dialog box and return to the Inbox window.

Figure 4-36

CHECK POINT

When you are going to be away from your computer and will be unable to respond to e-mail messages that you receive, the *Out of Office Assistant* is a great tool to use if you are running Outlook from a network setup that uses Microsoft Exchange. To set up the Out of Office Assistant to automatically respond to message senders until your return, just choose **Tools | Out of Office Assistant** and follow the onscreen directions to set up the assistant for the times you need it. Include your approximate return date as you create your out-of-office message response so that those who receive the automatic reply will know when to expect a message from you. Then follow through when you return to the office!

Working with Mail Attachments

As you become more familiar with e-mail, you will discover that not only can you create new e-mail messages, but you can also attach files created in other applications to e-mail messages and send them electronically. In addition, when you receive files attached to e-mail messages, you can open, save, edit, and print the files in much the same way that you open, save, edit, and print files on disk or in other software programs.

Task 15:
To Attach, Open, and Save Files Using E-Mail

Figure 4-37

1 Open the **Inbox** and create the new mail message shown in Figure 4-37, addressing it to your classmate.

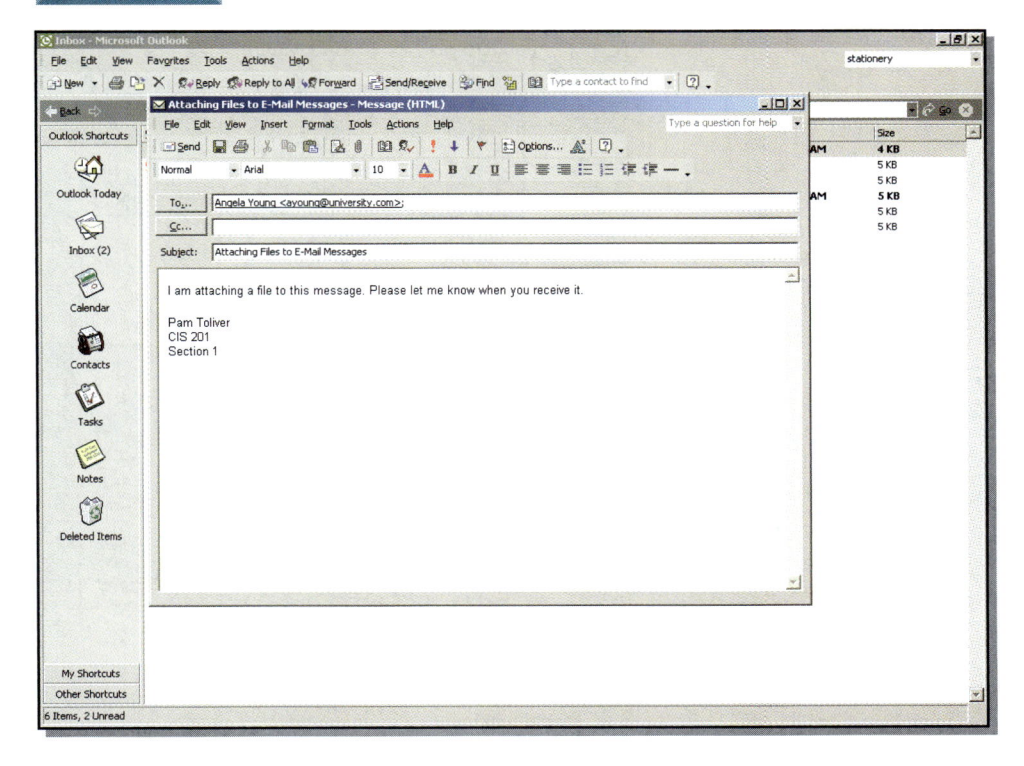

Working with Mail Attachments

2. Choose **Insert | File**, open the folder containing your student files, and click **e-Selections.doc**.

3. Click **Insert**.

Troubleshooting
If you do not have a copy of this file on your student disk, ask your instructor what file to attach.

Figure 4-38

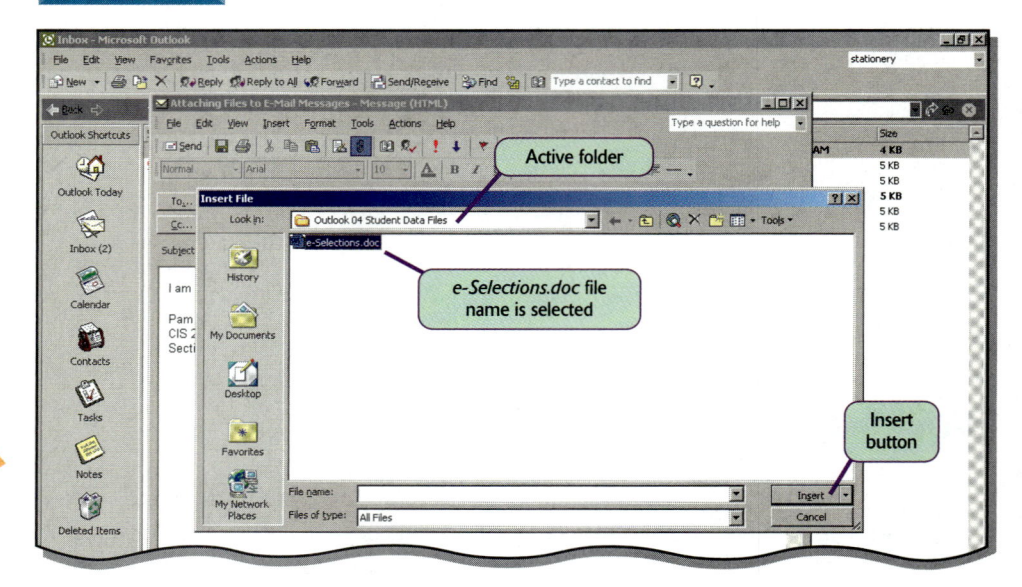

- Active folder
- e-Selections.doc file name is selected
- Insert button

Other Ways

To insert an attachment:
- Click the **Insert File** button on the Standard message toolbar.

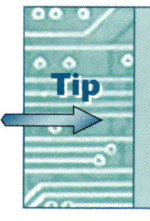

Tip
Attachments to e-mail messages that you create appear in different formats depending on the mail format that is active. When HTML or Plain Text is active, attachments appear as shown in Figure 4-39. When Rich Text is selected for the mail format, attachments may appear as icons in the body of the e-mail message.

4. Click the **Send** button.

Tip The time required to send the message depends on the size of the file you have attached. Because the file you used is small, you should receive e-mail quickly.

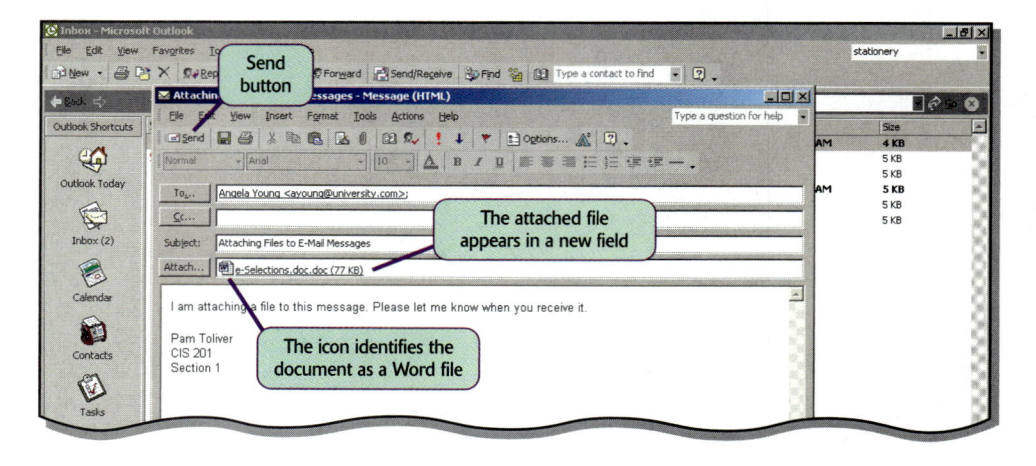

Figure 4-39

- Send button
- The attached file appears in a new field
- The icon identifies the document as a Word file

Corresponding Using Outlook Mail OU 4-31

5 Open the message containing the attachment that you receive from your classmate.

6 Double-click the attachment to open it.

Figure 4-40

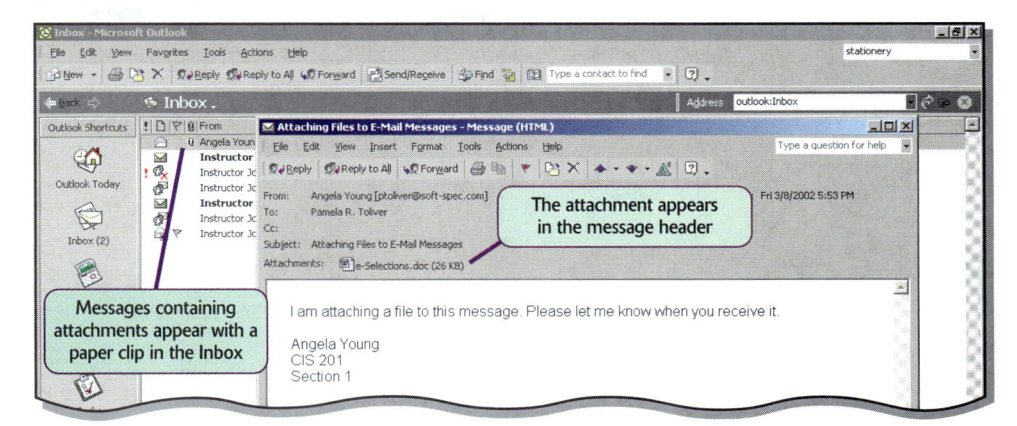

- Messages containing attachments appear with a paper clip in the Inbox
- The attachment appears in the message header

Troubleshooting If your computer is equipped with a virus-checking program that works automatically, the attachment will be checked for viruses. If your virus checker is initiated manually, it is a good idea to check attachments for viruses before opening them.

7 Select the **Save it to disk** option, if necessary, click **OK**, and save the file as **E-Mail e-Selections.doc**.

Figure 4-41

- Choosing Open creates a temporary file on the hard disk that is removed when you close the file
- Saving the file to disk and then opening and editing the file ensures that files you edit will be stored on your system

Tip Depending on the options you have set for your e-mail editor, Word may launch and display the attachment, bypassing the dialog box shown in Figure 4-41.

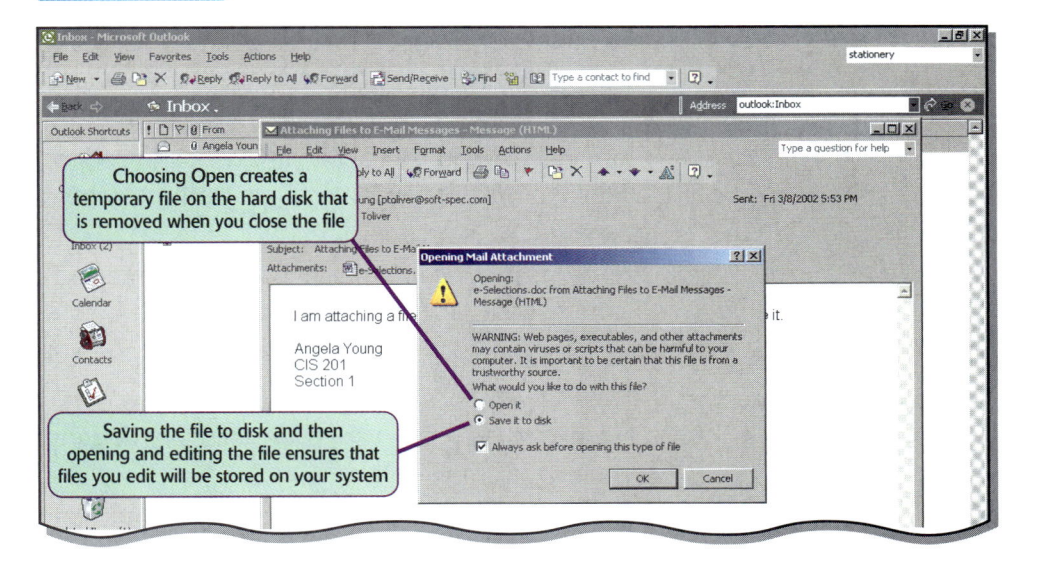

Troubleshooting Depending on how Outlook is set up on your computer, replying to a message that contains an attachment may not automatically attach the edited file to the response. As a result, it is safer to save the attachment as a separate file, edit it, and then attach it to your reply. If you double-click an attachment to open it directly from the e-mail message, edit it, and then save changes using the **File | Save** command, Outlook saves your edits to a temporary attachment file. After you close the file, you have no electronic copy stored on your computer or disk.

SUMMARY AND EXERCISES

SUMMARY

- The Outlook Inbox is a folder in which you receive items including e-mail messages, meeting requests, task assignments, and notifications.
- Messages received in your Inbox can be read, moved to another folder, deleted, replied to, forwarded to someone else, or marked with a flag for follow-up.
- You can set delivery options that identify a message as low, normal, or high importance; you can also request notification when a message has been read by the recipient.
- You can determine the type and status of an Inbox item from the icon located in a column to the left of the item. For example, a new e-mail is denoted by a closed envelope. After it is read, the icon changes to an open envelope.
- When replying to a Meeting Request, you can accept, decline, respond as tentative, or propose a new meeting time. After responding to a Meeting Request, the original request is automatically deleted from your Inbox.
- Many options can be set within Outlook to control things such as when Outlook checks for new messages, or if messages are sent immediately or queued to be sent later.
- Signatures include information (such as name and phone number) that is automatically added to the end of e-mails before they are sent.
- You can use the Find feature to search for messages that contain certain words or phrases.
- Outlook comes with a variety of stationery designs that can be used to format e-mail messages.
- Files, such as a Word document, can be attached to an e-mail before sending.

KEY TERMS & SKILLS

KEY TERMS
- attachment (p. 4-22)
- signature (p. 4-15)
- sort (p. 4-25)

SKILLS
- Attach, open, and save files using e-mail (p. 4-29)
- Change message format settings and create a signature (p. 4-16)
- Create an e-mail message (p. 4-19)
- Display the Inbox and identify Inbox features (p. 4-6)
- Format a new message using stationery (p. 4-22)
- Print Outlook e-mail messages (p. 4-15)
- Propose a new meeting time (p. 4-12)
- Retrieve and open e-mail (p. 4-7)
- Reply to and forward messages (p. 4-8)
- Respond to meeting requests (p. 4-10)
- Save messages (p. 4-14)
- Set e-mail options (p. 4-27)
- Set message tracking options and send the message (p. 4-21)
- Sort and find messages (p. 4-25)
- Use message flagging features (p. 4-24)

STUDY QUESTIONS

MULTIPLE CHOICE

1. What default folder is displayed by Outlook when there are no changes to a setting?
   a. Contacts
   b. Calendar
   c. Inbox
   d. Outlook Today

2. Which of the following icons appears beside new regular messages in the Inbox?
   a. ✉
   b. ✉
   c.
   d.

3. Which of the following icons appears beside tasks that are assigned?
   a. ✉
   b. ✉
   c.
   d.

4. Which of the following icons appears beside an e-mail message when an attachment is included with the message?
   a. ✉
   b. ❣
   c. 📎
   d.

5. To send a message to someone who did not receive the message originally, click
   a. **Reply**.
   b. **Reply to All**.
   c. **Send**.
   d. **Forward**.

6. When sending e-mail messages, you can set all the following *except*
   a. the time after which the message should not be delivered.
   b. the day and time the message should be sent.
   c. the importance of the message.
   d. the format in which the recipient receives the message.

7. To use the Out of Office Assistant, all of the following are true *except*
   a. Outlook must be run from a network setup.
   b. The network must use Microsoft Exchange.
   c. To access the Assistant, choose **Insert | Out of Office Assistant**.
   d. You follow onscreen directions to set up the Assistant.

8. Outlook provides all of the following file formats for saving messages *except*
   a. Word Document.
   b. Outlook Template.
   c. HTML.
   d. Text Only.

9. How many format styles are available for printing single messages?
   a. one
   b. two
   c. three
   d. four

10. When you click the **To** button on a new message window, the list of addresses shown is from the
   a. Inbox.
   b. Contacts.
   c. address book.
   d. personal list.

SHORT ANSWER

1. When viewing messages in the Inbox, how can you tell if a message has been read?
2. In what style of layouts can you print e-mail messages?
3. What happens to meeting requests after you respond to them?
4. What happens to meeting requests that you accept?
5. What is the name of the default e-mail editor?
6. What would you use to create a mail message on formatted "paper"?
7. What is the purpose of flagging messages?
8. How would you quickly sort messages alphabetically by sender?
9. What does requesting a read receipt guarantee?
10. When using the Find feature to locate messages, what part of the message does Outlook search?

FILL IN THE BLANK

1. The _____ command sends a response to the message sender only.
2. Click _____ to let a meeting organizer know that you cannot attend.
3. Use the _____ layout style to print a list of Inbox items.
4. To read mail, click Inbox on the Outlook Bar, and then select _____.
5. To automatically add text to each message you send, create a(n) _____.
6. The _____ page of the meeting request form shows possible free/busy times of meeting participants.
7. If the time for a meeting to which someone has invited you is not convenient for you, you can _____ for the meeting.

8. When inviting attendees to a meeting, you can also schedule conference rooms and equipment by adding them as _____.
9. *High* and *Low* are examples of message _____ settings.
10. To transmit a new e-mail message, click _____.

DISCUSSION

1. Why is it important to check the **To** field when you reply to a message?
2. Describe the Outlook features you prefer to use and why you choose to use them.
3. What is the difference between accepting a meeting request and sending a tentative acceptance?
4. Why should you save files attached to e-mail messages rather than open them directly from the e-mail message?

GUIDED EXERCISES

1 GONE—WELL SORT OF

As you have learned, the default setting for Outlook automatically removes meeting requests to which you respond from the Inbox. Do they simply disappear into thin air? No, Outlook moves them to your Deleted Items folder, where you can retrieve them from the trash and respond differently to the request when necessary. Follow these steps to retrieve a meeting request.

1. Launch Outlook and open the **Deleted Items** folder.

2. Double-click the **Meeting to Learn Outlook Account Setup Procedures** meeting request to which you have already responded.

3. Click the **Accept** button to accept the meeting request.

4. Display the calendar for the day on which the meeting is to occur, verify that Outlook added the meeting to your calendar, and print a copy of the calendar for the day.

5. Repeat the procedures outlined in Steps 1 (with the exception of launching Outlook again) and 2 to retrieve and open the meeting request and this time click the **Propose New Time** button.

6. Click the **Schedule** button to review available dates of meeting attendees, if available, and then select a time that is convenient for you, enter the time in the proposed new time area, and send the message.

7. Then check your schedule for the date of the original appointment and the date of the proposed meeting and print copies of the calendar for both dates.

2 PERSONALIZING MESSAGES

You have already learned how to create a signature that inserts your name, class, and section at the bottom of each message you send. Because some of the messages you send are related to personal business and others are related to work, you may need to insert different signature information on different messages. In Outlook, you can create numerous signatures, set the one you use most as the default signature, and insert other signatures manually. Follow these steps to create a personal signature and insert it into a new message.

1. Launch Outlook and open the **Inbox** folder.

2. Choose **Tools | Options | Mail Format** and click the **Signatures** button.

3. Click **New**, type *Your Name—Personal* as the signature title, click **Next**, and type and format information—name, telephone number, and so forth—you want to include in your personal signature.

4. Click **Finish** and then click **OK** twice.

5. Create a new e-mail message, delete the automatic signature that Outlook adds, choose **Insert | Signature**, and select your personal signature, if necessary.

6. Complete a short message to your instructor, letting her know that you have created your new signature. Click the **Options** button for the message, set the Read Receipt option for the message so that you will be notified when the instructor opens the message, and print a copy of the message before you send it.

7. Send another e-mail message to your own e-mail address, choose **Tools | Options | Mail Format** and select your personal signature from the Signature drop-down list to make it the default signature, click OK, and type a short note to yourself.

8. Click the **Send/Receive** button to retrieve the message you just sent, open the message you sent to yourself, choose **File | Save As**, select **Text** from the **Save as type** drop-down list, and click **Save** to save the message.

9. Finally, create another message to your instructor, ensure that it contains your personal signature, choose **Insert | File** and attach the text file that you saved in Step 8 to the message, print a copy of the message, and send it to your instructor.

ON YOUR OWN

The difficulty of these case studies varies: ⚑ are the least difficult; ⚑⚑ are more difficult; and ⚑⚑⚑ are the most difficult.

1 ET PHONE HOME

⚑ Because it is so easy to forget to phone home, why not start communicating with home via e-mail. Create a new e-mail message and format it using stationery. Then send the message to your parents or guardians. If they do not have e-mail, print a copy of the message and mail it to them. Print a copy of the message to turn in to your instructor. Then flag all messages in your Inbox that you have not yet responded to and set a due date for the follow-up for the following Saturday. Sort the Inbox by the Flag column and mark the flag complete after you reply to a message.

2 REACHING OUT TO BUSINESSES

⚑⚑ You may already have discovered that business Web sites often contain contact information for submitting e-mail messages to the business. Some businesses include a *Contact Us* link while other businesses provide an e-mail address to which requests for information can be sent. Search the Web for the Web site of a business related to your major area of study. Explore the Web site to locate the e-mail address to which you can send e-mail messages. Use the e-mail address to send a request for information, such as a catalog, list of services, and so forth, about the business. Format the message using plain text and request a return receipt for the message. Print a copy of the message you send. Then monitor the time it takes to receive a reply to your message and forward the first message you receive from the business to your instructor.

3 JUST ANOTHER MEETING

As you gain knowledge and experience with Outlook, you will discover that the ease and convenience of using Outlook to schedule meetings and invite attendees will spread to other facets of your life and become more popular with your friends and business associates. As a result, you need to practice sending and responding to such requests. Send a meeting request to a classmate or other person assigned by your instructor. The purpose of the meeting is to work on your Outlook project. Request a return receipt on the meeting request to ensure that you are notified when the recipient opens it. Set your e-mail options to display a notification message when new mail arrives. Then, when you receive the request proposed by your classmate, respond appropriately after reviewing your schedule. Propose an alternative time for the meeting and send the new time to the meeting organizer with a copy of your response to your instructor.

4 LOCATING UNIVERSAL INBOX SERVICES

Search the Internet for companies that market Universal Inbox services. Download the Web pages for three different companies that offer such services. Create a new e-mail message to your instructor with a Cc to yourself and attach the downloaded files to the message. Send the message with importance **High**. Open the files attached to the message you send yourself and print a copy of each attachment as well as a copy of the message.

5 REPORTING IN

Create a new e-mail message addressed to your instructor that outlines the functions you have discovered about Outlook e-mail that you believe you will use frequently. Explain how and why you believe knowledge of these functions will meet your needs as you work with e-mail. Save the message as a text only file named *Outstanding Inbox Features*.

Prepare a new signature that includes your name, class and section number, and the assignment due date. Format the signature text so that your name appears in one color and font style and the remaining signature lines are formatted using a different color and font style.

Then prepare another e-mail message to your instructor that includes your new signature that is formatted using the Marbled Desk stationery. Attach the *Outstanding Inbox Features* file to the message. Open the attachment before you send the message and print a copy of the attachment. Add text to the message that references the attachment. Print a copy of the e-mail message and request a return receipt to ensure that the instructor opens it before the due date. Then send the message.

Photospread credits pages 4-2 & 4-3
©Tony Stone: ©Edouard Berne, ©Fisher/Thatcher; ©FPG: ©Telegraph Colour Library 1998; ©Pearson Education; ©Lorraine Castellano

PROJECT 5

Recording Tasks and Writing Notes

Outlook features provide a wealth of different tools for communicating with others and for keeping you organized. Two features—Tasks and Notes—are specifically designed to help you electronically track activities and post reminders. In this project, you will learn the basics of maintaining a task list and working with electronic notes as well as advanced features such as assigning tasks and linking tasks and notes to Contacts.

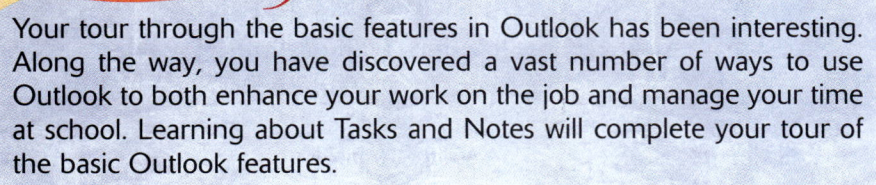

OBJECTIVES

After completing this project, you will be able to:

- Create task lists
- Update and modify tasks
- Change Tasks view and organize tasks
- Create and update recurring tasks
- Assign tasks and send task requests
- Track assigned tasks
- Print tasks
- Set task options
- Create and edit notes
- View, organize, and read notes
- Assign notes to contacts
- Set notes options
- Save, forward, and print notes

e-selections Running Case

Your tour through the basic features in Outlook has been interesting. Along the way, you have discovered a vast number of ways to use Outlook to both enhance your work on the job and manage your time at school. Learning about Tasks and Notes will complete your tour of the basic Outlook features.

Recording Tasks and Writing Notes e-Organizing:
Document Management Systems

Imagine a sea of paper stretching as far as the eye can see ... millions of pages ... printed on yellow, blue, green, orange, white, and black paper ... a sea that grows larger every day as multi-page documents are added to this sea of paper. Now imagine having to wade through that sea of paper document files to retrieve a particular document. I believe you get the picture ...

As today's businesses have become increasingly overwhelmed by the ever-growing number of electronic documents, they have started implementing Electronic Document Management Systems (EDMS).

What are (Electronic) Document Management Systems?

Electronic Document Management Systems, or EDMSs as they're also called, are commercial off-the-shelf software packages that store, retrieve, and manage "unstructured data", such as files, text, spreadsheets, images, sound clips, multi-media, and compound documents. EDMS software provides a fail-safe way to manage online paperwork and streamline business processes. EDMS programs enable users to store their documents in libraries, folders, and on servers in such a way that they are easy to retrieve. As each file is stored in an EDMS, a file profile is created that records the author, the typist, and other information about the document.

Document retrieval from an EDMS becomes almost instantaneous. With just the click of a couple buttons, time wasted hand shuffling through paper files (or wading through that sea of paper) looking for documents and then returning those files is eliminated. Users can search for a file using any profile field of information. Each EDMS program comes equipped with document management tools that track:

- File access
- File edits
- File versioning
- File security

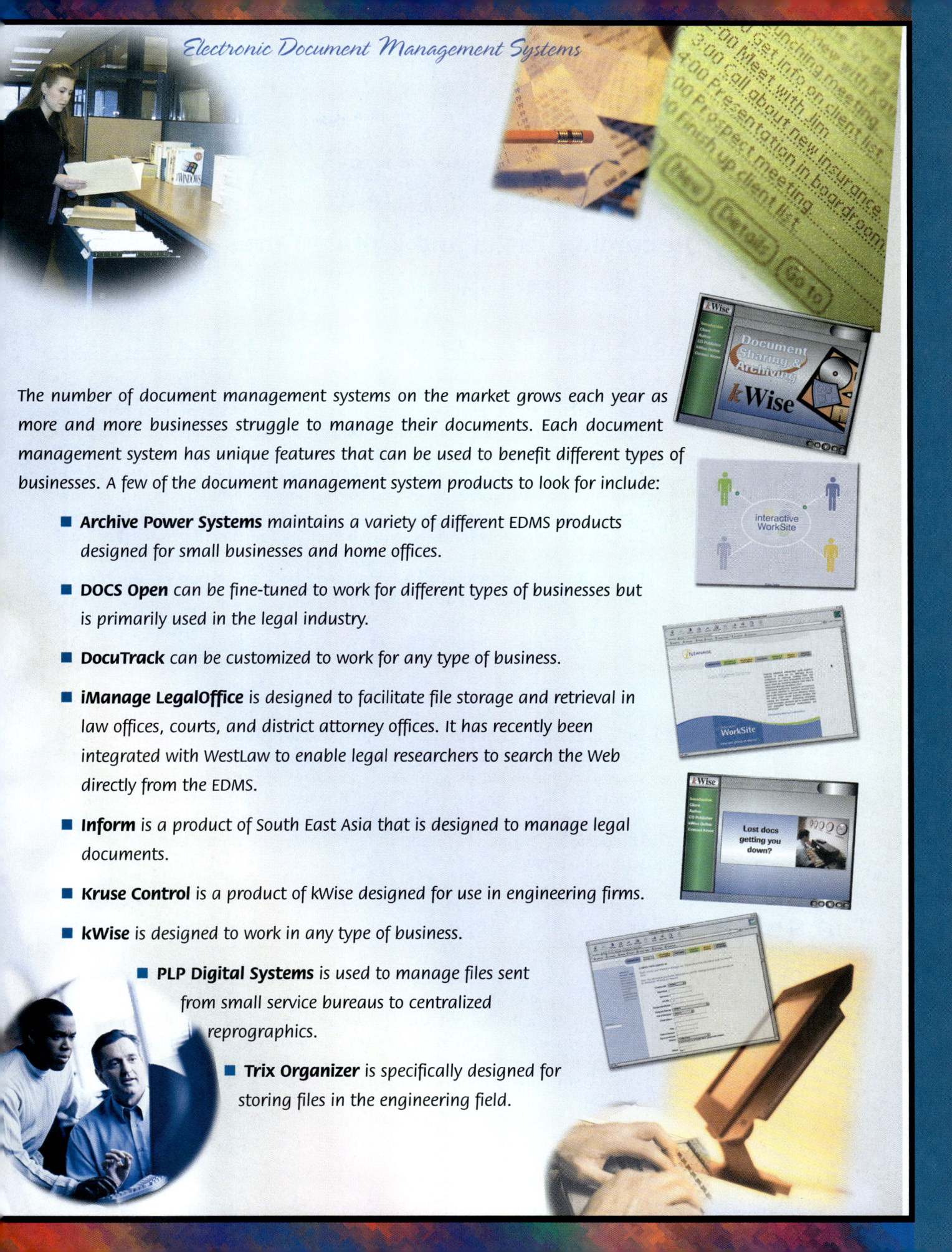

Electronic Document Management Systems

The number of document management systems on the market grows each year as more and more businesses struggle to manage their documents. Each document management system has unique features that can be used to benefit different types of businesses. A few of the document management system products to look for include:

- **Archive Power Systems** maintains a variety of different EDMS products designed for small businesses and home offices.

- **DOCS Open** can be fine-tuned to work for different types of businesses but is primarily used in the legal industry.

- **DocuTrack** can be customized to work for any type of business.

- **iManage LegalOffice** is designed to facilitate file storage and retrieval in law offices, courts, and district attorney offices. It has recently been integrated with WestLaw to enable legal researchers to search the Web directly from the EDMS.

- **Inform** is a product of South East Asia that is designed to manage legal documents.

- **Kruse Control** is a product of kWise designed for use in engineering firms.

- **kWise** is designed to work in any type of business.

  - **PLP Digital Systems** is used to manage files sent from small service bureaus to centralized reprographics.

    - **Trix Organizer** is specifically designed for storing files in the engineering field.

PROJECT 5

Recording Tasks and Writing Notes

The Challenge

Because of your hectic schedule, you have found that scheduling appointments in the Calendar folder helps you track the work- and school-related meetings and classes. You have also been scheduling appointments in the Calendar folder to track assignments and other tasks that you need to complete. As a result, your calendar is beginning to look like your desk when it was stacked with sticky notes and bits of paper on which you jotted down appointments and tasks you needed to complete. One of your coworkers has suggested that you might want to explore alternative features for tracking tasks and notes in Outlook, and Ms. Wright has requested that you keep someone in the company informed about the progress you make on different tasks to avoid duplication of effort.

The Solution

Outlook is becoming more and more important to you for managing your time and tasks. You are now comfortable with many of the Outlook features and have decided to plunge ahead of the class to explore the new features recommended by your coworker. You also need to send a progress report to Ms. Wright to let her know how you have progressed on tasks for which you are responsible. Because you are in your office at work, some of the customizations you made to Outlook on the computer lab computer will not appear.

The Setup

Before starting this Project, it is a good idea to reset some of the customizations you may have set as you worked your way through other Projects. Launch Outlook and follow the instructions identified in Table 5-1 to reduce the differences between the screen you see and the figures in this Project, keeping in mind that some differences are the result of network requirements for your installation.

Table 5-1 Outlook Settings

Feature	Setting
Office Assistant	Hide the Office Assistant.
Outlook Bar	Right-click an empty space on the Outlook Bar and select **Large Icons**.
Toolbars	Choose **Tools	Customize	Toolbars**, select the **Standard** toolbar, click **Reset**, click **Yes**, and click **Close** to restore the toolbar to its default settings.

Creating Task Lists

As you have already discovered, the TaskPad appears in a pane of the Calendar window for easy access. In addition, you can open the Tasks folder to display *tasks* as a table in a full-size Outlook window. The procedures used to record tasks are the same regardless of whether you enter the task in the Calendar TaskPad or open the Tasks folder. The New Task dialog box provides options for setting task due dates, reminders, and status reports and for recording notes about the task. When you open the Tasks folder, tasks appear as a simple list in a table layout.

Task 1:
To Record Tasks and Create Tasks Lists

Figure 5-1

1 Click the **Calendar** icon on the Outlook Bar to open the folder and display **February 2003** and **March 2003** in the Date Navigator.

2 Click **Click here to add a new task** in the TaskPad task entry bar, type **Send forms to John's new firm.** and press Enter to add the task to the list.

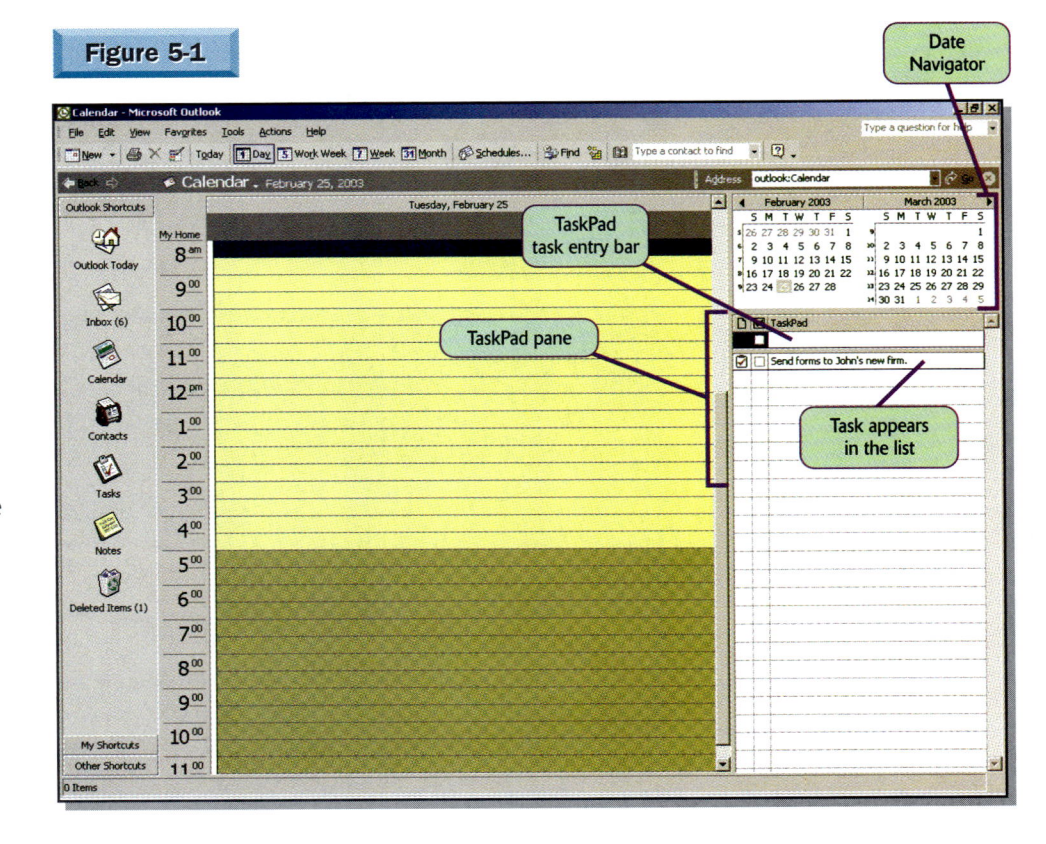

Creating Task Lists

3 Double-click the task entry bar to open a new task window and type the data shown in Figure 5-2 as follows:
- **Subject:** Notify Ms. Wright about class progress.
- **Due Date:** Place yesterday's date so that the task will be overdue.
- **Reminder:** Clear the Reminder check box if it is selected.

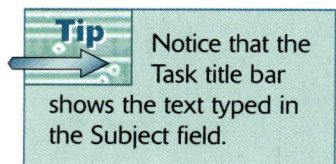

> **Tip:** Notice that the Task title bar shows the text typed in the Subject field.

Figure 5-2

Callouts: Task title bar • Save and Close button • Task progress and due date settings • Information in InfoBar • Person who created the task • Reminder check box is clear • Private check box

4 Click the **Save and Close** button to save and close the task window.

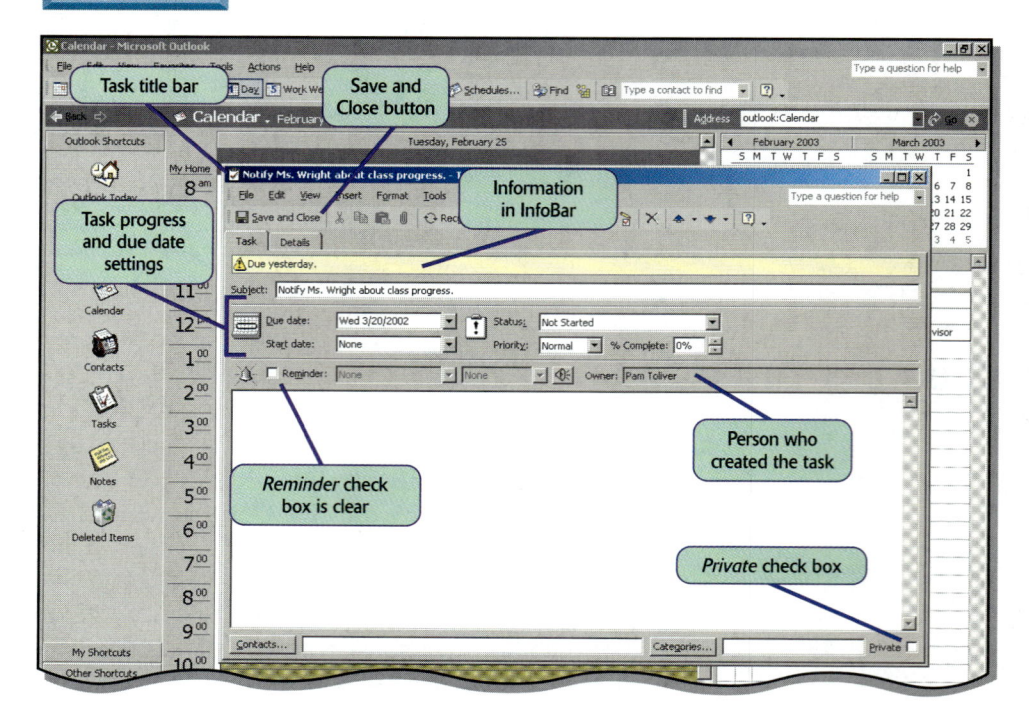

> **Tip:** Marking tasks **Private** enables you to view the task on your Outlook Calendar window but hides the task from others who have access to your task list.

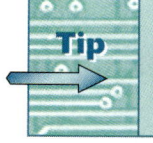

5 Review the new task in the TaskPad list.

Figure 5-3

Callout: Past-due tasks appear in red

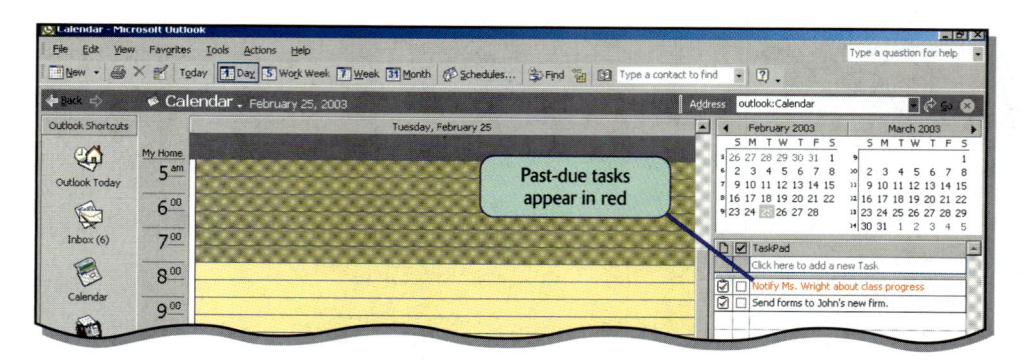

> **Tip:** If the week numbers are missing from your Date Navigator, choose **Tools | Options | Preferences**, click the **Calendar Options** button, and check the **Show week numbers in the Date Navigator** check box.

Updating and Modifying Tasks

One of the benefits of recording tasks electronically is the ease with which you can mark them completed. When tasks extend over several days or weeks, you can update the tasks to record your progress and send task updates to other users. When tasks are 100% complete, Outlook "draws" a line through the task. The next time you launch Outlook, only tasks that you have not yet completed appear in the TaskPad pane of the Calendar window. When you want to review all completed and pending tasks, open the Tasks folder.

Task 2:
To Edit and Update Tasks

1 Display the **Calendar** for February 2003 and March 2003 and select the check box beside the *Send forms to John's new firm.* task to mark it completed.

2 Click the Outlook Bar **Tasks** icon to open the Tasks folder.

3 Clear the check mark from the *Send forms to John's new firm.* task and double-click the clipboard icon at the left end of the task to open it in a separate window.

4 Double-click the value in the **% Complete** value box, type **50**, and then click the **Details** tab.

Figure 5-4

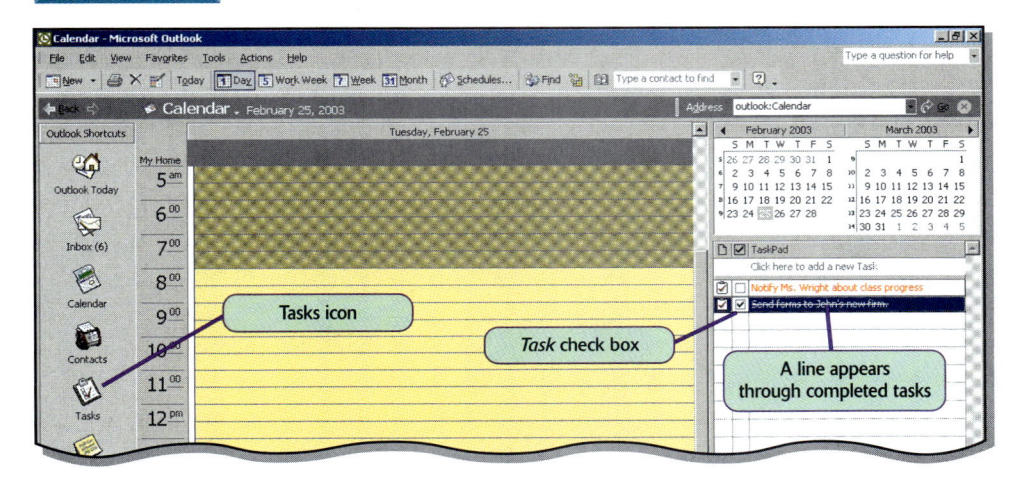

Figure 5-5

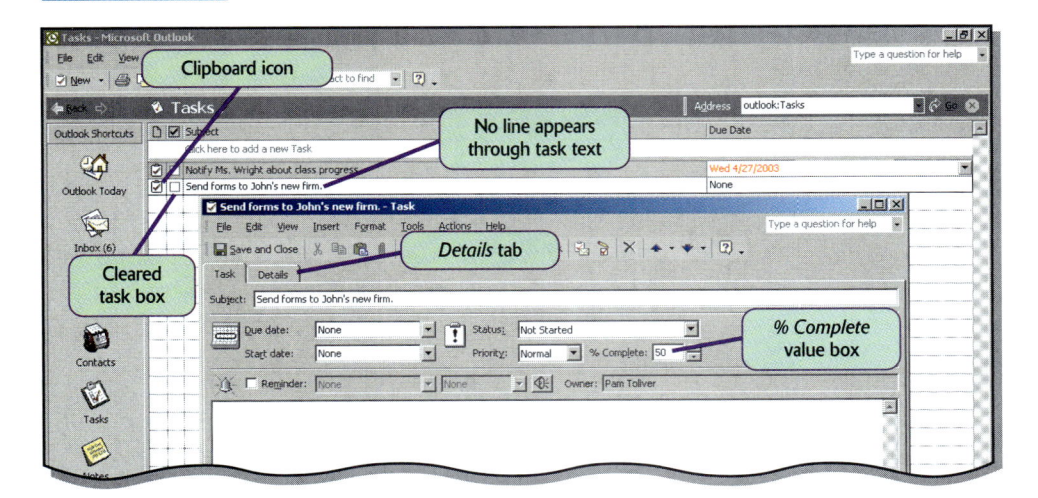

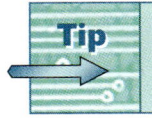

Tip You can also click the % Complete down arrow and select 25%, 50%, 75%, or 100% to change the percentage complete.

5 Select the value in the **Actual work** text box, type **3 hours**, and click the **Save and Close** ![Save and Close] button.

6 Click the **Subject** column heading button to sort the tasks alphabetically by subject.

Figure 5-6

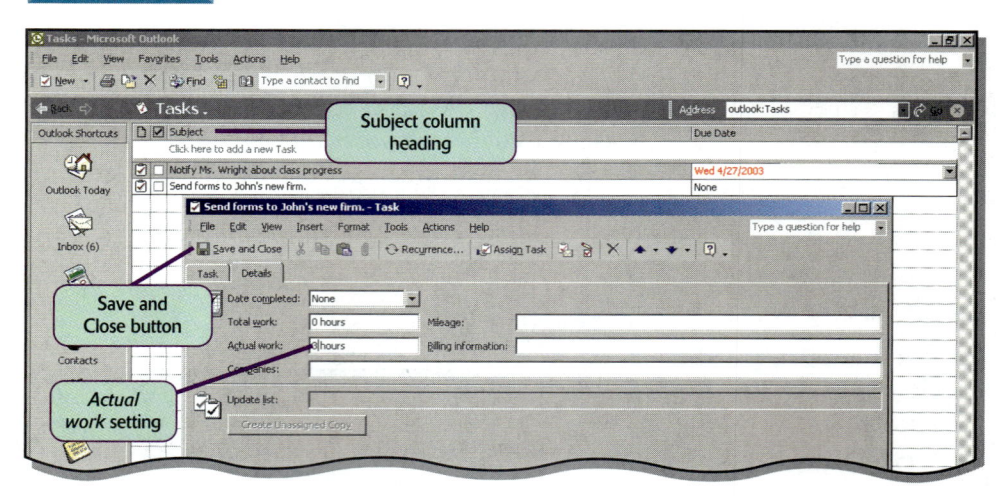

(Subject column heading; Save and Close button; Actual work setting)

7 Click the **Due Date** column heading to sort the tasks by the date they are due.

Figure 5-7

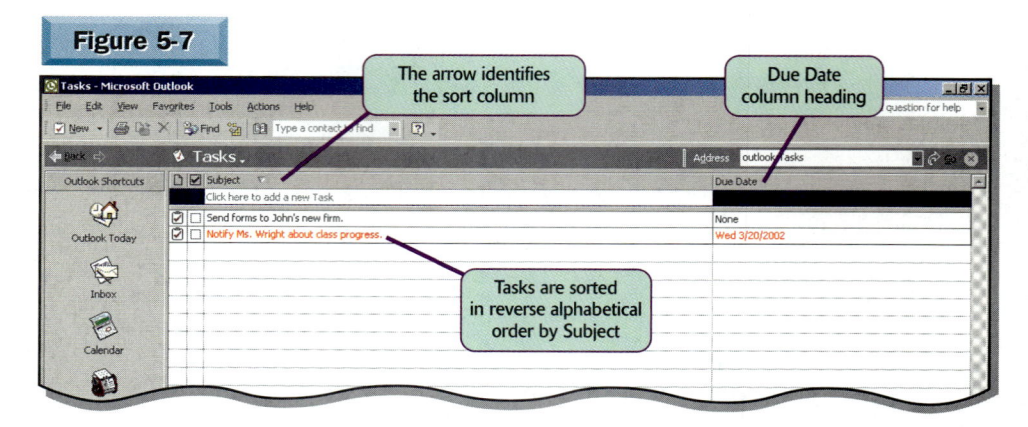

(The arrow identifies the sort column; Due Date column heading; Tasks are sorted in reverse alphabetical order by Subject)

Changing the Tasks View and Organizing Tasks

When the Tasks folder is open and all tasks are displayed, you can sort them by clicking the column heading button for the column on which you want to sort or by changing the Current View to display specific tasks. Outlook also contains an Organize tool that you can use to sort and organize items in each Outlook folder.

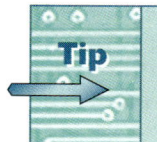

> **Tip** The views displayed on the Organize pane depend on the active folder and are the same views that appear on the Current Views list for the folder.

Task 3:
To Change Tasks View and Organize Tasks

1 Open the Tasks folder, if necessary, click the **Organize** button on the toolbar, and then click **Using Views** from the **Ways to Organize Tasks** pane.

2 Scroll to the bottom of the **Change your view** list and select **Task Timeline**.

3 Double-click the clipboard icon for the overdue task, change the **Due date** to April 27 of next year, and save and close the task.

4 Scroll back to the top of the **Change your view** list, select **Simple List** to restore the view, and click the **Organize** button again to hide the **Ways to Organize Tasks** pane.

Figure 5-8

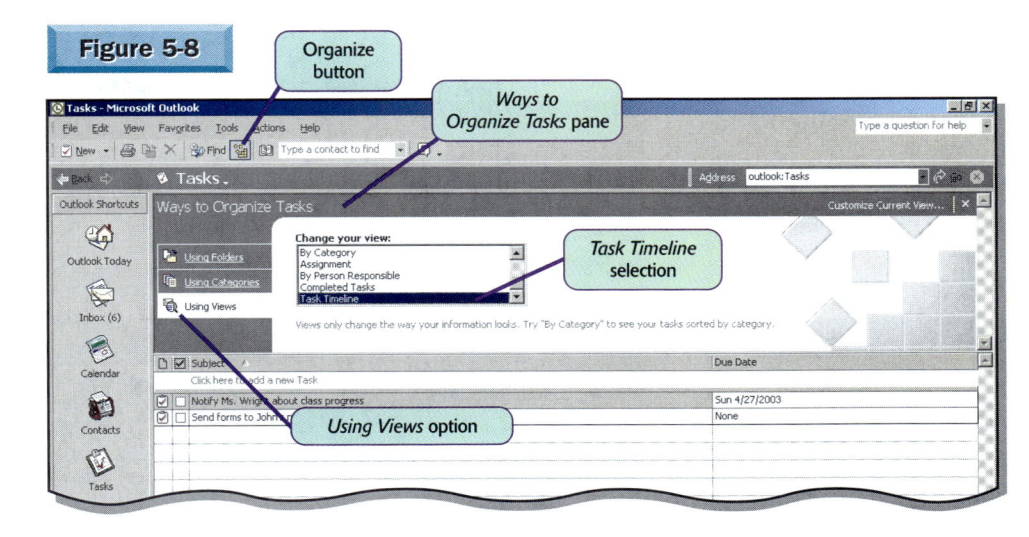

Callouts: Organize button; Ways to Organize Tasks pane; Task Timeline selection; Using Views option

Figure 5-9

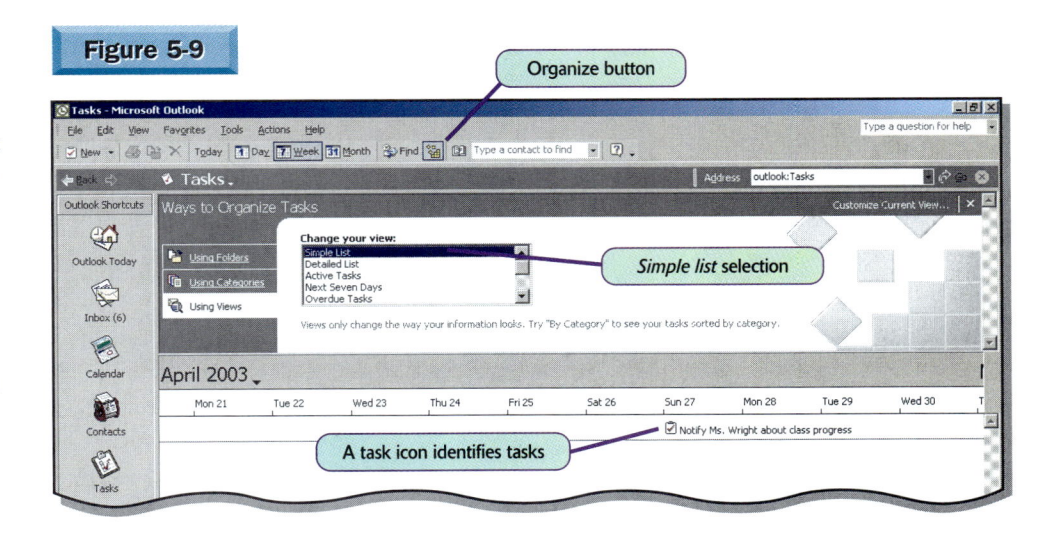

Callouts: Organize button; Simple list selection; A task icon identifies tasks

Creating and Updating Recurring Tasks

Recurring tasks are tasks that must be repeated at regular intervals. For example, you might be responsible for preparing monthly sales reports and want to be sure that Outlook reminds you each month. Outlook can even track recurring events that have varying dates and times. Once the first occurrence of the task is marked completed, Outlook will automatically enter the next recurring task based on either the specific day and time or a specified number of days from the completion date of the previous task. If you have worked with Outlook Calendar, you will find that many of the features required to record recurring tasks are the same as the features for recording recurring appointments.

Task 4:
To Create and Update Recurring Tasks

1 Open the **Tasks** folder and click the **New Task** ☑ New ▾ button to create a new task.

2 Click the **Recurrence** 🔄 Recurrence... button, set the recurrence options displayed in Figure 5-10, and click **OK**.

> **Troubleshooting**
> If other days of the week are selected, clear the check boxes so that only Friday is selected in the Recurrence Pattern section.

3 Complete the task shown in Figure 5-11 and save and close the task.

Figure 5-10

Callouts: New Task button; Recurrence button; Weekly recurrence pattern; Friday; Task start date; 13 occurrences

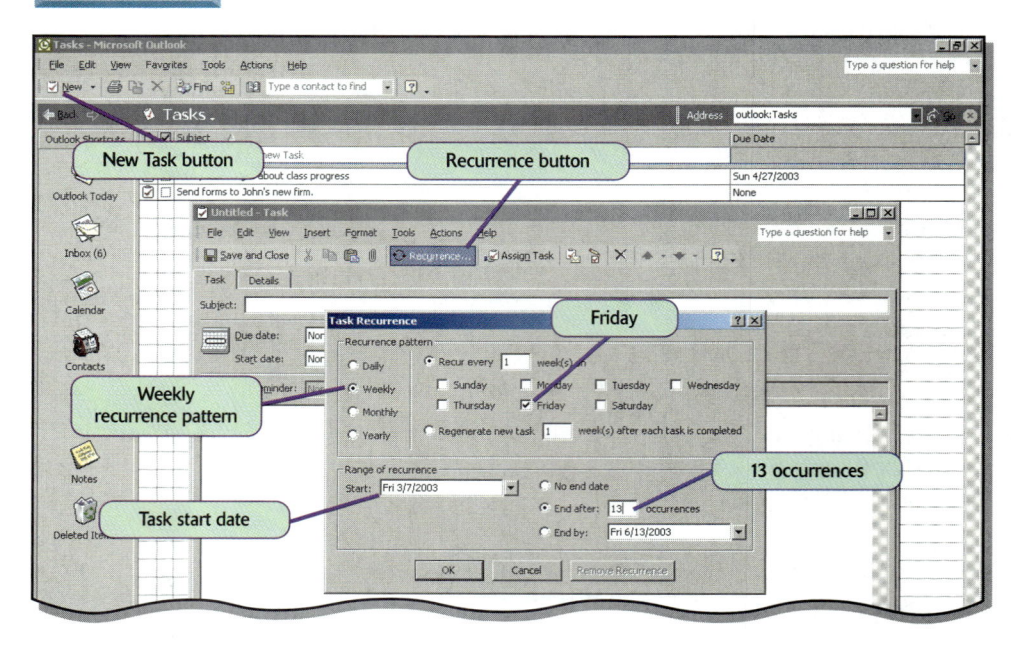

Other Ways

To open the New Task dialog box:
- Click the New Task button down arrow and select **Task**.
- Press Ctrl + N.
- Choose **Actions | New Task**.
- Choose **File | New | Task**.
- Press Ctrl + Shift + K.

Figure 5-11

Callouts: Selected *Reminder* check box; Recurrence information appears in the InfoBar; Task subject

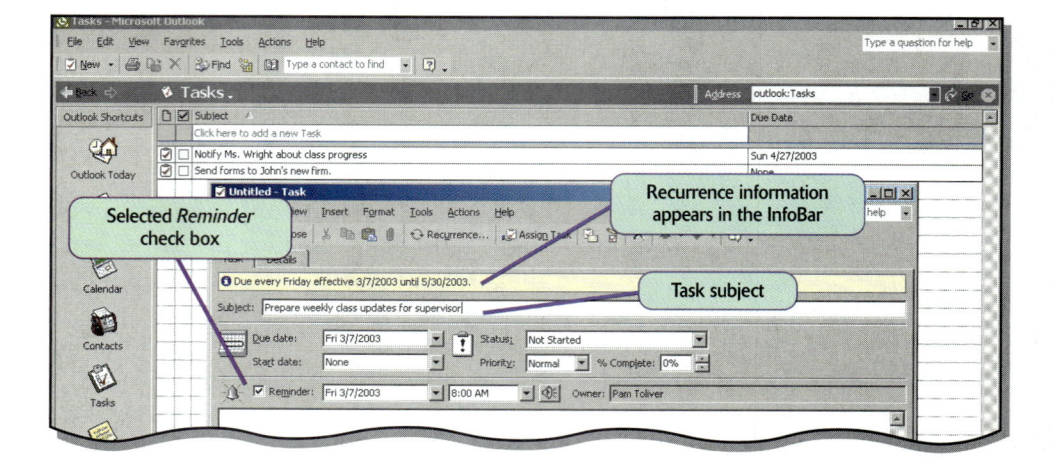

Recording Tasks and Writing Notes OU 5-11

4 Select the check box for the recurring task to mark it complete. When you mark a recurring task complete, Outlook adds the task to the TaskPad palette and changes the due date for the next recurrence of the task.

Figure 5-12

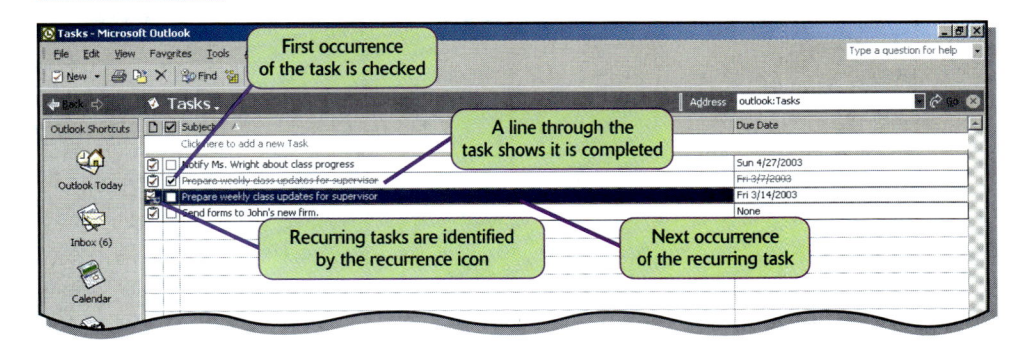

Callouts:
- First occurrence of the task is checked
- A line through the task shows it is completed
- Recurring tasks are identified by the recurrence icon
- Next occurrence of the recurring task

WEB TIP

Did you know you can start a business, find a job, travel safely, get college money, and more by searching out the information from government Web sites? One of the best kept secrets is how many useful sites there are. The challenge is steering people in the right directions. Search for the Web site govWorks, Inc., and see what information might be useful.

Assigning Tasks and Sending Task Requests

Tip The owner of a task is usually the person who creates the task. However, when the task creator assigns the task to another person who accepts the assignment, the person who accepts responsibility for completing the task becomes the task owner.

The Tasks feature enables you to create tasks for yourself as well as to assign tasks to others by sending a task request to the person you want to complete a task. Outlook sends task requests to the recipient's e-mail address, just as it did when you sent meeting requests from the Calendar. The functions associated with assigning tasks include

- Assigning tasks to others adds a *To* field to the New Task dialog box so that you can address the task to the person who will be responsible for its completion.
- When you assign tasks to others, they have the option of accepting or declining the task.
- Outlook places a copy of tasks you assign to others on your task list. These copies are updated automatically each time the person responsible for completing the task makes an update to the task.
- Only the person responsible for the task (the task owner) can make updates to the task.

Task 5:
To Assign and Send a Task Request

1 Click the **Tasks** icon on the Outlook Bar to open the **Tasks** folder and click the **New Task** ☑ New ▾ button to open a new Task window.

2 Type **Review computer project outline.** in the **Subject** text box, set the due date for a week from Friday, and click the **Assign Task** ☑ Assign Task button on the toolbar.

3 Click the **To** field and type the name of one of your classmates that appears in your Contacts folder.

4 Ensure that the **Keep an updated copy of this task on my task list** and the **Send me a status report when the task is complete** check boxes are selected and click **Send**.

5 Click **OK** to acknowledge the message.

> **Tip** Icons for assigned tasks appear with an open hand on the left of the clipboard icon to show that they are being "handed off" to someone else.

Figure 5-13

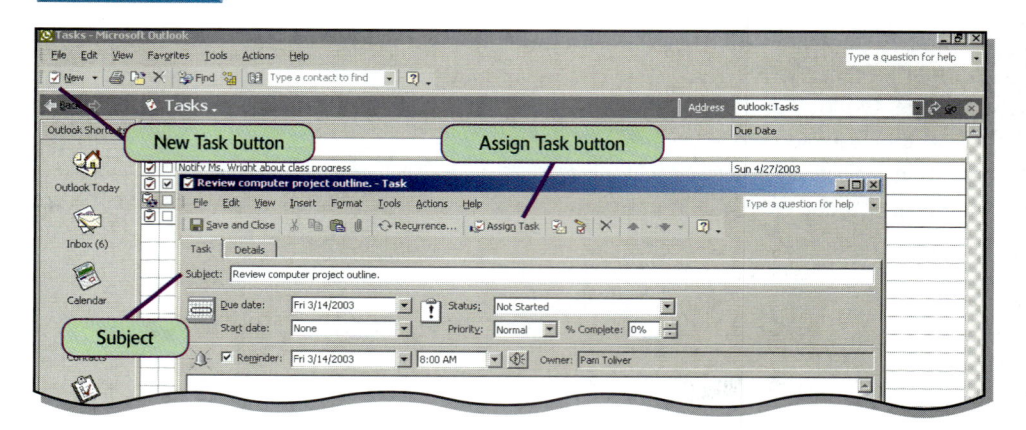

(screenshot showing New Task button, Assign Task button, and Subject)

Figure 5-14

(screenshot showing Send button, Keep an updated copy of this task on my task list check box, Send me a status report when the task is complete check box, To field, and Message window)

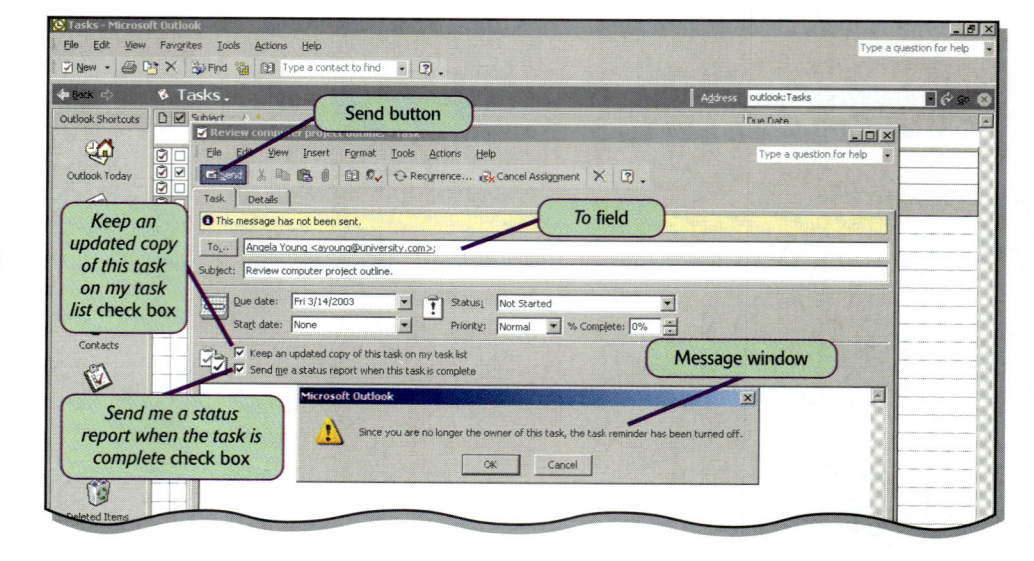

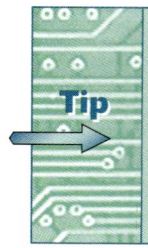

> **Tip** Outlook displays a message when you assign tasks to others telling you that the reminder has been turned off since you are no longer the owner of the task. When you assign a task to someone else, they become the temporary owner of the task. When they accept the task, they become the permanent owner. If they decline to accept the task, ownership is returned to you.

Responding to a Task Request

Tools for accepting, declining, or delegating task assignments appear when you view or open a task assignment message. The action Outlook takes depends on the response you make, as described in Table 5-2.

> **Tip:** You can assign tasks to other Outlook users outside of your network and to users who are not running Outlook on an Exchange Server. However, sharing tasks with users who are running other e-mail and desktop managers is limited.

Table 5-2 Task Assignment Responses

Response	Description/Action
Accept	Outlook assigns you as the owner of the task and places it on your task list. You are the only one who can record updates to the task. You can send updates periodically via e-mail to the person who assigned the task. Each time you make a change to the task status, Outlook automatically sends an update to the person who assigned the task.
Decline	Outlook automatically returns the task to the person who assigned it via e-mail so that they can complete the task themselves or assign it to someone else.
Assign Task	Outlook places a copy of the task on your task list as well as on the task list of the person who assigned the task to you. The person to whom you assign the task becomes the new task owner if they accept the task.

Task 6:
To Accept, Decline, or Delegate Tasks

1. Open the **Inbox** and open the message from your instructor that contains *Task Assignment* in the **Subject** field.

2. Click **Accept** and click **OK** to send without editing the response, if necessary.

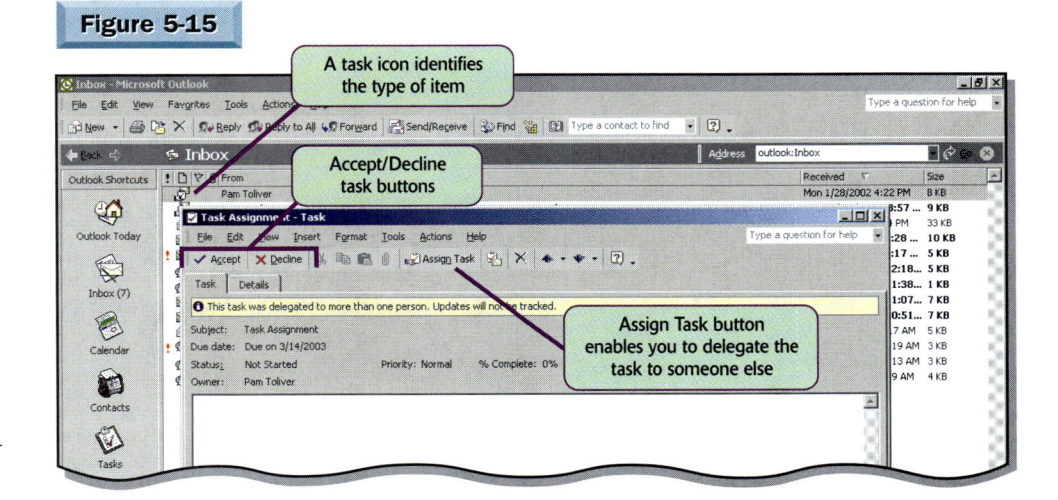

Figure 5-15

> **Tip:** After you accept or decline a task assignment, Outlook moves the task item from your Inbox folder to your Deleted Items folder.

3 Open the **Tasks** folder and review the assigned task format.

Figure 5-16

> **Tip**
> Notice that the icon for the task you assigned to your classmate is different from the icon for the task your instructor assigned to you and that you accepted.

The task you assigned a classmate appears in bold

The task your instructor assigned to you is also bold

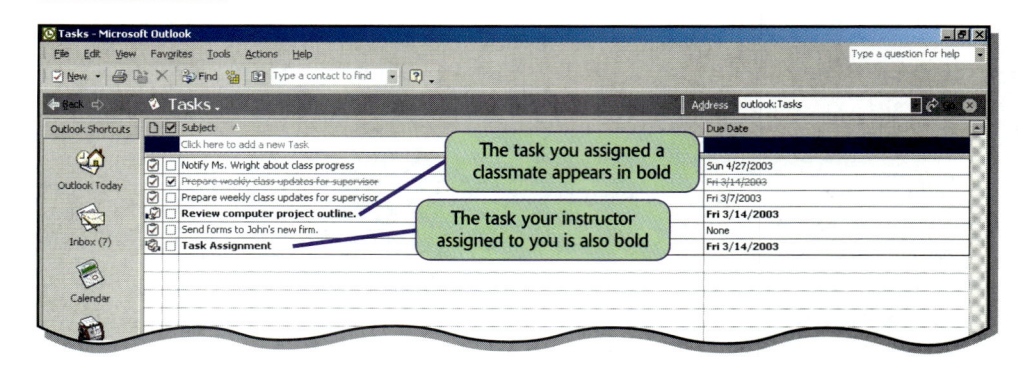

Sending Task Updates

As the person responsible for completing a task, you will want to keep the person who assigned the task to you up to date on your progress. Each time you make a change in the task status, Outlook automatically updates all copies of the task. If you wish to add a message to the update, you can send a manual task update.

Figure 5-17

Details tab

Send Status Report button

Actual work field

Task 7:
To Send Task Updates

1 Open the *Task Assignment* task that you accepted and change the status of the task to 50% complete.

2 Click the **Details** tab, type **2 hours** in the **Actual work** field, and click the **Send Status Report** button to send a report to the person who assigned the task to you.

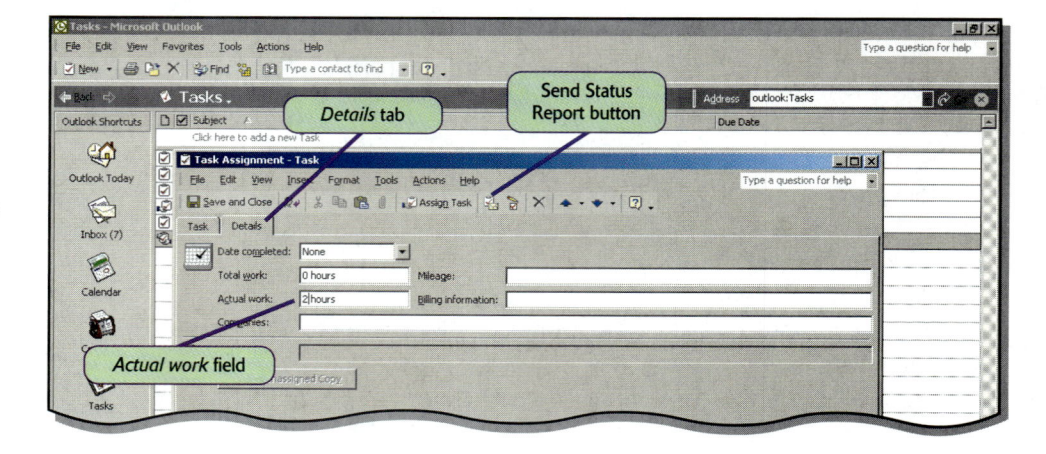

3 Type the information shown in Figure 5-18 in the message window.

4 Click the **Send** button and close the task.

Figure 5-18

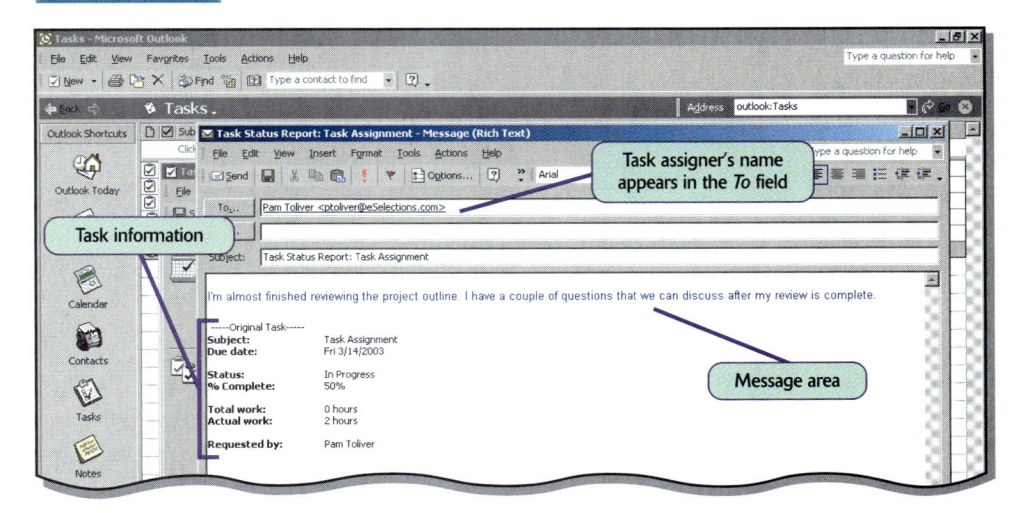

- Task assigner's name appears in the *To* field
- Task information
- Message area

Tracking Assigned Tasks

When you assign a task to someone else and select the option to keep an updated copy of the task on your task list, you receive an update automatically each time the task owner records a change in the task status. In addition, you can request an update on the task via e-mail or telephone when you fail to receive regular updates.

Task 8:
To Track Assigned Tasks

1 Open the task *Review computer project outline* that you sent to another classmate and review the task progress information.

2 Save and close the task.

Figure 5-19

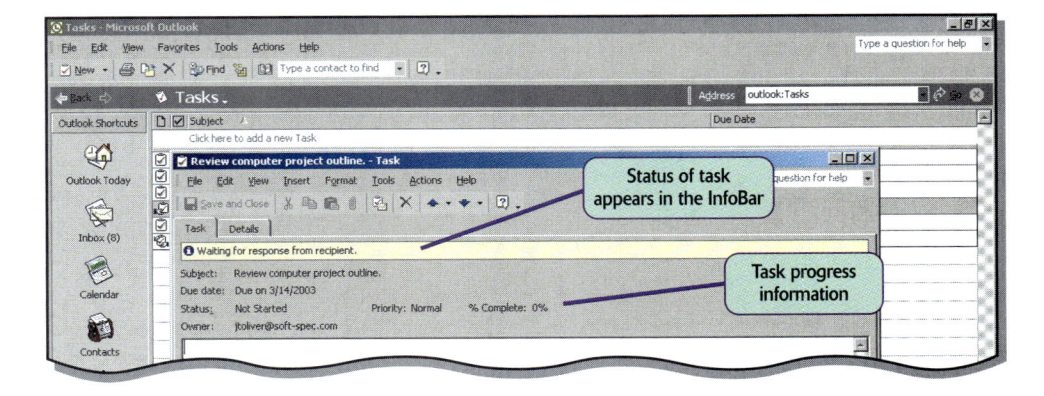

- Status of task appears in the InfoBar
- Task progress information

Tip When the task owner sends a task update, you can open the e-mail message you receive and review the updated task information.

CHECK POINT

Did you know that you can also forward information about tasks to users such as supervisors who are not officially associated with completing the task yet need to be kept aware of the task status? Regardless of whether you are the task owner or want to forward an update that you receive from the task owner, just open the task, choose **Actions | Forward**, and enter the e-mail addresses of those to whom you want to send the task information. The same *To, Cc,* or *Bcc* fields appear when you forward a task update that are available in an e-mail message. Once you identify the task recipients, you can send the message on its way.

Printing Tasks

Printing items in the Outlook Tasks folder enables you to print a list of tasks in table format or to print individual task items. Because of the different options available for each format, the Print dialog box opens regardless of what technique you use to issue the Print command.

Task 9:
To Print Task Items

1 Open the **Tasks** folder, select any task in the list, and click the **Print** button.

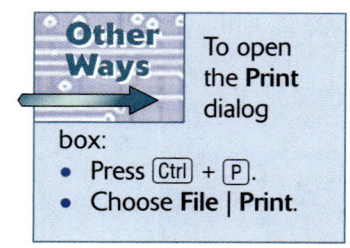

Other Ways — To open the **Print** dialog box:
- Press Ctrl + P.
- Choose **File | Print**.

2 Select the **Table** Style and click **Preview**.

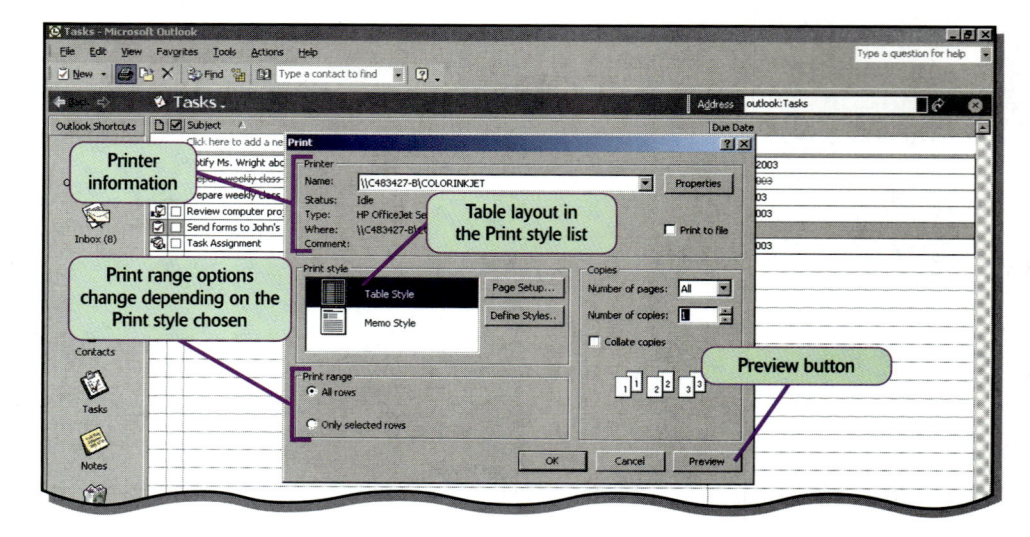

Figure 5-20

3. Press **Esc** to close the **Print Preview** window.

Figure 5-21

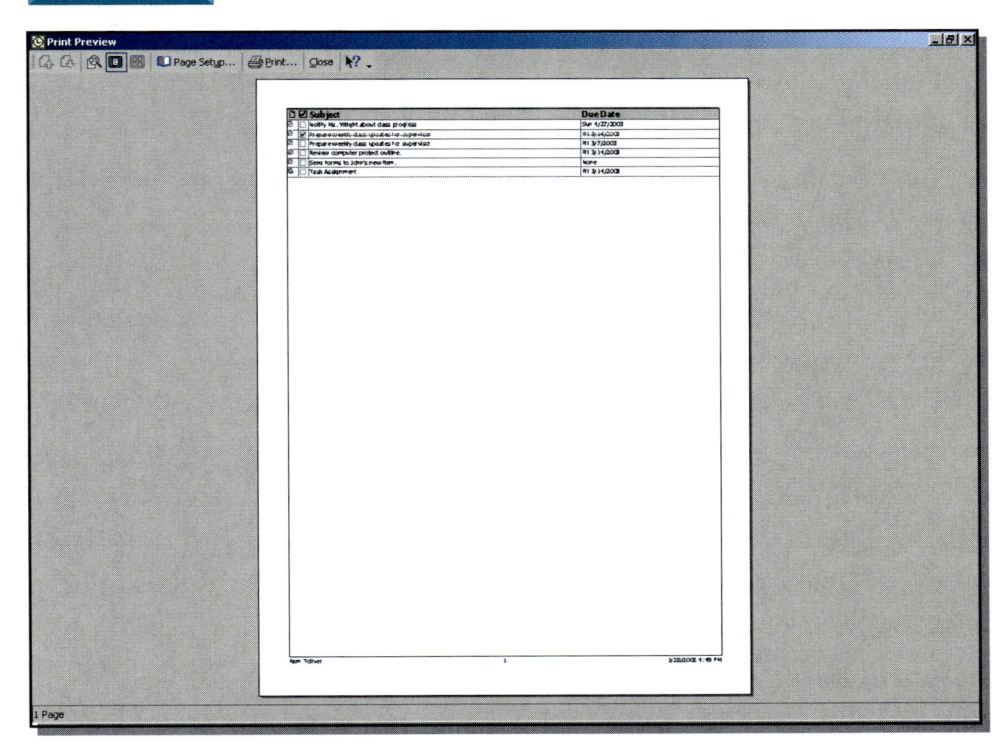

Tip Point to each tool on the Print Preview window toolbar to determine how it is used. Then click the toolbar buttons to switch between actual size and full page to change the view.

Setting Task Options

The work times and habits of Outlook users vary; therefore, Outlook contains tools for customizing these settings to better meet your needs. Using Task options enables you to control the display time of reminder notifications for tasks with due dates, select the color of overdue and completed task item text, and set options for assigned tasks and status reports. The default settings for task reminders with due dates is 8:00 A.M. and the default colors are used to identify overdue and assigned tasks and task updates.

Task 10:
To Set Task Options

1 Choose **Tools | Options**.

2 Click the **Reminder time** down arrow, select **10:00 AM**, and click the **Task Options** button.

Figure 5-22

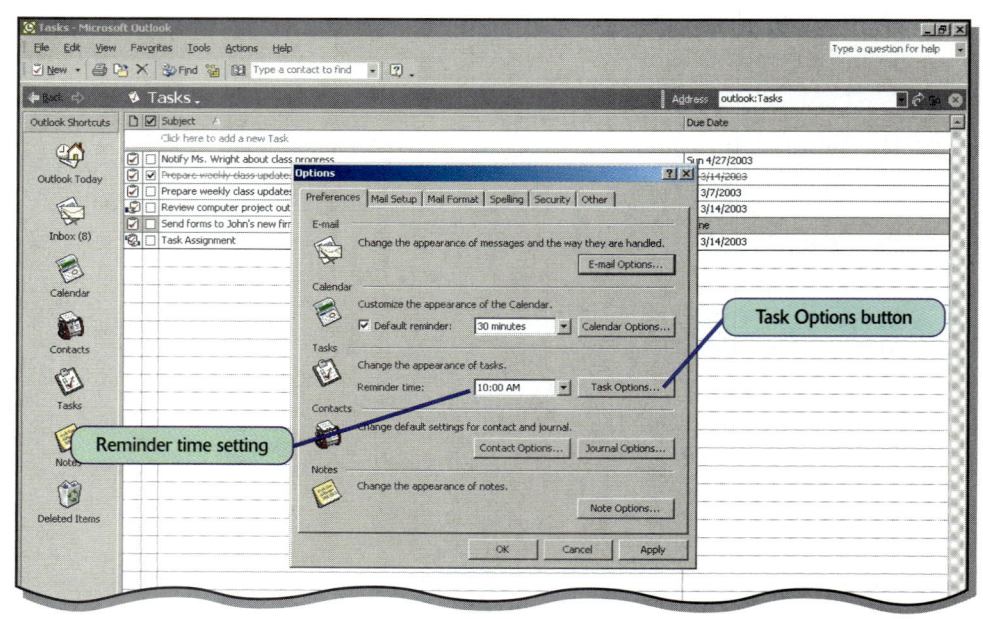

Task Options button

Reminder time setting

3 Select a different color from the **Overdue task color** list, select a different color from the **Completed task color** list, and click **OK** twice.

Figure 5-23

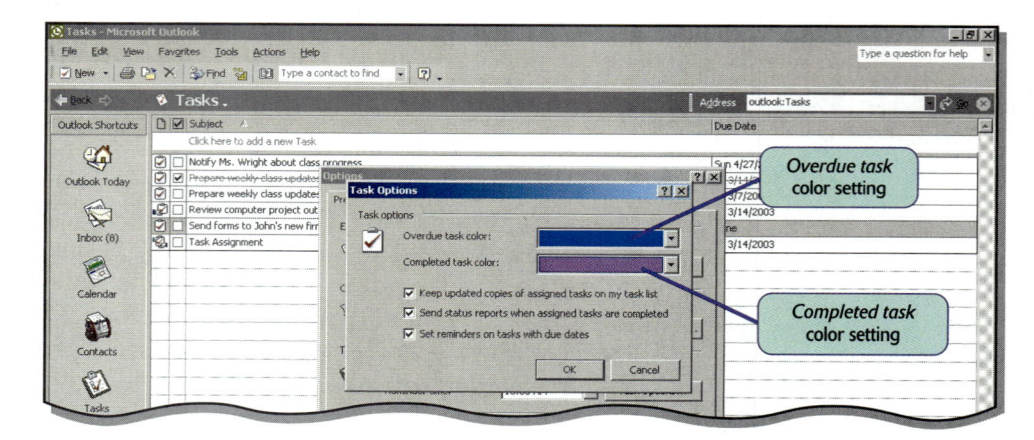

Overdue task color setting

Completed task color setting

4 Mark the *Send forms to John's new firm.* task completed.

Figure 5-24

Completed tasks are marked with the new color

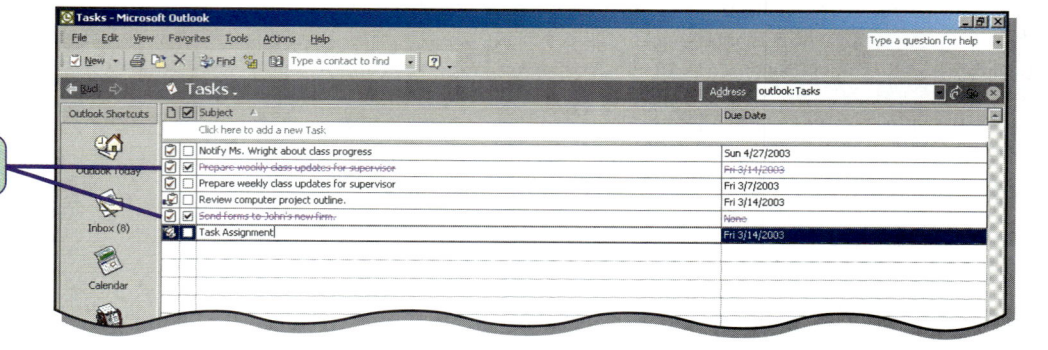

Recording Tasks and Writing Notes OU 5-19

WEB TIP

Most PDAs (Personal Digital Assistants), regardless of how sophisticated they are, contain tools for jotting down notes and tasks. Check out a few simple, inexpensive PDAs to see what features they contain.

Creating and Editing Notes

If you look around your office or home, you are almost certain to see a number of different *notes* on which you have jotted down reminders, phone numbers, or names. The electronic Outlook Notes feature can help you reduce the number of pieces of paper that clutter your life, and can be fun to use. By using Notes, you can store reminders and other pieces of information and "stick" them on the Outlook window just as you place "sticky notes" on so many things around you.

Task 11:
To Create Electronic Notes

1. Click the Outlook Bar **Notes** icon.

2. Click the **New Note** button and type **Don't forget to check with classmate about our project**.

3. Click the **Note close** × button.

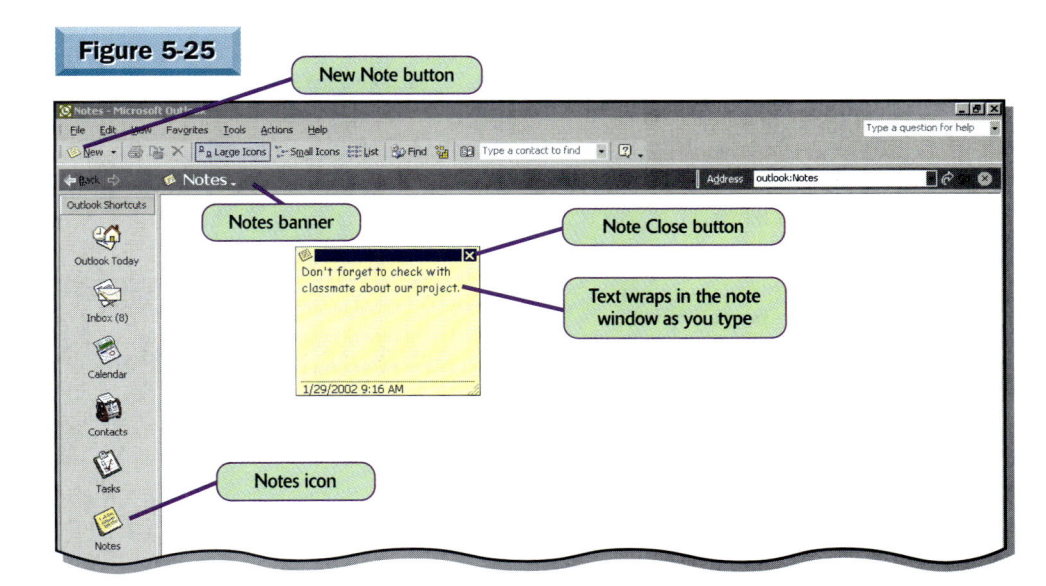

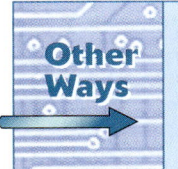

Figure 5-25

- New Note button
- Notes banner
- Note Close button
- Text wraps in the note window as you type
- Notes icon

Other Ways

To create a new note:
- Choose **File | New | Note**.
- Choose **Actions | New Note**.
- Press Ctrl + N.

4 Click a blank area of the window to deselect the note.

Figure 5-26

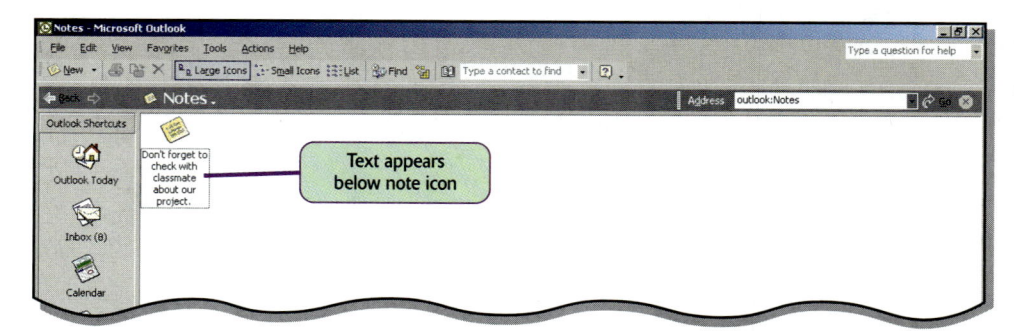

Text appears below note icon

> **Tip**
>
> Depending on the size of the monitor and the screen resolution, the full note text may be *truncated*—or abbreviated—so that only part of the note appears onscreen when the note is closed. To display all note text for truncated notes, point to the note, and the full note text will appear below it.
>
> Only text contained in the first paragraph of a note appears when the note is closed. As a result, text you type after pressing the Enter key can be viewed only by opening the note.

5 Click the **Small Icons** button on the Standard toolbar to reduce the size of the note.

6 Click the **Large Icons** button to restore the window.

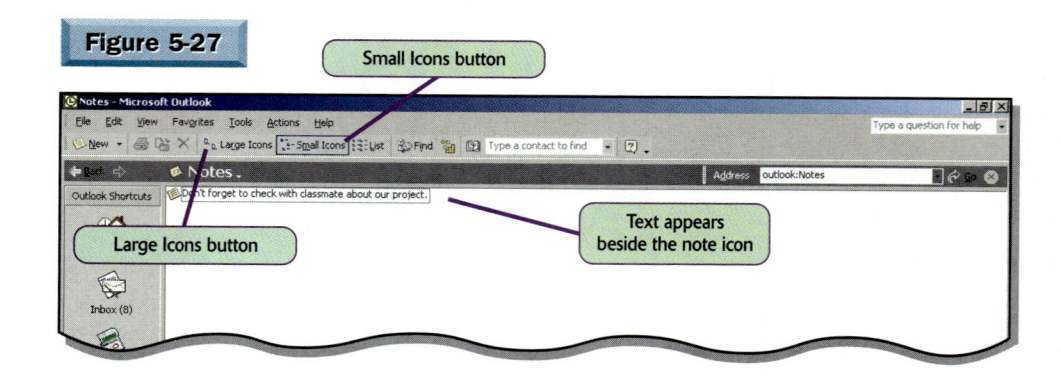

Figure 5-27

Small Icons button

Large Icons button

Text appears beside the note icon

Viewing, Organizing, and Reading Notes

As the number of notes on your Outlook desktop increases and the length of the notes get longer, text can appear in truncated form below the note icon. You can quickly identify the general context of each note, but to edit the note you must open it.

Task 12:
To View, Open, and Edit Electronic Notes

1 Double-click the note icon to open it and add text to create the note shown in Figure 5-28.

2 Close the note to save changes to the note.

Figure 5-28

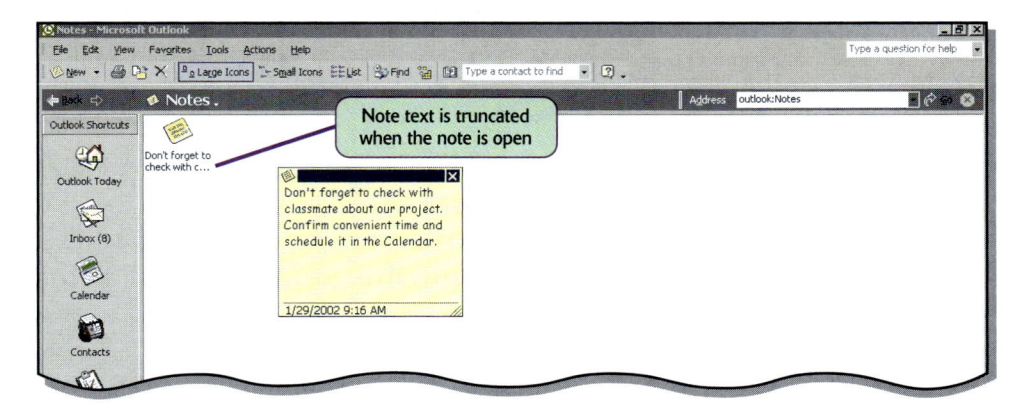

Note text is truncated when the note is open

Troubleshooting If the note window hides the note icon, drag the open note title bar to move the open note.

Assigning Notes to Contacts

Many of the notes you create will be reminders to discuss items with people who are listed in your Contacts folder. For example, if you are organizing a board of directors meeting and have recorded numerous notes concerning issues you want to discuss with the hotel event planner, you could assign the notes to the contact and quickly review all notes the next time you speak with the planner. Notes assigned to contacts appear on the Activities page of the contact listing.

Task 13:
To Assign Electronic Notes to Contacts

1 Open the electronic note you just edited, click the **Note menu** button to display the menu, and select **Contacts**.

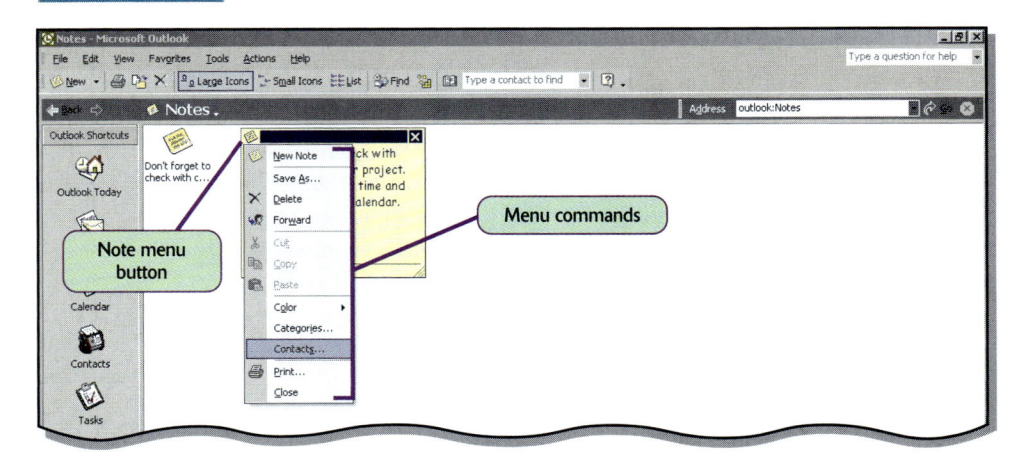

Figure 5-29

Note menu button

Menu commands

Assigning Notes to Contacts

2 Click the **Contacts** button and then click the **Contacts** folder, if necessary.

3 Select the listing for one of your classmates from the **Items** list, and click **OK**.

Figure 5-30

4 Click **Close** to close the note, and click the Outlook Bar **Contacts** icon.

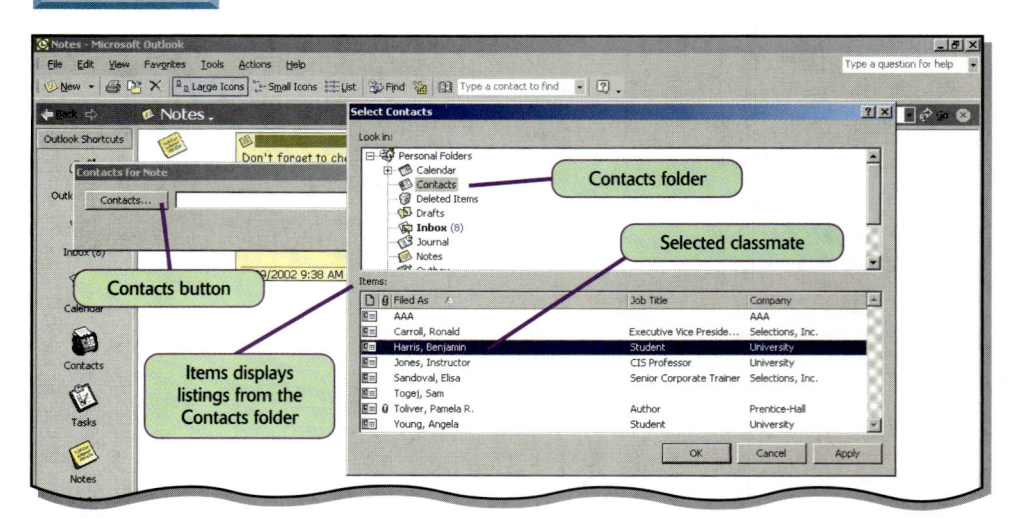

Figure 5-31

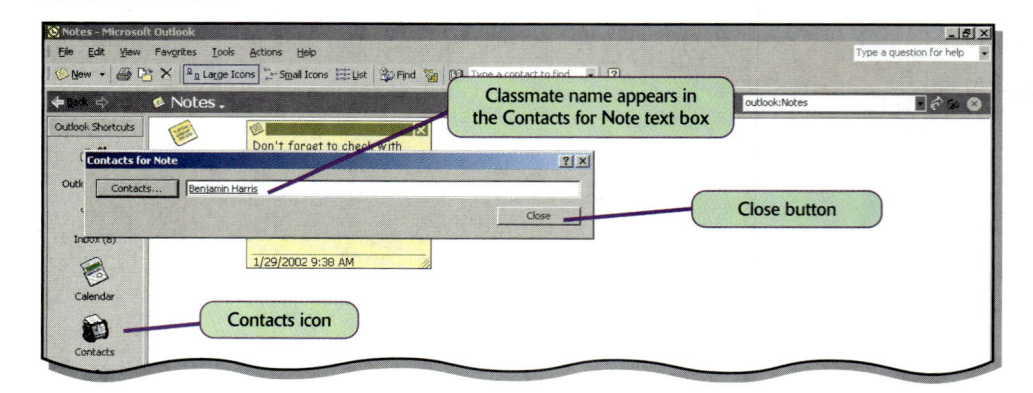

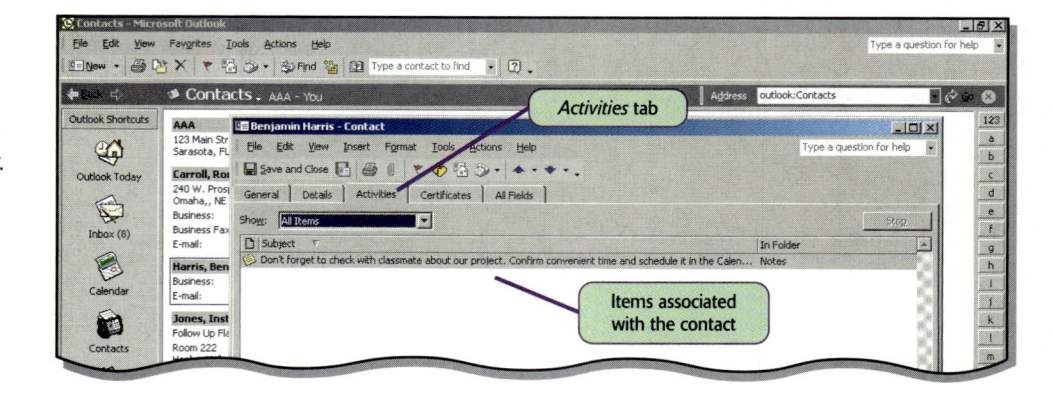

5 Open the contact listing for the classmate you chose for the note, and display the **Activities** page.

6 Close the contact and open the Notes folder.

Figure 5-32

Recording Tasks and Writing Notes   OU 5-23

Setting Notes Options

Outlook contains options that you can set to customize the color, size, and font of Outlook notes. Changes made to note options affect new notes you create after making the changes. However, when you open notes created before setting new color options, you might find that Outlook reformatted existing notes, too.

Task 14:
To Set Notes Options

1 Open the **Notes** folder, choose **Tools | Options** to open the Options dialog box, and click the **Note Options** button to open the Note Options dialog box.

2 Click the **Color** down arrow, select a note color, click the **Size** down arrow, and select **Large**.

3 Click the **Font** button to open the Font dialog box.

Figure 5-33

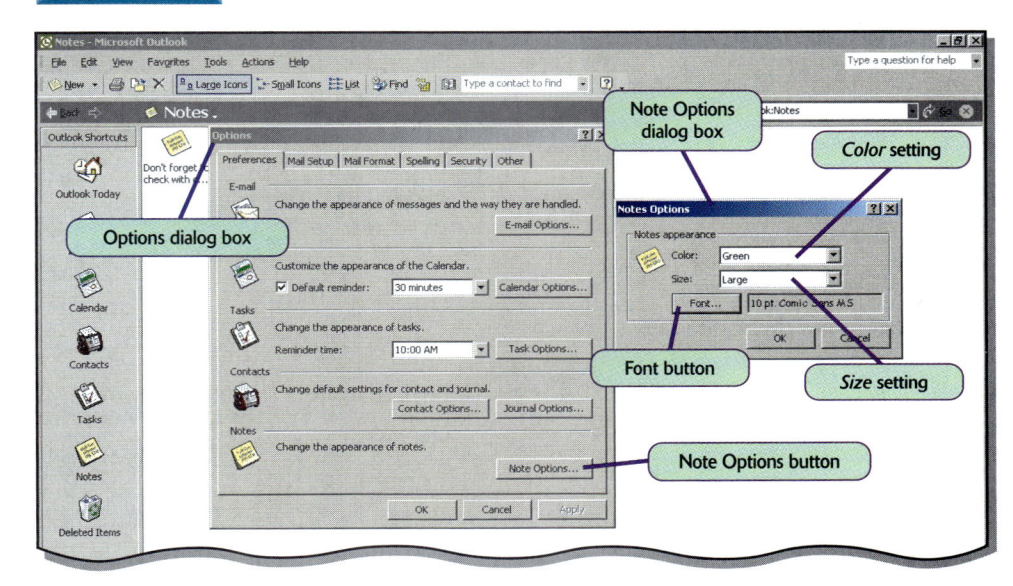

Tip Note background customization affects the background for new notes you create after changing the settings. Text color changes affect existing notes and new notes but only appears when the notes are open.

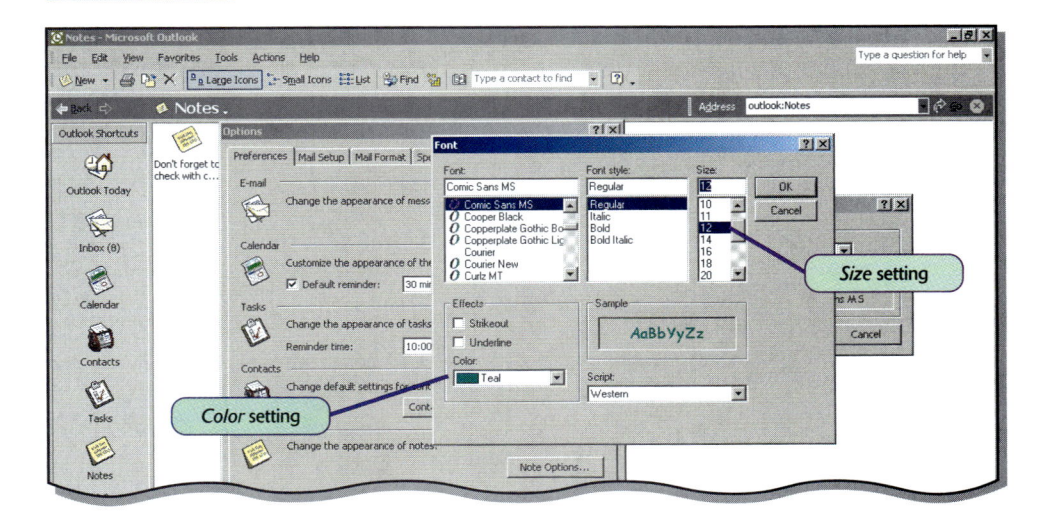

4 Select a different font color from the **Color** list, select **12** in the **Size** list, and click **OK** three times to close all open dialog boxes.

Figure 5-34

5 Create a new note and type **I have customized my notes format.**

6 Close the note.

> **Tip** New notes appear in the Notes folder before existing notes.

Figure 5-35

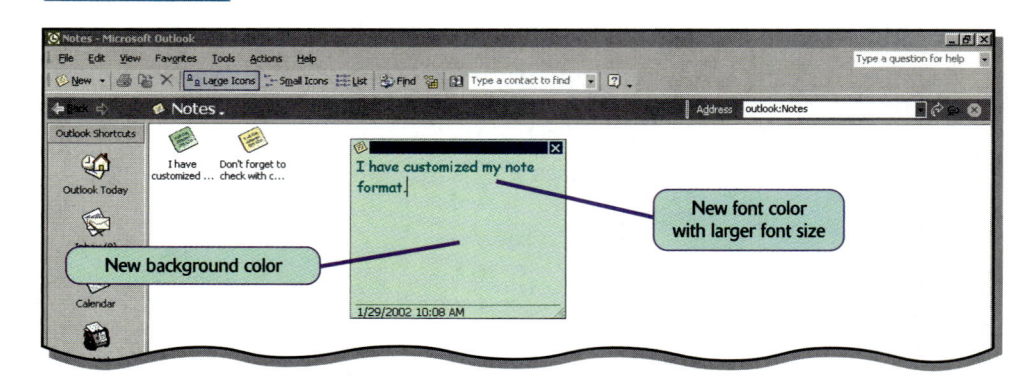

Saving, Forwarding, and Printing Notes

> **Tip** You can create a special folder to hold tasks related to specific projects or classes. Refer to Project 1 for information on creating new Outlook folders.

Notes you create are formatted to appear as Outlook notes only. While you can open and copy the text contained in a note and paste the text into other files, Outlook offers three different ways you can transfer notes from your Notes folder.

- Save notes in formats that are recognized by other programs.
- Forward the note electronically so that note recipients who use Outlook can place the electronic note in their Outlook Notes folder.
- Print notes.

Task 15:
To Share Electronic Notes

1 Open the **Notes** folder and select the note concerning the meeting with your classmate.

2 Click the **Note menu** button and select **Forward**.

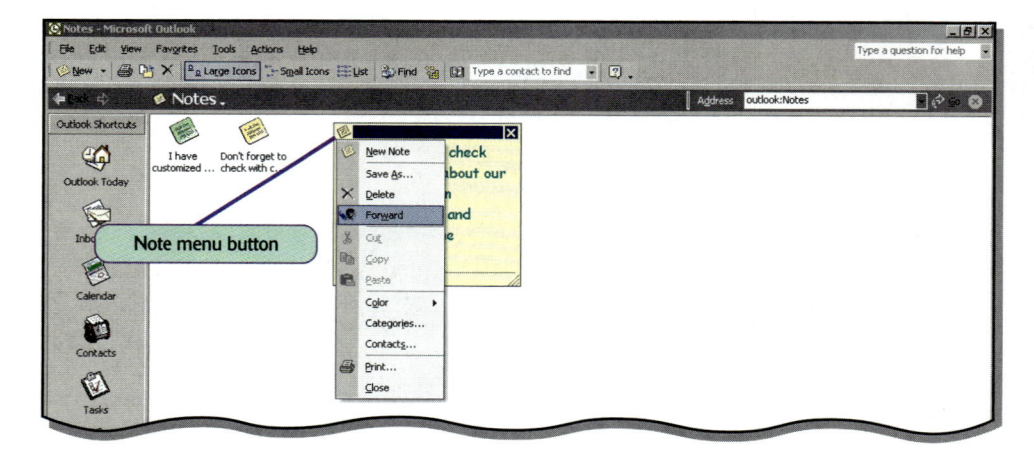

Figure 5-36

Recording Tasks and Writing Notes

OU 5-25

3 Address the message to the classmate to whom you assigned the note, type a short message, and click **Send**.

Figure 5-37

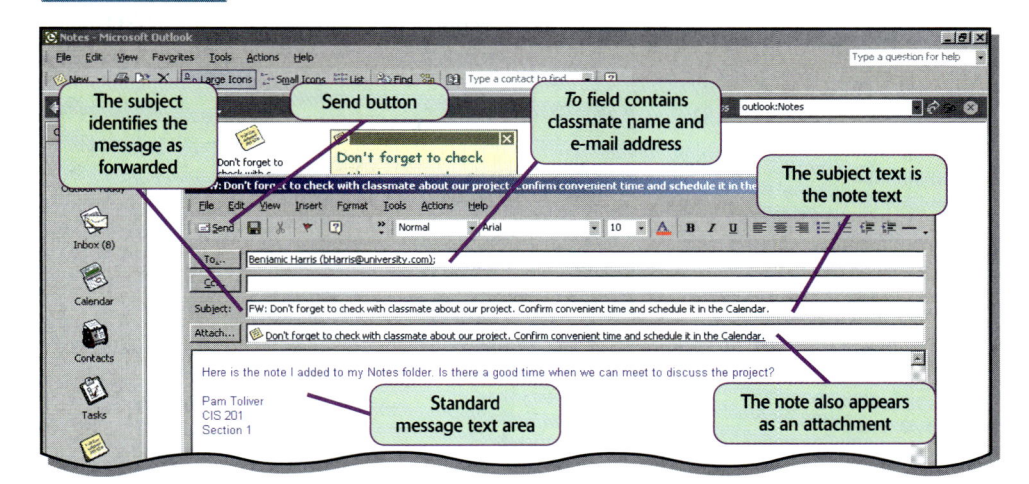

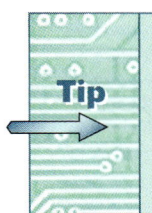

- The subject identifies the message as forwarded
- Send button
- *To* field contains classmate name and e-mail address
- The subject text is the note text
- Standard message text area
- The note also appears as an attachment

Tip: Attachments to e-mail messages appear in different formats depending on the mail format that is active. When HTML or Plain Text are active, attachments appear as shown in Figure 5-37. When Rich Text is selected for the mail format, attachments may appear as icons in the body of the e-mail message.

4 Select the note again, click the **Print** button to open the Print dialog box, review print options, and click **Cancel**.

Figure 5-38

- Printer information
- Notes print in only one Print style
- Print options
- Copy options

Tip: When you open the Print dialog box by clicking the Print button or choosing **File | Print**, the note closes automatically. If you display the Print dialog box using the [Ctrl] + [P] command, the note stays open.

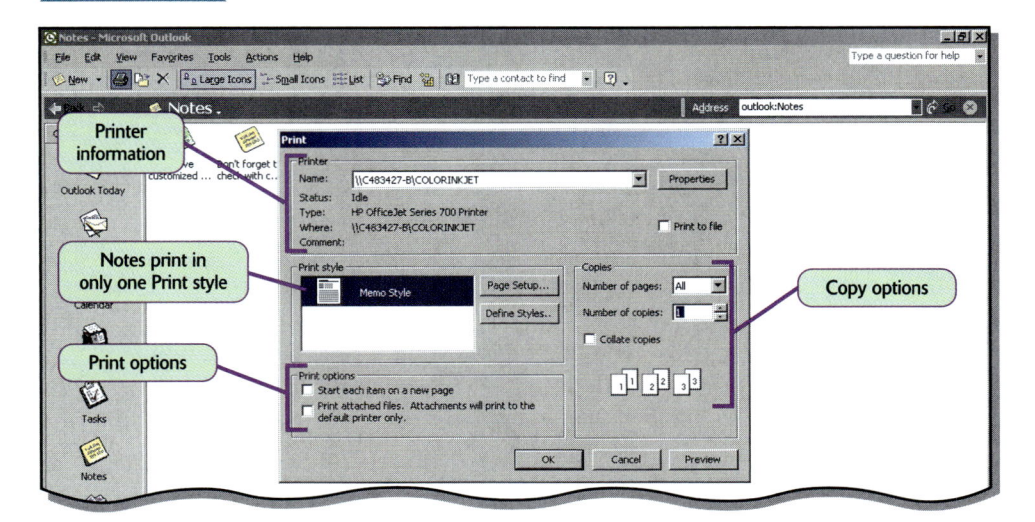

Saving, Forwarding, and Printing Notes

5 Select the note, if necessary, and choose **File | Save As**.

6 Type **Sample Note** in the **File name** text box, open the folder in which you want to save the file, and click **Save**.

Figure 5-39

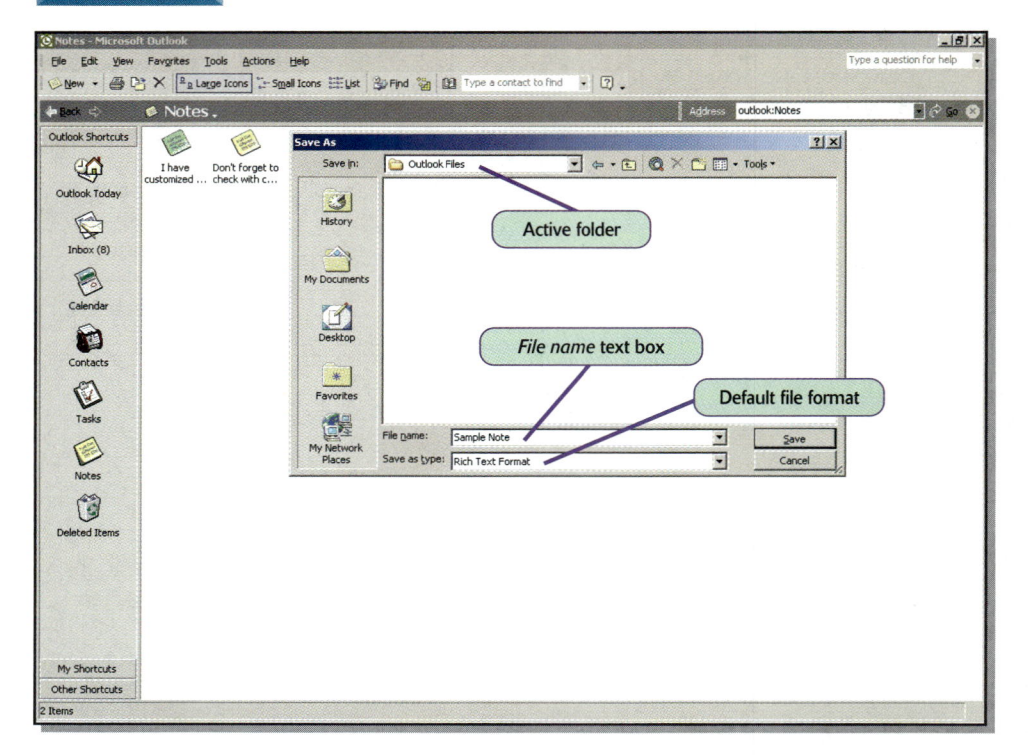

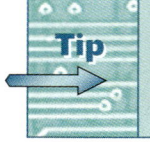

Tip Outlook places the original note text in the File name text box. Because text can be long and nondescriptive, it is usually better to change the file name to something more meaningful.

SUMMARY AND EXERCISES

SUMMARY

- Tasks and Notes are specifically designed to help you electronically track activities and maintain set reminders.
- The procedures used to record tasks are the same regardless of whether you enter the task in the Calendar TaskPad or display a new Tasks dialog box.
- When tasks extend over several days or weeks, you can update the tasks to record your progress and send task updates to other users.
- You can sort tasks in Tasks view by using the column heading or use the Organize Tool to sort and organize tasks.
- Recurring tasks are tasks that must be repeated at regular intervals and are recorded using the same basic procedures used to record recurring appointments.
- The Tasks feature enables you to create tasks for yourself as well as to assign tasks to others who may accept or decline the task.
- You receive an update automatically each time a person who accepts the tasks you assign records a change in the task status.
- Task options enable you to control the time that reminder notifications display for tasks with due dates, the color of overdue task item text, completed task color, and options for assigned tasks and status reports.
- The Notes feature enables you to add electronic "sticky note" reminders to your Outlook screen and to control the note color, size, and font that appear in the note.
- When you assign a note to a contact, the note appears on the Activities page of the contact listing.

KEY TERMS & SKILLS

KEY TERMS
- Notes (p. 5-19)
- recurrence (p. 5-10)
- tasks (p. 5-5)
- truncated (p. 5-20)

SKILLS
- Accept, decline, or delegate tasks (p. 5-13)
- Assign electronic notes to contacts (p. 5-21)
- Assign and send a task request (p. 5-12)
- Change tasks view and organize tasks (p. 5-9)
- Create electronic notes (p. 5-19)
- Create and update recurring tasks (p. 5-10)
- Edit and update tasks (p. 5-7)
- Print task items (p. 5-16)
- Record tasks and create tasks lists (p. 5-5)
- Send task updates (p. 5-14)
- Set notes options (p. 5-23)
- Set task options (p. 5-18)
- Share electronic notes (p. 5-24)
- Track assigned tasks (p. 5-15)
- View, open, and edit electronic notes (p. 5-21)

STUDY QUESTIONS

MULTIPLE CHOICE

1. The two feature windows that provide direct access for creating tasks are
   a. Inbox and Tasks.
   b. Contacts and Tasks.
   c. Calendar and Tasks.
   d. Notes and Tasks.

2. Completed tasks appear
   a. with red text.
   b. with a line drawn through them.
   c. in the TaskPad only.
   d. in the Deleted Items folder.

3. All of the following options can be set for tasks *except*
   a. due time.
   b. private.
   c. reminders.
   d. due date.

4. Which of the following might be marked to update a task?
   a. Time completed
   b. Name of person who completed the task
   c. The due date
   d. Hours worked on the task

5. The default task view displays
   a. a simple list.
   b. a detailed list.
   c. active tasks only.
   d. overdue tasks only.

6. To assign a task to someone else, click
   a. New.
   b. Recurrence....
   c. Assign Task.
   d. Send.

7. The task option set on the Outlook Options dialog box is
   a. reminder time for tasks with due dates.
   b. overdue task color.
   c. completed task color.
   d. update action.

8. The Outlook feature that resembles "sticky notes" is
   a. Tasks.
   b. Appointments.
   c. Contacts.
   d. Notes.

9. All of the following techniques can be used to transmit notes *except*
   a. saving a note in a different file format.
   b. forwarding notes.
   c. printing notes.
   d. replying to notes.

SHORT ANSWER

1. What happens when you double-click the **TaskPad** task entry field in Calendar?
2. How do you mark a task completed?
3. What are the basic increments available for marking the % of a task completed using the nudge buttons—the buttons containing arrows that appear beside the value box?
4. How do the task views displayed in the Organizer pane vary from those shown on the current view list?
5. How do you delegate an assigned task to someone else?
6. What do you do to track a task that you want someone else to complete?
7. What are the three options you can set for notes?

FILL IN THE BLANK

1. The _____ pane appears in the Calendar window to display tasks.
2. _____ tasks occur at regular intervals.
3. When you accept an assigned task, you become the task _____.
4. When you print a task list, the list appears in _____ format.
5. To access most Notes commands, click the _____.
6. Tasks assigned to you can be _____ or _____.
7. Notes assigned to contacts appear on the contact _____ page.

DISCUSSION

1. What might be considered the down side of assigning tasks?
2. Why would you want to assign a note to a contact?
3. How does assigning notes to contacts differ from assigning tasks?

GUIDED EXERCISES

1 FEELING THE POWER

Now that you know that you can use Outlook to create tasks for others, you might feel a power surge and decide you can use the tool to exercise that power. Let us see how it works by trying it out on your instructor. Follow these steps to give your instructor a due date for completing the grading of your last assignment.

1. Display the Calendar and double-click the TaskPad task entry bar.
2. Type Complete grading of last week's Outlook assignments in the **Subject** field.
3. Set a due date for the next class period and click the **Assign Task** button.
4. Add your instructor's e-mail address to the **To** field and click **Send**.

2 SELF-TASKING

Taking time to jot down all the little things that need to be accomplished during a given day can be well worthwhile. Marking them complete can be especially satisfying. Follow these steps to record a number of tasks:

1. Open the **Tasks** folder, click the **New Task** button on the toolbar, type Complete list of assigned tasks in the **Subject** field, select today's date in the **Due date** field, and save and close the task.
2. Repeat the procedures outlined in Step 1 to create new tasks for the tasks shown in Table 5-3.

Table 5-3 Tasks		
Task	**Due Date**	**Details**
Complete PowerPoint presentation for next week	Friday	
Send PowerPoint presentation for review to two associates	Friday	
Assign PowerPoint presentation review to two associates	Next Monday	Assign task to two classmates
Review presentation comments submitted by two associates and finalize the presentation	Next Tuesday	
Pick up bread on the way home	Today	Mark private

3 Mark the task *Complete list of assigned tasks* complete.

4 Create another new task, type **Meet with secretarial staff supervisor** in the **Subject** field, click the **Recurrence** button, and set the recurrence pattern for **Monthly** on the last Thursday of the month for 6 months.

5 Open the *Assign PowerPoint presentation review to two associates* task, click the **Assign** button, type the e-mail address of one of your classmates in the **To** field, and send the assignment.

6 Open the task assignment you receive from your classmate and click the **Accept** button to accept the task.

7 Click the Tasks Due Date column heading to sort the tasks by due date and print a copy of the list.

8 Open the assigned task you accepted, mark the task complete, send an update to the classmate who assigned it, and print a copy of the revised task list.

3 TRIP NOTES

Each trip you take requires preparation. Electronic notes provide a great tool for jotting down all the things you need to do to get ready for the trip. You have been working with a travel agent planning a trip to the Caribbean for the next school holiday and need to discuss with the agent several issues. Follow these directions to create a contact for the travel agent and record notes to discuss with the agent.

1 Click the **Contacts** button, click the **New Contact** button to open a new Contact form window, record the following information for the travel agent, and save and close the contact.
- Name: Ellen Reyborn
- Company: Aggie Travel Points
- Telephone Number: 202-555-8586
- E-mail Address: eReyborn@isp.com

2 Click the **Notes** icon on the Outlook Bar to open the Notes folder, click the **New Note** button, type **Find out what the weather will be like that time of year**, and close the note.

3 Repeat the procedures outlined in Step 2 to create individual notes containing the following text:
- Find out how many suitcases we are allowed.
- Check to see if American dollars are accepted.
- Try on summer clothing.
- Renew passport.
- Purchase sports equipment needed.

4 Open the electronic note **Find out what the weather will be like that time of year**, click the **Note menu** button to display the menu, and select Contacts.

5 Click the **Contacts** button and then click the **Contacts** folder, if necessary.

6 Select the listing for Ellen Reyborn from the **Items** list, and click **OK**.

7 Repeat the procedures outlined in Steps 4–6 to assign the *Find out how many suitcases we are allowed* and *Check to see if American dollars are accepted* notes to the same contact.

8 Choose **View | Current View | Notes List** to display a list of notes, press Ctrl + P to open the Print dialog box, select **Table** from the Style list, and print a copy of the notes.

9 Open the Contacts folder, open Ellen Reyborn's contact form, click the **Activities** tab, and print a copy of the activities.

ON YOUR OWN

> The difficulty of these case studies varies:
> ♩ are the least difficult; ♩♩ are more difficult; and ♩♩♩ are the most difficult.

1 ITSY-BITSY TASKS

♩ Sometimes, recording simple tasks in the TaskPad and setting a reminder is important to remind you to complete the simple task. Record a task to read an assignment for your classes and set a reminder for the day before the class for which the assignment is due. Then record a task to call your doctor or dentist to set up an appointment. Mark the task private. Print a copy of both tasks.

2 NOTING NOTABLES

♩ Notes provide a great way to jot down something you want to remember about a person. When you associate the note with a contact, it becomes even more valuable. Create a contact for one of your classmates, if you have not already done so. Then obtain information about the free evening schedule of the classmate. Create a note that lists the evenings the classmate is free and might be able to work on a project. Assign the note to the classmate's contact and print a copy.

3 THE GREAT PAYOFF

♩♩ Aren't paydays wonderful? Whether your payday reflects remuneration for a job well done or a check from home, letting Outlook remind you that it is payday can give you a lift. Record a *Don't forget—tomorrow's payday!* recurring task that occurs every two weeks on Saturday. Set the option to add the next occurrence to the task list for two weeks after you mark the previous occurrence complete. Set a reminder for the day before the appointment. Mark the first occurrence of the appointment complete and open the occurrence Outlook generates. Print a copy of the second occurrence.

4 FREE TASKING PROGRAMS

If you do not currently have a time management program such as Outlook on your home computer, you might be interested in searching for programs available from other companies and those that are offered free over the Internet. Search the Internet for time management products—both software and manual tools. Then create at least five new contacts containing information about the companies that offer free programs. Create separate notes to record the features of each program and assign the notes to the corresponding Contact. Print copies of the Notes List view and each company's contact Activities page. Change the note background color to dark gray and the font color to yellow and then forward the note containing the information about the program you like best to your instructor.

5 MULTITASKING TEST

The Board of Directors meeting is scheduled for two months from now. The list of tasks associated with planning a meeting can grow faster than you anticipate. As a result, it will often be necessary to distribute the tasks among others in your organization. Search the Web for information about planning a meeting, identify at least ten different tasks that must be accomplished and the timeline associated with performing each task. Then create a new folder named *Board of Directors Tasks*. Create a task list that records the tasks and use the timeline to determine the due date for each item. Sort the list of tasks by due date and print a copy of the tasks list in table format. Then assign at least one task to your class partner or a class group member. Accept the task assignment you receive from a classmate, sort the task list by subject, and print a copy of the revised task list.

Photospread credits pages 5-2 & 5-3
©Tony Stone: ©David Arky, ©Fisher/Thatcher; ©FPG: ©VCG 1998; ©Pearson Education; and ©Lorraine Castellano

PROJECT 6

Managing Outlook Files, Folders, and the Journal

Microsoft Outlook 2002 is known as a personal desktop organizer because of its unique capabilities for helping you organize and associate information from each Outlook feature with information contained in other Outlook features. How effectively you monitor computer activities depends, to a certain extent, on how efficiently you maintain your Outlook folders. In this project, you will learn how to use categories to manage Outlook items, create rules to manage folder items, create associations between items in different Outlook folders, track activities, and archive outdated items.

OBJECTIVES

After completing this project, you will be able to:

- Create and assign categories to items
- Sort items by categories
- Customize Outlook views
- Create rules to organize Outlook items
- Create associations between Outlook items and contacts
- Use the Journal
- Archive items

e-selections   Running Case

As an employee of e-Selections, you are finding that staying organized and maintaining up-to-date information through communication and time management is extremely important. Connecting different pieces of information to time management items and maintaining contacts is getting tougher as you delve more deeply into your job. Because of your computer class, you are staying one step ahead of the time management game. You are about to take one giant leap forward in managing Outlook information.

Help! I'm Being Attacked!

Recently, I experienced a rash of attacks on my home computer—attacks by people and places I've never heard of! I couldn't figure out why I was being attacked. All I knew was that, every once in a while, a little icon that usually sat quietly on my systray (the right end of my taskbar) would light up and start flashing. Then a window would pop open in the middle of my screen and display what looked like a robot dangling a bug from the end of its claws.

Now I don't have any national secrets stored on my computer, so why would someone want to attack it? The simple answer—because they can! And what's more, there are now virus writing kits on the market that make it easy to create new viruses and distribute them seamlessly to unsuspecting victims.

Common Virus Types

Since the advent of virus writing kits, there are typically three different types of viruses used to infect computers:

- **Worms,** such as the Anna virus, designed to spread through your computer system to attack and damage files.
- **Viruses,** such as the I Love You virus that hit more than 45 million computers, spread through e-mail programs, uploading, and downloading via the Internet.
- **Trojan horses,** more sophisticated programs that masquerade as seemingly innocent applications can be used to let hackers enter, search, and manipulate the computer system through the Internet.

Planning Protection

The marketplace is loaded with software products designed to help keep your computer safe from attack and invasion. Before deciding what product is best for you, consider these important factors:

- The operating system you're using. Protection products are geared to different types of operating systems—such

Protection products are geared to different operating systems

Don't let them succeed with attacks on your computer!

as Windows, Macintosh, or Linux. Most attack programs are designed to infiltrate computers using the Windows operating system.

- The type of Internet connection you have—broadband cable, DSL, or dial-up. Computers are only vulnerable when you are connected to the Internet, so broadband cable users who stay connected all the time are most vulnerable.

- Internet Protocol (IP) addresses can affect vulnerability. Internet Service Providers usually control a specific series of IP addresses that they distribute to users as they connect. By staying connected all the time, broadband cable users maintain the same IP address and become sitting targets.

Getting Protected

You can protect your computer against invasion using a simple approach of caution and protective software. On the caution side, experts shout, "Don't open suspicious e-mail attachments or messages from people unknown to you!" On the software side, consider the following:

- **Anti-virus software**—which detect and remove most viruses—should be installed on all networked computers—both dial-up and broadband connections. The programs check system files when you boot up and monitor the system continuously for virus-like activity. You should update your anti-virus software frequently to cover new viruses.

- **Firewall programs**—mainly for broadband connections—are effective against Trojan horses and prevent unauthorized access to computers by blocking data ports—the ports through which information passes between the computer and the Internet.

You can also install a number of hardware components to help protect your system—hardware that comes with no written guarantee, of course. I took the precautions recommended by the experts, so my system was protected against the invasions I experienced. Don't let them succeed with their attacks on your computer. Take the necessary precautions!

PROJECT 6

Managing Outlook Files, Folders, and the Journal

The Setup

Tasks you completed in previous projects, as well as the exercises and activities you have used Outlook to accomplish, affect what items are listed in your Outlook folders. As you complete the steps in this project, items pictured in the Figures may be different from those you see on your screen. In addition, customizations made to toolbars and other onscreen features may also be different. Items in Outlook folders should have no effect on Task steps required to complete the objectives.

The Challenge

Ms. Amber Wright, e-Administration Manager, was extremely pleased with your report that outlined some of the features and functions available in Outlook e-mail. She has assigned you the task of exploring and reporting on other tools that make managing information and associating Outlook items with other Outlook information more efficient.

The Solution

You have already learned a number of functions that you can include in your report to Ms. Wright. Advanced topics covered in the next few classes you take at the college will help you identify other features and functions that will be important to you and other e-Selections employees.

Creating and Assigning Categories to Items

Outlook comes with a default set of categories that enable you to group items—contacts, tasks, appointments, messages, and so on—from within Outlook folders to specific categories. By categorizing items, you can store them in their original folders yet display them in groups by category.

Assigning Categories to Outlook Items

The Categories field appears on the form for most Outlook items. You can assign a category to an Outlook item by typing the category in the Category field or by displaying the Master Category List and selecting the category or categories you want to assign to the item.

Task 1:
To Create New Categories and Assign Categories to Items

1 Open the **Contacts** folder and double-click the contact title bar for **Sam Togej** to open the contact.

Troubleshooting
If you have not yet created a contact for Sam Togej, create one using the information displayed in Figure 6-1.

2 Click in the **Categories** text box, type **Class Files**, save and close the contact.

3 Click the Outlook Bar **Notes** icon, click the **New Note** button to create a new note, and type **Send an agenda to Sam Togej**.

4 Click the Note menu button and select **Categories**.

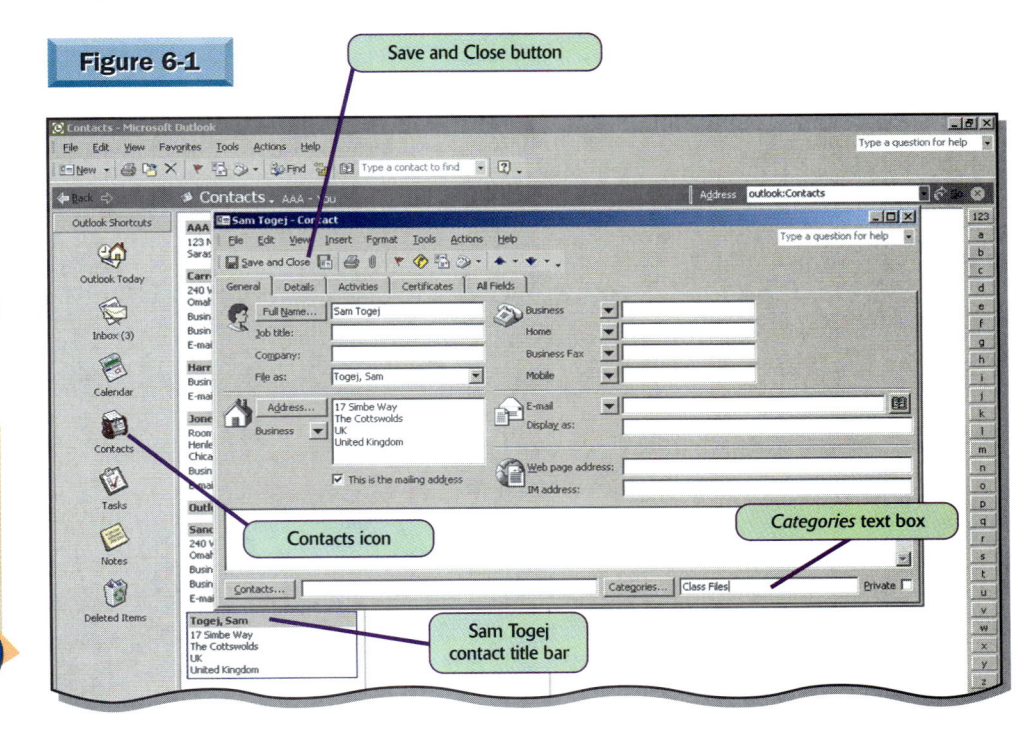

Figure 6-1

Callouts: Save and Close button; Contacts icon; Sam Togej contact title bar; Categories text box

Tip Outlook does not add category names you type in the Categories text box to the Master Category List.

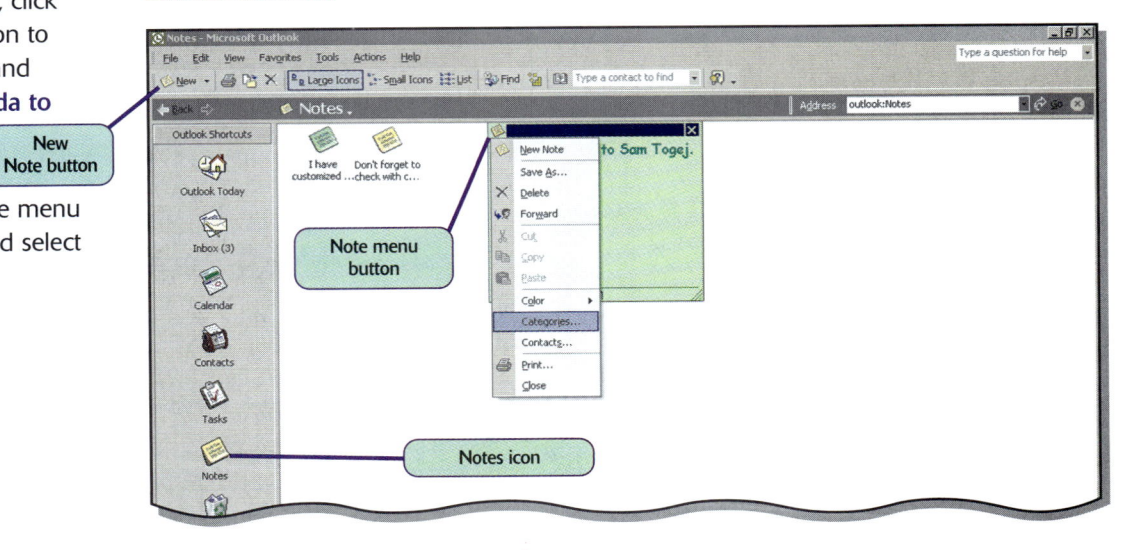

Figure 6-2

Callouts: New Note button; Note menu button; Notes icon

Creating and Assigning Categories to Items

5 Type **Class Files** in the **Item(s) belong to these categories** box and click **Add to List**.

Figure 6-3

> **Tip** Category names are not case sensitive—Outlook would consider *Class Files* and *class files* the same category.

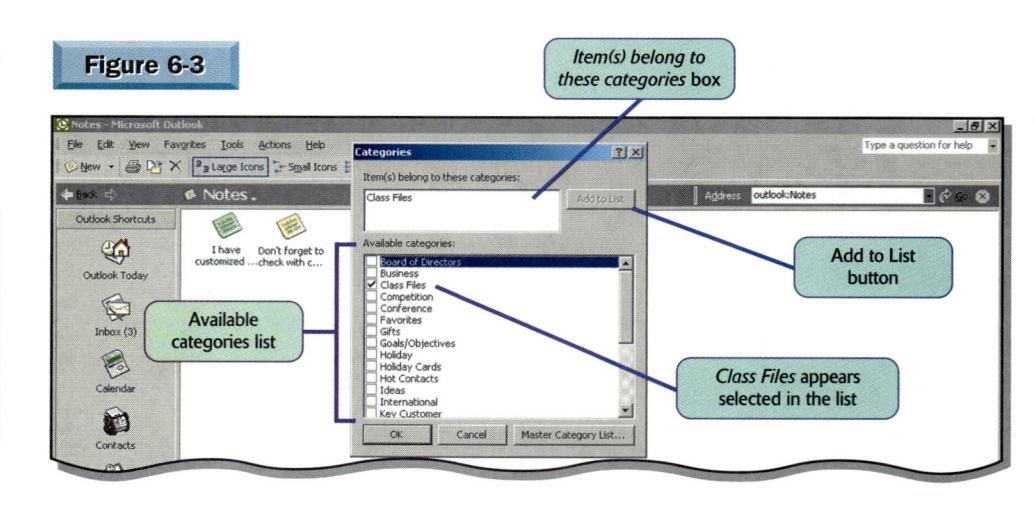

6 Click **OK** and close the note.

> **Tip** *Class Files* appears in the **Available categories** list after you click the **Add to List** button.

7 Switch to the **Inbox**, right-click a message from your instructor to display the shortcut menu, and select **Categories** to open the Categories dialog box.

Figure 6-4

8 Select the **Class Files** category and click **OK** to apply the category to the message.

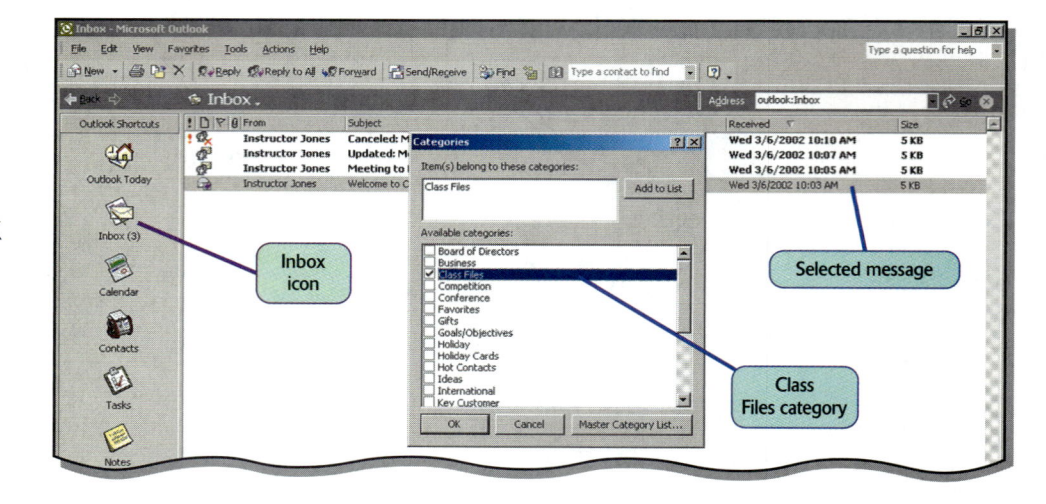

9 Click the **Calendar** icon on the Outlook bar, move to **April 2003** using the Date Navigator, select **April 8**, and enter the appointment shown in Figure 6-5.

Figure 6-5

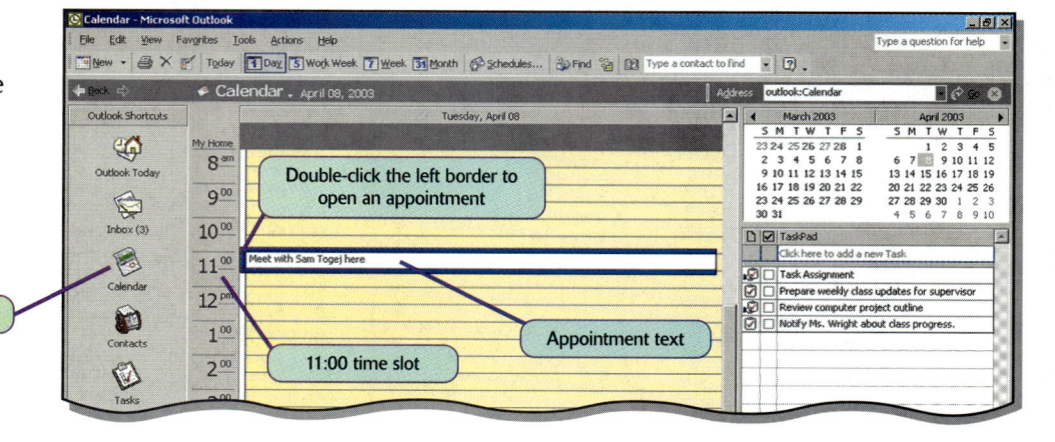

Managing Outlook Files, Folders, and the Journal

10 Open the appointment, click the **Categories** button, select the **Class Files** category check box, click **OK**, and save and close the appointment.

Figure 6-6

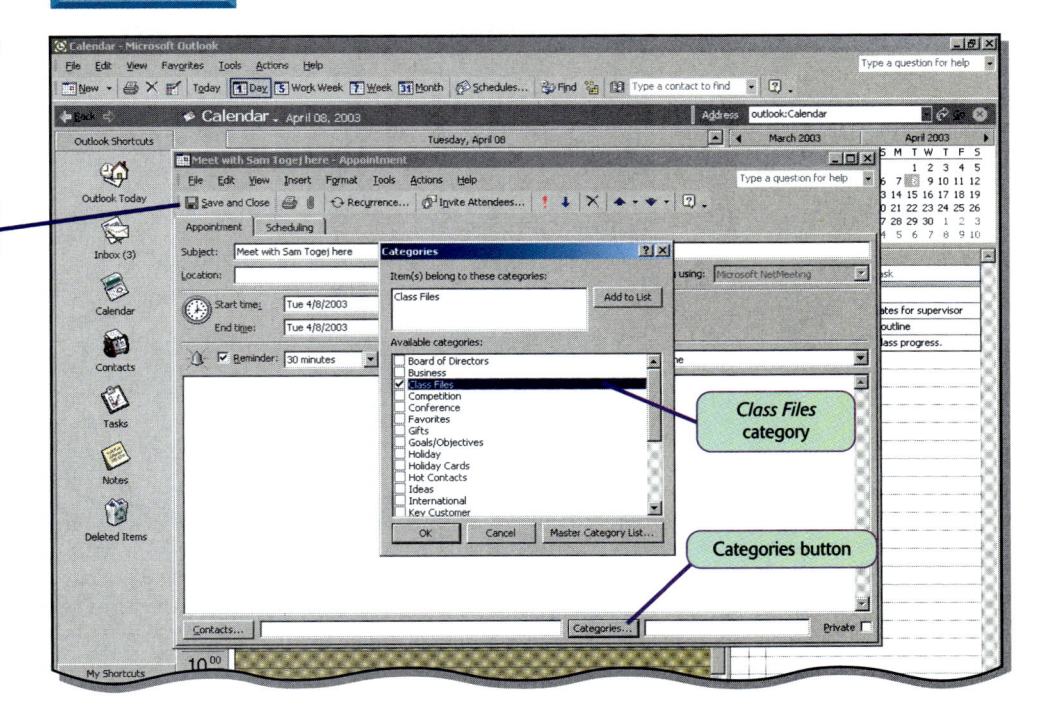

Save and Close button

Class Files category

Categories button

11 Click the **TaskPad** task entry bar, type **Prepare for meeting with Sam Togej**, and press Enter.

12 Right-click the task you just typed to display the shortcut menu, select **Categories** to open the Categories dialog box, select **Class Files**, and click **OK**.

Figure 6-7

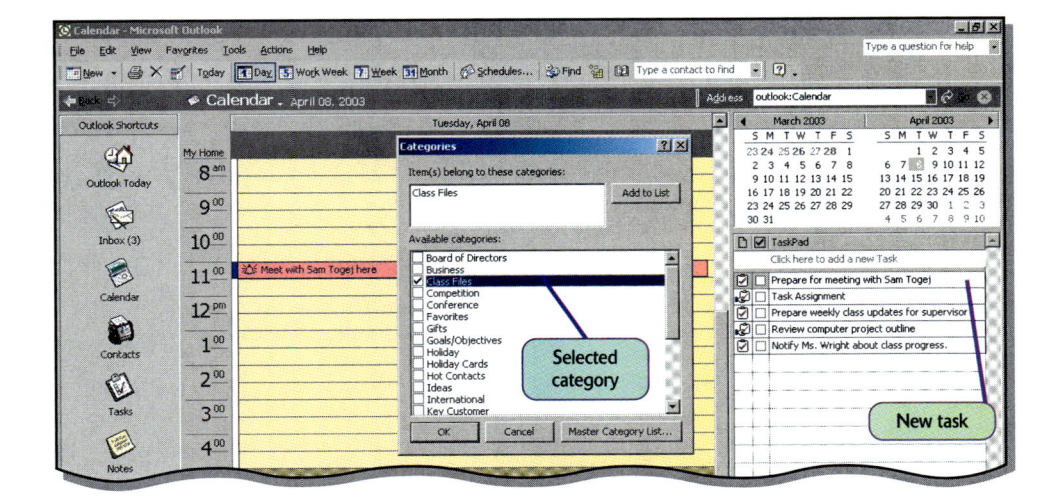

Selected category

New task

Modifying the Master Category List

The list of categories that comes with Outlook provides a good base of generic categories. However, many users will want to personalize the *Master Category List* to meet their specific needs. Outlook allows you to both add and remove categories from the Master Category List. You can modify the Master Category List by assigning categories to items as you did when you assigned the *Class List* category to the note in Task 1 or go directly to the Master Category List and create additional categories without assigning the categories to a particular item.

Task 2:
To Modify the Master Category List

1 Click the Outlook Bar **Inbox** icon and choose **Edit | Categories** to open the Categories dialog box.

2 Click the **Master Category List** button to open the Master Category List dialog box.

3 Type **Board of Directors** in the **New category** text box and click **Add**.

4 Repeat the procedures outlined in Step 3 to add the following categories: **Conference**, **Workshop**, **Family Activities**.

5 Select the **Family Activities** category and click **Delete** to remove the category from the Master Category List.

> **Tip** New categories appear alphabetically in the Categories list.

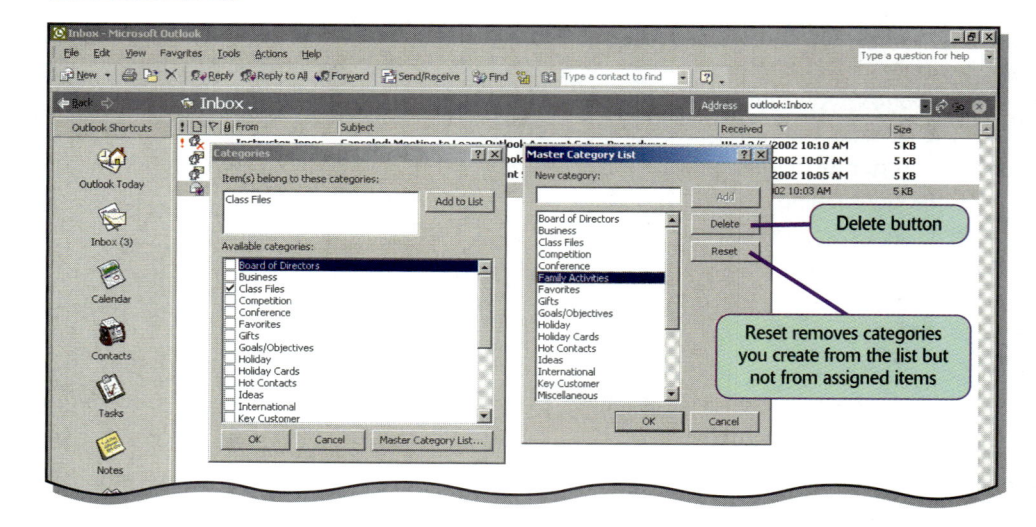

6 Repeat the procedures outlined in Step 5 to delete the **Board of Directors** category and then click **OK** twice to close the dialog boxes.

Figure 6-8

New category text box

Inbox icon

Add button

Master Category List button

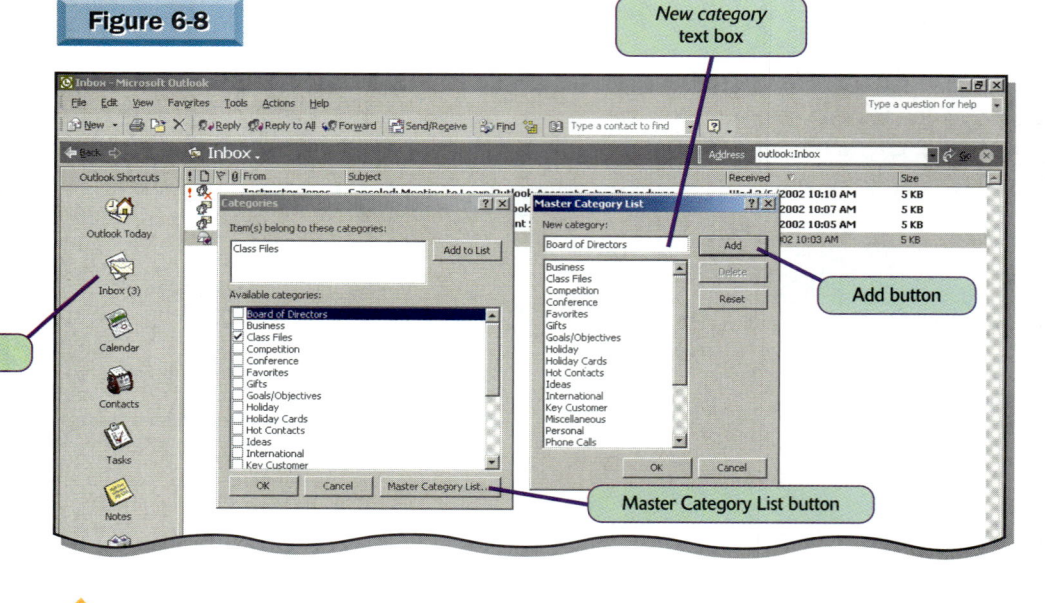

> **Troubleshooting** The **Categories** command is only available when an Outlook item—a message, note, appointment, and so forth—is selected. When the Inbox is open, a message is automatically selected. As a result, opening the Inbox ensures that an item (in this case, a message) was selected and that the *Categories* command was available.

Figure 6-9

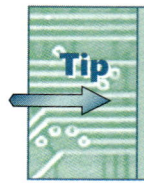

Delete button

Reset removes categories you create from the list but not from assigned items

> **Tip** *Reset* removes user-created categories from the Master Categories list and restores all original items to the list. *Delete* removes selected categories from the list. Personal categories applied to existing items are unaffected by *Reset* and *Delete*.

Managing Outlook Files, Folders, and the Journal

OU 6-9

WEB TIP

Did you know that computer viruses, like the flu, can greatly reduce productivity and cost companies billions of dollars? Scientists have analyzed the statistical incidence of hundreds of computer viruses and found that they live much longer than current theories predict—in some cases up to three years! Be sure to update your virus databases regularly by logging on to the virus product Web site and downloading the latest vaccines.

Sorting Items by Category

After assigning categories to Outlook items, you can sort items within a folder by category. In addition, you can search multiple folders by category using the *Find* feature.

Task 3: To Sort and Find Items by Category

1 Open the **Contacts** folder and choose **View | Current View | By Category** to change the folder view.

Figure 6-10

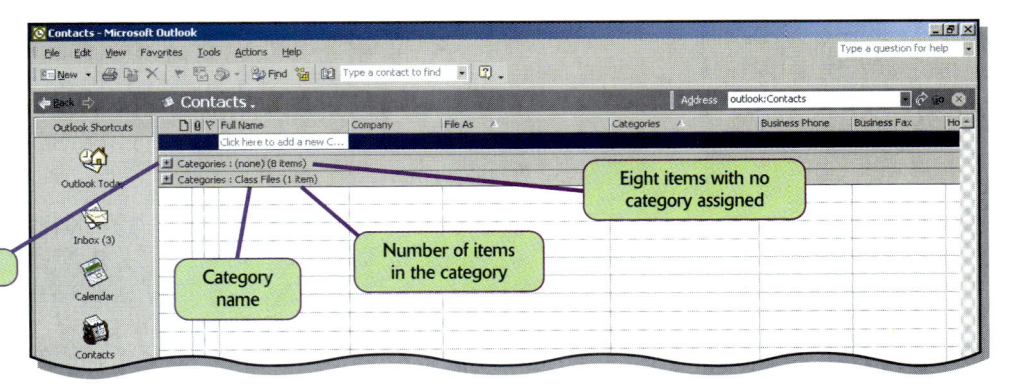

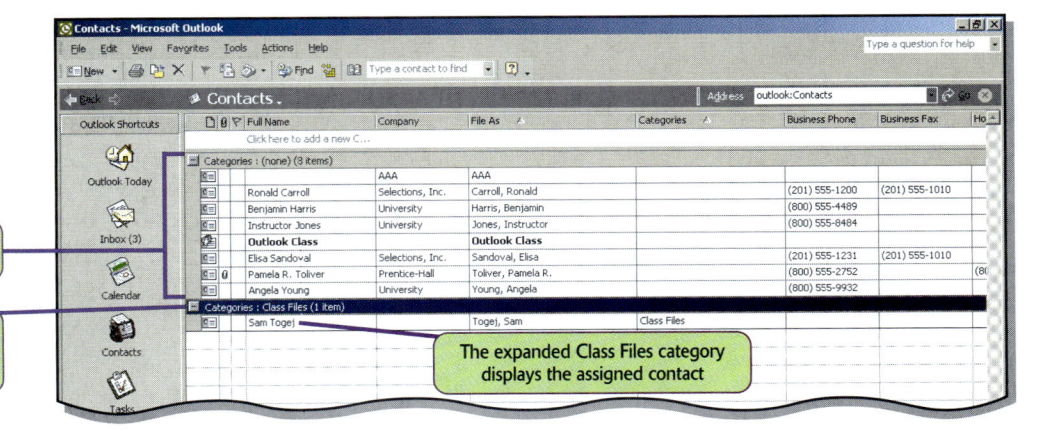

- Expand button
- Category name
- Number of items in the category
- Eight items with no category assigned

2 Click the Expand (+) button on the **Class Files** category bar and on the **(none)** category bar.

3 Review items listed below each category and then choose **View | Current View | Address Cards** to restore the default view.

Figure 6-11

- Contact items without assigned categories
- Expand button changes to the Collapse button
- The expanded Class Files category displays the assigned contact

Sorting Items by Category

4 Choose **Tools | Advanced Find** to open the Advanced Find dialog box.

5 Click the **Look for** down arrow, select **Any type of Outlook item**, and click the **More Choices** tab.

> **Tip** A message box may appear warning you that your actions will clear other search options. Click **OK** to clear the all search options or click **Cancel** to maintain the search and then manually edit search options individually.

Figure 6-12

6 Click the **Categories** button, select the **Class Files** check box from the category list, click **OK**, and click the **Find Now** button.

> **Tip** After Outlook locates items with Class Files as the category, you can double-click the item to open it directly from the Advanced Find dialog box.

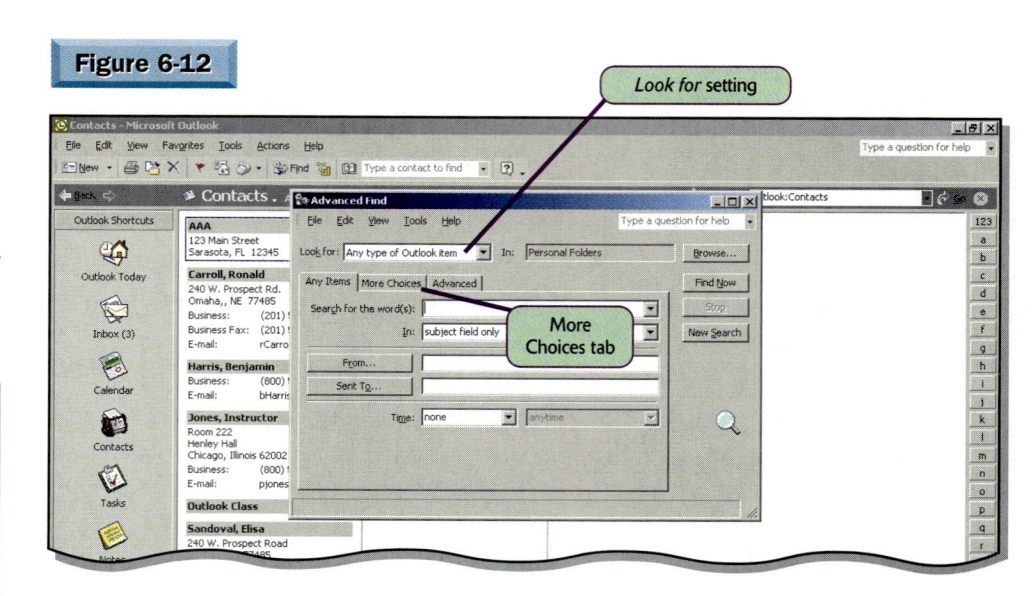

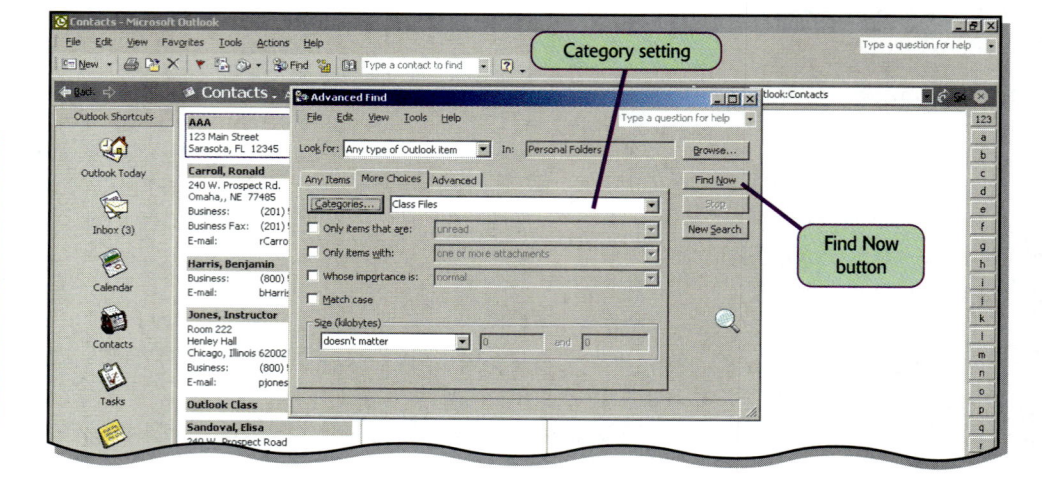

Figure 6-13

Managing Outlook Files, Folders, and the Journal

OU 6-**11**

7 Close the **Advanced Find** dialog box.

Tip You may need to maximize the **Advanced Find** window to display all the items.

Figure 6-14

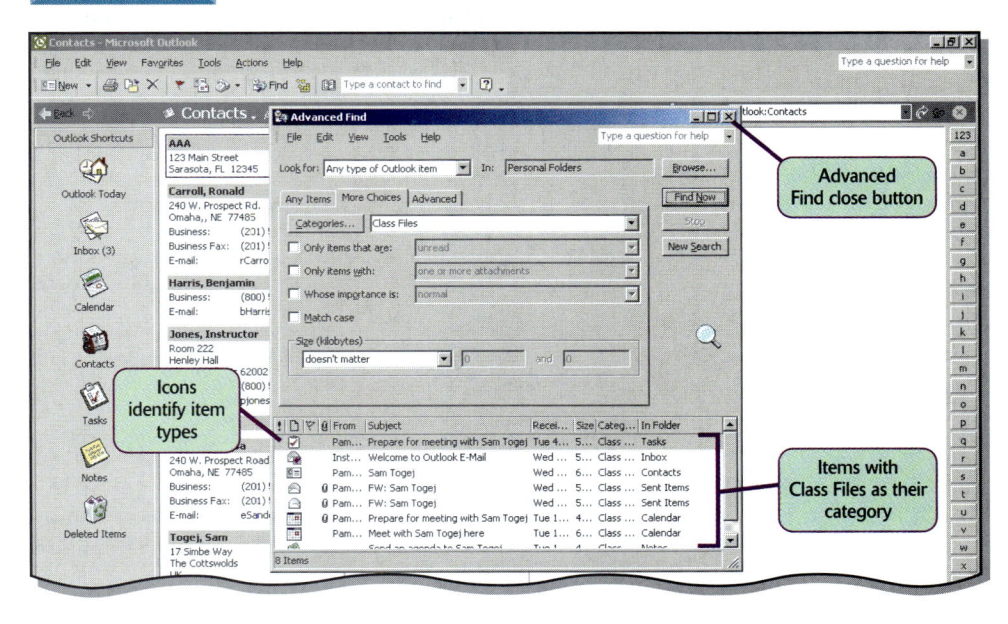

Customizing Outlook Views

The Current View list is a great way to filter Outlook folders to limit the items displayed to those you want to review, such as a list of items by a specific category or overdue items, and so forth. By using standard views available in each Outlook folder, you can display such items as active appointments, past due tasks, and new messages, simply by changing the view. When you have few items in a folder, filtering the view displays little difference. As the number of items in each folder grows, however, there will be times when you want to customize the folder view by filtering it, specifying the fields you want to include in the view, changing the arrangement of fields on screen, and so forth. The View Summary dialog box contains groups of tools that will help you customize views. Each group of tools found in the View Summary dialog box is described in Table 6-1.

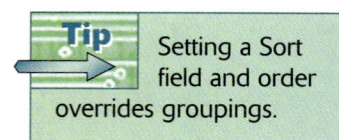

Tip Setting a Sort field and order overrides groupings.

Table 6-1 View Summary Tool Groups

Group	Tools and Uses
Fields	Select fields to appear in the view and the order in which they will appear
Group By	Select the items or fields to group items by. For example, you could group all messages in the Inbox by sender. When a group by field is set, group bars identify each separate group. You can display or hide items in each group by clicking the Expand (+) or Collapse (-) button.
Sort	Set the field on which you want to sort items in a folder and the order—ascending or descending—in which you want to sort them.
Filter	Set criteria, such as dates on which messages were received, contacts associated with specific companies, and so forth, to display only the items in the folder that meet the criteria.
Other Settings	Set font and style formatting for onscreen items such as row and column headings and grid lines.
Automatic Formatting	Set formatting for folder items such as *unread messages* in the Inbox, overdue or completed tasks, distribution list items, and folder-specific items.

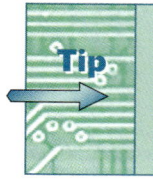

Tip The Current View list contains different views for each Outlook folder. However, you will use the same techniques to customize current views for the Calendar, Tasks, and Contacts that you use to customize the current Inbox view.

Task 4:
To Customize Outlook Folder Views

Figure 6-15

① Open the **Inbox** folder and choose **View | Current View | Customize Current View** to open the View Summary dialog box.

② Click the **Fields** button.

Tip Options and fields available in the View Summary dialog box vary depending on the folder that is open—Inbox, Contacts, Notes, and so forth—and the current view.

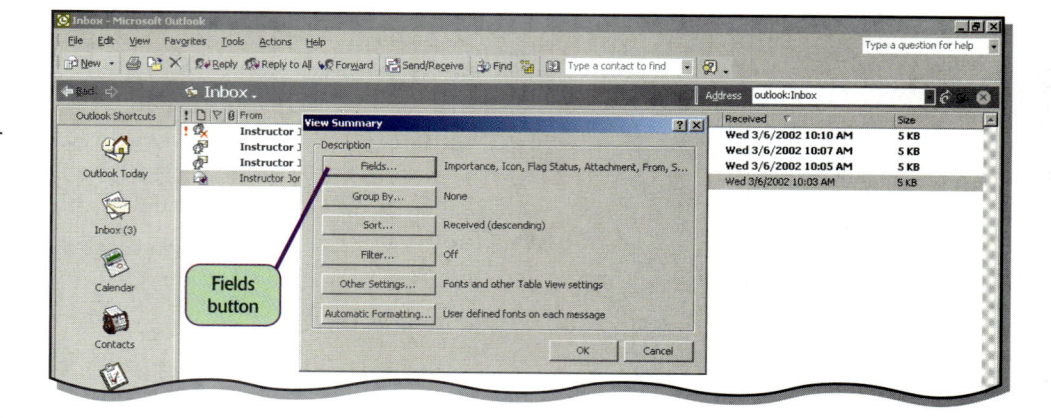

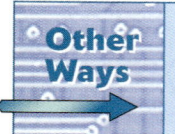

Other Ways
To display the View Summary dialog box:
- Scroll the window to display a blank area, right-click a blank area of the window, and select **Customize Current View**.

Managing Outlook Files, Folders, and the Journal   OU 6-13

3 Select the **Attachment** field in the **Show these fields in this order** list and click the **Move Down** button once to reposition the field.

4 Select the **Categories** field in the **Available fields** list, click **Add**, click the **Move Down** button until the field appears after **Received**, and click **OK** twice.

Troubleshooting
If you click the **Move Down** button too many times and the fields are out of order, click the **Move Up** button to position them correctly.

5 Review columns displayed in the Inbox.

6 Choose **View | Current View | Customize Current View** to open the View Summary dialog box again and click the **Other Settings** button.

7 Click the **Column Headings Font** button and select the font settings displayed in Figure 6-18 to change the font to 10 pt Tahoma bold, and click **OK** twice to return to the View Summary dialog box.

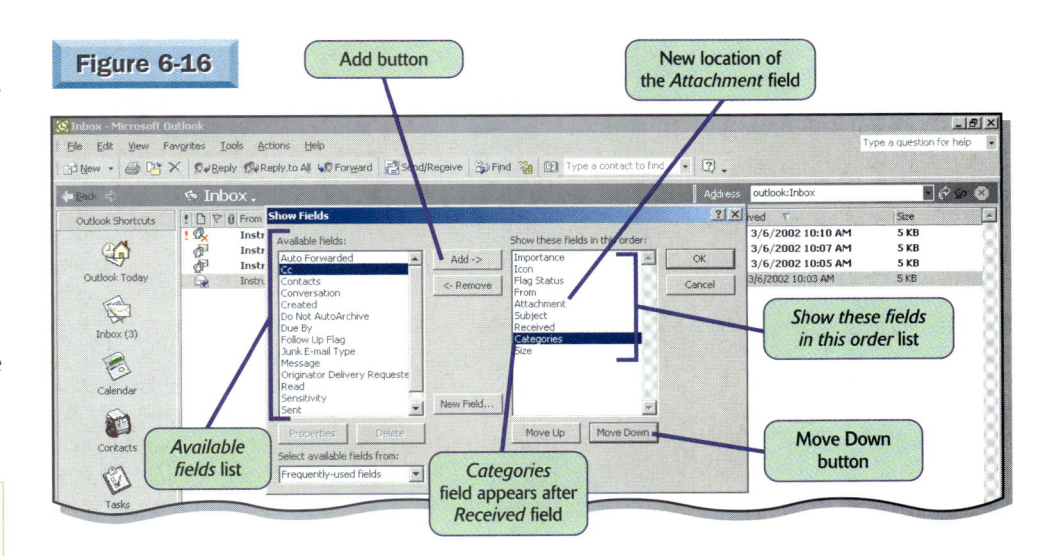

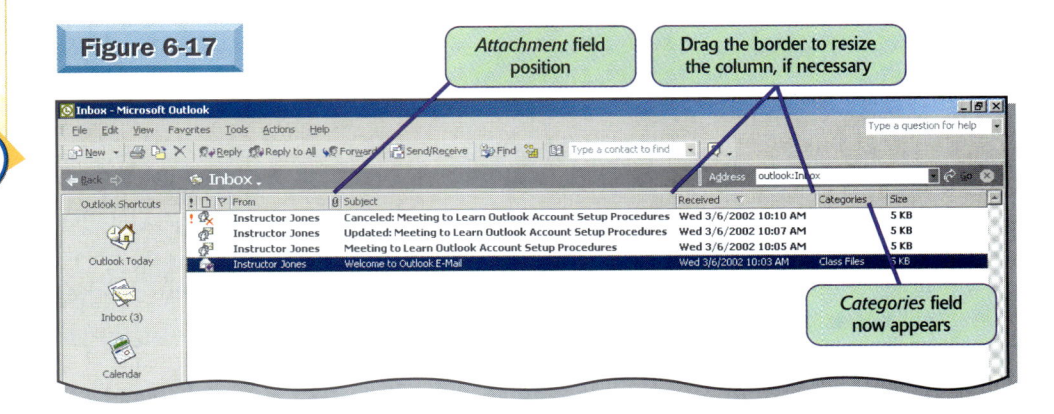

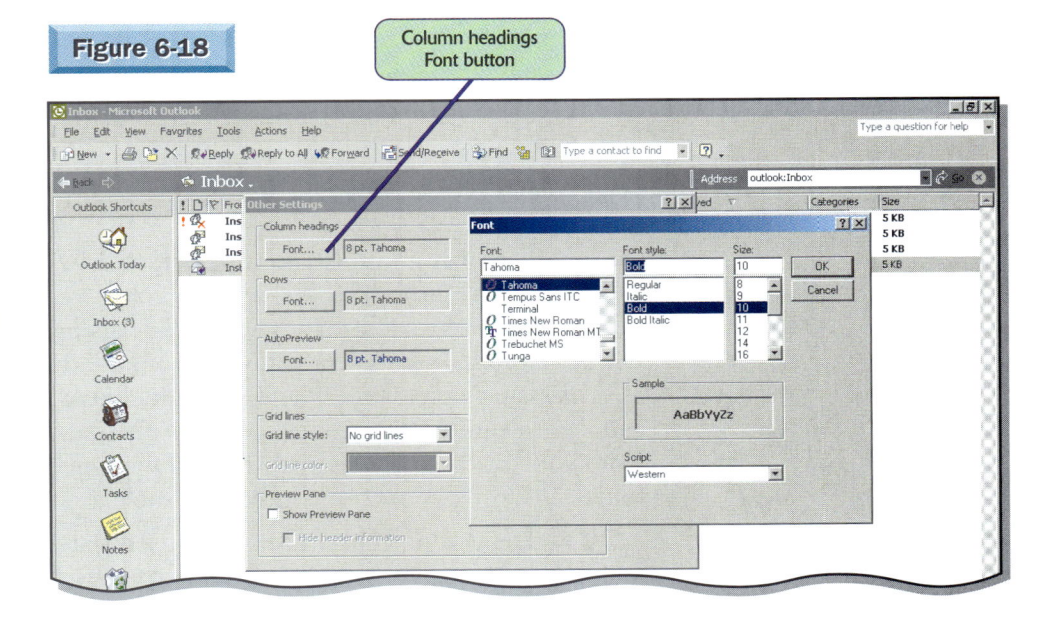

Figure 6-16

Figure 6-17

Figure 6-18

Tip: Font changes will be applied after you close the View Summary dialog box.

8 Click the **Filter** button and click the **More Choices** tab.

9 Click the **Size (kilobytes)** down arrow, select **between**, type the values shown in Figure 6-19 in the value boxes, and click **OK** twice.

Figure 6-19 — More Choices tab, Size setting, Value boxes

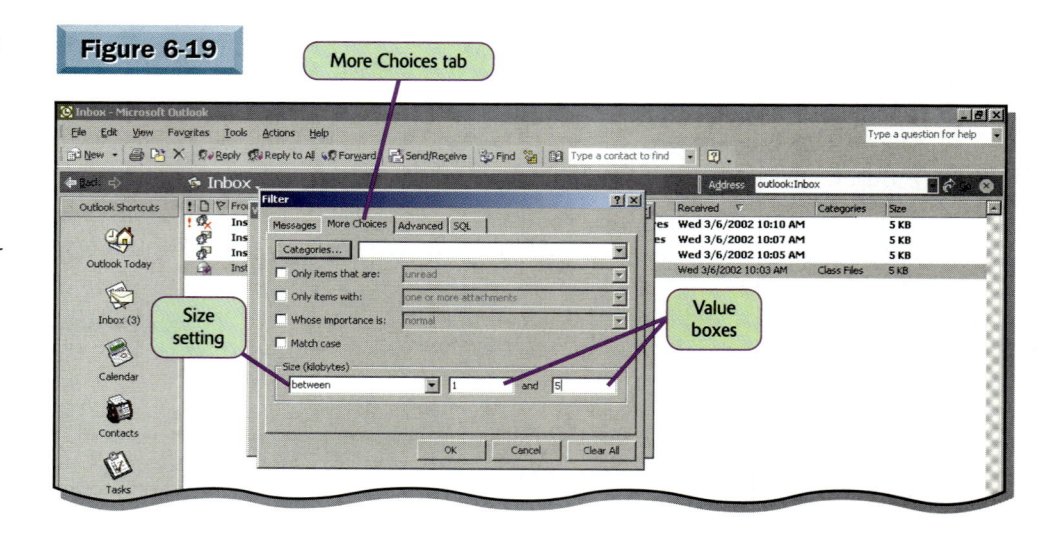

Tip Filtering messages using the value boxes displays only those messages that are between the size specifications you set.

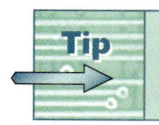

10 Choose **View** | **Current View** | **Customize Current View**, click the **Filter** button, click the **Clear All** button in the lower right corner of the dialog box, and then click **OK** twice to restore the view.

Figure 6-20 — Message list is filtered

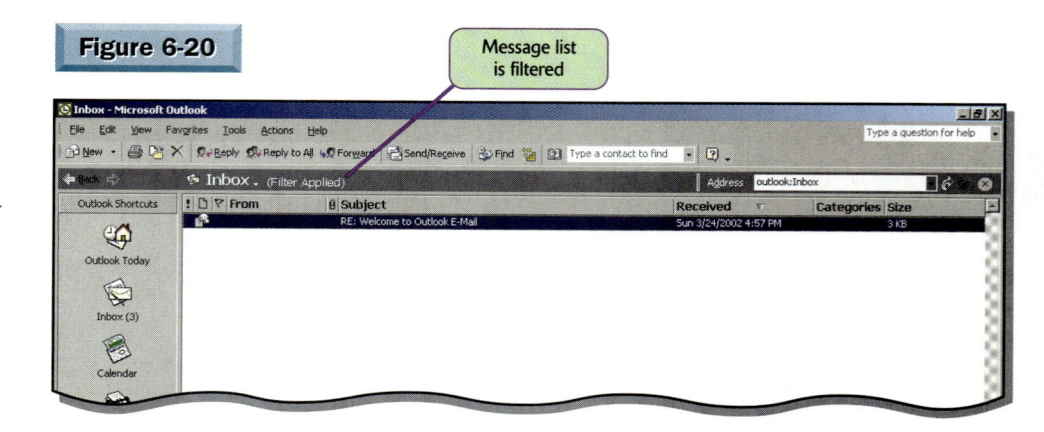

Creating Rules to Organize Outlook Items

Outlook contains a number of different tools that you can use to sift through items in your Outlook folders. You have already identified a few of these tools—categories, customizing views, and using advanced find—all tools that you manipulate manually. Outlook also contains tools that enable you to create *rules* that determine when Outlook should perform an action automatically. For example, you could create a rule that would color code all messages from your instructor when you receive them or send items to specific Outlook folders. The two most frequently used tools are as follows:

- The Outlook Organize tool is used to manually perform common tasks such as moving items to specific folders and creating rules that make decisions and perform actions based on criteria.
- The *Rules Wizard* assists you in creating and building rules to accomplish customized and complex tasks.

Using the Organize Tool

Features that appear in the *Organize pane* vary depending on the folder that is open. Table 6-2 provides an overview of the different tools displayed in the Organize pane for major Outlook folders.

Table 6-2	Organize Pane Tools
Folder	**Available Tools**
Inbox	Using Folders, Colors, and Views Setting Items as *Junk E-mail*
Calendar	Using Categories and Views
Contacts	Using Folders, Categories, and Views
Tasks	Using Folders, Categories, and Views
Notes	Using Folders and Views

Using the Organize tool to perform common tasks such as color coding messages and sending messages to specific folders will reduce the amount of time you spend trying to stay organized.

Task 5:
To Color Code Messages and Move Items to Folders

1 Open the **Tasks** folder, select the *Prepare for meeting with Sam Togej* task, and click the Organize button to open the Ways to Organize Tasks pane.

2 Click **Using Folders**.

3 Click the **Move task selected below to** down arrow, select **Calendar**, and click **Move**.

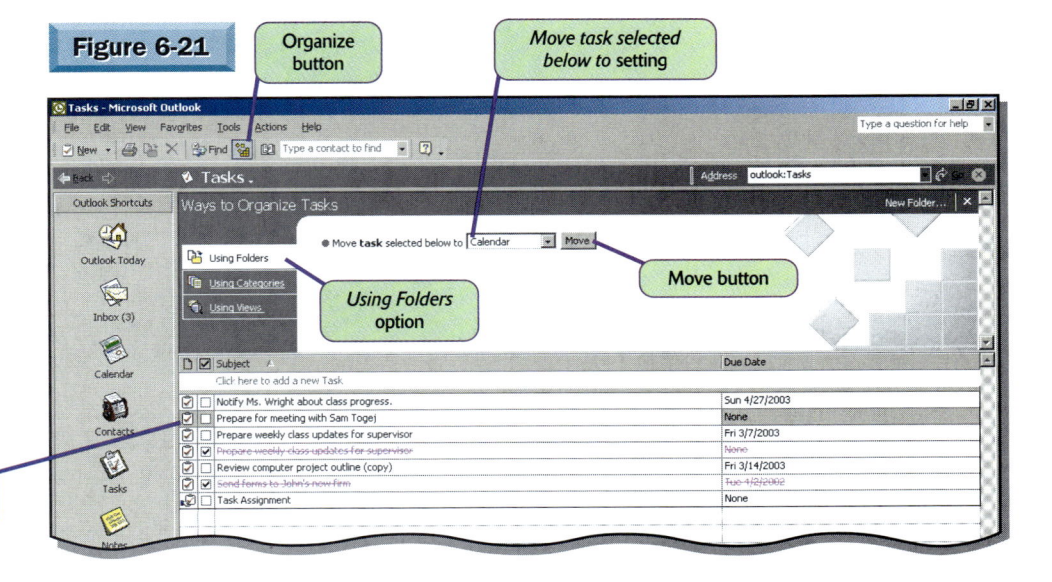

Figure 6-21

4 Enter the information and set the options shown in Figure 6-22, then save and close the appointment.

Figure 6-22

Tip Notice that the *Prepare for meeting with Sam Togej* task is no longer in the task pane. It appears in the Calendar folder.

The task appears in the notes area of the appointment dialog box

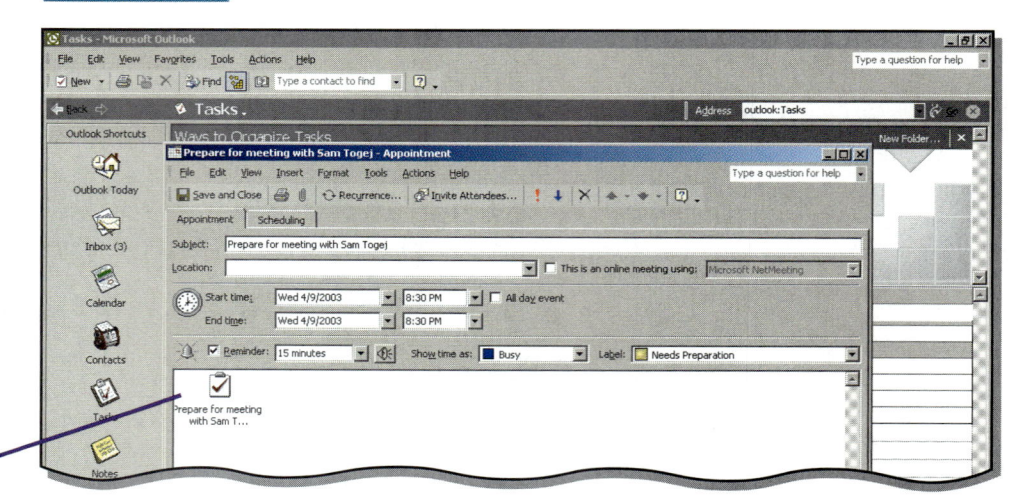

Tip The Organize pane closes when you switch to a different Outlook feature. As a result, you will have to click the **Organize** button each time you change to a different folder.

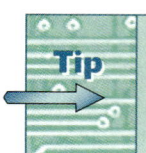

5 Open the **Inbox** folder, click the Organize button, and click the **Using Folders** link, if necessary.

Figure 6-23

Organize button

Using Folders link

Create a rule setting

Create button

Folder to send the message to

6 Select a message from one of your classmates, click the **Create a rule** down arrow and select **from**, ensure that the correct sender's name appears in the next text box, select your personal name folder from the text box list, and click **Create**.

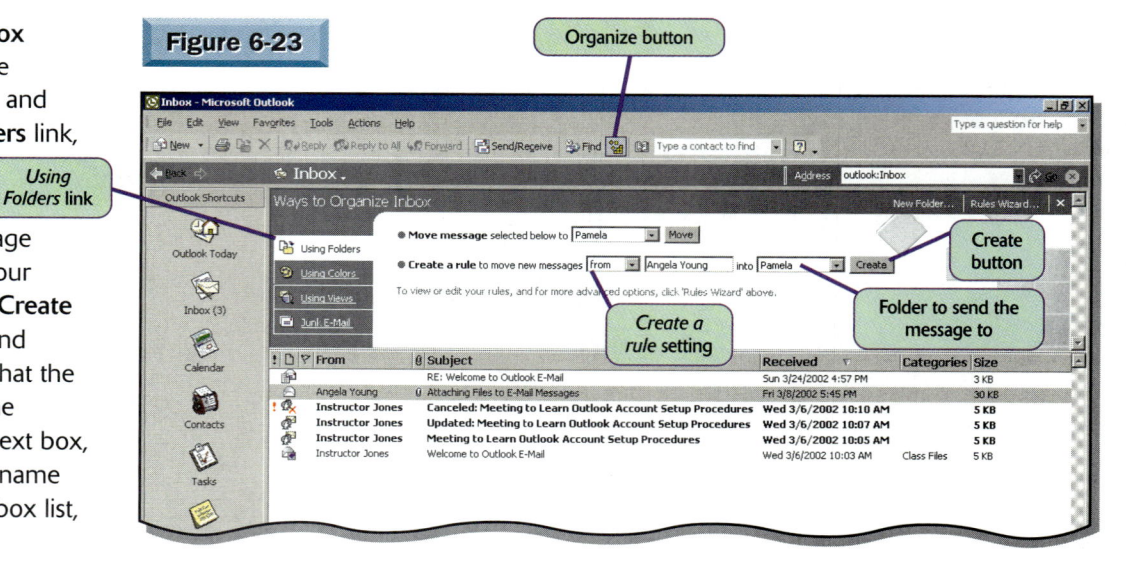

Troubleshooting If you have not yet created a personal folder, create a new Mail folder named *Your First Name* or follow your instructor's directions to determine where to place the items.

Managing Outlook Files, Folders, and the Journal

OU 6-17

7 Click **Yes** to run the rule on the contents of the folder.

Figure 6-24

Tip After this rule is created, all new e-mail messages you receive from the selected classmate will automatically be moved to the folder you selected.

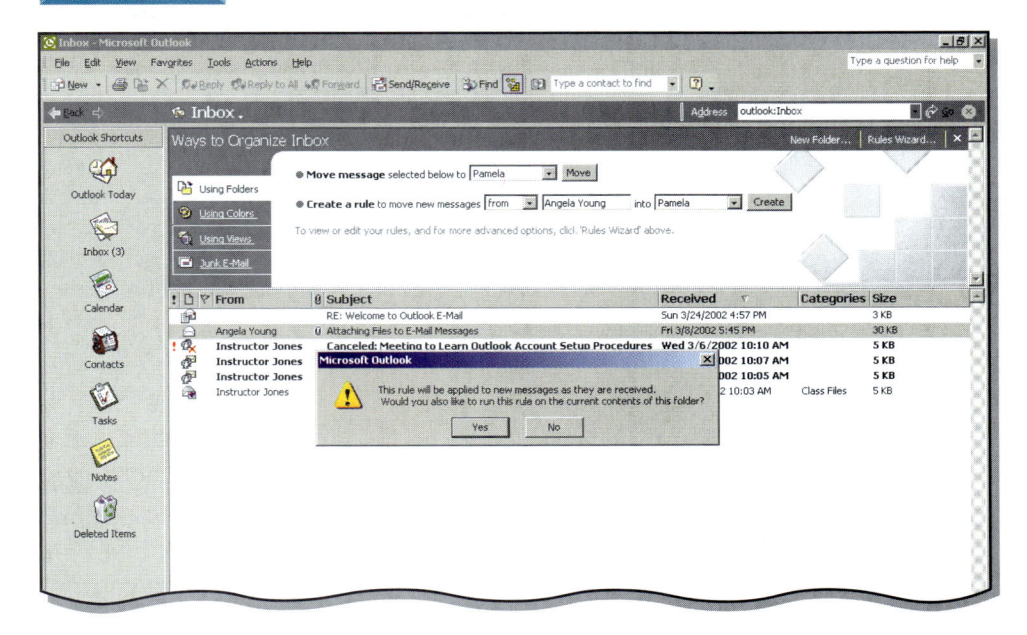

8 Click the **Using Colors** link in the Organize pane, select a message from your instructor, and select the settings shown in Figure 6-25, changing the color to the one you prefer.

Figure 6-25

9 Click **Apply Color** to display all messages from your instructor in the selected color.

Rule refers to messages from your instructor

10 Click the Organize button to close the Organize pane.

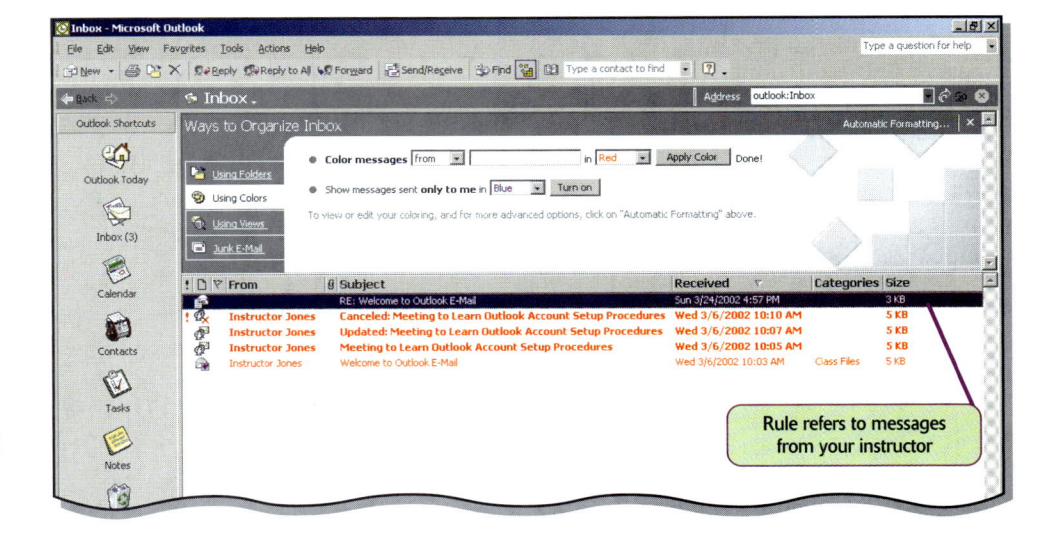

Tip After you create rules to color code messages from specific senders, all new messages that arrive from the senders will appear in the selected color.

CHECK POINT

It did not take long for "bulk mailers" to discover how they could save money by using e-mail to distribute their "business mail." As a result, program developers have initiated an automated way for you to move items from specific senders to the Junk Mail folder. Open the Inbox and select a message from the sender you want to add to the Junk Mail folder. Right-click on the message and select **Junk E-mail | Add to Junk Senders list**. After adding the sender to the junk e-mail list, all messages you receive from the sender will automatically be move to the Junk Mail folder. In addition, you can select messages containing Adult Content and send them to the Junk Mail folder using the same techniques.

WEB TIP

Did you know that Web portals are now able to notify subscribers each time a new message or a change is posted to specific Web sites and portals? Web portals have now been implemented by many corporations and agencies to help keep constituents up to date on corporate or agency happenings. Search the Internet for information about Web portals to learn more about how they are being used.

Creating Rules Using the Rules Wizard

The rule you created using the Organize pane is similar to the rules you can create using the Rules Wizard. However, the Rules Wizard enables you to set a number of different options for organizing e-mail messages. The following steps are required to build rules in Outlook:

1. Tell Outlook that you want to create a new rule.
2. Determine whether you want to create a rule using a template or start from scratch.
3. Set conditions that must be met for the rule to be applied.
4. Specify the action that should be taken when the conditions are met.
5. Identify exceptions to the rule.
6. Name the rule and turn it on.

Managing Outlook Files, Folders, and the Journal

OU 6-19

Task 6:
To Create an Inbox Rule Using the Rules Wizard

Figure 6-26

1 Open the Inbox folder, if necessary, and choose **Tools** | **Rules Wizard** to open the first Rules Wizard dialog box.

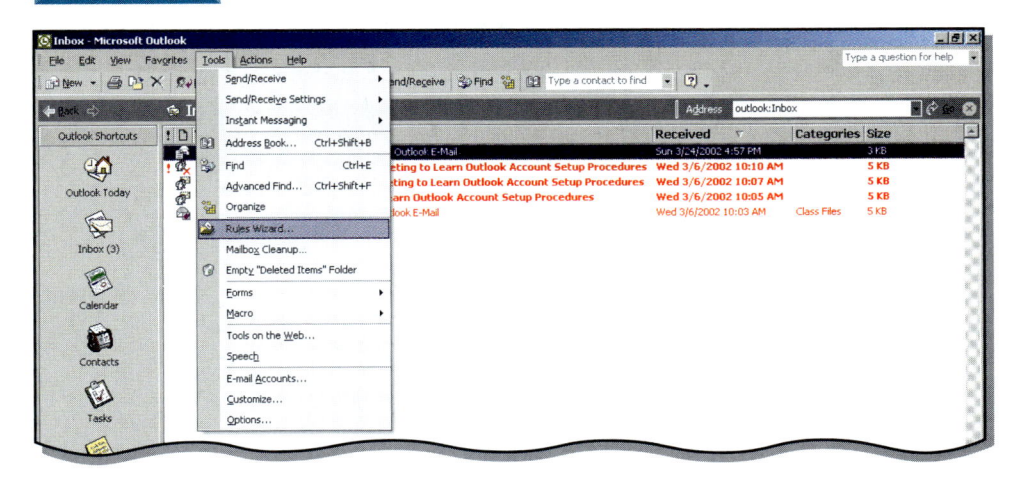

2 Click **New** to open the next Rules Wizard dialog box.

Figure 6-27

- Start creating a rule from a template option
- New button
- Existing rules created using Organize
- Selected rule description
- Template from which the rule will be created
- Template actions appear in the *Rule description* area

> **Troubleshooting**
> If the Office Assistant opens and offers help, click **No, don't provide help now** to close the Assistant.

3 Select the **Start creating a rule from a template** option and select **Notify me when important messages arrive** from the list of actions.

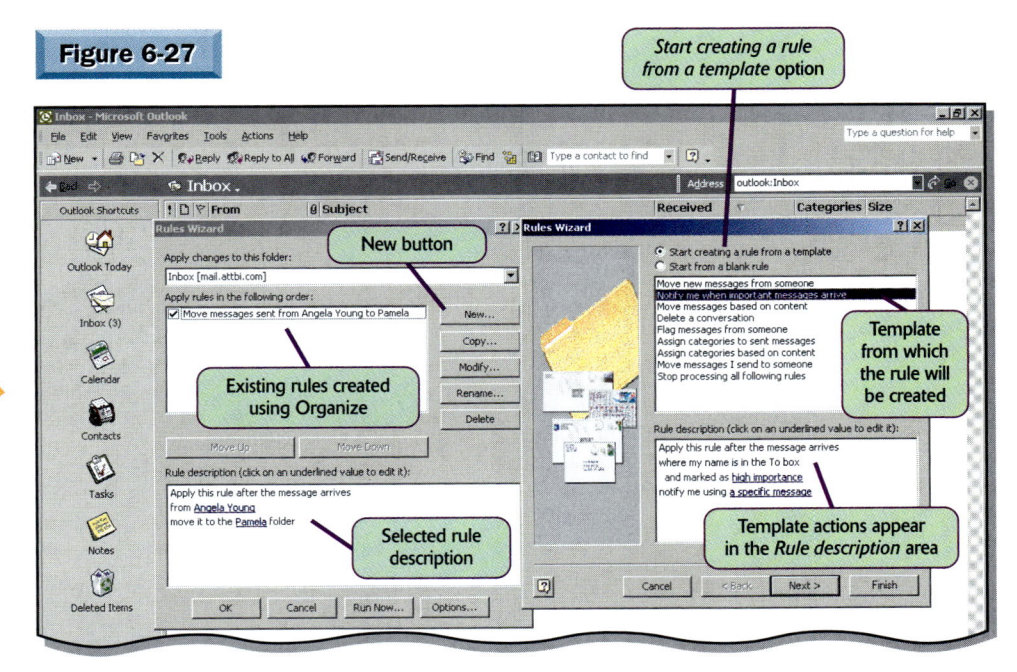

Tip Rules that are checked are "turned on" or active.

4 Click the **high importance** link in the **Rule description** area, select **High** from the **Specify the importance to look for** list, if necessary, and click **OK**.

Figure 6-28

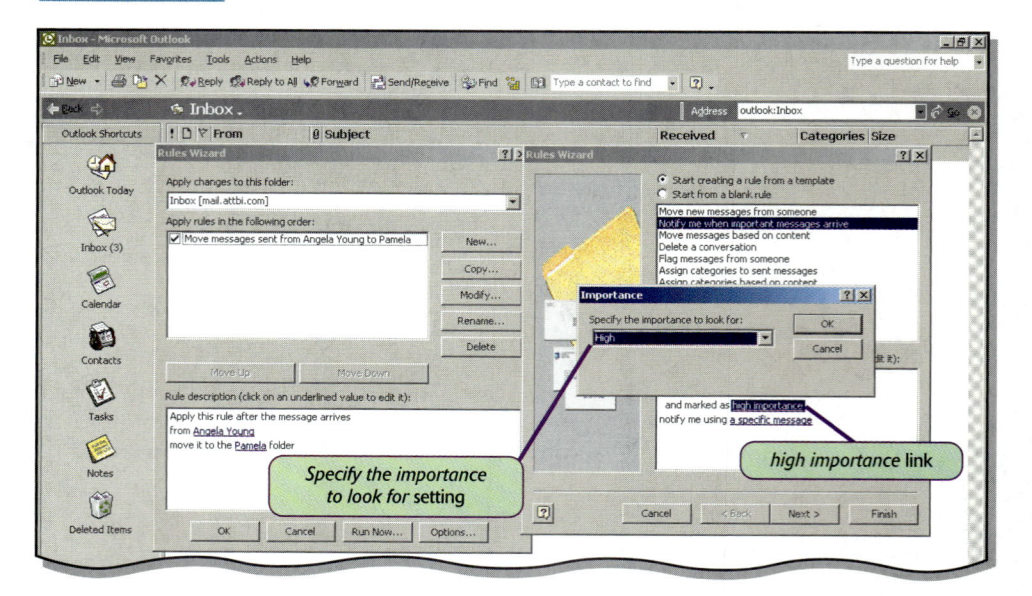

5 Click the **a specific message** link, type **You have received an important message.** in the **Specify a notification message** text box, and click **OK**.

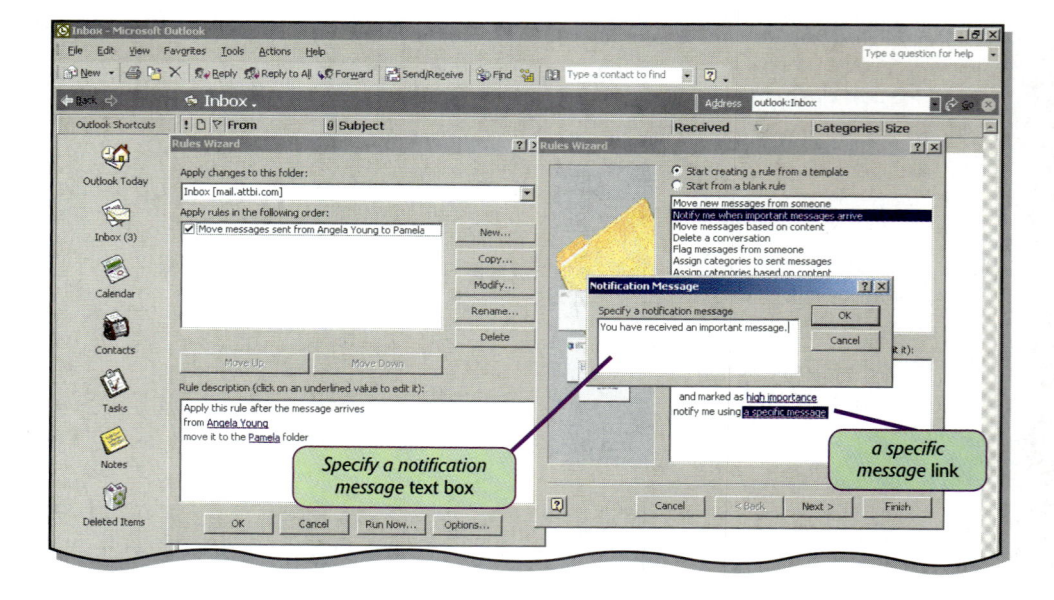

Figure 6-29

Managing Outlook Files, Folders, and the Journal

6 Click **Next**, select the **from people or distribution list** check box, and click the **people or distribution list** link in the **Rule description** text box.

7 Select your instructor's name from the Contacts list, click the **From** button, click **OK**, and then click **Next**.

8 Click **Next** again to accept the default **notify me using a specific message** option.

9 Select **except where my name is in the Cc box** and click **Next**.

Tip If you are the recipient of a copied e-mail message, the rule will not apply. Review options available in the Rules Wizard dialog boxes to become more familiar with the various criteria and actions you can set.

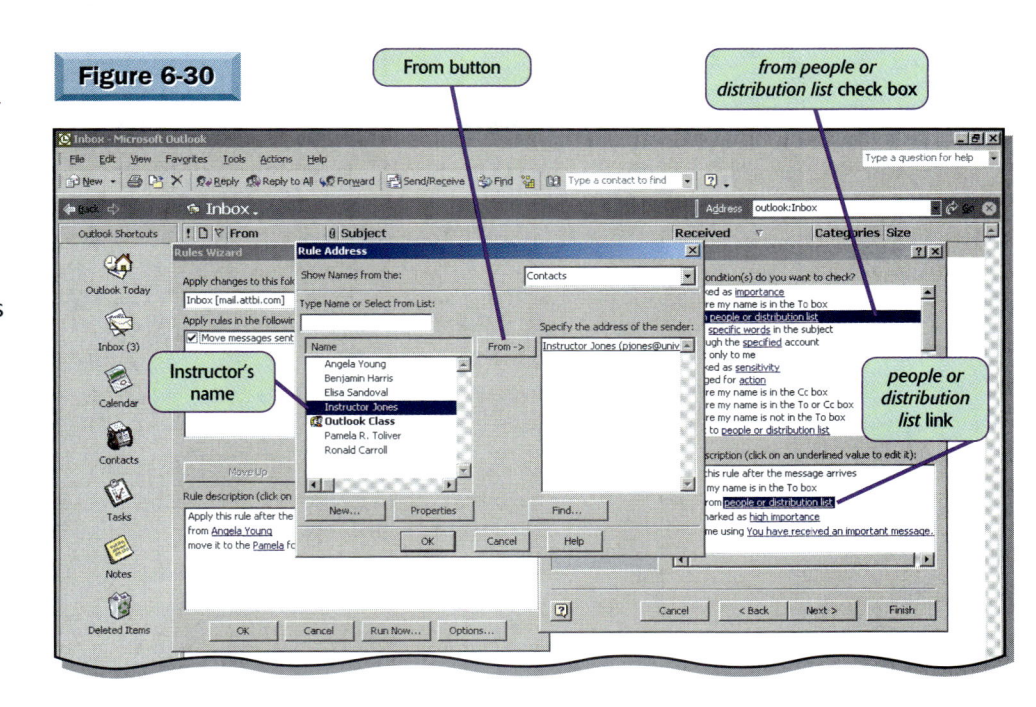

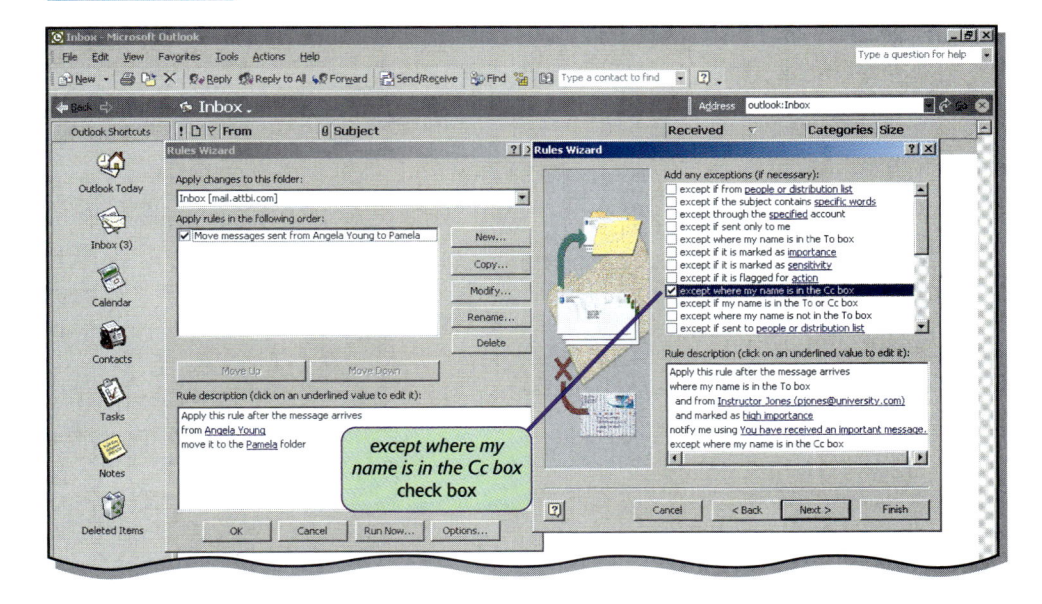

Figure 6-30

Figure 6-31

Creating Rules to Organize Outlook Items

10 Type **Messages from Instructor** and click **Finish** to save the rule.

Figure 6-32

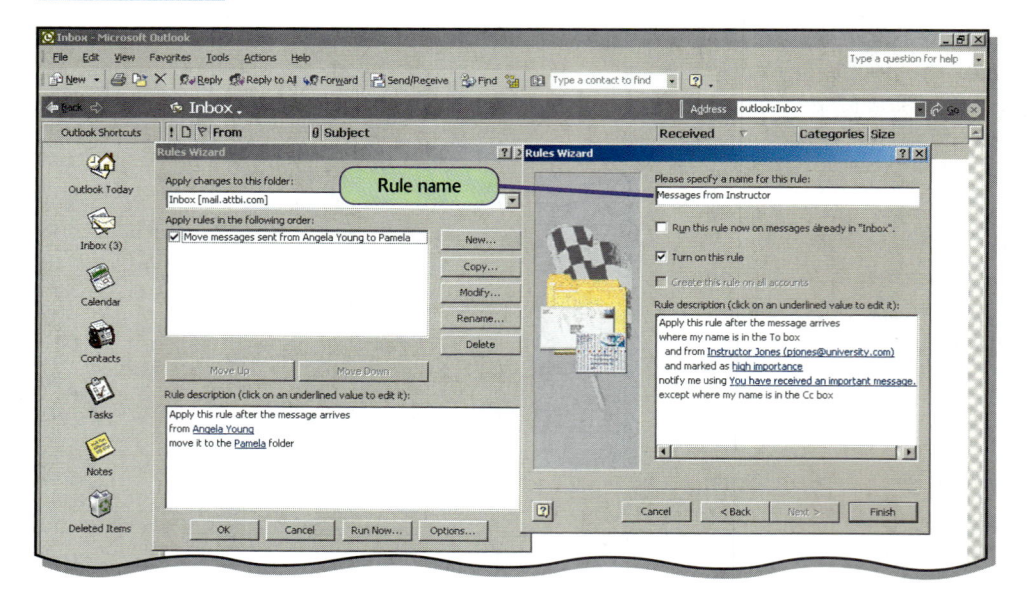

11 Click **OK** to close the Rules Wizard dialog box.

Figure 6-33

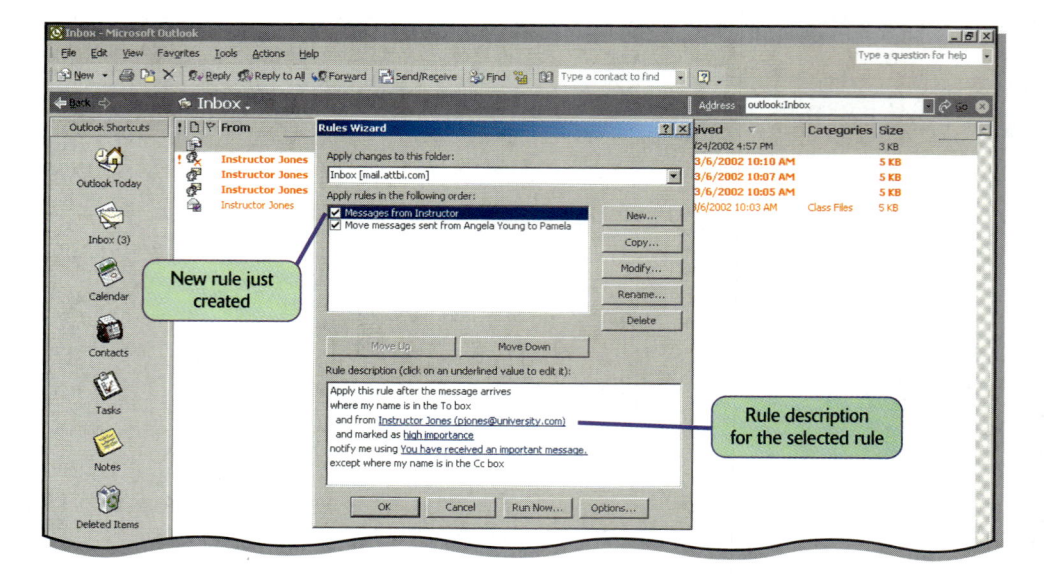

CHECK POINT

When the rules you create become obsolete or need editing, you can delete the rule or modify the rule settings using the **Rules Wizard** dialog box. Simply choose **Tools | Rules Wizard**, select the rule to delete or modify, and click the appropriate action button in the dialog box. If you are deleting a rule, Outlook presents a message asking if you are sure you want to delete it. If you are modifying the rule, follow the directions contained in Task 6 to reconstruct or select options.

Creating Associations between Outlook Items and Contacts

Many of the items you create in Outlook—e-mail messages, meeting requests, and so on—automatically *link* to the Activities page associated with a contact. For example, e-mails and meeting requests to and from your manager automatically link to your manager's contact information. However, there are certain items that Outlook does not automatically link because Outlook has no way to discern the relationship between the items. In such cases, you can link the related Outlook item manually. Linking creates an invisible connection between items in Outlook so that you can easily locate related items. For example, you might want to link e-mail messages sent to you from your manager's secretary to your manager.

Task 7:
To Link Outlook Items Manually

1. Open the **Contacts** folder and select the listing for one of your classmates.

2. Choose **Actions | Link | Items**.

Figure 6-34

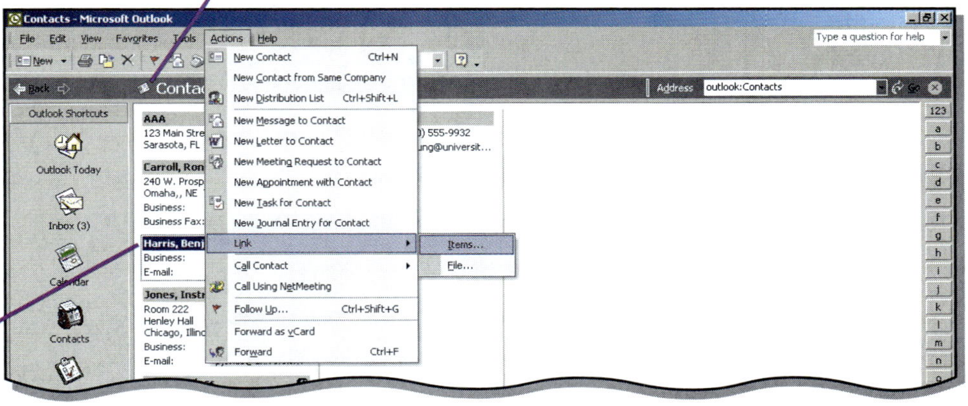

3. Click the **Inbox** folder in the **Look in** list, if necessary, select a message that you have received from your instructor, and click **OK**.

Figure 6-35

Tip The link between the message and the contact is completed.

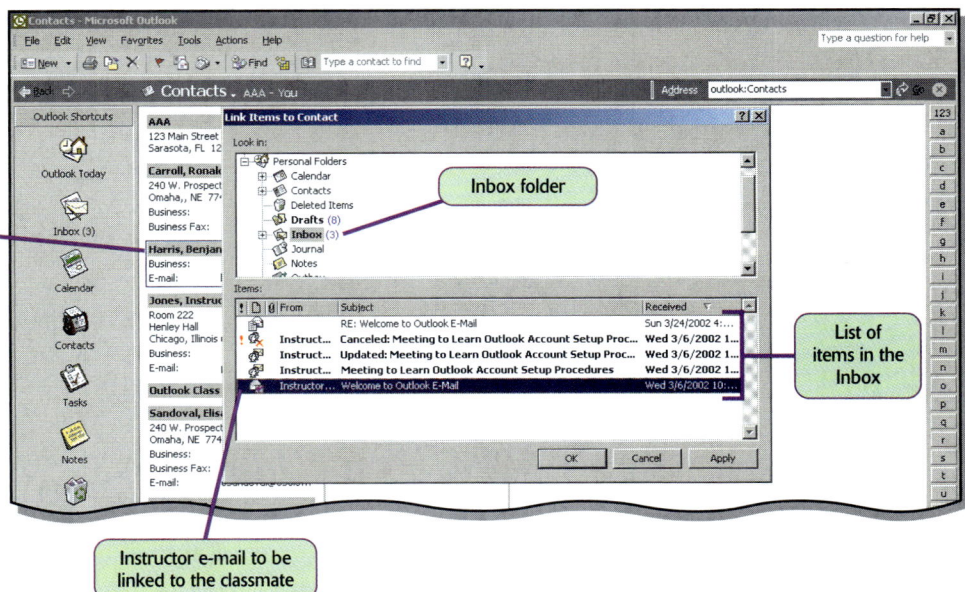

4 Open the contact for the classmate and click the **Activities** tab.

5 Choose **View | Current View | Customize Current View** to open the View Summary dialog box and click the **Fields** button.

6 Scroll the **Available fields** list, double-click the **From** and **To** fields to add them to the **Show these fields in this order** list, and click **OK** twice.

Figure 6-36

7 Close all message windows and/or dialog boxes.

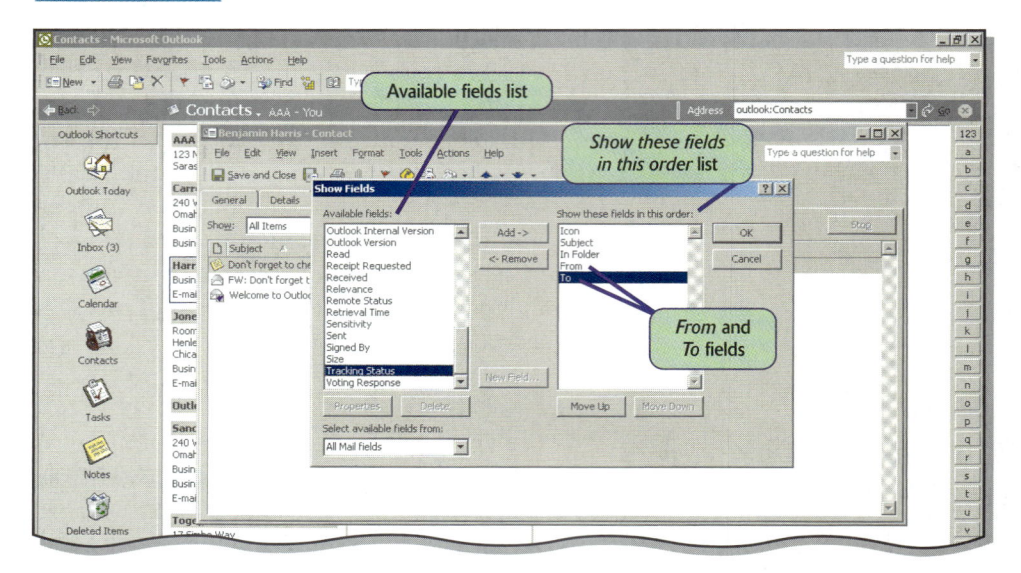

Figure 6-37

Using the Journal

The Outlook Journal records various actions in a timeline format which enables the user to view the recorded items from a "project management" point of view. The journal layout provides some simple project management features. For example, you could use the Journal to record notes about conversations with clients and include a contact name for each entry. You could then use the Outlook Find feature to search the Journal folder for all conversations for a specific client In addition, you could set the journal to automatically track e-mail messages and meeting requests sent to specific clients. By using these tools, you would be able to quickly create a detailed history of all correspondence with specific clients.

Managing Outlook Files, Folders, and the Journal

As you explore features in the Journal, you will discover that Outlook automatically assigns the journal entry types to each entry in the journal. For example, Outlook assigns *E-mail Message* to messages. You can customize the entry type to more accurately reflect the contents of e-mail messages to make them easier to locate. For example, when an e-mail message contains a request for data, you might want to change the journal entry type to *Data request*.

Setting Options to Track Journal Activities

When Outlook is installed on your computer, the Journal folder is created in the *My Shortcuts* group on the Outlook Bar. However, the Journal starts tracking activities only after you turn it on and set options regarding the types of items you want to track.

Task 8:
To Turn On and Set Options to Track Journal Activities

1 Choose **Tools** | **Options** to open the Options dialog box and click the **Journal Options** button to open the Journal Options dialog box.

2 Select all four Office XP items check boxes and click **OK** twice to close all dialog boxes.

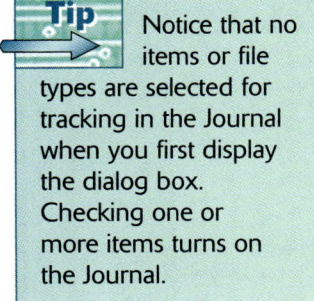

Figure 6-38

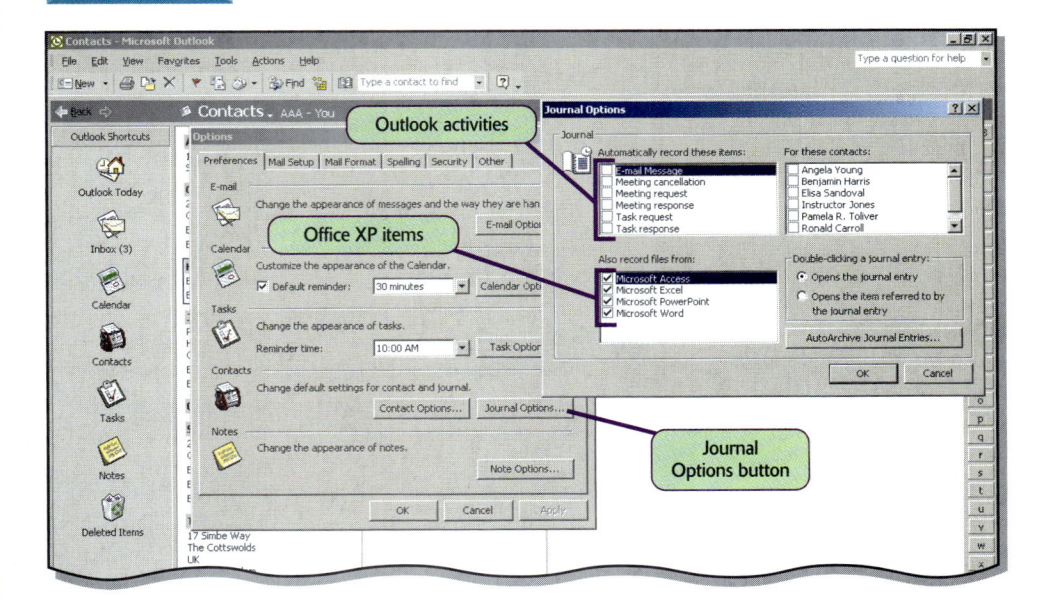

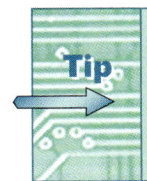

> **Tip** Notice that no items or file types are selected for tracking in the Journal when you first display the dialog box. Checking one or more items turns on the Journal.

> **Tip** The Activities list contains different types of activities that you can track for specific contacts. To record activities associated with specific contacts, select the activities in the Activities list and then select the contact or contacts for whom you want to track the activities in the **For these contacts** list.

3 Click the Outlook Bar **My Shortcuts** group button and then click the **Journal** icon to open the Journal folder.

Figure 6-39

My Shortcuts group button
Journal icon
Journal view

Troubleshooting
Selecting options and activities to be tracked by the Journal "turns on" the Journal feature. If the Journal has not yet been turned on, clicking the Journal icon in the Outlook Bar displays a message box that asks if you want to turn on the Journal feature. If the message box appears, click **Yes** and select the options to track in the dialog box displayed in Figure 6-39.

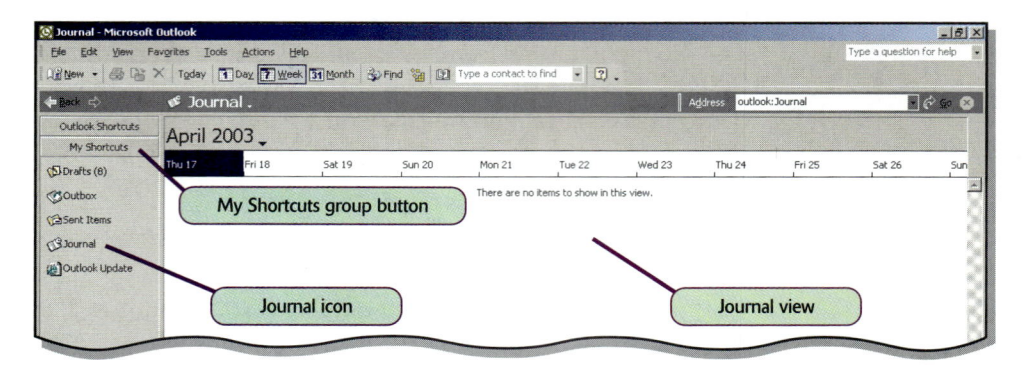

Creating Journal Entries

The Journal also serves as a tool that enables you to manually record events that you want to track in a timeline format, even items that occur outside the realm of the computer world, such as dates and times you spoke with clients on the telephone, dates you received correspondence, and time you spent performing professional services for a client.

Task 9:
To Record Journal Entries

Figure 6-40

New Journal Entry button
The subject appears in the title bar
Subject
Start date and time
Entry type text box
Company text box
Duration
Notes and other information

1 Open the **Journal** folder in the **My Shortcuts** group, if necessary, and click the New Journal Entry button.

2 Enter the data and set options shown in Figure 6-40 and then save and close the entry.

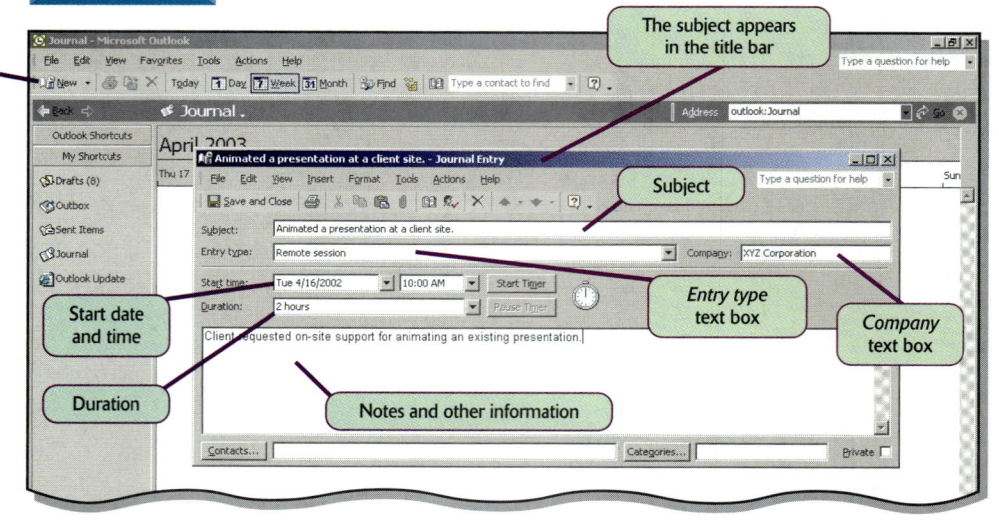

Tip
To record time required to complete a phone call or other activity, click the Start Timer button and record activity length.

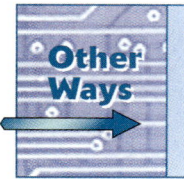

Other Ways
To create a new Journal entry:
- Double-click a blank area of the Journal pane below the bars.
- Right-click the blank area of the Journal pane and select **New Journal Entry**.

3 Click the **Expand** button to display the entry list and scroll using the horizontal scroll bar to display April 2003.

> Clicking the Expand button displays each remote session at the appropriate position on the timeline

Figure 6-41

- Date down arrow
- The Remote Session bar groups remote session items together

Tip The Journal groups items by entry type (e-mail message, phone call, remote session, and so forth) and program (Word, Excel, and so forth).

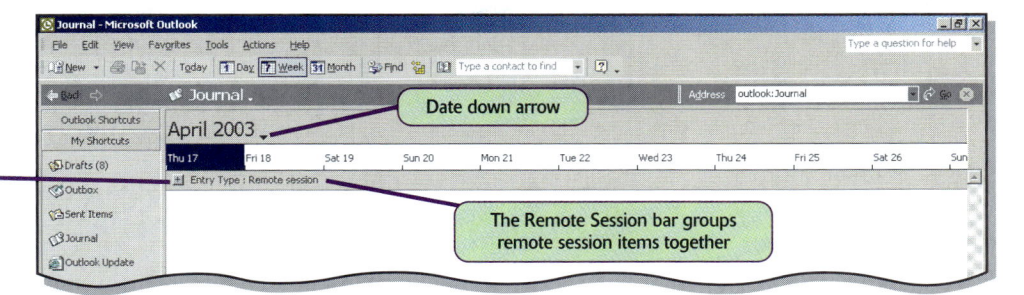

Other Ways

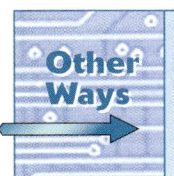

To display a different Journal month:
- Click the date down arrow and navigate to the appropriate month.
- Press Ctrl + G to open the Go To dialog box and then use the calendar palette to navigate to the month.

4 Click the **Collapse** button to close the entry list.

Figure 6-42

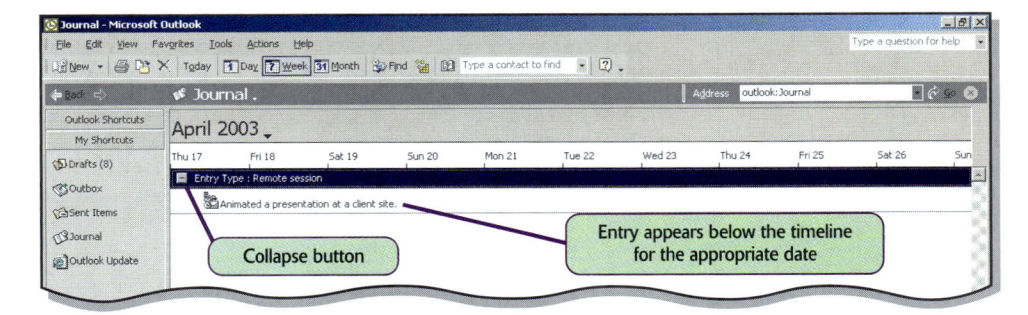

- Collapse button
- Entry appears below the timeline for the appropriate date

Assigning Contacts to Journal Entries

Options in the Journal Options dialog box enable you to track activities for selected contacts in the Journal. For example, you could select the contact for your instructor or supervisor and track meeting requests you receive from the contact in your Journal. Tracking the activities related to numerous contacts in the Journal folder crowds up the Journal and rapidly increases the amount of space the Journal folder requires on your computer. As a result, manually entering Journal activities would produce a more useful timeline and help lower the Journal size.

Task 10:
To Assign Contacts to Existing Journal Entries

1 Open the Journal folder, expand the Remote Session entries, and navigate to the April 11, 2003, entry you recorded in Task 9.

2 Double-click the entry to open it and click the **Contacts** button to open the **Select Contacts** dialog box.

3 Select your instructor's listing, click **Apply**, click **OK** to close the dialog box, and then save and close the entry.

> **Tip**
> To verify that the Journal entry was assigned to the contact, open the Contacts folder, open your instructor's listing, and click the **Activities** tab. The Journal activity should appear in the Activities list.

Figure 6-43

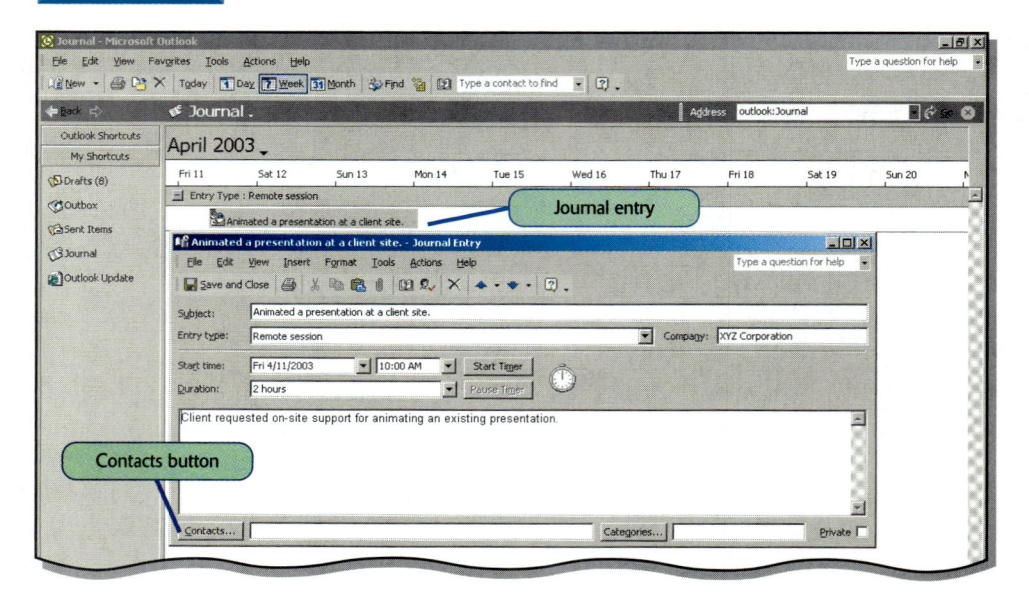

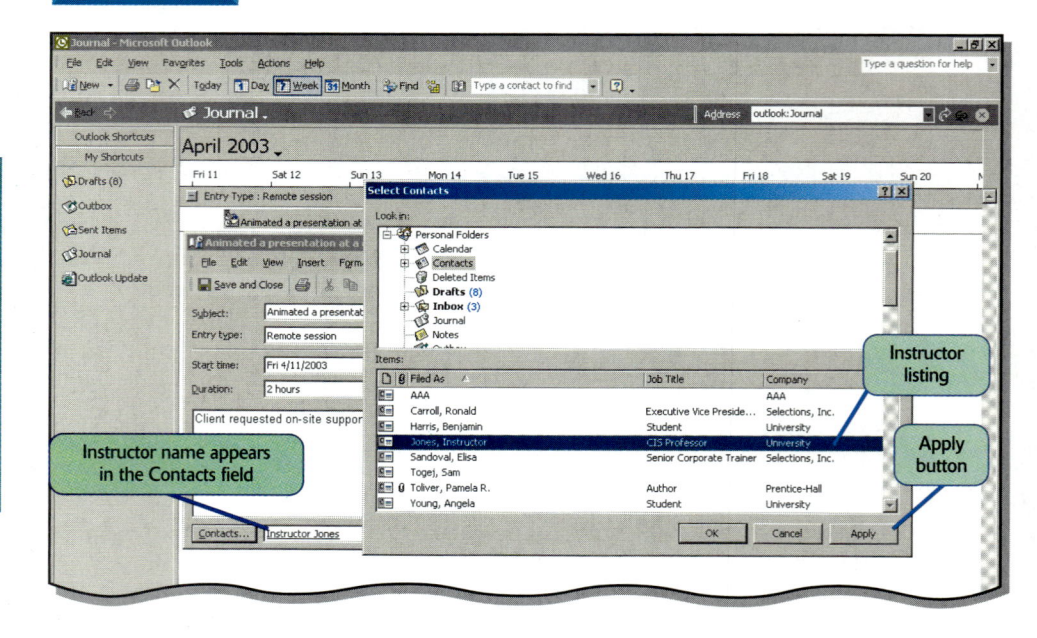

Figure 6-44

Modifying Journal Entry Types

The journal entry type (e-mail message, fax, phone call, and so forth) is assigned by the user when a manual journal entry is created and is automatically assigned by Outlook in an automated journal entry. Regardless of how the journal entry type was assigned, you can change the entry type by opening and editing the journal entry.

Task 11:
To Modify Journal Entry Types

Figure 6-45

1. Open the Journal folder, if necessary, navigate to the April 11, 2003, Journal activity you recorded in Task 9, and open it.

2. Click the **Entry type** down arrow, select **Microsoft PowerPoint**, and click the Save and Close **Save and Close** button.

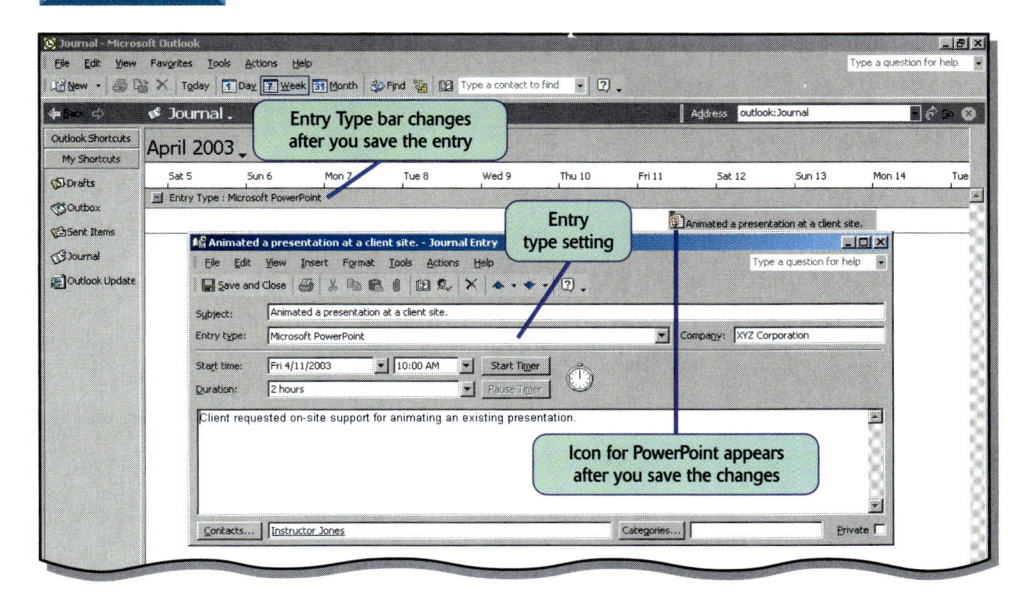

Tip: When you change the program associated with a journal activity, Outlook changes the icon associated with the activity and places the activity in the new group.

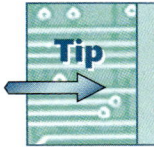

Archiving Items

As you work with Outlook, the amount of information contained in your Outlook folders grows. To maintain folders of manageable size, the Outlook AutoArchive feature automatically stores out-of-date items into a file called an *archive.pst*. Default settings in Outlook are designed to automatically archive files at regular, scheduled intervals, clearing out old and expired items. As a result, you will periodically receive a message box asking if you would like to *archive* files.

Archiving items

You can also archive items in different Outlook folders manually and select the items you want to archive. The default folders in which archived files are stored are determined by factors such as the operating system and network setup. You can choose both the filename and folder in which archived files are stored when you archive items files;archiving manually.

CHECK POINT

Tired of seeing the "Do you want to archive files now?" message?

AutoArchive is turned on by default to help you manage Outlook files. You can, however, change the default settings and disable AutoArchive so that only the items you archive manually are removed from your Outlook folders. Simply choose **Tools | Options,** click the **Other** tab, and click the **AutoArchive** button. Then clear the check mark in the **Run AutoArchive every** *n* **days** option and click **OK**. After turning off AutoArchive, it is up to you to keep your folders cleaned out!

Task 12:
To Archive Files

1 Click the Outlook Shortcuts group button on the Outlook Bar and click the **Inbox** icon to open the Inbox folder.

2 Click the **Received** column heading until the sort arrow points up to arrange the messages in chronological order and choose **File | Archive** to open the Archive dialog box.

3 Select last Friday's date from the **Archive items older than** drop-down list calendar and click **OK** to create the archive file.

Figure 6-46

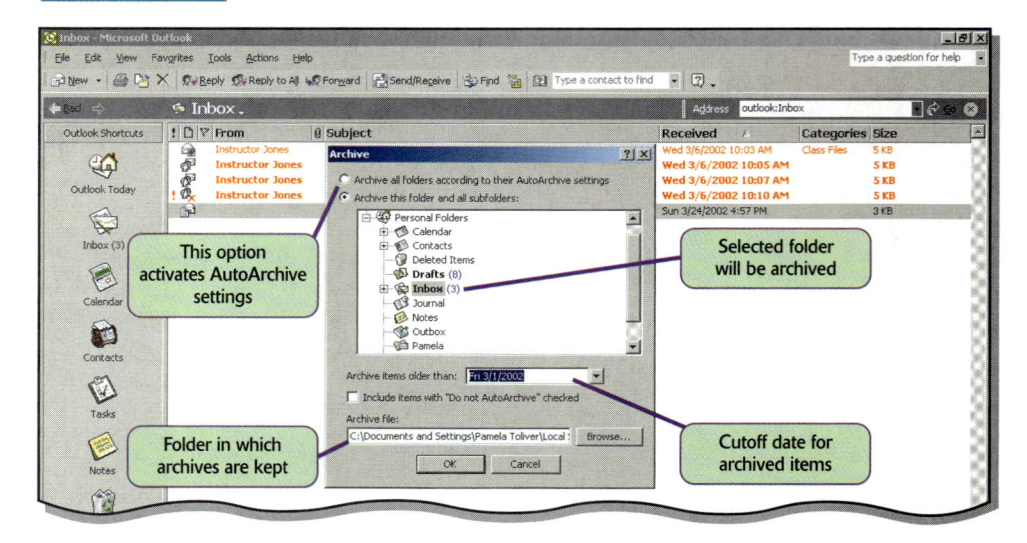

This option activates AutoArchive settings

Folder in which archives are kept

Selected folder will be archived

Cutoff date for archived items

Tip Notice that messages may change back to their default black color when you change views. The view customization that you made earlier in the project applies only to the view that was active at the time you customized the view.

Managing Outlook Files, Folders, and the Journal   OU 6-31

Restoring Archived Files

Archived items are removed from the Outlook folder in which they were originally stored. When you need to review items that were archived, you can open the archive file and select the folders or individual folder items you need and restore them to original folders.

Task 13:
To Restore Archived Items

1 Open the **Inbox** folder and choose **View | Folder List** to display a list of all Outlook folders.

2 Click the **Archive Folders** Expand (+) button to display a list of archived folders and then click the **Inbox** subfolder to display a list of archived messages.

3 Select all messages contained in the **Inbox** subfolder and drag the selected items to the **Personal Folders Inbox** to restore them.

4 Click the Outlook Bar **Inbox** icon to open the inbox to verify that archived messages were restored.

5 Close the **Folder List** pane.

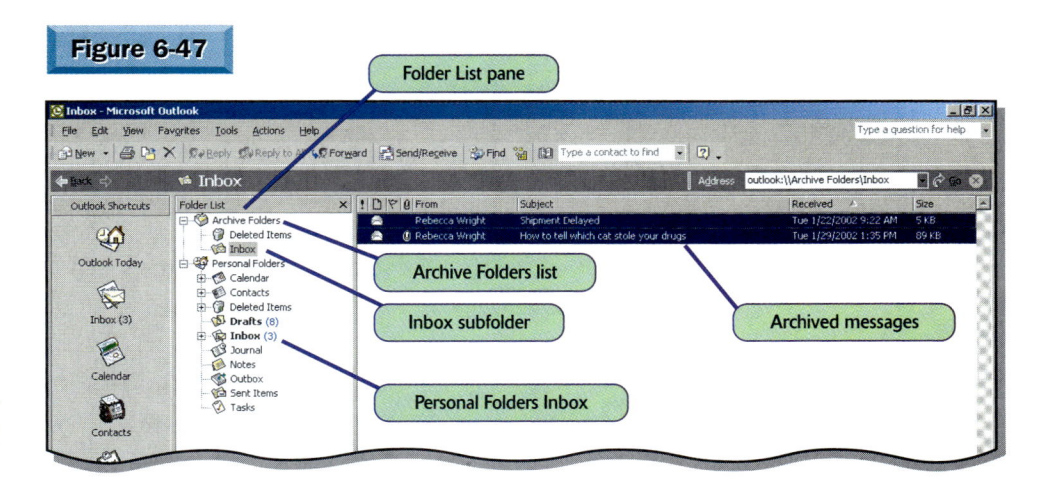

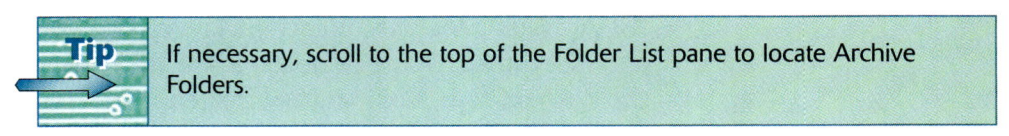

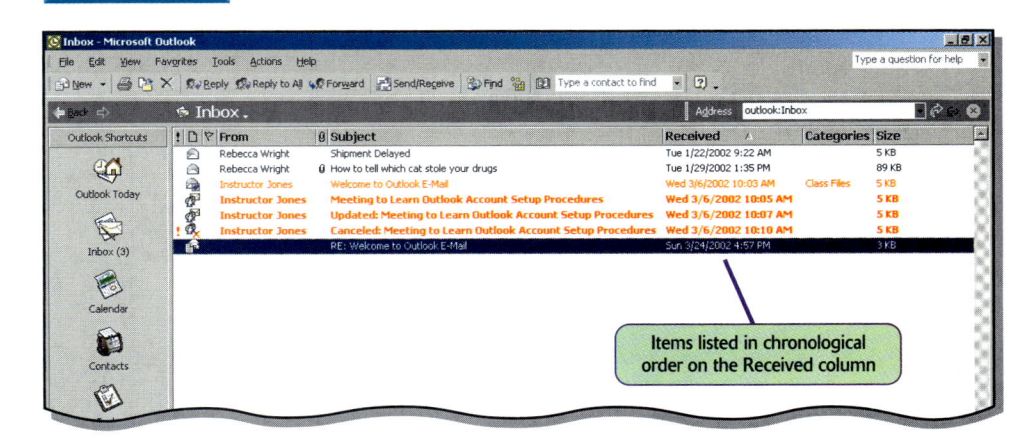

Figure 6-47

Folder List pane
Archive Folders list
Inbox subfolder
Archived messages
Personal Folders Inbox

Tip If necessary, scroll to the top of the Folder List pane to locate Archive Folders.

Figure 6-48

Items listed in chronological order on the Received column

SUMMARY AND EXERCISES

SUMMARY

- Assigning categories, such as Business or Personal, to Outlook items, such as e-mail messages and calendar entries, enhances your ability to organize and search for items within Outlook.

- It is possible to create associations between Outlook items and contacts in your contact list. For example, associate all e-mails, meeting requests, and calendar items related to your manager with your manager's contact in the contact list.

- You can customize Outlook views in many ways including but not limited to filtering by category and file size; sorting by sender or date; displaying fields such as Importance, Attachment, and Subject; and formatting font type and gridlines.

- The Activities page of a contact displays all Outlook items associated with that contact. Some associations are automatically created by Outlook and some are manually created.

- Rules are created to define how Outlook automatically organizes items. For example, a user may create a rule to move all e-mails with a particular subject into a specific folder as the e-mails are received.

- The Outlook Journal automatically tracks items generated by Outlook and other Office programs. Other items, such as conversations, are manually tracked within the Journal.

- The Outlook Archive feature eliminates out-of-date items from your Outlook folders. If needed, archived items can be restored.

KEY TERMS & SKILLS

KEY TERMS
archive (p. 6-29)
Junk E-Mail (p. 6-18)
link (p. 6-23)
Master Category List (p. 6-7)
Organize pane (p. 6-15)
rules (p. 6-14)
Rules Wizard (p. 6-18)

SKILLS
Archive files (p. 6-30)
Assign contacts to existing Journal entries (p. 6-28)
Color code messages and move items to folders (p. 6-15)
Create an Inbox rule using the Rules Wizard (p. 6-19)
Create new categories and assign categories to items (p. 6-5)
Customize Outlook folder views (p. 6-12)
Link Outlook items manually (p. 6-23)
Modify Journal entry types (p. 6-29)
Modify the Master Category List (p. 6-8)
Record Journal entries (p. 6-26)
Restore archived items (p. 6-31)
Sort and find items by category (p. 6-9)
Turn on and set Options to track Journal activities (p. 6-25)

STUDY QUESTIONS

MULTIPLE CHOICE

1. To add a category to the default Outlook collection of categories, access the
   a. File menu.
   b. Master Category List.
   c. Major Contacts List.
   d. Assign Category dialog box.

2. The Categories command appears on the
   a. Insert menu.
   b. Tools menu.
   c. Actions menu.
   d. Edit menu.

3. To locate items from all Outlook folders that are assigned to a category,
   a. change the current view to *By Category*.
   b. click the *Category* column heading button.
   c. you must use the *Advanced Find* feature.
   d. switch to Outlook Today.

4. To customize a view, you must first
   a. display the view you want to customize.
   b. choose **View** | **Current View** | **Customize Current View**.
   c. click the view **Design** button.
   d. choose **Tools** | **Options**.

5. You can customize each of the following view items using options in the View Summary dialog box *except*
   a. the view font.
   b. view fields.
   c. sort order.
   d. default folder view.

6. To limit the items displayed in an Outlook window, apply a
   a. sort order.
   b. filter.
   c. category.
   d. new folder.

7. You can organize the Contacts list using all the following tools in the **Organize** pane *except*
   a. junk contacts.
   b. folders.
   c. views.
   d. categories.

8. The organize feature that is available in the **Organize** pane for only the current mail folder is
   a. folders.
   b. categories.
   c. colors.
   d. views.

9. The Journal folder tracks activities associated with Microsoft programs and plots them in a
   a. table layout.
   b. dialog box.
   c. numeric layout.
   d. timeline layout.

10. Manually entered journal activities are made primarily to track
    a. activities of Microsoft Word.
    b. activities that do not involve the computer.
    c. activities associated with contacts.
    d. phone messages only.

SHORT ANSWER

1. What is the advantage of assigning categories to Outlook items?
2. When you create a new category in a folder item dialog box, does Outlook add the category to the master list?
3. Which of the Outlook folders contains items that cannot be assigned to categories?
4. What does color coding messages received from specific senders enable you to do?
5. How does the Organize tool enable you to organize messages using folders for e-mail messages?
6. Do all of the templates available in the Rules Wizard present the same options for creating rules?
7. What does it mean when the **Categories** command on the **Edit** menu is not available?
8. What is the easiest way to sort items in a folder by category?
9. What determines the path (drive and folder) location for storing an archive?
10. What happens if you try to use the Journal and there are no activities set?

FILL IN THE BLANK

1. Microsoft Outlook 2002 is known as a(n) _____ _____ _____.
2. You can assign _____ to most Outlook items to show item relationships.
3. The _____ feature streamlines the process for creating frequently used rules to manage folder items.
4. The Inbox contains features for filtering out unsolicited e-mail messages sometimes known as _____ _____.
5. To view or edit an existing rule or to set advanced rule options, use the _____ _____.

6. Items in other folders that are associated with contacts appear on the _____ page of the contact's dialog box.
7. Items associated with contacts are said to be _____ to the contact.
8. The _____ can track all activities involving Outlook and other Office XP programs.
9. The _____ command enables you to move out-of-date items from Outlook folders and store them so they can be restored if needed.
10. Instructions entered in Outlook that identify special handling for specific items are called _____.

DISCUSSION

1. What are some different categories that you believe should be added to the Master Category List to customize it to meet your needs?
2. Why would you use the Journal?
3. Which of the features described in this project do you believe you will use most? For what purposes will these features be most useful to you?

GUIDED EXERCISES

1 UN-CUSTOMIZING

The customizations you made to Outlook views in this project can be reversed and reset to restore the default fields and display information onscreen as it first appeared. Follow these steps to remove the fields and customizations you added earlier:

1. Open the **Inbox** folder and choose **View | Current View | Messages**, and then choose **View | Current View | Customize Current View**.

2. Click the **Fields** button, click the **Attachment** field in the **Show these fields in this order** list, and click the **Move Up** button once.

3. Click the **Categories** field in the **Show these fields in this order** list and click the **Remove** button.

4. Click **OK** and then click the **Other Settings** button.

5. Click the Column Heading **Font** button and change the font settings to 8 pt Tahoma Regular and click **OK**.

6. Click the **Group By** button and select **(none)** from the **Group Items by** drop-down list and click **OK**.

7. Click **OK** to close the **View Summary** dialog box.

2 CATEGORICALLY ORGANIZING CONTACTS

Knowing the ins and outs of assigning categories to items in different folders as you add them is great. You can quickly assign a category to numerous contacts at the same time by selecting the contacts and using the Organize feature. Follow these steps to assign the same category to selected contacts:

1. Open the **Contacts** folder, display the Address Card view, and create contacts for the Board of Directors listed in Table 6-3 if you have not already entered them, saving and closing each contact as you complete it.

   Table 6-3   Board of Directors Contact Information

Name	Address	Telephone	e-Mail
Donald Koontz	802 North Allen, Robinson, IL 62454	618-555-3964	dkoontz@isp.com
Norma Rule	Rt. 1, Box 884, Naperville, IL 60544	630-555-3384	nrule@isp.com
Tamara Patterson	448 Blarney Stone Way, Bloomington, IL 61704	630-555-2701	tpatterson@isp.com
Lee Lowell	2471 Spring Lane, Indianapolis, IN 46268	317-555-7521	llowell@isp.com
David Steele	889 Seventh Avenue, Pekin, IL 61554	309-555-3234	dsteele@isp.com
Pamela Ayers	18822 Flakewood Court, Little Rock, AR 72207	501-555-2807	payers@isp.com

2. Click the title bar of the first Board member contact, then press [Ctrl] and click the title bar of each additional member of the Board of Directors contact. As you press [Ctrl] and click each contact, Outlook highlights the title bar to identify selected contacts.

3. Click the **Organize** button on the toolbar, click the **Using Categories** link, type **Board of Directors** in the **Create a new category called** box, and click **Create**.

4. Choose **View | Current View | By Category** and verify that all selected contacts appear grouped into the same category.

5. Choose **View | Current View | Address Cards** to restore the view, and click the **Find** button to open the Find Bar.

6. Click the **Options** button on the Find Bar, select **Advanced Find**, click the **More Choices** tab, type **Board of Directors** in the **Categories** text box, and click **Find Now** to locate the contacts.

7. Close the Advanced Find dialog box and then close the Find Bar.

ON YOUR OWN

The difficulty of these case studies varies: ♩ are the least difficult; ♩♩ are more difficult; and ♩♩♩ are the most difficult.

1 REVIEWING ORGANIZATION OPTIONS

♩ The options available in the Organize pane vary between Outlook features. Review the different ways you can use the Organize pane in each Outlook feature—Inbox, Calendar, Contacts, Tasks, and Notes. Think of practical examples for each method of organization in each feature and list these examples in outline format, print a copy of the outline, and turn it in to your instructor.

2 PERSONALIZING CATEGORIES

♩ Each person who uses Outlook will have unique categories they want to use to sort items in different folders. From school to work to personal settings, planning these categories ahead will reduce the amount of time you spend editing later. Make a list of at least ten different categories you expect to use to sort items in different Outlook folders and type the list in an Outlook Note. Be sure to include custom categories that you would need to add to the Master Category List. Then e-mail the note to your instructor and print a copy of the note to use in class.

3 COLORIZING YOUR ORGANIZED WORLD

Colors make great ways to sort and identify so many things, and Outlook takes advantage of using colors to help you stay organized. For example, you can color code messages in the Inbox from people with whom you correspond regularly to help you quickly identify messages from these people. Identify at least three people with whom you correspond regularly by e-mail. Create a new folder for each of these people, format the folder to contain e-mail messages, and add the folders to the Outlook Bar. Then use the Organize pane to color code messages from each person using a different color and automatically move messages you receive from these people into the appropriate folder when new messages arrive. Open each folder and print a copy of the folder contents in Table style for each of the new folders. Then open the Rules Wizard dialog box and delete the three rules created using the Organize feature.

4 CREATING AND CATEGORIZING OUTLOOK ITEMS

Each of the items you record in Outlook can be associated with a contact, a task, an appointment, or an e-mail message. Assigning categories to each item you record makes sorting and locating items more efficient. Do you remember how you can color code calendar items using the label choices in the Appointment window? Label choices include *important, business, needs preparation*, and so forth. Labeling information stored in the Calendar can also make prioritizing items easier. However, labeling items does not help you perform a basic sort as categories do. Create the following items in Outlook, assign the appropriate label to each appointment, and type the label type in the **Categories** field of the appointment. Then change the Calendar view to **By Category** and print a copy of the table.

- A parent's, sibling's, or other close relative's birthday.
- The final exam date and time for this course—an important event!
- The starting date for next semester.
- The semester break—a great vacation!
- The weekend before your final exams—these will need preparation.
- 7 P.M. next Sunday evening—time to phone home.

5 REPORT TIME

Remember the report requested by Ms. Wright on the features in this project that you think will be most helpful to you? These features might also be useful to others in the company. Now that you have identified a number of useful tools, it is time to prepare the report. Review each of the features covered in this project—there are at least 13—and list each feature on a separate line of a new document file. Based on a scale of one to five with five being the most useful, rank each feature by how useful you believe it will be. For those ranked five, add a paragraph explaining how or why you believe it would be useful. Display the Journal Options dialog box, select your Instructor's contact listing, and turn on the E-mail activity for your instructor. Prepare your report and include it in an e-mail message to your instructor. Verify that the e-mail containing your report is recorded in the journal, record a new document journal entry with the subject *Prepared report for Outlook* for the date on which you prepared the file, link the file to your instructor's contact, and print a copy of the entry from the journal to submit to your instructor. Then open the entry for the e-mail message you sent to your instructor that transmitted the report and print a copy of that journal entry for your instructor.

6 RESPONDING TO THE RULES

The Inbox Assistant is a tool that is available to Outlook users who are connected to networks that are running Microsoft Exchange. When the Inbox Assistant is available, you can turn it on so that a message is automatically generated to notify people from whom you receive e-mail messages that you are away from the office and may not reply immediately. When the Inbox Assistant is unavailable, you can create a rule to generate an automatic message any time you receive an e-mail message. Create a new blank rule using the Rules Wizard that meets the following criteria:

- Checks messages when they arrive
- For messages received in a specific date span between yesterday and tomorrow
- Respond using the *mail.oft* form

Then send a message to your own e-mail address with *Rules Test* as the Subject. When the response to the message arrives, print a copy of the Inbox message list in Table style for your instructor. Then archive all messages that you received today, display the Archive Folders Inbox subfolder list and print a copy of the list in Table style. Restore the messages you want to keep, leaving the expendable messages in the archive.

Photospread credits pages 6-2 & 6-3
©FPG: ©Telegraph Colour Library 1998; ©Tony Stone: ©David Arky, ©Fisher/Thatcher; ©Mark Douet; ©Pearson Education; and ©Lorraine Castellano

FROM THE FILES

You Will Need
- ✔ e-Selections Background.jpg
- ✔ e-Selections.gif
- ✔ Sandoval Contacts.csv
- ✔ Special Message.csv

PROJECT 7

Integrating, Customizing, and Sharing Outlook Files

As you have discovered, Outlook is a powerful desktop management tool that offers many time saving, organizational, and communication features. In prior projects you learned to integrate information among Outlook features as well as how to customize Outlook features. As a part of Office XP, Outlook enables you to interact with other Office XP applications—Word, Access, Excel, and PowerPoint—and to share information with other users. In addition, you will find features in Outlook that you can use to customize Outlook forms. In this project you will learn how to enable others to view your Outlook folders, share contacts with other users, create Office XP files directly from Outlook, and create custom stationery and forms.

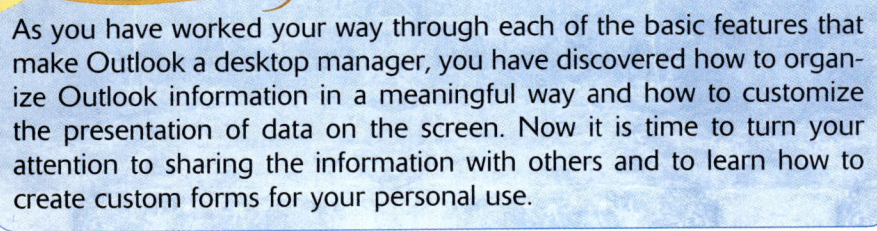

OBJECTIVES

After completing this project, you will be able to:

- Send, export, and import contacts
- Share Outlook folders
- Open folders belonging to other users
- Create Office XP files from Outlook
- Create e-mail stationery
- Create custom Outlook forms

e-selections Running Case

As you have worked your way through each of the basic features that make Outlook a desktop manager, you have discovered how to organize Outlook information in a meaningful way and how to customize the presentation of data on the screen. Now it is time to turn your attention to sharing the information with others and to learn how to create custom forms for your personal use.

Integrating, Customizing, and Sharing Outlook Files

To 'ping' or 'tiff' or 'jpeg' – that is the question…

Have the TIFF, PNG, JPG, PCX, and other acronyms got you down? Have you ever wanted to ask "Wot's'at?" when presented with a file with a unique file name extension? Or have you ever been asked to, "Save it as a graphic and send it to me."?

If you've ever experienced one of these situations, you know how challenging working with unusual file types can be. Because there are literally hundreds of different graphics file formats you can use, the task can become overwhelming.

Come on along—it's time to unravel the mystery surrounding some of the more commonly used graphics file formats. As these different file formats unfold, you'll realize that each graphics format has distinct and unique uses. You'll then be able to determine the format that best meets the needs of the task at hand.

File Format	Stands for	Description
.bmp	Windows Bitmap	A commonly used file format on PCs that can be read by most programs.
.cgm	Computer Graphics Metafile	Another basic file format used on PCs that can be read by most programs.
.gif	CompuServe Graphics Interchange Format file	A file format of graphics added to documents that are uploaded to the CompuServe Information Service. It is the most common graphics format found on the Internet.
.jpeg .jpg	Joint Photographic Experts Group	A compressed file format that identifies and discards information that the human eye can't see. An image saved in the .jpg format may not be identical to the original image; however, the difference between the two is usually indistinguishable.

jpeg

Each graphics format has distinct and unique uses...

bmp

File Format	Stands for	Description
.pcx	PC Paintbrush	Zsoft created this file format for its PC Paintbrush software. It can be used by all PC computers.
.pdf	Adobe Acrobat Portable Document Format	A file format commonly used to store completed documents on Web sites in a format that cannot be edited.
.png	Portable Network Graphic	A compressed file format that some experts believe will replace .gif as the most widely used format for the Internet.
.tiff .tif	Tagged-Image File Format	A format that produces very large files and high-quality images. It is used to exchange documents between different software and platforms.
.wmf	Windows Metafile	A file format used by Windows programs to exchange graphics.

The next time you're asked to save something as a graphic, you'll at least go into the task armed and ready. If you choose to use one of the other hundreds of graphics file formats, you're on your own . . .

tiff

wmf

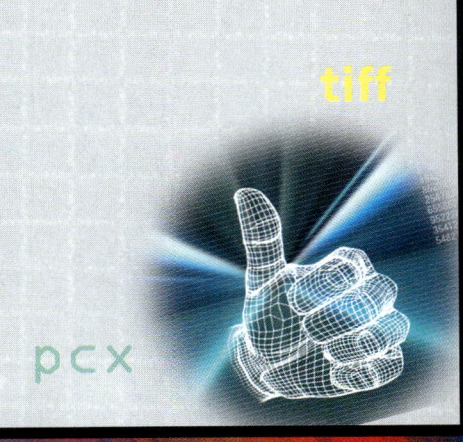

pcx

PROJECT 7

Integrating, Customizing, and Sharing Outlook Files

The Setup

While there is no definitive way to ensure that the settings on your computer will match those pictured in this Project, there are some settings that can be checked to reduce the number of differences. Most of these reflect Outlook defaults with no customizations or custom folders. Active settings are described in Table 7-1.

Table 7-1	Outlook Settings
Feature	**Setting**
Default Launch Feature	Inbox: Choose **Tools**	**Options**	**Other**	**Advanced Options**	**General Settings**	**Startup in this folder** and select Inbox, if necessary.
Outlook Bar setting	Large icons: Right-click the Outlook Bar and select **Large icons**.
Office Assistant	Hide the Office Assistant: Right-click the Office Assistant and select **Hide**.
Toolbars	Choose **Tools**	**Customize**	**Toolbars**, select the **Standard** toolbar, click **Reset**, click **Yes**, and click **Close** to restore the toolbar to its default settings.

The Challenge

Because you have been working while attending your Outlook class, you have maintained two separate e-mail accounts, one at school and one at work. Now that the class is winding to a close, it is time to identify ways that you can copy contacts from your school account to your work account without retyping them. Ms. Wright has also asked you if you have learned how to set up Outlook accounts so that the administrative assistants at e-Selections can access their manager's folders to schedule appointments and track task progress. She also wonders if there is a way to use contact information in other Office files. Finally, she would like for you to create the e-Selections stationery and form displayed in Figure 7-1.

Figure 7-1

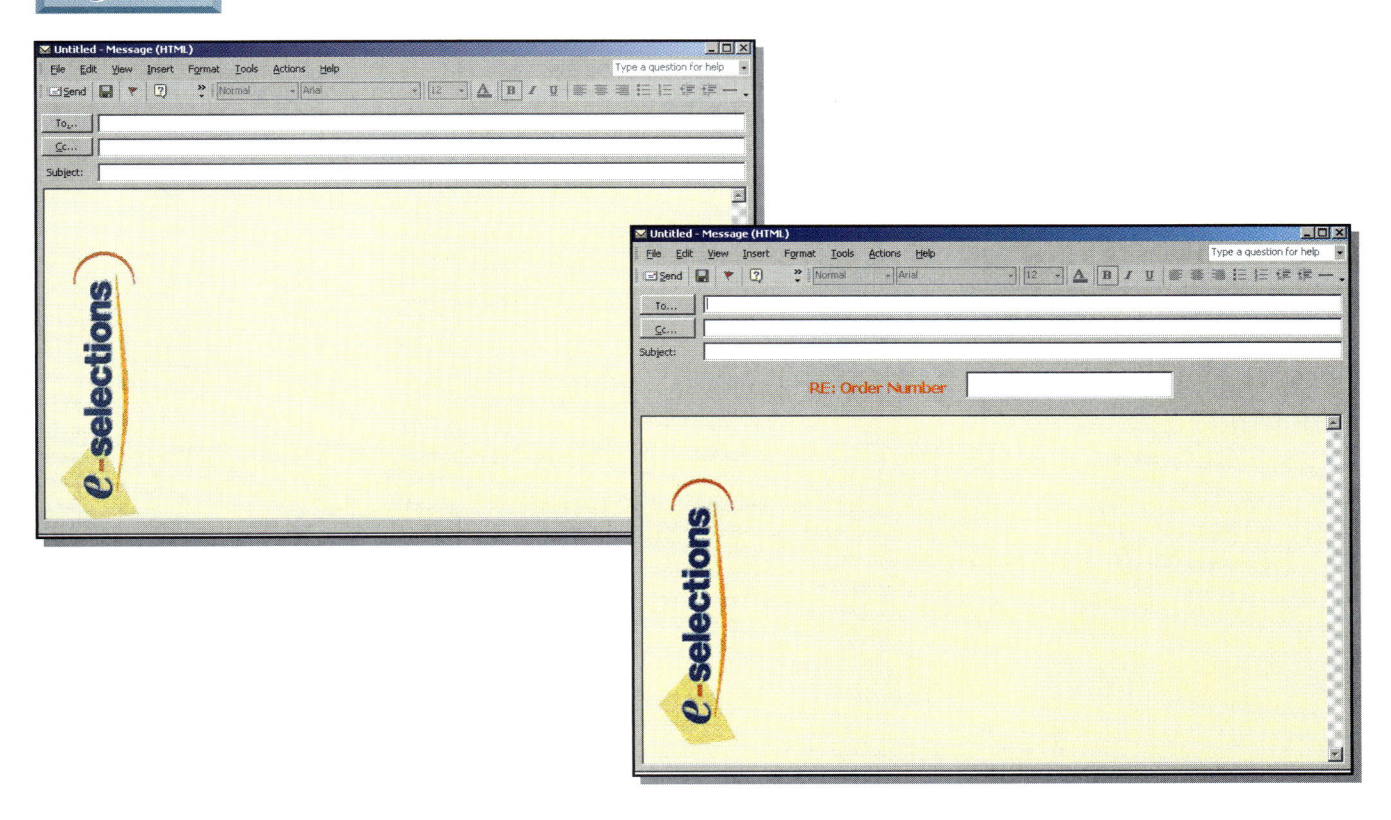

The Solution

Outlook offers a number of different ways you can move your school contacts to your work machine. You will also be able to change Outlook folder options so that others connected to the network can access the folders. Outlook's connection to other Office XP applications enables you to create other files directly from Outlook. Because the instructor has left the format for the custom stationery and *form* up to each student, you will be able to use class time and Outlook tools to create and customize the stationery and forms she has requested.

Sending, Exporting, and Importing Contacts

Maintaining contacts in separate locations is potentially time consuming. Outlook offers various ways to move or copy contact information from one computer or network to another:

- E-mail the contact to another e-mail address. Outlook sends the contact listing as a *vCard*—the Internet standard for creating and sharing virtual business cards—so that you can simply add it to the Contacts folder on the receiving computer.
- Export contacts from one computer and import them into another.
- Create the contact using the **From** information of e-mail you receive.
- Export data from Outlook to another Office application.

E-mailing Contacts from Outlook

Troubleshooting
If you have not yet created a contact for Sam Togej, use the information shown in Figure 7-2 to create one or select a different contact listing, as directed by your instructor.

You can attach a selected contact to an e-mail message and send it to another computer or to an e-mail recipient using special tools built into Outlook. When you send a contact from the Contacts folder, Outlook attaches a copy of the contact with a .vcf extension so that the recipient can open and save it in their Contact folder.

Task 1:
To E-Mail and Export Contacts

1. Launch Outlook and open the **Contacts** folder.

2. Click the contact listing for *Sam Togej* to select it and choose **Actions | Forward as vCard** to open a new message window.

3. Address the message to your own e-mail address, type the message shown in Figure 7-2, and click Send to send the message.

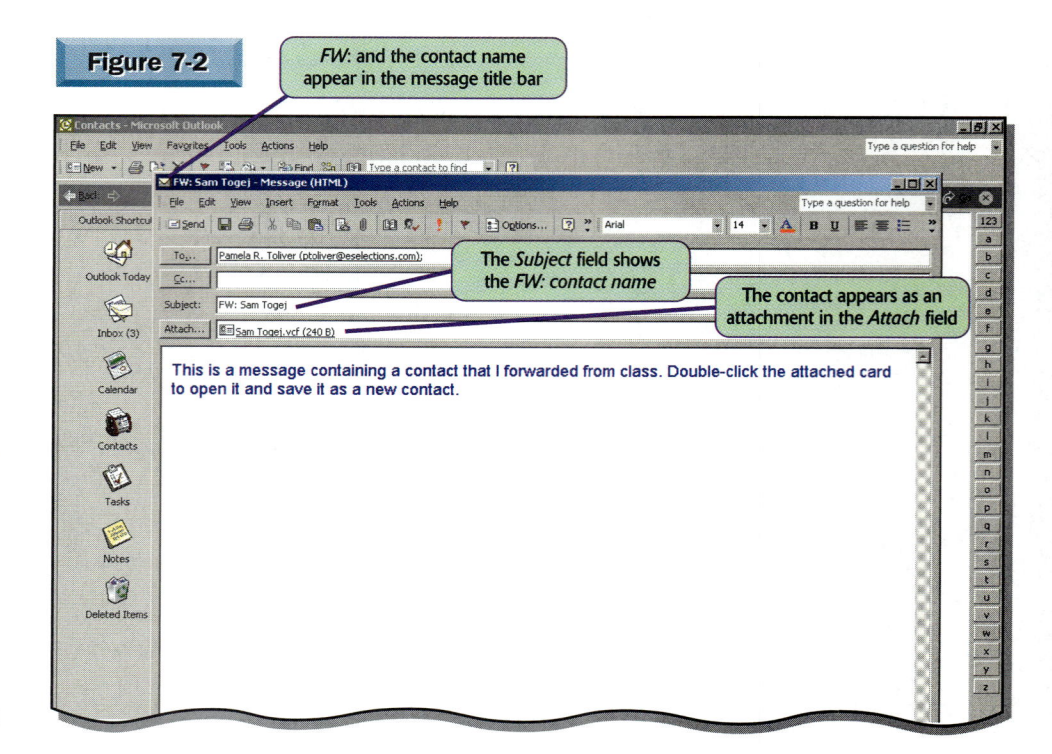

Figure 7-2

- *FW*: and the contact name appear in the message title bar
- The *Subject* field shows the *FW: contact name*
- The contact appears as an attachment in the *Attach* field

Exporting Contacts to a File

When you want to transfer a complete list of contacts to another computer or create a backup copy of your contacts, you can export the contacts to a file. Contacts exported to a file can then be imported and saved on a different computer.

Integrating, Customizing, and Sharing Outlook Files

OU 7-7

Task 2:
To Export Contacts to a File

1 Choose **File | Import and Export** to open the Import and Export Wizard.

2 Select **Export to a file** from the **Choose an action to perform** list and click **Next**.

Figure 7-3

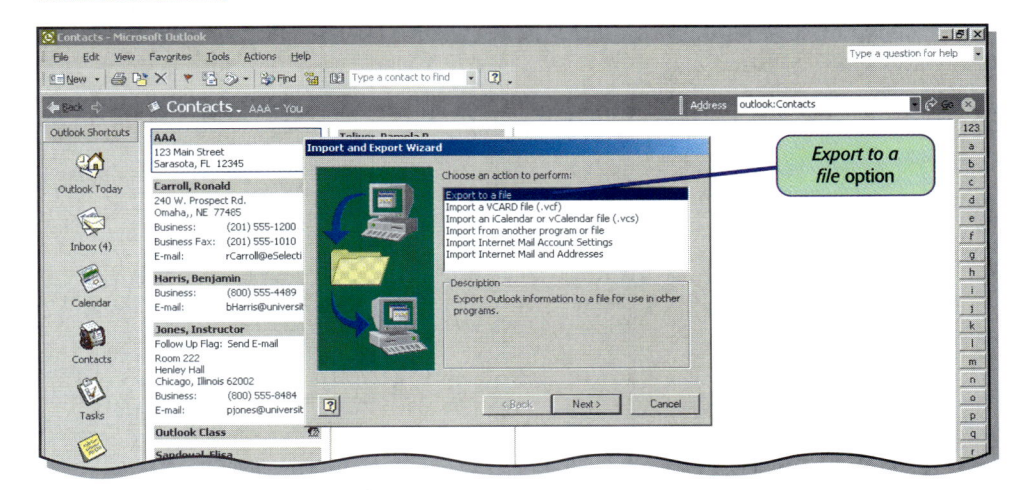

Export to a file option

Troubleshooting If the Office Assistant offers help, click **No, don't provide help now** in the Office Assistant dialog box to close the Office Assistant.

3 Select **Comma Separated Values (Windows)** from the **Create a file of type** list and click **Next**.

Figure 7-4

Comma Separated Values (Windows) option

Troubleshooting
If the necessary translator has not been installed on your computer, a message box may appear asking if you want to install it. If you have the necessary Office XP disks, follow the directions in the dialog box and click **Yes** to install the translator. If you are in a lab, follow the direction of your instructor to continue.

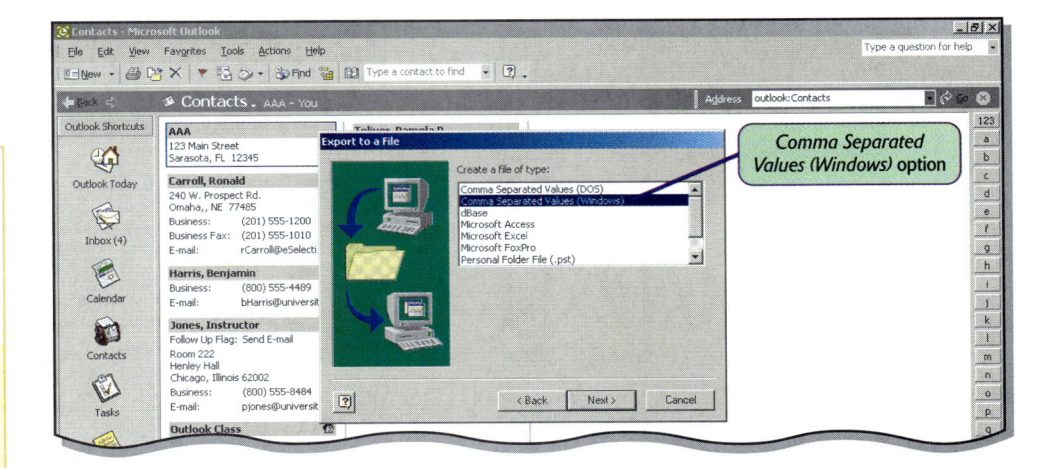

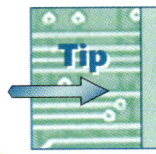

Tip Selecting *comma separated values* as the file type simply tells Outlook to place a comma between fields of information contained in each listing. The file you create will have a *.csv* file extension.

Sending, Exporting, and Importing Contacts

4 Select the **Contacts** folder from the **Select folder to export from** list, if necessary, and click **Next**.

Figure 7-5

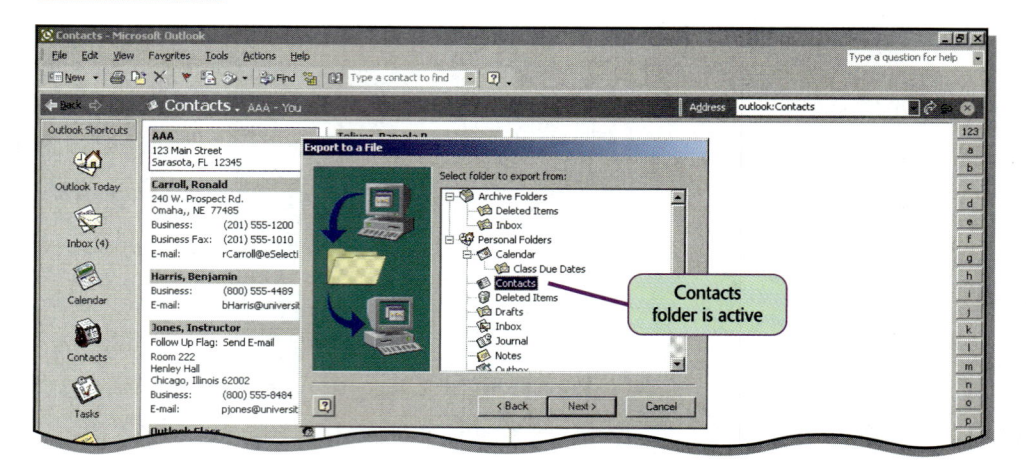

5 Click **Browse**, open the drive and folder in which you want to store the file, and type **My Class Contacts** in the **File name** text box.

6 Click **OK** to close the Browse dialog box and then click **Next**.

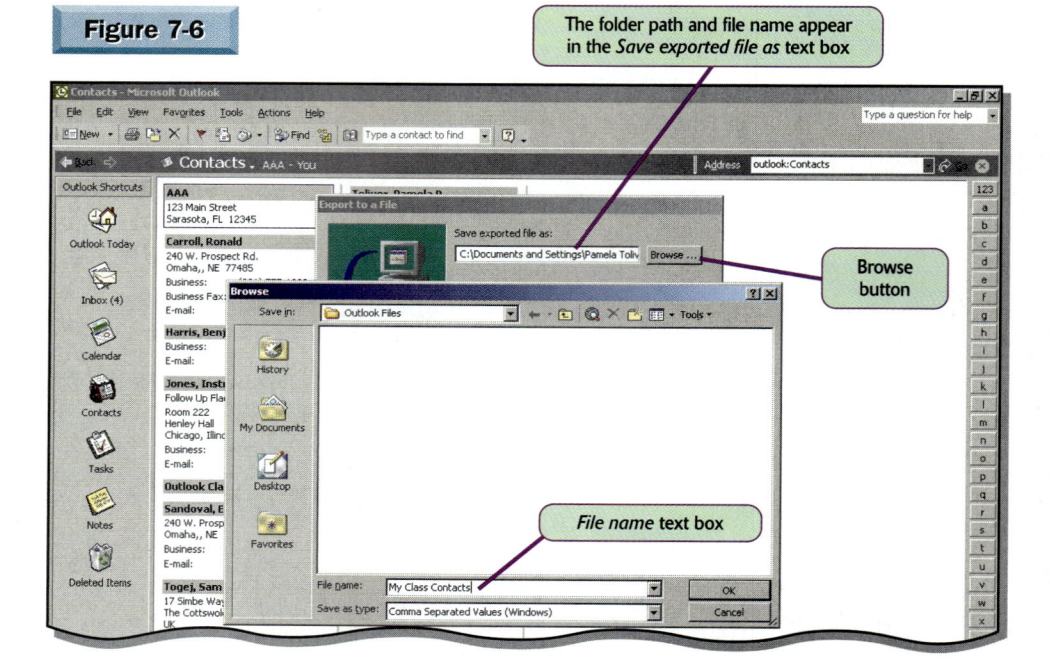

Figure 7-6

7 Click **Finish** to export the contact items.

Figure 7-7

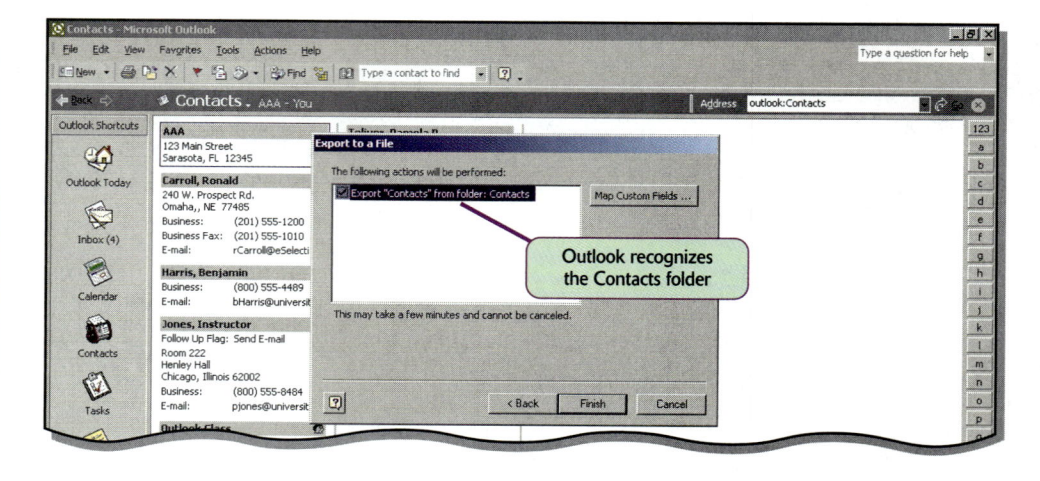

Tip The Import and Export Progress window appears until the action is complete. The more contacts you have stored in the folder, the longer the export process takes.

CHECK POINT

Because you are exporting items from the Contacts folder to a file that will contain the same types of items that require the same field names, you do not need to change the field mappings to connect or match the fields. If you were exporting the items to a file that you could use in a different application or from a folder that contains custom fields, click the Map Custom Fields button and pair fields in the Contacts folder items by dragging them to the appropriate field names in the new file, following the directions in the **Map Custom Fields** dialog box.

Saving vCards as Contacts

After you send contacts from Outlook via e-mail, recipients can add them to their Contacts folder by simply opening them and saving them.

Task 3:
To Save vCards as Contacts

1 Display the **Inbox** and open the message containing *FW: Sam Togej* in the **Subject** field that you received.

2 Point to the attachment, right-click to display the shortcut menu, and select **Open** from the shortcut menu.

Figure 7-8

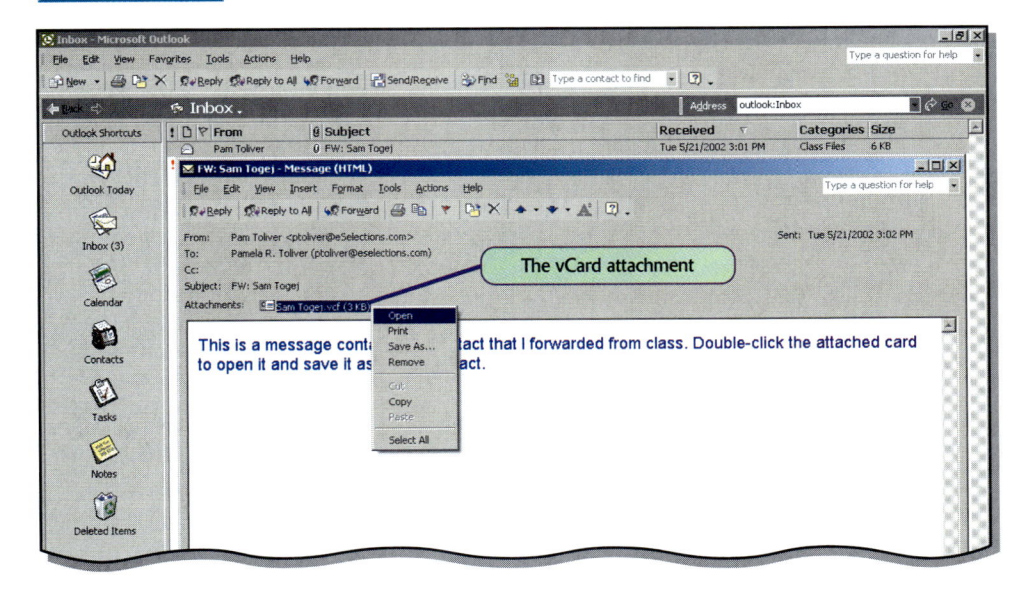

The vCard attachment

Other Ways

To open an attachment:
- Double-click the attachment.

Sending, Exporting, and Importing Contacts

3 Choose **Open it** from the warning message, if necessary, and click **OK** to open the contact.

Tip When an attachment comes from an outside source, it is a good idea to scan the attachment for viruses before opening it.

Figure 7-9

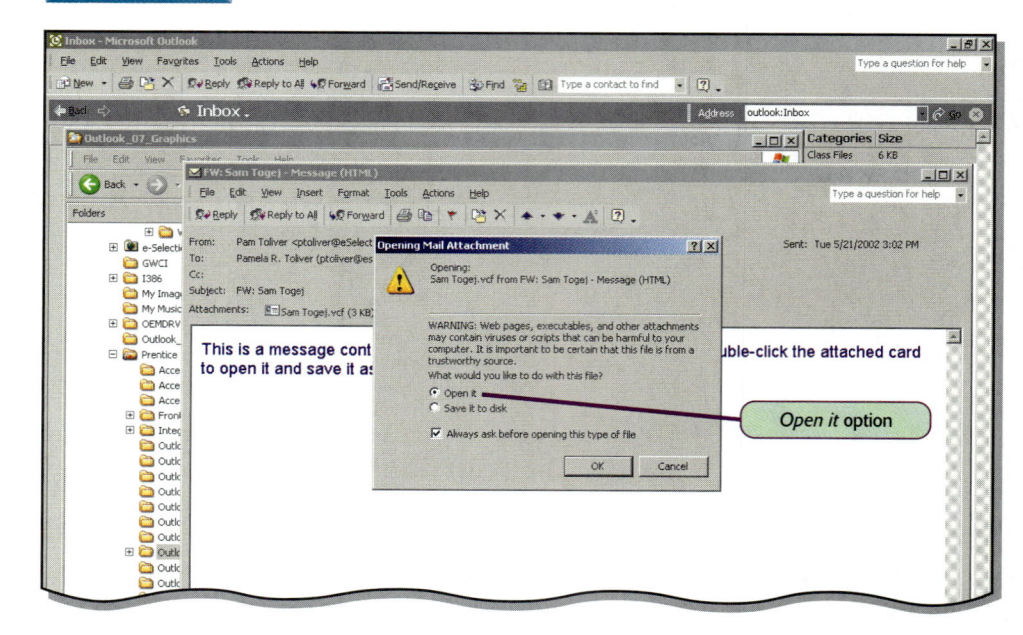

Open it option

4 Click the Save and Close **Save and Close** button to save the contact in your Contacts folder and close the message, if necessary.

5 Select **Add this as a new contact anyway** and click **OK**.

6 Close the message, if necessary, and display Contacts.

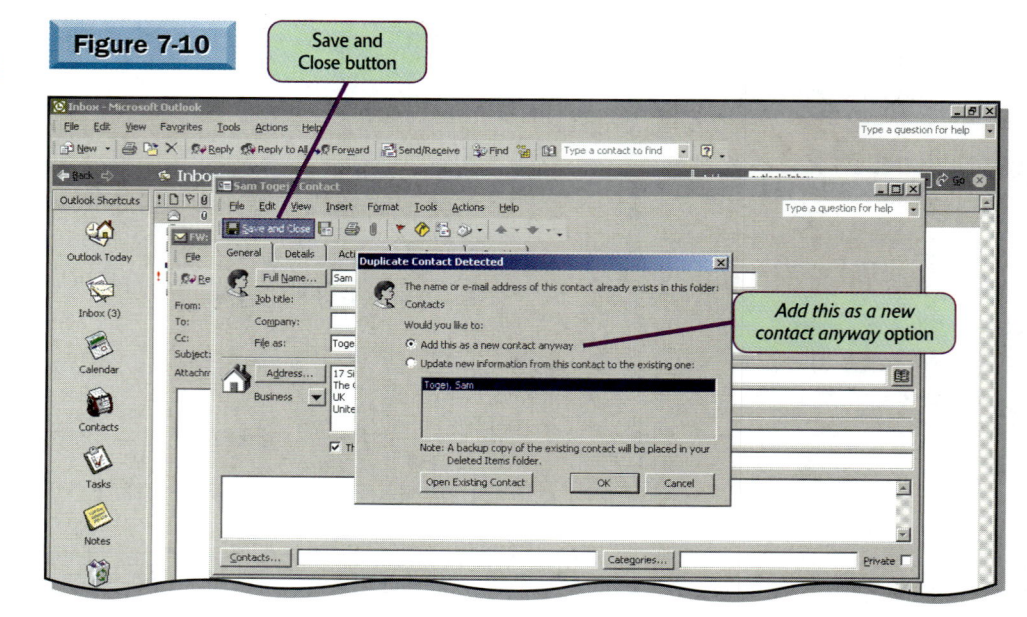

Figure 7-10

Save and Close button

Add this as a new contact anyway option

Tip Notice that you now have two contacts for Sam Togej.

Integrating, Customizing, and Sharing Outlook Files   OU 7-**11**

> **Tip** Some e-mail programs other than Outlook, such as Lotus Notes or GroupWise, can recognize contact listing formats exported from Outlook.

Importing Contacts from Files

Files created by exporting contacts can easily be imported into the Outlook Contacts folder on another computer. By importing a different set of contacts in Task 4, some contacts will be duplicated while others will be new listings. Importing your own exported contact file would duplicate all listings.

Task 4:
To Import Contacts from a File

1 Choose **File | Import and Export**, select **Import from another program or file**, and click **Next**.

Figure 7-11

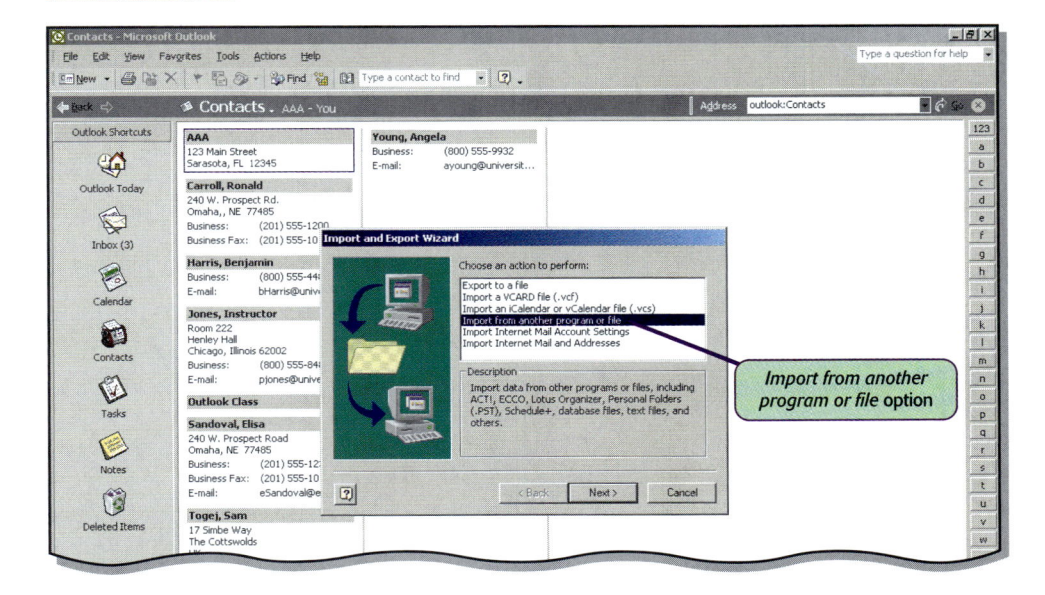

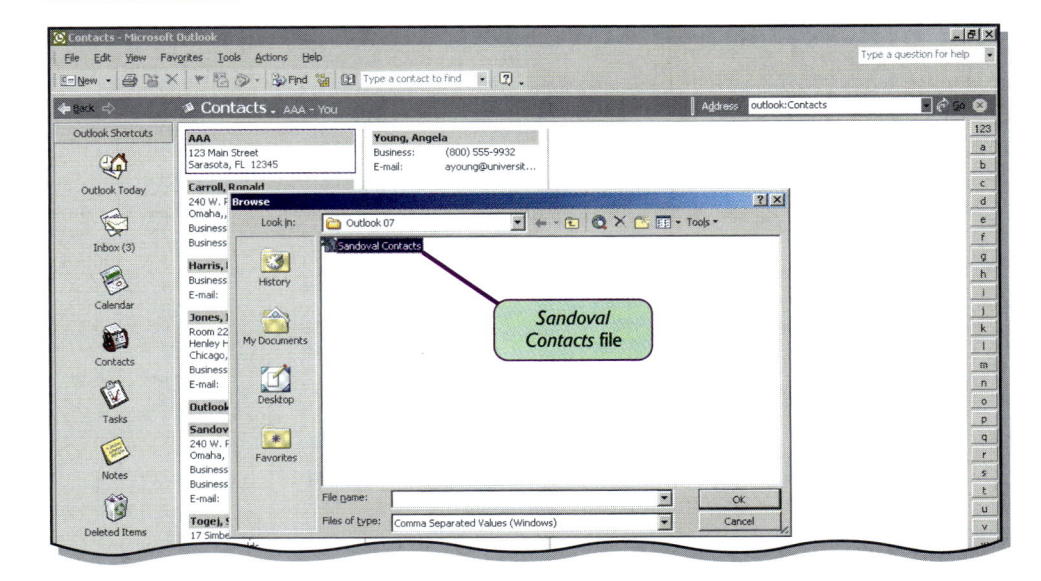

2 Select **Comma Separated Values (Windows)** and click **Next**.

3 Click **Browse**, open the drive and folder containing your student files, select the **Sandoval Contacts.csv** file, and click **OK** to select the file.

Figure 7-12

OU 7-12 Sending, Exporting, and Importing Contacts

4 Click **Next** twice to accept default settings and place the new listing in the **Contacts** folder, and then click **Finish** to import new contacts.

5 Delete duplicate listings from the Contacts folder.

> **Tip** The duplicate entries you see will be different from those shown in Figure 7-13 because of the entries already contained in your Contacts folder. To delete a contact, right-click the contact title bar and select **Delete**.

Figure 7-13

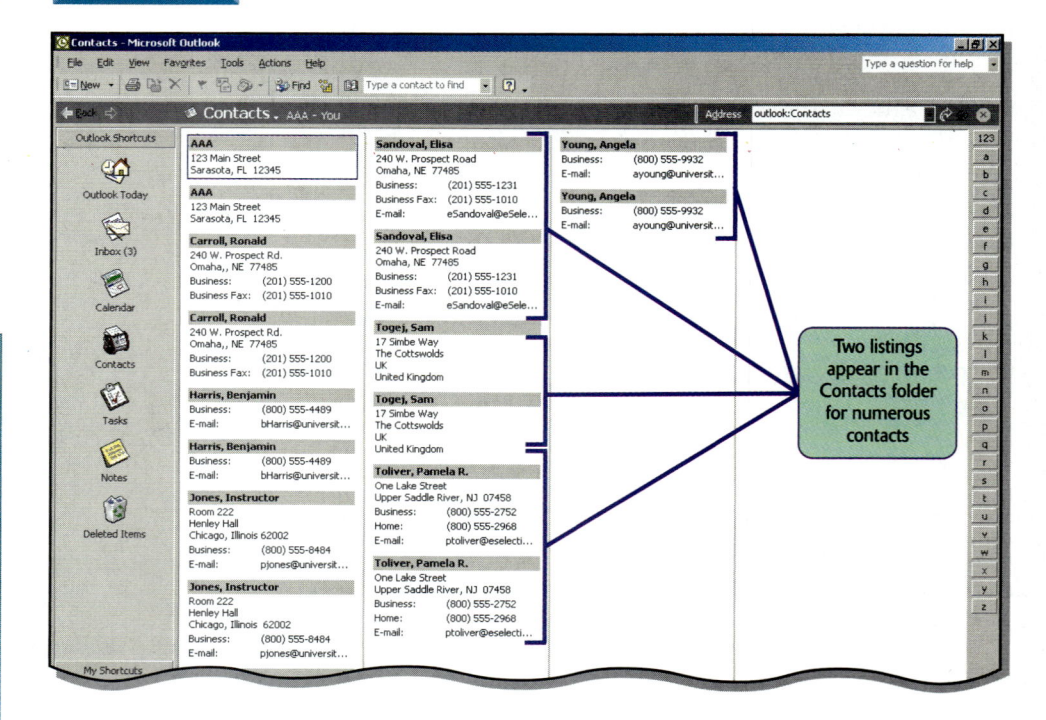

Creating Contacts from E-Mail

E-mail you receive is also a great source for creating contacts. When you receive an e-mail from someone you want to add to your Contacts folder, you can select the information in the *From* field and use it to create a new contact.

Figure 7-14

Task 5:
To Create a Contact from an E-Mail Message

1 Open the **Inbox** folder and open a message, preferably from someone you have not added to Contacts.

2 Right-click the sender's name in the **From** field at the top of the message and select **Add to Contacts** to create a new contact.

3 Complete the contact information, save and close the contact, and close any open Outlook items.

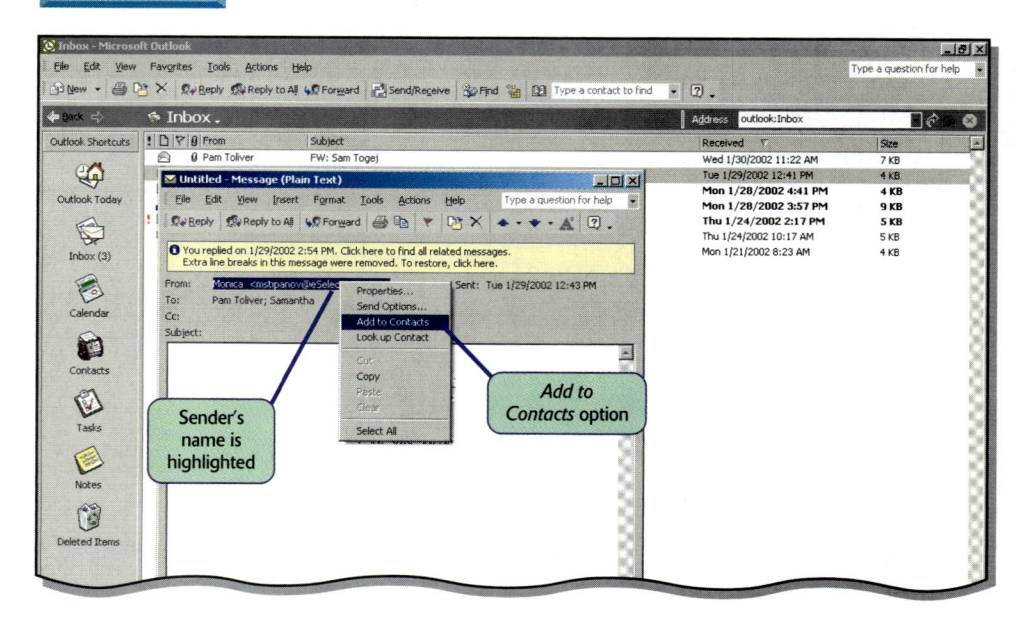

CHECK POINT

In Task 1, you learned how easy it is to export contacts to a file so that you can import them into the Contacts folder on another computer. You can use the same command to export items from other Outlook folders as well. The type of file you create depends on the information you are exporting and the application in which you want to use the data. Simply choose **File | Import and Export**, select the type of file you want to create from the **Create a file of type** list, select the Outlook folder that contains the data you want to export, and identify the drive and folder on which you want to store the file. Outlook will do most of the exporting work for you and ask you questions along the way. When the export is complete, be sure to open the new file in the application to which you sent it to see how it looks.

By the same token, you can import data from other files into Outlook and store the data in one of the default folders or in a custom folder. Simply follow the instructions provided in Task 4 to open an Access file, an Excel file, or another file and place the data in the folder of your choice. It is a great way to add a list of people from an Access database to your Contacts folder!

Sharing Outlook Folders

> **Tip** Until now, Figures in this Project have shown contacts and other items available from Outlook installed on a stand-alone computer that was not connected to a network. Figures in this section show contacts and other items available from a networked version of Outlook. As a result, the items will be different.

Office assistants often maintain the calendar, update tasks in the task list, and perform other functions that require access to a supervisor's Outlook folders. As a result, Outlook provides two different approaches for granting access to folders:

- Assigning *delegates* to access folders
- Setting folder properties to share the folder

Assigning Delegates to Access Folders

Those to whom you, the *owner*, grant folder access are called *delegates*, and you can select the folders to which each delegate should have access. In addition, you can select the *access level* you want each delegate to have. A delegate's access level controls the actions he or she can perform. These levels and rights that apply to delegates are identified in Table 7-2.

Table 7-2	Owner and Delegate Access Rights
Level	**Rights**
Owner	Create, read, modify, and delete all items; create subfolders; and grant, modify, and delete permission levels for delegates
Author	Read and create all folder items, modify and delete items the author creates in the folder, and send items to others on behalf of the owner
Editor	Includes all the rights of the author; in addition, can modify and delete owner-created items
Reviewer	Read folder items

Sharing Outlook Folders

Troubleshooting To assign delegates and set delegate *permissions*, you must be connected to a network that is running a Microsoft Exchange server. If you are not connected to a network, follow the direction of your instructor for information on how to proceed.

Task 6:
To Assign Delegates and Set Delegate Permissions

1 Display the Outlook window, choose **Tools | Options**, click the **Delegates** tab, and click the **Add** button to add a new delegate.

Tip The listings shown on this network will be different from those shown on your network.

Figure 7-15

Delegates tab
Add button

2 Select a classmate's name from the **Type Name or Select from List** box and click **Add** to add the name to **Add Users** list.

3 Click **OK** to close the **Add Users** dialog box and open the **Delegate Permissions** dialog box.

Tip To select multiple names, press Ctrl as you click each name. The permissions you set will apply to all delegates.

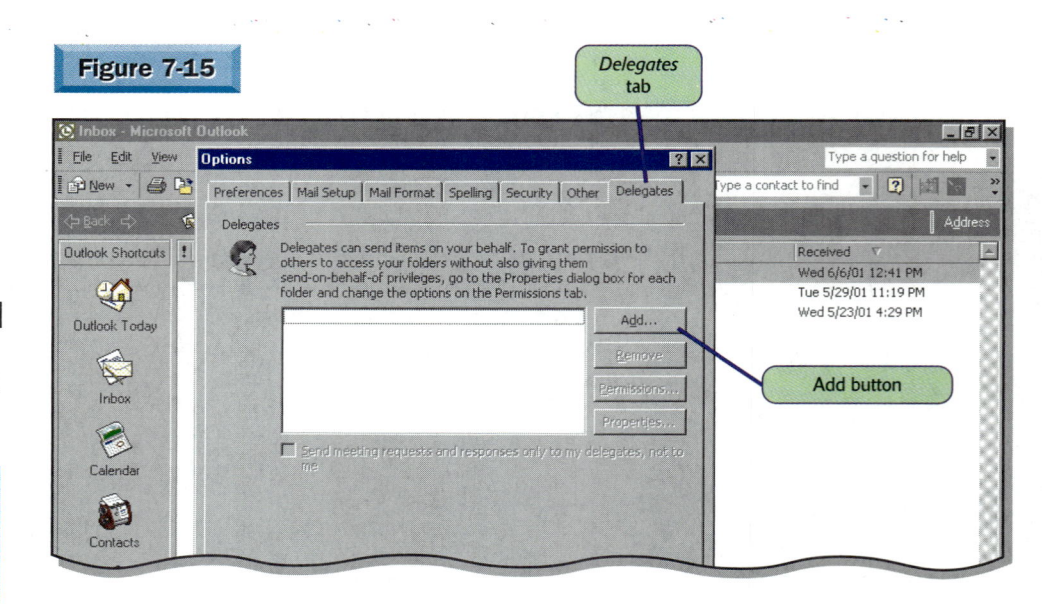

Figure 7-16

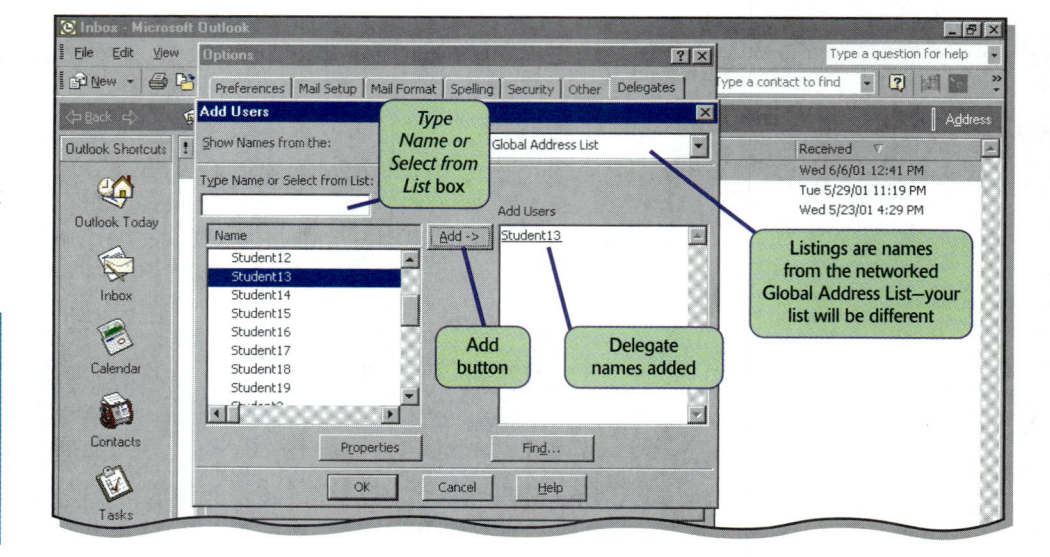

Type Name or Select from List box
Add button
Delegate names added
Listings are names from the networked Global Address List—your list will be different

Troubleshooting If the Delegate Permissions dialog box fails to open automatically, select the user to whom you want to assign permissions and click the **Permissions** button on the Delegate page of the Options dialog box.

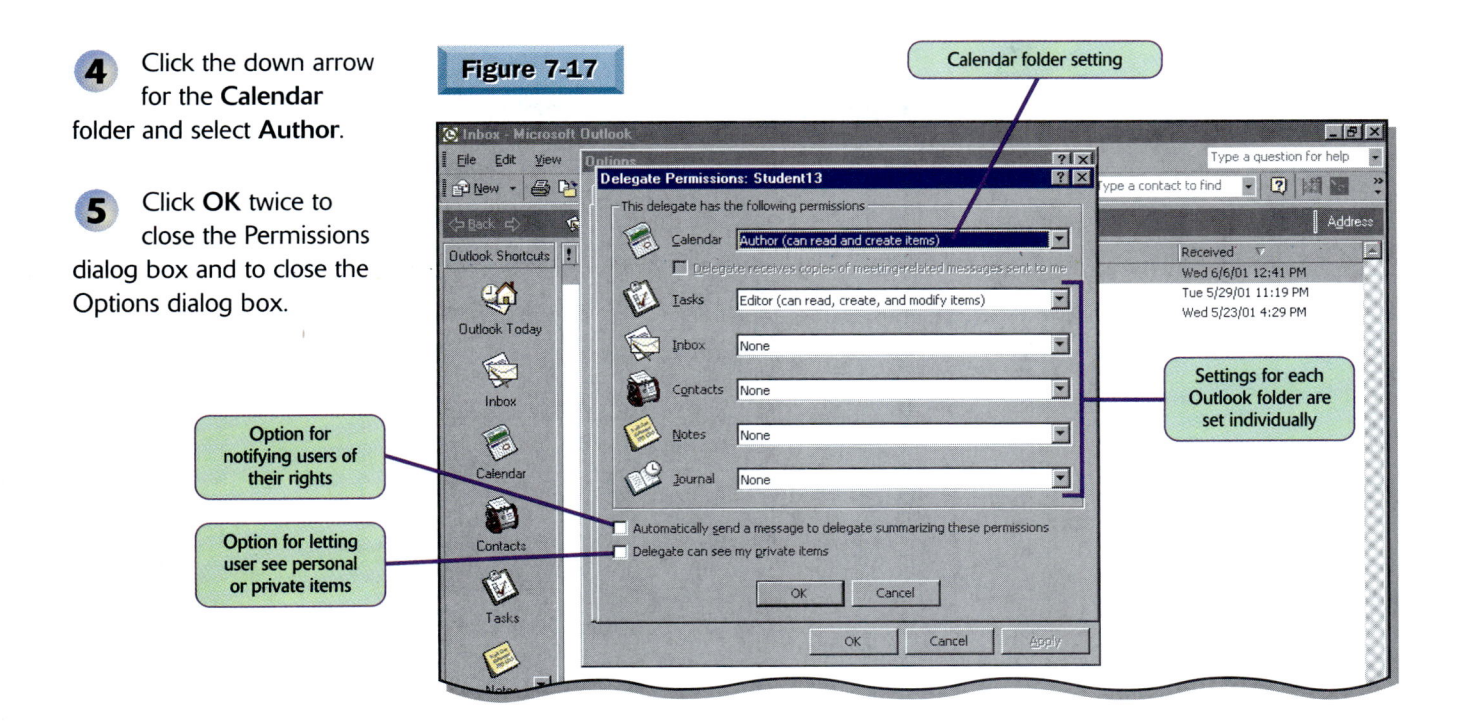

Integrating, Customizing, and Sharing Outlook Files

4 Click the down arrow for the **Calendar** folder and select **Author**.

5 Click **OK** twice to close the Permissions dialog box and to close the Options dialog box.

Figure 7-17

- Calendar folder setting
- Option for notifying users of their rights
- Option for letting user see personal or private items
- Settings for each Outlook folder are set individually

WEB TIP

Is Big Brother watching? While state laws differ, generally employers have the right to peruse your inbox without your knowledge. By mid-2001, 74 percent of all companies had initiated electronic monitoring of employees. In some cases, companies monitor only the sites their employees visit on the Internet while others check computer hard disks, e-mail messages, voice messages, phone conversations, or a combination of all these systems. Still others monitor employee performance electronically using video cameras!

Setting Folder Permissions

Assigning delegates to access folders typically provides sufficient folder access options. However, the owner of the folder can set additional access options by changing the folder properties. Setting permissions by changing folder properties enables users with rights to your folders to add them to their Folder List and, therefore, to their Outlook bar for easy access. Setting folder permissions enables you to select access levels that contain different options, as defined in Table 7-3.

Table 7-3 Folder Permissions Rights

Level	Rights
Owner	Total control of all items and subfolders in the folder and authority to grant rights and set permissions
Publishing Editor	Create, read, modify, and delete all items and files. Create subfolders but neither own the items nor be a contact that is notified of entries and changes, as an owner would be.
Editor	All rights associated with Publishing Editor except the right to create subfolders
Publishing Author	Create and read items and files, create subfolders, and modify and delete their own items.
Author	All rights associated with Publishing Author except the right to create subfolders
Nonediting Author	Create, read, and delete their own folder items but cannot edit items belonging to others
Reviewer	View and read items in the folder
Contributor	Create items only, without viewing other items in the folder
Custom	Perform only the activities selected by the folder owner
None	See the folder only, not folder items

Task 7:
To Set Folder Permissions

1 Choose **View | Folder List** to display the **Folder List**, if necessary.

2 Right-click the **Tasks** folder in the **Folder List**, select **Properties**, and click the **Permissions** tab.

3 Click the **Add** button to select users to whom you want to assign permissions.

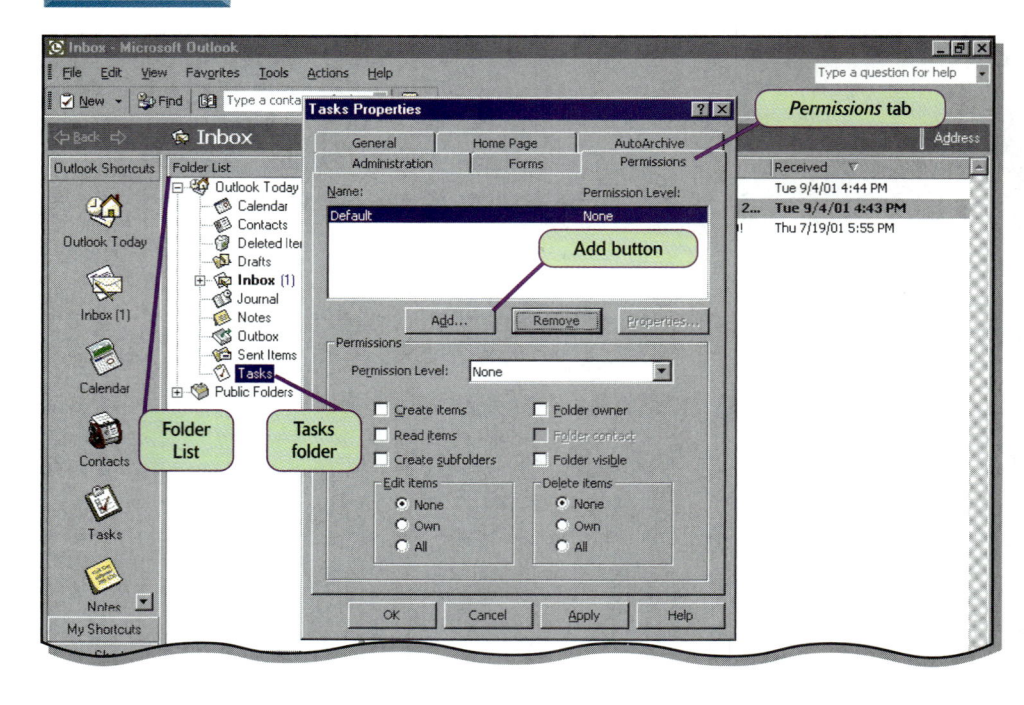

Figure 7-18

Integrating, Customizing, and Sharing Outlook Files OU 7-17

4 Select the name of the user designated by your instructor, click **Add** to add the name to the **Add Users** list, and click **OK** to close the **Add Users** dialog box.

Figure 7-19

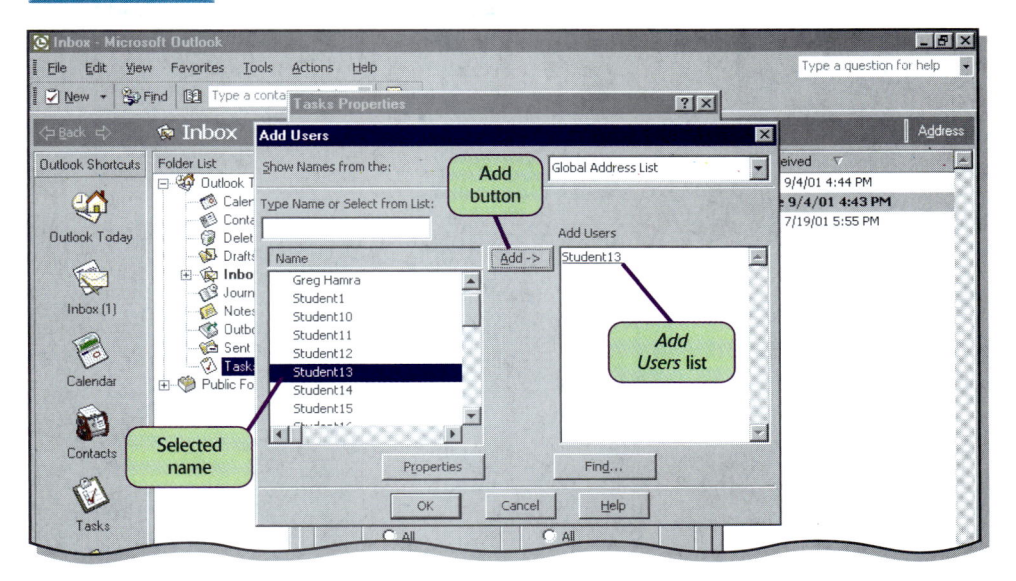

5 Select the name of the person for whom you want to set permissions, click the **Permission Level** down arrow, and select **Reviewer**.

> **Tip** Because you selected the **Tasks** folder originally, the permissions you set apply to the Tasks folder only.

6 Click **Apply** to set the permission level and then click **OK** twice to close the **Permissions** dialog box and to close the **Options** dialog box.

Figure 7-20

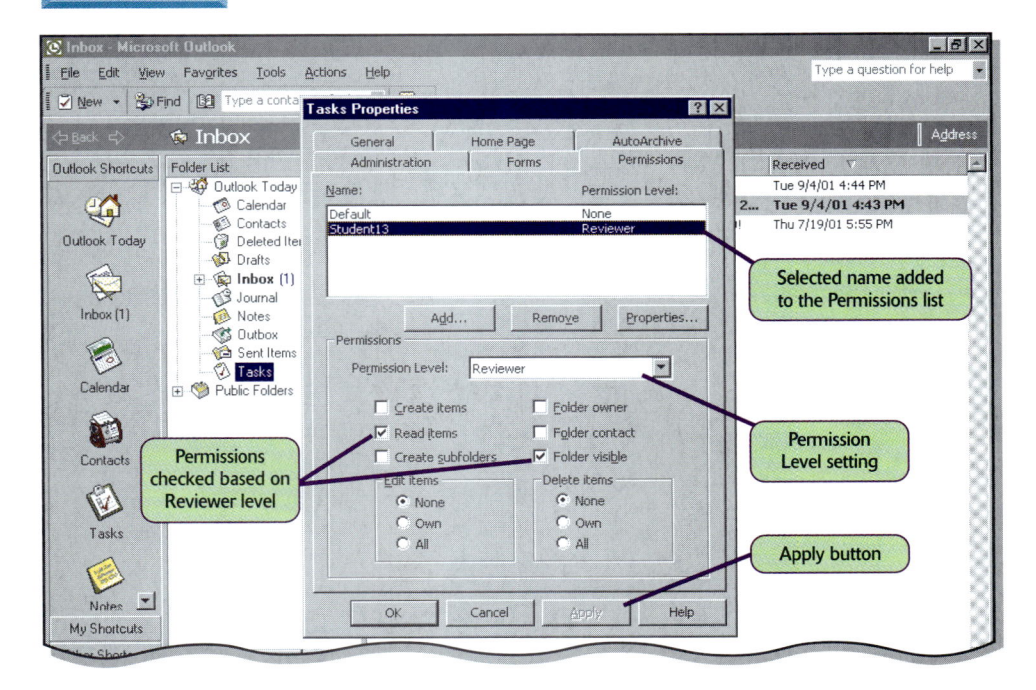

Opening Folders Belonging to Other Users

Now that you have set permissions for a classmate to access two of your folders—one as a delegate and one by setting folder permissions—those users have access to your folders. When they are logged on and connected to the network, they can open your folders and display folder contents directly from Outlook on their networked computers.

Opening Folders as a Delegate

If you have been assigned delegate rights to another user's folders, you can open the folder and display it in a separate window on your computer desktop.

Tip: Before opening another user's folder, the other user must have previously appointed you as a delegate and set delegate permissions for you.

Task 8:
To Open Another User's Folder

1 Choose **File | Open | Other User's Folder** and click the **Name** button.

Figure 7-21

2 Scroll the list of users until the folder owner's name appears, select the folder owner's name, and click **OK**.

Troubleshooting
If the user whose folder you are opening has not set permissions for you to access the folder, Outlook displays a message advising you that you do not have rights to the folder. Click **OK** to continue and then ask the other person to assign you delegate permissions.

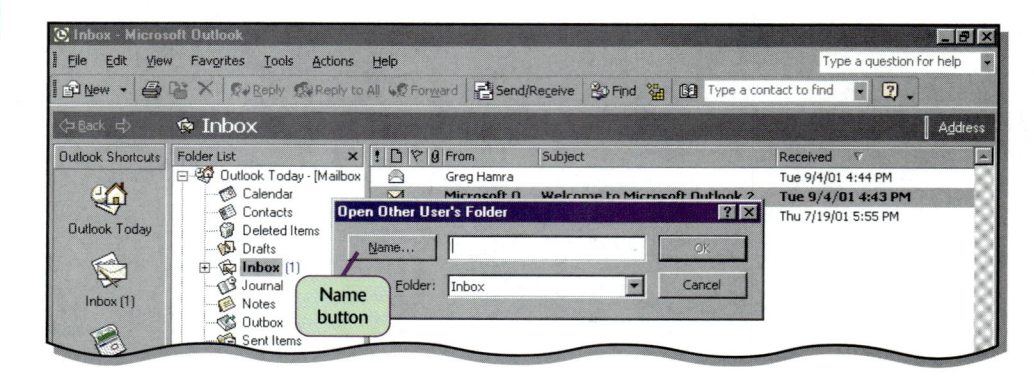

Figure 7-22

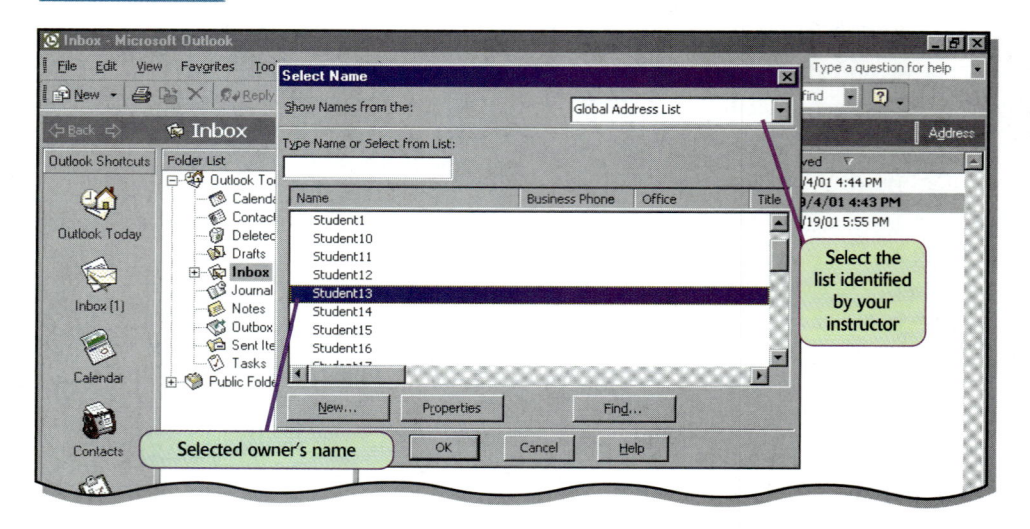

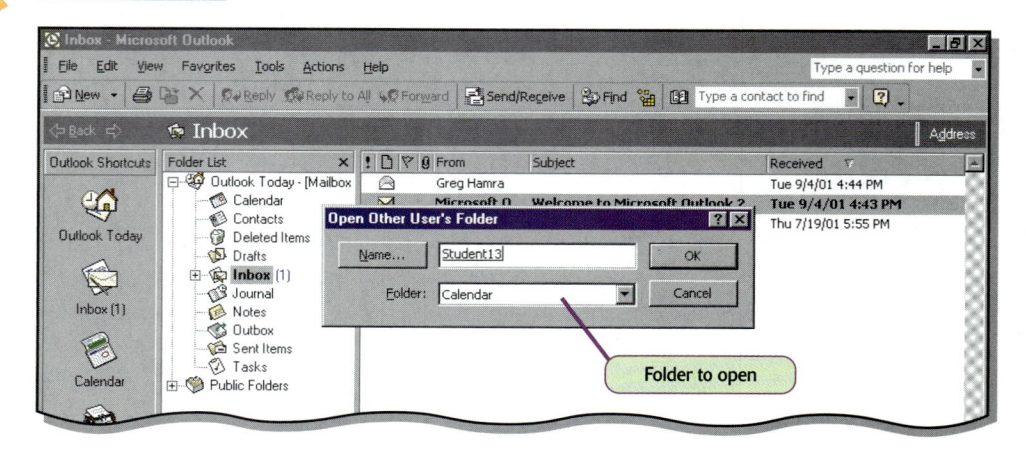

3 Click the **Folder** down arrow and select **Calendar** to open the other user's Calendar folder.

4 Click **OK**.

Figure 7-23

Integrating, Customizing, and Sharing Outlook Files

OU 7-19

5 Close the other person's Calendar and then close the Folder List.

> **Tip** Notice that there is no name on Student13's Calendar window. Juggling appointments to the correct schedule when you have multiple Calendar windows open can be a challenge!

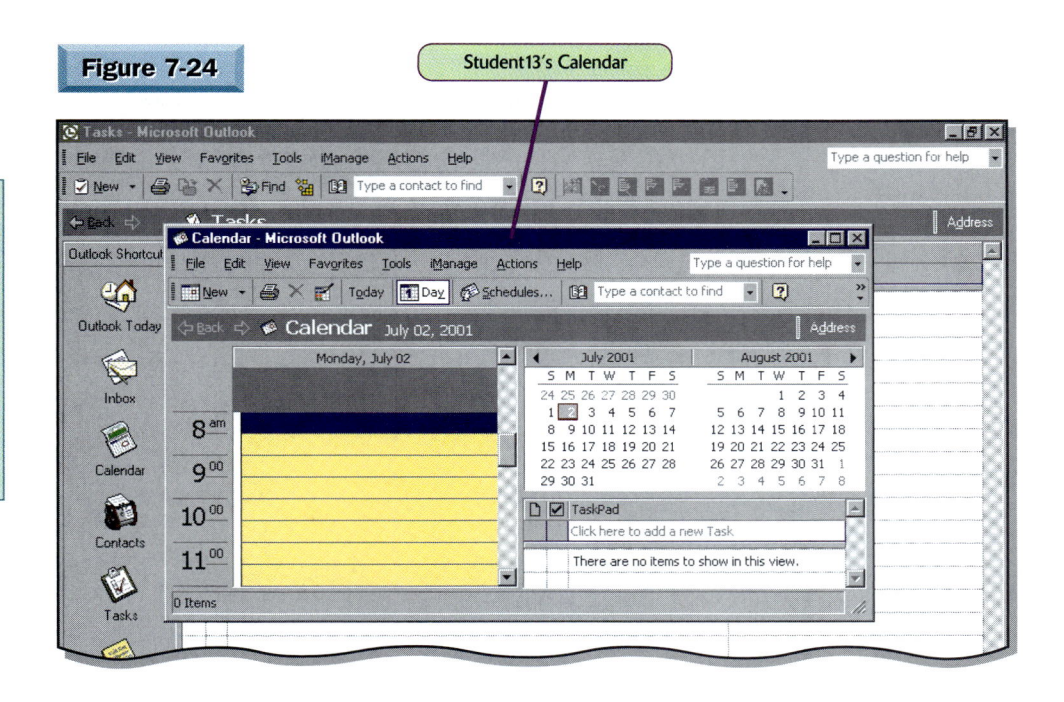

Figure 7-24

Student13's Calendar

Creating Office XP Files from Outlook

Outlook allows you to create new Excel, Word, and PowerPoint files directly from the Outlook menu. You can also select a contact from the Contacts folder and create a new letter to the contact.

Creating New Blank Office XP Files from Outlook

Using Outlook as a launching pad, you can create new Excel, Word, and PowerPoint files. To create a new file using one of these applications, the application must be installed on the computer you are using.

Task 9:
To Create a New PowerPoint File from Outlook

1 Display the Outlook program window and choose **File | New | Office Document**.

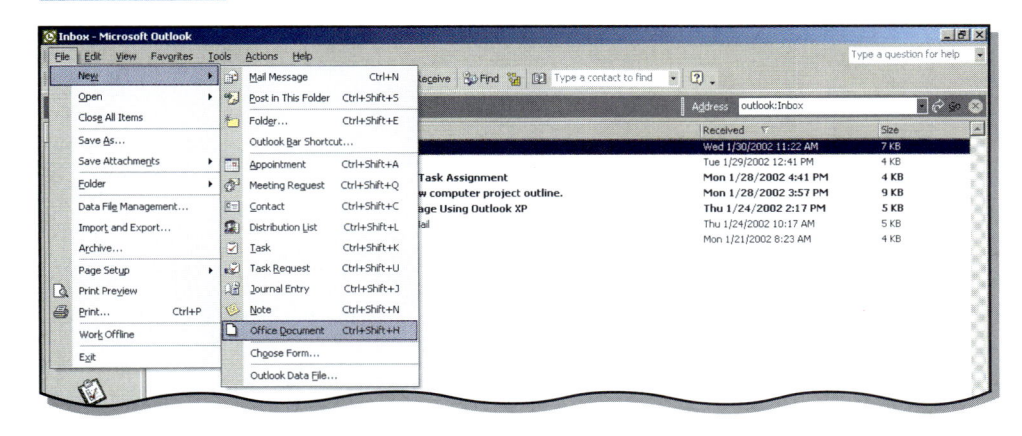

Figure 7-25

> **Other Ways** To create a new Office document from Outlook:
> - Press Ctrl + Shift + H

OU 7-20 Creating Office XP Files from Outlook

2 Double-click the **Microsoft PowerPoint Presentation** icon.

Figure 7-26

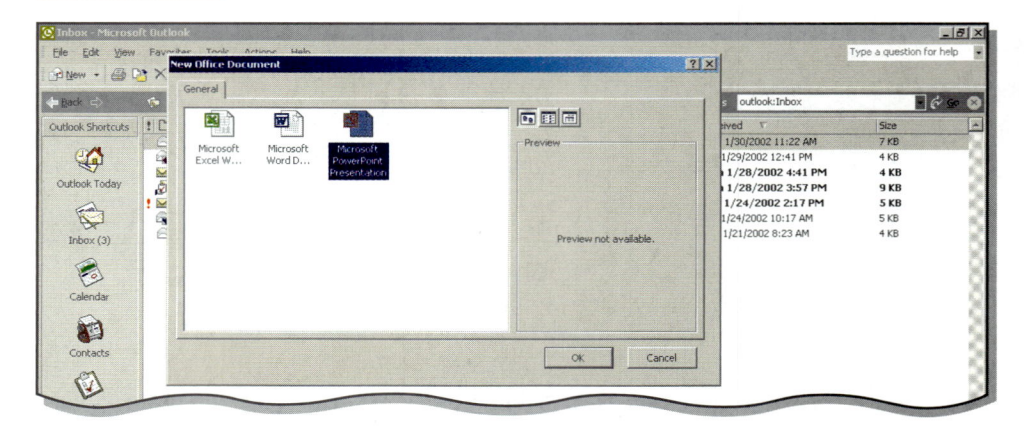

3 Type **Microsoft Outlook 2002 Presentation**, press Ctrl + Enter, and type **by** *Your Name*, substituting your real name where appropriate.

4 Save the file using the file name *My Outlook Presentation* in your student folder and then exit PowerPoint.

Figure 7-27

- PowerPoint launches
- Slide Layout task pane opens
- Text in placeholders
- Slide 1 thumbnail
- Slide 1 in a new presentation appears

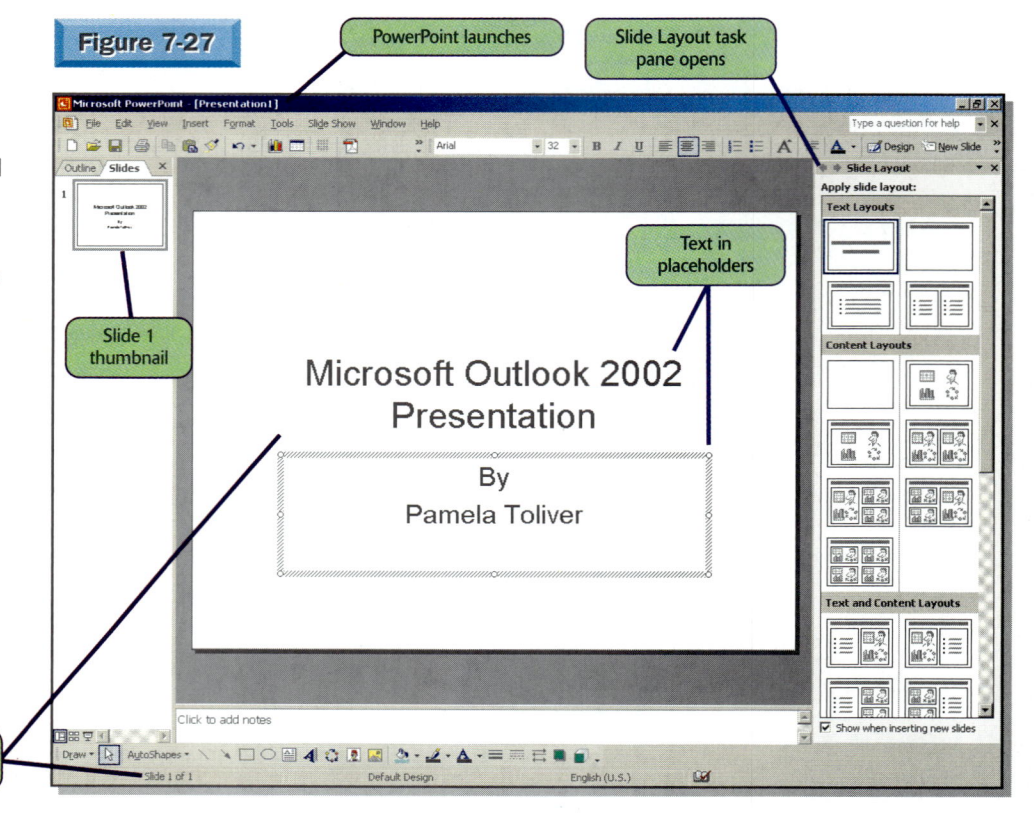

Integrating, Customizing, and Sharing Outlook Files　　OU 7-**21**

Creating a Letter to an Outlook Contact

When you need to create a letter to someone in your Contacts list, you can use the Contact listing to generate the letter. Outlook starts Word and enters the information it finds in Contacts and then Word presents Wizard pages for entering other pieces of information for the letter.

Task 10:
To Create a New Letter to an Outlook Contact

1 Open the **Contacts** folder and select the contact listing for **Elisa Sandoval**.

2 Choose **Actions | New Letter to Contact**.

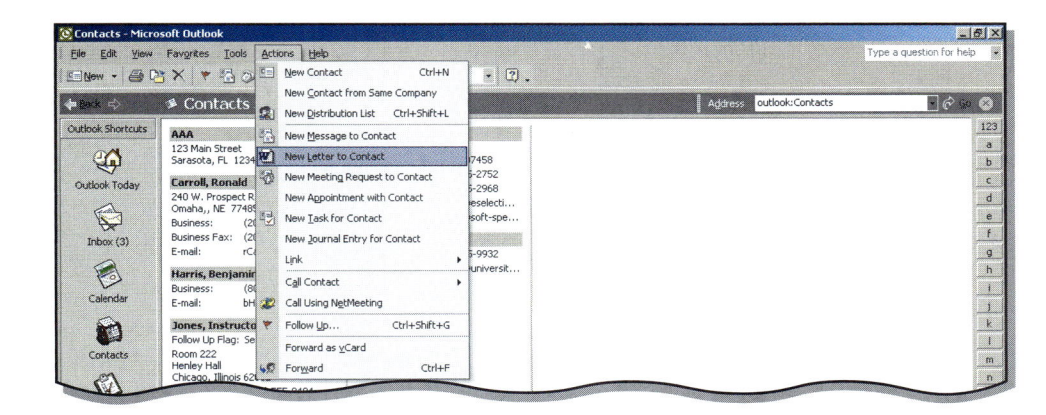

Figure 7-28

Troubleshooting If the Office Assistant opens and offers help, right-click the assistant and select **Hide** to close it.

3 Select the **Date line** check box, select **Professional Letter** from the **Choose a page design** drop-down list, and click **Next**.

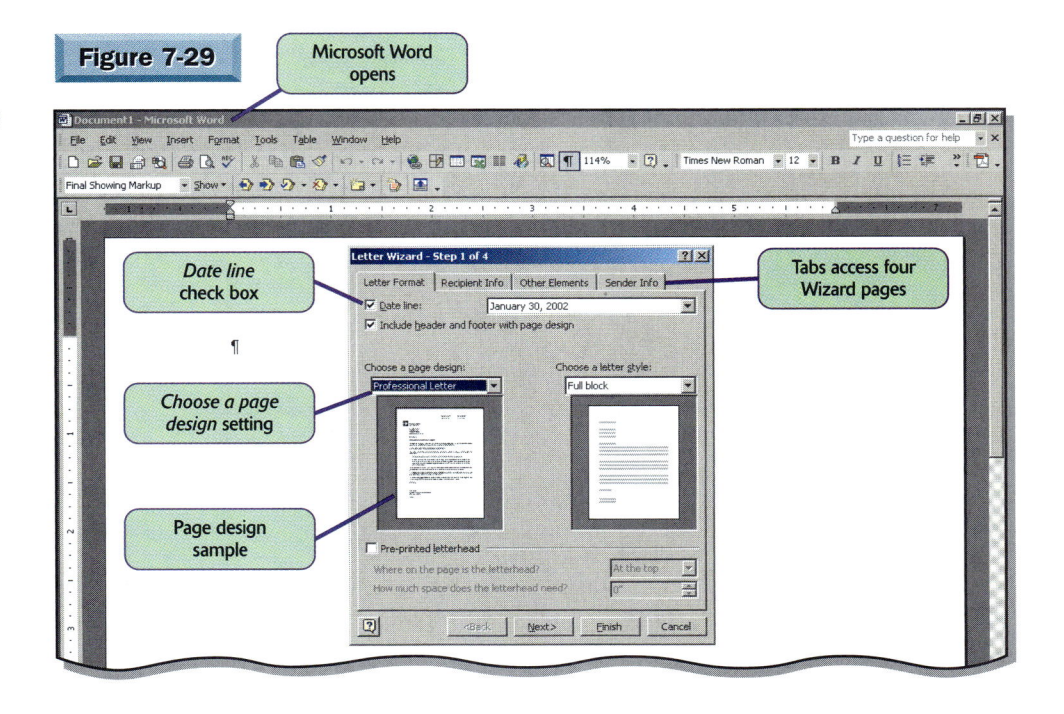

Figure 7-29

Microsoft Word opens

Date line check box

Choose a page design setting

Page design sample

Tabs access four Wizard pages

Creating Office XP Files from Outlook

4 Type **Dear Ms. Sandoval:** in the **Salutation** text box and click **Next**.

Figure 7-30

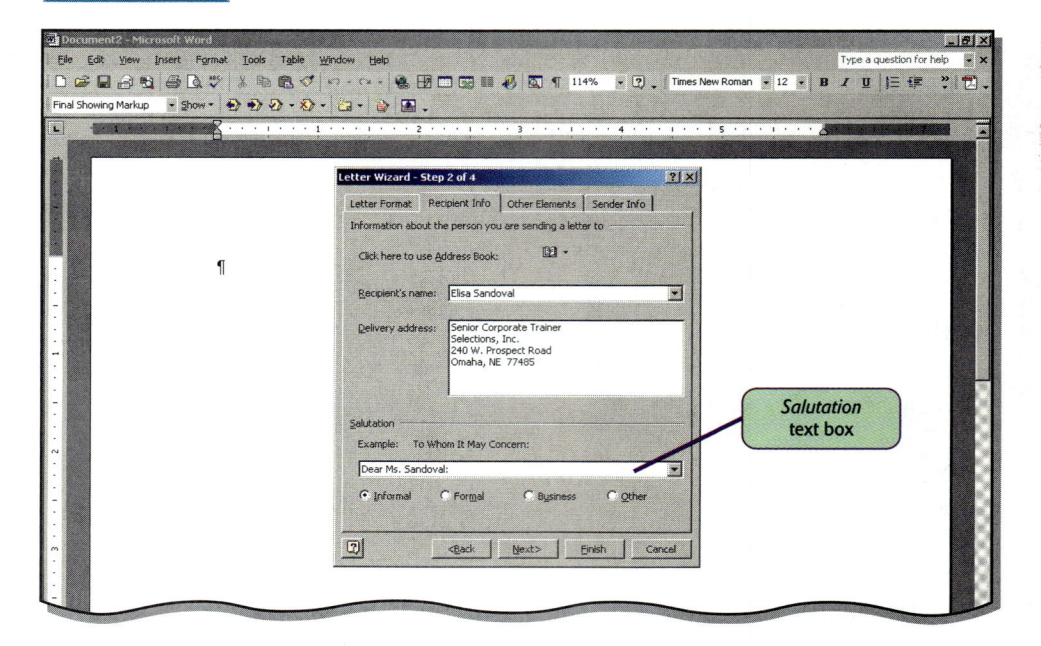

5 Select the **Reference line** check box, select **RE:** from the drop-down list, click in the **Reference line** text box after the RE:, type **Outlook Class**, and click **Next**.

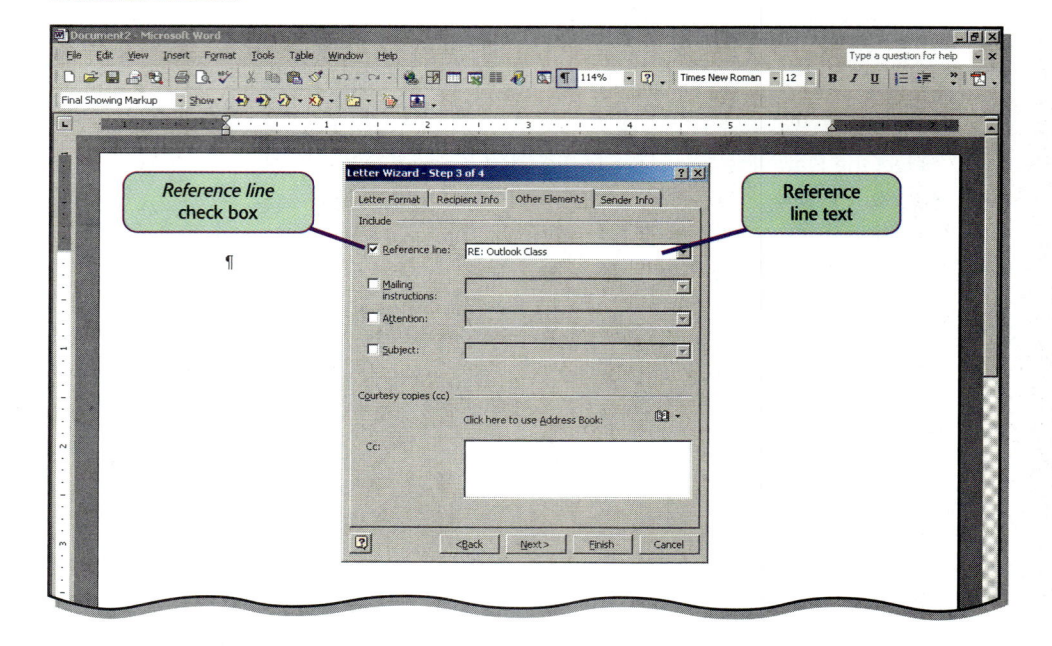

Figure 7-31

6 Type your personal information in the **Sender's name** and **Return address** boxes, select a **Complimentary closing** from the drop-down list, and type your school name in the **Company** text box.

Figure 7-32

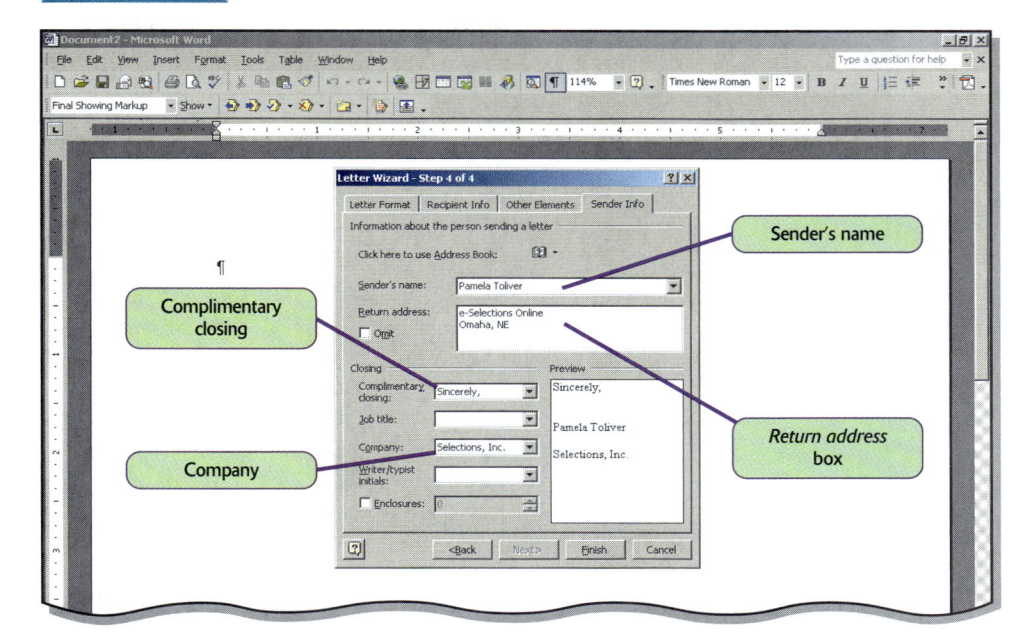

7 Click **Finish**, type the message shown in Figure 7-33 to Ms. Sandoval, and save the file on a floppy disk or in the folder identified by your instructor using the file name **Sandoval Letter**.

Figure 7-33

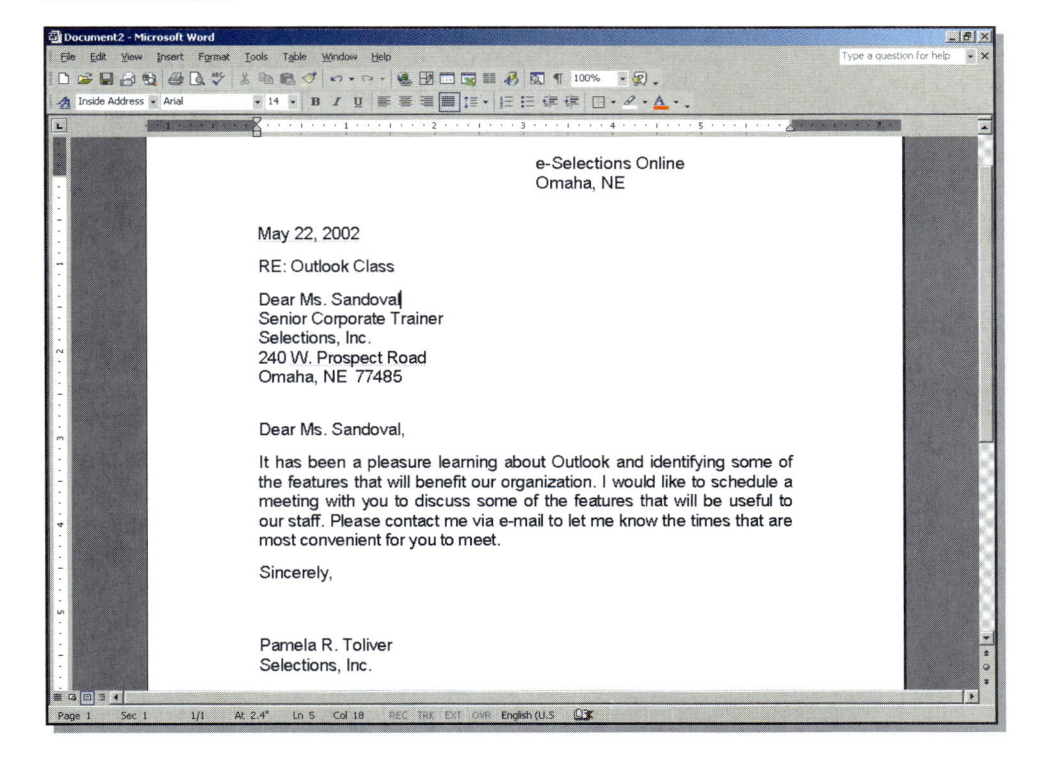

Creating E-Mail Stationery

CHECK POINT

One of the most frequently used Outlook integration tasks in Corporate America is creating form letters using Outlook contacts as the data source. Outlook 2002 enables you to quickly and efficiently merge contacts with a Word 2002 document and generate form letters. When you use listings in the Contacts folder to create merge letters, Outlook creates a temporary mail merge source file containing the listings and launches Word 2002 so that you can complete the merge letter, insert merge fields, and finish the merge. While the Wizards in both Outlook and Word guide you through the mail merge process, a basic understanding of the terminology associated with mail merges and experience working with merges increases your chances of success.

Tip To learn more about mail merge terminology and procedures, launch Word, search for help on mail merge, and review the information in the **About mail merge for form letters and mass mailings** topic.

Creating E-Mail Stationery

As you might have discovered, Outlook comes with a box of stationery that you can use to format e-mail messages you send to others. Outlook also provides you with tools for creating and personalizing your own stationery when you use the HTML mail format. You can use these tools to create and format the stationery Ms. Wright requested.

Task 11:
To Create Custom E-Mail Stationery

1. Choose **Tools | Options | Mail Format**.

2. Click the **Stationery Picker** button and then click **New**.

Troubleshooting
If the **Stationery Picker** button is unavailable, click the **Compose in this message format** down arrow and select **HTML**.

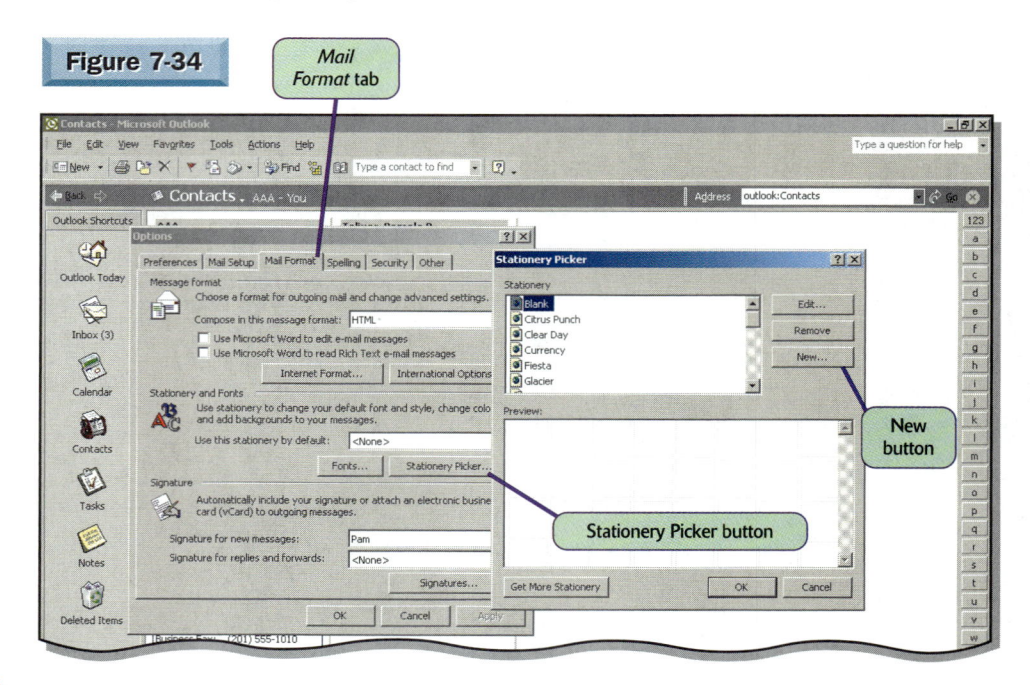

Figure 7-34

Integrating, Customizing, and Sharing Outlook Files

3 Type *Your Initials* **e-Selections** in the **Enter a name for your new stationery** text box, select the **Start with a blank stationery** option, and click **Next**.

Figure 7-35

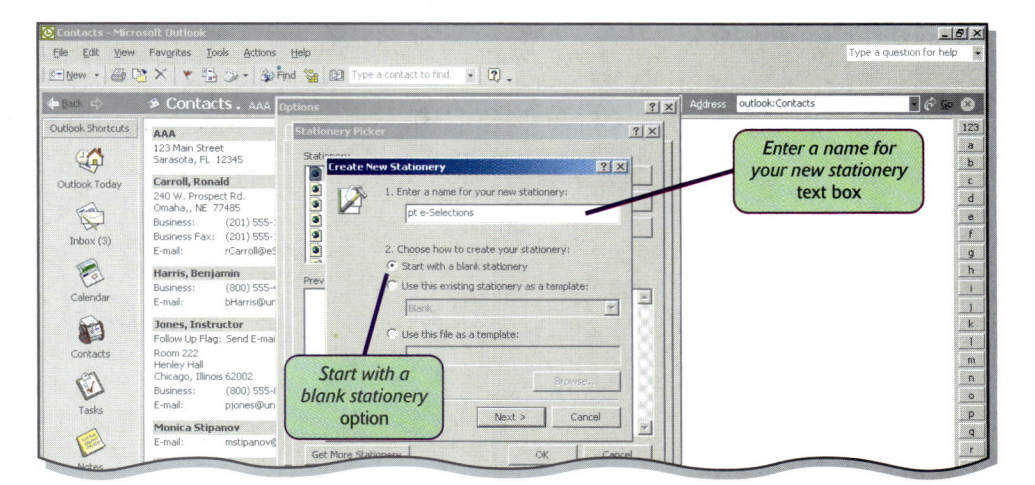

4 Select the **Picture** option and click **Browse** to open the Background Picture dialog box.

5 Open the drive and folder containing your student files, select the *e-Selections.gif* file, and click **Select**.

6 Click the **Change font** button, select **Arial**, **Bold**, and **12** from appropriate font format lists, and click **OK** four times to close all open dialog boxes.

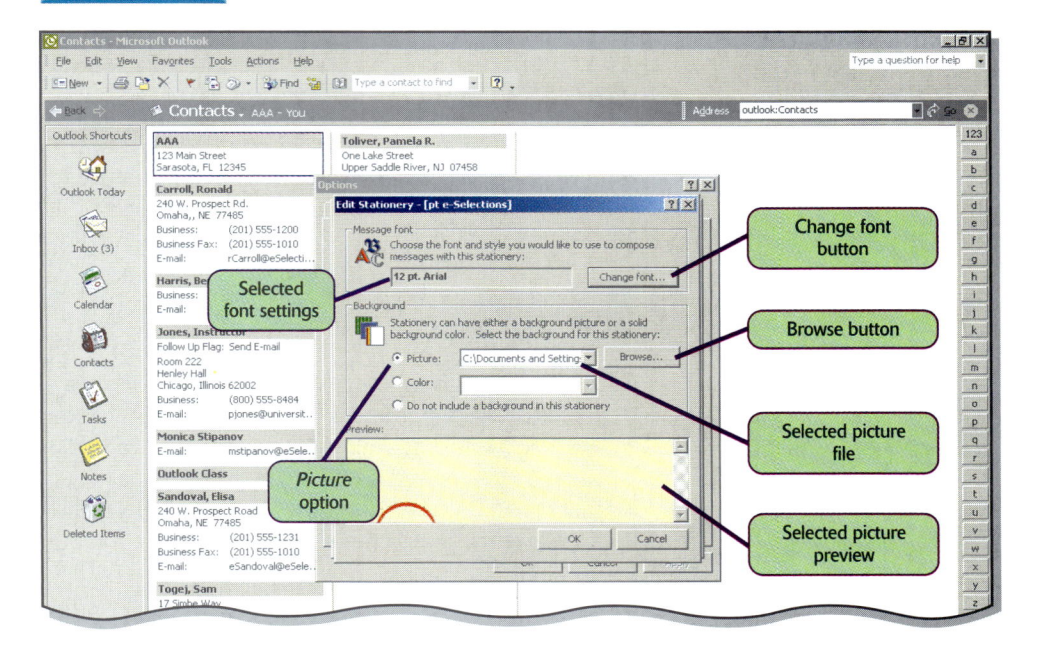

Figure 7-36

Creating E-Mail Stationery

7 Open the **Inbox** folder and click the **New Message** button.

8 Close the message without saving it.

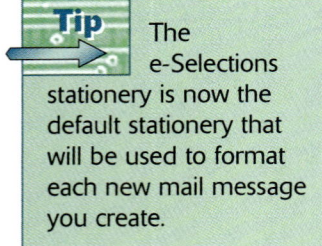

Tip The e-Selections stationery is now the default stationery that will be used to format each new mail message you create.

Figure 7-37

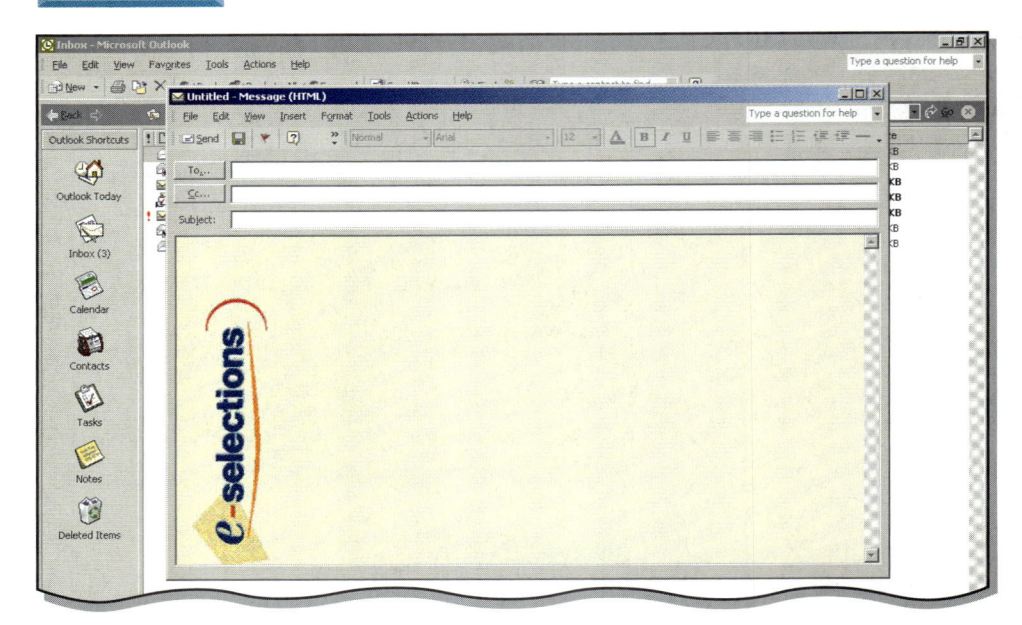

Troubleshooting If your signature block is still active or overlays the graphic on the new stationery, choose **Tools | Options | Mail Format**, select **None** from the **Signature for new messages** drop-down list, and click **OK**.

CHECK POINT

Tip If Word is not designated as your e-mail editor, another program such as FrontPage may open for editing the signature. To ensure that these steps operate as expected, you may also want to select **Rich Text** as the message format.

When you plan to use custom stationery for your e-mail messages, you may have to adjust the alignment and position of the signature that you plan to use. If you are using Word as your e-mail editor, you can adjust the position of the signature using Word tools. If you are using Outlook as your e-mail editor, editing the signature is a bit more complex, even though you will still use Word to make the adjustments. To edit the signature:

1. Choose **Tools | Options | Mail Format**.
2. Select the signature to edit and then click the **Signatures** button.
3. Click the **Edit** button and then click the **Advanced Edit** button.
4. Click **Yes** in response to the message that you will be opening an editor that is not part of Outlook.
5. Press [Enter] two or three times, select the entire signature including the blank lines, and adjust the indent position using the Word ruler or press [Tab] several times to indent each line of the signature. When you type text in a new e-mail message, text will now be aligned at the new indent position.
6. Save and close the signature.

After you have adjusted the signature settings, switch back to Outlook and click **OK** twice to save the signature edits. The next time you use the signature in a message, you will see the difference.

Integrating, Customizing, and Sharing Outlook Files   **OU 7-27**

Creating Custom Outlook Forms

The stationery you designed for your e-mail messages changed the look of the message area without changing the information the form contained. Each item you create in Outlook—a new contact, a new task, a new message, and so forth—is designed to hold specific pieces of information. When you create a new item, you enter information into different fields contained on a *form*—a predesigned layout of fields that hold item information.

Outlook forms are generic in nature; therefore, organizations often choose to add fields of their own which contain information unique to their business. For example, Ms. Wright has requested that you include an order number field in all e-mails from e-Selections. The Outlook *toolbox* contains tools for creating or modifying Outlook forms. You can use these tools to create the custom message form Ms. Wright has requested. New Outlook forms are based on existing Outlook forms that you edit and save as new forms.

Task 12:
To Create a Custom Message Form

Figure 7-38

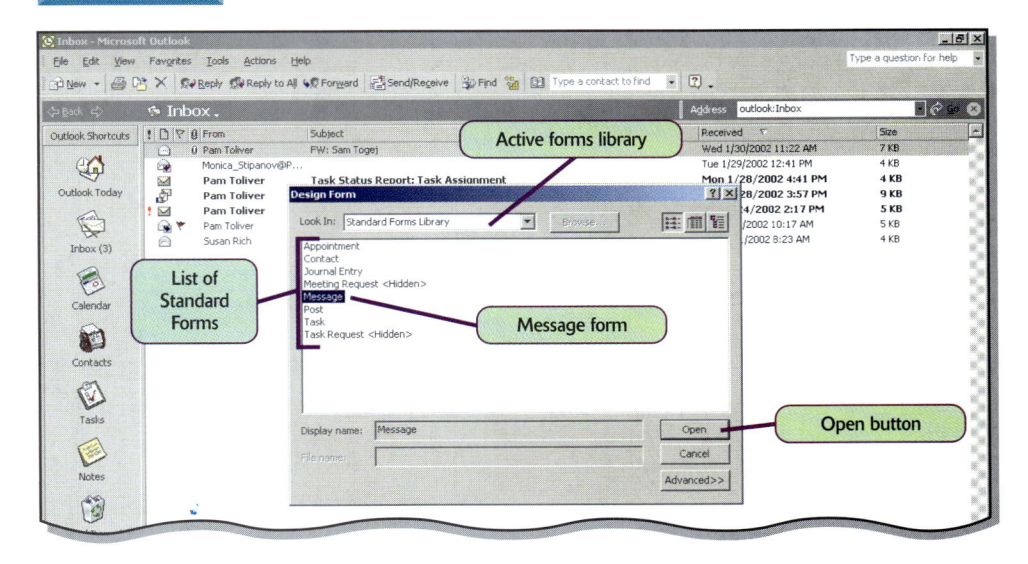

(Screenshot of Outlook Inbox with Design Form dialog box showing: Active forms library, List of Standard Forms, Message form, and Open button labels)

1 Display the Outlook window and choose **Tools | Forms | Design a Form** to open the Design Form dialog box.

2 Select **Message** from the list of form types and click **Open**.

> **Tip** Because you set the e-Selections stationery as the default message form for new messages, it appears in the Design window.

> **Other Ways** To display the form design view:
> - Create a new item using the standard Outlook form and then choose **Tools | Forms | Design This Form**.

Creating Custom Outlook Forms

3 Click the Control Toolbox button to display the Toolbox and position the Toolbox as shown in Figure 7-39.

> **Tip**
> The Field Chooser appears when the design window is opened and lists fields frequently displayed on forms

4 Click the large message area below the Subject area of the form to select it and drag the top center sizing handle down to open a blank area above the message box.

Figure 7-39

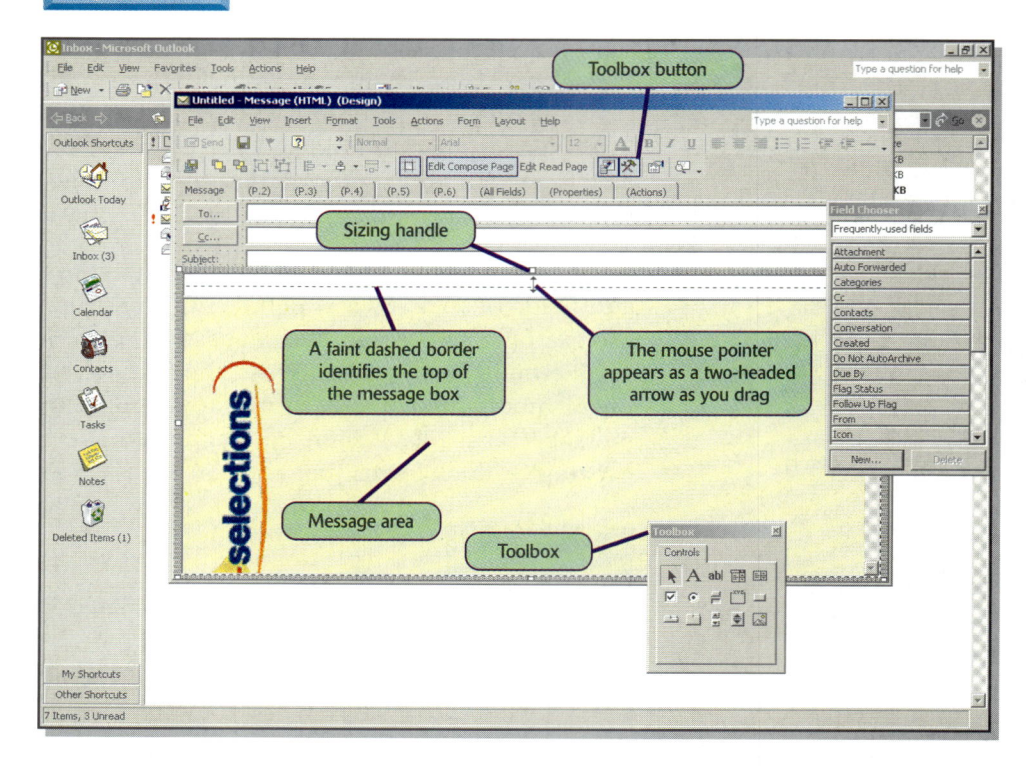

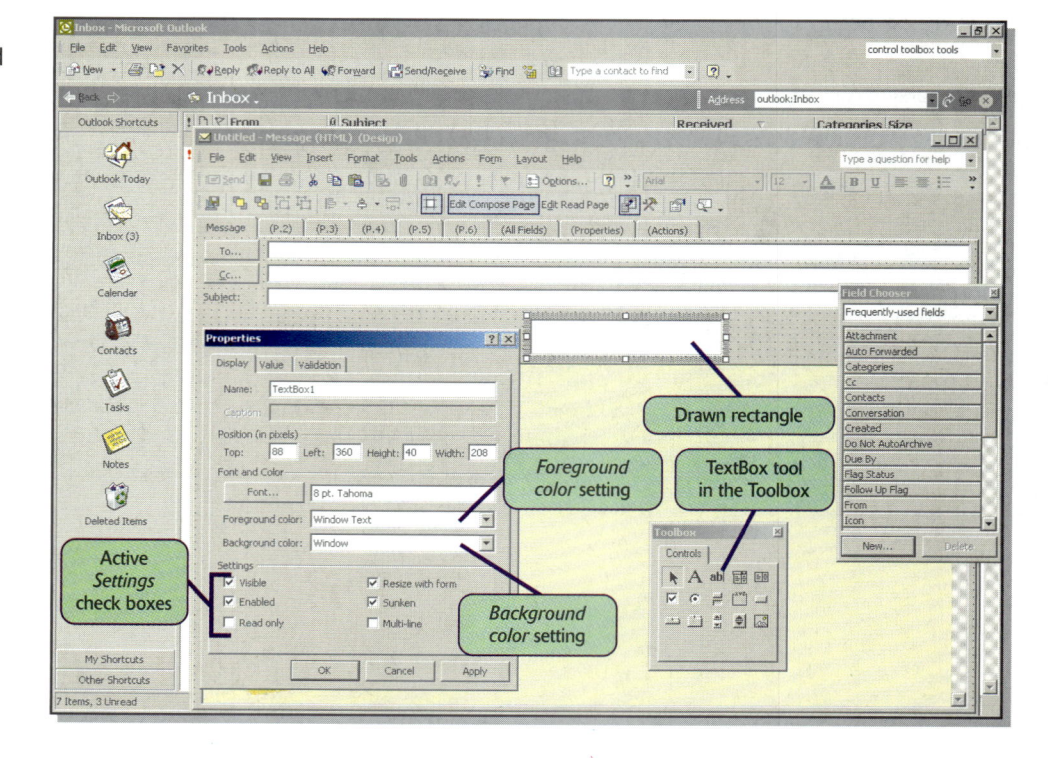

Labels: Toolbox button, Sizing handle, A faint dashed border identifies the top of the message box, The mouse pointer appears as a two-headed arrow as you drag, Message area, Toolbox

5 Click the **TextBox** tool, point to the upper center of the area above the message box, and drag the crosshair to form a rectangle similar to the one shown in Figure 7-40.

6 Right-click the new text box, select **Properties**, click the **Display** tab, if necessary, set the properties shown in Figure 7-40, and click **OK**.

Figure 7-40

Labels: Drawn rectangle, Foreground color setting, TextBox tool in the Toolbox, Background color setting, Active Settings check boxes

Integrating, Customizing, and Sharing Outlook Files

OU 7-29

6 Click the **Label** **A** tool in the Toolbox and draw a rectangle similar to the one shown in Figure 7-41, right-click the label rectangle to display the shortcut menu, and select **Properties** to open the Properties dialog box.

7 Double-click the **Caption** field, type **RE: Order Number**, and change position settings to those shown in Figure 7-41.

8 Click the **Font** button, select the following font settings, and then click **OK**:
- Font style: select **Bold**
- Size: select **12**
- Color: select **Red**

Figure 7-41

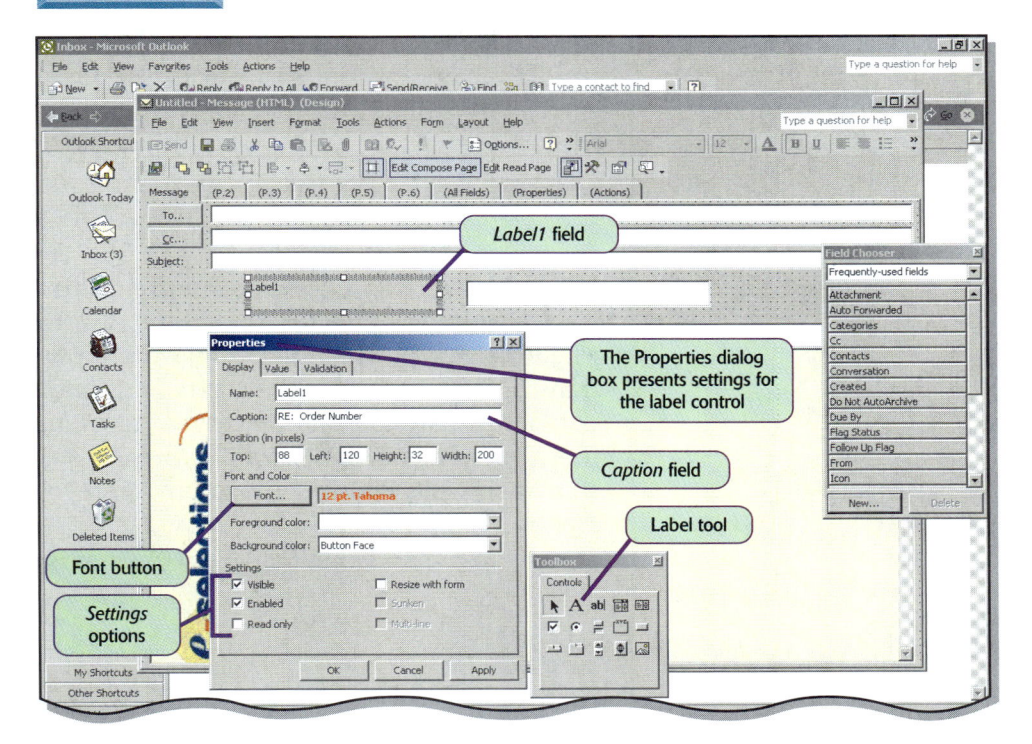

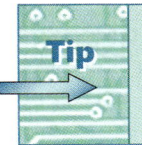

Label1 field

The Properties dialog box presents settings for the label control

Caption field

Label tool

Font button

Settings options

> **Tip** Outlook numbers new Label boxes consecutively as you add them. If you delete a box, the label number is lost and the numbering continues with the next label box you add to the form.

9 Click **OK** and adjust the size of the label box so that it is just big enough for the text it contains.

10 Click the Publish Form button and type **e-Selections Order Reference Form** in the **Display name** text box.

11 Click **Publish**, click **Yes** to save the form in a format that others can use, close the Design window, clicking **No** to close the window without saving.

Figure 7-42

Publish Form button

Display name text box

Publish button

> **Tip** Outlook stores the form in the Personal Forms Library.

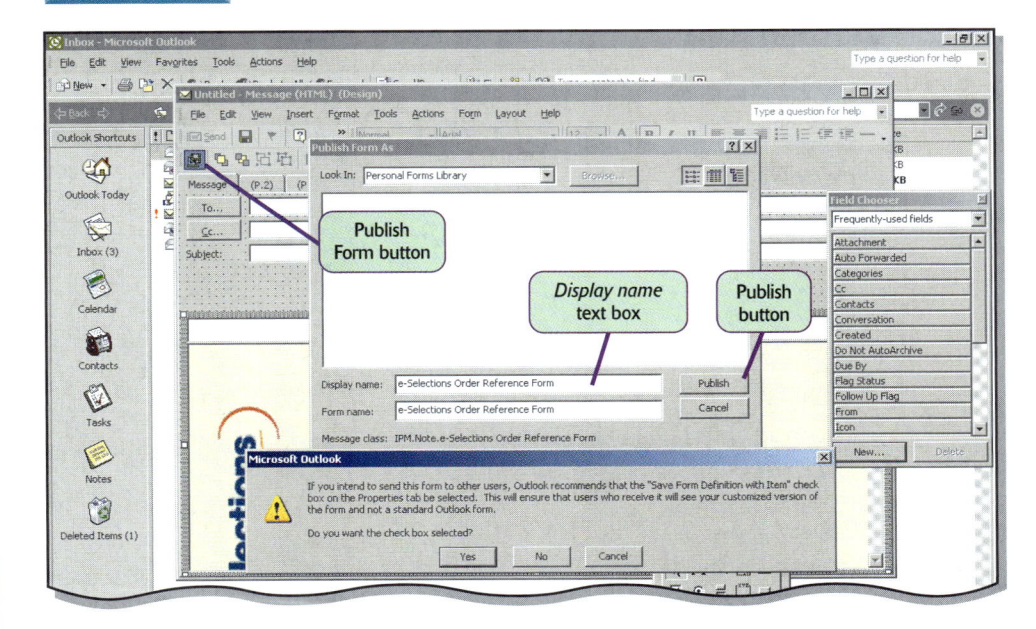

Using a Custom Form

After you create a custom form, you can use it to create new Outlook items. You now have a custom form to use when sending a message related to e-Selections business.

WEB TIP

Have you ever considered how those forms you complete when you register products or order something over the Internet are used? It might be worth your while to think about the information you are transmitting electronically. Much of this information goes into large databases that others can access. As a result, you may find out that these forms are designed with gathering data in mind. Perhaps you should carefully consider the information you volunteer when completing Web forms.

Task 13:
To Use a Custom Form

1 Display the Outlook Inbox, if necessary, and choose **Tools | Forms | Choose Form**.

2 Click the **Look in** down arrow and select **Personal Forms Library**.

3 Select the **e-Selections Order Reference Form** and click **Open**.

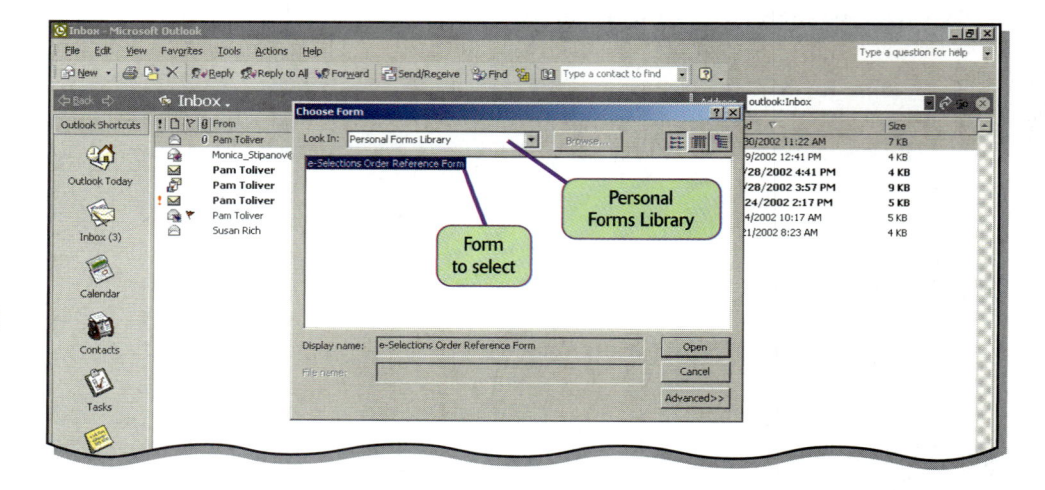

Figure 7-43

Integrating, Customizing, and Sharing Outlook Files

4 Click the **RE: Order Number** text box and type **1234** to confirm that you can enter order numbers on the form.

Figure 7-44

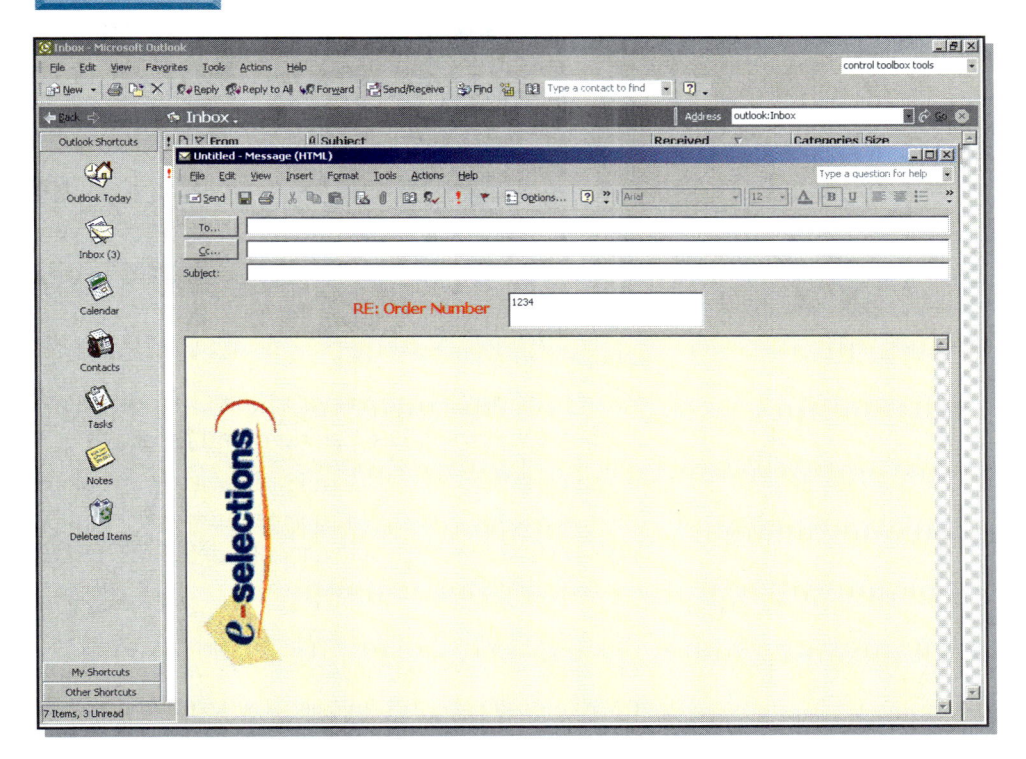

5 Close the message without saving it.

CHECK POINT

Do you recall how to set the default e-mail stationery? Now that you have reached the end of this project, you might want to set the default stationery to something other than the e-Selections stationery. Choose **Tools | Options | Mail Format**, click the **Use this stationery by default** down arrow, and select the stationery you want to use.

SUMMARY AND EXERCISES

SUMMARY

- Contact information is easily shared with other users and copied from one computer to another. It can be sent as an attachment to an e-mail, exported to a file, or copied from the *From* field of an e-mail message.
- You are defined as the owner of the Outlook items contained in your Outlook folders such as Calendar and Inbox.
- As the owner of your Outlook folder items, you have total control of these items, including giving other users access at various permission levels by assigning specific users as delegates or by assigning certain permissions to a specific folder.
- Outlook is a part of the Microsoft XP suite of software and integrates data with other XP applications by creating new Word, Excel, and PowerPoint files from Outlook or using the Contact information in Outlook to create form letters in Word.
- User-created stationery allows you to personalize your e-mail messages with your choice of graphics, backgrounds, and other formatting choices and use the stationery as the default message format or open it on an as-needed basis.
- The Outlook form design feature gives you the capability to create user-defined forms that contain custom fields to hold such information as order numbers, proposal date, fee per hour, materials cost, and so forth.

KEY TERMS & SKILLS

KEY TERMS

access level (p. 7-13)	Editor (p. 7-13)	Publishing Editor (p. 7-16)
Author (p. 7-13)	form (p. 7-5)	Reviewer (p. 7-13)
comma separated values (p. 7-7)	Nonediting Author (p. 7-16)	toolbox (p. 7-27)
Contributor (p. 7-16)	Owner (p. 7-13)	vCard (p. 7-5)
delegates (p. 7-13)	permissions (p. 7-14)	

SKILLS

Assign delegates and set delegate permissions (p. 7-14)
Create a contact from an e-mail message (p. 7-12)
Create a custom message form (p. 7-27)
Create a new letter to an Outlook contact (p. 7-21)
Create a new PowerPoint file from Outlook (p. 7-19)
Create custom e-mail stationery (p. 7-24)
E-Mail and export contacts (p. 7-6)
Export contacts to a file (p. 7-7)
Imports contacts from a file (p. 7-11)
Open another user's folder (p. 7-18)
Save vCards as contacts (p. 7-9)
Set Folder Permissions (p. 7-16)
Use a custom form (p. 7-30)

STUDY QUESTIONS

MULTIPLE CHOICE

1. Outlook makes it possible to share contact listings between computers using all of the following techniques *except*
   a. e-mailing a contact.
   b. copying and pasting a contact.
   c. exporting contacts to a file.
   d. creating a contact from e-mail messages received.

2. To e-mail a virtual business card, choose
   a. **Actions | Forward as vCard**.
   b. **File | Export**.
   c. **Tools | Forward a Contact**.
   d. **File | Send**.

3. To save a contact that you receive in an e-mail message,
   a. save the message.
   b. import the contact.
   c. open the attached contact and save it.
   d. forward the message to yourself.

4. All of the following are roles you can assign to Outlook folder delegates *except*
   a. Owner.
   b. Author.
   c. Editor.
   d. Reviewer.

5. Folder reviewers can
   a. grant access rights to other users.
   b. create subfolders.
   c. edit and delete folder items.
   d. read folder items.

6. The command to open another user's folder appears on the
   a. **Actions** menu.
   b. **Insert** menu.
   c. **File** menu.
   d. **Window** menu.

7. Delegates can open
   a. all of the other user's folders.
   b. only the folders they have permission to open.
   c. only the Calendar folder.
   d. the user's Outlook Today.

8. Outlook contains tools for creating new Office XP files for all applications *except*
   a. Word.
   b. Excel.
   c. PowerPoint.
   d. Access.

9. To create a letter to a contact, what Outlook folder must be open?
   a. Inbox
   b. Calendar
   c. Contacts
   d. Tasks

10. Personalized stationery can be used to format e-mail messages when
    a. Word is the e-mail editor.
    b. mail messages are formatted as HTML.
    c. mail messages are formatted as rich text.
    d. you select the stationery from the Forms List.

SHORT ANSWER

1. What is the extension for files exported as comma separated values?
2. What page of the **Options** dialog box displays stationery options?
3. What is the difference between Outlook stationery and Outlook signatures?
4. What view is active when you are customizing a form?
5. What does the Forms Toolbox hold?
6. What are properties?
7. After you complete a new or custom form, how do you save it?

FILL IN THE BLANK

1. To save contacts in a file for use on a different computer, _____ the contacts.
2. To add contacts stored in a file to the Contacts folder on a different computer, _____ the contacts.
3. Create a new contact for the sender of an e-mail message using information contained in the _____ field of the message you receive.
4. Grant other users access to Outlook folders by naming them as _____.
5. Select a _____ format to create new e-mail messages formatted with a different message background.
6. Create a custom _____ to add new fields to hold folder item information.
7. The person who creates subfolders in another user's folder is the _____ of the subfolder.
8. The Forms list appears on the _____ menu.
19. To add text to a form, use the _____ tool.
10. _____ is the application used to edit the format or position of a signature on Outlook stationery.

DISCUSSION

1. What is the difference between vCards and comma separated values?
2. What is the difference between delegates and permissions?
3. What uses can you think of for creating custom e-mail stationery?
4. When would you normally want to create a form for a folder rather than use stationery?

GUIDED EXERCISES

1. DECORATING A MESSAGE FORM USING GRAPHICS

The message form you created for e-Selections contained a new field but used the stationery you assigned to your e-mail messages. The stationery then becomes part of the custom form. Instead of using stationery to format the e-mail message background, you can add a graphic to create a message form similar to the one shown in Figure 7-45 and use the custom form instead of the stationery.

Figure 7-45

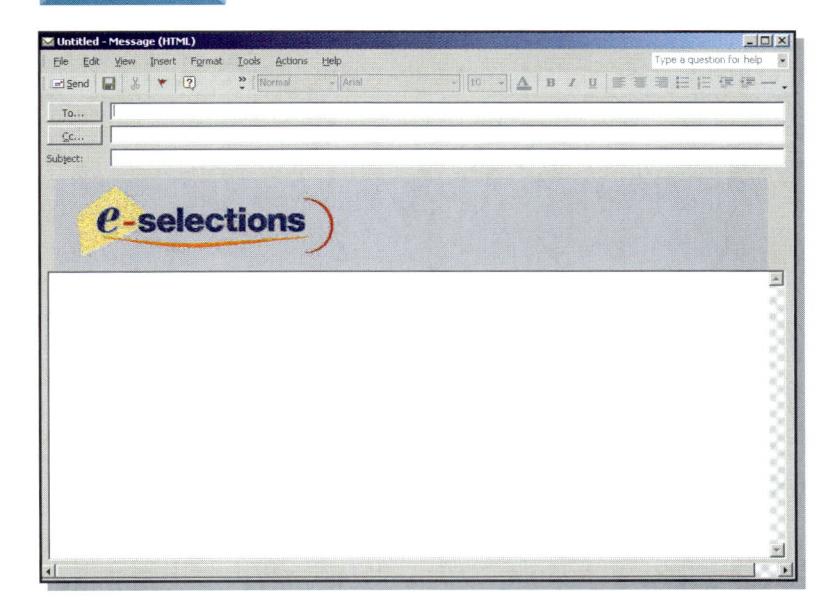

Follow these instructions to complete the form:

1. Choose **Tools | Options | Mail Format**, select None from **the Use this stationery by default** drop-down list, and click **OK**.

2. Choose **Tools | Forms | Design a Form**, select **Message** from the forms list, click **Open**, and move the **Field Chooser** list box to the bottom right corner of the window, if necessary.

3. Click the **Control Toolbox** icon to open the Toolbox, if necessary.

4. Click in the large area below the Subject to select the message area and drag the top center sizing handle down to open a blank area above the message box.

5. Click the **Image** button in the Toolbox, drag a rectangle to hold the picture shown on Figure 7-45, right-click the image box, and select **Advanced Properties**.

6 Double-click the Picture property row of the **Properties** dialog box to open the **Load Picture** dialog box.

7 Open the folder containing your student files and double-click *e-Selections Background.jpg*.

8 Click each of the properties identified below and select the **settings** from the drop-down list at the top of the **Properties** dialog box:
- **BorderStyle** property: **None**
- **AutoSize** property: **-1-True**
- **PictureAlignment** property: **3 - BottomLeft**

9 Click the **Apply** button to apply the settings and close the **Properties** dialog box.

10 Adjust the size of the message area to accommodate the graphic.

11 Click the **Publish Form** button to publish the form, type **e-Selections Message** in the **Display name** text box, click **Publish** to publish the form, and click **Yes** to save the form in a format that others can use.

12 Close the **Form Design** window without saving changes.

13 Choose **Tools | Forms | Choose a Form**, select the Personal Forms Library, and select the new form.

2 EXPORTING AN E-MAIL MESSAGE

E-mail messages and items from other folders can be exported using the same basic techniques you used to export listings from the Contacts folder. You can use these techniques to export messages in your school Inbox to copy them to your home or dorm computer. Follow these instructions to export messages:

1 Open the Inbox folder and select **File | Import and Export**.

2 Select **Export to a file** from the **Choose an action to perform** list and click **Next**.

3 Select **Comma Separated Values (Windows)** from the **Create a file of type** list and click **Next**.

4 Select **Inbox** from the **Select folder to export from** list and click **Next**.

5 Click the **Browse** button, select the drive and folder to which you want to export the messages, type **School Messages** in the **File name** text box, click **OK**, and then click **Next**.

6 Review the actions listed in the **Export to a File** dialog box to ensure that Inbox is identified as the folder to export from and click **Finish**.

3 IMPORTING MAIL MESSAGES

After you export messages to a file, you can import the messages into the same Outlook folder on another computer. Follow these instructions to import a special message into your Inbox folder.

1. Choose **File | Import and Export**, select **Import** from another program or file, if necessary, and click **Next**.

2. Select **Comma Separated Values (Windows)** from the **Select file type to import from** list and click **Next**.

3. Click **Browse**, open the drive and folder containing your student files, select the *Special Message.csv* file, ensure that the **Allow duplicates to be created** option is selected, and click **Next**.

4. Select **Inbox** from the **Select destination folder** list, click **Next**, and then click **Finish**. The **Import and Export Progress** window displays import progress. Outlook removes the date of imported messages and places them at the bottom of the Inbox when it is sorted by received date with the most recent messages at the top.

5. Scroll down the Inbox messages to locate the message you imported and open and review the message.

ON YOUR OWN

The difficulty of these case studies varies: ▶ are the least difficult; ▶▶ are more difficult; and ▶▶▶ are the most difficult.

1 ASKING PERMISSION

▶ Have you ever heard the phrase, *It's easier to beg forgiveness than to ask permission*? While this statement may be true in many cases, it is difficult to apply to Outlook. Outlook limits access to your folders to those to whom you grant access. As a result, they must have permission before accessing your Outlook folders. Delegate access rights that will enable your Instructor to access all your Outlook folders except your Inbox. Be sure to set the option to have Outlook notify your Instructor of the access rights you have set up.

2 GETTING CAUGHT IN FORMS ON THE WEB

▶ Many sites you visit on the Internet or World Wide Web use forms to gather information. Search the Web for forms different organizations use to compile information and download copies of at least five different forms that are formatted in different degrees of complexity and design. Print a copy of each form.

3 VIRTUAL CARDING

Sending virtual business cards is so easy, you will find it an efficient way to exchange information between business associates. Forward your personal contact listing to your instructor and ask your instructor to send a personal vCard back so that you have it for your records. When you receive the card, open it and save it in your Contacts folder. Create a PowerPoint presentation directly from Outlook. Include in the presentation at least three slides: a title slide, a slide that contains instructions for how to open a vCard you receive, and a slide that contains instructions on how to e-mail information as a vCard. Print a copy of the presentation. Forward your contact information as a vCard to others with whom you communicate via e-mail regularly and attach the presentation to an e-mail message. Ask recipients to forward their contact information to you. Print a copy of the message you send along with at least one response you receive. Create at least three contacts from e-mail messages you have received from others who use an e-mail program other than Outlook. Identify the name of their e-mail program in the Notes area of the contact and print copies of each contact you create.

4 EXPORTING AND IMPORTING

Each Outlook folder contains unique information that you might find useful if saved in a different format. Export your Calendar folder contents and your contacts to files formatted as Microsoft Excel spreadsheets. Start Excel and open the exported files to see the results of the export. Print copies of each spreadsheet and turn them in to your instructor.

5 HOLIDAY STATIONERY

Designing e-mail stationery to use for each of the holidays is a great way to spread some holiday cheer each time you communicate via e-mail. Design and create a custom stationery for the next holiday you celebrate or the holiday identified by your instructor. Then create a new e-mail message to your instructor using the stationery and print a copy of the message.

6 FORMULATING PERSONAL FORMS

Creating stationery and forms is a great way to identify yourself, your business, or your school in e-mail messages so that the recipient knows at a glance where the message originated. Create a personal stationery that contains a picture and at least two additional custom fields. Set the stationery as the default stationery, print a copy of the stationery, and use it to send a message to your instructor. Then create an e-mail message form that contains a picture of your school logo, a text box containing your name on the form, and your school name. Print a copy of the form and send a message to your instructor using the new form.

Photospread credits pages 7-2 & 7-3
©Tony Stone; ©Robert Daly; ©Pearson Education; and ©Lorraine Castellano

PROJECT 8

Using Outlook with the Internet

Interfacing with the Internet increases the versatility of Outlook. Not only can you communicate with people using e-mail, but Outlook provides services that enable you to

- "Chat" using instant messaging
- Share your schedule
- Use newsreaders
- Schedule and conduct online meetings
- Access mail remotely
- Import and export data between Outlook and other mail applications.

As you explore these features, keep in mind that most of these features connect you to the Internet—and be careful what information you provide.

OBJECTIVES

After completing this project, you will be able to:

- Save a calendar as a Web page
- Share free and busy schedules
- Assign folder home pages
- Send and receive information using a newsreader
- Schedule NetMeetings
- Use Outlook Instant Messaging
- Set up remote mail
- Set security

e-selections Running Case

The class you have been taking has only one week left and you're beginning to panic because there seems to be so many additional features you want to explore. Many of these features revolve around interfacing with the Internet and learning how you can share information outside of your immediate company network. You had better get busy.

Hello room, anyone want to chat!

Messaging Mania!

*"Teens are addicted to it.
Executives can't live without it."*

instant message: You've got mail

Even the U.S. Navy has come to appreciate the benefits of instant messaging (IM)—the ability to send brief text notes directly to buddies, colleagues or even strangers across the room or half way around the world on virtually anything with Internet access: PC, laptop, handheld, mobile phone or pager.

John Yaukey of the Gannett News Service seems to have a handle on the growing popularity of instant messaging. How about you? Have you experienced the wonders of one of the hottest applications on the Internet? According to Forrester Research, a third of all Americans are using an instant messaging application at least once a week instead of calling on the phone. Although the concept is similar to e-mailing messages back and forth, there are a number of marked differences:

- Instant messaging programs identify your 'buddies' who are online while e-mail messages are stored until the recipient logs on and collects them.

- You can chat only with those people who are currently logged on—instant messages go right to their target and if the target is missing, the message bounces right back at you.

- Those with whom you want to chat must be using the same instant messaging program you are using—e-mail is delivered to recipients regardless of what e-mail program they are using.

- Messaging is quieter then telephoning—you can send messages during a meeting (or class!)—without others knowing.

- Size for most instant messages is limited to make the exchange faster.

Instant messaging programs are easy to set up, they are free, and most work in both Windows and Macintosh environments. Most provide features for transmitting pictures and documents or other files along with message text. Five of the most popular programs include:

Here is that vital information you have been awaiting...

Bill we are all meeting tomorrow at 10am in Joan's office

- AOL Instant Messenger (AIM)—currently has more than 65 million users—and you can use the service without subscribing to AOL.

- MSN Messenger—alerts you when the correspondent is composing a response to your message.

- Yahoo! Messenger—integrates with other Yahoo! features, such as the Yahoo! auction and Yahoo! calendar and is available for Palm and PocketPC handhelds as well as Web-enabled phones.

- ICQ (I seek you)—currently has more than 75 million users and is popular worldwide, provides a cozy environment, and is available for Palm and PocketPC devices.

- Odigo—one of the newest services and one that permits chatting with people using AIM, Yahoo! or ICQ. Odigo is considered a playful program because you can select a graphic or cartoon to represent yourself or change settings to reflect your mood. It also offers a version to use with Web-enabled mobile phones.

While many of the IM services provide access and voice messaging features, the focus of IMs is in text messaging. As you increase your instant messaging skills, you'll find that you can juggle several conversations at the same time. You'll also discover that some of the programs provide chat rooms where more than two people can chat with each other at the same time—and getting a word in edgewise in a chat room discussion can be a challenge!

One of the hazards of using an instant messaging service is that others know when you connect—almost instantly. If they are lying in wait for you to log on, you may find yourself ambushed and drawn into a "conversation" when you're trying to get some work done or simply want to check your messages.

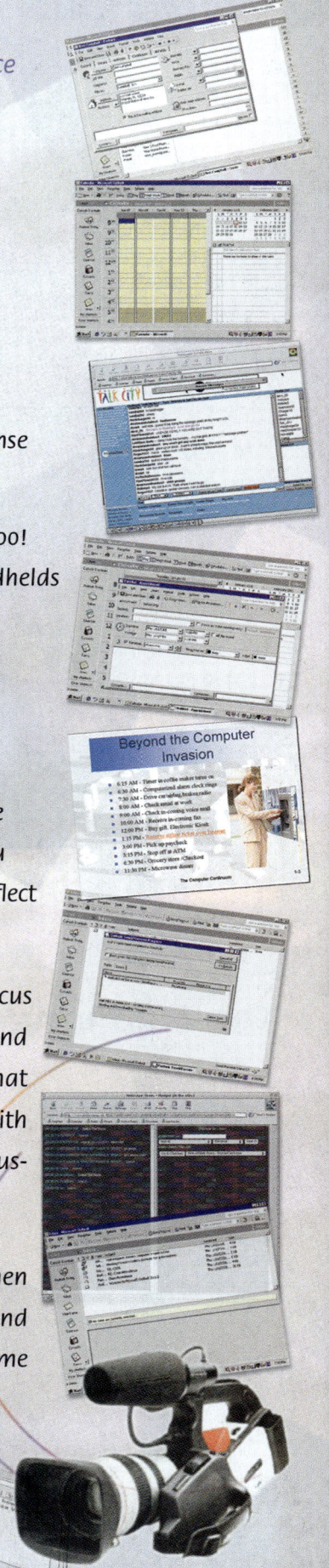

Joe cool writes> Buffy, so where are you from...

PROJECT 8

Using Outlook with the Internet

The Setup

Most of the figures in this project reflect default Outlook settings with few customizations and custom folders. If your computer setup contains customizations, what you see onscreen will be different from features displayed in the figures. Active settings are described in Table 8-1.

Table 8-1	Outlook Settings
Feature	**Setting**
Default Launch Feature	Inbox: Choose **Tools**	**Options**	**Other**	**Advanced Options**	**General Settings**	**Startup in this folder** and then select **Inbox**, if necessary, to change the launch feature
Outlook Bar Setting	Large icons: Right-click a blank area of the Outlook Bar and then select **Large icons**
Office Assistant	Hide the Office Assistant: Choose **Help**	**Hide the Office Assistant**
Toolbars	Choose **Tools**	**Customize**	**Toolbars**, select the **Standard** toolbar, click **Reset**, click **Yes**, and click **Close** to restore the toolbar to its default settings.

The Challenge

Many of the clients you work with at e-Selections use different e-mail systems and applications. As a result, you often find yourself reverting to Internet access to communicate, transmit files, share information, and so on. You believe that if those outside the company could access your calendar and schedule, you could reduce the number of messages required to set up meetings. In addition, Ms. Wright would like for you to explore Outlook features that will enable corporate personnel who travel to connect to the network system when they are away from the office. She would also like for you to identify ways to conduct online meetings using Outlook features.

The Solution

Features in Outlook enable you to communicate with others over the Web and will have you up and running in no time. You can use these features to save your calendar as a Web page and post your schedule to the Internet as well. In addition, you'll find a number of different tools designed for conducting online meetings: NetMeeting, NetShows, and instant messaging. Finally, you can explore Outlook's remote access features and learn how to connect, synchronize files, and perform other tasks while connected remotely.

Saving a Calendar as a Web Page

Saving your calendar as a Web page enables you to post it to the Internet or a Web site and is a great way to make your calendar available to others. In addition, when the calendar is posted on the Web, you can access it when you are away from the office. When you save your calendar as a Web page, you can review it using the latest versions of most browsers.

WEB TIP

Before you can actually publish a calendar on a Web site, you need to know the Web site address to which you want to post the calendar. You will also have to have access rights to post items on the site. The Web address is formatted using the following parameters: Protocol://page.domain.domain type. The protocol for Web folders will be http://.

Task 1:
To Save a Calendar as a Web Page

1 Launch Outlook, open the **Calendar** folder, and then choose **File | Save as Web Page**.

2 Click the **Start date** down arrow, select the first day of next semester from the calendar palette, click the **End date** down arrow, and then select the last day of next semester from the palette.

3 Type *Your Name's Calendar* in the **Calendar Title** text box, substituting your real name where appropriate, and then click the **Browse** button to open the Calendar File Name dialog box.

4 Open the Web folder or drive and folder in which you want to publish the calendar.

5 Type *YourName's NextSemester* at the end of the path in the **File name** text box, substituting your name and the next semester where appropriate, and then click **Select**.

> **Tip** Type the file name with no spaces. Calendar names that you save as Web pages cannot contain spaces.

Figure 8-1

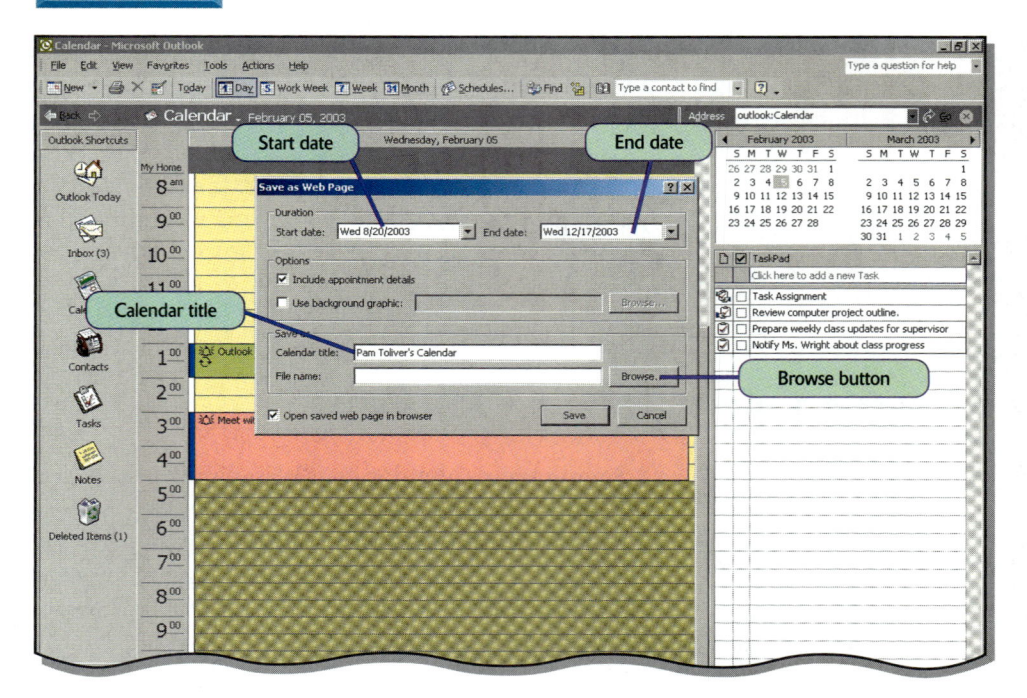

Figure 8-2

Troubleshooting If you are saving to a Web folder, a path that identifies the location of the folder may appear in the **File name** text box. Select the path and then press Delete to remove it.

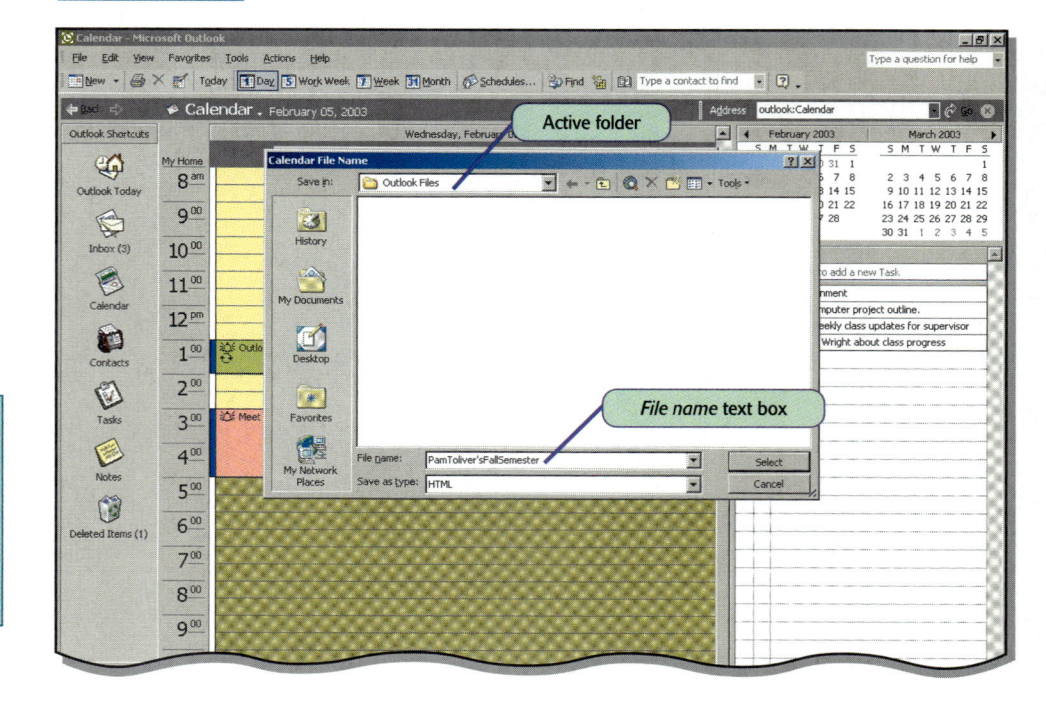

Using Outlook with the Internet

OU 8-7

6 Click **Save** to save the calendar and then display it in your default browser.

Figure 8-3

Troubleshooting
If the file name you typed contains spaces, Outlook displays a message box advising you that either the file name or path is invalid. Click **OK** to acknowledge the message and then edit the file name.

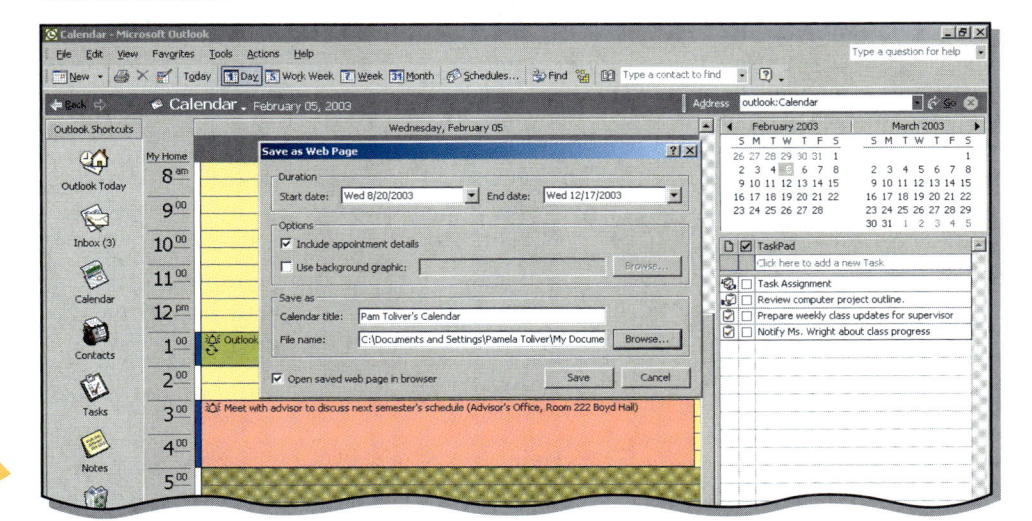

7 Close the Browser window.

Figure 8-4

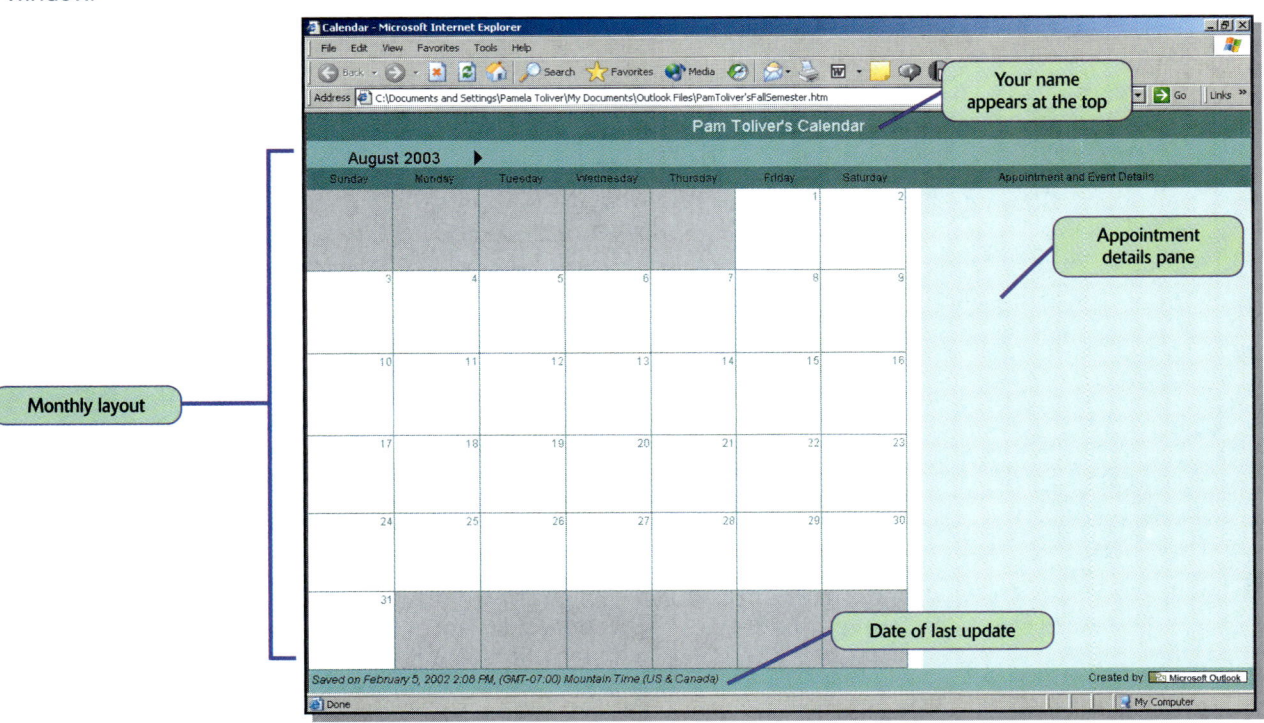

Your name appears at the top

Appointment details pane

Monthly layout

Date of last update

Sharing Free and Busy Schedules

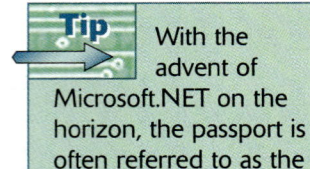

> **Tip**: With the advent of Microsoft.NET on the horizon, the passport is often referred to as the .NET Passport.

Microsoft offers a service through which you can share your free and busy schedule so that others can view the schedule and use it to determine the best times to schedule meetings. The service is free, and the process of setting Outlook up so that you can use the *Free/Busy Service* is a multistep process:

- Set up a passport account to access the Microsoft Office Internet Free/Busy Service
- Set free and busy options
- Join and publish to the Microsoft Office Internet Free/Busy Service
- Authorize access to your Free/Busy schedule
- View the schedules of others

Setting up a Passport Account

In conjunction with some of the features Microsoft makes available to its customers, they have initiated a passport program to enable users to log on to the services. You log on to the Microsoft Internet Free/Busy Service using your *passport*—the free logon name and password you set up when you register with the passport service—to access posted schedules. If you currently have an MSN or Hotmail account, you can use it as your passport. If not, you need to set up a passport.

Connect to the Microsoft Web site at www.Microsoft.com, type **passports** in the **Search for** text box at the top of the left Web page pane, and click **Go** to search for information about Passports. Follow the onscreen directions as well as the directions of your instructor to sign up for your personal passport. It's free of charge.

Setting Free/Busy Options

Before you publish your free/busy schedule, it is important to set the options that identify the dates you want to publish and how often you want to publish the schedule. Publishing dates that span too far ahead requires more frequent updates than short periods of time. Outlook limits the number of months you can publish to 36. You can publish updates to the calendar as frequently as you want.

Using Outlook with the Internet

Task 2:
To Set Free/Busy Options

1 Open the Outlook Calendar folder, choose **Tools | Options**, and then click the **Calendar Options** button to open the Calendar Options dialog box.

2 Click **Free/Busy Options** button to open the Free/Busy Options dialog box.

Figure 8-5

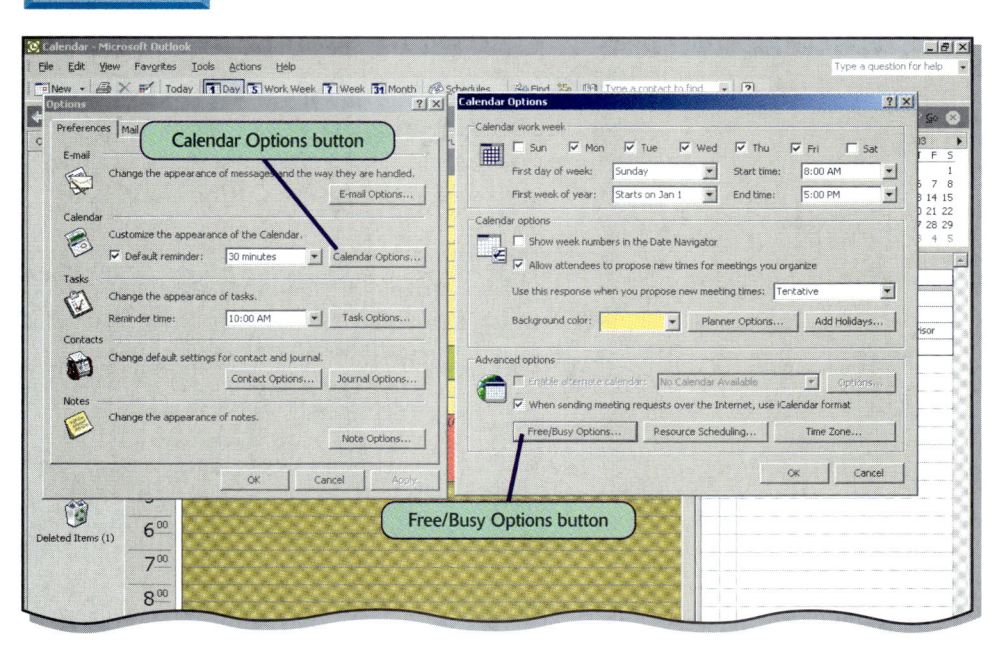

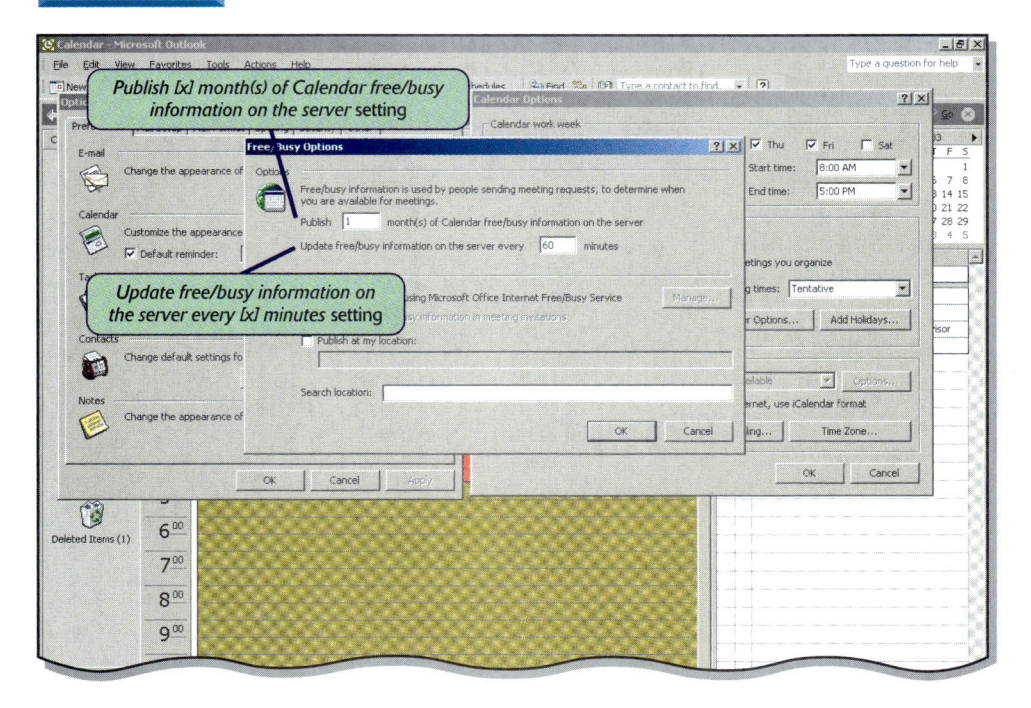

3 Type 1 in the **Publish [x] month(s) of Calendar free/busy information on the server** box.

4 Type **60** in the **Update free/busy information on the server every [x] minutes** box.

5 Click **OK** three times to close all open dialog boxes.

Figure 8-6

Joining and Publishing to the Microsoft Office Internet Free/Busy Service

To use the Microsoft Office Internet Free/Busy Service, you must first join the service and identify the person or people with whom you want Microsoft to share your schedule. There are a number of ways you can join the service, but the easiest way to join is by setting options in Outlook.

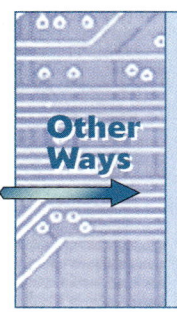

Other Ways

To join the Microsoft Office Internet Free/Busy Service:
- Select **Yes** in the message box that appears when you try to schedule a meeting with a user whose schedule Outlook cannot access.
- Click an invitation link in an e-mail from another member of the service.
- Access the service Web site at http://freebusy.office.Microsoft.com/freebusy/freebusy.dll.

Task 3:
To Join the Internet Free/Busy Service and Publish a Schedule

Figure 8-7

1 Open the Outlook Calendar folder, choose **Tools | Options | Calendar Options**, and then click the **Free/Busy Options** button to open the Free/Busy Options dialog box.

2 Select the **Publish and search using Microsoft Office Internet Free/Busy Service** check box and then click the **Manage** button to launch Internet Explorer.

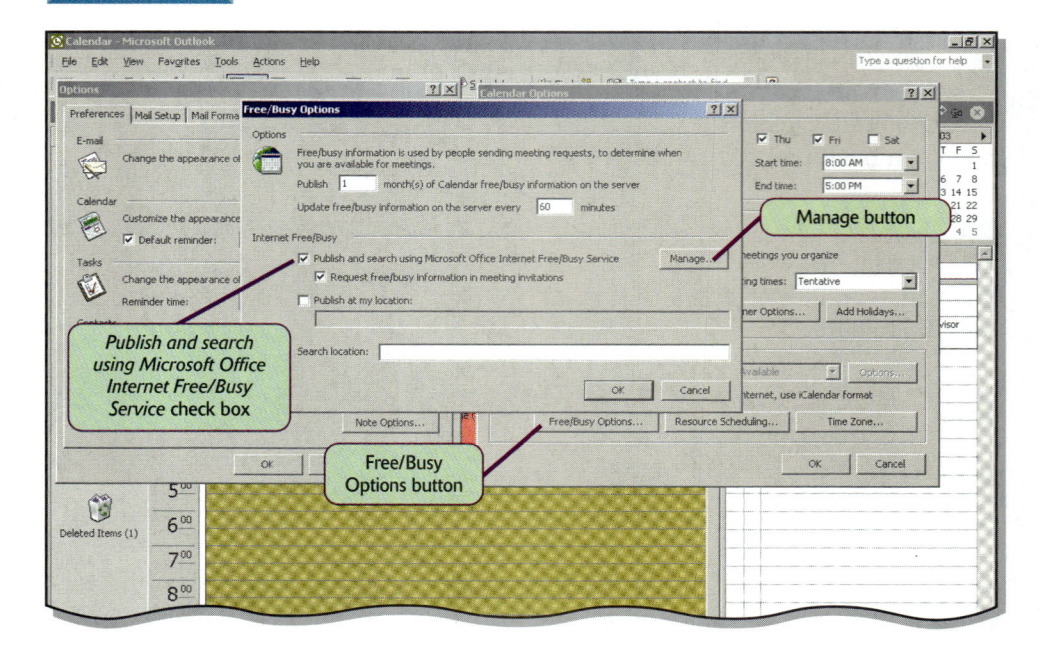

Troubleshooting If you have not yet set up a passport account, the Passport Wizard will start and guide you through account setup when you click the **Manage** button. Follow the onscreen directions to set up your account and then continue.

If a screen appears advising you that your e-mail address is not shared, you have not yet entered the e-mail address associated with your Outlook Calendar folder. Click the **Edit your Passport sign-in profile**, enter the e-mail address you use to receive e-mail in Outlook, enter your password, if necessary, click **OK**, and then click the **Home** link on the left pane of the Web page to continue.

Using Outlook with the Internet　　　OU 8-11

Troubleshooting If a **Sign In** dialog box appears, type your full passport e-mail address in the **E-mail address** text box and your password in the **Password** text box, click **Sign In**, and then click **OK** to continue.

3 Review the information on the **Welcome to the Microsoft Office Internet Free/Busy Service** page and click **Continue** at the bottom of the Welcome page to display the **Terms of use** page.

Figure 8-8

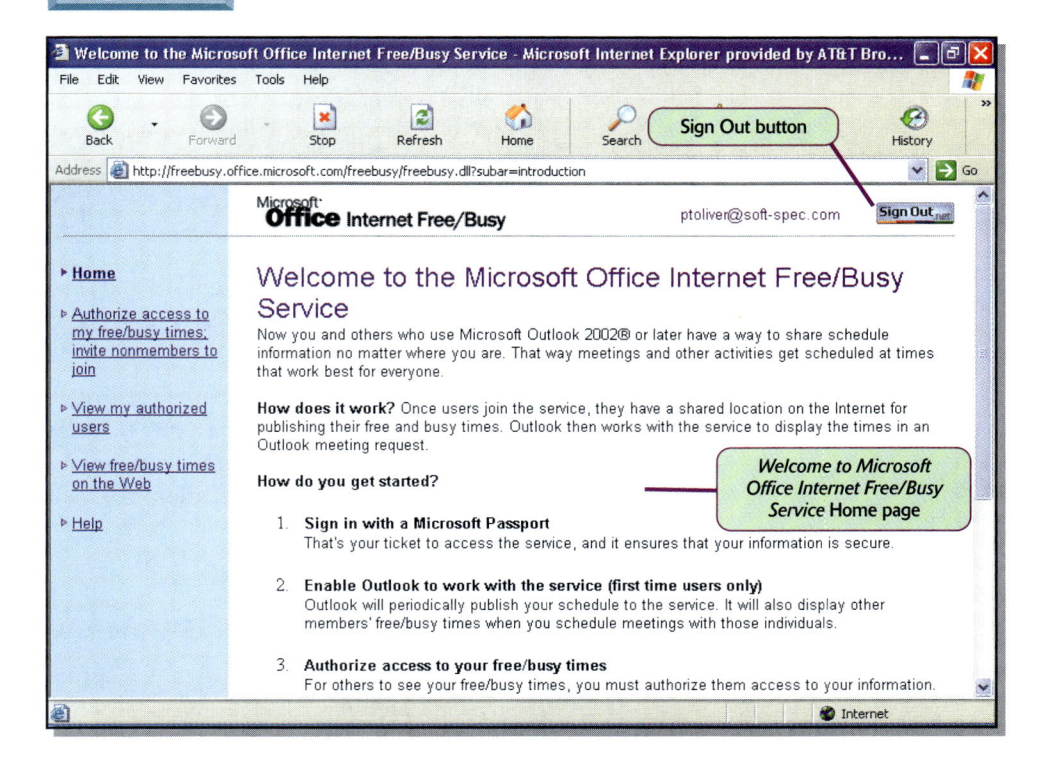

Sign Out button

Welcome to Microsoft Office Internet Free/Busy Service Home page

4 Review the **Terms of use** information and then click **Yes, I agree** to join the service.

5 Click the **Home** link in the left pane to display the **Welcome to Microsoft Office Internet Free/Busy Service** Home page again.

6 Switch back to Outlook and then click **OK** three times to close all open dialog boxes with new settings active.

Figure 8-9

Home link

Yes, I agree link

Tip Add the Free/Busy site to your **Favorites** list for easy access.

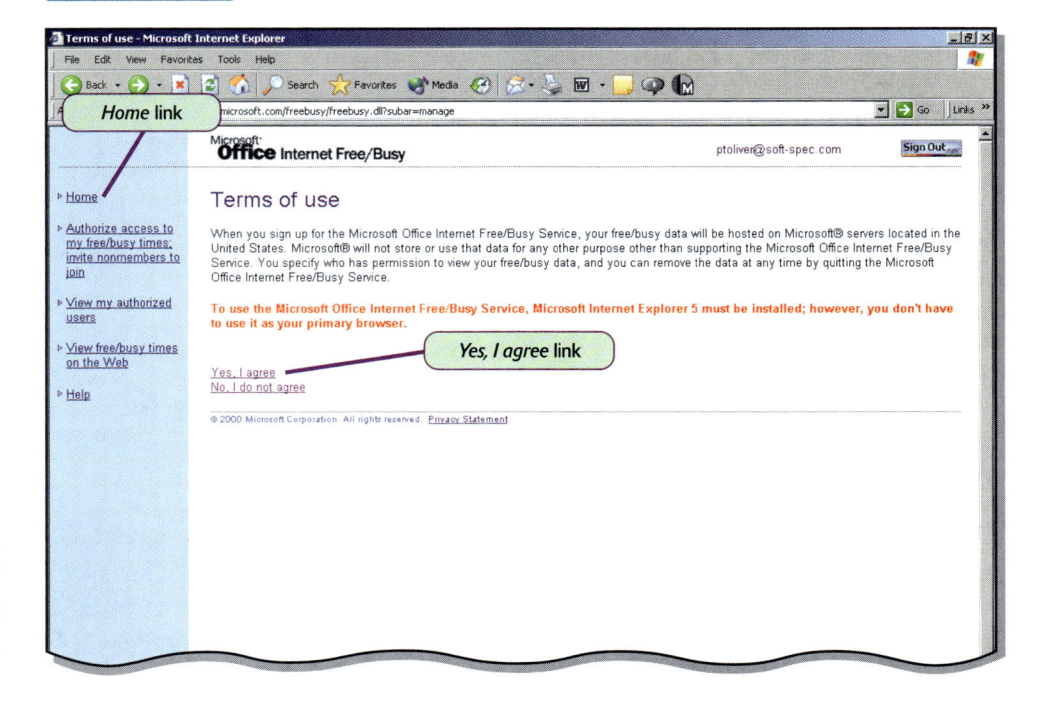

> **Troubleshooting** If you have already reviewed the Terms of use and have clicked the **Yes, I agree** link, a screen to authorize and invite others to join the Free/Busy Service will appear when you click **Continue**. That's okay—continue with Step 6 to get back on track.

CHECK POINT

After you join the Free/Busy Service, Microsoft will send you an e-mail welcoming you to the service and providing additional information about the service and about effectively using it. Be sure to read the information carefully—it will contain information about procedures that have been updated since this book was written.

Authorizing Access to Schedules

After you have successfully set up Outlook to post your schedule to the Free/Busy Service, and have posted your schedule, you can identify those who should have access to your schedule. You can also invite others to join the service so that you can view their schedules.

Task 4:
To Authorize Access to Your Schedule

1. Switch back to the Internet Explorer window and then click the **Authorize access to my free/busy times; invite nonmembers to join** link in the left site frame.

2. Click the **Address book** link.

Figure 8-10

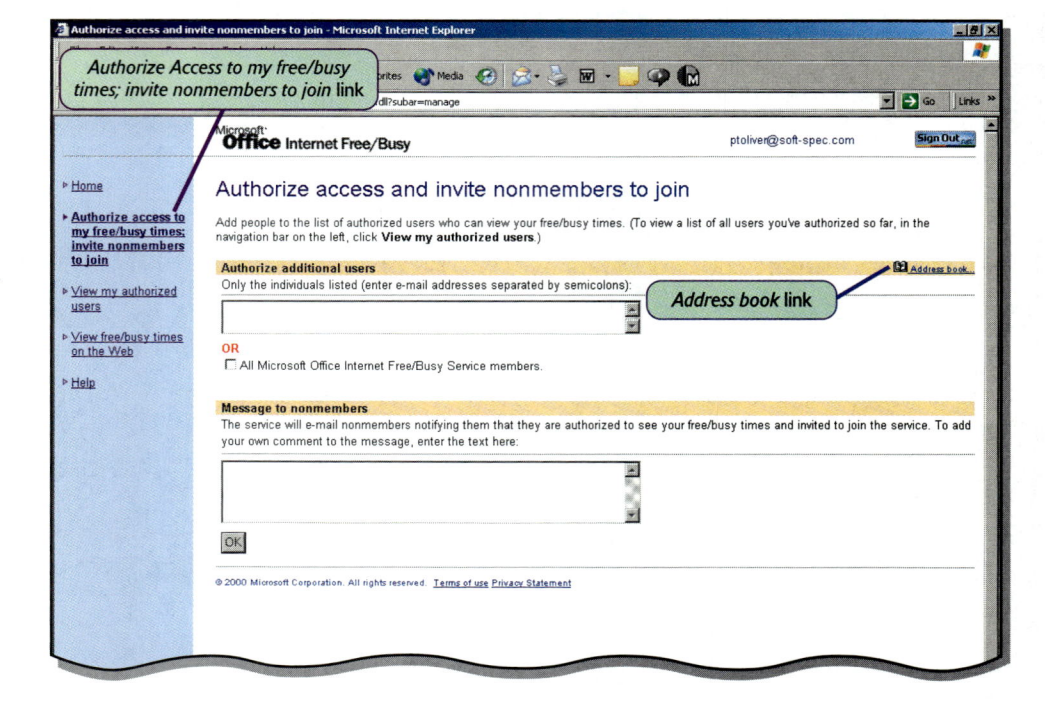

> **Troubleshooting** If you close the Internet Explorer window at the end of the last task, open the Outlook Calendar folder, choose **Tools | Options | Calendar Options | Free/Busy Options**, click the **Manage** button and then sign in to the service.

Using Outlook with the Internet

3 Select the contacts for two of your classmates, your instructor, and yourself (as well as others who should have access to your schedule), click the **To** button to move them to the selected names list, and then click **OK**.

Figure 8-11

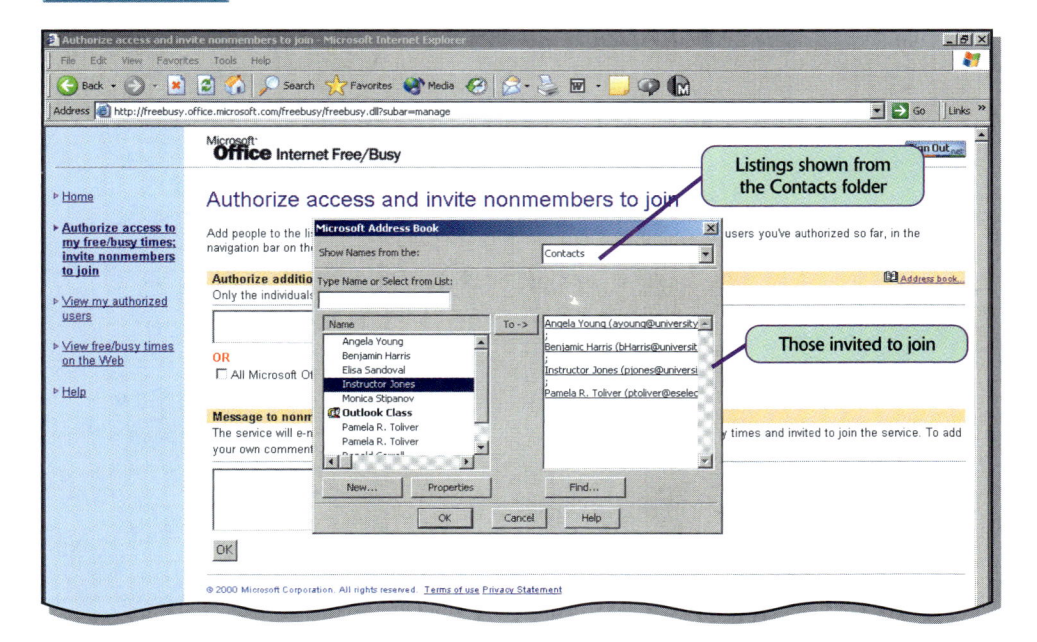

4 Position the insertion point in the **Message to nonmembers** text box and then type the text you want Microsoft to send to nonmembers with the invitation to join the Free/Busy Service.

5 Click **OK**.

6 Click **Sign Out** and then close the Internet Explorer.

Figure 8-12

Troubleshooting

A Microsoft Outlook message may appear, advising you that a program is trying to access e-mail addresses and asking if you want to allow this. Because you are selecting the names of users who can access your Free/Busy schedule, click **Yes**.

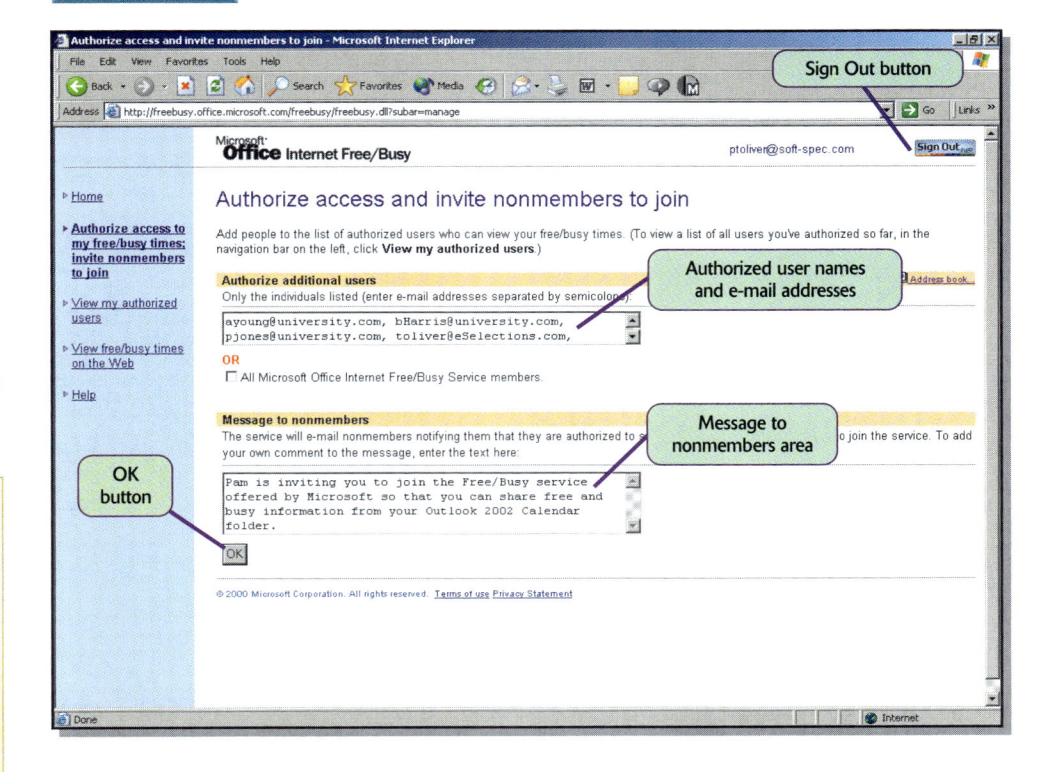

Reviewing Posted Schedules

When you connect to the Free/Busy site, you can view the free and busy schedules of those members who have authorized access to you. Tools displayed on the Free/Busy schedule page enable you to select the date and time you want to view.

Figure 8-13

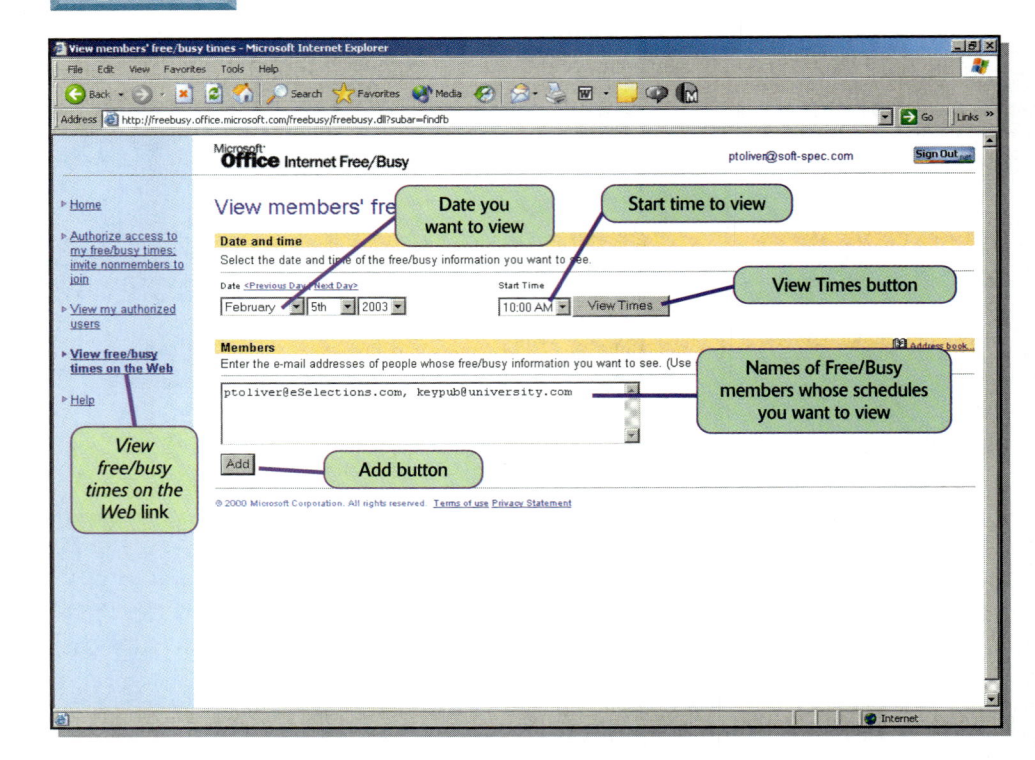

Task 5:
To View a Free/Busy Schedule

1. Choose **Tools | Options | Calendar Options | Free/Busy Options**, click the **Manage** button to launch Internet Explorer, and then sign in to the service.

2. Click the **View free/busy times on the Web** link in the left site frame.

3. Select or type the name of the person whose schedule you want to review and then click **Add**.

4. Click the **Date** down arrow and select the date you want to check, click the **Time** down arrow and select the time you want to check, and then click **View Times**.

Other Ways

To access the Free/Busy site if you have saved the Free/Busy site as a favorite:
- Launch Internet Explorer, choose **Favorites**, select the favorite listing you used to save the sign in page, and sign in.

5 Click **Sign Out** and then close the Internet Explorer.

Figure 8-14

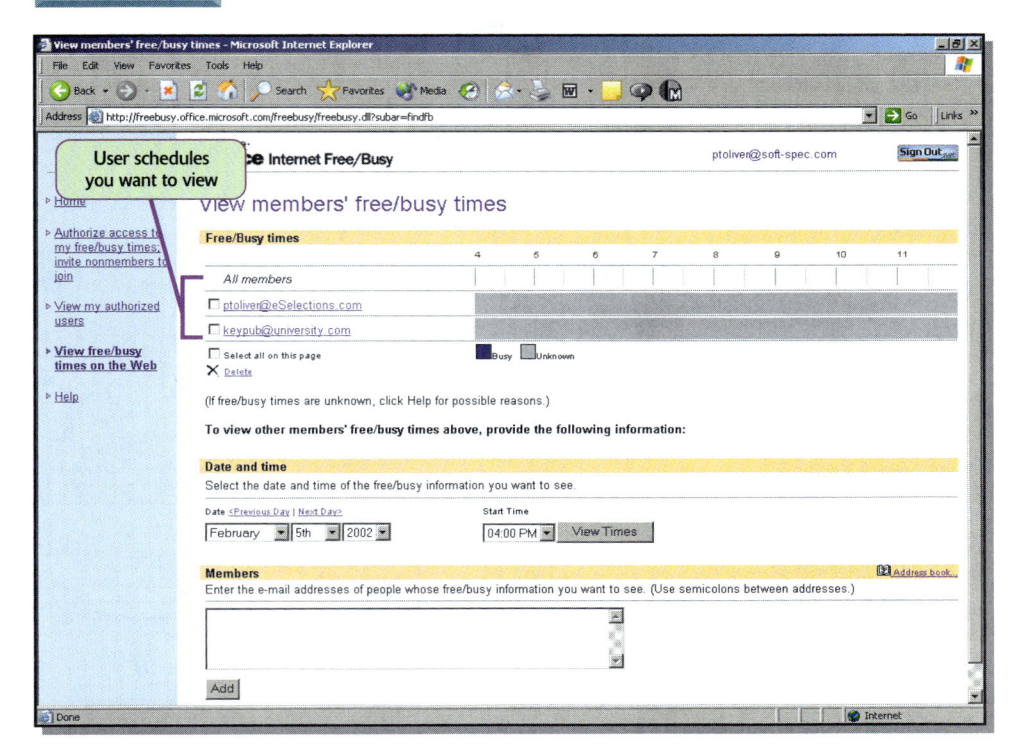

Assigning Folder Home Pages

Outlook contains special browser features found in Internet Explorer that enables you to view Web sites without leaving Outlook. Using these features, you can assign a home page to an Outlook folder. Folders to which a home page is assigned display the home page each time you open the folder. To view original folder contents, you can remove the home page from the folder.

Task 6:
To Assign a Home Page to the Notes Folder

1 Open the **Inbox** folder in Outlook, right-click the Notes icon in the Outlook Bar, and then select **Properties** from the shortcut menu.

2 Click the **Home Page** tab in the Notes Properties dialog box.

3 Type **www.prenhall.com** in the **Address** text box, select the **Show home page by default for this folder** check box, and then click **OK**.

4 Click the Notes icon in the Outlook Bar to open the folder.

5 Right-click the **Notes** folder icon again, select **Properties**, click the **Home Page** tab, clear the check mark in the **Show home page by default for this folder** check box, and then click **OK** to reset the Notes folder.

Figure 8-15

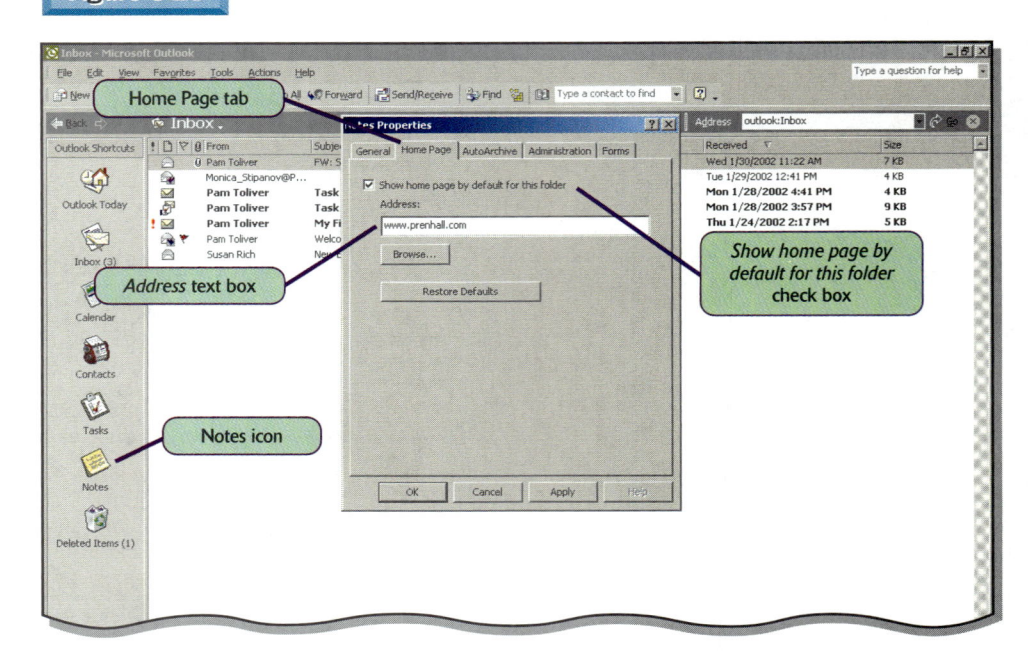

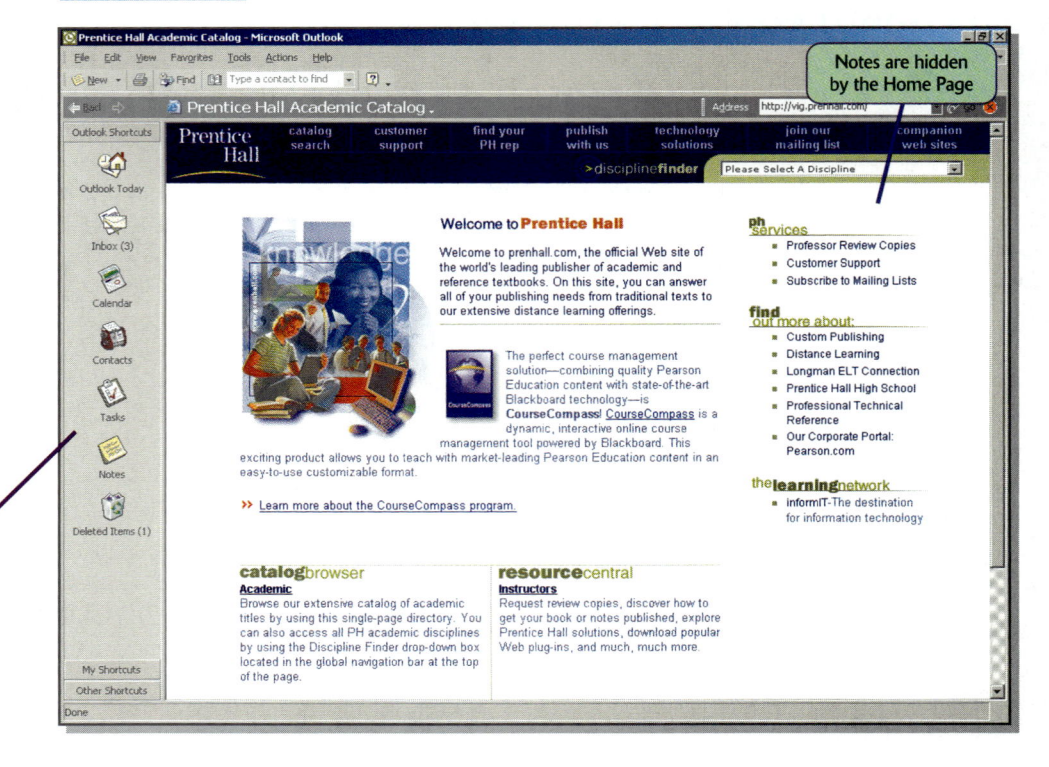

Callouts: Home Page tab; Address text box; Notes icon; Show home page by default for this folder check box

Figure 8-16

Callouts: Notes are hidden by the Home Page; Outlook bar is still active

Sending and Receiving Information Using a Newsreader

WEB TIP

Newsgroups provide a great way to get help on topics related to using the Internet and computer hardware, and tips for using many computer software programs. All you have to do is locate the newsgroup that you think would most likely address the topic, post a question or plea for help, and then sit back and hope someone with the answer sees the message and responds!

The Internet contains a wide variety of topic-specific messages containing information posted by different people to *news servers*—computers maintained by companies, interest groups, and so forth. Information posted on these servers is generally accessible to anyone with access to the newsgroup. *Newsreaders* are Internet tools that enable you to access newsgroup information and post replies to messages you find there. You can establish membership in many of these different newsgroups and gain access to their newsreaders without charge.

Subscribing to a Newsgroup

Outlook, by default, has established access to the Outlook Newsreader on the Internet. You can use the Outlook Newsreader or set up a different newsreader to access the newsgroups most useful to you. After you connect to the Outlook Newsreader, you will need to *subscribe* to—sign up for or join—the newsgroup you want to view to have access to messages.

CHECK POINT

The first time you connect to a newsgroup, the Internet Connection Wizard may appear, asking for the name you want to display on the news server. Many members use pseudonyms when they access newsreaders in order to maintain privacy. To set up your Internet connection for the newsreader, follow these steps:

1. Choose **View | Go To | News** and then click **Set up a Newsgroups account**.

2. Type the name you want to display in the **Display name** text box and then click **Next**.

3. Type your e-mail address in the **E-mail address** text box and then click **Next**.

4. Follow onscreen Wizard prompts to complete your connection information, reading each screen carefully.

5. Click **Finish** and click **Yes** to see a list of newsgroups.

6. Select the newsgroup you want to subscribe to and then click the **Subscribe** button for each newsgroup you want to join.

7. Click **OK** to close the Newsgroup Subscriptions dialog box.

Task 7:
To Subscribe to a Newsgroup

1 Launch Outlook, if necessary, open the **Inbox** folder, and then choose **View | Go To | News** to launch the Outlook Newsreader.

> **Troubleshooting**
> If the Internet Connection Wizard appears, follow the direction of your instructor to get connected or follow the steps outlined in the Check Point presented just before this task to get connected.

2 Click the **Subscribe to Newsgroups** link to open the **Newsgroup Subscriptions** dialog box.

3 Type **24** in the **Display newsgroups which contain** text box to narrow the list of newsgroups, select **24hoursupport.helpdesk**, and then click **Subscribe** to subscribe to the newsgroup.

> **Tip** The number of newsgroups available on each server varies—there are more than 17,000 newsgroups shown in the Outlook Newsgroup. New newsgroups are added frequently, so the list you see will be different from the one shown in Figure 8-18.

Figure 8-17

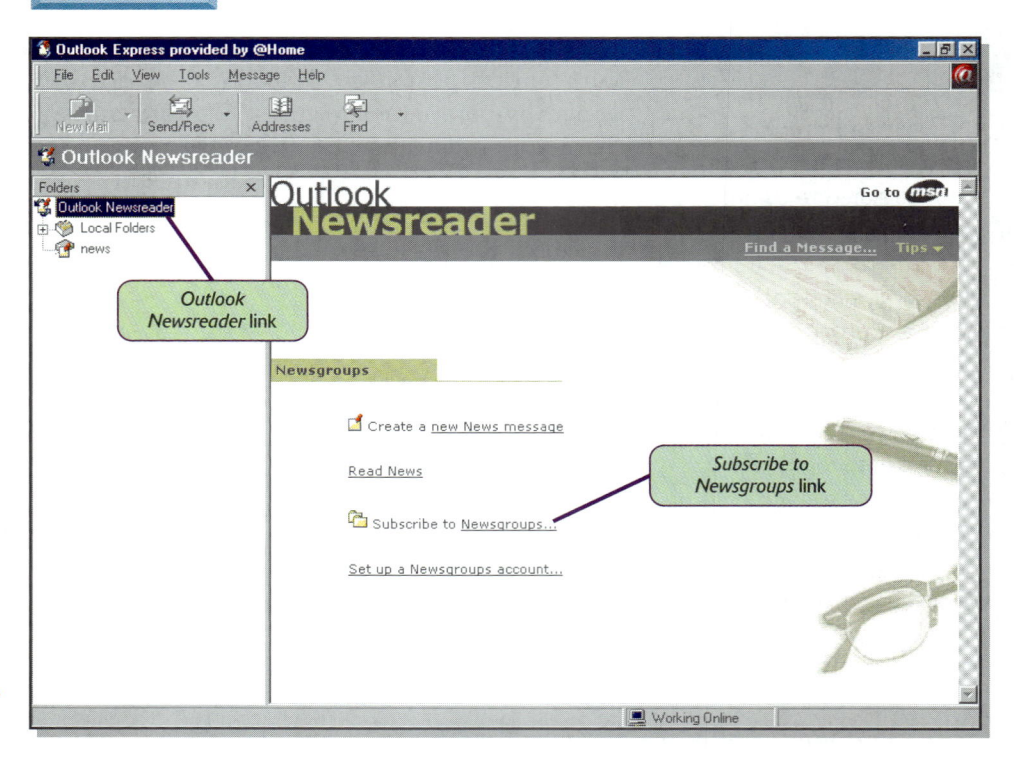

Outlook Newsreader link

Subscribe to Newsgroups link

> **Troubleshooting** If the Outlook Newsreader window shown in Figure 8-17 does not appear, click the Outlook Newsreader link on the Folders pane.

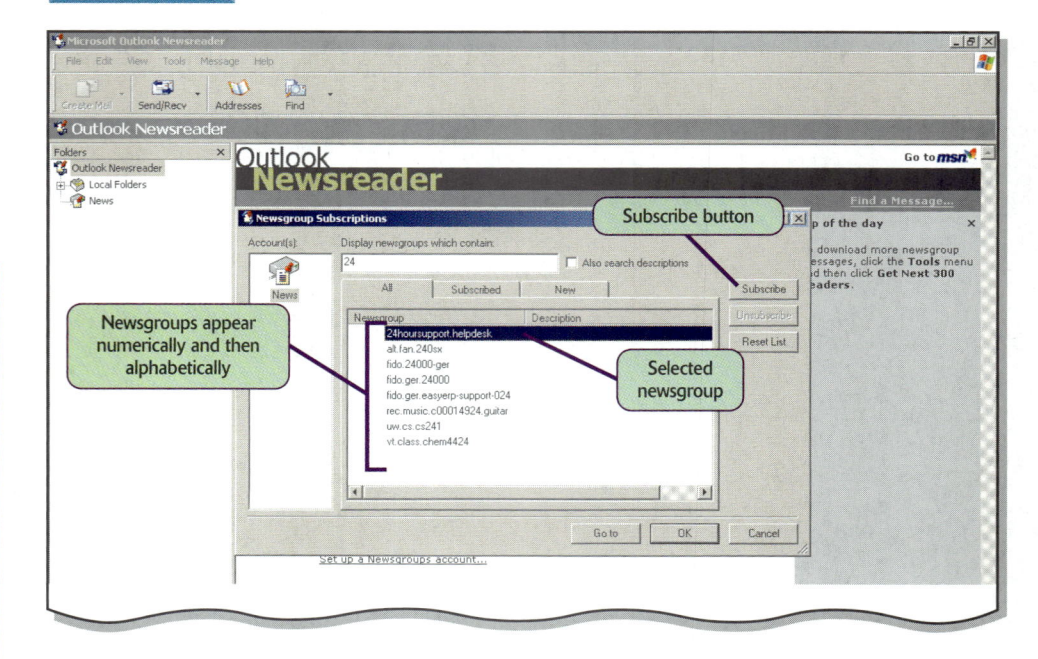

Figure 8-18

Subscribe button

Newsgroups appear numerically and then alphabetically

Selected newsgroup

Using Outlook with the Internet

OU 8-19

Troubleshooting If the **24hoursupport.helpdesk** newsgroup is unavailable, select a different newsgroup following the direction of your instructor.

4 Click **Go to** to view newsgroup messages.

Figure 8-19

Troubleshooting
If your ISP requires you to login to use a newsreader, a **Logon** dialog box will appear. Enter the appropriate information and click **OK** to continue.

An icon appears beside subscribed newsgroups

Go to button

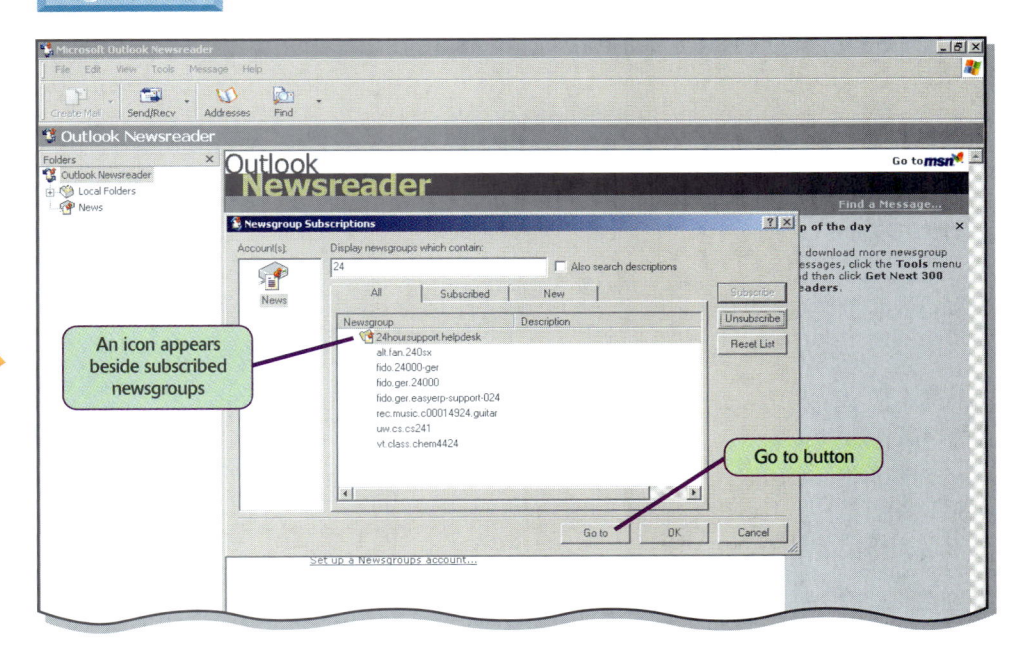

5 Close the Newsreader window.

Figure 8-20

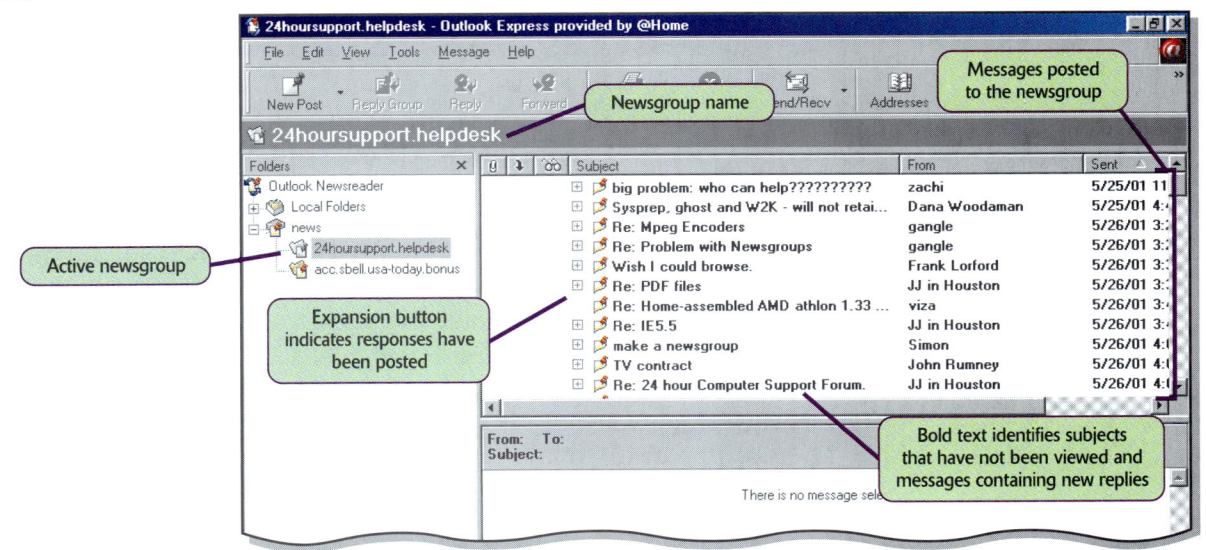

Newsgroup name

Messages posted to the newsgroup

Active newsgroup

Expansion button indicates responses have been posted

Bold text identifies subjects that have not been viewed and messages containing new replies

Opening and Reading a Newsgroup Message

After you have subscribed to a newsgroup, you can open messages contained in the newsgroup that are of interest to you. You can then respond to messages by posting responses on the newsgroup site where all members can read them or by replying directly to the individual who posted the message. Replies to the person who posted the message are sent as e-mail messages and do not appear in the newsgroup.

Task 8:
To Open and Read Newsgroup Messages

1. Double-click a message to open it.

2. Close the message and then close the Outlook Newsreader window.

Figure 8-21

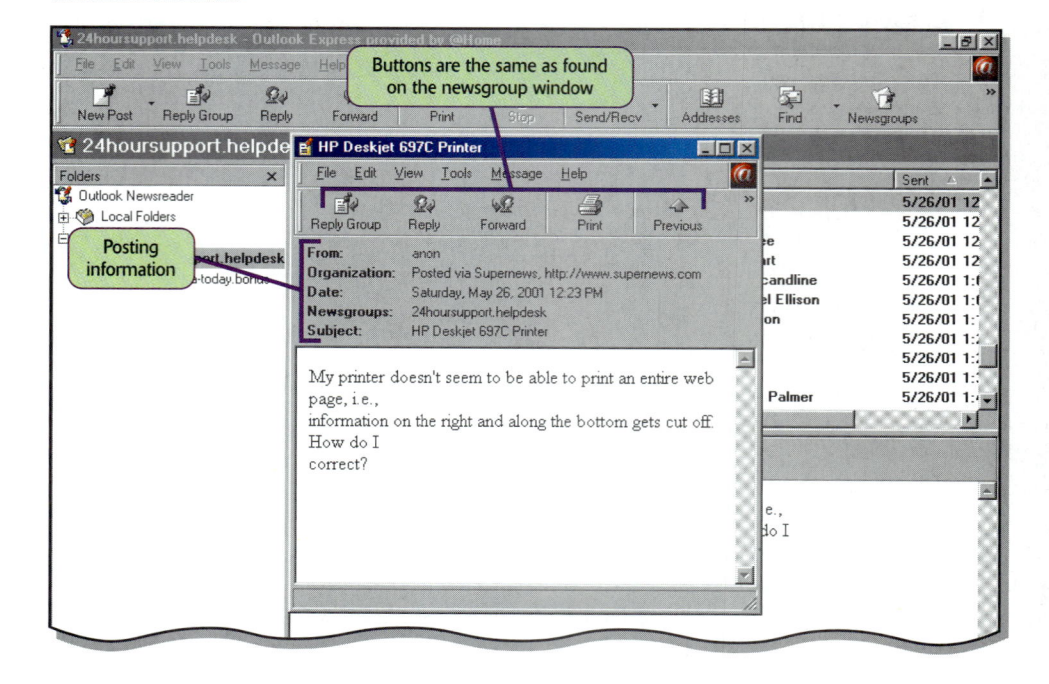

Scheduling NetMeetings

Traditionally, setting up meetings and inviting others to attend those meetings centers around attendees coming together at the same time and same place. Outlook enables you to schedule meetings to occur *online* so that those attendees who are located at different sites may participate without traveling to the meeting site. The same basic procedures are involved in setting up online meetings that you use to schedule traditional meetings. *NetMeeting* is a Microsoft program than is used to conduct the online meeting.

Using Outlook with the Internet

OU 8-21

Task 9:
To Schedule an Online Meeting Using NetMeetings

1 Open the Outlook **Calendar** folder and then click the New Appointment **New** button.

2 Click **Invite Attendees** and then type the e-mail addresses of your instructor and two classmates in the **To** field.

3 Type the information, select the options, set the dates and times identified in Figure 8-22, and then click **Send**.

Figure 8-22

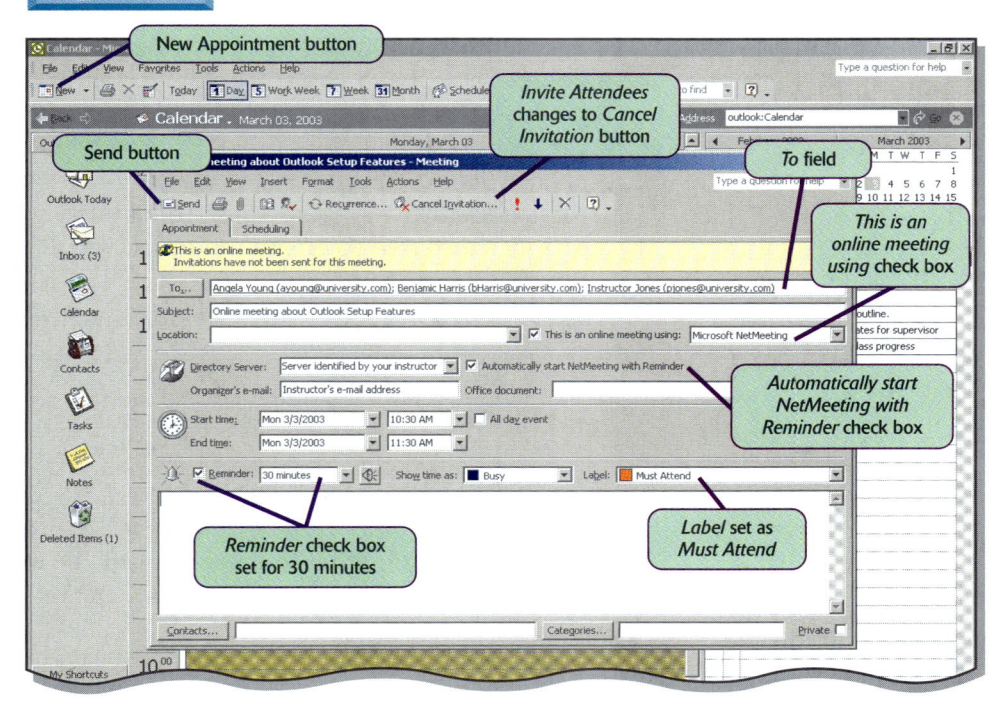

Callouts: New Appointment button; Send button; Invite Attendees changes to *Cancel Invitation* button; To field; This is an online meeting using check box; Automatically start NetMeeting with Reminder check box; Reminder check box set for 30 minutes; Label set as Must Attend

CHECK POINT

There is more to conducting a successful NetMeeting than simply scheduling it. You have to plan it far enough in advance that those who should attend have ample time to respond to the invitation. After invitations are accepted, the meeting automatically appears in the recipient's Calendar folder. If you set the reminder option when you scheduled the meeting, an automatic reminder will appear onscreen to remind attendees of the meeting. Tools on the **Reminder** window will help meeting attendees connect to the online meeting.

Using Outlook Instant Messaging

Instant messaging services have been around for a number of years and enable users to communicate live with others who are online at the same time and have the service running. Microsoft Outlook 2002 contains an instant messaging feature that you can use to communicate with contacts, determine if a contact is online, and set controls that allow others to see when you are online and available for online chatting.

WEB TIP

It would be easy to confuse instant messaging with other Web terms. For example, have you run across the term *blog* yet? Some people confuse blogs with chat. It helps to think of blogs as online diaries rather than online chats. Blogs are thoughts or musings posted and shared via the Internet as *Weblogs*—diary-like entries about a given topic added to a Web site on a regular basis. The term *Weblog* was simply shortened to create the term *blog* and people who post them are called *bloggers*.

Enabling Instant Messaging

Unless the installation of Outlook 2002 on your computer has been customized, the instant messaging feature is "enabled"—turned on—by default so that you are automatically logged on to the service each time you launch Outlook. You can check the setting and enable instant messaging or turn off the feature at any time.

Task 10:
To Enable Instant Messaging in Outlook

1 Close any open items to return to the Outlook main window and choose **Tools | Options | Other** to display the **Other** page of the dialog box.

2 Select the **Enable Instant Messaging in Microsoft Outlook** check box, if necessary, to enable instant messaging and then click **OK**.

Figure 8-23

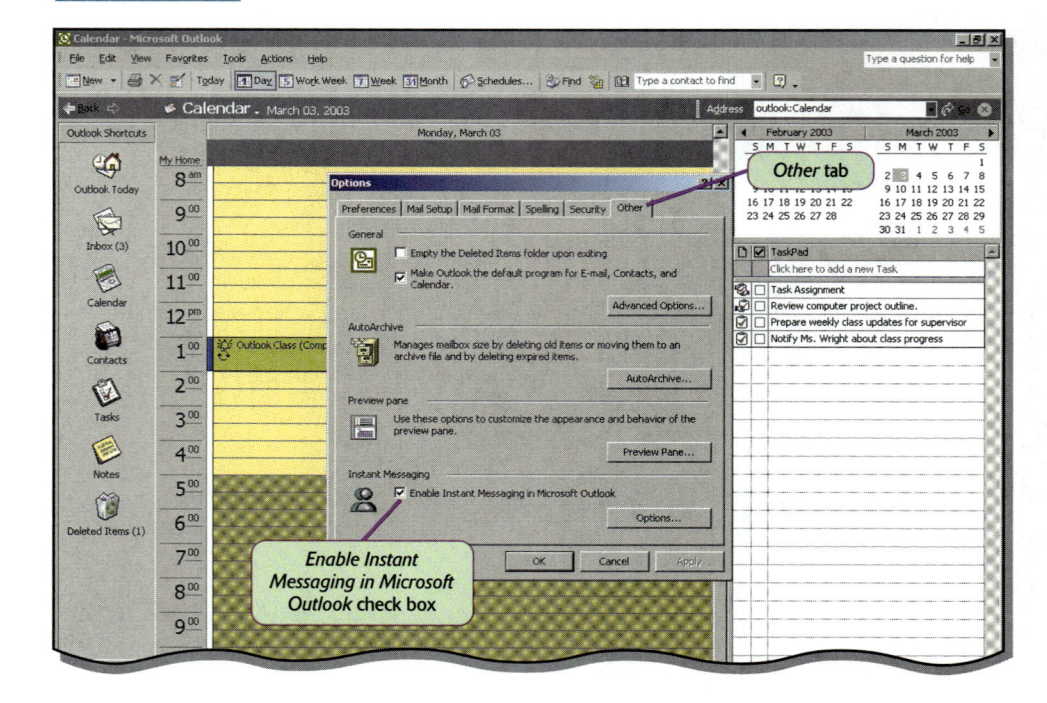

Using Outlook with the Internet

OU 8-23

Sending Instant Messages

You will find an *IM address* field—a field you can use to record the instant messaging address—on the General page of the contact listing for each contact you add to the Contacts folder. When you type the IM address in the field, the instant message status of a contact appears in the InfoBar—the yellow banner at the top of the contact form. If the contact is online and has instant messaging enabled, you can communicate in "real time"—instantly—by sending the contact a message. If they have added your IM address to the contact listing in their Contacts folder, they can determine whether you are online, too. When you want to be available to "chat," launch the Windows Messenger.

Task 11:
To Activate Instant Messaging and Send a Message

1 Launch Outlook, if necessary, choose **Tools | Instant Messaging | Log on**, type your Passport information in the appropriate fields of the **.NET Messenger Service** dialog box, and then click **OK** to launch the Windows Messenger.

2 Minimize Outlook and then double-click the **Microsoft Messenger** icon on the taskbar to launch the Windows Messenger.

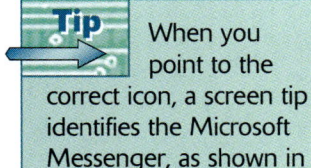

Figure 8-24

Microsoft Messenger icon

Tip When you point to the correct icon, a screen tip identifies the Microsoft Messenger, as shown in Figure 8-24.

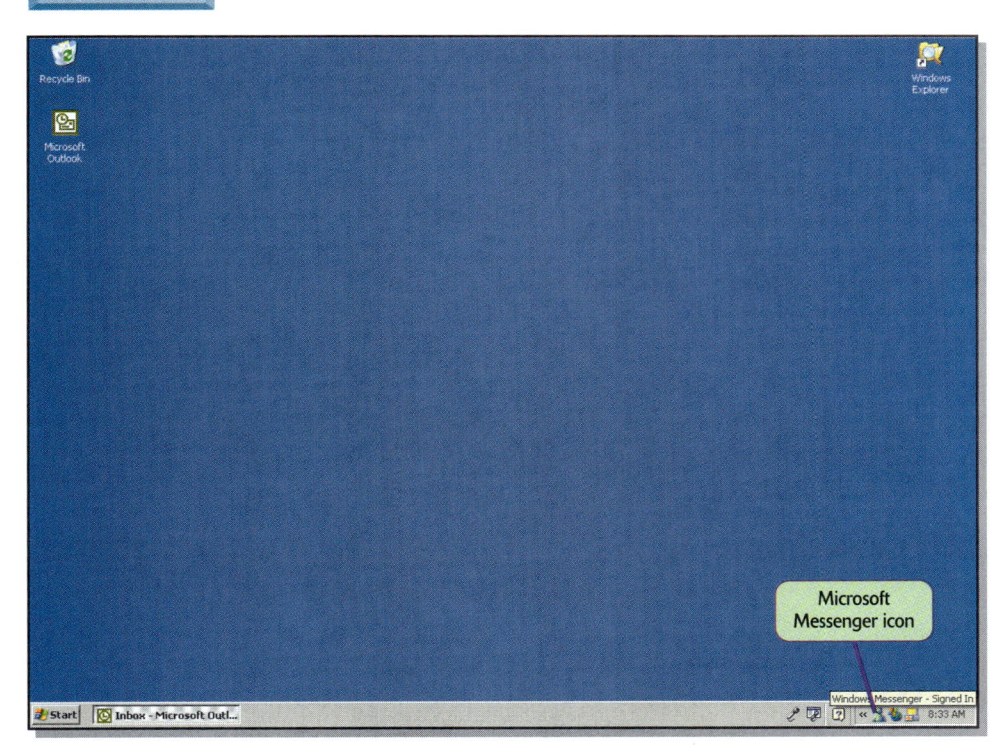

Troubleshooting Depending on the settings active on your computer, the Windows Messenger may activate automatically each time you sign on to the computer. If **Log off** is active on the **Tools | Instant Messaging** menu and **Log on** is inactive, it means the Windows Messenger is already running and you can skip Step 1.

Troubleshooting A message box may open and list those who have added you to the contact lists. Select the option for the communication setting you want to activate for the person identified and click **OK**.

Sending Instant Messages

3 Double-click the name of the online contact to whom you want to send a message and review the features of the **Conversation** window.

> **Tip** Follow the direction of your instructor for the name of the classmate to whom you should send the message so that all class members will receive a message.

Figure 8-25

4 Type the message shown in Figure 8-26 and then click **Send**.

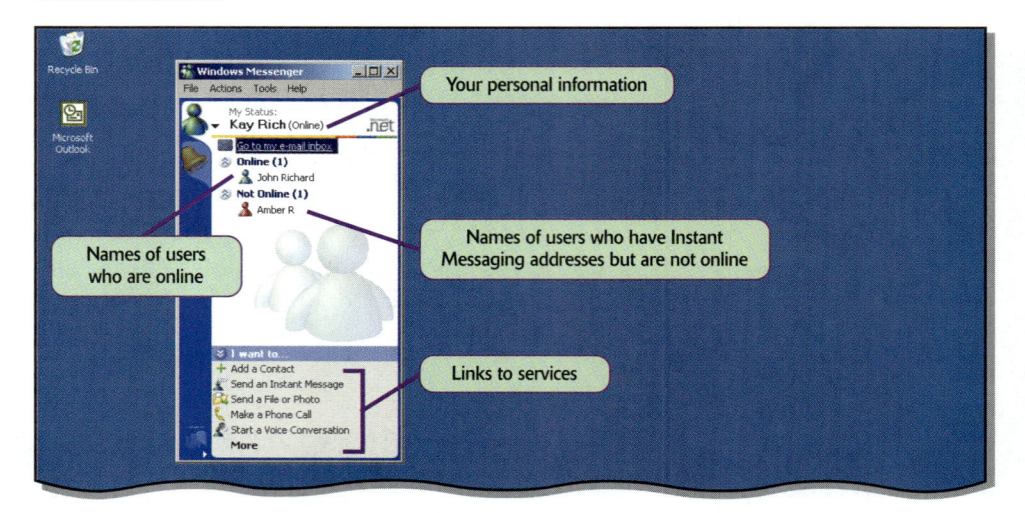

Figure 8-26

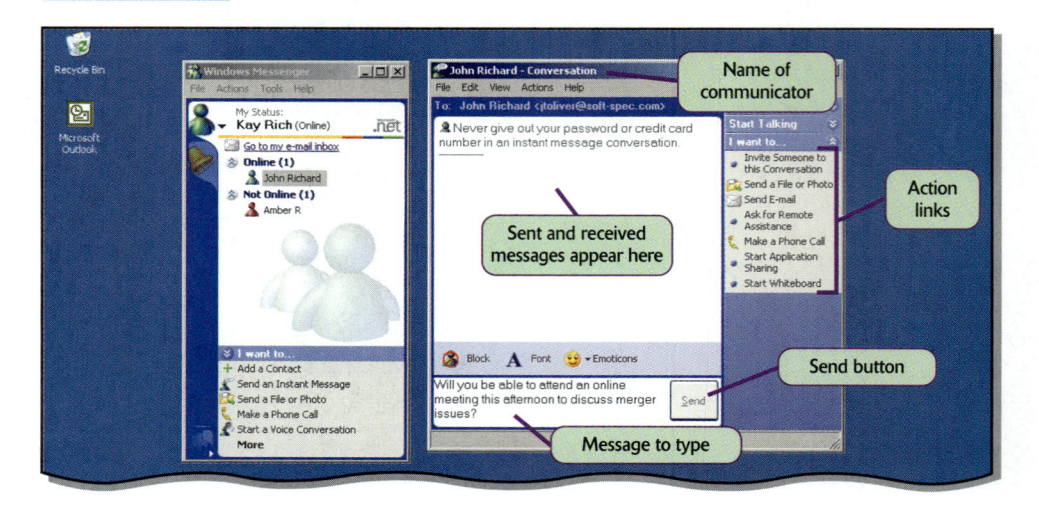

5 Type a response to the message you receive and then click the **Send** button.

6 Close the **Conversation** window and then close the **Windows Messenger** window.

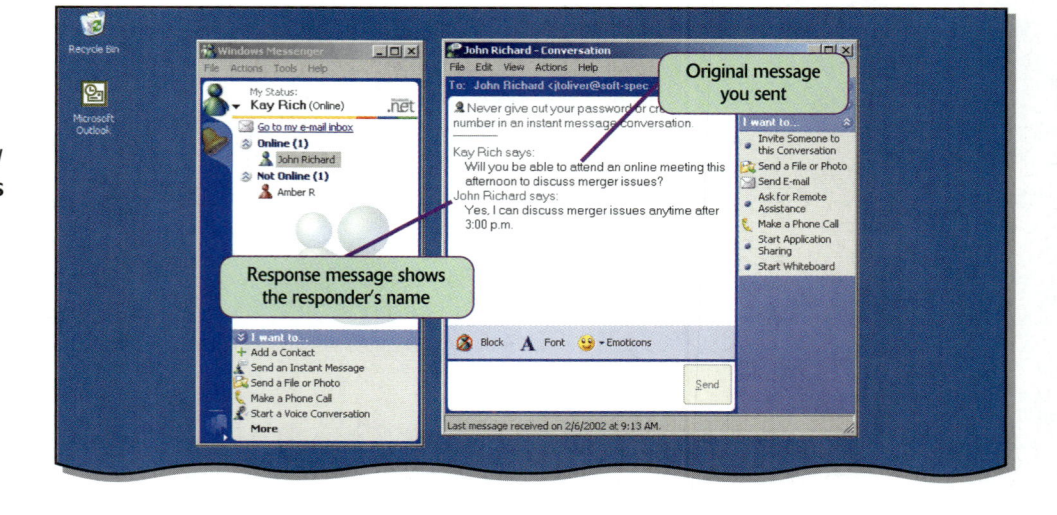

Figure 8-27

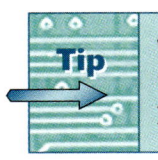

> **Tip:** When you close the **Windows Messenger** window, a message appears telling you that the program will continue to run in the taskbar so that you can receive instant messages.

CHECK POINT

There is so much more to the instant messaging service than is covered in Task 11. Explore the features available to locate how to

- Block messages from selected contacts
- Send an automatic response when you are away from your desk
- Add additional names to your contact list
- Call or page a contact

Using Remote Mail

Maintaining Outlook files when you are part of a network on which Outlook information is stored can be challenging—especially when you travel. Connecting remotely to your network Outlook account enables you to check mail and store information from Outlook on your laptop in such a way that the information automatically updates between your laptop and desktop computers. Preparing your laptop computer for use *offline* is important to the success of offline use as well as for successful synchronization after you return to the office. Consider three separate stages for working remotely:

1. Prepare to work offline or remotely by creating and specifying folders for offline use and synchronizing folders from the network
2. Switch to offline mode and then return to online mode
3. Connect remotely and *synchronize* information

Each of these stages requires preparation that will enable you to work efficiently.

CHECK POINT

To connect remotely using a modem and telephone line connection from a home computer or from a laptop, you need to establish a dial-up network connection on a home computer or laptop. To create the connection, you must have access to My Computer and follow these steps:

1. Double-click **My Computer** on the desktop.

> **Other Ways**
> To open the My Computer window:
> - Right-click the **Start** button, select **Explore**, scroll to the top of the **Folders** pane, and then click **My Computer**.

2. Double-click the **Dial-Up Networking** icon to open the **Dial-Up Networking** dialog box and then double-click the **Make New Connection** icon.

3. Type a connection name in **Type a name for the computer you are dialing** and then click **Next**.

4. Type the area code and telephone number in appropriate text boxes, select an appropriate setting from the **Country or region code** list, if necessary, click **Next**, and then click **Finish**.

> **Tip** If you are using Windows XP, you must have access to the Control Panel.

> **Tip** If you are using Windows XP, click the **Start** button, select **Control Panel**, click **Network and Internet Connections**, click **Create a connection to the network at your office**, select **Dial-up connection**, and then click **Next**.

Creating and Specifying Offline Folders

Creating folders to hold the Outlook information that you plan to review offline will enable you to synchronize—duplicate or update—the information after you reconnect to the network. Outlook requires special folders containing an *.ost* extension. You will need to establish the folders on your laptop or the computer you plan to use to connect remotely. This procedure must be performed while you are connected to the network.

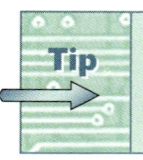

> **Tip** Because it is necessary to connect to the Microsoft Exchange Server to complete these tasks, Figures shown for the remaining tasks in this book will appear different from other figures.

Using Outlook with the Internet

Task 12:
To Create and Specify an Offline Folder

Figure 8-28

1. Connect to the network and launch Outlook.

2. Choose **Tools | E-Mail Accounts**, select **View or change existing e-mail accounts**, and then click **Next**.

3. Select the **Microsoft Exchange Server** listing and then click **Change**.

4. Click the **More Settings** button, click the **Advanced** tab, click **Offline Folder File Settings**, and then type the drive, folder, and file name you want to use for your offline files.

5. Click **OK**, click **Next**, and then click **Finish**.

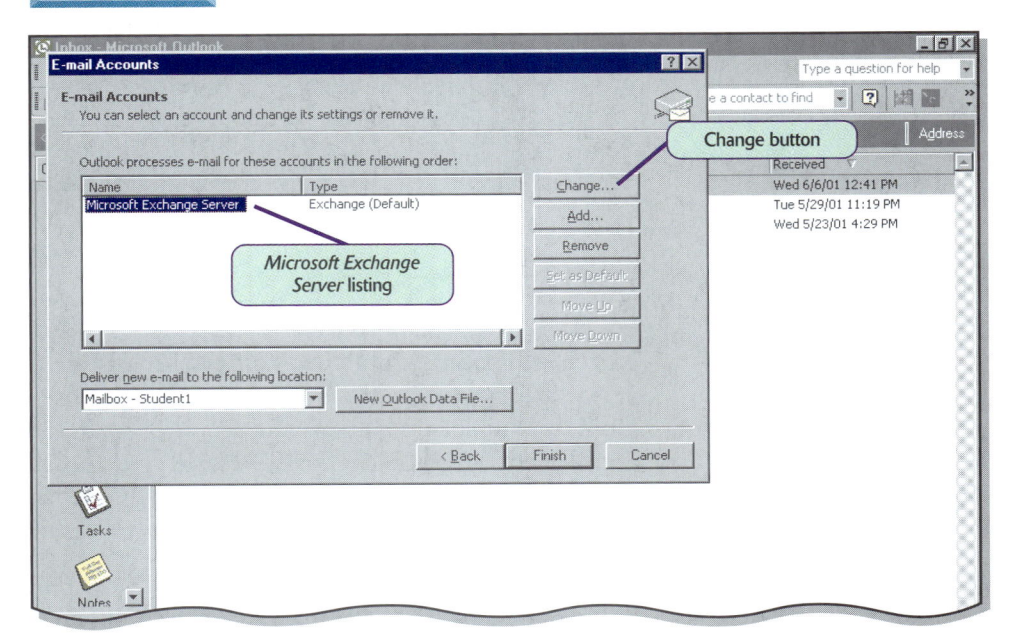

Figure 8-29

Troubleshooting
Special permissions must be set by the system administrator to allow you to set up offline folders. If you do not have the appropriate permission, the **Offline Folder File Settings** button will not appear. Click **Cancel** to continue.

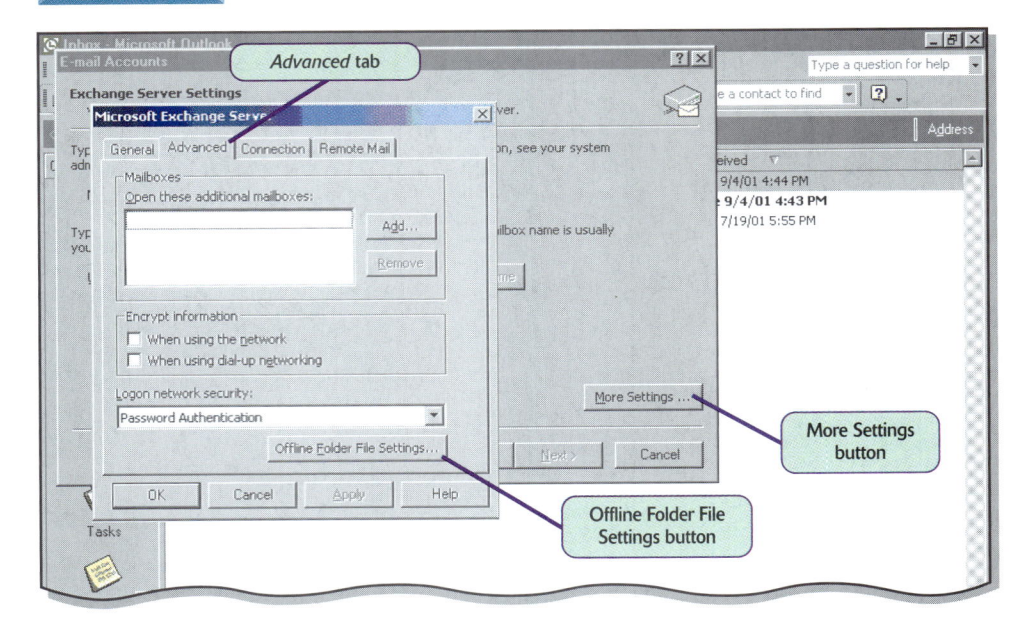

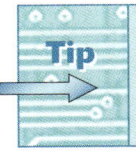

Tip Only one offline folder can be created for each Outlook profile. As a result, if an offline file has already been established for your profile, you will not be able to change the setting. Click **Cancel** to continue.

Using Remote Mail

> **Tip:** Outlook automatically makes the Inbox, Outbox, Deleted Items, Sent Items, Calendar, Contacts, Tasks, Journal Notes, and Drafts folders available for offline use. If you want to use other Outlook folders while you are working offline, you can designate the folder for offline use by selecting the folder in the Folder List pane and choosing **Tools | Send/Receive Settings | Make This Folder Available Offline**.

Synchronizing Folders

After you have established folders for offline use, you can synchronize—in effect, duplicate—entries from Outlook folders on the network to the offline folders you set up. When you synchronize folders, Outlook checks the folder on the network and the offline folder and transfers data between the computers to update files in both locations. To download the folder information to the offline folder you have set up, you need to synchronize the folders.

You can set up Outlook to automatically synchronize files or synchronize the files manually. If you synchronize manually, you can select to synchronize a selected folder, all folders, or a send/receive group of folders.

Task 13:
To Synchronize All Folders

1 Connect to the network using a remote dial-up connection or connect your computer directly to the network using a network connection.

2 Launch Outlook and then choose **Tools | Send/Receive | Send and Receive All** to synchronize all Outlook folders.

Figure 8-30

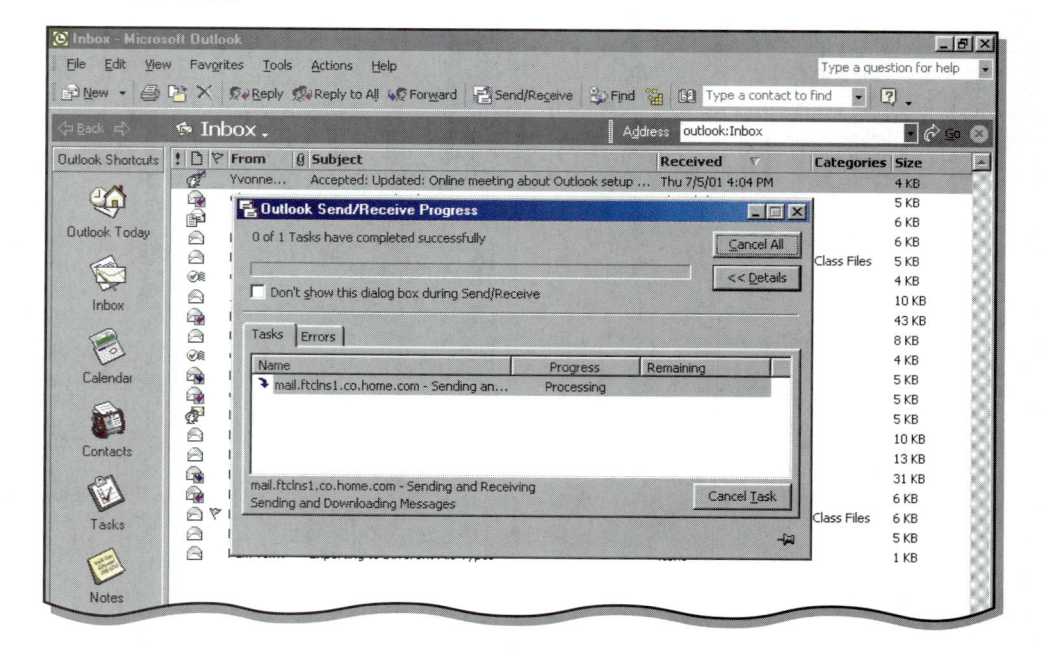

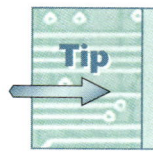

> **Tip:** Whether you connect to the network remotely or directly using the network cable, the procedures for synchronizing are the same. As a result, when you connect, you can synchronize Outlook folders.

Switching between Online and Offline Modes

When you work remotely, you typically tie up a telephone line so that callers receive a busy signal when you are connected and working online—while connected to the network. Working offline—working on a computer without being connected to a network—while you are connected to the network at the office prevents messages from arriving in your Inbox folder while you are working. You can switch between online and offline modes quite easily in Outlook.

Task 14:
To Switch Between Online and Offline Mode

1 Choose **File | Work Offline** while connected to the network.

2 Choose **File | Work Offline** again to remove the checkmark from the menu option.

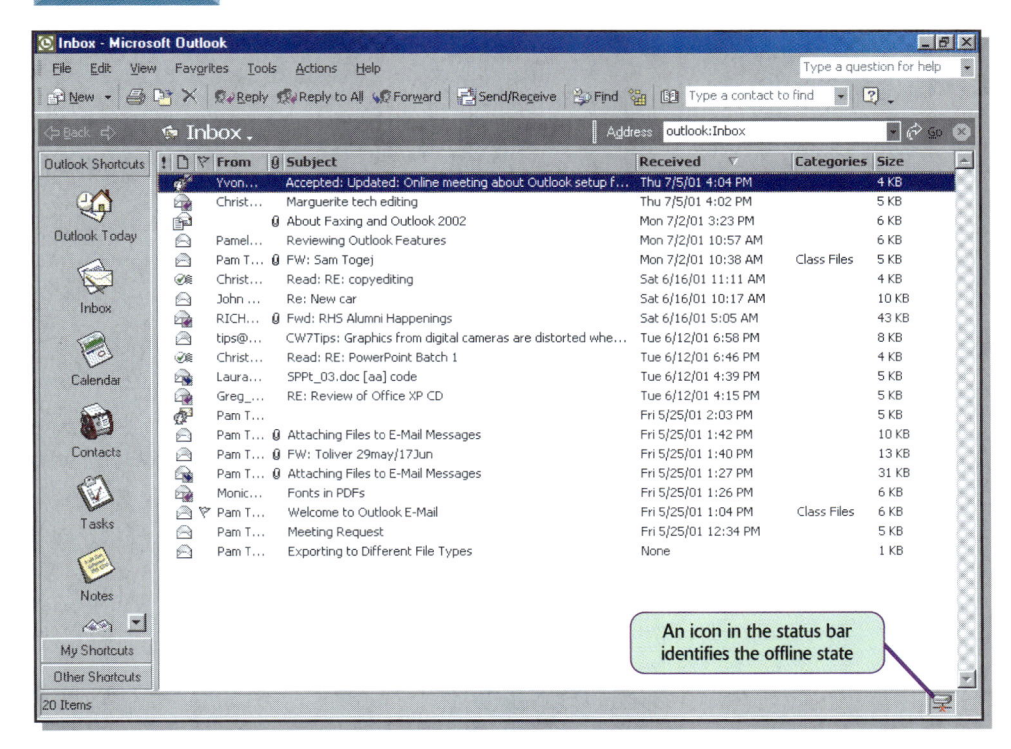

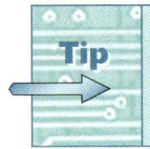

Figure 8-31

An icon in the status bar identifies the offline state

Tip: A checkmark beside a menu item identifies the feature as active. Removing the checkmark "turns off" the feature and the icon disappears from the status bar.

Setting Security

There are a number of reasons you might want to set security on your computer:

- Protect your computer against viruses
- Authenticate messages
- Ensure that only the intended message recipient can read a message

The procedures you must follow and the settings you set depend on the type of security you want and the reason you are implementing security.

Modifying Security Zone Settings

Viruses are known bugs that attack files on your computer and affect the way your computer operates. Viruses can infect your computer from e-mail attachments, through files you download from the Internet, and from mail messages you receive, such as the ILOVEYOU and Melissa viruses. To protect computers on a network, network administrators generally implement different levels of security. You can change the security zone settings on your computer to help protect the computer against infection.

Task 15:
To Modify Security Zone Settings

1 Open the Inbox folder and then choose **Tools | Options** to open the Options dialog box.

2 Click the **Security** tab, click the **Zone Settings** button, read the warning message that appears, and then click **OK**.

Figure 8-32

3 Click the **Internet** icon and then click the **Default Level** button, if necessary, to display the security level slide bar.

4 Drag the slide bar down one notch, click **Yes** in response to the warning, and then review the protection description for the **Medium-low** setting.

Tip If the **Default Level** button is inactive, it means that the slide bar is already displayed. It becomes inactive after you click it.

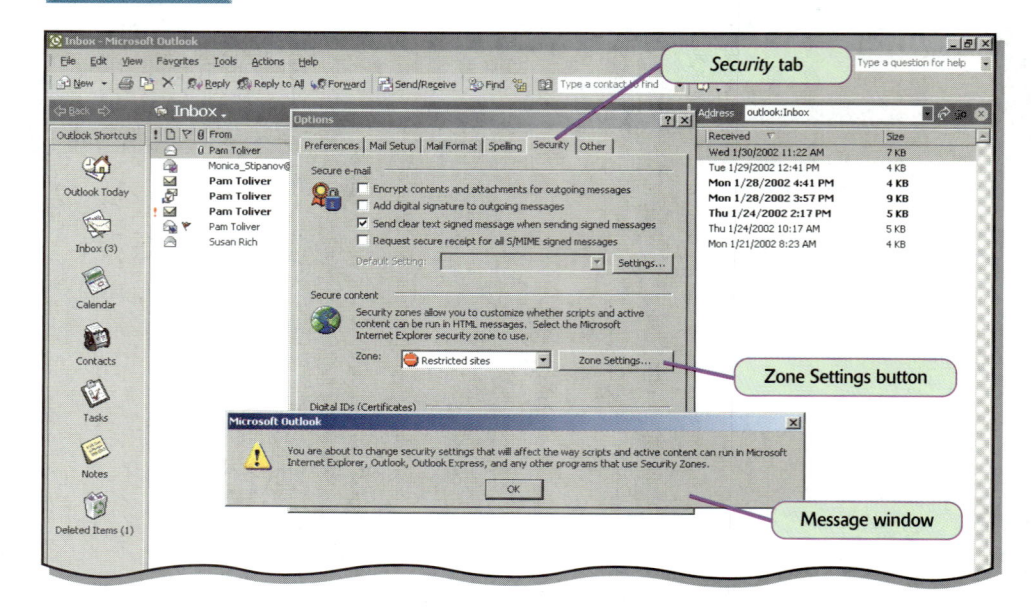

Figure 8-33

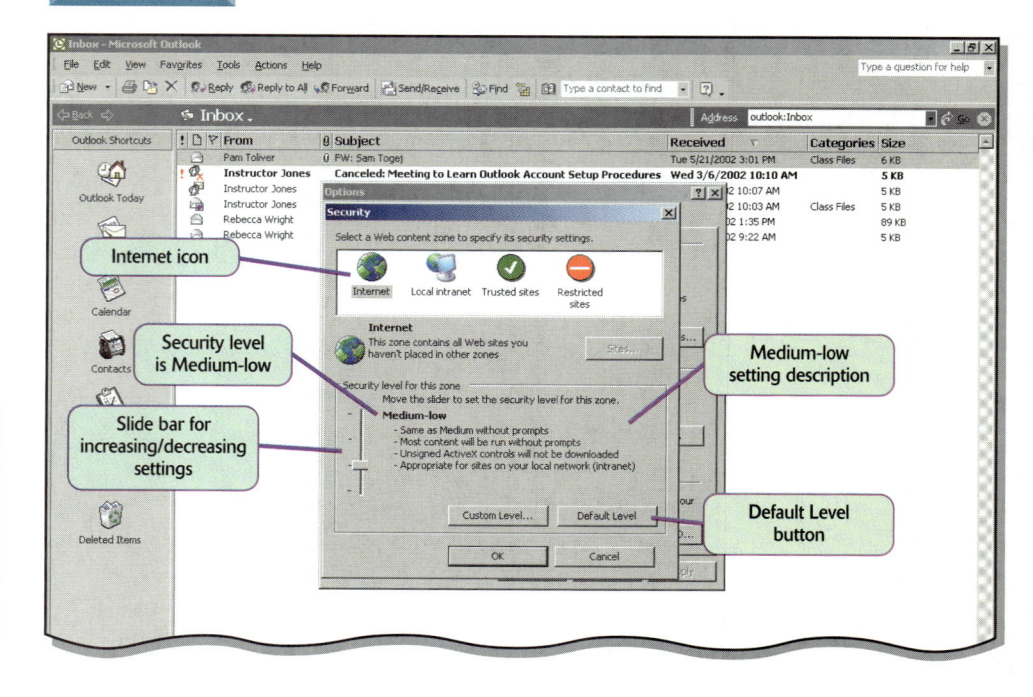

Using Outlook with the Internet

5 Click the **Default Level** button to reset the zone to Medium.

6 Click the **Restricted Sites** icon, review screen settings, and then click the **Sites** button to view a list of restricted sites.

> **Tip** The Sites button becomes available after you click the **Restricted Sites** icon.

Figure 8-34

7 Click **Cancel** and then click **OK** twice to close all dialog boxes.

> **Tip** To add a site to the restricted list, type the URL for the Web site in the **Add this Web site to the zone** text box and then click **Add**.

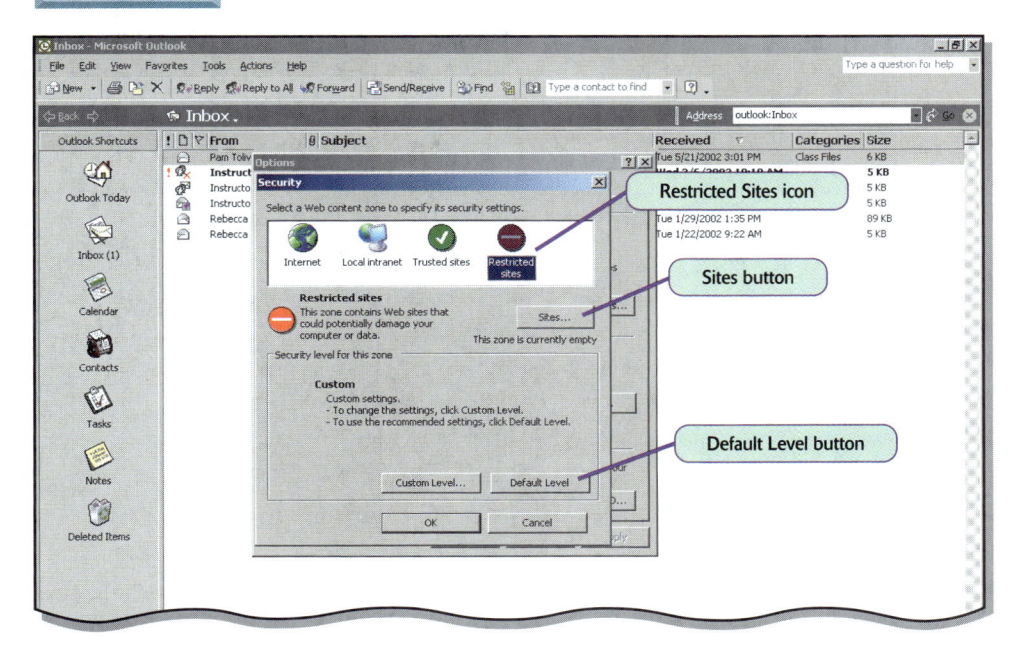

Figure 8-35

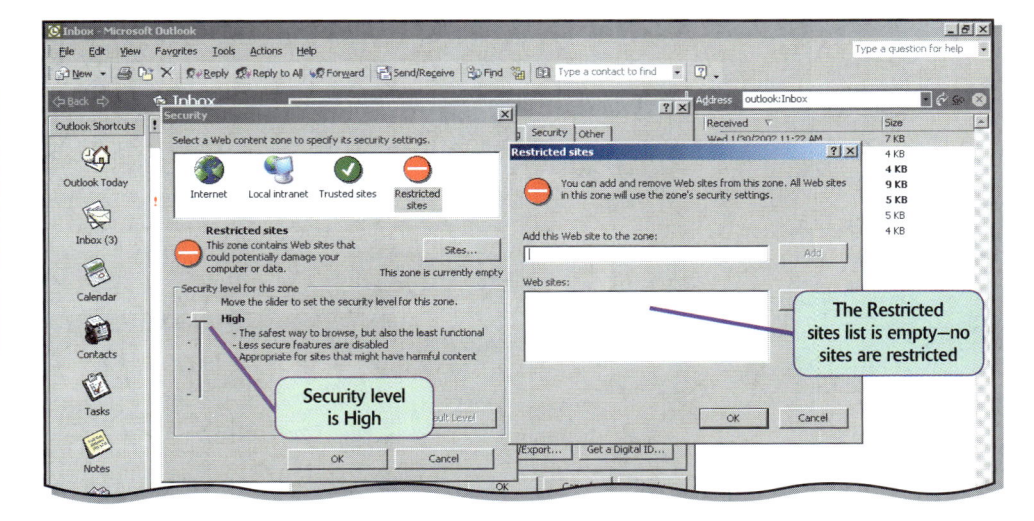

Setting up Secure E-Mail

Securing e-mail messages you send authenticates the message so that message recipients know that the message came from you and helps protect messages so that only the intended recipients can read them. Several terms are important to users who want to secure e-mail messages they send, as described in Table 8-2.

Table 8-2 Secure E-Mail Terminology

Feature	Description
Digital ID	A personalized code used to authenticate messages sent from your computer. Digital IDs cost about $1,000.
Digital signature	Attached to e-mail messages before you send them to attach the digital ID to the message.
Private key	A code that stays on the sender's computer and is attached to messages that are digitally signed to authenticate the message.
Public key	A code that is carried in a certificate which is attached to digitally signed messages. The public key is saved on recipient computers to enable them to decipher messages you send.
Certificate	An item attached to digitally signed messages that holds the public key.
Encryption	Encoding messages so that they appear garbled and are unreadable to anyone other than the intended recipients.

Obtaining a Digital ID

To secure e-mail messages, you must first obtain a digital ID. In addition, if you plan to send encrypted messages, you need a copy of the digital IDs of message recipients. After you obtain the digital IDs of message recipients, you can add the IDs to the recipients' contact listings. The average cost for a digital ID is $1,000.

Task 16:
To Obtain a Digital ID

1 Choose **Tools | Options | Security** and then click the **Get a Digital ID** button.

Figure 8-36

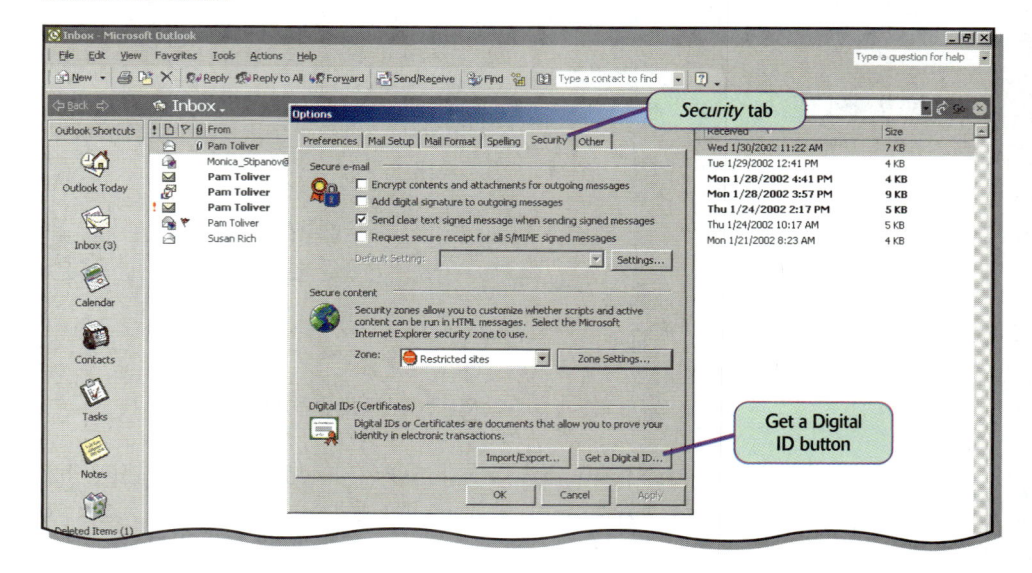

Using Outlook with the Internet   OU 8-33

2 Review the information about digital IDs and the companies that issue them.

Figure 8-37

3 Close the browser and then close the **Options** dialog box.

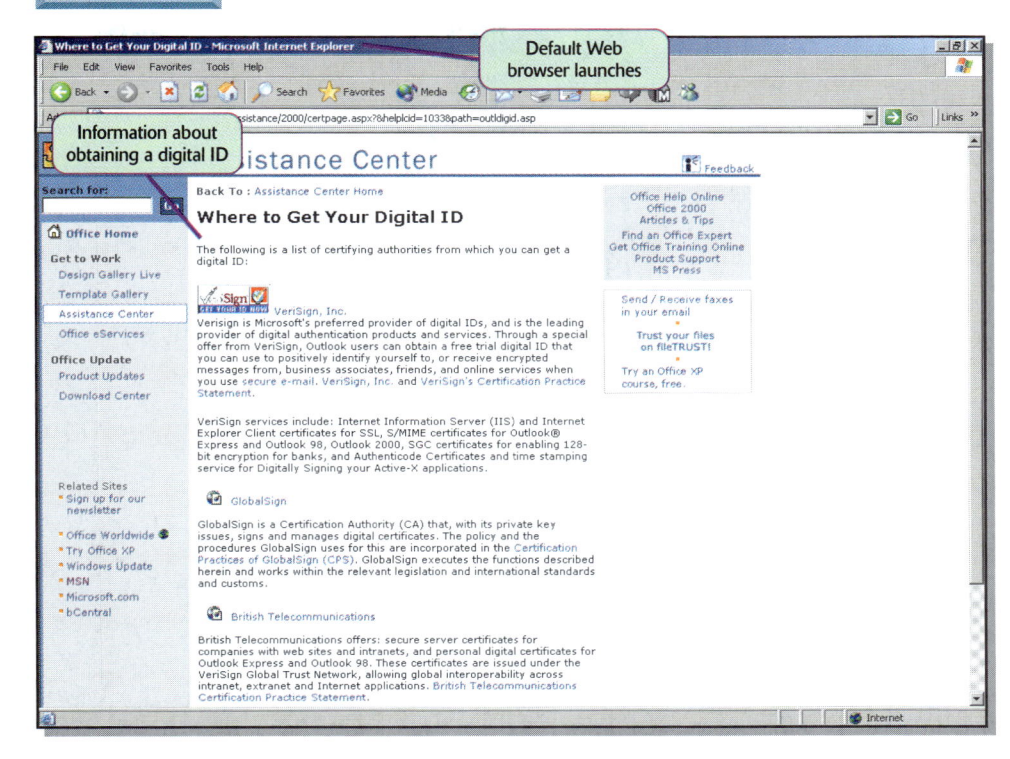

Digitally Signing or Encrypting Messages

After you obtain a digital ID, you can digitally sign or encrypt messages by attaching the certificate containing the codes to messages you send.

Task 17:
To Send Secure E-Mail

Figure 8-38

1 Open the **Inbox** folder and then create a new mail message.

2 Click the **Options** button on the message toolbar to open the Message Options dialog box and then click the **Security Settings** button to open the Security Properties dialog box.

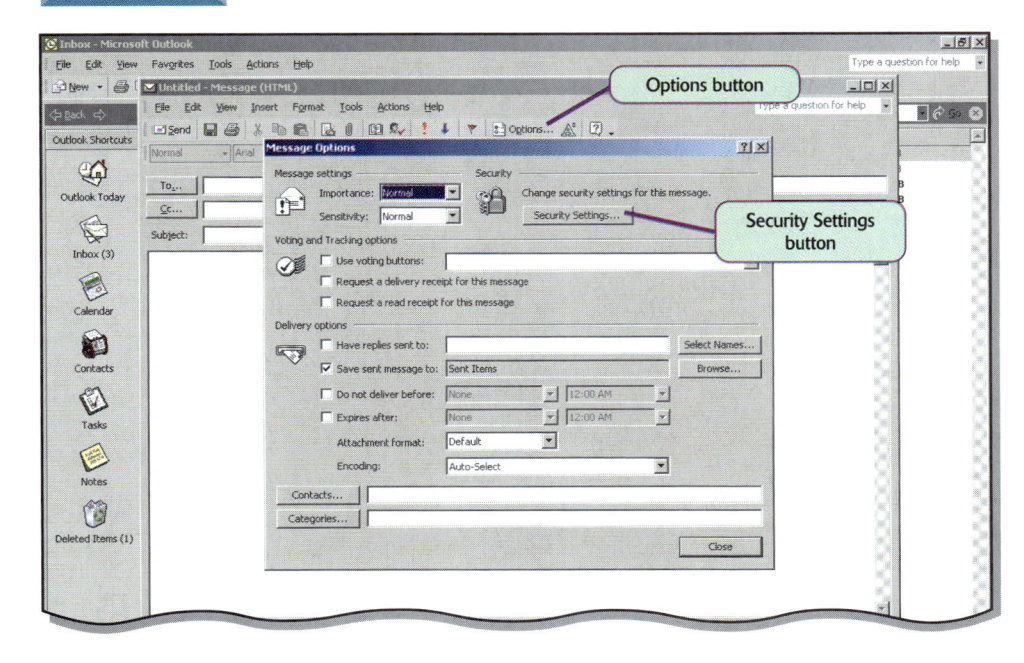

Other Ways

To display the Message Options dialog box:
- Choose **View | Options**.

3 Review options in the Security Properties dialog box, click **Cancel**, and then click **Close**.

4 Close the message without saving it.

Tip Use tools in the Security Properties dialog box to change the security level setting of the message.

Figure 8-39

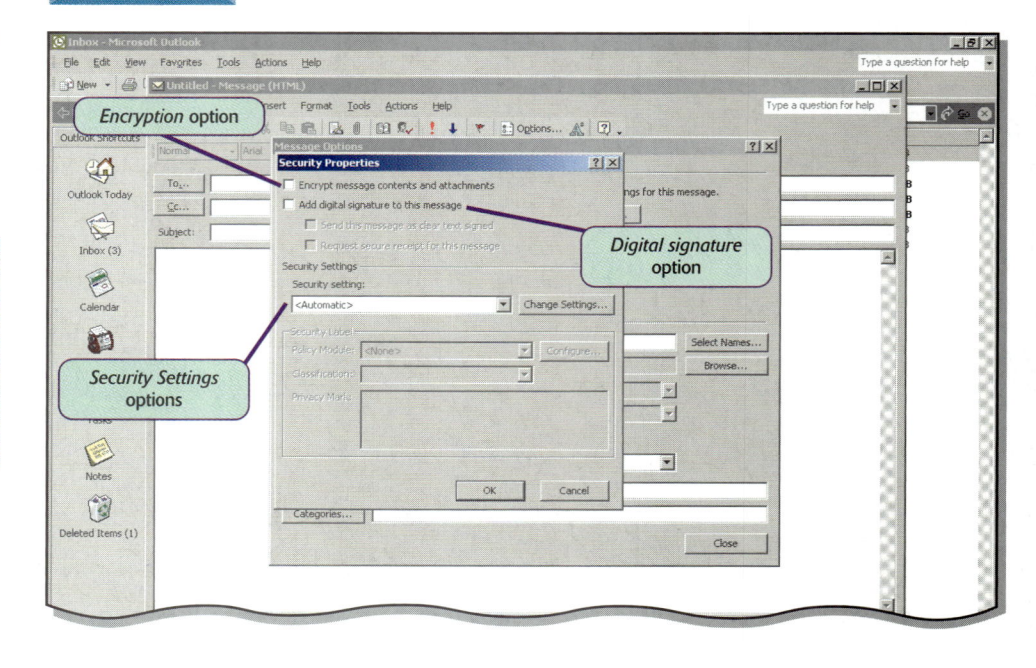

SUMMARY AND EXERCISES

SUMMARY

- When you save your calendar as a Web page, you can review it using the latest versions of most browsers.
- Microsoft offers a service through which you can share your free and busy schedule so that others to whom you grant access can view the schedule and use it to determine the best times to schedule meetings.
- A passport login is required to log on to the Microsoft Internet Free/Busy Service.
- Outlook folder home pages enable you to view Web sites without leaving Outlook.
- News servers are computers maintained by companies, interest groups, and so forth that enable interested users to share information and post replies to messages you find there.
- Outlook enables you to schedule meetings to occur online so that attendees located at different sites may participate without traveling to the meeting site.
- Outlook's instant messaging feature enables you to communicate with contacts, determine if a contact is online, and set controls that allow others to see when you are online and available for chatting.
- Before traveling, you can set up Outlook on a laptop computer so that you can connect remotely to your office network, check e-mail, and synchronize Outlook folders.
- Outlook provides access to security tools that you can use to change the security zone settings on your computer to help protect the computer against viruses and unauthorized access.
- Outlook provides features that authenticate messages so that message recipients know that the message came from you and helps protect messages so that only the intended recipients can read them.

KEY TERMS & SKILLS

KEY TERMS

bloggers (p. 8-22)
blogs (p. 8-22)
Free/Busy Service (p. 8-8)
IM address (p. 8-23)
instant messaging (p. 8-21)
NetMeeting (p. 8-20)
newsreaders (p. 8-17)

news servers (p. 8-17)
offline (p. 8-25)
online (p. 8-20)
passport (p. 8-8)
subscribe (p. 8-17)
synchronize (p. 8-25)
Weblog (p. 8-22)

SKILLS

Activate instant messaging and send a message (p. 8-23)
Assign a home page to the notes folder (p. 8-16)
Authorize access to your schedule (p. 8-12)
Create and specify an offline folder (p. 8-27)
Enable instant messaging in Outlook (p. 8-22)
Join the Internet Free/Busy Service and publish a schedule (p. 8-10)
Modify security zone settings (p. 8-30)

Obtain a digital ID (p. 8-32)
Open and read newsgroup messages (p. 8-20)
Save a calendar as a Web page (p. 8-6)
Schedule an online meeting using NetMeetings (p. 8-21)
Send secure e-mail (p. 8-33)
Set Free/Busy options (p. 8-9)
Subscribe to a newsgroup (p. 8-18)
Switch between online and offline mode (p. 8-29)
Synchronize all folders (p. 8-28)
View a Free/Busy schedule (p. 8-14)

STUDY QUESTIONS

MULTIPLE CHOICE

1. Protocols for Web folders appear in which of the following formats?
   a. html
   b. http:\\
   c. ftp://
   d. http://

2. The command used to save calendars in a format that can be used on the Web is
   a. **File | Save As**.
   b. **File | Save**.
   c. **File | Save as Web Page**.
   d. **Format | Web Page**.

3. A free/busy schedule can be posted for up to
   a. 3 years.
   b. 60 minutes.
   c. 2 months.
   d. 36 days.

4. The number of days of posted free/busy schedules you can view is limited to
   a. 1.
   b. 2.
   c. 7.
   d. 30.

5. Home pages can be assigned to all Outlook folders except the
   a. Inbox.
   b. Calendar.
   c. Contacts.
   d. Instant Message.

6. Internet tools for accessing newsgroup information are called
   a. news services.
   b. newsreaders.
   c. news servers.
   d. newsgroups.

7. Microsoft tools for conducting online meetings include all the following *except*
   a. NetMeeting.
   b. NetShow.
   c. NetOnline.
   d. Instant Messaging.

8. To connect remotely to network Outlook folders, you need all of the following *except*
   a. secure ID.
   b. modem.
   c. phone line.
   d. dial-up networking connection.

9. Setting Outlook security requires
   a. a secure Internet connection.
   b. digital ID.
   c. virus scanning software.
   d. new security zone.

10. The default Internet security setting is
    a. low.
    b. medium-low.
    c. medium.
    d. high.

SHORT ANSWER

1. Who can view your free/busy schedule after you post it?
2. How do you display folder contents when a home page is assigned for the folder?
3. How does the command to switch from online to offline differ from the command used to switch from offline to online?
4. Are there costs associated with obtaining digital signature IDs?
5. What is the difference between a private key and a public key?
6. What does a security certificate contain?
7. How do you post messages to newsgroups?
8. What is the difference between instant messaging and online meetings?

FILL IN THE BLANK

1. To post free/busy information to the service, you must obtain a login and password called a(n) _____.
2. Set up Free/Busy options by setting options for the _____ folder.
3. Topic-specific messages containing information posted by different people are stored on _____ _____.
4. To view topic-specific messages stored on servers, you must _____ to the server.
5. _____ means to connect to an instant messaging service and conduct an online conversation with another user who is online.
6. Messages from Outlook that you want to read while disconnected from the network are stored in _____ folders.
7. To update items in Outlook folders between a laptop or remote computer and the network, connect to the network and _____ Outlook folders.
8. Messages that appear to be garbled and are unreadable are usually _____.

DISCUSSION

1. What are some advantages to saving your Outlook calendar as a Web page and posting it to a Web site?
2. What is the difference between saving a calendar as a Web page and posting free and busy information?
3. What are the names of some recently discovered computer viruses?
4. Under what circumstances might you want to obtain a digital ID and use it?

Photospread credits pages 8-2 & 8-3
©FPG: ©VCG 1998; ©Pearson Education; and ©Lorraine Castellano

Glossary

Access level Controls set to identify the actions a delegate to Outlook folders can perform.

Archive Moving out-of-date items into a file at regularly scheduled intervals to clear out old and expired items.

Attachment Files created in other applications that are attached to e-mail messages and sent electronically. Files attached to e-mail messages you receive can be opened, saved, edited, and printed.

Attendees People invited to attend a meeting.

Author An access level that enables the delegate to read and create all folder items, modify and delete items the author creates in the folder, and send items to others on behalf of the owner.

Calendar An Outlook folder designed to hold scheduled appointments and meetings.

Calendar banner The folder banner for the Calendar folder that appears at the top of the Calendar window to identify the folder that is open.

Categories A keyword or phrase used to keep track of, sort, filter, or group items stored in different Outlook folders.

Certificate The item attached to digitally signed messages that holds the public key.

Comma separated values A file type that uses commas to separate fields of information contained in each listing.

Conditional formatting Formatting automatically applied to a folder item display based on rules created. For example, you could set a rule that automatically formats meetings by labeling the meeting as Important.

Contacts The Outlook folder designed to hold listings of information about business and personal contacts on a Rolodex™-type file for easy access.

Contributor An access level that enables the delegate to create items only without viewing other items in the folder.

Date Navigator A pane in the Calendar window that displays a full-month palette for one or more months, depending on the size of the pane, and that is used to navigate to different months and dates.

Delegates Those to whom an Outlook folder owner grants folder access.

Deleted items The Outlook folder designed as a wastebasket to hold "thrown out" items that you can retrieve, if desired, as long as the wastebasket has not been emptied.

Digital ID A personalized code used to authenticate messages sent from your computer.

Digital signature Signatures used to electronically attach digital IDs to e-mail messages.

Distribution list An entry in the Contacts folder that contains a collection of related contacts—people who work for the same company, associates who work in a department, and so forth—and enables you to send an e-mail message to all individuals contained in the list.

Editor An access level that enables the delegate to read and create all folder items, modify and delete items the author creates in the folder, send items to others on behalf of the owner, and modify and delete owner created items.

E-mail The abbreviation for electronic mail that you can send via a computer.

Encryption Encoding messages so that they appear garbled and are unreadable to anyone other than the intended recipients.

Events In Outlook, all-day activities recorded in the Calendar.

Index

Symbols

- (Collapse) button, OU 6-9, OU 6-12
    displaying remote sessions, OU 6-27
+ (Expand) button, OU 6-9, OU 6-12
    recording activity lengths, OU 6-27
    restoring archived items, OU 6-31
24hoursupport.helpdesk newsgroup, OU 8-18–19

A

accepting
    invitations, OU 8-21
    meetings, OU 4-10–13
    tasks, OU 5-11–14
accessing
    Calendar window, OU 3-5
    calendars remotely, OU 8-5
    information on news servers, OU 8-17
    Microsoft web site, OU-11
    newsreaders, OU 8-17
    Outlook features, OU-5–8
    posted schedules, OU 8-8
access rights
    authorizing
        e-mail addresses, OU 8-13
        Free/Busy Service. See Free/Busy Service, schedules
    delegates
        assigning to folders, OU 7-13–15
        opening folders, OU 7-18–19
    folder permissions, OU 7-15–17
    granting to folders, OU 7-13–15
    modifying permission levels, OU 7-13
    options for notifying users, OU 7-15
    owners and delegates, OU 7-13
    posting calendars, OU 8-5
    setting security, OU 8-29
        e-mail, OU 30–32
        security zone settings, OU 30–31
    viewing posted schedules, OU 8-14

account setup
    Internet newsgroups, OU 8-17
    Free/Busy Service, OU 8-10–12
    Passport, OU 8-8, OU 8-10
actions, undoing (Undo Delete command), OU 2-9
Actions menu commands
    Add or Remove Attendees, OU 3-21
    Cancel Meeting, OU 3-22
    Decline and Propose New Time, OU 4-12
    Follow Up, OU 2-18, OU 4-24
    Forward, OU 5-16
        as vCard, OU 7-6
    Link Items, OU 6-23
    New All Day Event, OU 3-13
    New Appointment, OU 3-9
    New Letter to Contact, OU 7-21
    New Mail Message, OU 4-19
    New Mail Message Using, More Stationery, OU 4-22
    New Meeting Request, OU 3-18
    New Message to Attendees, OU 3-23
    New Note, OU 5-19
    New Recurring Appointment, OU 3-16
    New Task, OU 5-10
    Reply, OU 4-9
    Tentative and Propose New Time, OU 4-12
activating
    features with checkmarks, OU 8-29
    instant messaging, OU 8-22–25
    Journal tracking, OU 6-25–26
    settings for Free/Busy Service, OU 8-11
    Windows Messenger, OU 8-23
Active Appointments view (Calendar), OU 1-22
Active date, OU 3-5–6
active view, OU 3-5–6
activities
    automatically recorded by Outlook, OU 2-21
    modifying entry types, OU 6-29
    recording length, OU 6-26
    tracking, OU 6-25
        contacts, OU 2-21, OU 6-27
        setting options, OU 6-25–26

Activities list, OU 6-25
    verifying Journal entries, OU 6-28
Activities tab (personal contact listing), OU 2-21
Add Holidays (Calendar option), OU 3-26
Add or Remove Attendees command (Actions menu), OU 3-21
Add to Junk Sender list command (Junk E-mail), OU 6-18
Add Users dialog box, OU 7-14, OU 7-17
Address Book, OU 2-6, OU 2-14
address box (Calendar), OU 3-5–6
address information, validating entries, OU 2-8
adjusting signature placement, OU 7-26
Adult Content messages, OU 6-18
Advanced E-mail Options dialog box, OU 4-27–28
Advanced Find command (Tools menu), OU 6-10, OU 6-14
Advanced Find dialog box, OU 6-10–11
    More Choice tab, OU 1-27
Advanced Options dialog box, OU 1-7
Advanced toolbar (View menu), OU 2-10
alignment, paragraphs, OU 4-20
anchoring folders, OU-9–10
Answer Wizard (Help window), OU-12
applications
    creating files, OU 7-19
    e-mail programs, OU 7-11
    exporting data, OU 7-5
    grouping Journal entry types, OU 6-27
    modifying entry types, OU 6-29
    newsgroups as resources, OU 8-17
applying
    advanced sort techniques, OU 2-11–13
    conditional formatting to appointments, OU 3-28–29
Appointment dialog box, OU 3-9, OU 3-19, OU 6-16
Appointment Recurrence dialog box, OU 3-16
Appointment toolbar, OU 3-22
appointments
    Active Appointments view, OU 1-22
    applying conditional formatting, OU 3-28–29
    automatically recording tasks, OU 2-21
    Calendar, OU-4
    Categories command (Edit menu), OU 6-8
    copying, OU 3-15
    default setting, OU 3-9
    displaying, OU 1-4
    filtering folders, OU 6-11
    grouping items, OU 6-4
    manipulating, OU 3-14–15
    moving, OU 3-14
    opening, OU 6-6
    Outlook Today, OU-4
    printing, OU 3-23–25
    recurring, OU 3-16–17
    removing cancellations, OU 3-14
    scheduling, OU 3-8–12
        all day events, OU 3-13–14
    setting reminders, OU 3-11–12
    storing, OU-9
    tracking, OU 3-4
archiving items, OU 6-29–31
    disabling AutoArchive, OU 6-30
    restoring archived files, OU 6-31
asking questions (Help), OU-11–14
    Ask a Question tool, OU-3, OU-11–12
    Office Assistant, OU-13–14
Assign Task response, OU 5-13
assigning
    categories to items, OU 6-4–9
    contacts to Journal entries, OU 6-27–28
    delegates for folder access, OU 7-13–15
    entry types, OU 6-25
    folder home pages, OU 8-15–16
    notes to contacts, OU 5-21–22
    task ownership, OU 5-12
    tasks, OU 5-11–15
associations between Outlook items and Contacts, creating, OU 6-23–24
attachments, OU 4-22
    alternate file formats, OU 5-25
    certificates, OU 8-33
    checking
        before opening, OU 7-10
        for viruses, OU 4-31
    digital signatures, OU 8-32
    e-mail messages, OU 4-29–31, OU 7-6
    manipulating, OU 4-29–31
    methods of virus infection, OU 8-30
    opening vCards, OU 7-9
    private keys, OU 8-32

attendees, meetings
    invitations, OU 3-23
    scheduling, OU 3-20
authenticating messages, OU 8-31–32
author level (access rights), OU 7-13, OU 7-15–17
authorizing access
    e-mail addresses, OU 8-13
    Free/Busy Service. *See* Free/Busy Service
    schedules, OU 8-12–13
AutoArchive feature, OU 6-29
    default setting, OU 6-30
    turning off, OU 6-30
Automatic Formatting command (Edit menu), OU 3-28

B

Back button, OU-3–4, OU-8
background
    Calendar, OU 3-27
    notes, OU 5-23–24
Background Picture dialog box, OU 7-25
Bcc field (task message), OU 5-16
blocking messages, OU 8-25
blogs/bloggers, OU 8-22
Browse dialog box, OU 7-8
browsers
    displaying calendars, OU 8-7
    Internet Explorer features, OU 8-15
    reviewing calendars, OU 8-5
bulk mailers, OU 6-18
business cards (vCards), OU 7-5
buttons. *See also* **toolbars**
    adding to toolbars, OU 1-16–19
    removing, OU 1-19
    shortcut groups, OU-4

C

Calendar, OU-4, OU-8, OU 3-1, OU 3-4–8
    accessing as delegate, OU 7-18
    adding holidays, OU 3-27
    advanced options, OU 3-26
    authorizing access, OU 8-12
    availability for offline use, OU 8-28
    customizing, OU 3-25–29
        applying conditional formatting to appointments, OU 3-28–29
        backgrounds, OU 3-27
        launch features, OU 1-7
        view, OU 6-12–14
    displaying
        and navigating, OU 3-4–8
        reminders, OU 3-11
        time zone changes, OU 1-20
    e-mail address association, OU 8-10
    meeting placement, OU 8-21
    mouse pointer shapes, OU 3-10
    moving items, OU 6-16
    Organize pane tools, OU 6-15
    printing, OU 3-23–25
    saving as Web pages, OU 8-5–7
    setting options, OU 3-25–27, OU 8-9
    spaces in names, OU 8-6
    views available, OU 1-22–23
Calendar Banner, OU 3-5–7
Calendar File Name dialog box, OU 8-6
Calendar icon (Outlook Bar), OU 6-6
Calendar Options dialog box, OU 3-25–26, OU 8-9
Cancel Meeting command (Actions menu), OU 3-22–23
cancelled messages, markings for, OU 4-10
cascading menu, displaying with mouse pointer, OU 1-18
case sensitivity for category names, OU 6-6
categories
    assigning, OU 6-4–9
    category names, OU 6-9
        case sensitivity, OU 6-6
    deleting from lists, OU 6-8
    modifying, OU 6-7–9
    resetting, OU 6-8
    sorting, OU 6-9–11
    tools, OU 6-14
Cc field
    e-mail messages, OU 4-18
    task messages, OU 5-16
certificates
    attaching to messages, OU 8-33
    public keys, OU 8-32
chatting (instant messaging), OU 8-21–25

Check Address dialog box, OU 2-8
Check Phone Number dialog box, OU 2-7
checking
    contact information, OU 2-7–8
    e-mail editor settings, OU 4-9
    messages, OU 4-7–8
Choose Contact dialog box, OU 2-14–15
Clipboard
    content limitations, OU 1-24
    contents, OU 1-24
Clippit, OU-13
Close button (Help window), OU-14
closing
    Outlook Newsreader, OU 8-20
    Windows Messenger, OU 8-24–25
Collapse (-) button, OU 6-9, OU 6-12
    displaying remote sessions, OU 6-27
colors
    archiving defaults, OU 6-30
    changing, OU 6-17
    color coding messages, OU 6-14–18
    forms
        customizing, OU 7-29
        setting, OU 7-28
    setting notes options, OU 5-23–24
    task reminder defaults, OU 5-17
columns, resizing, OU 6-13
comma separated values, OU 7-7, OU 7-11
commands
    Actions menu
        Add or Remove Attendees, OU 3-21
        Cancel Meeting, OU 3-22
        Decline and Propose New Time, OU 4-12
        Follow Up, OU 2-18, OU 4-24
        Forward as vCard, OU 7-6
        Forward, OU 5-16
        Link, Items, OU 6-23
        New All Day Event, OU 3-13
        New Appointment, OU 3-9
        New Letter to Contact, OU 7-21
        New Mail Message Using, More Stationery, OU 4-22
        New Mail Message, OU 4-19
        New Meeting Request, OU 3-18
        New Message to Attendees, OU 3-23
        New Note, OU 5-19
        New Recurring Appointment, OU 3-16
        New Task, OU 5-10
        Reply, OU 4-9
        Tentative and Propose New Time, OU 4-12
    adding to menus, OU 1-16–19
    Edit menu
        Automatic Formatting, OU 3-28
        Categories, OU 6-8
        Cut/Copy/Paste, OU 1-24
        Undo Delete, OU 2-9
        Undo, OU 2-13
    File menu
        Archive, OU 6-30
        Exit, OU-15
        Folder, New Folder, OU 1-9
        Import and Export, OU 7-7, OU 7-11, OU 7-13
        New Appointment, OU 3-9
        New Distribution List, OU 2-19
        New Folder, OU 1-9
        New Meeting Request, OU 3-18
        New, Mail Message, OU 4-19
        New, Task, OU 5-10
        Note, OU 5-19
        Open, Other User's Folder, OU 7-18
        Print Preview, OU 2-16
        Print, OU 2-15–17, OU 4-15, OU 5-16, OU 5-25
        Save as Web Page, OU 8-6
        Save As, OU 5-26
        Save, OU 2-6, OU 4-14, OU 4-31
        Work Offline, OU 8-29
    Format menu
        Font, OU 4-20
        Paragraph, OU 4-20
    Help menu
        Office on the Web, OU-11
        Show the Office Assistant, OU-13
        Show, OU-12
    Insert menu
        File, OU 4-30
        Signature, OU 4-18
    Junk E-mail menu
        Add to Junk Sender list, OU 6-18
    removing, OU 1-19
    Start menu
        Microsoft Office Application Recovery, OU-15
        Outlook, OU-3

Tools menu
  Advanced Find, OU 6-10
  Customize, OU 1-16–17
  E-Mail Accounts, OU 8-27
  Find, OU 1-26, OU 2-14
  Forms, Choose Form, OU 7-30
  Forms, Design a Form, OU 7-27
  Instant Messaging, Log Off, OU 8-23
  Instant Messaging, Log On, OU 8-23
  Options, Advanced, OU 1-7
  Options, Calendar Options, OU 1-20–21, OU 3-26–3-27, OU 8-9–10
  Options, Calendar Options, Free/Busy Options, OU 8-12–14
  Options, Contact Options, OU 2-22
  Options, Delegates, OU 7-14
  Options, E-Mail Options, OU 4-27
  Options, E-Mail Options, Advanced E-Mail Options, OU 4-11, OU 4-27
  Options, Journal Options, OU 6-25
  Options, Mail Format, OU 4-16, OU 4-23, OU 7-24–26, OU 7-31
  Options, Note Options, OU 5-23,
  Options, Other, OU 1-7, OU 6-30, OU 8-22
  Options, Preferences, OU 5-6
  Options, Security, OU 8-30–32
  Out of Office Assistant, OU 4-29
  Rules Wizard, OU 6-19, OU 6-22
  Send/Receive Settings, Make This Folder Available Offline, OU 8-28
  Send/Receive, Send and Receive All, OU 4-7, OU 8-28
View menu
  Current View, OU 1-22
  Current View, Active Appointments, OU 3-24
  Current View, Address Cards, OU 6-9
  Current View, By Category, OU 6-9
  Current View, By Company, OU 2-11
  Current View, Customize Current View, OU 2-11, OU 6-12–14, OU 6-24
  Current View, Day/Week/Month, OU 1-23, OU 1-27, OU 3-25
  Current View, Message Timeline, OU 1-23
  Folder List, OU 6-31, OU 7-16
  Go To, Go To Date, OU 3-7
  Go To, News, OU 8-17–18
  Options, OU 8-33–34
  Preview Pane, OU 1-22–23, OU 4-6
  Toolbars, Advanced, OU 2-10
Company field (Contacts), OU 2-8
computer viruses. See viruses
computers
  digital IDs, OU 8-32
  hardware, newsgroups as resources, OU 8-17
  methods of virus infections, OU 8-30
  .ost folders, OU 8-26
  private keys, OU 8-32
  protecting
    from viruses, OU 4-6
    on networks, OU 8-30
  public keys, OU 8-32
  remote access, OU 8-26
  software programs, OU 8-17
conditional formatting. See formatting
conditions, setting, OU 6-18
connections
  creating for remote access, OU 8-26
  linking items, OU 6-23
  remote access, OU 8-25–26
  setting delegate permissions, OU 7-14
  setting up for newsreaders, OU 8-17
  tools for online meetings, OU 8-21
contacts
  assigning notes, OU 5-21–22
  assigning to Journal entries, OU 6-27–28
  authorizing access, OU 8-13
  automatic sorting, OU 2-23–24
  automatically recording tasks, OU 2-21
  availability for offline use, OU 8-28
  blocking messages, OU 8-25
  business contacts, OU-4
  categories. See categories, OU 6-5–7
  Company field, OU 2-8
  Contacts folder, OU-4
  copying, OU 2-23–24
  creating, OU 2-5–8
    associations, OU 6-23–24
    contact letters, OU 7-21–24
    from e-mail, OU 7-12–13
    from vCards, OU 7-9–10
    letters, OU 7-19
  customizing
    launch features, OU 1-7
    views, OU 6-12

data fields, OU 2-6
deleting, OU 7-12
duplicate entries, OU 7-12
e-mailing, OU 7-6
editing, OU 2-9–10
exporting, OU 7-5–9
finding, OU 2-10, OU 2-13–15
flagging for follow-up, OU 2-17–18
Full Name field, OU 2-7, OU 2-10
grouping items, OU 6-4
importing, OU 7-11–12
instant messaging, OU 8-21–25
integrating information, OU 2-13
item information, OU 7-27
linking items manually, OU 6-23
maintaining, OU 7-5–13
merging, OU 7-24
online contacts, OU 8-24
opening Contacts folder, OU 3-8
Organize pane tools, OU 6-15
printing, OU 2-15–17
recording notes, OU 6-24
saving vCards, OU 7-9–10
sending information, OU 7-6
setting options, OU 2-22
sorting
 advanced techniques, OU 2-11
 categories, OU 6-9
 views, OU 2-10–13
storing Access files, OU 7-13
tracking activities, OU 2-21, OU 6-25
verifying Journal entries, OU 6-28
View Summary Filter group, OU 6-12
Contacts By Location view, OU 2-22
context-sensitive help, question mark button, OU-10
contributor (level), folder permissions rights, OU 7-16
Control Panel, setting up remote access, OU 8-26
conversations
grouping entry types, OU 6-27
instant messaging, OU 8-21–25
modifying entry types, OU 6-29
recording, OU 6-24
 activity lengths, OU 6-26
 date/time, OU 6-26

Copy button (Standard toolbar), OU 1-24, OU 3-15
copying
appointments, OU 3-14–15
contacts, OU 2-23–24
information, OU 7-5
text, OU 1-24
Create New Folder dialog box, OU 1-9, OU 1-18
Create New Signature dialog box, OU 4-16
Create Signature dialog box, OU 4-16–17
.csv file extension, OU 7-7
Current View command (View menu), OU 1-22, OU 2-11
Active Appointments, OU 3-24
Address Cards, OU 6-9
By Category, OU 6-9
By Company, OU 2-11
Customize Current View, OU 2-11, OU 6-12–14, OU 6-24
Day/Week/Month, OU 1-23, OU 1-27, OU 3-25
Message Timeline, OU 1-23
Current View list
customizing views, OU 6-12
filtering folders, OU 6-11
custom level, folder permissions rights, OU 7-16
custom forms, using, OU 7-30–31
Customize dialog box, OU 1-18–19
Options tab, OU 1-16
Toolbars tab, OU 1-17
customizing
active view settings, OU 2-12
Calendar, OU 3-25, OU 3-28
 setting options, OU 3-25–27
contact options, OU 2-22
e-mail stationery, OU 7-24–26
forms, OU 7-27–31
impact on notes, OU 5-23–24
launch features
 changing default feature window, OU 1-7–8
meeting request removal options, OU 4-11
menus, OU 1-15
 adding commands, OU 1-16–19
 changing settings, OU 1-16
 setting options, OU 1-16

Outlook Bar
   adding groups, OU 1-11–12
   changing shortcut icon size, OU 1-15
   manipulating groups, OU 1-11
   repositioning folders, OU 1-11–13
Outlook Today, OU 1-4–6, OU 1-11
Outlook views, OU 6-11–14
toolbars, OU 1-15
   adding buttons, OU 1-16–19
views, OU 2-22, OU 6-14
windows
   sizing feature panes, OU 1-24–26
cutting text (Edit, Cut/Copy/Paste commands), OU 1-24, OU 3-15

D

daily appointment palette, OU 3-5–9
daily calendar palette, OU 3-8–9
Daily Calendar view, mouse pointer shapes, OU 3-10
data
   checking, contact information, OU 2-7
   exporting, OU 7-5
   importing, OU 7-13
   storing, OU 7-30
   storing remotely, OU 8-25
   synchronizing, OU 8-28
Data request entry type (Journal), OU 6-25
Date Navigator, OU 3-5–10, OU 3-17, OU 3-27, OU 5-5, OU 6-6
   missing week numbers, OU 5-6
date palette, OU 3-7
dates
   recording, OU 6-26
   scheduling NetMeetings, OU 8-21
   selecting viewing parameters, OU 8-14
   setting free/busy options, OU 8-8
   setting viewing parameters, OU 8-14
   View Summary Filter group, OU 6-12
Day/Week/Month view (Calendar), OU 1-22
decision making rules, OU 6-14
Decline (request response), OU 4-10–13
   declining tasks, OU 5-11–14
Decline and Propose New Time command (Actions menu), OU 4-12

defaults. *See also* settings
   archiving files, OU 6-29
   AutoArchive feature, OU 6-30
   changing default feature window, OU 1-7–8
   customizing launch window, OU 1-7–8
   instant messaging, OU 8-22
   sets of categories, OU 6-4
   setting e-mail stationery, OU 7-31
Delegate Permissions dialog box, OU 7-14
delegates
   assigning to folders, OU 7-13–15
   opening folders, OU 7-18–19
delegating tasks, OU 5-11–15
Delete button, OU 6-8
Deleted Items folder, OU-4
   Accept response, OU 4-10
   availability for offline use, OU 8-28
   Decline response, OU 4-10
   meeting request, OU 4-13
   task assignment responses, OU 5-13
   Tentative response, OU 4-10
deleting
   appointments, OU 3-14–15
   author access rights, OU 7-13
   boxes, OU 7-29
   buttons, OU 1-19
   categories from lists, OU 6-8
   commands, OU 1-19, OU 2-9–10, OU 7-12
   delegate permission levels, OU 7-13
   owner access rights, OU 7-13
   rules, OU 6-22
delivery options, setting for messages, OU 4-20
Design Form dialog box, OU 7-27
desktop organizer, Web availability, OU 1-11
desktop shortcuts, Outlook, OU-3
Dial-Up Networking connections, OU 8-25–29
dialog boxes, OU 2-6
   Accept response to meeting request, OU 4-10
   Add Users, OU 7-14, OU 7-17
   Advanced E-mail Options, OU 4-27–28
   Advanced Find, OU 6-10–11
      More Choices tab, OU 1-27
   Advanced Options
      Right-to-left tab, OU 1-7

Appointment, OU 3-9, OU 3-19, OU 6-16
Appointment Recurrence, OU 3-16
Archive, OU 6-30
Background Picture, OU 7-25
Browse, OU 7-8
bypassing display, OU 4-31
Calendar File Name, OU 8-6
Calendar Options, OU 3-25–26, OU 8-9
Categories, OU 6-6–8
Check Address, OU 2-8
Check Name, OU 2-7
Check Phone Number, OU 2-7
Choose Contact, OU 2-14–15
Create New Folder, OU 1-9, OU 1-18
Create New Signature, OU 4-16
Create Signature, OU 4-16–17
Customize, OU 1-8–19
   Options tab, OU 1-16
Decline response to meeting request, OU 4-10
Delegate Permissions, OU 7-14
Design Form, OU 7-27
Dial-Up Networking, OU 8-26
display options for Calendar features, OU 3-25
E-Mail Options, OU 4-27
Flag for Follow Up, OU 2-18, OU 4-23–24
Free/Busy Options, OU 8-9–10
Go To, OU 3-7, OU 6-27
installing translators, OU 7-7
Invited Event, OU 3-22
Journal Options, OU 6-25–27
Logon, OU 8-19
Map Custom Fields, OU 7-9
Master Category List, OU 6-8
Meeting, OU 3-19
Message Options, OU 4-21, OU 8-33–34
.NET Messenger Service, OU 8-23
New All Day Event, OU 3-13
New Appointment, OU 3-8
New Entry, OU 3-19
New Task, OU 5-10–11
Newsgroup Subscriptions, OU 8-17–18
Note Options, OU 5-23
Notes Properties, OU 8-16
Office Assistant, OU 7-7
   deactivating, OU-14

Options
   Calendar, OU 1-20–21, OU 3-25–27, OU 8-9–10
   Delegates, OU 7-14–17
   E-Mail, OU 4-26–27
   Journal, OU 6-25
   Note, OU 5-23
   Other, OU 1-7, OU 8-22
   Security, OU 8-30–33
Page Setup, Card Styling, OU 2-16
Permissions, OU 7-15–17
Print, OU 2-15, OU 3-23–24, OU 4-15, OU 5-16, OU 5-25
Properties, OU 7-29
Propose New Time, OU 4-10–12
question mark button, OU-10
Reminder, OU 3-12
Rules Wizard, OU 6-19–22
Security Properties, OU 8-33–34
Select Attendees and Resources, OU 3-19–21
Select Contacts, OU 6-28
Select Folder, OU 1-5
Select Members, OU 2-19
Select Names, OU 4-19
Sign In, OU 8-11
Sort, OU 2-11
Tentative response to meeting request, OU 4-10
Tracking Options dialog box, OU 4-28
Untitled Distribution List, OU 2-19
View Summary, OU 2-10–12, OU 6-11–13, OU 6-24

digital Ids/signatures
average cost, OU 8-32
certificates, OU 8-32
digital signatures, OU 8-33
message recipients, OU 8-32
obtaining, OU 8-32–33
private keys, OU 8-32
public keys, OU 8-32
signing messages, OU 8-33–34

displaying
bypassing dialog boxes, OU 4-31
Calendar, OU 3-5
Calendar window, OU 3-4–8
cascading menus with mouse pointer, OU 1-18
contents of others' folders, OU 7-18

features previously viewed, OU-4
fields on forms, OU 7-28
Folder List, OU-9–10
form design view, OU 7-27
groups by category, OU 6-4
home pages, OU 8-15
Inbox, OU 4-5–6
incomplete tasks, OU 5-7
information on forms, OU 7-27
items, OU 6-12
Master Category List, OU 6-5
menu commands, OU 1-16
messages saved in alternate file formats, OU 4-14
messages within size specifications, OU 6-14
Outlook Today, OU-9, OU 1-4
question, OU-13
distribution lists, OU 2-24
    automatically recording tasks, OU 2-21
    creating, OU 2-19–20
    View Summary Automatic Formatting group, OU 6-12
downloading
    information, OU 8-28
    methods of virus infection, OU 8-30
    virus vaccines, OU 6-9
Drafts folder, OU-5–6
    availability for offline use, OU 8-28
drives
    company monitoring, OU 7-15
    exporting items, OU 7-13
duplicate entries, OU 7-11–12
duplicating information, OU 8-26

E

e-mail, OU 4-30, OU 7-6. *See also*
    attachments
        addresses
            adding to Junk Senders list, OU 6-18
            authorizing access, OU 8-13
            maintaining contact information, OU 7-5
            scheduling online meetings, OU 8-21
            setting up newsgroup access, OU 8-17
            sharing, OU 8-10
            Sign In dialog box, OU 8-11
        automatically recording tasks, OU 2-21
        blank lines in signatures, OU 4-17
    business mail, OU 4-7, OU 6-18
    company monitoring, OU 7-15
    creating and sending, OU 4-18–20
    digital signatures, OU 8-32
    direct replies, OU 8-20
    displaying, OU 1-4
    editors, OU 4-8
        bypassing dialog boxes, OU 4-31
        checking settings, OU 4-9
        FrontPage, OU 7-26
        Microsoft Word, OU 4-15, OU 7-26
        opening, OU 7-26
        Outlook, OU 4-18, OU 7-26
    formatting, OU 7-24
    From field, OU 7-5, OU 7-12
    grouping entry types, OU 6-27
    Inbox, OU-4
    integrating contact information, OU 2-13
    linking with contacts, OU 6-23
    methods of virus infection, OU 8-30
    modifying entry types, OU 6-29
    netiquette, OU 4-18
    organizing with Rules Wizard, OU 6-18
    Outlook Today, OU-4
    printing, OU 4-15
    receiving task status updates, OU 5-15
    remote access, OU 8-25–29
    retrieving and opening, OU 4-7–8
    rules for copied, OU 6-21
    securing, OU 8-31–34
    security terminology, OU 8-32
    sending contacts, OU 7-6
    sending securely, OU 8-33–34
    sending vCards, OU 7-9
    setting options, OU 4-26–29
    stationery
        creating, OU 7-24–26
        setting as default, OU 7-31
    storing, OU-9
    Subject field, OU 4-23, OU 7-9
    tasks distribution, OU 5-11
    tracking, OU 6-24
    using to create contacts, OU 7-12–13
    welcome from Microsoft, OU 8-12
E-Mail Accounts command (Tools menu), OU 8-27
E-mail Message entry type (Journal), OU 6-25

E-mail Options dialog box, OU 4-27
Edit menu commands
    Automatic Formatting, OU 3-28
    Categories, OU 6-8
    Cut/Copy/Paste, OU 1-24
    Undo Delete, OU 2-9
    Undo, OU 2-13
editing
    contacts, OU 2-9–10
    entry types, OU 6-29
    meeting participants, OU 3-21–22, OU 4-13
    notes, OU 5-19–20
    passports, OU 8-10
    rules, OU 6-22
    signatures with Outlook, OU 7-26
    tasks, OU 5-7–8
editor level (access rights), OU 7-13, OU 7-16
editors (e-mail). *See* e-mail, editors
electronic notes, OU 5-19. *See also* notes
electronic monitoring, OU 7-15
enabling, instant messaging, OU 8-22
encrypted messages, OU 8-32–34
entry types
    assigning, OU 6-25
    grouping items, OU 6-27
    modifying, OU 6-29
events, OU 3-8
    recording with Journal, OU 6-26
    scheduling and labeling, OU 3-13–14
Excel. *See* Microsoft Excel
Exchange Server, OU 5-13
exiting Outlook, OU-15
Expand (+) button, OU 6-9, OU 6-12
    recording activity lengths, OU 6-27
    restoring archived items, OU 6-31
exporting
    contacts, OU 7-5–13
    data, OU 7-5
    matching field names, OU 7-9
    timing considerations, OU 7-8
extending appointment end times, OU 3-15

F

Favorites list, OU 8-11, OU 8-14
faxes, modifying entry types, OU 6-29
feature window, changing defaults, OU 1-7–8

Field Chooser, OU 7-28
fields (forms)
    comma separated values, OU 7-7
    contact information, OU 2-6
    customized forms, OU 7-27
    displaying on forms, OU 7-28
    From field (e-mail), OU 7-5, OU 7-12
    holding information, OU 7-27
    IM address, OU 8-23
    matching names while exporting, OU 7-9
    out of order, OU 6-13
    Subject field (e-mail), OU 7-9
    View Summary Field group, OU 6-12
Fields group (View Summary), OU 6-12
File command (Insert menu), OU 4-30
file formats, OU 7-7
    e-mail attachments, OU 4-30
    extensions, OU 4-14
        .csv, OU 7-7
        .html (.htm), OU 4-14
        .txt, OU 4-14
        .vcf, OU 7-6
    saving messages, OU 4-14
File menu
    Archive, OU 6-30
    Exit, OU-15
    Folder, New Folder, OU 1-9
    Import and Export, OU 7-7, OU 7-11–13
    New
        Appointment, OU 3-9
        Distribution List, OU 2-19
        Folder, OU 1-9
        Mail Message, OU 4-19
        Meeting Request, OU 3-18
        Task, OU 5-10
    Note, OU 5-19
    Open
        Other User's Folder, OU 7-18
    Print Preview, OU 2-16
    Print, OU 2-15–17, OU 4-15, OU 5-16, OU 5-25
    Save as Web Page, OU 8-6
    Save As, OU 5-26
    Save, OU 2-6, OU 4-14, OU 4-31
    Work Offline, OU 8-29

files, OU 6-31, OU 7-7. *See also* archived files; file extensions
- archive.pst, OU 6-29
- archiving, OU 6-29–31
- contacts
  - *exporting, OU 7-6–9*
  - *importing, OU 7-11–12*
- creating
  - *Office XP files, OU 7-19–24*
  - *PowerPoint files, OU 7-19–20*
- formats. *See* file formats
- mail merging, OU 7-24
- maintaining on network, OU 8-25
- manipulating via e-mail, OU 4-29–31
- methods of virus infection, OU 8-30
- names
  - *archive settings, OU 6-30*
  - *spaces within, OU 8-7*
- offline files, OU 8-27

Filter group (View Summary), OU 6-12

filtering
- folders with Current View list, OU 6-11
- messages, OU 6-12–14

Find a Contact text box (Standard toolbar), OU 2-14–15

Find button
- Outlook toolbar, OU 4-26
- Standard toolbar, OU 1-26

Find command (Tools menu), OU 1-26, OU 2-14

Find feature, OU 1-26–27, OU 2-13, OU 6-9. *See also* searching
- Activities page as alternative, OU 2-21
- searching
  - *capabilities, OU 4-25*
  - *Journal folder, OU 6-24*

Flag for Follow Up dialog box, OU 2-18, OU 4-23–24

flagging
- contacts for follow-up, OU 2-17–18
- keyboard shortcut, OU 2-18
- messages for follow up, OU 4-23–25
- red flag icon, OU 4-23

folder banners, OU 3-5–6

Folder command (File menu), OU 1-9

Folder List, OU 7-15–16, OU 7-19
- displaying, OU-9–10

Folder List Close button, OU-10

Folder List command (View menu), OU 6-31, OU 7-16

Folder List pane, OU 6-31, OU 8-28

folders, OU 8-5. *See also* offline folders; Web folders
- adding to Outlook Bar, OU 1-8–14
- anchoring, OU-9–10
- archive settings, OU 6-30
- assigning home pages, OU 8-15–16
- author deletion rights, OU 7-13
- changing views, OU 6-9
- Contacts, printing from, OU 2-15–17
- containing custom fields, OU 7-9
- creating, OU 1-8–11
  - *for offline use, OU 8-25*
- customizing views, OU 6-12–14
- designating for offline use, OU 8-28
- exporting items, OU 7-13
- filtering views, OU 6-11
- Find feature, OU 1-26
- formatting items, OU 6-12
- granting access, OU 7-13
- grouping items, OU 6-4
- interconnected nature, OU 2-21
- junk mail, OU 6-18
- maintaining, OU 6-30
- messages to specific, OU 6-15
- moving items, OU 6-14–18
- My Documents, default location, OU 4-14
- My Shortcuts, OU-5–6
- opening, OU-6
  - *others' folders, OU 7-17–19*
- options synchronizing, OU 8-28
- organizing items, OU 6-14–18
- .ost extension, OU 8-26
- Outlook Shortcuts, OU-4, OU-8
- Outlook Today, OU 1-5
- owner permissions rights, OU 7-16
- permissions rights, OU 7-16
- repositioning, OU 1-11–13
- restoring archived files, OU 6-31
- searching, OU 6-9
- setting permissions, OU 7-15–17
- sharing, OU 7-13–17
- shortcut groups, OU-4, OU-9
- sizing considerations, OU 6-29

storing
  data, OU 7-13
  items, OU 1-8
  shortcuts, OU 1-11
 synchronizing, OU 8-28
 verifying selected, OU 1-6
 View Summary tool groups, OU 6-12
follow up
 flagging contacts, OU 2-17–18
 flagging messages, OU 4-23–25
Follow Up command (Actions menu), OU 2-18, OU 4-24
Font command (Format menu), OU 4-20
fonts
 changing, OU 4-20, OU 6-13
 customizing e-mail stationery, OU 7-25
 customizing forms, OU 7-29
 setting notes options, OU 5-23–24
 View Summary Other Settings group, OU 6-12
foreign language symbols, OU 1-21
form letters, OU 7-24
Format menu
 Font, OU 4-20
 Paragraph, OU 4-20
formats, OU 4-14–15. *See also* file formats; message formats
 e-mail program support, OU 7-11
 HTML, OU 7-24
 Journal timeline format, OU 6-26
 Rich Text, OU 7-26
 saving forms, OU 7-29
 Web addresses, OU 8-5
formatting
 active view settings, OU 2-12
 applying to appointments, OU 3-28–29
 changing font settings, OU 4-20
 changing paragraph settings, OU 4-20
 e-mail stationery, OU 7-24
 messages with stationery, OU 4-22–23, OU 7-26
 setting notes options, OU 5-23
 View Summary Automatic Formatting group, OU 6-12
 View Summary Other Settings group, OU 6-12
forms, OU 7-30. *See also* custom forms
 creating custom, OU 7-27–31
 customizing, OU 7-28–29
 displaying information, OU 7-27
 publishing, OU 7-29
 setting colors, OU 7-28
 using customized, OU 7-30–31
Forms command (Tools menu)
 Choose Form, OU 7-30
 Design a Form, OU 7-27
 Design This Form, OU 7-27
Forward as vCard command (Actions menu), OU 7-6
Forward button, OU-3–4
Forward command (Actions menu), OU 5-16
forwarding
 messages, OU 4-8–9
 notes, OU 5-24–26
 standard messages, OU 4-8–9
 task status updates, OU 5-16
Free/Busy Options (Calendar options), OU 3-26
Free/Busy Options dialog box, OU 8-9–10
Free/Busy Service, OU 8-8
 authorizing access, OU 8-13
 home page, OU 8-11
 joining and publishing to, OU 8-10–12
 joining, OU 8-10–13
 posting schedules, OU 8-12
 schedules
  posting, OU 8-12
  setting options, OU 8-8
  sharing, OU 8-8–15
  viewing, OU 8-14–15
 setting options, OU 8-8–9
 setting up passport accounts, OU 8-8
 tools displayed, OU 8-14
From field (e-mail), OU 7-5, OU 7-12
FrontPage, e-mail editor, OU 7-26
Full Name field (Contacts), OU 2-7, OU 2-10

G

gathering data, OU 7-30
Global Address List, OU 7-14
Go To command (View menu)
 Go To Date, OU 3-7
 News, OU 8-17–18
Go To dialog box, OU 3-7, OU 6-27
granting access
 owner access rights, OU 7-13
 owner permission rights, OU 7-16

grid lines, OU 6-12
group buttons, OU-4
    My Shortcuts, OU-5
Group By group (View Summary), OU 6-12
grouping
    items, OU 6-4, OU 6-12
    items by entry type, OU 6-27
    messages, OU 6-12
    remote sessions, OU 6-27
groups
    customizing Outlook Bar, OU 1-11
    moving modified activities, OU 6-29
    storing shortcuts, OU 1-11
    View Summary tool groups, OU 6-12
GroupWise e-mail program, OU 7-11

H

Hang Manager, OU-15
headings, OU 6-12
helpdesk newsgroup (24hoursupport), OU 8-18–19
Help menu commands
    Office Assistant, OU-12–14
    Office on the Web, OU-11
    Show, OU-12–13
Help window
    Ask a Question, OU-11–12
    Close button, OU-14
    context-sensitive help, OU-10
    features, OU-12
    getting, OU-10–11
Hide button, OU-12
hiding
    items, OU 6-12
    Office Assistant, OU-14
    tasks from others, OU 5-6
holidays, adding to Calendar, OU 3-27
home pages
    assigning to folders, OU 8-15–16
    Free/Busy Service, OU 8-11
Hotmail accounts, OU 8-8
    HTML format, e-mail attachments, OU 4-30, OU 5-25
    stationary, OU 7-24
    saving messages, OU 4-14

I

icons
    active features, OU 8-29
    assigned tasks, OU 5-12
    changing sizes, OU 1-15
    displaying alternate file formats, OU 5-25
    message identification, OU 4-6
    recurring tasks, OU 5-11
    red flag, OU 4-23
    shortcuts, OU 1-11
ILOVEYOU virus, OU 8-30
IM address, OU 8-23–24
Import and Export command (File menu), OU 7-7, OU 7-11–13
Import and Export Progress window, OU 7-8
Import and Export Wizard, OU 7-7
importing
    contacts, OU 7-5–13
    data, OU 7-13
    holidays to Calendar, OU 3-27
Inbox, OU 4-5–6
    archiving files, OU 6-30
    assigning categories to items, OU 6-6
    assigning home pages, OU 8-16
    availability for offline use, OU 8-28
    creating contacts from e-mail, OU 7-12
    creating rules, OU 6-19
    customizing
        launch features, OU 1-7
        customizing views, OU 6-12
    dealing with junk mail, OU 6-18
    displaying, OU 4-5–6
    formatting items, OU 6-12
    grouping messages, OU 6-12
    linking items manually, OU 6-23
    meeting request removal, OU 4-11
    message delivery, OU 8-29
    modifying security zone settings, OU 8-30
    opening, OU 6-8
    Organize pane tools, OU 6-15–16
    preview pane, OU 1-22–23
        opening/closing, OU 1-22–23, OU 4-6
        e-mail viruses, OU 4-6
    printing items, OU 4-15
    restoring archived items, OU 6-31
    saving vCards, OU 7-9
    sending secure e-mail, OU 8-33

subscribing to newsgroups, OU 8-18
using custom forms, OU 7-30
views available, OU 1-22–23
Inbox icon (Outlook Bar), OU 6-8, OU 6-30–31
indenting signatures, OU 7-26
Index (Help window), OU-12
Insert File button (Standard message toolbar), OU 4-30
Insert menu
File, OU 4-30
Signature, OU 4-18
insertion point, positioning, OU 3-10
installing translators, OU 7-7
instant messaging, OU 8-21–25
sending, OU 8-23–24
enabling, OU 8-22
Internet
access to Outlook Newsreader, OU 8-17
fast connections, OU 3-6
form usage, OU 7-30
free connections, OU 2-10
methods of virus infection, OU 8-30
Microsoft Web site, OU-11
monitoring access, OU 7-15
newsgroups as resources, OU 8-17
posting calendars, OU 8-5
setting up newsreader connections, OU 8-17
tools, OU 8-17
variety of messages, OU 8-17
Web portals, OU 6-18
Weblogs, OU 8-22
Internet Connection Wizard, OU 8-17–18
Internet Explorer
authorizing access, OU 8-12
browser features, OU 8-15
displaying messages, OU 4-14
launching, OU 8-10, OU 8-14
Internet Free/Busy Service, OU 4-12. *See also* Free/Busy Service
Internet Service Provider (ISP), OU 4-7, OU 8-19
invitation links, OU 8-10–13, OU 8-21
Invited Event dialog box, OU 3-22
ISP (Internet Service Provider), OU 4-7, OU 8-19
items
archiving, OU 6-29–31
assigning categories, OU 6-4–9
author creation rights, OU 7-13

Categories command (Edit menu), OU 6-8
creating associations, OU 6-23–24
discerning relationships, OU 6-23
exporting, OU 7-13
finding, OU 1-26–27
grouping by entry type, OU 6-27
linking manually, OU 6-23–24
moving to folders, OU 6-14–18
printing Inbox items, OU 4-15
printing task, OU 5-16–17
restoring archived, OU 6-31
rules for organizing, OU 6-14–22
View Summary, OU 6-12

J

joining
Free/Busy Service, OU 8-8–13
newsgroups, OU 8-17
Journal, OU-5, OU 6-24–29
assigning contacts, OU 6-27–28
availability for offline use, OU 8-28
creating, OU 6-26–27
modifying entry types, OU 6-29
recording, OU 6-26–27
searching, OU 6-24
setting options to track activities, OU 6-25–26
space considerations, OU 6-27
tracking activities, OU 6-26
using, OU 6-24–29
Journal icon (Outlook Bar), OU 6-26
Journal Options dialog box, OU 6-25–26
junk e-mail, adding addresses to Junk Senders list, OU 6-18

K

keyboard shortcuts
creating
folders, OU 1-9
distribution lists, OU 2-19
Journal entries, OU 6-26
meeting requests, OU 3-18
new e-mail messages, OU 4-19
note, OU 5-19
Office documents, OU 7-19

Cut/Copy/Paste, OU 1-24, OU 3-15
displaying
   Flag for Follow Up dialog box, OU 4-24
   Journal months, OU 6-27
   Print dialog box, OU 4-15
exiting Outlook, OU-15
Find feature, OU 1-26
flagging items, OU 2-18
forwarding messages, OU 4-9
opening
   Appointment dialog box, OU 3-9
   Appointment Recurrence dialog box, OU 3-16
   attachments, OU 7-9
   Go To dialog box, OU 3-7
   New Task dialog box, OU 5-10
   Print dialog box, OU 2-15, OU 3-23, OU 5-16
   reply window, OU 4-9
retrieving e-mail messages, OU 4-7
saving contact information, OU 2-6
selecting multiple items, OU 7-14

L

labeling
   Calendar
      all-day events, OU 3-13–14
      applying conditional formatting to appointments, OU 3-28
      form labels, OU 7-29
laptops, using remote mail, OU 8-25–29
Large Icons button (Standard toolbar), OU 5-20
launch features, setting, OU 1-7–8
launching
   Internet Explorer, OU 8-10, OU 8-14
   Outlook, OU-3
   Outlook Newsreader, OU 8-18
letters, creating, OU 7-19–24
linking items with contacts, OU 6-23–24
logging on
   Free/Busy Service, OU 8-8
   instant messaging, OU 8-22
   ISP newsreader requirements, OU 8-19
Logon dialog box, OU 8-19
Lotus Notes e-mail program, OU 7-11

M

mail merge, OU 7-24
mail servers, OU 4-7
Map Custom Fields dialog box, OU 7-9
marking
   cancelled messages, OU 4-10
   contacts for follow-up, OU 2-17–18
   tasks private, OU 5-6
mass mailings, OU 7-24
Master Category List, OU 6-8
   Categories text box, OU 6-5
   displaying, OU 6-5
   modifying, OU 6-7–9
Master Category List dialog box, OU 6-8
Maximize button, OU-3
Meeting dialog box, OU 3-19
meetings, OU 8-20. *See also* **online meetings**
   automatically records tasks, OU 2-21
   Calendar, OU-4
   canceling, OU 3-22–23
   editing participants, OU 3-21–22, OU 4-13
   icon identifying cancellations, OU 4-6, OU 4-10
   icons identifying responses, OU 4-6
   labeling, OU 3-28
   requests/invitations, OU 4-8
      Accept response, OU 4-10–13
      creating and sending, OU 3-18–20
      customizing removal options, OU 4-11
      Decline response, OU 4-10–13
      icons identifying, OU 4-6
      linking with contacts, OU 6-23
      opening and responding, OU 4-7–11
      proposing new meeting times, OU 4-10, OU 4-12–13
      removal from Inbox, OU 4-11
      responses, OU 4-10
      Tentative response, OU 4-10–11
      tracking, OU 6-24, OU 6-27
   scheduling, OU 3-14, OU 3-18–20
   sending updates, OU 3-21–22
   setting reminder option, OU 8-21
Melissa virus, OU 8-30
menus
   commands. *See also* commands
      adding, OU 1-16–19
      displaying, OU 1-16
      removing, OU 1-19

changing menu settings, OU 1-16
customizing, OU 1-15
setting menu options, OU 1-16
merging contacts, OU 7-24
message boxes
    additions to contact lists, OU 8-23
    clearing search options, OU 6-10
    creating forms, OU 7-28
    customizing forms, OU 7-28
    folder permissions rights, OU 7-18
    installing translators, OU 7-7
    sharing schedules, OU 8-10
    spaces in file names, OU 8-7
    turning on Journal feature, OU 6-26
Message Options dialog box, OU 4-21, OU 8-33–34
messages, OU 4-6, OU 8-20
    Adult Content, OU 6-18
    authentication, OU 8-31–32
    automatic selection, OU 6-8
    blocking, OU 8-25
    cancelled messages, markings for, OU 4-10
    Categories command (Edit menu), OU 6-8
    checking for and opening, OU 4-7–8
    checking To field, OU 4-9
    color coding, OU 6-15–18
    creating customized forms, OU 7-27–29
    default colors, OU 6-30
    displaying within size specifications, OU 6-14
    E-mail Message entry type, OU 6-25
    encoding, OU 8-32
    encrypted, OU 8-33–34
    filtering folders, OU 6-11
    filtering, OU 6-12–14
    flagging for follow up, OU 4-23–25
    formats, OU 4-14
        modifying, OU 4-15–18
    formatting with stationery, OU 4-22–23, OU 7-26
    forwarding standard, OU 4-8–9
    grouping, OU 6-12
    grouping items, OU 6-4
    icons, OU 4-6–7
    item information, OU 7-27
    methods of virus infection, OU 8-30
    moving to folders, OU 6-17
    offline mode, OU 8-29
    opening and responding, OU 4-7–13
    posted to newsgroup, OU 8-19
    posting responses, OU 8-20
    posting to newsgroups, OU 8-17
    private keys, OU 8-32
    reading securely, OU 8-29, OU 8-32
    replying, OU 4-8, OU 8-20
    rules for color coding, OU 6-14
    saving in different file formats, OU 4-14
    sending to folders, OU 6-15
    sending, OU 4-20–21, OU 8-23–25
    setting tracking options, OU 4-20–21
    sorting and searching, OU 4-25–26
    storing in Inbox, OU 4-5
    types stored, OU 4-8
    variety on Internet, OU 8-17
    View Summary Automatic Formatting group, OU 6-12
    View Summary Filter group, OU 6-12
    Web portal notification, OU 6-18
Messages view (Inbox), OU 1-22
Microsoft Access, OU 7-13
Microsoft Excel, OU 4-14
    creating new files, OU 7-19
    grouping entry types, OU 6-27
    storing files, OU 7-13
Microsoft Exchange, Out of Office Assistant, OU 4-29
Microsoft Exchange Server, OU 8-26–27
Microsoft Messenger, OU 8-23
Microsoft Office Application Recover command (Start menu), OU-15
Microsoft Office Exchange, OU 7-14
Microsoft Office Internet Free/Busy Service, OU 4-12
Microsoft Outlook. *See* **Outlook**
Microsoft PowerPoint, OU 4-14
    creating files, OU 7-19–20
    modifying entry types, OU 6-29
Microsoft Web site, OU-5, OU 8-8–10
    accessing, OU-11
Microsoft Word, OU 4-14
    adjusting signature placement, OU 7-26
    creating contact letters, OU 7-21
    creating new files, OU 7-19
    displaying messages, OU 4-14

e-mail editor, OU 4-15
grouping entry types, OU 6-27
mail merging, OU 7-24
merging letters, OU 7-24
wizard, OU 7-21, OU 7-24
Microsoft.NET, OU 8-8
modems, OU 8-26
monitoring of e-mail, OU 7-15
More Choices tab (Advanced Find dialog box), OU 1-27
mouse pointer
black bar, OU 1-13, OU 1-18
carrying X, OU 1-17
displaying cascading menus, OU 1-18
four-headed arrow, OU 3-10–11, OU 3-14, OU 3-17
I-beam, OU 3-10
plus sign, OU 1-17, OU 2-23, OU 3-15
selection arrow, OU 3-10
shape meanings, OU 3-10
shapes, OU 3-10
two-headed arrow, OU 1-5, OU 1-25, OU 3-10, OU 3-15, OU 7-28
moving
activities to new groups, OU 6-29
appointments, OU 3-14–15
information, OU 7-5
items to folders, OU 6-14–18
messages to folders, OU 6-17
text, OU 1-24
MSN accounts, OU 8-8
My Computer
opening window, OU 8-26
setting up remote access, OU 8-26
My Documents, default folder location, OU 4-14
My Shortcuts, OU-4–5, OU 6-25–26
adding folders, OU 1-8
displaying folders, OU-9
Drafts, OU-5–6
folders and features, OU-5
Journal, OU-5, OU 6-26
Outbox, OU-5
Outlook Bar, OU-5, OU 1-10
Outlook Update, OU-5
Sent Items, OU-5

N

names
customizing display format, OU 2-22
Full Name field
entering in, OU 2-7
sorting by, OU 2-10
naming rules, OU 6-18
navigating
Back button, OU-4
Calendar, OU 3-4–8
date palette, OU 3-7
Forward button, OU-4
identifying, OU-4
Outlook Bar, OU-4
.NET Messenger Service dialog box, OU 8-23
.NET Passport, OU 8-8
netiquette, OU 4-18
NetMeetings, OU 8-20
scheduling, OU 8-20–21
networks. *See also* **dial-up network connections**
access rights, OU 7-13
accessing others' folders, OU 7-17
administrators, OU 8-30
archive settings, OU 6-30
maintaining files, OU 8-25
manipulating information, OU 7-5, OU 8-26
protecting computers, OU 8-30
setting delegate permissions, OU 7-14
synchronizing data, OU 8-28
synchronizing folders, OU 8-25
working offline settings, OU 8-29
New All Day Event dialog box, OU 3-13
New Appointment command (Actions menu), OU 3-9
New Appointment dialog box, OU 3-8
New button (Standard toolbar), OU 4-18
New command (File menu)
Appointment, OU 3-9
Distribution List, OU 2-19
Mail Message, OU 4-19
Meeting Request, OU 3-18
Task, OU 5-10
New Entry dialog box, OU 3-19
New Folder command (File menu), OU 1-9
New Letter to Contact (Actions menu), OU 7-21

New Mail Message command (Actions menu), OU 4-19
    Using More Stationery, OU 4-22
New Meeting Request (Actions menu), OU 3-18
New Message button (Outlook toolbar), OU 4-19
New Message to Attendees command (Actions menu), OU 3-23
New Note command (Actions menu), OU 5-19
New Recurring Appointment command (Actions menu), OU 3-16
New Task dialog box, OU 5-10–11
news servers, OU 8-17
newsgroups
    accessing information, OU 8-17
    establishing membership, OU 8-17
    helpdesk, 24hoursupport, OU 8-18–19
    numbers available, OU 8-18
    opening and reading messages, OU 8-20
    posted messages, OU 8-19
    posting questions, OU 8-17
    pseudonyms, OU 8-17
    subscribing to, OU 8-17–19
Newsgroup Subscriptions dialog box, OU 8-17–18
newsreaders
    accessing, OU 8-17
    Internet tools, OU 8-17
    ISP login requirements, OU 8-19
    manipulating information, OU 8-17–20
Next button, OU-8
Next month, OU 3-5–7
none level, folder permissions rights, OU 7-16
nonediting author level, folder permissions rights, OU 7-16
Note command (File menu), OU 5-19
Note Options dialog box, OU 5-23
notes, OU-4, OU 5-5, OU 5-19
    assigning home page, OU 8-16
    assigning to contacts, OU 5-21–22
    Categories command (Edit menu), OU 6-8
    creating and editing, OU 5-19–20
    customization impact, OU 5-23–24
    customizing views, OU 6-12
    Organize pane tools, OU 6-15
    recording, OU 6-24
    setting options, OU 5-23–24
    truncation, OU 5-20–21
    working with, OU 5-20–21, OU 5-24–26
Notes icon (Outlook Bar), OU 6-5, OU 8-16
Notes Properties dialog box, OU 8-16

O

Office Assistant, OU-11–14
    Clippit, OU-13
    creating contact letter, OU 7-21
    exporting contacts to files, OU 7-7
    hiding, OU-14
    Rules Wizard, OU 6-19
    Shortcut menu, OU-14
Office Assistant dialog box, OU 7-7
Office on the Web command (Help menu), OU-11
Office Safe Mode, OU-15
Office XP
    Ask a Question, OU-11
    creating files, OU 7-19–24
    installing translators, OU 7-7
offline files, OU 8-27
offline folders
    creating and specifying, OU 8-26–28
    profile restrictions, OU 8-27
    setting up, OU 8-27
    synchronizing data, OU 8-28
offline mode, switching to, OU 8-25, OU 8-29
online, OU 8-20–21
    switching to online mode, OU 8-25, OU 8-29
online chats (instant messaging), OU 8-21–25
online diaries, OU 8-22
online meetings
    scheduling, OU 8-20–21
    tools for connecting, OU 8-21
Open, Other User's Folder command (File menu), OU 7-18
opening
    appointments, OU 6-6
    attachments, OU 7-9
    Calendar, OU-8
    contacts, OU 2-9–10
    e-mail, OU 4-7–8
    e-mail editors, OU 7-26

files using e-mail, OU 4-29–31
folders
  Calendar, OU 8-10
  Contacts, OU 3-8
  other users' folders, OU 7-17–19
Inbox, OU 6-8
keyboard shortcuts
  Appointment Recurrence dialog box, OU 3-16
  Print dialog box, OU 2-15, OU 3-23
meeting requests, OU 4-7–13
messages, OU 4-7–13
My Computer, OU 8-26
newsgroup messages, OU 8-20
reply window, OU 4-9
vCard attachment, OU 7-9
options, OU 4-20. *See also* **tracking options**
  comma separated values, OU 7-7
  folder access, OU 7-15
  for communication settings, OU 8-23
  modifying rules, OU 6-21
  notifying users of rights, OU 7-15
  printing Inbox items, OU 4-15
  reminder option, OU 8-21
  replying to standard messages, OU 4-8
  resizing feature panes, OU 1-24–26
  responding to meeting requests, OU 4-9
  Rules Wizard, OU 6-18
  setting, OU 1-22–24
    for Calendar, OU 3-25–27
    for contacts, OU 2-22
    for e-mail, OU 4-26–29
    for Free/Busy Service, OU 8-8–9
    for notes, OU 5-23–24
    for tasks, OU 5-17–19
    for tracking, OU 6-25–26
    free and busy, OU 8-8
  synchronizing, OU 8-28
  View Summary dialog box, OU 6-12
  viewing private items, OU 7-15
  working offline settings, OU 8-29
Options command (Tools menu)
  Calendar Options, OU 1-20–21, OU 3-27, OU 8-9–10
    Advanced, OU 3-26
    Free/Busy Options, OU 8-12–14
  Contact Options, OU 2-22

  Delegates, OU 7-14
  E-Mail Options, OU 4-27
    Advanced E-Mail Options, OU 4-11
  Journal Options, OU 6-25
  Mail Format, OU 4-16, OU 4-23, OU 7-24–26, OU 7-31
  Note Options, OU 5-23
  Other, OU 1-7, OU 6-30, OU 8-22
  Preferences, OU 5-6
  Security, OU 8-30
Options dialog box
  Calendar, OU 3-25
  Delegates, OU 7-14–17
  E-mail, OU 4-26
  Journal, OU 6-25
  Note, OU 5-23
  Other, OU 1-7, OU 8-22
  Security, OU 8-30–33
Options tab (Customize dialog box), OU 1-16
Organize button (Organize pane), OU 6-17
Organize pane
  available tools, OU 6-15
  creating rules, OU 6-18
  Organize button, OU 6-17
  switching features, OU 6-16
Organize tool, OU 5-8, OU 6-14
  using, OU 6-15–18
organizing
  items with rules, OU 6-14–22
  notes, OU 5-20–21
  Rules Wizard options, OU 6-18
  sorting items into folders, OU 1-8
  tasks, OU 5-8–9
.ost folder extension, OU 8-26
Other Settings group (View Summary), OU 6-12
Other Shortcuts, OU-4
  group button, OU-6
Out of Office Assistant command (Tools menu), OU 4-29
Outbox, OU-5
  availability for offline use, OU 8-28
Outlook, OU 8-22
  accessing features, OU-5–8
  desktop shortcuts, OU-3
  e-mail editor, OU 4-18
  editing signatures, OU 7-26

exiting, OU-15
  features, OU-4
  recovery, OU-15
Help button, OU-13
launching, OU-3
Notes, OU 5-19
Organize tool, OU 5-8
printing e-mail messages, OU 4-15
tasks automatically recorded, OU 2-21
  time zone settings, affect on other programs, OU 1-19
updating, OU-5
warning messages, setting reminders, OU 3-11
wizard, OU 7-24
Outlook Bar, OU-3–8
  accessing Calendar window, OU 3-5
  adding folders, OU 1-8–11
  adding groups, OU 1-11–12
  creating shortcuts, OU 1-11–14
  customizing, OU 1-11
  features and folders, OU-4
    My Shortcuts, OU-5
  folder access options, OU 7-15
  icons
    Calendar, OU-8, OU 6-6
    changing size, OU 1-15
    Inbox, OU 6-8, OU 6-30–31
    Journal, OU 6-26
    Notes, OU 6-5, OU 8-16
    Outlook Today, OU 1-5
  manipulating groups, OU 1-11
  My Shortcuts, OU-5, OU 1-10, OU 6-25–26
  opening folders, OU-6
  Other Shortcuts, OU-6
  Outlook Class, OU 1-13
  repositioning folders, OU 1-11–13
  Scroll Down button, OU-7
  Scroll Up button, OU-7
  shortcut groups, OU-9
    Outlook Shortcuts, OU-4
Outlook Class, OU 1-13
Outlook Newsgroup, OU 8-18
Outlook Newsreader, OU 8-17–18
  closing, OU 8-20
  launching, OU 8-18
Outlook Shortcuts
  Calendar, OU-4, OU-8
  Contacts, OU-4

Deleted Items, OU-4
displaying folders, OU-9
Inbox, OU-4
Notes, OU-4
Outlook Today, OU-4, OU-8
repositioning folders, OU 1-13
Tasks, OU-4, OU-8
Outlook Today, OU-4
  customizing launch window, OU 1-7–8
  customizing, OU 1-4–6, OU 1-11
  displaying, OU-9
  resizing, OU-10
Outlook toolbar
  Find, OU 4-26
  New Message, OU 4-19
Outlook toolbox, OU 7-27–29
  creating forms, OU 7-28
Outlook Update, OU-5
overriding groupings, OU 6-12
owner level (access rights), OU 7-13–16

P

Page Setup, Card Styling dialog box, OU 2-16
paging contacts, OU 8-25
pane borders, OU 3-5–6
Paragraph command (Format menu), OU 4-20
paragraphs, changing settings in messages, OU 4-20
passports
  account setup, OU 8-8, OU 8-10
  activating instant messaging, OU 8-23
  editing, OU 8-10
  .NET Passport, OU 8-8
  personal, OU 8-8
  searching for information, OU 8-8
passwords, OU 8-8
  editing passports, OU 8-10
  Sign In dialog box, OU 8-11
pasting text, OU 1-24, OU 3-15
path selection, OU 8-6–7
PCMCIA card, OU 3-25
PDA (Personal Digital Assistant), OU 3-6, OU 3-25, OU 5-19
permission settings
  delegates, OU 7-14–15, OU 7-18
  folders, OU 7-15–17
  system administrator, OU 8-27

Permissions dialog box, OU 7-15–17
personal contacts
    Activities tab, OU 2-21
    Contacts, OU-4
Personal Data Assistant (PDA). *See* PDA
personal distribution lists. *See* distribution lists
Personal Folders Inbox, OU 6-31
personal folders, OU 6-16
Personal Forms Library, OU 7-29–30
personalizing
    categories, OU 6-7–9
    e-mail stationery, OU 7-24–26
phone calls
    company monitoring, OU 7-15
    grouping entry types, OU 6-27
    instant messaging, OU 8-25
    modifying entry types, OU 6-29
    recording activity lengths, OU 6-26
phone numbers, validating entries, OU 2-7
Plain Text format for e-mail attachments, OU 4-30, OU 5-25
Planner Options (Calendar option), OU 3-26
portals, OU 2-15
posting
    calendars, OU 8-5
    questions to newsgroups, OU 8-17
    replies to newsgroups, OU 8-17
    responses, OU 8-20
    schedules, OU 8-12
        reviewing, OU 8-14–15
PowerPoint. *See* Microsoft PowerPoint
preview pane, OU 1-22–23
    opening/closing, OU 1-22–23, OU 4-6
    e-mail viruses, OU 4-6
Previous month arrow (Calendar), OU 3-5–7
Print button (Standard toolbar), OU 3-23
Print dialog box, OU 2-15–17, OU 3-23–24, OU 4-15, OU 5-16, OU 5-25
Print Preview command (File menu), OU 2-16
Print Preview toolbar, OU 2-16, OU 3-24
printing
    appointments, OU 3-23–25
    bypassing Print dialog box, OU 4-15
    calendar options, OU-14
    Calendar, OU 3-23–25
    displaying help, OU-14
    e-mail messages, OU 4-15

    from Contacts folder, OU 2-15–17
    Inbox items, OU 4-15
    notes, OU 5-24–26
    tasks, OU 5-16–17
privacy
    gathering data, OU 7-30
    marking tasks for, OU 5-6
    newsgroup pseudonyms, OU 8-17
    viewing options, OU 7-15
private keys, OU 8-32
product registration, OU 7-30
profiles, offline folder restrictions, OU 8-27
Programs command (Start menu), OU-3
progress of tasks
    recording, OU 5-7–8
    sending, OU 5-14–15
properties
    folder access options, OU 7-15
    folder permissions rights, OU 7-16
    setting for forms, OU 7-28–29
    setting to view home pages, OU 8-16
Properties dialog box, OU 7-29
Propose New Time response, OU 4-10–13
protocol for Web folders, OU 8-5
pseudonyms in newsgroups, OU 8-17
public keys (secure e-mail), OU 8-32
publishing
    calendars, OU 8-5
    forms, OU 7-29
    schedules, OU 8-10–12
    setting free/busy options, OU 8-8
    to Free/Busy Service, OU 8-8–12
Publishing Author level, folder permissions rights, OU 7-16
Publishing Editor level, folder permissions rights, OU 7-16
Pushpin (folder list), OU-9

Q-R

questions, asking (Help), OU-11–14
question mark button (dialog boxes), OU-10
Quick Launch toolbar, OU-3

reading
    folder permissions rights, OU 7-16
    messages securely, OU 8-29–32
    newsgroup messages, OU 8-20

notes, OU 5-20–21
owner access rights, OU 7-13
reviewer access rights, OU 7-13
real time communication, OU 8-23
receiving
information using newsreaders, OU 8-17–20
instant messages, OU 8-25
recording
contact activities, OU 6-25
conversations, OU 6-24
events with Journal, OU 6-26
Journal entries, OU 6-26–27
task progress, OU 5-7–8, OU 5-14
tasks, OU 5-5–6
tasks automatically, OU 2-21
recovery features, OU-15
Recurrence button, OU 5-10
recurring
appointments, OU 3-16–17
tasks
recurrence icon, OU 5-11
updating, OU 5-9–11
registration with passport service, OU 8-8
relationships between items, OU 6-23
Reminder dialog box, OU 3-12
reminders
audio signal, OU 3-11–12
controlling notifications, OU 5-17–18
flagging, OU 2-17
setting, OU 3-10–12
remote access, OU 8-25–29
connecting via Dial-Up Networking, OU 8-26
creating and specifying online folders, OU 8-26–28
Journal entries, OU 6-27–28
posting calendars on the Web, OU 8-5–7
switching between online/offline modes, OU 8-28
synchronizing folders, OU 8-28
removing. *See* **deleting**
replacing text, OU 1-24
Reply command (Actions menu), OU 4-9
replying to messages, OU 4-8–9
newsgroup messages, OU 8-20
meeting requests, OU 4-9–13
repositioning folders, OU 1-11–13

Reset button, OU 6-8
resizing
columns, OU 6-13
windows, OU-7, OU-10
Resource Scheduling (Calendar option), OU 3-26
resources, OU 3-18
responses
Accept, OU 4-10–13
task assignments, OU 5-13
Assign Task
task assignments, OU 5-13
Decline, OU 4-10–13
task assignments, OU 5-13
instant messaging, OU 8-24
meeting invitations, OU 3-18, OU 3-21
meeting requests, OU 4-7–11
proposing new meeting times, OU 4-12–13
messages, OU 4-7–13
posting, OU 8-20
Propose New Time, OU 4-10, OU 4-13
sending automatic, OU 8-25
tasks, OU 5-11, OU 5-13
Tentative, OU 4-10–11
Restore Down button (message window), OU 4-8
restoring archived files, OU 6-31
restricted sites, adding to list, OU 8-31
retrieving e-mail, OU 4-7–8
returning after Back button, OU-4
reviewer level (access rights), OU 7-16–17
reviewing
calendars, OU 8-5
information offline, OU 8-26
messages, OU 4-5
posted schedules, OU 8-14–15
task progress, OU 5-15
Rich Text format (rtf), OU 7-26
e-mail attachments, OU 4-30, OU 5-25
Right-to-left tab (Advanced Options dialog box), OU 1-7
Rolodex™. *See* **contacts**
rules
building requirements, OU 6-18
color coding messages, OU 6-14, OU 6-17
copied e-mail messages, OU 6-21

creating
   with Rules Wizard, OU 6-18–22
   with templates, OU 6-18–19
deleting, OU 6-22
editing, OU 6-22
identifying exceptions, OU 6-18
modifying settings, OU 6-22
naming, OU 6-18
organizing items, OU 6-14–22
Rules Wizard, OU 6-14
   creating rules, OU 6-18–22

S

Save As command (File menu), OU 5-26
Save as Web Page command (File menu), OU 8-6
Save command (File menu), OU 2-6, OU 4-14, OU 4-31
saving
   calendars as Web pages, OU 8-5–7
   files using e-mail, OU 4-29–31
   forms, OU 7-29
   messages in file formats, OU 4-14
   notes, OU 5-24–26
   vCards as contacts, OU 7-9–10
   to Web folders, OU 8-6
schedules, OU 8-8. *See also* **free/busy schedules**
   accessing, OU 8-8
   authorizing access, OU 8-12–13
   publishing, OU 8-10–12
   reviewing posted, OU 8-14–15
   viewing others', OU 8-12
scheduling
   appointments, OU 3-8–10, OU 3-12–14
     all day events, OU 3-13–14
   checking free time, OU 3-20
   meetings involving others, OU 3-18–20
   NetMeetings, OU 8-20–21
   recurring appointments, OU 3-16–17
Scroll Down/Up buttons, OU-7
Search button, OU-13
searching, OU 1-26, OU 6-24. *See also* **Find feature**
   contacts, OU 2-10, OU 2-13–15
   Find feature, OU 1-26–27

items, OU 1-26–27
items by category, OU 6-9–11
Journal folder, OU 6-24
matching text case, OU 1-27
messages, OU 4-25–26
options for, OU 6-10
passport information, OU 8-8
security
   gathering data, OU 7-30
   e-mail, OU 8-31–34
   implementing different levels, OU 8-30
   newsgroup pseudonyms, OU 8-17
   setting, OU 8-29–34
   viewing options, OU 7-15
   zone settings, OU 8-34
     changing, OU 8-30
     modifying, OU 8-30–31
Security Properties dialog box, OU 8-33–34
Select Attendees and Resources dialog box, OU 3-19–21
Select Contacts dialog box, OU 6-28
Select Folder dialog box, OU 1-5
Select Members dialog box, OU 2-19
Select Names dialog box, OU 4-19
Send/Receive, Send and Receive All command (Tools menu), OU 4-7, OU 8-28
Send/Receive Settings/Make This Folder Available Offline command (Tools menu), OU 8-28
sending
   author access rights, OU 7-13
   automatic responses, OU 8-25
   contacts, OU 7-5–13
   e-mail messages, OU 4-18–20
   information using newsreaders, OU 8-17–20
   instant messages, OU 8-23–25
   meeting requests, OU 3-18–20
   meeting updates, OU 3-21–22
   messages, OU 4-20–21, OU 8-23–25
     to folders, OU 6-15
   secure-e-mail, OU 8-33–34
   task requests, OU 5-11–15
   task updates, OU 5-14–15
   vCards via e-mail, OU 7-9
Sent Items folder, OU-5
   availability for offline use, OU 8-28

settings, OU 6-14, OU 6-29, OU 8-30. *See also* security, zone settings; size settings
- activating for Free/Busy Service, OU 8-11
- changing, OU 4-20
- checking e-mail editor, OU 4-9
- customizing
  - *name formats, OU 2-22*
  - *Outlook, OU 4-7*
- instant messaging, OU 8-22
- modifying for rules, OU 6-22
- options for communication, OU 8-23
- Windows Messenger, OU 8-23
- working offline, OU 8-29

sharing
- e-mail address, OU 8-10
- folders, OU 7-13–17
- free/busy schedules, OU 8-8–15
- notes, OU 5-24–26

shortcut groups, OU-4
- My Shortcuts, OU-5–6
- Other Shortcuts, OU-6
- Outlook Shortcuts, OU-4

shortcuts
- assigning categories to items, OU 6-6–7
- changing icon size, OU 1-15
- changing time zones, OU 1-21
- creating, OU 1-11
- icons, OU 1-11
- opening attachments, OU 7-9
- Outlook Bar, OU-4
  - *creating, OU 1-13–14*
- removing buttons from toolbar, OU 1-19
- storing in separate folders, OU 1-11

Show button (Help window toolbar), OU-12
Show the Office Assistant command (Help menu), OU-13
Sign In dialog box, OU 8-11
signature blocks, OU 7-26
Signature command (Insert menu), OU 4-18
signatures, OU 4-15
- adjusting placements, OU 7-26
- automatic inclusion, OU 4-19
- creating, OU 4-15–18
- editing, OU 7-26
- indenting lines, OU 7-26
- location in message, OU 4-18

signing up. *See* joining

size settings
- customizing forms, OU 7-29
- displaying messages, OU 6-14

Small Icons button (Standard toolbar), OU 5-20
Sort dialog box, OU 2-11
Sort group (View Summary), OU 6-12

sorting
- advanced techniques, OU 2-11–13
- categories, OU 6-9–11
- contacts automatically, OU 2-23–24
- contacts by view, OU 2-10–11
- items into folders, OU 1-8
- messages, OU 4-25–26
- tasks alphabetically, OU 5-8
- View Summary Sort group, OU 6-12

spaces
- calendar names, OU 8-6
- file name restrictions, OU 8-7

specifying offline folders, OU 8-26–28
spell checker, OU 4-15
Standard toolbar, OU 3-5–6
- Find a Contact, OU 2-14–15
- Find, OU 1-26
- Large Icons, OU 5-20
- New, OU 4-18
- Print, OU 3-23
- Small Icons, OU 5-20
- text manipulation, OU 1-24
- Today button, OU 3-8

Start menu commands
- Microsoft Office Application Recovery, OU-15
- Programs, Outlook, OU-3

Start Time button, OU 6-26

stationery
- creating, OU 7-24–26
- formatting messages, OU 4-22–23
- setting as default, OU 7-31

Stationery Picker button, OU 7-24
status bar, OU 8-29

storing
- appointments, OU-9
- archived files, OU 6-30
- data, OU 7-13, OU 7-30, OU 8-25

files, OU 7-13
forms, OU 7-29
items in folders, OU 1-8
mail messages, OU-9, OU 4-5
shortcuts in separate groups, OU 1-11
tasks, OU-9
subfolders
owner access rights, OU 7-13
owner permissions rights, OU 7-16
Subject field (e-mail message), OU 4-23, OU 5-6, OU 7-9
subscribing to newsgroups, OU 8-17–19
switching
features, OU 6-16
modes, OU 8-25, OU 8-29
symbols, foreign language, OU 1-21
synchronizing folders, OU 8-28
system administrator, OU 8-27

T

TaskPad, OU 3-5–6, OU 5-5, OU 6-7
adding task to palette, OU 5-11
displaying incomplete tasks, OU 5-7
tasks, OU-4, OU 5-5
accepting, OU 5-12
assigning, OU 5-11–15
automatically recorded by Outlook, OU 2-21
availability for offline use, OU 8-28
changing view, OU 5-8–9
creating, OU 5-5–6
recurring tasks, OU 5-9–11
customizing
launch features, OU 1-7
views, OU 6-12
declining, OU 5-12
displaying, OU 1-4, OU 5-7
reminders, OU 3-11
filtering folders, OU 6-11
grouping items, OU 6-4
hiding from others, OU 5-6
icon identifying new, OU 4-6
item information, OU 7-27
lists
creating, OU 5-5–6
tasks copied automatically, OU 5-11
marking private, OU 5-6
Organize tool, OU 6-15
organizing, OU 5-8–9
Outlook Today, OU-4
owners
determining, OU 5-11
sending automatic updates, OU 5-15
special functions, OU 5-12
permissions rights, OU 7-17
printing, OU 5-16–17
recording date/time performed, OU 6-26
recording progress, OU 5-7–8, OU 5-14
recording, OU 5-5–6
recurring, OU 5-9–11
recurrence icon, OU 5-11
requests
Accept response, OU 5-13
Assign Task response, OU 5-13
Decline response, OU 5-13
responding, OU 5-13
sending, OU 5-11–15
responding, OU 5-11–14
reviewing progress, OU 5-15
Rules Wizard, OU 6-14
sending updates, OU 5-14–19
sorting alphabetically, OU 5-8
storing, OU-9
Tasks folder, OU-4
tracking assigned, OU 5-15–16
updating and modifying, OU 5-7–8
View Summary Automatic Formatting group, OU 6-12
telephone numbers, validating entries, OU 2-7
templates
creating rules, OU 6-18–19
formatting messages, OU 4-15
Tentative response, OU 4-10–11
Tentative and Propose New Time command (Actions menu), OU 4-12
Terms of use information, OU 8-11–12
text, cutting/copying/pasting, OU 1-24, OU 3-15
Text Only format
alternate file formats, OU 4-14
Microsoft Word, OU 4-15
Time Zone (Calendar option), OU 3-26

time zones
    adding, OU 1-20–21
    affect on other programs, OU 1-19
    changing shortcut, OU 1-21
    setting, OU 1-19–21

timelines
    computer activities, OU-5
    Journal activities, OU 6-27
    recording, OU 6-26

times
    changing for all day events, OU 3-13
    extending appointments, OU 3-15
    recording activity length, OU 6-26
    scheduling NetMeetings, OU 8-21
    setting viewing parameters, OU 8-14

title bar, Calendar, OU 3-5–6
To field (task messages), OU 4-9, OU 5-11–12, OU 5-15–16
Today button (Standard toolbar), OU 3-8
toolbars
    Appointment, OU 3-22
    buttons
        adding, OU 1-16–19
        removing, OU 1-19
    customizing, OU 1-15–16
    message toolbar, Propose New Time, OU 4-12
    Outlook
        Find, OU 4-26
        New Message, OU 4-19
    Print Preview, OU 2-16, OU 3-24
    Quick Launch, OU-3
    Standard
        Find, OU 1-26
        Find a Contact, OU 2-14–15
        Large Icons, OU 5-20
        New, OU 4-18
        Print, OU 3-23
        Small Icons, OU 5-20
        text manipulation, OU 1-24
    Standard message, Insert File, OU 4-30

Toolbars, Advanced command (View menu), OU 2-10
tools
    AutoArchive feature, OU 6-29
    connecting to online meetings, OU 8-21
    customizing stationery, OU 7-24
    e-mail editors, OU 7-26
    e-sending contact information, OU 7-6
    Free/Busy schedule page, OU 8-14
    Journal for recording events, OU 6-26
    newsreaders, OU 8-17
    Organize tool, OU 5-8, OU 6-15–18
    Outlook folders, OU 6-14
    Outlook toolbox, OU 7-27–29
    PDAs, OU 5-19
    Task options, OU 5-17
    tracking, OU 6-24
    View Summary, OU 6-12

Tools menu
    Advanced Find, OU 6-10
    Customize, OU 1-16–17
    E-Mail Accounts, OU 8-27
    Find, OU 1-26, OU 2-14
    Forms
        Choose Form, OU 7-30
        Design a Form, OU 7-27
        Design This Form, OU 7-27
    Instant Messaging
        Log Off, OU 8-23
        Log On, OU 8-23
    Options
        Calendar Options, OU 3-27, OU 8-9–10
        Calendar Options button, OU 1-20–21
        Calendar Options, Advanced, OU 3-26–27
        Calendar Options, Free/Busy Options, OU 8-12–14
        Contact Options, OU 2-22
        Delegates, OU 7-14
        E-Mail Options, OU 4-27
        E-Mail Options, Advanced E-Mail Options, OU 4-11
        Journal Options, OU 6-25
        Mail Format, OU 4-16, OU 4-23, OU 7-24–26, OU 7-31
        Note Options, OU 5-23
        Other, OU 1-7, OU 6-30, OU 8-22
        Preferences, OU 5-6
        Security, OU 8-30–32
    Out of Office Assistant, OU 4-29
    Rules Wizard, OU 6-19, OU 6-22
    Send/Receive
        Make This Folder Available Offline, OU 8-28
        Send and Receive All, OU 4-7, OU 8-28

tracking
    activities for selected contacts, OU 6-27
    appointments, OU 3-4
    assigned tasks, OU 5-15–16
    contact activities, OU 2-21, OU 6-25
    e-mail messages, OU 6-24
    setting for messages, OU 4-20–21
    setting options, OU 6-25-26
Tracking Options dialog box, OU 4-28
transferring notes, OU 5-24–26
translators, OU 7-7
truncated note text, OU 5-20–21
turning on. *See* **activating**

U

Undo command (Edit menu), OU 2-13
Undo Delete command (Edit menu), OU 2-9
Unread Messages view (Inbox), OU 1-22
Untitled Distribution List dialog box, OU 2-19
updating
    calendars, OU 8-8
    free/busy information, OU 8-9
    information, OU 8-25–26
    Outlook, OU-5
    recurring tasks, OU 5-9–11
    sending for meetings, OU 3-21–22
    sending tasks, OU 5-14–15
    tasks, OU 5-7–8
URLs (Uniform Resource Locators)
    adding to restricted sites list, OU 8-31
    address box, OU 3-6
Using Categories link (Organize pane), OU 6-15
Using Colors link (Organize pane), OU 6-15–17
Using Folders link (Organize pane), OU 6-15–16
Using Views link (Organize pane), OU 6-15

V

value boxes, filtering messages, OU 6-14
vCards, OU 7-5
    saving as contacts, OU 7-9–10
.vcf file extension, OU 7-6
verifying
    folders selected, OU 1-6
    Journal entries, OU 6-28

View menu
    Current View, OU 1-22, OU 2-11
        Active Assignments, OU 3-24
        Address Cards, OU 6-9
        By Category, OU 6-9
        By Company, OU 2-11
        Customize Current View, OU 2-11, OU 6-12–14, OU 6-24
        Day/Week/Month, OU 1-23, OU 1-27, OU 3-25
        Message Timeline, OU 1-23
    Folder List, OU 6-31, OU 7-16
    Go To
        Go To Date, OU 3-7
        News, OU 8-17–18
    Options, OU 8-33–34
    Preview Pane, OU 1-22–23, OU 4-6
    Toolbars, Advanced, OU 2-10
View Summary dialog box, OU 2-10–12, OU 6-11–13, OU 6-24
viewing
    folder permissions rights, OU 7-16
    free/busy schedules, OU 8-14–15
    notes, OU 5-20–21
    restricted sites, OU 8-31
    schedules, OU 8-8, OU 8-12
    setting parameters, OU 8-14
    Web sites, OU 8-15
views
    Calendar, OU 1-22–23
    changing, OU 1-22–26, OU 6-9
        Tasks view, OU 5-8–9
    colors and archived files, OU 6-30
    Contacts By Location, OU 2-22
    customizing, OU 2-12, OU 6-11–14
    Daily Calendar, OU 3-10
    displaying form design, OU 7-27
    filtering, OU 6-11
    Inbox, OU 1-22–23
    sorting contacts by, OU 2-10–13
virtual business cards, OU 7-5
viruses
    checking attachments, OU 4-31, OU 7-10
    ILOVEYOU virus, OU 8-30
    lifespan, OU 6-9
    methods of infection, OU 8-30
    setting security, OU 8-29
    spreading via preview pane, OU 4-6

W-X-Y-Z

warning messages, setting reminders in Outlook, OU 3-11
Ways to Organize Tasks pane, OU 6-15
Web address formats, OU 8-5
Web folders
    path selection, OU 8-6
    protocol, OU 8-5
Web pages
    editing passports, OU 8-10
    saving calendars as, OU 8-5–7
    spaces in calendar names, OU 8-6
Web portals, OU 6-18
Web sites
    adding to restricted list, OU 8-31
    address box, OU 3-6
    downloading virus vaccines, OU 6-9
    Favorites list, OU 8-11, OU 8-14
    joining Free/Busy Service, OU 8-10
    message notification, OU 6-18
    Microsoft, OU-5, OU 8-8
    obtaining personal desktop organizer, OU 1-11
    portals, OU 2-15
    posting calendars, OU 8-5
    usefulness of government sites, OU 5-11
    viewing, OU 8-15
    Weblogs, OU 8-22
Weblogs, OU 8-22
windows
    Calendar features, OU 3-5–6
    displaying others' folders, OU 7-18
    resizing, OU-7, OU-10
        panes, OU 1-24–26
Windows Messenger, OU 8-23–25
Windows XP
    Outlook desktop shortcut, OU-3
    setting up remote access, OU 8-26
wizards
    Import and Export Wizard, OU 7-7
    Internet Connection Wizard, OU 8-17–18
    mail merging, OU 7-24
    Microsoft Word, OU 7-21
    Passport Wizard, OU 8-10
    Rules Wizard, OU 6-14, OU 6-18–22
    setting up newsgroup access, OU 8-17
Word. *See* Microsoft Word
WordPad, displaying messages, OU 4-14
World Wide Web. *See* Web folders; Web pages; Web sites
Work Offline command (File menu), OU 8-29